THE WELLCOME-MARSTON ARCHAEOLOGICAL RESEARCH EXPEDITION
TO THE NEAR EAST
VOLUME III

LACHISH III

(TELL ED-DUWEIR)

THE IRON AGE

TEXT

THE WELLCOME-MARSTON ARCHAEOLOGICAL RESEARCH EXPEDITION
TO THE NEAR EAST

LACHISH III

(TELL ED-DUWEIR)

THE IRON AGE

BY

OLGA TUFNELL

WITH CONTRIBUTIONS BY

MARGARET A. MURRAY

AND

DAVID DIRINGER

TEXT

PUBLISHED FOR
THE TRUSTEES OF THE LATE SIR HENRY WELLCOME
BY THE
OXFORD UNIVERSITY PRESS
LONDON   NEW YORK   TORONTO
1953

c

233138 Theol.

PRINTED IN GREAT BRITAIN

TO THE MEMORY OF

SIR CHARLES MARSTON

IN GRATITUDE FOR

HIS ENCOURAGEMENT OF

BIBLICAL RESEARCH

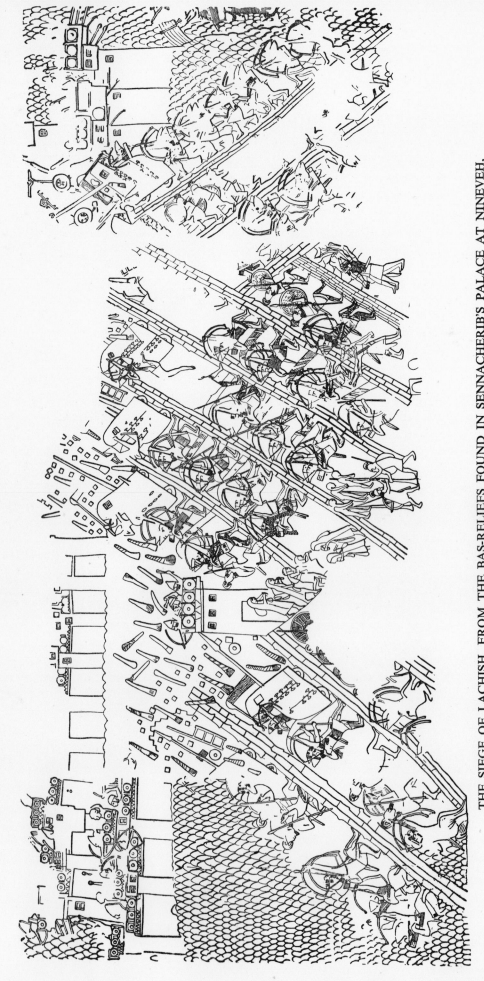

THE SIEGE OF LACHISH, FROM THE BAS-RELIEFS FOUND IN SENNACHERIB'S PALACE AT NINEVEH, NOW IN THE ASSYRIAN GALLERY, BRITISH MUSEUM

PREFACE

THE series of publications, *Lachish I* to *IV*, is designed to cover all aspects of the excavations at the site of Tell ed-Duweir which took place between 1932 and 1938, under the leadership of the late J. L. Starkey. It cannot, however, be sufficiently emphasised that all the work in those years was in the nature of a preliminary clearance to prepare and clear ground for dump heaps, and that the main task on the mound was just beginning at the time of Mr. Starkey's death. The chronological, cultural, linguistic, and architectural problems which it was hoped to solve are mostly unanswered, and the subsequent preparation of the reports has been hampered, not only by inconclusive results, but by the loss of our leader and much unavoidable delay.

Lachish I (1938), "The Lachish Letters", gave the account of the ostraca found in the guardroom at the city gate, whose ceramic and architectural associations are more fully described in the present book. It contained full-scale photographs of Ostraca I–XVIII, accompanied by facsimile line drawings prepared from the originals by Lankester Harding. The text was written by Harry Torczyner, Bialik Professor of Hebrew in the University of Jerusalem. J. L. Starkey and Lankester Harding added notes on the discovery, and Alkin Lewis described the composition of the ink. The book was seen through the press by the authors, but the date of publication, early in 1938, coincided so closely with J. L. Starkey's untimely death that he never saw the finished work.

Lachish II (1940), "The Fosse Temple", contains a complete account of three superimposed structures which were the centre of a religious cult from the sixteenth (or fifteenth) to the thirteenth century B.C. The contents and conclusions are frequently referred to in the present volume. Begun in the summer of 1938 by the joint authors, Olga Tufnell, Charles H. Inge, and Lankester Harding, it was published in the autumn of 1940. Theodor Gaster summarised the readings by various experts of the archaic inscriptions, and Miss Barbara Parker provided a note on cylinder seals.

Lachish III (1953), "The Iron Age". The scope of the present book is shown in the List of Contents. While it deals chiefly with the three periods of the Iron Age, from 1200 B.C. to the conquest of Alexander, these broad limits do not preclude the inclusion of some discoveries of later date, a list of coins from the site, and a description of part of the Roman road from Beit Jibrin (Eleutheropolis to Gaza) on which Eusebius, the fourth-century divine, noted the position of *Lakeis*. Two tomb groups and some sherds and scarabs from the mound, belonging, perhaps, to the first decades after 1200 B.C., are reserved for the next volume, as they are so much closer to the cultural affinities of the Bronze Age.

Lachish IV, "The Bronze Age". The fourth and last volume of the series is in course of preparation. It is hoped to include in it all the remaining material from the site, which was first occupied, as far as present research has shown, in the Early Bronze Age, contemporary with the cultural phase encountered at Jericho, Tomb A, Tell Beit Mirsim J, "Pre-Semitic" Gezer, and elsewhere. A summary of the results obtained from the stratified section appeared in the Quarterly Statement of the Palestine Exploration Fund for October, 1950. The tomb contents of all the periods to the end of the Bronze Age will be presented as individual groups.

When, after the war, I undertook to produce the third and fourth volumes of the series, the task seemed more simple than it proved. Work was unavoidably suspended for months at a time, and there may still be other difficulties and delays ahead.

Had it not been for the firm and constant encouragement of the Wellcome Trustees, I could not have achieved even this amount, and as the whole work grows to completion, my sense of indebtedness to them will be shared, not only by those who have helped to produce the books, but by all who seek for knowledge of the past.

O. T.

CONTRIBUTORS

FIELD WORK

The names of the staff and those visitors who undertook supervision of field work or other duties are given below, but the list would not be complete without grateful mention of the presence of Mrs. Starkey and her children in camp during several seasons.

It would be the wish of all concerned to record the splendid service over many years of the Arab staff and workers. While it is impossible to mention them all, SULTAN BAKHYT from Quft, Egypt, acted as Foreman, and SALIM MUHAMMED, HASSAN AWAD EL-QUTSHAN, ABD EL-KARYM ES-SALAAMEH and the three brothers, SALMAN, SULEYMAN and ABDULLA ALY, were among those who left their homes in South Palestine each year to join the Expedition.

J. L. STARKEY, 1932–1938

L. HARDING, 1932–1936
R. RICHMOND BROWN, 1932–1937
C. H. INGE, 1932–1938
MISS O. TUFNELL, 1932–1938
W. B. K. SHAW, 1932–1935
H. W. PUMMELL, 1933–1938
DONALD BROWN, 1932–1935
MR. and MRS. H. DUNSCOMBE COLT, 1932–1933
H. H. McWILLIAMS, 1932–1933
L. UPTON WAY, 1932–1933
R. M. COX, 1933–1934
MISS E. DYOTT (Mrs. W. B. K. Shaw), 1934–1935
G. I. GOULDEN, 1934–1935

J. RICHMOND, 1934–1935
H. V. BONNEY, 1935–1938
A. LEWIS, 1935–1936
MISS L. McNAIR SCOTT (Mrs. Murray-Thriepland), 1935–1936
G. B. GARDINER, 1935–1936
MR. and MRS. E. F. WARREN HASTINGS, 1936–1938
J. S. KIRKMAN, 1936–1938
MISS B. H. PARKER, 1936–1937
MISS J. CROWFOOT (Mrs. Payne), 1936–1937
MISS M. V. SETON WILLIAMS, 1937–1938
MISS NINA CUMING, 1937–1938
N. SHIAH, 1938

FIELD SURVEY, PLANS AND DRAWINGS

The original field survey was made by MR. SHAW, the Expedition's surveyor from 1932 to 1935. MR. GOULDEN took his place in 1935 until the following season, when MR. BONNEY joined the Expedition. The latter prepared most of the plans for publication, and additional drawings have been made by MR. S. P. HOWES, MR. L. J. F. YELL, MISS MINA GREENHILL, MRS. A. GELL, MR. H. M. STEWART and MR. NICHOLAS THOMAS.

PHOTOGRAPHY

MR. RICHMOND BROWN was the Expedition's photographer from 1932 to 1937, and most of the views on Plates 1–26 are his work. In the final year MISS SETON WILLIAMS, MR. C. RAAD and MR. SCHWEIG, Official Photographer to the Government of Palestine Department of Antiquities, completed the photographic records of the Expedition. Though most of the objects were photographed in camp and are reproduced in this publication from the excellent field records, supplementary photographs were made in London by MR. M. B. COOKSON, Official Photographer to the Institute of Archaeology, and MR. S. W. MICHIELI of the Wellcome Research Institution. MR. I. A. MacDONALD photographed the scaraboid, Fig. 35.

REPAIR AND RECONSTRUCTION OF POTTERY

Miss Olive Starkey, of the Institute of Archaeology, was again responsible for the repair and reconstruction of the pottery collections, and it is due to her great care and technical ability that the vessels are now fully restored. Dr. H. Plenderleith of the British Museum Laboratory extended the facilities of his department on many occasions for the treatment of fragile objects.

TEXT

Dr. Margaret A. Murray gave the Expedition the benefit of her profound knowledge of Egyptian hieroglyphs in the elucidation of the scarabs, seals and amulets.

Dr. David Diringer is responsible for the summary and conclusions on all the Early Hebrew epigraphic material from the site, and prepared the bibliography of all references to the Lachish Letters which have been made by other scholars.

Sir J. D. Beazley and Miss J. Du Plat Taylor provided notes on the Attic wares found in the post-exilic buildings.

Miss Seton Williams examined and compared the beads, the metal and the limestone altars, besides giving much assistance in the early stages of the preparation of this book.

Miss Linda Melton has compiled lists, checked statistics, prepared the text for publication, and made the Index. Her help has been of the greatest value throughout the final stages.

For astringent comment on literary style, the author is much indebted to Mr. C. E. Vulliamy, who has patiently perused both manuscript and proof. Miss K. M. Kenyon has kindly read the section on pottery in Part IV. Many colleagues and friends, too numerous to name, have given generous help and encouragement. Members of the Wellcome Foundation have responded most courteously to varied requests, and their expert knowledge, allied to the high standard observed at the Oxford University Press, has eased many typographical problems.

IDENTIFICATIONS

Professor F. E. Zeuner, Mr. L. A. Lacaille and Mr. P. M. Game identified geological specimens, and Mr. D. Baden-Powell contributed notes on fossil and more recent shells.

To supplement Mr. D. L. Risdon's report in Biometrika, Volume 31, 1939 (The Study of the Cranial and other Human Remains from Palestine excavated at Tell-ed-Duweir) Dr. I. G. Cunnison measured the skulls found after that publication had appeared. Miss Madeleine Giles (Mrs. Smith) made the comparisons and prepared the report for publication, under the supervision of Dr. J. C. Trevor of the University Museum of Archaeology and Ethnology, Cambridge.

The late Miss D. M. A. Bate prepared the report on the animal remains found in the ossuary groups, and Miss J. E. King identified other specimens.

Miss Virginia Grace, of the Institute of Advanced Studies, Princeton, U.S.A., examined the inscriptions on the Rhodian jar handles, and dated them in accordance with her classification.

Mr. D. B. Harden, of the Ashmolean Museum, Oxford, reported on the glass objects found on the site.

Mr. Kirkman applied himself indefatigably to the cleaning and identification of the coins and prepared the list for publication.

Mr. A. Reifenberg, of the Soil Science Laboratory, The Hebrew University, Jerusalem, supplied the report which is quoted on p. 246.

GOVERNMENT OF PALESTINE UNDER BRITISH MANDATE, DEPARTMENT OF ANTIQUITIES, JERUSALEM

During six seasons' work, the Expedition received generous help and encouragement from all officials connected with the Department. MR. E. T. RICHMOND was succeeded as Director of Antiquities by MR. R. W. HAMILTON, and throughout their years of office they extended all facilities to every member of the Expedition.

MR. J. H. ILIFFE, Keeper of the Palestine Museum, made the annual division of antiquities with great consideration and care.

UNIVERSITY OF LONDON, INSTITUTE OF ARCHAEOLOGY

Since 1936 the Expedition has occupied rooms at St. John's Lodge, Regent's Park, which were most generously made available by the Director, Dr. R. E. M. Wheeler, and Committee of the then newly founded Institute of Archaeology.

From that time onwards, members of the Expedition have enjoyed the expert advice and helpful co-operation of the Professorial, Administrative and Technical staff of the Institute, and these unique facilities have solved many practical difficulties and eased many burdens. When war ended, the expansion and growth of the Institute activities made many new claims on space; the Wellcome Trustees and the Expedition staff therefore owe a special debt of gratitude to the present Director, Professor V. Gordon Childe, who has allowed the Expedition to remain in much-needed premises through the crucial years of publication. In recognition, the type specimens, photographs and records are to be presented to the University of London, Institute of Archaeology, and will form part of the University collections.

CONTENTS

LIST OF ILLUSTRATIONS

15

(*For Pictorial Summary of Levels I–VI see p. 102.*)

BIBLIOGRAPHY WITH ABBREVIATIONS

AAA   Annals of Archaeology and Anthropology, University of Liverpool. (Liverpool, 1908–1940).

AASOR   Annual of the American School of Oriental Research. (New Haven, 1920–).

AG   PETRIE, F.: Ancient Gaza, I–IV. BSAE LII–LVI. (London, 1931–1934).

AJA   American Journal of Archaeology, Archaeological Institute of America. (Concord, 1885–).

Amulets   PETRIE, F.: Amulets. (London, 1914).

Anthedon   PETRIE, F., and ELLIS, J. C.: Anthedon. BSAE LVIII. (London, 1937).
Antiquity. (Gloucester, 1927–).

APEF   Annual of the Palestine Exploration Fund. (London, 1911–).
Archaeologia. (London, 1849–).
The Archaeology of Palestine: ALBRIGHT, W. F. (London, 1949).
Arslan Tash: THUREAU-DANGIN, F., BARROIS, A., DOSSIN, G. and DUNAND, M. (Paris, 1931).

AS   GRANT, ELIHU, and WRIGHT, G. E.: Rumeileh, 'Ain Shems Excavations, Vols. I–V. (Haverford, 1931–1939).

BASOR   Bulletin of the American School of Oriental Research.

BDS   PETRIE, F.: Buttons and Design Scarabs. BSAE XXXVIII. (London, 1925).
Biblical Researches in Palestine: ROBINSON, E. (London, 1856).
Biometrika. See under Risdon.

BM   BLISS, F. J., and MACALISTER, R. A. S.: Excavations in Palestine. (London, 1902).
Bogazköy: BITTEL, K. and GUTERBOCK, H. G. (Berlin, 1935).

BP I   PETRIE, F., and TUFNELL, O.: Beth-pelet I. BSAE XLVIII. (London, 1930).

BS   GRANT, ELIHU: Beth-shemesh. (Haverford, 1929).

B-S   ROWE, ALAN: Beth-Shan, Vol. I. (Pennsylvania, 1930.) FITZGERALD, G. M.: Vol. II, Pt. II (1930).
ROWE, ALAN: Vol. II, Pt. I (1940). FITZGERALD, G. M.: Vol. III (1931).

BZ   SELLERS, O. P.: Citadel of Beth-Zur. (Philadelphia, 1933).

CAH   Cambridge Ancient History. (Cambridge, 1928–).

Carchemish   WOOLLEY, C. L.: Carchemish: Part II, The Town Defences. (London, 1921).

CFBA   VAN BUREN, E. DOUGLAS: Clay Figurines of Babylonia and Assyria. Yale Oriental Series XVI. (London, 1930).
La Civilisation Primitive en Italie: MONTELIUS, O. (Stockholm, 1895–1910).

Corinth   BRONEER, O.: Corinth, Vol. IV, Pt. II, Terracotta Lamps. (Harvard, 1930).

CPP   DUNCAN, J. G.: Corpus of Palestinian Pottery. BSAE XLIX. (London, 1930).

Déchelette   DÉCHELETTE, JOSEPH: Manuel d'Archéologie Préhistorique, Celtique et Gallo-Romaine. (Paris, 1924).

DP   Denkmäler Palästinas: WATZINGER, C. (Leipzig, 1935).
Excavations at Dura-Europos, Sixth Season, 1932–1933: ROSTOVTZEFF, M. I., BELLINGER, A. R., HOPKINS, C., and WELLES, C. B. (Yale, 1936).

FFSV   PETRIE, F.: Funeral Furniture of Egypt; Stone and Metal Vases. (London, 1937).

FGO   BLINKENBERG, C.: Fibules Grecques et Orientales. (København, 1926).
Fouilles de Sialk, Vol. II, Musée du Louvre: GHIRSHMAN, R. (Paris, 1939).
Fouilles de Tepe-Giyan, Musée du Louvre: CONTENAU, G., and GHIRSHMAN, R. (Paris, 1935).

19

FPGK	MULLER, V.: Frühe Plastik in Griechenland und Kleinasien. (Augsburg, 1929).
FS	VAN INGEN, W.: Figurines from Seleucia on the Tigris. (London, 1939).
	Géographie de la Palestine: ABEL, F.-M. (Paris, 1933 and 1938).
Gerar	PETRIE, F.: Gerar. BSAE XLIII. (London, 1928).
Gezer	MACALISTER, R. A. S.: The Excavation of Gezer, 1902–1905 and 1907–1909, Vols. I–III. (London, 1912).
GSCE	GJERSTAD, E.: The Swedish Cyprus Expedition, Vols. I–IV. (Stockholm, 1934–1937).
Hama	RIIS, P. J.: Les Cimetières à Crémation. (København, 1948).
HIC	PETRIE, F., and DUNCAN, J. G.: Hyksos and Israelite Cities. BSAE XII. (London, 1906).
	History of Egypt: PETRIE, F. (London, 1905).
HG	Historical Geography of the Holy Land: SMITH, G. ADAM. (London, 1915).
	Hittite Seals: HOGARTH, D. G. (Oxford, 1930).
IKG	PETRIE, F.: Illahun, Kahun and Gurob. (London, 1871).
ILN	Illustrated London News.
	Iraq, British School of Archaeology in Iraq. (London, 1934–).
	Journal of the Royal Anthropological Institute. (London, 1900–).
	Kurzes Bibelworterbuch: GUTHE, C. E. (Berlin, 1903).
L. I	TORCZYNER, H., HARDING, L., LEWIS, A., and STARKEY, J. L.: The Lachish Letters. (Oxford, 1938).
L. II	TUFNELL, O., INGE, C. H., and HARDING. L.: The Fosse Temple. (Oxford, 1940).
Lahun II	PETRIE, F., BRUNTON, G., and MURRAY, M. A.: Lahun II. BSAE XXXIII. (London, 1923).
	Man, Royal Anthropological Institute. (London, 1912–).
Manuel	BARROIS, A. G.: Manuel d'Archéologie Biblique. (Paris, 1939).
M. I	LAMON, R. S., and SHIPTON, G. M.: Megiddo I. (Chicago, 1939).
M. II	LOUD, GORDON: Megiddo II. (Chicago, 1948).
Memphis I	PETRIE, F., and WALKER, J. H.: Memphis I. BSAE. XV. (London, 1908).
	Mission Archéologique en Arabie: JAUSSEN and SAVIGNAC. (Paris, 1909–1922).
MMC	BLISS, F. J.: A Mound of Many Cities. (London, 1894).
MRMC	MAY, H. G., and ENGBERG, R. M.: Material Remains of the Megiddo Cult. (Chicago, 1935).
MS	Mélanges Syriens, Vols. I and II. (Paris, 1939).
MT	GUY, P. L. O., and ENGBERG, R. M.: Megiddo Tombs. (Chicago, 1938).
Naukratis I	PETRIE, F.: Naukratis I. (London, 1886).
NS	NEWBERRY, P. E.: Scarabs. (London, 1906).
ODU	PETRIE, F.: Objects of Daily Use. BSAE XLII. (London, 1927).
OIC	Oriental Institute Communications, University of Chicago.
OIP	Oriental Institute Publications, University of Chicago. (Chicago, 1924–).
	The Other Side of the Jordan: GLUECK, NELSON. (New Haven, 1945).
PAC	PETRIE, F.: Arts and Crafts of Ancient Egypt. (London, 1909).
PEQ	Palestine Exploration Fund Quarterly Statement. (London, 1869–).
PPS	DEBEVOISE, N. C.: Parthian Pottery from Seleucia on the Tigris. (Ann Arbor, 1934).
PSC	PETRIE, F.: Scarabs and Cylinders. BSAE XXIX. (London, 1917).
	Painted Tombs in the Necropolis of Marissa: PETERS, F. and THIERSCH, H. (London, 1905).
PTW	PETRIE, F.: Tools and Weapons. BSAE XXX. (London, 1917).
QB	BRUNTON, G.: Qau and Badari III. BSAE L. (London, 1930).

QDAP	Quarterly of the Department of Antiquities, Palestine. (Jerusalem, 1931–1946).
	Rapport préliminaire sur sept campagnes de fouilles à Hama en Syrie: INGHOLT, HARALD. (Copenhagen, 1940).
	Revue Biblique. (Paris, 1932–).
RES	ROWE, ALAN: A Catalogue of Egyptian Scarabs in the Palestine Archaeological Museum. (Cairo, 1936).
	Report on the Excavation of the Roman Fort at Richborough, Kent: BUSHE-FOX, J. P. (Oxford, 1928).
Risdon	RISDON, D. L.: A Study of Cranial and other Human Remains from Palestine excavated at Tell Duweir. (Biometrika 31, London, 1939).
S	REISNER, G. A., FISHER, C. S., and LYON, D. G.: Harvard Excavations at Samaria, Vols. I–II. (Cambridge, Mass., 1924).
	Schweich Lectures, The Religion of Ancient Palestine in the Light of Archaeology: COOK, A. S. (London, 1925).
Soli	WESTHOLM, A.: The Temple of Soli. (Stockholm, 1936).
SS III	CROWFOOT, J. W., and KENYON, K. M.: Sebastiyeh-Samaria, Vol. III. (In preparation).
	Stratigraphie Comparée et Chronologie de l'Asie Occidentale: SCHAEFFER, C. F. A. (London, 1948).
STTN	BADÈ, W. F.: Some Tombs of Tell en-Nasbeh discovered in 1929. (Berkeley, 1931).
SW	SELLIN, E. and WATZINGER, C.: Jericho. (Leipzig, 1913).
	Syria, Revue d'Art et Archéologie. (Paris, 1920).
Tanis	PETRIE, F.: Tanis I. (London, 1885.) Tanis II. (London, 1888).
TBM	See AASOR.
TCHP	THOMPSON, H. A.: Two Centuries of Hellenistic Pottery. Hesperia, Vol. III, No. 4. (Athens, 1934).
TFN	LEGRAIN, LÉON: Terracottas from Nippur. (Pennsylvania, 1930).
TH	PETRIE, F.: Tell el-Heṣi (Lachish). (London, 1891).
TMTH	CATON-THOMPSON, G.: The Tombs and Moon Temple of Hureidha. (London, 1944).
TN I	McCOWN, C. C.: Tell en-Nasbeh. (Berkeley, 1947).
TN II	WAMPLER, J. C.: Tell en-Nasbeh: The Pottery. (Berkeley, 1947).
UCL	University of London, University College, Edwards Library.
	Westminster Historical Atlas. (Philadelphia, 1945).
Vroulia	KINCH, K. F.: Fouilles de Vroulia (Rhodes). (Berlin, 1914).
Vrokastro	HALL, E. H.: Excavations in Eastern Crete. (Philadelphia, 1914).
ZAS	Zeitschrift für Ägyptische Sprache.
ZAW	Zeitschrift für die Alttestamentliche Wissenschaft.
ZDPV	Zeitschrift des Deutschen Palästina-Vereins. (Leipzig, 1895–1943).

BIBLIOGRAPHY OF THE LACHISH OSTRACA

1938

ALBRIGHT, W. F.: The Oldest Hebrew Letters. BASOR 70, pp. 11–17.

DUSSAUD, R.: Le Prophète Jérémie et les lettres de Lakish. Syria XIX, pp. 256–271.

ELBOGEN, I.: Review in Monatschrift für die Geschichte der Wissenschaft des Judenthums LXXXII pp. 198–203.

ELLIGER, K.: Die Ostraca von Lachis, Palästinajahrbuch des deutschen evangelischen Instituts für Altertumswissenschaft des Heiligen Landes zu Jerusalem XXXIV, 1938, pp. 30–58.

GINSBERG, H. L.: Lachish Notes. BASOR 71, pp. 24–27.

GORDON, C. H.: Notes on the Lachish Letters. BASOR 70, pp. 17–18.

HARRIS, Z. S.: The Lachish Letters. Journal of Biblical Literature LVII, pp. 437–439.

HEMPEL, J.: Die Ostraka von Lakiš. ZAW N.S. XV, pp. 126–139.

JACK, J. W.: The Lachish Letters, their Date and Import. An Examination of Professor Torczyner's View. PEQ LXX, pp. 165–187; The Lachish Letters. Expository Times XLIX, pp. 380–381.

JOÜON, P.: Lachish. Revue des Études Sémitiques, pp. 84–88.

KAHLE, P.: Review, Zeitschrift der Deutschen Morgenländischen Gesellschaft XCII, pp. 271–276.

REIDER, J.: The Lachish Letters. Jewish Quarterly Review N.S. XXIX, pp. 225–239.

YEIVIN, S.: The Lachish Letters (in Hebrew). Bulletin of the Jewish Palestine Exploration Society VI, pp. 1–7.

1939

ALBRIGHT, W. F.: A reëxamination of the Lachish Letters. BASOR 73, pp. 16–21.

BIRNBAUM, S.: The Lachish Ostraca. PEQ LXXI, pp. 20–28, 91–110.

BURROWS, M.: Journal of Religion XIX, pp. 272–276.

CANTINEAU, J.: Review, Archiv für Orientforschung XII, pp. 386–388.

CASSUTO, U.: Monatschrift für die Geschichte der Wissenschaft des Judenthums LXXXIII, pp. 389–400: this article was not published owing to war conditions, but it has appeared as an offprint and is quoted by Torczyner and others.

DE VAUX, R.: Les Ostraka de Lâchis. Revue Biblique XLVIII, pp. 181–206.

DOSSIN, G.: Signaux lumineux au Pays de Mari. Revue d'Assyriologie XXXVI, pp. 174–186.

ELLIGER, K.: Zu Text und Schrift der Ostraka von Lachis. ZDPV LXII, pp. 63–89.

GIBSON, D. J.: Chronology of the Book of Jeremiah and the Lachish Letters.

JIRKU, A.: Lag das alte Lakiš auf dem Tell ed-Duweir ? ZAW N.S. XVI, pp. 152–153.

SELMS, A. VAN: De brieven van Lakiš. Jaarbericht Ex Oriente Lux VI, pp. 84–88.

STUMMER, F.: Briefe auf Tonscherben aus der Zeit des Propheten Jeremias. Das Heilige Land in Vergangenheit und Gegenwart (Cologne), pp. 34–39.

THOMAS, D. WINTON: The Lachish Letters. Journal of Theological Studies XL, pp. 1–15.

VACCARI, A.: Le lettere di Lachis. In margine al libro di Geremia. Biblica XX, pp. 180–199. Lettere dell' antica Palestina in margine alla Bibbia, Civiltà Cattolica, 1939, pp. 121–134, and 224–232.

VELLAS, B. M.: Τὰ νέα ὄστρακα τῆς Λάχης, (Athens).

VINCENT, A.: Les Lettres de Lachis. Journal des Savants, pp. 61–68.

ZOLLI, I.: Le lettere di Lakhish. Religio, pp. 81–84.

1940

ALBRIGHT, W. F.: Review, Kirjath Sepher XVI, pp. 310–312.

BALAZS, G.: Egy feltárt bibliai város ("An excavated Biblical city") a Lachisi (Tell ed-Duweir). Ásótások archeológiai és epigráfiai eredményei (Budapest), pp. 63–104.

BENTZEN, A.: Lakis brevere . . . Gads Danske Magazin XXIV, pp. 49 sqq.

GINSBERG, H. L.: Lachish Ostraca New and Old. BASOR 80, pp. 10–13.

HAMMERSHAIMB, E.: Lachish brevere. Dansk Theologisk Tidsskr.

HROZNÝ, B.: Review, Archiv Orientální, pp. 303–304.

PEDERSEN, J.: Review, Der Alte Orient XXXIX, pp. 144–152.

THOMAS, D. WINTON: The Site of Ancient Lachish: The Evidence of Ostracon IV from Tell ed-Duweir. PEQ LXXII, pp. 148–149.

TORCZYNER, H.: Te'udoth Lakish: Mikhtabirim miyemê Yermiyahû ha-nabî (Jerusalem).

1941

ALBRIGHT, W. F.: The Lachish Letters after Five Years. BASOR 82, pp. 18–24.

MICHAUD, H.: Le témoignage des Ostraca de Tell Duweir concernant le prophète Jérémie. Revue des Études Sémitiques, pp. 42–60.

1942

CHAPIRA, B.: Les lettres de Lakiš. Revue des Études Sémitiques, pp. 105–173.

JACK, J. W.: Lachish Letters. Expository Times LIII, p. 193; Lachish: Thy Servant a Dog. Ibid., p. 369.

OUDENRIJN, M. A. VAN DEN: Les fouilles de Lākîš et l'étude de l'Ancien Testament. (Fribourg en Suisse.)

1943

DIRINGER, D.: On Ancient Hebrew Inscriptions Discovered at Tell ed-Duweir (Lachish): The Lachish Ostraca Nos. XIX–XXI. PEQ LXXV, pp. 89–99 and Pls. V–VI.

DRIVER, G. R.: Notes on Some Recently Recovered Proper Names. BASOR 90, p. 34.

1944

LANE, J. and MILLER, M. S.: Encyclopedia of Bible Life. (New York.)

ORLINSKY, H. M.: Journal of Biblical Literature LXIII, p. 43, n. 34.

1945

ALBRIGHT, W. F.: Postscript to Professor May's Article. BASOR 97, p. 26.

MAY, H. G.: Lachish Letter IV: 7–10. BASOR 97, pp. 22–25.

ORLINSKY, H. M.: A Rejoinder (to Torczyner's Abbreviation or Haplography?). Journal of Biblical Literature LXIV, pp. 400–402.

TORCZYNER, H.: Abbreviation or Haplography? op. cit., p. 399; Yes, Haplography! op. cit., pp. 545–546.

1946

THOMAS, D. WINTON: "The Prophet" in the Lachish Ostraca (London). The Lachish Ostraca: Professor Torczyner's latest views. PEQ LXXVIII, pp. 38–42; Jerusalem in the Lachish Ostraca. Op. cit., pp. 86–91.

1947

ALBRIGHT, W. F.: Review, BASOR 105, p. 15.

MIDDLETON, R. D.: Review, Theology L, p. 273; Expository Times LVIII, p. 292.

1948

GINSBERG, H. L.: An Aramaic Contemporary of the Lachish Letters. BASOR 111, p. 24.

1950

THOMAS, D. WINTON: Ostraca XIX–XXI from Tell ed-Duweir (Lachish). In Essays and Studies presented to Stanley Arthur Cook, Cambridge Oriental Series No. 2.

THOMAS, D. WINTON: The Lachish Ostraca (in Hebrew), Melilah III.

ABBREVIATIONS

AE	bronze	gs.	glass	pk.	pink
am.	amethyst	gy.	grey	Pl.	Plate
AR	silver	gz.	glaze	pol.	polished
AV	gold	in.	inside	pst.	paste
bf.	buff	irr.	irregular	pt.	part
bk.	black	H.	hard fire	rd.	red
bl.	blue	LB	Late Bronze Age	Rm.	Room
bn.	brown	LI	Late Iron Age	S.	soft fire
bur.	burnish	lmst.	limestone	sca.	scarab
cm.	cream	lt.	light	spi.	spiral
cn.	carnelian	M.	medium fire	str.	structure
con.	concentric	MB	Middle Bronze Age	veg.	vegetable
dec.	decoration	MI	Middle Iron Age	vert.	vertical
dk.	dark	mot.	mottled	wh.	wheel
EI	Early Iron Age	NP	not published	wt.	white
Fe	iron	out.	outside	yw.	yellow
gn.	green	p.	page		

NOTES

Levels I–VI indicate the stratigraphical divisions of the mound numbered from the top downwards, as far as they were examined up to the close of excavations in 1938.

"Houses I, II or III", with a room or area number, correspond to Levels I, II or III in the stratification of the mound.

Grid references are given in front of room numbers, e.g., H.17: 1087. H.17 refers to the Grid Plan on Pl. 108, while 1087 refers to the room or area numbered on Pl. 114.

References to NE., NW., SE., and SW. corners in the Plate Descriptions indicate that the objects concerned were found on the slopes of the mound outside the lines of fortification.

The letters "D/X" indicate that the object concerned was found on the surface of the mound.

The excavations around the mound were divided into areas described as Cemetery Areas 100, 200, 500, 700, 1000, 4000, 6000 and 7000. Numbers not used in this series were to be allocated to intervening areas which either proved sterile or were not excavated in 1932–1938. Where area numbers are given as locus numbers in the Plate Descriptions, e.g. "500", it means that the object concerned was found on the surface in that area. The distribution of Cemetery Area numbers is noted on Pl. 108.

The pottery forms throughout the publication are numbered to correspond with the sequence 1–700 on Pls. 78–103. An asterisk against the number denotes that the vessel has been photographed, and the appropriate plate number is given below.

Figures in brackets denote the number of specimens from a particular locus or of a particular type.

In cases where more than one Field Number is given, the first is that of the type specimen, and the following numbers are those of other examples, originally listed as separate types, which are now amalgamated owing to similarity of form.

The letters "PM" prefacing a number indicate that an example of the object concerned was acquired by the Department of Antiquities of the Government of Palestine under British Mandate, and is now in the Palestine Museum, Jerusalem.

The name "Colt" indicates that an example of the object concerned was allocated to H. Dunscombe Colt in 1932–1933, and is now in the United States of America.

INTRODUCTION

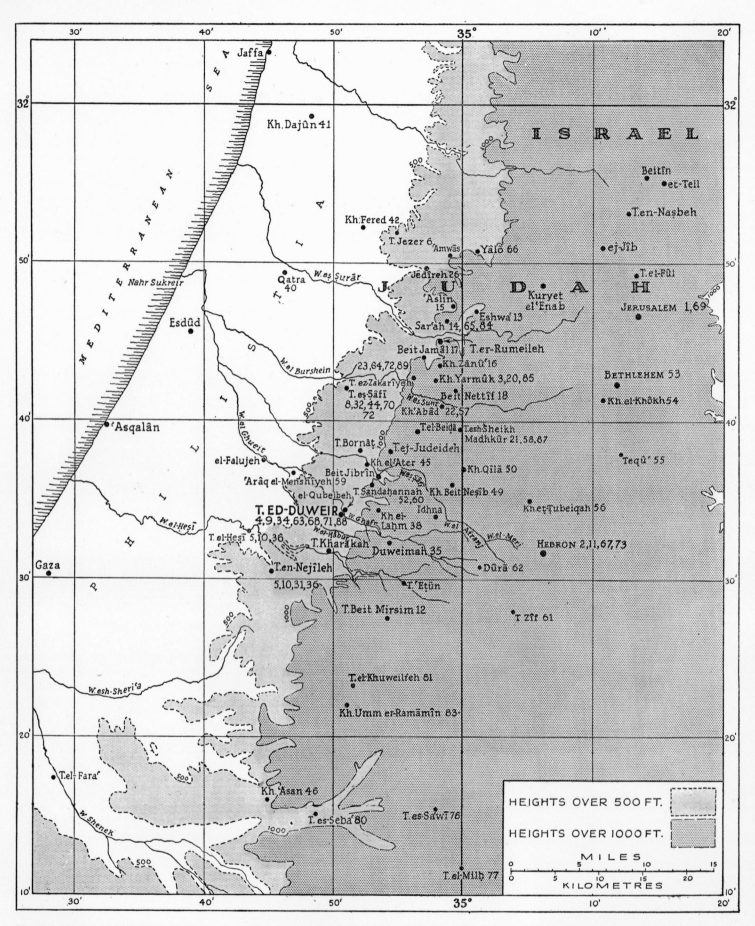

MAP OF PALESTINE WITH ARABIC NAMES OF SOME IRON AGE SITES MENTIONED IN THE BIBLE

PRESENT IDENTIFICATIONS OF SOME IRON AGE SITES

REFERENCES TO LACHISH AND ASSOCIATED TOWNS IN TOPOGRAPHICAL
PASSAGES OF THE BIBLE

No. on map	Revised Version	Hebrew Bible (when differing from R.V.)	MODERN PLACE NAMES Arabic
	Joshua X: 5 f.:		
1	Jerusalem	Yerûshalaim	El-Qûds
2	Hebron	Ḥebrôn	El-Khalîl
3	Jarmuth	Yarmûth	Kh. Yarmûk
4	Lachish	Lakîsh	Tell ed-Duweir
5	Eglon		Tell el-Ḥesi *or* Tell en-Nejîleh
6	Gezer		Tell Jezer
	Joshua X: 28–43:		
7	Makkedah	Maqqedah	?
8	Libnah		Tell eṣ-Ṣâfî *or* Tell Bornāt
9	Lachish		see 4
10	Eglon		see 5
11	Hebron		see 2
12	Debir		Tell Beit Mirsim
	Joshua XV: 33–44:		
13	Eshtaol		Eshwa‘
14	Zoreah	Sor‘ah	Sar‘ah
15	Ashnah		‘Aslin
16	Zanoah	Zanoaḥ	Kh. Zānû’
17	En-gannim	‘Ein Gannîm	Beit Jamâl (?)
18	Tappuah	Tappuaḥ	Beit Nettîf
19	Enam	‘Einam	?
20	Jarmuth		see 3
21	Adullam		Tell esh-Sheikh Madhkûr
22	Socoh	Sokoh	Kh. ‘Abbâd
23	Azekah	‘Azeqah	Tell ez-Zakarîyeh
24	Sharaim	Sha‘arayim	?
25	Adithaim	‘Adithayim	?
26	Gederah		Jedîreh
27	Gederothaim		?
28	Zenan	Ṣenan	?
29	Hadashah	Ḥadashah	?
30	Migdal-Gad		?
31	Dilean	Dile‘n	Tell en-Nejîleh (?)
32	Mizpeh	Miṣpeh	Tell eṣ-Ṣâfî (?)
33	Joktheel	Yoqtheel	?
34	Lachish		see 4, 9

No. on map	Revised Version	Hebrew Bible (when differing from R.V.)	Arabic
35	Bozkath	Boṣqath	Duweimah (?)
36	Eglon		see 5, 10
37	Cabbon	Kabbon	?
38	Lahmam	Laḥmam	Kh. el-Laḥm (?)
39	Kithlish		?
40	Gederoth		Qaṭra
41	Beth-Dagon		Kh. Dajûn (?)
42	Naamah	Na'amah	Kh. Fered (?)
43	Makkedah		see 7
44	Libnah		see 8
45	Ether	'Ether	Kh. el-'Ater
46	Ashan	'Ashan	Kh. 'Asan
47	Jiphtah	Yiptaḥ	?
48	Ashnah		Idhna
49	Nezib	Neṣîb	Kh. Beit Neṣîb
50	Keilah	Qe'îlah	Kh. Qîlā
51	Achzib	Akzib	Tell el-Beiḍā (?)
52	Mareshah		Tell Sandaḥannah
	II Chronicles XI: 5–10:		
53	Beth-lehem	Beît-leḥem	Beit Laḥm
54	Etam	'Îtam	Kh. el-Khôkh
55	Tekoa	Teqôa'	Tequ'
56	Beth-zur	Beît-ṣûr	Kh. eṭ-Ṭubeiqah
57	Shoco	Sôkô	see 22
58	Adullam		see 21
59	Gath		'Arâq el-Menshîyeh (?)
60	Mareshah		see 52
61	Ziph	Zîph	Tell Zîf
62	Adoraim	Adôrayim	Dûrā
63	Lachish		see 4, 9, 34
64	Azekah		see 23
65	Zorah		see 14
66	Aijalon	Aiyalôn	Yâlō
67	Hebron		see 2, 11
	II Kings XVIII–XIX, II Chronicles XXXII, Isaiah XXVI–XXXVIII:		
68	Lachish		see 4, 9, 34, 63
69	Jerusalem		see 1
70	Libnah		see 8
	Jeremiah XXXIV: 7:		
71	Lachish		see 4, 9, 34, 63, 68
72	Azekah		see 23, 64
	Nehemiah XI: 15–30:		
73	Kirjath-arba (Hebron)	Qiryath ha-Arba'	see 2, 11, 67

No. on map	Revised Version	Hebrew Bible (when differing from R.V.)	Arabic
74	Dibon	Dimonah	?
75	Jekabzeel (Kabzeel)	Yeqabṣeel	?
76	Jeshua (Shema)	Yeshua'	Tell es-Sa'wī
77	Moladah		Tell el-Milḥ
78	Beth-phelet (-paleṭ, -peleṭ)	Beît-Peleṭ	Tell el-Fara *or* Tell esh-Sheri'ah
79	Hazar-shual	Ḥaṣar Shû'al	?
80	Beersheba	Beer Sheba'	Tell es-Seba'
81	Ziklag	Ṣiqlag	Tell el-Khuweilfeh (?)
82	Mekonah		?
83	En-rimmon	'Eîn Rimmon	Kh. Umm er-Ramāmîn
84	Zareah		see 14, 65
85	Jarmuth		see 3, 20
86	Zanoah	Zanoaḥ	?
87	Adullam		see 21, 58
88	Lachish		see 4, 9, 34, 63, 68, 71
89	Azekah		see 23, 64, 72

Place-Names. The list of places is given in order of the Old Testament Books, and should be read with reference to the map on p. 28, where the numbers follow the modern Arabic names of the sites as identified in the *Westminister Historical Atlas to the Bible Géographie de la Palestine* by Père F.-M. Abel was also consulted.

The list gives three parallel readings in English, Hebrew and Arabic transliteration, based on the established system, but wherever inconsistencies in spelling are discovered in the main text, it should be assumed that the principle defended by T. E. Lawrence in *Revolt in the Desert* has prevailed.

THE EXPEDITION—METHODS AND AIMS

> The man who knows and dwells in history adds a new dimension to his existence; he no longer lives in the one plane of present ways and thought, he lives in the whole space of life, past, present and dimly future.
>
> PETRIE: *Methods and Aims.*

FROM the first, it was recognised that a long-term programme of excavation was required to deal with the formidable mound of Tell ed-Duweir. Yet J. L. Starkey saw it as part of his wide intention to seek the sources of foreign influences which had imposed themselves on Palestinian culture in all periods, and he was prepared to move in the direction indicated by the results from this first essay.

He looked for a settlement north of the Wadis Ghuzzeh and Sheriah, and within the region of the Philistine Pentapolis, for he was hoping to gain fresh light on the origins of the Sea Peoples and to find contacts with Egypt and Mesopotamia in the earliest times.

In the spring of 1932 he became interested in two sharply contrasted sites, 'Araq el-Menshîyeh (Tell Areini), on the edge of the coastal plain, at the junction of the two main branches of the Wadi Ghueit, and Tell ed-Duweir, in the foothills which divert the course of a smaller tributary of the same great artery from east to west.

Tell Areini was a small mound based on a promontory in the alluvial plain, where ancient buildings would have been made of brick. Tell ed-Duweir was four times the size of Tell Areini, and it was clear from the outset that the whole site was encumbered with large stones.

On his return to England that summer Starkey approached Sir Henry Wellcome and obtained the interest of Sir Charles Marston, Sir Robert Mond and Mr. H. Dunscombe Colt. He discussed with them the relative value and importance of both sites, and it was typical of Sir Henry that he at once agreed to support the more extensive plan.

It was thus that the Wellcome–Colt Archaeological Research Expedition set out in October 1932. The following year Mr. Colt withdrew to undertake fresh excavations at Esbeita, and after Sir Henry's death in 1936 Sir Charles Marston increased his financial support and his name was included in that of the Expedition.

Like other more ancient structures on the site, the modern camphouse was built of mud and stones, and the walls were faced with white lime plaster from the calcined breaches of the city. Year by year the camp grew in extent around three sides of an open court (Pl. 7: 1), and from that commanding position near the south-west corner of the mound the course of the Wadi Ghafr could be followed as it winds into the hidden recesses of the Hebron hills.

Exposed to the onslaught of wind and rain, it was not surprising that the corrugated iron roofs of the buildings did not always withstand the winter gales. At such times the comfort of a wood fire was a reminder that fuel was once easily obtained in the vicinity. Except for a stunted lote tree (*Zizyphus Spina Christi*) on the north-east side of the mound (Pl. 11: 1), which is sacred to the villagers of Qubeibeh, who will not willingly approach it after dark, there are now no trees in the neighbourhood, where Sennacherib's war artist once saw the luxuriant vine, olive and fig.

In an attempt to stem the erosion of the slopes, acacia and almond seedlings were planted round the camp, and for a few weeks each spring, scarlet anemones, wild tulip and narcissus, cyclamen and stock evoked the brief but brilliant illusion of an English garden.

The grove, the garden and the house did not long survive the closing of the camp in 1938. The local guards left in charge with an Egyptian foreman were powerless to withstand attack from a marauding band, and when part of the buildings was burnt in a second raid, their position became untenable.

The railway equipment was sold at the time of Rommel's advance to Egypt, and the villagers cleared all that was left of stores and equipment.

Equipment and Methods

Apart from the survey of the Concession Area described on p. 38, the first consideration was the proper provision of cleared space for dump heaps. This is especially important where mechanical equipment is employed, in order to ensure that tracks are laid at the correct gradient for the trucks, in the best positions to serve all sections of the work.

By 1938 Starkey had achieved his primary intention to clear the escarpment and lower slopes of the mound at three main points: the north-west corner (Cemeteries 100 and 200), the north-east corner (Cemeteries 4000 and 6000) and the south side (Cemetery 7000).

The area finally cleared at the north-west corner covered 3,900 square metres, or $1\frac{1}{4}$ acres, but owing to the presence of the Fosse Temple, it was not in full use as a dumping ground until 1935, when the steel chute[1] on the slope above was put into operation (Pl. 1: 1).

A similar chute was erected in 1936 to take the debris from the Great Shaft depression, and a track was laid from it along the flank of the south side to the dumping ground over Cemetery 7000. These chutes could be moved in sections and set up at other necessary points.

Through the generosity of Sir Robert Mond, light railway equipment was acquired, including 650 metres of 500-mm. gauge track, eight double-sided tipping wagons (Pl. 25: 6) and three platform wagons for stones.[2] Another mechanical contrivance was the Priestman Orange Peel Grab.[3]

These were, however, merely mechanical aids to speed and efficiency, and a source of pride and encouragement to the workers. They could not replace the patient skill and integrity of the men, and the sharp eyes and industry of the boys and girls working behind them, for the success of an excavation will always be due in the main to the ready co-operation of the workers. It is not enough to pay a flat daily wage to secure their interest: they must share in the benefits of careful method and appreciate its necessity. They enjoy competition, and will exert their skill to trace the line of a crumbling wall, or to recover a fragile vessel. They measure their achievement by reward, and the Expedition tried to ensure that this should be just and generous. Rates of pay, between 1932 and 1938, were 2*s.* a day for skilled men, somewhat less for unskilled labour, and an average of a shilling a day for each child.

A 10-metre section was allotted to each gang (Pl. 7: 2). When a tomb or building encroached on more than one section, the proceeds were shared between the principals—the pickmen. The less skilled diggers who filled the baskets, and the children who carried them, were rewarded for anything overlooked by the leaders.

As a final insurance, the debris from all tombs was put aside and was often sieved twice, once through large-mesh sieves, dry, and, if there were small beads, through fine-mesh sieves dipped in water.

Unskilled labour was drawn from two main sources—the villagers of Qubeibeh ibn Awad and the Bedu of the Ajjulyn tribe (Beersheba district). There was also a nucleus of trained Bedu from south of Gaza, most of whom had begun as basket boys and grown in the course of years to be most skilful workers. Two Egyptians from Quft, trained by Professor Sir Flinders Petrie, acted as foremen under a member of the staff in charge, but they had no part in the engagement, payment or dismissal of labour.

---

[1] Supplied by Messrs. F. Braby & Co., Ltd.

[2] Supplied by Messrs. Decauville of Belgium and R. Hudson, Ltd.

[3] Supplied by Messrs. W. Jones, Ltd.

THE SITE AND ITS NEIGHBOURS

HALF-WAY between Jerusalem and Gaza, the site stands athwart the Wadi Ghafr on its eastward course from Dura in the Hebron hills. The rocky barrier of the mound diverts the wadi along its eastern slope to the north-east corner (Pl. 2: 1) where the watercourse passes between the ancient city and the village of Qubeibeh ibn Awad (el-Qubeibeh), still less than a century old, on an adjoining spur (Pl. 18: 3). Beyond the village of Falujeh, where the quick descent of the river bed is checked as it approaches the plain, the wadi is merged in the greater tributaries of the Wadi el-Ghueit, which gathers the copious winter rainfall of the hills and squanders it, with the scarce earth of the valleys, in the sea.

The Wadi el-Ghueit is one of the great arteries flowing from east to west across the land between Carmel and Sinai, scoring deep furrows in the land which obstruct all movement north and south and promote it between the coast and the hills. Both ancient and modern roads therefore conform to the same well-beaten tracks, and while the foot-hills remain isolated and remote, the ceaseless traffic of trade and the recurring tide of territorial ambition move along the easier highways of the coast.

If the traveller goes to Tell ed-Duweir by the modern motor road from Gaza or Jerusalem, he will see nothing of the site until he turns off the main track, when its steep sides are visible at close range through a gap in the hills. If he uses the older and more direct way, following the line of the Roman road between north and south, the only landmark he will see at a distance is the cairn of the building which once crowned the tell, just visible above the surrounding plateau.

The full height of the mound is only exposed to view from the escarpment of the surrounding plain; founded on a natural promontory, it rises from the middle of a green, well-tilled basin, and stands nearly 40 metres above the valley, as a result of man's occupation through the centuries.

Eighteen acres (73,200 sq.m.) are enclosed within the upper scarp, and there is a pronounced tilt from east to west, so that much of the surface is conveniently displayed to an observer standing on the eastern edge of the plain. The base covers 39 acres, and is still spreading, through slow denudation of the upper slopes, though these are only slightly scarred, for the contours have been preserved by at least two stout girdles of stone which were only partly visible before excavation.

The mound is rectangular in plan, and the gradient of the slope is almost uniform on all four sides. At the south-west corner, however, an isthmus joins the tell to the southern plateau and forms the only natural line of approach, of which full advantage was taken by those who planned the system of defence.

From the highest point, the whole breadth of the country is spread out. On the east, the barrier of the Hebron hills extends in ever decreasing hummocks towards the plain, where these old hill formations, almost drained of strength and vitality, are buried under a rich emerald and brown carpet. This long, narrow coastal strip, where the agricultural future of the country lies, is firmly divided from the sea by a menacing line of sand-dune, which threatens the fertility of the land, both north and south, as far as the eye can see.

Within these boundaries, certain landmarks are outstanding.

Three and a half miles to the north-east is Tell es-Sandaḥannah, at the entrance to the Wadi eṣ-Ṣafi and the Wadi el 'Afranj, which lead to the vicinity of Hebron, marked by a white *weli*, the only building visible on the hills. Indeed, the narrow gorge is the reason for the unbroken existence of that town, which has guarded the the best means of access to the hill country (*ha-har*) from the foot-hills (*ha-Shpĕhēlah*) from the earliest times.[1]

The inhabitants of both the foot-hills and the plain were equally concerned to protect their end of this vital channel, and sites such as Tell Bornāt (Bronze Age and Iron I), Judeideh (Iron II), Sandaḥannah (Hellenistic)

---

[1] On the definition of these terms, which actually mean "the mountain" and "the plain", see G. A. Smith, HG, pp. 202 f.

and Beit Jibrin (Roman) have each in turn succeeded to the guardianship of the route. Tell ed-Duweir is well placed to control the parallel southern line along the Wadi Ghueit, and could also, in case of need, support, during the Jewish period, the smaller garrisons overlooking the pass.

The next key-point westward is also visible from Tell ed-Duweir. It is now known as 'Arâq el-Menshîyeh, and it lies some five miles away, marked by the domed tomb of Sheykh el-Areini on its summit, and pointing the easiest route to the south and to the sea. It holds a position of considerable strategic importance, since it commands the junctions of the Wadis el-Hābûr and Ghafr, and is accessible, through the valley of a tributary, to traffic using the Wadi eṣ-Ṣafi. The prominent scarp of Tell eṣ-Ṣafi, white or shining, as its name implies, is about ten miles to the north.

Tell ed-Duweir, then, is almost midway between Hebron and the sea at 'Asqalan, and it could control communication east and west. It was not, perhaps, of main strategic importance, for the best route north and south lay along the plain, and those making for Jerusalem would, if conditions were normal, use the Wadi es-Surar. During the Iron Age, however, there was no political unity between the people of the foot-hills and the plain, and the secondary route passing Tell ed-Duweir linked a chain of natural strongholds fortified by Rehoboam and maintained by his successors: Tell es-Sandaḥannah, Tell ej-Judeideh (both visible from Tell ed-Duweir), and beyond them, Tell ez-Zakarîyeh and Tell er-Rumeileh ('Ain Shems). All these mounds are identified with towns which played prominent parts in the history of Judah, and if size is any criterion, Tell ed-Duweir must have been the most important of them.

Excavations have shown that all these sites were occupied during the Iron Age, and valuable comparative material can be obtained from a study of the published reports, fully listed in the bibliography.

Towards the south, other important mounds must be considered in relation to Tell ed-Duweir. Tell Beit Mirsim, in a valley on the route between Beit Jibrin and Beersheba (Tell es-Seba), eight miles south-east of our site, has been intensively excavated for the American Schools of Oriental Research between the years 1926–1932 by Professor W. F. Albright. Seven miles west is the magnificent mound of Tell el-Ḥeṣi, where the first sectional excavation of a Palestinian site was made by the late Sir Flinders Petrie in 1890 and continued by the Rev. F. J. Bliss in the following year. Near by is the equally imposing mound of Tell en-Nejîleh, still untouched by the spade. On etymological grounds, it has some claim to represent Eglon, an identity also given by some scholars to Tell el-Ḥesi. Comparable in size to Tell Jezer and Tell ed-Duweir in the Bronze Age, there was only a fort covering less than an acre on Tell el-Ḥesi in the following period, a change which would be in keeping, if it is Eglon, with its lost importance as one of the five cities of the Amorites, for the name is missing from later historical record. Alternatively, there should be massive Iron Age defences if it were the site of Lachish, as proposed in the early years of exploration.

Twenty-five miles south-west, nearer the coast, is Tell Jemmeh, where an important section was cut through the mound by Sir Flinders Petrie on his return to Palestine in 1926.

The five great trading cities of the Philistine League were no doubt larger, but of these only Gaza ($\frac{3}{4}$ mile across), and 'Asqalan (400 m. × 260 m.) are certainly identified, while the old city of Ashdod is buried in the sands. The list given below tells its own story, while the following section will establish the position of Lachish among the strongholds of Judah.

On geographical and historical grounds, it therefore seems justifiable to identify the mound of Tell ed-Duweir with the ancient city of Lachish.

Sizes of Some Iron Age Sites

	Approximate acreage of summit		Approximate acreage of summit
Tell Jezer (Gezer)	18	Tell Beit Mirsim	7½
Tell ed-Duweir (Lachish)	18	Tell er-Rumeileh ('Ain Shems)	7
Tell Muteselim (Megiddo)	13	Tell ej-Judeideh	6½
Jerusalem	11½	Tell ez-Zakarîyeh (Azekah)	5
Tell eṣ-Ṣafi	9	Tell el-Ḥesi	1
Tell en-Naṣbeh	8		

GEOLOGY AND USE OF STONE

"The Structure and Evolution of Palestine" by Leo Picard (Bulletin of the Geological Department, Hebrew University, Jerusalem, Vol. IV, Nos. 2–4, 1943) is the source from which the information contained in the following notes is taken, and to which those who need to supplement it should refer. Fig. 12 on p. 52 of that work is reproduced (Fig. 1) by kind permission of the author. It is a particularly fortunate section for the purpose of

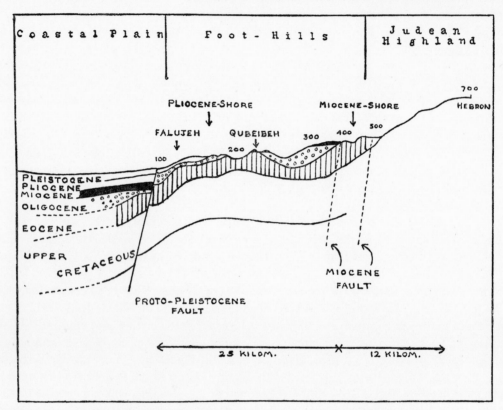

FIG. 1. Section through Tertiary deposits of Palestine at Qubeibeh

the present volume, for it shows a simplified cross-section from Hebron to the Coastal Plain, passing through the village of Qubeibeh, and makes clear the relationship of the Tertiary deposits (Eocene, Oligocene and Miocene) which exist at Tell ed-Duweir.

Professor Picard interprets the palaeogeology of the region as follows:

"The section demonstrates the position of the littoral Vindebonian, consisting of gravel and coarse calcareous sandstone, resting with sharp angular discordance on the truncated Oligo-Eocene beds. To make this position clearer, the thickness of the Miocene is exaggerated in the drawing (black in Fig. 12). In the exposures the Miocene is often eroded to the lowest gravel basis. This basis is the former Middle-Miocene abrasion plain; the foot-hill 'pene-plain' is, thus, a marine plain of denudation. Viewed from the Coastal region, this plain usually appears as an even skyline, which, however, shows a slight dip of about 1·6, or, at 12 km. distance, a gradual rise from 200 to 400 m. above sea level. The plain was thus tilted in post-Miocene times.

"As demonstrated previously, we have no clear proof that the Upper Eocene or Oligocene sea encroached upon the highest parts of the Judaean highland." (Op. cit., p. 51.)

In many places the Miocene capping rests directly on the Eocene stratum, but the late G. S. Blake was able to establish the presence of marine Oligocene at certain places in Southern Judaea. This, in Palestine, mostly lies buried below the Mio-Pilo-Pleistocene of the Coastal Plain.

36

In the section exposed at the north-west corner of Tell ed-Duweir (Grid Square D.5 on Pl. 108), four miles south-west of Beit Jibrin, the same series can be seen, and it is described by G. S. Blake in "The Stratigraphy of Palestine and its Building Stones" (Printing and Stationery Office, Jerusalem, No. 3, Palestine) on pp. 27 f.:

"The best exposure is to be seen below Tell Duweir, where Mr. Starkey has uncovered the following section:

	Metres
Crystalline limestone with numerous fossils showing in parts hard round concretions of hard *Operculina* limestone	10
Yellow marly chalks	6
Hard bedded chalk	2
Hard bedded mizzi with abundant *Operculina* passing into chalk conglomerate with blocks of foreign stone	2–4
Massive chalk (exposed)	

"The passage beds from conglomerate to mizzi are composed largely of *Operculina* and other foraminifera. In their passage upwards the beds become hard, containing less foraminifera and more molluscan remains. The conglomerates contain large blocks of chalks and hard crystalline limestone. The size and shape of these blocks suggest the near presence of an old sea cliff.

"Mr. Starkey states that the marls contain well-preserved Pectens and other fossils. In this respect and in general lithological character they resemble the strata of the Ramle quarry. In the broken beds of the Ramle quarry it was difficult to give a sequence; fragments of the foraminiferal beds are found there. It is evident from the Qubeibeh conglomerates that the foraminifera advanced along the shore line with the transgression of the sea and formed the main sediment which was followed by a more general type.

"It seems probable that these beds lie exposed in patches generally covered with nari over a belt 6 to 10 kms. wide, but the fact that at Iraq el Manshiya, chalk with flints come to the surface and form part of the high Pliocene shore line extending through Summeil, Balin and Dhennabeh, indicate the broken (faulted) condition of an otherwise rather featureless plain."

It is the nari crust which has so frequently collapsed when left as a roof to a cave or tomb on the escarpments around Tell ed-Duweir, while the underlying chambers were cut in the Eocene deposits. Professor Picard defines the term *nari* as follows:

"*Nari* (Arabic *nar*, fire). Name introduced by Blanckenhorn (1905, p. 117) for the 'Deckelstein' of Fraas (1867, p. 202). Nari is a calcareous surface crust consisting mainly of pure $CaCO_3$, which covers the soft and mostly calcareous rocks. Its origin has been thought to be caused by rainwater, which penetrates into the calcareous rocks and dissolves the lime of the rock. Then by the influence of sunrays, a retrogressive process starts and raises this limy water by capillary force into fine channels and veins up to the surface of the rock, forming there a cover or crust. The nari crust therefore depends greatly on Mediterranean climatic conditions. It is only observed in Palestine, in such regions where sufficient rainfall governs. For Palestine, Picard (1932, p. 213) noted a rain figure of 300 mm. per annum as minimum for the development of nari. Nari is therefore missing in the more arid parts of the country and has no stratigraphic meaning."[1]

Below the nari crust in the section cut in Grid Square D.5 there is the hard bedded *mizzi*—an Arabic name meaning "the excellent", and at 6 m. from the surface, yellow chalky marls are encountered, which are described locally as *howr*. At 10 m. the crystalline limestone containing many fossils is reached.

The Uses of the Stone

The varieties of limestone available to local builders and craftsmen at all times were naturally employed as the chief building material.

Nari was too friable, pitted and uneven to be valuable, but it was used quite extensively in the later building period. Mizzi was eminently suitable, and could be quarried from the slopes of the mound and hoisted to the top without much difficulty. Further study of the constructional methods of the great podium of Palaces A, B and C in relation to the quarries with unfinished blocks which were found mostly on the north side of the mound, e.g. Nos. 4006, 4025, 4032, 4035, 6021 and 7001, would no doubt reveal the source of the stone for each subsequent enlargement of the structure. Better quality stone was used for Palace A than for Palace B (cf. Pl. 19: 1–3), and greater care was taken with the dressing of the surface, but nothing was achieved at Tell ed-Duweir comparable to the masonry of Megiddo or Samaria.

---

[1] "Synopsis of Stratigraphic Terms in Palestinian Geology" by L. Picard, Bulletin of Geological Department, Hebrew University, Jerusalem, Vol. II, 1938, No. 2).

From the marks of the tool used to disengage and dress the blocks, it is inferred that a short-handled pick was used (Pls. 9: 5; 10: 3), but no such tools or appliances have come to light in the excavations. Tool marks were particularly clear and fresh in the lower part of the Great Shaft, and there also quarrying methods could be studied.

It is somewhat surprising that a soft-quality limestone was used for the steps leading to Palace C on the east side. On the lime-surfaced pavement adjoining the latest flight of steps there were piles of chips from the final dressing, showing that the stones were finished in position, but the very nature of the stone would make frequent replacement necessary, and there are actually two earlier flights incorporated into the last set, which was hardly completed before the destruction of Level III (Pl. 18).

METHOD OF SURVEY

W. B. K. Shaw planned the field survey, and carried out the work until 1935. It was subsequently continued on the same lines by G. I. Goulden and H. V. Bonney. Mr. Shaw has written the following notes on the method used:

"In the valley below the mound and encircling it, a ring of permanent survey points was established at such a distance from the foot of the tell that they were unlikely to come within the area of excavation or be covered with waste earth. These points were marked by nails set in blocks of concrete or in outcrops of rock and were inter-visible. Round the upper edge of the tell, a second ring of points was established, each being visible from at least two of the permanent points in the valley. Starting from a base measured between two of the permanent points in the valley, a theodolite triangulation network was built up to include the inner and outer rings. The rectangular co-ordinates of each point were then calculated with reference to an origin at the most westerly point.

"As had been anticipated, some of the inner ring of points had to be moved from time to time, but they were easily re-established from the points in the valley.

"The detailed, large-scale survey of the excavations was carried out from two or three of the above-mentioned points, plotted from their co-ordinates at a suitable scale onto a plane-table sheet. Most of the survey was done by plane-table intersections or by single rays and tape measurement. The scale used was normally 1/200.

"Levels were referred to a datum (257·8 metres above sea level) at a Palestine Survey Department station on the ridge west of the tell. From this point levels were established at various convenient points around the tell from which the detailed levelling of the excavations was carried out."

In addition to the survey of the tell itself, the Concession Area was surveyed to a scale of 1/1000, with contours at 3-metre intervals, and from these plans a scale model of the tell and its surrounding valleys was made. This is now at the Institute of Archaeology in London.

IDENTIFICATION OF THE SITE

1841–1856 (Biblical Researches in Palestine, Vol. II, pp. 46–47). E. Robinson visited the site of *Um Lakis*, a mound of late ruins in the maritime plain, ten miles due west of Tell ed-Duweir, in order to satisfy himself of the fallacy of any proposed resemblance of the name to Lachish, but except at that spot he was unable to identify any traces of an ancient site which might have been Lachish or Libnah.

1878 (PEQ, p. 20). C. R. Conder agreed that *Um Lags* (as it is pronounced) was an entirely late settlement, and he proposed Tell el-Hesi. He saw in the name a corruption of Lachish, the Hebrew *kaph* being changed into the guttural. (See also Survey of Western Palestine Memoirs, Vol. III, p. 261.)

1890 (Lachish, p. 19). Flinders Petrie upheld Conder's identification and he traced a resemblance between the Lachish Reliefs and the configuration of Tell el-Hesi.

1894 (A Mound of Many Cities, p. 139). W. F. Bliss accepted the identity of Tell el-Hesi with Lachish somewhat guardedly. His excavations revealed deposits dating from the Early Bronze Age to 500–400 B.C., but they did not provide any further dating evidence. Indeed, the discovery of a tablet in cuneiform script mentioning Zimrida of Lachish in the text would suggest that the city was elsewhere (Tell el-Amarna Letter 333, J. A. Knudtzon—Die el Amarna Tafeln; notes and registers by Otto Weber and Erich Ebeling, 1915).

1903 (Kurzes Bibelwörterbuch, p. 382). Guthe suggested the region of Duweimah.

1929 (ZAW VI, p. 3, note 2). W. F. Albright questioned the identity of Tell el-Ḥesi and Lachish, and he proposed Tell ed-Duweir:

"For a number of years the writer has maintained this identification, which is so evident that several other topographers have accepted it. The Onomasticon (Os. 274, 9. 135.22) states that Lachish was a village in the seventh mile from Eleutheropolis to the Negeb (Daroma). This general location suits the Biblical references to the place remarkably well, while Tell el-Hesy does not. Tell Duweir is easily four times as large as Tell Hesy, which is altogether too small to represent an important Jewish town like Lachish. Moreover, Tell Hesy is nearly twice as far away from Beit Jibrin as is allowed by Onomasticon for Lachish. For its identity with Eglon, cf. Bulletin No. 15, p. 7 ff. While Tell Duweir is only five miles by road from Beit Jibrin, there are a number of Byzantine sites in the immediate neighbourhood which could be identified with the Lachish of that period referred to by Eusebius. Hirbet ed-Duweir is the most prominent site, situated about six miles by road from Eleutheropolis."

1931 (ZDPV 54, No. 3, pp. 113–117). G. Beyer notes that out of the fifteen cities fortified by Rehoboam, thirteen of the identifications of sites are considered certain. Only Lachish and Gath were, until recently, a subject of controversy, although Beyer states that "there is a general agreement that both places were situated in the south-west of this system of fortification, that is, in the south of the hill country of Judah, or even farther west in the plain". Lachish, he suggested, should be identified either with Beit ʿAuwa or with Tell ʿEtun, and he proposed that the population had migrated to Beit ʿAuwa in the period between Jeremiah XXXIV: 7 and Eusebius.

1931 (Joshua Judges, pp. 172 f.). J. Garstang wrote:

"Lachish . . . is to be identified in all probability with an ancient mound of exceptional size and appearance called Tell el Duweir. . . . It is true that Lachish is more familiarly associated in the minds of English readers with the small mound called Tell el Hesy . . . but this identification seems to be ill-founded. Tell el Hesy is a site of small importance, incompatible with the position accorded to Lachish in contemporary history; and the fact that a letter from the King of Lachish has been found at Tell el Hesy seems opposed to the identity of these two places. The position, moreover, is at variance with the statement of *Onomasticon* that *Lakeis*, the Roman city which had replaced that of earlier history, lay at the seventh milestone, that is, six full miles from *Eleutheropolis* in the direction of *Daroma*. The former is found at Beit Jibrin, the present road centre of the vicinity; the latter near the coast, well to the south of Gaza. It is true that a main road leads by Tell el Hesy towards Gaza, but if this had been meant it would surely have been so stated; whereas Tell el Duweir lies on the line of route towards Tell Sharieh and thence across to the Negeb westward to *Daroma*. Following the Roman road, which first led southward from Eleutheropolis for some two miles and thence westward, the prescribed distance of six miles brings one exactly to the Roman and Byzantine ruins lying to the southeast of Tell el Duweir, which indicate the city of Lachish at the time when the notes for the *Onomasticon* were compiled, a correspondence which seems conclusive."

1931 (Historical Geography of the Holy Land, 25th ed., p. 229 f.). George Adam Smith mentioned both the claims of Tell el-Ḥesi and Tell ed-Duweir and he noted that during the Latin kingdom of Jerusalem the city's successor at *Um Lakis* was held by the Order of the Hospitallers.

1940 (PEQ, p. 148). D. Winton Thomas wrote:

"The aim of this note is not to discuss the general question of the site of ancient Lachish—which in the last half century has been identified with at least four different localities—but only to contest the claim made by Torczyner that lines 9–13 of Ostracon IV 'give positive proof that Tell ed-Duweir, where the letters were found, really is the site of ancient Lachish. . . .' It may be pointed out, in the first place, that it cannot be regarded as certain that the sender of this letter had Tell ed-Duweir, and not some other place, in mind when he wrote that he and his fellows were watching the signal-stations of Lachish. There is indeed nothing in the lines in question to forbid the supposition that both Tell ed-Duweir and Lachish were signal-stations and that the military governor of Tell ed-Duweir commanded all three stations—Tell ed-Duweir, Lachish and Azekah—and perhaps also some others. Again, no great weight need be attached to the fact that the letter was found at Tell ed-Duweir. We know nothing of its 'history' prior to its discovery there. Even if its original destination was, in fact, Lachish—and we do not know for certain that it was—it could still be argued that it might have been brought to Tell ed-Duweir later.

"Our conclusion, then, must be that this letter—the only one, incidentally, in which Lachish is mentioned—does not in itself provide sufficient evidence to prove that Tell ed-Duweir marks the site of ancient Lachish. We may, indeed, go further and say that while there are good grounds for believing that Tell ed-Duweir is to be identified with Lachish, the evidence of Ostracon IV is of too uncertain a character to warrant its use even as an additional argument in favour of the identification."

LITERARY SOURCES

Lachish was already a very important place before the Iron Age, as is seen both from the excavations and frequent references to the city in the Tell el-Amarna Letters. Pre-Iron Age sources will therefore be examined in *Lachish IV* (19th–13th centuries B.C.), as well as the etymological value of the name. Here it is sufficient to note that its origin appears to be pre-Semitic, although many scholars have tried to explain it as a Semitic root.

There is no doubt that the city maintained its pre-eminent position to the end of the Jewish monarchy, and this is amply confirmed by both Biblical and Assyrian contemporary sources. In order to keep Biblical references together, those sources which refer to the Hebrew conquest have been included.

Five kings of the Amorites formed a league against Joshua:

". . . the king of Jerusalem, the king of Hebron, the king of Jarmuth, the king of Lachish, the king of Eglon, gathered themselves together and went up, they and all their hosts and encamped before Gibeon and made war against it." (Joshua X: 5).

After the defeat of this coalition, Japhia, King of Lachish, with the other kings, was hanged at Makkedah, and Joshua advanced southwards:

"And the Lord delivered Lachish into the hand of Israel, which took it on the second day, and smote it with the edge of the sword, and all the souls that were therein." (Joshua X: 32).

"Then Horam king of Gezer came up to help Lachish; and Joshua smote him and his people, until he had left him none remaining." (v. 33).

"And from Lachish Joshua passed unto Eglon . . . and they took it on that day, and smote it with the edge of the sword . . . according to all that he had done to Lachish." (v. 34–35).

At the beginning of the first millennium, Lachish was included among fifteen cities fortified by Rehoboam:

"And he fortified the strongholds and put captains in them, and store of victual, and of oil and wine."
"And in every several city he put shields and spears and made them exceeding strong . . ." (II Chronicles XI: 11–12).

A century later:

"Now after the time that Amaziah did turn away from following the Lord, they made a conspiracy against him in Jerusalem; and he fled to Lachish: but they sent to Lachish after him and slew him there." (II Chronicles XXV: 27; cf. II Kings XIV: 19).

From the Assyrian annals, Sennacherib's campaign is very closely dated to 700 B.C., and it is also described in II Kings, II Chronicles, and Isaiah:

"Now in the fourteenth year of King Hezekiah did Sennacherib king of Assyria come up against all the fenced cities of Judah and took them." (II Kings XVIII: 13).

"And Hezekiah king of Judah sent to the king of Assyria to Lachish saying, I have offended; return from me; that which thou puttest on me will I bear. . . .

"And Hezekiah gave him all the silver that was found in the house of the Lord. . . .

"And the king of Assyria sent Tartan and Rabsaris and Rabshakeh from Lachish to king Hezekiah with a great host against Jerusalem." (II Kings XVIII: 14, 15, 17).

The account in Chronicles does not admit that the cities were taken—the phrase is "thought to win them for himself", and adds a note in brackets, "(but he *himself laid siege* against Lachish and all his power with him)" (II Chronicles XXXII: 1, 9).

In the Royal Correspondence of the Assyrian Empire, J. Waterman includes a letter (Vol. I, Letter 218) from one Nergalballit to the king:

"As for the Philistines, from whom the king my lord has organised a contingent of 5 troops (and) given them to me, now they are before me. They are *stationed* in the city of Lachish. . . ."

The passage may have been written after the capture of the city by Sennacherib in 700 B.C., or some twenty-five years later when Eserhaddon campaigned against Egypt. Anyhow, it shows that Lachish, like Megiddo and Ammon, and probably other chief cities, was under Assyrian control in the seventh century B.C.—an unpleasant fact which would not be emphasised in Biblical record.

The collapse of Assyrian power in 612 B.C. gave the cities of Palestine a short respite, but the Babylonians lost little time in regaining control. Nebuchadrezzar led two campaigns, one in 598 and another between 589 and 587 B.C. It is probably to the second of these that the following passage refers:

"When the king of Babylon's army fought against Jerusalem, and against all the cities of Judah that were left, against Lachish, and against Azekah: for these defenced cities remained of the cities of Judah." (Jeremiah XXXIV: 7.)

Old Testament References to Lachish

Joshua X: 5
   ,,   X: 32–35
   ,,   XII: 11
   ,,   XV: 39
II Kings XIV: 19
   ,,   XVIII: 14, 17
   ,,   XIX: 8

II Chronicles XI: 9
   ,,   XXV: 27
   ,,   XXXII: 9
Nehemiah XI: 30
Isaiah XXXVI: 2
   ,,   XXXVII: 8
Jeremiah XXXIV: 7
Micah I: 13

PART I
HISTORY AND ARCHAEOLOGY

CHAPTER 1

SURVEY OF RESULTS

> When a thing is old, broken, and useless, we throw it on the dust-heap, but when it is sufficiently old, sufficiently broken, and sufficiently useless, we give money for it, put it into a museum, and read papers over it which people come long distances to hear.
>
> SAMUEL BUTLER: *Notebooks*

THE growth, prosperity and decay of a single community, seen in its products and possessions, and viewed in relation to near and distant neighbours, is an absorbing study.

In the varied assembly of objects recovered from a site of great extent, interest is not confined to things of value and beauty—though there are many such—but can be focused equally on the contents of the dust-heap. These may be old, broken and useless, but they promote understanding of a broad outline of economics and events which will establish the position of any place in the contemporary scene.

Six years' work has amply justified the choice of Tell ed-Duweir as a site for excavation, and the Wellcome Expedition presents in the accounts which follow a close and detailed study of daily life in a chief city of Judah. Reoccupied on an increasing scale after the death of Solomon, when his kingdom was divided into the separate states of Israel and Judah, the city described in the present volume, which was almost certainly the site of ancient Lachish, continued to be an important centre of trade and communication until its destruction by Nebuchadrezzar about 586 B.C.

Following closely on a previous partial burning, the date of that event is equated on the site with a widespread destruction by fire, which had charred the roads and approaches to the city, caused great breaches in the walls, and covered the few poor houses of the period, Level II, in a deep layer of ash.

Working backwards in time, the site retained similar evidence of an earlier conflagration, causing the destruction of a much larger district of shops and houses south of the citadel, which was itself burnt from inside during the same catastrophe. Both from Assyrian and Biblical sources it is known that the Assyrian king Sennacherib "and all his force with him" laid siege to Lachish, and the burning of the city at Level III is therefore attributed to his campaign which, according to recent opinion, occurred in 700 B.C.

Two archaeological reasons support the date. The commonest class of bowl (B.13) in Level III had a thick "folded" rim and was usually burnished inside, and that form did not appear at Samaria until after the historic destruction in 722 B.C. Allowing for the fact that the pottery of any level normally represents the last phase of use, it would leave two decades in which such bowls became popular at Lachish, before that city also fell to the Assyrians.

Nearly every house of Level III contained one or more large storage jars, the handles of which were impressed with a "royal" stamp, which Dr. Diringer has divided into three classes on the basis of epigraphic development (see Chapter 10).

It will be seen that the majority of the stamps belong to the intermediate class, which is very close to, if not indistinguishable from, the script of the Siloam Tunnel inscription. Though that commemorative record bears no date, it may well belong to the reign of Hezekiah, who was responsible for hydraulic constructions in Jerusalem. The predominance of stamps in class ii among those accumulated on the site would seem to weight the evidence in favour of Sennacherib's campaign rather than that of Nebuchadrezzar more than a century later. Moreover, the majority of "royal" stamps found at Tell en-Naṣbeh at the northern extremity of Judah, which became an important place in the seventh and sixth centuries, belonged to the latest epigraphic class.

Charcoal and ash also marked the end of the fourth level of occupation above bed-rock (Level VI, from ground surface) in the stratified sections of the mound exposed on the north-east and west sides (pp. 71–74), and the same layer appears to indicate the immediate cause of the destruction of the Fosse Temple.

In the publication of *Lachish II*, a date about 1223 B.C. was suggested for this event, but it may have occurred a decade or so after rather than before 1200 B.C., in view of the presence of one scarab of Rameses III on disturbed Bronze Age debris near the citadel,[1] but the final conclusion on this matter must await publication of the Bronze Age tomb groups in *Lachish IV*, and does not affect the argument, for it is clear that a date after 1200 B.C. is the starting-point of the present series.

There is, indeed, evidence of a gap in occupation and time separating the painted wares so variously represented in the structures of the Fosse Temple, which may survive in decadent form through the early decades of the twelfth century, from the red hand-burnished wares which are characteristic of the new series. The alternative reasons for the break are discussed in Chapter 2.

In the trial cut at the south-east corner of the citadel which penetrated a building attributed to Level V (pp. 80 ff.), such hand-burnished pottery was ubiquitous; in all but the earliest tomb groups of the Iron Age series and in the foundation levels of the upper city wall of Level IV (pp. 72–74), the quantity and extent of burnish were less remarkable.

Four large burial deposits, Tombs 218, 224, 1002 and 106, provide a consecutive but partially contemporary series of ceramic and other material, which is supplemented by the contents of smaller groups. The contents of tombs can be related to some extent to those of the houses in Levels III and II, and the result of the examination is set out on p. 50 with the approximate dates of the principal groups. It will be seen that from the terminal date for Level II, *c*. 586 B.C.—the only one which is relatively secure—the four main groups reach back towards the middle of the tenth century B.C.

Two groups stand apart and a little before the main series. Cave 6024 contained varied and unusual objects which should perhaps be viewed as the apparatus and trial pieces of a craft or crafts. Isolated from the large tombs of the period, both in position, condition and contents, the rock-hewn Tomb 521 was the burial-place of a small family or group which had remained undisturbed by human agency. The iron knives and the large trident, as well as the dependence of the pottery on metal prototypes, suggest that this family, at least, had close associations with those people who were responsible for the introduction of iron and its products to south Palestine.

In the earlier part of the main series—Tombs 218 and 223—bangles and bracelets of iron were almost as numerous as those of bronze; but in the groups which follow, where ceramic development shows only slight change, iron was rarely used for personal ornaments. Though less common than in the flourishing days of Solomonic trade, gold, electrum and silver were still occasionally used for trinkets, but towards the end of the eighth century it is noteworthy that iron was reserved for tools and weapons and even bronze and silver were in short supply.

The survey which follows is an attempt to assemble the ceramic and other elements of each phase in the period of maximum use.

c. 1150–925 B.C.

At some time between these dates a striking change had occurred in the ceramic products of Tell ed-Duweir. The initial stages are not so far apparent at the site, and the final developments, as represented in Level V, have only been tentatively sounded. However, Cave 6024 and Tomb 521 must be close in time to the new source of influence, for they contained more than 90 per cent. of the pottery with red hand-burnish, which was applied in imitation of the polished surface of metal vessels.

---

[1] Cf. closure of necropolis at 'Ain Shems, contemporary with Stratum IVb, which contained a scarab of Rameses III (AS V, p. 125); and Megiddo Stratum VII, where an ivory was found bearing the same cartouche (OIP vol. LII, Pl. 62).

On the other hand, some bowls, and especially the lamps, show an unbroken progression from Bronze Age tradition, and there are other elements which suggest that the incoming culture did not entirely displace the wares and forms which had been popular in the thirteenth century.

On the evidence of this one site, a closer dating for the two groups which precede the main series is not easy to achieve, but the absence of Philistine painted pottery in both suggests one of two things: either the groups are later than the extinction of such wares, or these never penetrated in quantity to the site. In view of the presence of Philistine pottery at places which are further inland,[1] the second alternative, if correct, would suggest that Tell ed-Duweir as a closely guarded stronghold was perhaps less vulnerable to influence from the Coastal Plain.

The reference in II Chronicles to Rehoboam's action in commissioning cities for defence in Judah may give a misleading impression that Lachish was unoccupied at that time, but it is proposed to adopt the approximate date of his accession, 925 B.C., for the beginning of the main tomb series, when there was apparently a marked increase in the cemetery population of the city.

c. 925–800 B.C.

In the contents of Tombs 218, 223 and 116, there is a reduction to 61 per cent. of the total in the amount of hand-burnish on bowls. Jugs, dippers and jars were also among the offerings, but lamps were infrequently provided, which may suggest that the new-comers were still in process of adopting local customs. Towards the end of the period iron was no longer used extensively for personal ornaments.

At no time in the following years were the contacts with Egypt so close, and Dr. M. A. Murray has shown that they were largely confined to the Delta region of Lower Egypt. Scarabs with the royal name of *Mn-ḫpr-Rʿ*, together with others bearing the name and titles of the god Amen (*Ymn*) were characteristic (Pl. 43), with faience amulets of Isis and Sekhmet (Pls. 34–36). At the same time, plain scaraboid seals, engraved with designs of ostriches, horses and men, were popular (Pl. 44), and other objects of non-Egyptian provenance were decorated bone gavels and rods (Pl. 37).

During the use of Tombs 224 and 1004 the amount of hand-burnish declined to 33 per cent., less of the surface was treated, and the first experiments in wheel-finished burnish were made. Lamps had become an important element in funerary equipment, and jugs with a round base had doubled in popularity.

Cheaper materials—bone, paste and glass—were displacing harder stone for seals and beads, which were also reduced in size, and there was little fresh enterprise in scaraboid design.

The first phase of the present survey therefore presents a steady social and economic decline, in which the new metal and its associated minerals, haematite and ochre, were less plentiful.

c. 800–700 B.C.

In compensation for the limitation of supplies, an important technical discovery speeded production in the largest industry of the time. Pottery had been made on the wheel for many centuries, but it was not until the last half of the ninth that a means was devised to burnish on the wheel. This logical and simple step had far-reaching effects, resulting in a larger output of standardised shapes and in a marked decrease of quality. Wherever the details of manufacture have been adequately recorded, the change from hand to wheel-burnished surfaces, which on the evidence from Duweir and Samaria came into general use about 800 B.C., will provide an invaluable means of synchronisation with the pottery from other sites.

Tomb 1002 covered most of the eighth century and contained in all layers at least 34 per cent. of wheel-burnished bowls, and so striking a reversal of the situation shows how quickly the new technique had spread. At this time wheel-burnish was largely confined to bowls, while among a variety of jugs—outnumbering the bowls by three to one—a high standard of workmanship was maintained, which seemed to owe something to Phoenician inspiration.

---

[1] Cf. Tell Beit Mirsim, Phase B₂ (AASOR XXI–XXII, p. 1) and 'Ain Shems, Stratum III (AS V, p. 10).

Perhaps the most striking change in ceramic development occurred in the upper layers of the tomb, when black-burnished juglets with handles attached to the neck (Class D.7) were replaced by their smaller poorly made successors with handles attached to the rim (D.8). At the same time, the first disk-based lamps made their appearance, and both these significant developments have been noted elsewhere (pp. 282, 301).

Nearly every household possessed one or more large storage jars. The distinctive form of the period was beautifully made of a hard metallic ware, and it is to similar jars that the numbers of handles with impressed royal stamps undoubtedly belonged. One vessel with a "royal" stamp and two with "private" signet impressions affixed while the clay was soft were reconstructed from crushed fragments (PEQ, April–July, 1941, Pl. X) and the seal readings are discussed in Chapter 10. It is on the epigraphic progression of the Early Hebrew characters on the "royal" stamps that the date is based for the destruction of the city at Level III.

c. 700–c. 586 B.C.

After Sennacherib's attack, few people were able to repair their homes in the wrecked city. The ruined palace on the citadel was not rebuilt, and if an administrative centre existed, it has not yet been found.

Some rooms attributed to the occupation of city Level II, with Tombs 106, 109, 114, provide the material which covers the seventh century, though it is likely that Tomb 106 was already open for burials before the destruction dated to 700 B.C. The sharp rise in the relative numbers of lamps to bowls in the tomb groups was more marked by the end of the period, when they had doubled in quantity, with high-footed, coarsely made bases as the predominant feature. Jugs were as common as bowls, and among the former, decanters of standard size represent a third of the total (Class J.8). Dippers survived in use (Classes D.4 and D.5b) with some imitations of imported juglets (Class D.6b), but they were outnumbered by black-burnished juglets (D.8). This range of pottery is to be seen in the rooms of Level II, augmented by a variety of storage jars. On one such vessel there was a spirited design of ibex (Pl. 50) and this attempt in a period when decorative art was rare emphasises the latent talent of at least one individual.

In a room of city Level II, and particularly in the burnt guardroom of the final phase, ostraca or sherds with writing in ink on them were found, which are now known as the Lachish Letters. They have been discussed by those competent to interpret and judge their meaning (L. I and Bibliography on pp. 21 f.). Through illegibility the text may withhold a vital word—the name of the prophet in Letter III for instance, or the complete introductory formula in Letter XX—which, had they been complete, might have provided a fixed point in history. There can be no doubt, however, of the interest of the whole correspondence, and if nothing else had been found on the site, these letters written in the time of Jeremiah would have been a rich reward.

c. 450–150 B.C.

According to the Scriptures, the deportation soon after 586 B.C. of useful and important members of the population to Babylon left the cities of Judah almost deserted. There are, indeed, no houses which can certainly be attributed to the sixth and early fifth centuries at Lachish, and it was not until the exiles were beginning to return, about 450 B.C., that there is much evidence of activity.

They did not come in numbers, for only a few houses were built within the walls, but communal pride, or the need for a Persian centre of administration, caused the people to build a spacious Residency on the burnt platform of the citadel. The new building (Pl. 119) was not, however, designed to a Persian plan, but was related to the buildings of Strata III–II at Megiddo (M. I, Fig. 89) and to other constructions of Syro-Hittite inspiration. In use during the latter part of the fifth and part of the fourth centuries B.C., the Residency was one of the last public buildings of note, and its position on the summit of the mound was not disputed, for later builders chose open ground to the east for the Solar Shrine and the adjoining pillared building.

The armies of Alexander and of the rival Hellenistic dynasties left little mark except for scattered coins; as the district settled under Seleucid control, Tell Sandaḥannah, site of Mareshah—nearest and oldest rival to

Lachish—achieved regional supremacy as the newly planned city of Marissa. But the road system of the Roman province which converged on Beit Jibrin eventually robbed Marissa of control.

In conclusion of this survey, it may be observed that the goods and chattels of daily life and the standard containers of food and drink, described in Part IV, show more speed and less skill in manufacture, offset by a growing shortage of imports and supplies and almost complete abstention from the decorative arts. Denied the enjoyment of painting, sculpture and design through poverty, or possibly religious scruples, many inhabitants of Lachish had a working knowledge of the Early Hebrew script, of which the ostraca, clay seal impressions and jar stamps give ample testimony.

The introduction of that alphabet, which, in a closely related form, was inherited by the Western world, did nothing to promote material prosperity in Judah, but its use led to diffusion of thought and to a new freedom of literary expression. In recording the Books of Kings and Chronicles, Isaiah and Jeremiah, the authors and compilers dwell on the spiritual progress or defeat of the people, and offer exhortation and consolation to those living among the distractions of foreign influence and long-established idolatry, of which the excavations provide some concrete examples. It is, therefore, against the background of the Bible that the discoveries gain a special, and indeed compelling, interest.

Approximate Dates of Principal Groups

Date	Level	Groups on Consolidated Chart	Other tombs, caves, pits and buildings	Graves
A.D. 400		(Tomb 106)	4021	
			215, 217, 220	
			4035	
B.C. 400			506, 515, 522	
	I		523, 534	
			1007, 1009, (4005)	
450		Houses I		525
			227	
				180, 183–186
550			109, 114, 1010	
586	II		505, 7002	
597				
650	II		513	4007
		Houses II		
		Tomb 106		
		(Tomb 120)	(107, 108, 116, 117)	
700			526	132
			4010	
750	III			
		Houses III		160, 191, 229
800		Tomb 1002	219	4026, 4027
		Tomb 1004		
				147, 152, 154, 159
850		Tomb 224	230, 507	167, 169, 182
		Tomb 116		
900	IV?			
		Tomb 218	6006	189, 192, 193, 194
		Tomb 120	107, 108, 117	196
950		Tomb 223	118, 4005	110
	V?			
1000		Tomb 521		
		Cave 6024		
1050				
1200	VI	Destruction of city Level VI		

Tombs which have a period of re-use have their numbers repeated in brackets.

CHAPTER 2

THE CULTURAL BACKGROUND

THE SITE IN RELATION TO HISTORY

> For the cities which were formerly great, have most of them become insignificant; and such as are at present powerful, were weak in olden time. I shall therefore discourse equally of both, convinced that human happiness never continues long in one stay. HERODOTUS, Book I: 5.

IF it is accepted that the deserted mound of Tell ed-Duweir is the site of Lachish, a chief city of Judah, the information from the excavations may be used to supplement the references to the place which are found in the literary sources. The present book is not concerned with the earliest history of the site, but it should be noted that the Tell el-Amarna correspondence of the mid-fourteenth century, written in cuneiform, makes it clear that Lachish was important by that time.

Excavations have shown that the natural advantages of the site had been fully exploited during the previous millennium and that the large and flourishing open settlement which occupied the surrounding spurs was dwindling and concentrating on the fortified mound. A section cut during the first season at the north-east corner recorded at least four phases of occupation prior to the destruction of the last Bronze Age city (PEQ, October, 1950, pp. 81 ff.). The final two phases are generously supplemented by the contents of the Fosse Temple,[1] which was founded on the disused fosse or moat of the Middle Bronze Age. Enlarged twice during about three centuries of use, this Canaanite sanctuary, with all its equipment and offerings, was burnt at the same time as the sixth Level of the city.

Destruction of Level VI, c. 1200 B.C.

Counting the strata from the surface downwards, a thick burnt layer represents the end of the sixth recognisable level. It extends to the temple at the foot of the north-west slope, which also contained some products of Egyptian and Aegean culture, influenced to some extent by the art of Syrian craftsmen, besides abundant but less distinguished wares of local manufacture.

Above the sealing of charcoal and ash, there is little but surface humus in the northern parts of the mound, while to the south there are overlying remains belonging to later phases of Jewish history.

The reasons for the fall of the city of Level VI—and of other cities of this period—which marked the close of the Bronze Age, are among those problems of history which are as yet unsolved. Three alternatives may be considered:

1. Despite periods of weak control and neglect, Egypt had been the undoubted suzerain of southern Canaan since the sixteenth century; the route to the north had to be maintained and garrisoned for Pharaoh's armies and messengers, and any threat to the city-states along it was a challenge to Egypt. In the thirteenth century, Rameses II, Merneptah and Rameses III were successively menaced by related movements of peoples from the north and west, and insurrections along the vital coast road to the north were suppressed with a firm hand.

If the city at Level VI was destroyed in an Egyptian punitive campaign, the presence of a burnt carnelian scarab in the constructional filling near the centre of the mound, bearing the name of Rameses II, and another of Rameses III in the same locality, suggest that Level VI survived at least to the beginning of the latter's reign (1198–1167 B.C.), when Aegean peoples were striding down the coasts of Syria and Palestine to meet defeat at last on the Egyptian border.

---

[1] *Lachish II.*

51

2. Lachish, in view of its isolated position, may have escaped from the general campaign, but other potential enemies had begun to settle along the coastal plain and to press their claims for territory inland whenever the chance arose. If the Philistines, to whom the country owes its modern name, were responsible for the fall of Level VI, it is difficult to believe that they failed to establish a permament settlement on such a valuable site, where, apart from a few sherds in a cave and two tombs containing anthropomorphic coffins, there is so far no trace of their distinctive culture.

3. The date of the Israelite invasion cannot be synchronized by reference to events or persons known from non-Biblical sources. On the initial incursion into Hebron, spies of Moses were impressed by the strength and prosperity of the land, and brought back a majority report which advised against attack, but Joshua, who was with them, supported a policy of aggression which was to culminate years later in the successful defeat of the Amorite League, which included Japhia, king of Lachish, among its five members. Egyptian weakness and local anarchy were essential to success, and historians suggest that these conditions prevailed in the first quarters of the fourteenth and twelfth centuries respectively. Both periods are marked by some interruption in the normal accumulation of rubbish in the stratified section at Tell ed-Duweir; there is an interval at 31 ft. above bed-rock (*c.* 1400 B.C.), and there is, as already mentioned, the thick layer of burning at 36 ft., which is equivalent to ground surface at 249 m. above sea level at the northern end of the mound.

Wherever the Late Bronze Age city of Level VI has been exposed, wherever contemporary tombs have been excavated, Egyptian influence and that of the Aegean world is to be seen, appearing also in the varied products of the Fosse Temple. No iron was found in any of these contexts, though references to its use are quite common in the Books of Joshua and Judges.

Whatever the reason for the fall of Level VI may prove to be, the destruction undoubtedly marked the close of a most prosperous phase in the city's history.

Partial Desertion, 1150–1000 B.C.

The political and economic situation in Canaan during the twelfth and eleventh centuries is obscure, for material remains are scarce and imperfectly known.

Not all the population could have been exterminated, nor is it certain that a wide gulf—in time or tradition —divided the known Bronze Age culture and its painted wares from the methods of the Iron Age, when—among later changes—ceramic design and technique was based on an imitation of metal vessels, which were accompanied by weapons and ornaments of iron.

Without appreciable delay, some cities were reoccupied: at Tell Beit Mirsim[1] and 'Ain Shems,[2] for instance, houses were rebuilt on the ashes of destruction. The same may prove to be the case at Lachish. There are, indeed, a few rubbish pits in the central part of the mound, whose contents appear to be analogous to phase B_1 at Tell Beit Mirsim, which followed the burning of the Bronze Age city C at that site very closely.

A large clearance of the ground down to the Bronze Age destruction would be necessary at Tell ed-Duweir to confirm the apparent desertion of the site for a century or more. It can only be said at present that the population was much restricted during that time, and certainly did not occupy the western edge of the mound, for the West Section through the stratification, at 37–34 ft. or 256 m. above sea level, was devoid of characteristic sherds other than Bronze Age fragments.

Level V, c. 1000–900 B.C.

In the first renewal of building activity on the mound, the ruin of the Bronze Age palace, of which only the north-west corner has been seen, was enclosed in a solid block or platform of large stones, laid in even courses, and forming a magnificent structure which still survives to a considerable height. The earth-filled interior possibly illustrates the method of construction of a "millo" such as David built at Jerusalem, for both the

---

[1] AASOR XXI–XXII, § 23.   [2] AS V, p. 12.

Hebrew word and its Assyrian equivalent can be translated as "filling". On the massive podium, 32 m. square, which is known in this book as Palace A, stood the first Iron Age building, of which no part of the brick super-structure now remains intact.

If the palace precincts were enclosed at that time, a thick brick wall running east and west under and parallel to the south face of Palace B–C may have been the first line of defence. Most of the wall is covered by the south end of the later buildings, and any structures between the wall and Palace A are also hidden for the same reason.

Whether or not the east–west wall formed part of an earlier defensive system, it was certainly related to a brick building which was described by J. L. Starkey as a "government storehouse".[1] Built at the same time, the rooms projected southwards from the wall and were exposed in a trial cut near the south-east corner of Palace C. They contained a high proportion of hand-burnished wares, comparable to pottery from phases B_2 and B_3 at Tell Beit Mirsim, Periods I and II at Tell el-Fûl, and Stratum V at Megiddo.

It is evident that unless further excavations take place the connexion between the rooms and the podium of Palace A cannot be established or denied, for the construction of Palace A could have begun at any time after the destruction of the Level VI city, and the contents of the filling have not yet been sufficiently explored. Both Palace A and the storerooms are therefore provisionally attributed to Level V.

Until the establishment of the United Monarchy, literary sources do not record any building activity in southern Judah, and from about 1000 B.C. the schemes planned by David and carried out by Solomon were largely confined to the new capital of Jerusalem, though Solomon also fortified several main points on his trade routes.

However, the security achieved through Solomon's unique position as a merchant prince trading to mutual advantage and on equal terms with neighbouring powers was hardly complete when the division of the kingdom made it essential to prepare and maintain frontier forts in Judah against aggression from all sides. Solomon's son was fully aware of the prime importance of defence, and Lachish is named among fifteen cities commissioned and equipped in the first years of Rehoboam's reign (II Chronicles XI: 11, 12):

"And he fortified the strong holds, and put captains in them, and store of victual, and of oil and wine.
"And in every several city he put shields and spears, and made them exceeding strong, having Judah and Benjamin on his side."

It was not long before the strongholds were put to the test, for in the fifth year of Rehoboam, about 920 B.C., Shishak,[2] the Libyan founder of the Egyptian xxiind dynasty, came up against Jerusalem, taking the "fenced" cities of Judah on his way (II Chronicles XII: 2–4). Lachish is not mentioned in either the Egyptian or Biblical record of this incident, an omission which may imply that it was not on the route to Jerusalem, though it is unlikely that an experienced commander would leave a military garrison unsubdued in the rear. By his sub-mission to Shishak, Rehoboam forfeited his father's treasure but kept his throne, and there is a special reference to prosperity in Judah during the remainder of his reign (II Chronicles XII: 12). The prevalence of cowrie shells and other non-indigenous objects in certain tomb groups of the period suggests that some of Shishak's army, which included Libyans and Nubians, may have settled in the district.[3]

Levels IV–III, c. 900–700 B.C.

Taking advantage of a further peaceful decade after his accession shortly before 900 B.C., Asa, Rehoboam's grandson, built "fenced" cities with "walls and towers, gates and bars" in Judah (II Chronicles XIV: 7). Con-tinuing his father's policy, Jehoshaphat garrisoned the strongholds and built fortresses and "cities of store", sending teachers among the people to spread knowledge of the Law, and gaining through his wise and sober policy the respect and tribute of his neighbours (II Chronicles XVII).

The reigns of Rehoboam (seventeen years), Asa (forty-one years) and Jehoshaphat (twenty-five years) were

---

[1] PEQ, 1937, p. 237; AASOR XXI–XXII, § 10.
[2] W. F. Albright argues for a date about 918 B.C. (AASOR XXI–XXII, p. 37, note 13).   [3] See Tomb 218.

periods of expansion and activity in Judah, only checked by Shishak's aforementioned invasion about 920 B.C. and by the defeat of his successor at Mareshah, c. 895 B.C.

If Palace A was the work of Rehoboam, the brick wall to enclose the rapidly expanding city may be attributed to Asa. As exposed in the West Section, it was based upon rubbish containing some burnished sherds which represent a later phase of development than that of the sherds in the rooms of the government store building. The great enlargement of the citadel to the south, described as Palace B, could be the work of Jehoshaphat, who took away the high places and the groves from Judah and apparently increased the responsibilities of the local "prince" or governor.

The combined attacks of the Philistines from the west and the Arabians from the east (II Chronicles XXI: 16–17) put the well-established kingdom of Judah on the defensive, and internal dissension during the minority of Joash, c. 842 B.C., caused Judah and Jerusalem to succumb to the onslaught of a small Syrian army which, as a matter of policy, wrecked Jehoshaphat's system of decentralised control, destroying "all the princes of the people from among the people" (II Chronicles XXIV: 23).

Warned by events, Amaziah, on coming to the throne, mobilised a picked force from Judah and led them successfully against the Edomites, which encouraged him to challenge Joash of Israel, by whom he was ignominiously defeated at Beth-shemesh. Amaziah's acceptance of Edomite gods fostered conspiracy against him in Jerusalem "and he fled to Lachish: but they sent to Lachish and slew him there" (II Chronicles XXV). His choice of refuge may indicate the religious sympathies of the town.

Reviewing the accounts of building activity in Judah, recorded in II Chronicles, which gives more detail than the parallel account in Kings, the reigns of Azariah (Uzziah) and his son Jotham stand out as a period of peace and expansion covering the first half of the eighth century. A successful campaign against the Philistines enabled Azariah to build cities in the plain and towers in the desert, and to dig many wells. He encouraged agriculture and husbandry throughout the land, and did not neglect to strengthen the fortifications of Jerusalem and to equip and train an efficient army (II Chronicles XXVI). Jotham, his son, "built cities in the mountains of Judah, and in the forests he built castles and towers" (II Chronicles XXVII: 4).

On the accession of Ahaz, the Philistines took their revenge for Ahaziah's destruction of the walls of Gath, Jabneh and Ashdod by attacking cities in the plain, including Beth-shemesh, and in repeated raids the Edomites took captives from Judah. Failing in his appeal for temporal help from Assyria, Ahaz turned to the powerful gods of Damascus and made high places to serve them "in every several city of Judah" (II Chronicles XXVIII).

Judah was weak and dependent when Hezekiah succeeded his father a few years before the final fall of Samaria in 722 B.C. Hezekiah, then the most active monarch on the Assyrian march towards the Nile, prepared for the defence of Judah. Among other precautions all external water supplies to Jerusalem were blocked (II Kings XX: 20, II Chronicles XXXII: 4, 30, Isaiah XXII: 9, 11), and it was probably this feat which was commemorated in the Siloam Tunnel by an Early Hebrew inscription (PEQ, 1882, pp. 122 f.).

In view of Sennacherib's eventual siege of Lachish, it is probable that measures of defence may have included the unfinished construction of the Great Shaft, which was presumably begun in an effort to supplement an inadequate water supply within the city. Structural alteration and repairs to the citadel had certainly been made on several occasions since the construction of Palace B. The strip C, along most of the east side, was apparently in existence by the earlier half of the eighth century. Attached to its eastern face were three sets of superimposed steps leading up to the building from the plaster court which surrounded the whole building. On a rise of the earliest flight, among other drawings and devices, were the first five letters of the Hebrew alphabet, scratched in a style of script which has been dated on epigraphic grounds to the late ninth or early eighth century. Are they indeed contemporary with Jehoshaphat's scheme for mass education?

The phase or phases of occupation in the houses around Palace B–C, ascribed to Level IV, cannot be isolated, subdivided or described until the overlying buildings of Level III have been removed. The poorer section of the community—soldiers and shopkeepers, with their families—lived in these houses south of the

54

palace and kept the shops near the city gate; it is the contents of their burnt homes which afford a clear picture of domestic life at the end of the eighth century.

In the last decades prior to the destruction of Level III, red burnished wares had largely disappeared, iron was only used for weapons of defence, and scarabs and beads which had been common in earlier burials, were scarce and poorly made.

Destruction of Level III, c. 700 B.C.

It will be recalled that J. L. Starkey tentatively assigned the earlier burning of the road and shops to the threat to Judah's independence in 597 B.C. (PEQ, 1937, p. 175 and p. 236), but more detailed study of the pottery does suggest that the gap between the contents of city Levels III and II is greater than was at first supposed.

If it is agreed that the wholesale destruction of Level III was the result of Sennacherib's attack, the pictorial record of the siege of Lachish found on the bas-reliefs in his palace at Nineveh will portray the state of the defences at that time, which are aptly described by Sir A. H. Layard:

"During the latter part of my residence at Mosul a chamber was discovered in which the sculptures were in better preservation than any before found at Kouyunjik. Some of the slabs, indeed, were almost entire, though cracked and otherwise injured by fire; and the epigraph, which fortunately explained the event portrayed, was complete. These bas-reliefs represented the siege and capture by the Assyrians, of a city evidently of great extent and importance. It appears to have been defended by double walls, with battlements and towers, and by fortified outworks. The country around it was hilly and wooded, producing the fig and the vine. The whole power of the great king seems to have been called forth to take this stronghold. In no other sculptures were so many armed warriors seen drawn up in array before a besieged city. In the first rank were the kneeling archers, those in the second were bending forward, whilst those in the third discharged their arrows standing upright, and were mingled with spearmen and slingers; the whole forming a compact and organised phalanx. The reserve consisted of large bodies of horsemen and charioteers. Against the fortifications had been thrown up as many as ten banks or mounts, compactly built of stones, bricks, earth and branches of trees, and seven battering-rams had already been rolled up to the walls. The besieged defended themselves with great determination. Spearmen, archers, and slingers thronged the battlements and towers, showering arrows, javelins, stones and blazing torches upon the assailants. On the battering-rams were bowmen discharging their arrows, and men with large ladles pouring water upon the flaming brands, which, hurled from above, threatened to destroy the engines. Ladders, probably used for escalade, were falling from the walls upon the soldiers who mounted the inclined ways to the assault. Part of the city had, however, been taken. Beneath its walls were seen Assyrian warriors impaling their prisoners, and from the gateway of an advanced tower, or fort, issued a procession of captives, reaching to the presence of the king, who, gorgeously arrayed, received them seated on his throne. . . . Above the head of the king was the following inscription, 'Sennacherib, the mighty king, king of the country of Assyria, sitting on the throne of judgment, before (or at the entrance of) the city of Lachish (Lakhisha). I give permission for its slaughter.'" (Nineveh and Babylon, p. 148.)

The city on the mound, drawn by Lankester Harding from the original slabs in the British Museum, is reproduced as the frontispiece of this book.

Excavation at Tell ed-Duweir has shown that during the ninth and eighth centuries B.C. the city was surrounded by two lines of defence, an upper wall of brick following the edge of the escarpment, and a lower wall or revetment of stone half-way down the slope. Both walls were planned with recessed panels, but the regularity and size of the recesses was governed by the contours of the underlying rock: in the Assyrian relief two walls with recessed panels are shown. Moreover, an isolated tower is depicted low down on the slope: this represents, perhaps, the bastion at the south-west corner, which appears to have been a free-standing block, unattached to the lower revetment in its earliest phase. On and near the roadways leading to the city were the missiles of the attack: iron arrowheads used by the bowmen engaged in the assault, stone slingshots used by the rear rank of slingers, a spearhead, and part of a bronze crest mount worn by a spearman—all embedded in a thick layer of ash which spread out over the road.

It is clear from the details of the reliefs that, after a stubborn defence, Lachish fell and made submission to the Assyrian king encamped in person before the city, though accounts in the Old Testament do not admit its capture. The Taylor Prism,[1] Sennacherib's official record of the campaign, records the fall of forty-six cities in Judah, and though Lachish is not mentioned by name, that number would presumably include all the effective strongholds, with the exception of Jerusalem alone, which was besieged but proved to be impregnable.

Conditions on the site leave no doubt that the destruction of Level III was the outcome of a fierce struggle. The upper city wall of Levels IV–III was demolished to within a metre of its own foundations; the gateway through it lay buried under the brick of its towers; the walls of shops and houses leading from it into the city were partly destroyed, and the contents of the rooms were covered by burnt brushwood and fallen beams from the roofs. Denudation has largely cleared the ground between the road and the citadel, but the same conditions prevailed among the houses which remained high on the slopes of the earth ramp south of the palace.

The entire superstructure of Palaces B–C collapsed, or was pulled down, about the time of the destruction, and lay where it had fallen, spreading out over the stairway and court to the east. Nothing remained intact of the brick walls, and the plan of the interior cannot be reconstructed from the remaining burnt patches of plaster floor.

No attempt was made by the inhabitants who had survived to recover the modest possessions and household equipment which lay under the widespread layer of burnt ash, and there was little effort to clear away the accumulation of ruins, except in the region of the upper city wall. Along the short length which survives in the low-lying area by the gate, the bottom courses of the brick construction were used as the basis for a stone wall with rubble filling. That wall, with an inner gate, became part of the fortifications in use during Level II.

Level II, c. 700–586 B.C.

The general level of occupation was a metre or more above the floors of Level III, and the intervening space was filled with bricks, stones and ash, sealing the contents of the underlying city. The street of shops which had lined the road was replaced by an open space, and only one or two houses of the crowded dwellings south of the citadel was repaired and reoccupied.

Besides the building of a new stone city wall, alterations were made in the plan and method of approach. In the preceding town, the main inner gate under the brick tower lay mostly inside the upper city wall; in Level II, though the wall and inner gate were rebuilt on the existing line, the outer gate was thrust out to meet the lower revetment, across the massive block of the Bastion.

From the southern approach the outer gate led into an intervening space, and the road then turned east across a cobbled surface to the inner gate. The largest of several small rooms between the gates was open to the road on its north side. Described, on account of its position, as the guardroom, it had been built over the original square bastion, whose north-east and south-east corners were seen below its foundations.

In plan and construction, therefore, the gateways of Level II were simple, though they gained in strength from the method of approach at right angles across an enclosed space. Assyrian influence on defence systems in the early seventh century may have dictated the change, for a letter exists from the Assyrian governor of Lachish to his king at Nineveh concerning Philistine levies assembled at Lachish, and other fortresses, such as Megiddo, were similarly controlled.

Alternatively, the new wall may have been constructed by Manasseh on his return from captivity in Babylon, when he renounced the idolatries of his earlier years, built a wall round Ophel and put captains of war in all the fenced cities of Judah (II Chronicles XXXIII: 11–14). His son, Josiah "while he was yet young" carried the reforms still farther, destroying the sacred groves and breaking the graven images (II Chronicles XXXIV: 3 and II Kings XXIII: 8).

It is therefore to the century before the accession of Josiah, c. 640 B.C., that the pottery figurines of the mother goddess, and other models, which were found in the last two large tombs in the series are most likely to belong (Chapter 12).

---

[1] Ancient Records of Assyria II, by J. W. Breasted and W. R. Harper, 1906, pp. 239–240.

About this time, too, according to Herodotus,[1] the Scythians, forced south by the pressure of northern nomads, extended their raids as far as Egypt, dominating much of Asia for a quarter of a century. Bronze fibulae (p. 393) and triple-bladed arrowheads (p. 386) are perhaps among the few relics of their occupation, or influence, at Lachish.

Egyptian claims to control Judah were dispelled by the Babylonian victory at Carchemish in 604, and the conqueror Nebuchadrezzar, while receiving tribute from Judah after the first siege and capture of Jerusalem in 597, still attempted to keep the royal line of Josiah on the throne. However, Zedekiah's defection and revolt, made with the connivance of Egypt, brought the full weight of Babylon against Jerusalem and "against all the cities of Judah that were left, against Lachish and against Azekah: for these defenced cities remained of the cities of Judah" (Jeremiah XXXIV: 7).

Despite the careful reconstruction of adequate fortifications at Lachish in the seventh century, very few houses of the period appear to have been built inside the city, and no trace of the administrative centre has so far come to light.

The contents of a row of ramshackle rooms, east of the ruined palace, provide all that is known so far of living conditions during the last decades of pre-exilic occupation. The pottery found there maintained some earlier traditions of form, though wheel-burnished decanters had become the standard jug. A successful but rare attempt at artistic expression was preserved on the surface of a storage jar, on which was incised a design of two ibexes devouring a lotus, a popular Bronze Age theme which is otherwise unknown in so late a context.

Notwithstanding the poor character of the rooms, two inscribed sherds were associated with them; the earlier fragment (Ostracon XXI) was found under the floor, and a large part of a storage jar stood on it, inscribed in a slightly later form of the same Early Hebrew script (Ostracon XX). The main collection of inscribed sherds, written in a contemporary hand by various scribes, as already mentioned, was recovered near the entrance to the city (L. I, Ostraca I–XVIII). Eighteen out of the twenty-one Lachish Letters were found embedded in burnt ash in the guardroom within the Bastion. The clear hand in which they are written leaves no doubt that at least in the last phase before the destruction of Level II the city was occupied by those who had fully mastered their own language and script. Ostracon XIX, found in the burnt debris low on the slopes at the south-west corner, is inscribed in an earlier style, current, perhaps, about the time of the burning of Level III.

On at least two later occasions the gate area was attacked and the approaches were covered in ash. Inside the city gate two superimposed roadways were distinguished, passing over and coalescing on the heap of the fallen brick tower, which was scored with the ruts of chariot wheels.[2] While denudation and the slope of the roads up to the gate make it extremely difficult to follow the succession of events, the interval between the destructions must have been unusually short: on historical grounds the first partial burning may be due to Nebuchadrezzar's campaign against Jehoiakim in 597, and this was followed in 588–586 by severe reprisals against the rebel Zedekiah, culminating in the complete destruction of Jerusalem.

The effects of the Babylonian onslaught were no less severe at Lachish. Masonry, consolidated into a chalky white mass streaked with red, had flowed in a liquid stream over the burnt road surface and lower wall, below which were piled charred heaps of burnt timber. In the angle below the north wall of the Bastion and the west revetment, breaches which had been hurriedly repaired with any material available were forced again; indeed, evidence of destruction by fire was not difficult to find anywhere within the circuit of the walls. Whether all the damage was done at the time of attack is uncertain. In the case of Jerusalem, the burning of the temple, the palace and the houses was the result of a systematic policy put into force by the troops a month after the capitulation, and the same method may have been used at Lachish. It is perhaps too much to suggest that the incomplete inscription on the jar, Ostracon XX, found in the burnt debris of a room east of the palace, which begins with the word *b t sh y t*, "in the ninth"—if it can be explained as an abbreviated form of "in the ninth

---

[1] Book I, § 106.

[2] The upper and lower road surfaces marked Road 1072 were

not defined when Starkey attributed the burning of Road 1087 to Nebuchadrezzar's campaign in 597 B.C.

year"—may be construed into confirmation of the historic date for the siege of Jerusalem in the ninth year of Zedekiah.

Desertion of the site, c. 586–450 B.C.

With the destruction of the walls and battlements, and the death and removal of a great part of the already depleted urban population, there was no incentive to rebuild or reoccupy the city, and there are no structures which can be attributed with certainty to the remainder of the sixth century.

The brief interlude of Gedaliah's rule, which had seemed to introduce new order and hope into the administration of a stricken land, is represented at Lachish by a seal impression from a papyrus document, bearing the name Gedaliah and the administrative title, "He who is over the House", which was only conferred on dignitaries of major importance.

The empire built by the enterprise of Nebuchadrezzar soon crumbled in the hands of his successors. To meet commitments nearer home, Nabonidus withdrew his army from Palestine about 553 B.C., for the spectacular rise of Persia placed Babylon on the defensive, and, to the delight of all subject nations, that proud capital fell in 538 B.C.

Inaugurating a policy new to conquerors in the Near East, Cyrus, king of Persia, authorised the rebuilding of the Temple at Jerusalem in 536 B.C., among other enlightened measures to restore religious liberties. At the same time he extended his dominion southwards, and his son, Cambyses, completed the conquest of Egypt by 525 B.C., leaving Persian rule unchallenged in the Nile Valley for forty years. In consequence, the supply routes through intervening territory were kept open, and Palestine was grouped with Syria, Phoenicia and Cyprus in the fifth satrapy of the empire of Darius. In the sixth year of his reign, c. 515 B.C., despite two decades of delay and opposition, the Temple at Jerusalem was completed and worship was resumed.

After an interval of sixty years about which nothing is known from Bible sources, Nehemiah undertook the refortification of Jerusalem; he allocated the responsibility for building a section of the wall to each group or guild, thereby completing the work in less than two months. "Now the city was large and great; but the people were few therein and the houses were not builded" (Nehemiah VII: 4). The same situation would have confronted the people when they dispersed to reoccupy the cities between Bethel and Beersheba.

Level I, c. 450–c. 150 B.C.

Among the places where some of the Judaeans settled at that time, "Lachish and the fields thereof" is mentioned in the same verse with Zanoah, Adullam and Azekah (Nehemiah XI: 30). Scholars disagree whether this Second Return took place in the reign of Artaxerxes I, c. 448 B.C., or in the seventh year of Artaxerxes II, in 397 B.C.

The spacious Residency at Lachish, with its courts and columns, its reception halls and living-rooms, was a public rather than a private building. It was founded directly on the razed site of Palace C, destroyed two and a half centuries earlier, and there appears to have been no intervening occupation. The sherds in the rooms included a proportion of Attic wares, which are dated on Greek analogies from the mid-fifth to the mid-fourth centuries, and the typical dishes and fragments of jars can be matched at most contemporary sites along the Coastal Plain. Neither the pottery nor the plan suggests direct Persian influence, and the architectural affinities, at least, are closer to Syro-Hittite inspiration. Planned on a scale which would seem to be beyond the resources of returning exiles, the existence of the building does postulate an organised urban control.

It is, of course, possible that the Residency was planned when Darius organised the satrapies, but there is no archaeological evidence for a date in the sixth century. It seems more probable that the settlement of many towns and villages in southern Palestine after the Second Return caused the authorities to set up new centres, with a Resident at Tell ed-Duweir, perhaps, to control the northern part, and another at Tell Jemmeh—where there was a similar building—to control the southern part of the Persian province.

In contrast to the careful plan and interior finish of the Residency, it should be noted that poor masonry was used in the construction of the walls, and also for perfunctory repairs to the fortifications and gate. The only other buildings within the city were two or three houses, planned without method or symmetry, and built without care.

Since the collapse of the Babylonian empire, southern Judah had been overrun by Edomite and other Arabian nomads. They have left little trace of their presence round Tell ed-Duweir, except for a few burials and scattered deposits of crude altars, one of which was inscribed in Aramaic.

The Jewish settlement at Lachish seems to have lingered on for about a century, during the revolt of Egypt and the weakening control of Persia. When Alexander the Great, having occupied Syria, moved south to the conquest of Egypt in 332, the site must have been largely deserted, and only a few coins bear witness to some trade with his passing troops.

After Alexander's death the fifth satrapy was divided as a result of rival pretensions among his generals: Ptolemy Lagi secured Egypt and Palestine, while Seleucus took Syria and set up a capital at Antioch—a division of territory which continued until Antiochus III finally added Palestine to the Seleucid empire in 198 B.C. The change from Ptolemaic to Seleucid control of the district around Tell ed-Duweir is very clearly reflected in the coins found on the surface, for among them only the first four Ptolemies were represented, while there were no coins of the Seleucid dynasty prior to those of the conqueror, Antiochus III.

During his reign and that of his successor two buildings of some interest and importance were in use on the south-east side of the mound, not far from the Great Shaft, which had been filling up with rubbish and silt ever since it was abandoned. Both buildings may have been in existence before the Seleucid conquest. The larger of the two is described as the Solar Shrine, because the east–west orientation, the presence of an altar, and various other features suggest a ritual significance, associated, perhaps, with those Syro-Persian cults which were to find favour in the Greco-Roman world.

So near to the Great Shaft that its south wall was in danger of collapsing into that depression was another structure, similarly oriented, which closely preserved the best traditions of Israelite buildings. At the western end of the main court the large chamber beyond was divided from north to south by eight squared pillars joined by a low stylobate, and the floor of the inner part was cobbled. Against the middle of the west wall was a trough or manger, and close to it, buried in the floor, was a large commemorative scarab of Amenhetep III, of the fifteenth century B.C.

By the time that both buildings fell into disrepair, during the second century, control of the district had finally passed to nearby Mareshah (Tell Sandaḥannah), renewed by the vigour of Sidonian colonists, while Lachish, once her formidable rival, was left desolate.

Final desertion

There was no rebuilding on the site from that time onward, nor any trace of occupation for half a century. Of the early Maccabean kings, only Alexander Jannaeus is represented by two coins, though it was under his rule that the Judaean kingdom achieved its greatest expansion. Roman provincial control from 63 B.C. did not leave any mark, and coins of the Julian emperors Augustus, Tiberius, Claudius and Nero cease at A.D. 68, a date which coincides with the revolt against Rome and the subsequent destruction of Jerusalem in A.D. 70.

Coins of Antoninus Pius, Lucius Verus, Geta and Alexander Severus exist from the second and third centuries A.D., after which there is another blank period until the establishment of the Byzantine empire.

During the first three-quarters of the fourth century A.D. Palestine enjoyed a rare interlude of peace. Agriculture and trade flourished round the important road centre of Eleutheropolis, where the main routes from Jerusalem to Gaza crossed the best means of access from Hebron to the plain.

When Eusebius travelled south early in the century, he went from Eleutheropolis (Beit Jibrin) and passed *Lakeis* at the seventh milestone. That line is still marked by stones protruding from the surface and excavations were made at two points on the far side of the valley, north of Tell ed-Duweir. A few hours' work revealed a cambered road, flanked by a footpath and a drainage channel, and on it were found many coins dating from the first three-quarters of the fourth century. By then the old city was already ruined, but Eusebius would have seen an open village to the south, the site of which, at Khirbet Duweir, is marked by piles of fourth-century pottery.

Thereafter, coins dating from the fifth, sixth and seventh centuries A.D. reflect in some degree the measure of security. The whole period of Arab rule between the eighth and thirteenth centuries is unrepresented, and the transfer of control from Baghdad to Cairo in the fourteenth century made little difference to the locality. Indeed, from the days of Nehemiah onwards, the words of Job were applicable to the solitary few who tilled the fields around Lachish: "And he dwelleth in desolate cities, and in houses which no man inhabiteth, which are ready to become heaps" (Job XV: 28).

FORTIFICATIONS AND BUILDINGS

The Fortifications

In the foot-hills of Judah where stone and lime are easily available and soil for brick-making is scarce, constructional tradition and style were not seriously affected by the passage of time. Methods were dependent on practical considerations, and were designed to take advantage of natural features and supplies, to overcome the effects of constant exposure, and above all to resist attack.

Complying with these requirements, the walls around Tell ed-Duweir were based on a sloping glacis or revetment of immense boulders, merging into vertical sections built of smaller stones. The complete circuit was crowned by recessed walls of brick, and all parts above ground were covered with white lime plaster frequently renewed. As an additional protection, buttresses were built against the outer face, and the intervening spaces were filled with packed stones and earth.

Whether the builders of the Iron Age made use of Bronze Age masonry must remain in doubt, but it is not impossible, for the revetment on the north-east side was so low on the outer slope of the mound that the city deposits against which it rested contained no sherds later than Middle Bronze Age II (PEQ, October, 1950, Pl. XIII). On the west side, however, the six-metre city wall, at least, was certainly of Iron Age origin, and the foundations of the lower revetment on that side have yet to be investigated.

The relationship of all component parts of the fortifications and approach roads in so far as it is at present understood is set out in Chapter 4.

The earlier phases may include the podium of Palace A (Fig. 5) and buildings such as the brick "government storehouse" to the south-east (Fig. 4), forming, perhaps, the stronghold of Level V, followed after a short time by the six-metre wall and brick gate-towers, with some parts of the lower revetment and Bastion (Pls. 109, 111, 114).

The rebuilding in stone of the "government storehouse" on the ruined walls of the brick construction may be contemporary with the city deposits of Level IV which are as yet unexcavated.

Apart from alterations and repairs, the city wall of Level IV–III continued in use until the destruction of the city at Level III. In the limited reconstruction of the city's defences at Level II, a completely new stone wall was built on the stump of the six-metre brick wall, and a gateway on a new plan was set over the Bastion. That gate and its guardrooms were soon subjected to destruction and were buried in a thick layer of ash.

When the Residency of the fifth century was founded on the site of Palace A–C, the city wall was possibly rebuilt or extensively repaired, but the masonry was poor and was too near the surface to be well preserved.

If the details of the Lachish relief are reliable and have been correctly interpreted, two circuits existed when the Assyrians attacked the city; they would correspond with the six-metre wall and the lower revetment on the west side, and both defences in plan and pictorial presentation have recessed panels. In the bas-reliefs, an isolated tower is depicted low on the slope, and this unusual feature may be matched on the site by the Bastion in its earliest phase, before it was incorporated into the lower line of the revetment in the seventh century.

Disregarding comparisons with fortifications in the southern kingdom or elsewhere which are certainly earlier than the Iron Age,[1] features in common are found at Tell el-Fûl, Tell Beit Mirsim, 'Ain Shems, Tell eṣ-Ṣafi and Tell en-Naṣbeh, in fact at most of the sites where excavations have taken place.

Outside Judah, similarities with Samaria, Megiddo and Carchemish are discussed in detail in Chapter 4; the contemporary system of Assyrian defence is well illustrated at Khorsabad and Zencerli.

The Buildings

Apart from the citadel, of which the remaining platform or podium is described in Chapter 3, and the post-exilic buildings which are examined in Chapter 6, there are two other structures which require special mention.

Near the south-east corner of the citadel stout stone walls projected southwards from the great east–west wall which almost bisects the mound. Though the plan of this stone building was incomplete through denudation (K.15: 1034), it was itself founded on an earlier brick construction, the plan of which, as partially exposed, is given in Fig. 4. Both buildings originally consisted of long chambers side by side, which, if completed by a room of similar size at right angles to the denuded ends, would form the simplest form of the so-called "hilani" building. Albright remarked on the ambiguity of the word, and considered Starkey's term "government storehouse" as a happier description (AASOR XXI–XXII, § 10 and PEQ, 1937, p. 237). "It can hardly be accidental", wrote Albright, "that we have a number of Palestinian buildings composed of parallel rooms of comparable proportion, all dating from about the tenth century B.C." In his view, they compare with building plans from Boghazköy, the Hittite capital, between 1500 and 1200 B.C.

West of the government storehouse, among many less spacious dwellings, one house, H.15: 1003 (Fig. 9), had apparently been repaired and re-used before the final catastrophe in 586 B.C. The characteristic feature of the plan is a row of monolithic stone pillars across the main axis of the room.

Albright noted the earlier occurrence of such pillars in house plans of northern sites (AASOR XXI–XXII, § 35), but their structural use—if any—is obscure. Sometimes one block is balanced on another, and in such cases the lack of tenon and mortice joint would limit their capacity to take weight or strain. Albright connects them with the weaving industry carried on in many buildings at his site of Tell Beit Mirsim, and there is no doubt from the number of clay loom weights on the floor that weaving was done in room H.15: 1003 at Tell ed-Duweir.

Employed in the stables of Megiddo as tethering posts for horses (M. I., p. 35), such pillars had other uses as well; that they served in some way to admit light and air through the spaces between them has also been suggested, but the evidence from Duweir offers no further explanation of their use.

The best preserved house with pillars was in Grid Square R.16: 10–21 (Pl. 123); it was apparently built after the destruction of Level II, and was not finally abandoned until the second century B.C. Comparisons for the plan from other sites are given in Chapter 6. Reminiscent of the best building period of the Jewish monarchy, the house cannot have served as a stable, for the cobbled space at the west end beyond the pillars is only two metres wide, which would be insufficient for animals of normal size.

North of the pillared house, and conforming to the same east–west axis, there was another building which cannot fail to be associated with some form of worship (Pl. 121). Overturned near some steps leading to the sanctuary was a stone altar bearing symbols of the solar cult, and for this and other reasons the building is described as the Solar Shrine. The date of construction is as yet unknown, but it can hardly be contemporary with the Residency of the fifth to fourth century, for it remained in use until the reign of Antiochus the Great. It would seem more probable that the Solar Shrine was erected during the period of Seleucid control early in the second century B.C.

---

[1] See A.-G. Barrois, Manuel, pp. 210 ff.; C. Watzinger, Denkmäler Palästinas, pp. 51 ff., and W. F. Albright, AASOR XVII, § 38; XXI–XXII, § 8, note 6.

PEOPLE AND DOMESTIC ANIMALS

Captives of Lachish, from the bas-reliefs found in Sennacherib's palace at Nineveh

In the long procession which moves towards the Assyrian king seated on his throne at Lachish, the artist of these valuable reliefs has shown the submission of all sections of the population.

At the head of the procession, in the upper row, are six bearded men in plain, long tunics, with the three foremost figures kneeling in supplication. Behind the Assyrian officers who guard them, two other prisoners are being questioned, and they are followed by men and women carrying sacks and leading children by the hand. A light, two-wheeled wagon drawn by oxen is piled with large bundles secured by cords. A woman drives the cart, while another nurses a baby and a child is perched on the sacks (Fig. 2).

Fig. 2. Procession of captives (reproduced by permission of the Trustees of the British Museum)

In the lower register of the relief male prisoners are subjected to torture and death, and the procession of people carrying sacks and flasks is completed by yet another loaded wagon in the rear. Behind, Assyrian soldiers remove plunder from the city, and a laden camel is urged on by native drivers. While the chief men, guarded by officers of rank at the head of the procession, are bareheaded and have curly hair and beards, the prisoners who follow wear turbans with fringed ends and short belted tunics. Women and girls wear plain robes and cloaks hanging to the ground.

The artist has differentiated between the leaders of the city and the rank and file, a distinction which would be accounted for if the governor and his military and civil staff were appointed from Jerusalem. That the civil population joined the troops in defence of the city is shown by the presence on the battlements of men with turbans, and the Judaean forces are distinguished from their enemies by their pointed casques, quite different from the plumed helmets of the Assyrians (see Frontispiece). There is much similarity between the dress of the eighth-century B.C. inhabitants of Lachish and that of Arab villagers in Palestine today, who still wear turbans and belts with woven fringed ends.

Anthropometric studies

The mortal remains of those who did not long survive the siege or its effects were buried with scant ceremony in several pits.[1] It was estimated that there were originally about 1,500 skulls, and some 700 were brought to England for study, an arduous task covering several years which was undertaken and published by D. L. Risdon.[2]

---

[1] Ossuaries 107, 108, 116, 117, 120.

[2] Biometrika XXXI, Parts I, II, July, 1939. The collection was presented to the British Museum (Natural History), apart from a representative series in the Palestine Archaeological Museum, and two trepanned skulls in the Wellcome Historical Medical Museum, London.

It is shown in his report that there were "few aged specimens" in the collection and "the population was considerably younger than such as is normally found in ancient or recent cemeteries."[1] The hypothesis that the bones were cleared from an existing cemetery is, in Risdon's opinion, unacceptable, both because of the lack of aged people and the high proportion of immature skeletons which are normally too easily damaged to survive more than one removal.

Risdon notes that the closest connexions of the Lachish collection are with series of Lower Egyptian type, and he infers that the population of the Palestinian town was entirely or almost completely of Egyptian origin.

While agreeing that the cranial characters are indeed similar, Sir Arthur Keith[2] challenged Risdon's conclusion that the population of Lachish was derived from Egypt. He would prefer to see, in the peoples of the Palestinian coast and the Egyptian Delta, members of the same Mediterranean family of peoples. Sir Arthur's personal observations led him to recognise a dark-complexioned, narrow-headed type among the present-day population of the Delta and south Palestine, and he asked whether they represent a remnant of the Philistines and of the people who inhabited Lachish. "In the recognition of race, variety or species," he wrote, "naturalists depend—not so much on measurements—as on certain distinctive marks or characters. Mr. Risdon notes among the Lachish people two characters which are non-Egyptian—namely, extreme narrowness and prominence of the bridge of the nose, and the curvature of the cheekbones. From these characters alone I should have suspected that the Lachish people were racially different from the Egyptians."

Sir Arthur's remarks are strikingly illustrated by the pottery portrait head which dates from the end of the Bronze or beginning of the Iron Age.[3] Black painted eyebrows meet on the bridge of the straight nose, which is extremely prominent. Another characteristic is the small moustache.

While five centuries separate this head from the ossuary deposits at Duweir, it is interesting to find that the type persisted in these skulls, and may even be found among the present population of the Fertile Crescent.

Since the publication of Risdon's report, other cranial remains were added to the series. They were examined by students of the Duckworth Laboratory, University Museum of Archaeology and Ethnology, Cambridge, and the results of their work are given in Appendix A. Though the new series of some twenty individuals includes some burials which took place in the tenth to ninth centuries B.C., it has not been possible to discover any racial differences in the earlier skeletons.

In a study of the Racial Relationships of the Ancient and Modern Populations of Egypt and Nubia,[4] Dr. A. Batrawi discusses the results obtained by Risdon.

A female cranium suggestive of osteomyelitis, and that of a male showing signs of hydrocephaly, represent diseased conditions, and there are eight skulls which are clearly artificially deformed, but Risdon does not consider it possible to assert that any were intentionally so treated in childhood.

Three trepanned skulls in the collection were described by Dr. T. Wilson Parry,[5] who said that they were the first specimens exhibiting evidence of this surgical operation to have been found in Asia.

Domestic Animals

Among the animal bones which overlay the human remains in the ossuary pits, the late Miss D. M. A. Bate recognised five species (Appendix A): the ox, camel, medium-sized horse and several skulls of domestic dog and pig. The first three animals figure on Sennacherib's Reliefs, but Miss Bate noted a distinct difference between the long-horned ox depicted there and the small horn cores of the actual skulls. If the oxen on the reliefs were indigenous to Lachish, the inhabitants must, in her opinion, have possessed two races of cattle.

Curiously enough, the domestic pig is best represented in the deposits, and all the skulls were deformed by pachyostosis, particularly on the frontal portion, though the domestic pig of today, which is kept hygienically,

---

[1] Ibid., p. 104.
[2] PEQ, 1940, pp. 7–12.
[3] PEQ, 1938, Pl. XXIII, Fig. 2—to be published in *Lachish IV*.

[4] Royal Anthropological Journal LXXVI, Pt. II, 1946.
[5] Man, 1936, pp. 233–234.

is not subject to this pathological condition. It cannot be said that the animal bones were spread with deliberate intention to defile the human remains below; indeed, the reasons for the deposits remain obscure.

It is eventually hoped to make a comparative study of the Lachish crania in the light of recent discoveries, and in relation to the recorded measurements of both ancient and modern populations in the Near East. Meanwhile, the detailed measurements and statistics are brought to life by the fortunate preservation at Nineveh of the graphic account of a war correspondent attached to the victorious Assyrian army, which provides a rare and delightful picture of the aspect and dress, the animals and transport of the people of Lachish.

RELIGION AND BURIAL

The burial-places and their contents which are described in Part III do not provide a clear picture of the rites and customs which accompanied the disposal of the dead during the period of the Jewish monarchy. Knowledge of the subject is not greatly increased from Biblical sources, for the references which occur there are mostly incidental and obscure. However, a comparison of the Old Testament with the results of excavation is more illuminating, for it reflects the difference between orthodox belief or policy emanating from Jerusalem and the deep-rooted practice of the common people.

Although the inhospitable hills of Judah yield a bare living to men and beasts, their formation provides the shelter of innumerable caves for both the living and the dead. In a land where soil was always scarce and valuable, the purchase price of four hundred silver shekels which Abraham is said to have paid for the cave of Machpelah shows the importance to the patriarch of a permanent burial-place, the traditional site of which at Hebron is still known and venerated (Genesis XXIII, XLIX: 29–32).

In the patriarchal age, as excavations have shown, a tomb of circular or two-lobed construction was usual. By gradual stages the latter chambers lost their distinctive character, as the equal halves merged into one, cut to a rectangular pattern. Low benches or recesses round the walls gave place to higher square-cut benches on each side of the entry, which was approached by a flight of steps.

The later course of this development is illustrated in the tombs at Tell Fara (BP II, p. 32 and Pl. LX) from the reign of Rameses I, c. 1300, to that of Pasebkhanu in the mid-eleventh century B.C. In this connexion, the earliest tomb plans at Duweir (Tombs 521 and 6006) present a more advanced stage in the process of transformation (Tomb 6006, Fig. 31) which is in keeping with the later phase of ceramic development.

Family tradition and the limitations of space ensured that burial-places of irregular or archaic shape sometimes continued in use, but occasionally alterations and enlargements appear to have been made to conform with newer trends.

Whatever transitional developments took place, and they may have differed in the hill country and in the plain, it is clear that by the seventh century a standard type of tomb had emerged and was in use throughout Judah, containing square chambers of similar dimensions, each provided with rock benches. A new feature was a circular well or repository driven through the rock behind the bench to the same depth as the floor. At Tell ed-Duweir this recess was consistently on the east side of the tomb (Figs. 21–23, 25, 27); at 'Ain Shems it was usually on the south-west (APEF II, Pls. V and VI). If the orientation had significance, it may have contributed to practical ventilation of the tomb through an oblique shaft, as found in Tomb 1 at 'Ain Shems, an explanation which would obviate any necessity to seek a ritual purpose. The construction of Tomb 14 at 'Ain Shems, dated to the sixth century B.C. by Grant and Wright (AS V, p. 77), maintains a high standard of cutting which is not to be found in Tomb 217 at Tell ed-Duweir (Fig. 23). It is possible that accuracy of plan and precision of cutting declined after the Babylonian conquest, and Tomb 217, with its irregular benches and inaccurate angles, may illustrate the general demoralisation which affected the surviving population.

It was not until the settlement of Sidonian colonists at Tell Sandaḥannah in the second century B.C., that the proper disposal of the dead in worthy family sepulchres once more became a matter for community pride, resulting in the elaborate painted tombs of Marissa,[1] which have no counterpart at Tell ed-Duweir.

Methods of Burial

Turning from the tombs to their contents, only Tomb 521 contained burials which were relatively undisturbed, with two bodies extended on a bench and burnished pottery vessels near them. An iron trident and iron knives (Pls. 40: 7 and 56: 38; 56: 22, 26, 27), which are best matched in the products of the Iron Age culture of Europe, indicate that in the equipment of the tomb new elements and influences were at work.

Apart from this isolated and unique tomb, only two methods of burial were observed at Tell ed-Duweir: interments in caves or pits, which contained many skeletons in extraordinary confusion, and individual graves cut in the soil or rock, which rarely contained more than one body.

On and around the ruins of the Fosse Temple, thirty-one graves were discovered, cut in the soil which had spread from the slopes of the mound to cover the deserted building. Unlike the cave burials, they were relatively undisturbed. Only a few bowls and dippers, with an occasional storage jar, were provided in each grave, for in most cases the poverty of the deceased, or strict observance of the Mosaic Law, had denied him the customary offerings. If poverty denied the shelter of a family vault, it also preserved the body from desecration, and this was further secured, perhaps, by the known sanctity of the temple site. Local memory retained the knowledge of its position for several centuries, attested by the crowd of burials near the ruined walls.

The earlier burials in the neighbourhood were oriented north and south, and about a dozen graves made at a later time, with shafts and coverings of stone slabs, were dug directly over them and oriented east and west. Absence of offerings—except for two jugs of identical form—restricts speculation about the occupants, whose method of burials is rather similar to that of the fifth to fourth century series at 'Athlit (QDAP II, pp. 41 et seq.) and the so-called "Philistine" graves at Gezer (Gezer I, pp. 289–300).

On the mound itself, long after the desertion of the city, nearly two hundred graves were cut in the low-lying area inside the ancient gateway, but apart from an east–west orientation, there is no indication of their date.

As the Old Testament affirms in countless passages, deprivation of burial was a dire calamity and a constant threat, and it was at all times a meritorious obligation to perform that office for the dead.

Among the incidents where such acts are recorded, the story of the man of God from Judah is of interest (I Kings XIII). Not only was the place of burial chosen and prepared for use, but its position on the mount above Bethel was marked by a monument which survived more than two centuries, for this tomb alone was spared when Josiah turned himself and "spied the sepulchres that were there in the mount, and sent and took the bones out of the sepulchres, and burned them upon the altar and polluted it" (II Kings XXIII: 16).

Strict observance of the Law should have condemned those who touched the bones or bodies of the dead to a period of expiation, but no record survives to show that those who took part in the wholesale removal of bones to defile the high places and the groves were deterred or affected by that ordinance.

Gaining ground with each adversity, and losing strength in times of peace and plenty, reform in Judah and Jerusalem was a long-established barometer of public feeling. In a reign of more than half a century, which was distinguished for idolatry, Manasseh's change of heart and attempts at reform only occurred after exile in Babylon (II Chronicles XXXIII: 11–17), but it was the energy and force of his grandson Josiah which really struck at the ancient centres of the cults wherever they were found.

That Lachish escaped all retribution at this time seems unlikely, when in the lifetime of the prophet Micah a century earlier, the city was "the beginning of sin to the daughter of Zion" (Micah I: 13), but what that sin was neither the Scriptures nor the site have revealed.

It is not to be expected, therefore, that the cemeteries of Lachish contained the bodies of the orthodox, unless their burials are represented by the poorly equipped and less disturbed graves near the Fosse Temple, for offerings

---

[1] Painted Tombs in the Necropolis of Marissa, by F. Peters and H. Thiersch.

to the dead, with which most tombs were provided, were in themselves apparently contrary to the Law (Deuteronomy XXVI: 14).

There are not a great many unmistakable signs of idolatrous practice. Amulets and scarabs of Egyptian deities do not always signify more than good-luck charms (Pls. 34, 35, 36, 43, 44), and the bone rods and gavels have yet to be proved to be the apparatus of rhabdomancy (Pl. 37).

However, the pottery figures so generally identified with Astarte or Ashtoreth—Queen of Heaven—as *dea nutrix*, are more certainly of cult or votive use and are associated with models of beds and chairs, her attribute, the dove, and pottery rattles (Pls. 27, 28, 29). Confined to the last large tomb groups and to the rooms of Level III–II, the smiling, once-painted faces framed in stiff rows of curls and cast from a mould give place in the latest phase to the merest indications of features pinched up by hand. The bodies in both cases were roughly modelled, with the hands supporting the full and prominent breasts, and the torso was finished in a plain pillar base (Pls. 27, 31).

No link has yet been found between these pillar-base figurines, which do not occur in tomb groups at Tell ed-Duweir prior to the eighth century, and the plaque figurines of the goddess offering her breasts, which are sometimes found in groups of the Late Bronze Age. That gesture became common in figurines of Assyrian make early in the ninth century, which suggests a recrudescence of a common influence, which spread eventually from the Syrian coast to the Aegean world by the middle of the eighth century B.C. (see p. 377).

It is uncertain whether the crude pillar figurines are like the household gods or idols described as *teraphaim* in the story of Rachel's theft from her father (Genesis XXXI: 34). They were small enough to be hidden under her as she sat on the camel trappings, but in another, much later, tale of feminine guile they were described as large enough to simulate the body of a sleeping man (I Samuel XIX: 13).

Specifically condemned with idols and other abominations by Josiah, the *teraphaim* had a special and time-honoured place among the people. If Josiah's edicts were rigorously applied by everyone in Judah, they should have been pounded to dust and scattered on the graves like other symbols of idolatry (II Kings XXIII: 6), but the drastic effects of sudden reforms are seldom found to be lasting.

It is unlikely that the rotund zoomorphic vessels which occur sporadically in groups of all periods have a religious significance, but some rite of superstition may animate the realistic models of a bareback horseman, which are occasionally associated with other pottery models of the eighth to seventh centuries. Whether they are to be connected with the nomad hordes who were in control of Asia in the second half of the seventh century must remain in doubt.[1] In sharp contrast to them are the bearded horsemen of the following centuries, riding on smaller steeds, fully caparisoned, and dressed in cloaks and pointed hoods.

Found chiefly on open ground near the city gate, these and other broken pottery models of men and women (Pl. 33) are certainly later than the destruction of Level II in 586 B.C. With them were many plain tapering pillars of varying height, and some were decorated with scratched geometric designs. An incomplete inscription on a square-shaped altar of a type familiar from Tell Jemmeh and elsewhere has been dated independently on epigraphic grounds by Professor Dupont-Sommer to about 450 B.C. (p. 358). The votive or ritual purpose of such altars is established by their presence in the tombs and Moon Temple of Hureidha, a site which was probably occupied during the fifth and fourth centuries B.C.[2] Apart from these deposits, nothing has been found which could be connected with a religious purpose at the time of the reoccupation of the site at Tell ed-Duweir.

Burials of the period are also rare, but the small group oriented east and west near the Fosse Temple may be contemporary. A similar grave near the city gate, in which two people were buried, was devoid of objects, though a fine seal found near by and a deep bowl above the stone slab covering may have some connexion.[3]

---

[1] Herodotus, Book I, § 106.

[2] Cf. The Tombs and Moon Temple of Hureidha, by G. Caton-Thompson.

[3] For comparisons with Grave 525, see Gezer I, pp. 289–294; M. I, pp. 92–97; and 'Athlit (QDAP II, pp. 41–104).

LETTERS AND DOCUMENTS

By DAVID DIRINGER, D.LITT.

The importance of the epigraphic material found at Tell ed-Duweir cannot be overestimated, either from the point of view of North Semitic epigraphy in general, or in relation to other discoveries at the site. It should be emphasised, moreover, that only the topmost layers of less than a quarter of the surface-area were examined, and further excavations—if political and financial conditions permit—may result in even more important finds.

It is well known that the epigraphic remains of ancient Israel are scarce. In explanation, it is suggested that the ancient Hebrews possessed none of that genius for "imperial conquest", for administration on a large scale, or for civic order, which inspired the great and numerous monumental inscriptions of the ancient world. Another theory is that there were inscriptions in early Hebrew Palestine, but these have not been allowed to survive, because, from the standpoint of later Judaism, the religious and general outlook of the pre-exilic Hebrews was essentially unorthodox. Alternatively, the majority of the inscriptions may have been destroyed in the many invasions and occupations of Palestine by hostile armies.

It must also be remembered that until recent times, excavations in Palestine were not conducted in accordance with strictly scientific methods, and many small inscriptions may have been lost. It was assumed that most contemporary documents, and particularly all the literary works, were written on papyrus, imported from Egypt, or on parchment, and in the damp soil of Palestine no papyrus could be expected to survive unless preserved in exceptional circumstances, like the Dead Sea Hebrew Scrolls recently discovered.

Although the excavations at Tell ed-Duweir remain incomplete, the epigraphic finds confirm at least the last two theories. It is now reasonable to suppose that there were many Early Hebrew inscriptions, but that the vast majority were destroyed through the agency of man or by the action of time and climate.

Indeed, it is highly probable that the Lachish Letters, which were found in the burnt debris, are only a small part of a large collection of correspondence and other documents. Much of the inscribed material found at Tell ed-Duweir could have escaped notice, and the seal impressions—smaller than a farthing and much the same colour as the soil—would probably have been lost. Four impressions of seals, with the marks of papyrus on the back, provide the first proof that this writing material was employed in Palestine, thus confirming the indirect references of the Bible.

Apart from these general results, there are other facts which must be taken into consideration.

For instance, the five letters of the Early Hebrew alphabet, scratched on the steps of the palace, and possibly belonging to the late ninth or early eighth century B.C., are among the earliest known examples of the alphabet in its conventional order, and they may be the outcome of systematic teaching. Is this connected with the instruction given by those, whom "in the third year of his reign" Jehoshaphat "sent to his princes to teach in the cities of Judah"? (II Chronicles XVII: 7).

The jar handle stamps do not offer many new names or words, nor do they present any new contribution to the knowledge of epigraphy, but their great number has made it possible to examine their significance. Comparison with the Siloam Tunnel inscription attributed to the last years of the eighth century B.C. provides one of the few examples which show how epigraphy can be utilised for Biblical research. Moreover, the possibility of dating the "royal" jar handle stamps may solve some archaeological problems, both at Tell ed-Duweir and at other sites in southern Palestine.

Prior to the discovery of the Tell ed-Duweir ostraca, only one Early Hebrew inscription, in the narrow sense of the term, was known with continuous text. This was the aforementioned Siloam inscription, containing six lines. The Lachish ostraca provide about a hundred lines of more or less readable Hebrew of pre-exilic times, and may be considered the earliest personal documents extant written in the language of the Bible. Their contribution to the knowledge of Early Hebrew epigraphy, language, proper names and so forth, as well as to Old Testament study, is so great that Professor D. Winton Thomas stated at the time that no more valuable discovery had ever been made in Biblical archaeology.

From the point of view of palaeography, the Lachish ostraca represent the climax of the development of the Early Hebrew current hand, while the Siloam inscription and the jar handle stamps are good specimens of the monumental style of writing. The recently discovered Early Hebrew fragments found with the Dead Sea Scrolls are evidence that a third style of script existed, which can be considered the literary hand of early Israel. The term Early Hebrew (with capitals), also known as Phoenician Hebrew or Canaanite Hebrew, is applied to the script and inscriptions of pre-exilic Israel in contrast to the term Square Hebrew, which denotes the predecessor of the Hebrew characters as used in modern print.

The inscribed weights have added to the knowledge of early Hebrew metrology, and they demonstrate the importance of the city as a commercial centre, while the seals and impressions provide new material for the study of proper names and titles, and are, as well, fine products of intaglio engraving.

Finally, even the two small Aramaic inscriptions in cursive and monumental style are not without value, increased by the apparent lack of sixth-century remains in south Palestine. They illustrate the diffusion of the Aramaic script in the fifth century B.C., and are the latest Semitic inscriptions from the site.

There are no other inscriptions of the fifth and fourth centuries, a period which covers the occupation of the Residency.

A few Rhodian stamps from Greek wine jars date the upper filling of the Great Shaft to the second quarter of the third century B.C., but including those found on the surface there were only eight, in marked contrast to 350 examples from the crowded town of Marissa at Tell Sandaḥannah near by. The series from Greece and the Aegean which Miss Virginia Grace has studied differs in detail from stamps found in south Palestine. When full comparisons are made, it may prove that choice wine reached Lachish and Marissa from emporia on the Syrian coast.

PART II
THE CITY

CHAPTER 3

THE STRATIFICATION OF THE SITE

THE MOUND: WEST SECTION

TOWARDS the end of the first season a cross-section was cut through the upper levels of tell debris north of the Bastion. There was a twofold reason for the investigation: it was hoped to examine the foundations of the Iron Age city walls, which are described in detail on pp. 87–93, and also to complete the history of the stratification which had been exposed in section from Early Bronze Age III to Late Bronze Age II (or III), near the north-east corner of the city. In this latter section the contents of the successive strata record an almost continuous occupation of the mound from that period, which was terminated, as elsewhere on the site, by a violent con-flagration, marked by a thick layer of burning close to the surface. It was therefore necessary to look somewhere else for the debris of the Iron Age occupation, and this was found to be nearly 7 metres deep along the west side. The position of the trench can be seen on Pl. 1: 1 and Pl. 2: 2, and the sectional plan is on Pl. 109.

The two trenches together provide a continuous stratification of tell debris with a total depth of 17 m., after a deduction of 60 cm. has been made to allow for an overlap of two layers common to both cuttings. The soil was removed in layers of 30 cm. at a time, and the sherds and other contents were kept separately without any sorting until the completion of the task. The layers were numbered from 1 to 56, beginning at the lowest level on bed-rock.

On the evidence of the potsherds, the sections presumably cover a period dating from the Early Bronze Age III, third millennium B.C., to the return from the Babylonian exile, in the reign of Cyrus the Persian, c. 538 B.C. This date can perhaps be extended by nearly a hundred years, for Lachish is mentioned among the towns of Judah reoccupied in Nehemiah's time, and his return is dated to about 445 B.C. Seventeen metres of debris had therefore been deposited in about two thousand years.

On this calculation, which is subsidiary to stratigraphical analysis, each layer of 30 cm. should represent an average period of about thirty-five years. The general correctness of this estimate at Tell ed-Duweir over a long period is supported by the finding of a scarab of Amenhetep II (1447–1420 B.C.) and of xviiith dynasty pottery in the thirtieth layer from the top, for which the estimate of thirty-five years for each layer, calculated from the time of Nehemiah, gives a fifteenth-century date.

A summary of the contents of the north-east and west sections has been published in the Palestine Explora-tion Quarterly for October, 1950; a full account of the north-east trench, with a diagram to scale of the strati-fication, will be published in *Lachish IV*. In the present volume it is only proposed to deal with the West Section.

The cutting was about 2 metres wide, and measured nearly 7 metres from the tell surface to a point in the stratification (at 33–36 ft.) where Late Bronze Age sherds were found in soil blackened by fire.

Examination of the area was suspended at about 255·60 m. above sea level, where the presence of a burnt layer was fully established which corresponded in intensity and content with the deposit at the top of the north-east cutting, and with Structure III of the Fosse Temple (L. II).

The potsherds found in the West Section, which penetrated behind the inner line of the brick and stone revetment, may have been partially disturbed when the Iron Age defences were built. The stratification is therefore not entirely reliable, though nothing was found which was obviously incongruous. The sherds were all small and indeterminate, and it was not until the full sequence of pottery form in the tomb groups had been worked out that the significance of the few recognisable rims and sections became less obscure.

71

INTERPRETATION OF OCCUPATIONAL LEVELS I–VI

The absence of recognisable floor levels in the West Section precluded the establishment of any distinct division between the layers. It was therefore necessary to reach some result by means of a sherd count, for few fragments were large enough to be accurately related to complete forms in the tomb series. Whenever possible, pottery class numbers, followed by the type numbers, are given under the appropriate headings in the Analysis of Pottery Fragments in the West Section on pp. 75 f. which shows the contents of the trench, layer by layer.

Level I. Surface at 262 m. above sea level (56–52 ft.)

The Analysis shows a predominance of storage jar fragments made of soft orange paste (Class S.3, type 488), at or near the present ground surface. Similar sherds were only found at Tell ed-Duweir on and in the floors of the post-exilic Residency, which was in use from about 450 B.C. to the following century—a date based on the presence of Attic sherds. Pieces of mortaria (Class B.14, types 565, 566) were recognised, and part of a Rhodian jar.

The orange paste jars and mortaria are typical of Stratum II at Tell Abu Hawam (QDAP IV, p. 4, Fig. 3) dated between the late sixth and early fourth centuries B.C. For other references see Chapter 9: Storage Jars, type 488.

The living level of the period was at or above 261·44 m.—the level of the latest remaining doorsill of the inner gate (Pl. 112 and Fig. 8)—which agrees with the presence of the majority of orange paste jar fragments above that height.

Level II. 261·04–260·14 m. (51–48 ft.)

Few sherds were found in the upper 2 ft., and only one recognisable bowl form, Class B.11, type 62.

Excavations within the city showed that the space close to the gate was clear of houses in the last pre-exilic phases, which accounts, perhaps, for the lack of debris in the section. The inner gate threshold of Level II was set at 260·38 m. (Pl. 111 and Fig. 8), over a metre below the post-exilic doorsill. Fortunately the threshold at 260·38 m. belongs to the gate through the stone wall of Level II, which was also exposed in the West Section (Pl. 109). Under the stone piers of the gate, the upper surface of the end of a brick wall was partially uncovered (Pls. 111, 114), which can confidently be identified with the brick wall of Level III, also exposed in the West Section (Pl. 109). The ground surface of Level II should be above the junction of the walls at 260 m., and seems to occur at about 260·44 m., where sherds of metallic reddish-grey pottery were most plentiful. These storage jar fragments are similar to those on which the Lachish ostraca were inscribed (Level II guardroom), though there are no rims to establish the connexion beyond doubt. The metallic ware is also close in appearance to that of the vessels bearing stamped jar handles, typical of Level III, so it is natural to find such fragments in both periods.

The necessary clearance of the fallen part of the brick city wall of Level III, before the construction of the stone wall of Level II, may have removed some of the accumulated rubbish of both Levels III and II.

Levels III–IV. 259·84–257·88 m. (47–41 ft.)

Without further excavation it is not possible to say where the 2 metres of debris attributed to Levels III–IV should be divided. That they represent at least two stages is indicated by more than one phase of building among the houses which were destroyed at the end of the Level III city, and the connexion between these houses and the West Section is amply demonstrated by the similarity of the pottery. Pl. 114 shows the relation between the houses built on either side of the road leading from the gate in Grid Squares G.17/18 and the exposed portions of the brick wall on the edge of the mound.

The West Section to the north of the gate exposed the same wall, which is based on one course of stone at 257·88 m. (Pl. 109).

The total accumulation of rubbish from the foundation of the wall to the top of the remaining part is 2·12 m. From the fact that the brick wall was apparently a free-standing structure, faced on the inner side by orthostats (one of which is seen in section on Pl. 109), it would appear that, unlike the lower revetment at the north-east corner, the rubbish accumulated after the building of the wall. If the rough-and-ready calculation which held good for the two sections as a whole were applied to the 7 ft. of deposits which appear to have accumulated prior to the destruction of Level III in *c.* 700 B.C., the multiplication of 35 years by 7 ft. gives 945 B.C. as the approximate date of the wall.

While the calculated date is not incompatible with the foundation of the wall by Rehoboam or his immediate successors, there are but few sherds in or near the foundations of the wall which are comparable to those in the trial cut at the south-east corner of the citadel (see description of Level V on pp. 80–83), where there is much

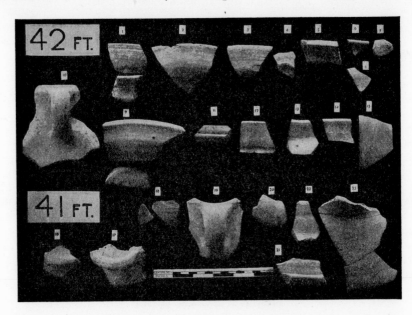

Fig. 3. Sherds from the West Section

more hand burnish of better quality. In that earlier phase of occupation the city did not apparently extend to the western edge.

In a total of at least 1,450 sherds recovered from the West Section, the proportion of thirty hand-burnished pieces and only eight burnished on the wheel is small. The first sherds to show hand burnish on red slip were at 257·14 m.; pieces with signs of hand and wheel finish were at 258·04 m., and bowl rims of Classes B.2, 3, 6, 7 and 13 were all in a singularly rich layer at 258·34 m. (42 ft.).

The characteristic sherds in the intervening metre of debris are fragments of shapes which can be matched in the pottery of the Fosse Temple, and the few pieces of burnish among them are small and indistinctive. The unburnished wares are coarse, with a rough surface, and it is a matter of speculation if they represent a phase of occupation after the destruction of the Bronze Age city and Fosse Temple, comparable to phase B_1 at Tell Beit Mirsim, or if the sherds are merely the accumulated rubbish from the destruction of Level VI.

In any case, the proportion of sherds above the bottom of the section (256·24–255·94 m.) which showed signs of burning did not exceed 12 per cent. in any one foot.

Contents at 258.34 m. (42 ft.)

No.	Description	Comparisons
1	2 bowl fragments. Exterior below rim grooved. Dk. bn., grits[3]. M. fire. Dk. bn. slip unevenly applied, dull finish.	Pl. 105: 10

No.	Description	Comparisons
2	1 fragment slightly carinate bowl, bn. S. fire, red slip in. and below carination out. Horizontal hand burnish similar to 9 fragments at S. wall, except for lack of slip on exterior.	B.3
3	1 bowl fragment. Bn., grits[1], M. fire. Bn. slip and horizontal hand burnish all over.	B.3
4	9 fragments thin-walled bowl, including most of the base, sunk centre inside. Pk., gy. core, M. fire, traces slip and burnish inside.	B.6, type 91?
5	1 fragment bowl rim, bn. M. fire, red slip and horizontal hand burnish in. and over rim, self burnish out.	B.7, type 48? SS III, Fig. 1: 3, Period I, 880 B.C. Tell Jemmeh, FL 186 AASOR IV, Pl. 26: 27, Tell el-Fûl III AASOR XXI–XXII, Pl. 72: 7, Tell Beit Mirsim A₁
6	1 small fragment bowl rim, slightly inverted. Bn. S. fire, red slip and burnish in. and over rim.	
7	1 fragment bowl with part of vestigial handle. Pk., gy. core, M. fire. Red slip in.	
8	3 bowl fragments. Pk., gy. core, light red slip in., even wheel burnish in.	AASOR XXI–XXII, Pl. 72A, Tell Beit Mirsim A₂
9	5 fragments forming complete section. Pk., gy. core, fine limestone grits. M. fire. Burnt patches.	B.13, type 628
10	3 fragments including rim and handle. Bn., grits[3]. S. fire, buff slip.	J.4, type 168 AASOR XXI–XXII, Pl. 68: 8, Tell Beit Mirsim A
11	2 fragments cooking pot rim. Fine red, H. fire, red slip.	AASOR XXI–XXII, Pl. 72: 2B, Tell Beit Mirsim A₁
12, 13, 14	Storage jar rims. Coarse bn. M. fire, flint and limestone grits.	S.4, type 512 S.5, type 515 S.5, type 516
15	5 fragments jug, form unknown. Pk., gy. core, H. fire, light bn. slip irregularly burnished.	

Contents at 258.04 m. (41 ft.)

No.	Description	Comparisons
16	Semi-ring base. Pk., grits[1], M. fire.	
17	Ring base. Buff, gy. core, grits[1], M. fire. Lime repairs to cracked base.	
18	Bn. M. fire. Reddish slip in., irregular burnish. Horizontal self burnish out.	
19	Pk., gy. in., grits[3], M. fire. Buff slip out. Oval section handle.	J.2, type 208?
20	Bn., grits[1], M. fire. Reddish slip out., traces burnish.	D.3, type 296?
21	Pk., gy. core, grits[1]. M. fire. Wet-smoothed.	PS, type 330?
22	Bf., grits[1], M. fire. Wet-smoothed.	S.1, type 476
23	Bn., grits[2], M. fire. Rough out.	S.5, type 515

Level V

See p. 80.

Level VI. 256·84–255·94 m. (37–34 ft.)

Below 257 m. the fragments tended to be grey, rather than brown or pink, and were sometimes finished with a cream slip. There were no identifiable Iron Age forms, and comparatively few sherds of any kind until the proportion of Late Bronze Age II forms became overwhelming in the burnt deposits at the bottom of the trench at 256 m. The wares at that point were brown to buff, with grits and straw tempering, usually medium fired and often with a grey or black central core. They are comparable to the sherds in Structure III of the Fosse Temple, and to those found on the surface levels in the north-east section.

As the desired connexion with the north-east section had been achieved, excavations were carried no farther on the west side.

Analysis of Pottery Fragments in the West Section

Metres above sea level	Feet over rock	Bowls (B)	Hand burnish unless marked "w" (wheel)	Cooking pots (CP) Dippers (D) Jugs (J) Lamps (L) Chalices (Ch) Pilgrim flasks (PF) Potstands (PS)	Handles Oval	Handles Rib	Storage jars (S) S.1–S.5	S.7	S.3	Total	% burnt	Bronze Age	Remarks
262·54	56	B.14: 566	—	J.8 handle	—	1	2	—	1	6	—	1	LEVEL I. Top of stone city wall, Levels I–II.
262·24	55	—	—	—	3	4	7	—	7	22	—	—	
261·94	54	7	—	—	1	1	6	—	18 (1 Rhodian?)	33		1	
261·64	53	B.14: 565	—	CP: 692? (D) 1	—	—	9	3	4	19	10·5	2	
261·34	52	—	—	—	—	2	S.2: 509–10	1	—	4	—	—	Level I inner gate doorsill at 261·44 m.
261·04	51	B.11: 62	(B) 1 (B) 1 w (J) 2	(D) 1	3	—	11	—	1	21	4·8	3	LEVEL II
260·74	50	1 disk base	—	(B) 2 (J) 2	1	—	7	—	—	13	—	1	
260·44	49	—	(J) 1	(B) 1 (D) 20	1	1	60	27	—	112	2·7	6	
260·14	48	—	(B) 1	J.5: 190	—	—	4	3	1	10	—	1	Level II inner gate doorsill at 260·38 m. Base of stone city wall, Level II, at 260 m. on brick wall.
259·84	47	B.13: 628	B.3: 26? B.3: 26 (B) 2 (B) 1 w	(J) 1 ring base L.7–8: 150 (J) 2 handles	—	—	5	2	—	10	—	1	LEVEL III
259·54	46	1 disk			2	—	46	12	2	70	5·7	3	
259·24	45	B.13: 83	B.13: 631 w B.13: 629? w (B) 5 (B) 1 self bur.	D.3: 296 PF: 431?	2	1	34	10	—	50	8·0	—	
258·94	44	B.2: 588 3 red slip 3 disk base		CP: 442?	3	—	130 and S.4: 478	1	—	152	5·9	6	
258·64	43	1 ring base	(B) red slip, irr. bur. in.	(D) soft pk. red slip (J) disk base	—	—	36	1	—	40	10·3	4	* Goblet fragment LB II.

Analysis of Pottery Fragments in the West Section—*continued*

Metres above sea level	Feet over rock	Bowls (B)	Hand burnish unless marked "w" (wheel)	Cooking pots (CP) Dippers (D) Jugs (J) Lamps (L) Chalices (Ch) Pilgrim flasks (PF) Potstands (PS)	Handles Oval	Rib	Storage jars (S) S.1-S.5	S.7	S.3	Total	% burnt	Bronze Age	Remarks
258·34	42	B.6: 91? 1 disk base 1 ring base B.13: 628 (B) plain rim, vestigial handle	(B) 8 (B) 3 w	J.4: 168 (J) 7 (J) 1 handle (CP) 8	1	—	164 and S.4: 512 S.5: 515-16	4	—	204	12·3	3	LEVEL IV
258·04	41	(B) 2 ring bases	(B) 1 hand and wheel	J.2: 208 D.3: 296 PS: 330 (CP) 4	2	—	67 and S.1: 476 S.5: 515	—	—	81	6·2	6	Base of brick city wall at 257·88 m.
257·74	40		(B) 2	J.5: 189 (J) 1 handle (D) 1 base (CP) 1 base Ch: 159?	3	—	78 and S.1: 476 S.5: 516	—	—	90	3·3	2	5 frags. at 41-40 ft. of jar stamped circles and notches.
257·44	39	(B) 1 ring base	—	J.4: 176 (CP) 2	3	—	98	—	—	105	3·8	15	Includes L. II: 387, 389 milk bowl; bn. self bur. frag. in LB style
257·14	38	(B) 3 ring bases	(B) 3	(J) 1 (CP) 3	6	1	140 and S.5: 516	—	—	155	8·4	12	
256·84	37	(B) 1 ring base	—	—	2	—	40	—	—	43	7·0	1	LEVEL VI Ware gy. not bn. M. fire. Some cm. slip.
256·54	36	(B) 1 ring base	—	—	—	—	71	—	—	72	8·3	1	Ware as above.
256·24	35	—	—	—	—	1	101	—	—	103	14·4	16	L. II: 21, 30, 50, 90-91, 95-96, 151, 162, 303, 364, 387
255·94	34	—	—	(D) 1	—	—	38	—	—	39	28·2	8	L. II: 30, 34, 49, 95, 100

* *Note*: The rim section of a goblet or "tazza" is made of white marble, i.e. calcium carbonate, often incorrectly called Egyptian alabaster. Cf. I. Ben-Dor, Palestinian Alabaster Vases, QDAP XI, p. 97.

THE UNEXCAVATED BRONZE AGE CITY

At nearly all points where excavation penetrated below the Iron Age levels, a thick layer of black earth and ash was exposed. It was undisturbed at the top of the section near the north-east corner and was seen 6·50 m. down in the West Section at 256 m. above sea level (p. 74). It was also observed near the south-east corner of Palace B–C, where a surprising quantity of fine decorated sherds—both local and imported—with many fragments of best quality alabaster and faience vases was found. A well-cut carnelian scarab of Rameses II, and a steatite example engraved with the name of the same king associated with his predecessor, Seti I, fix the general horizon of the deposit (to be published in *Lachish IV*). There is no doubt, from the similarity of the contents, that the burning was contemporary with the destruction of the Fosse Temple described in *Lachish II*, and that it was presumably due to the same widespread calamity.

The layer of burning around the citadel did not remain undisturbed, for the builders of the Iron Age cut into it to lay the foundations of their walls and piled it to form a glacis against the lower courses of the palace-fort. A sectional cut at the south-east corner of Palace B–C demonstrated the method of throw from north to south. It was confirmed by the discovery of some twenty-five fragments of a bowl inscribed in hieratic, the pieces of which lay at various levels on the surface of the ramp. See Pl. 16: 4, extreme right foreground, for the position of the area, K.16: 1031. The hieratic inscription (F. No. 6240) will be published in *Lachish IV*.

Very little can be said about the configuration, fortifications and plan of the Late Bronze Age town. At that time it would seem that the highest point within the walls was east of the citadel, where the burnt layer is seen immediately below the plaster court of the late Jewish period. However, further excavation may show that the glacis made by the Iron Age builders extends round the east and north sides, and in that case the true living level of the underlying city may be lower.

In order to keep the gate and roadway clear and unobstructed at all times, the rate of accumulation would have been slow in those areas in comparison with the rest of the site. Moreover, in common with Oriental cities today, the gate was likely to continue in use over several centuries.

No trace of a Bronze Age defence wall has yet been seen, though there were remains of a structure made of kiln-fired bricks near the north-east corner of the mound (Pl. 11: 2).

It was evident that the Iron Age fort had been built directly on the mound formed by the destruction of a large brick building beneath. Wherever excavation had penetrated to the base of the constructional filling of the first Iron Age building Palace A, brick walls a metre and a half wide were revealed, faced with thick white lime plaster. The room space between was filled with burnt brick, representing, no doubt, the collapse of the superstructure.

The same building was also observed below the north-west angle of Palace A, and this corner, at least, was founded directly on that of the earlier building. Pl. 19: 7 shows the exploratory trench which revealed the usual thick black deposit containing Ramesside sherds, and fragments of gold leaf and faience, running under the lowest course of stones. After clearing a mass of fallen brick, the corner of a plastered building built of red kiln-fired bricks was exposed. Close by in the debris was part of an octagonal column and a dressed stone, and both should probably be associated with the earlier building.[1] The brick constructions of the burnt Ramesside city should belong to building level VI.

At the diagonally opposite corner of Palace B–C another incursion was made into the Late Bronze Age city. Pl. 16: 6 shows the section cut through the plastered court at the south-east corner, exposing the foundations of the Palace C wall. Separated from the foundations by about a metre of debris, three parallel lines of brick wall were exposed, running in under the wall of Palace C, but not in alinement with it. The average height of the walls, as preserved, was 60 cm. and the top of the walls were 266·07 to 266·70 m. above sea level, with foundations from 265·54 to 266·10 m. Compare the level of the exposed corner of the burnt brick structure immediately below the north-west corner of Palace A, which is preserved at 266·70 m.

---

[1] The column, F. No. 7233, from Grid Square K.11, is now in the Palestine Museum (PM.38.775).

Though there is nothing to show that the Late Bronze Age main building was directly connected with the brick rooms 2002–2003 at the south-east corner, it can perhaps be said that the Late Bronze administrative centre covered at least as much ground as the later Iron Age palace.

The store chambers, K.15: 2002–2003, lie under the plastered court K.15: 1033, and the relation of the plan to the later storehouse to the south is seen in Fig. 4. The sherds in the rooms are typical of Structure III in the Fosse Temple, and include a Mycenean fragment and parts of coarsely made milk bowls. Many pieces are

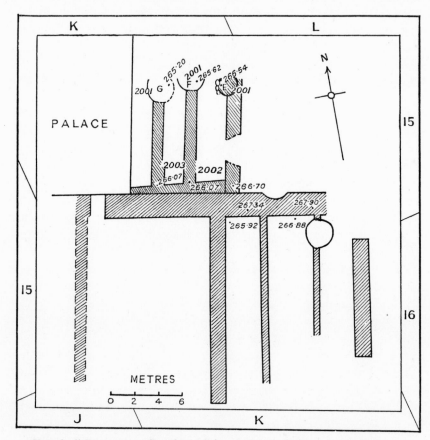

FIG. 4. "Government Storehouse" in relation to Bronze Age buildings

decorated in red with palmettes, zigzags and bands of red and white. Several are burnt, but there were no signs of burning in the rooms or in the section under Palace C wall. After the disuse of the building, several pits, K.15: 2001: A–G, were cut through the walls from an Iron Age occupation level at 266·50 m., and the contents are more fully described in the notes on Level V (pp. 80 f.). Before the close of excavations in 1938 the section was filled in to prevent the seepage of water into the lower levels of the city.

THE IRON AGE CITADEL

There are three separate building phases for the construction of the platform on which the Iron Age palace-forts were founded (Fig. 5), and there are various alternatives for the order of construction.

Palace A may have been demolished before Palace B was planned, or it may have remained standing during the occupation of that addition. The strip C was merely an extension of B, and could not have constituted a building on its own, though for purposes of identification it is described as Palace C in this book.

Palace A was built on podium A.

Palace B was built on podium B or on A and B.

Palace C was built on strip C and B, or reconstructed at the date of strip C on podiums A and B and C.

PALACE A

It was noted in the foregoing paragraphs that the earliest Iron Age podium of Palace A was founded directly on the ruins of the Ramesside building.

In order to provide a flat surface and a solid basis for the citadel it was necessary to encase and build up the sides of the brick ruin beneath. The resulting platform or podium, forming a block 32 m. square, still stands on the west side, to a height of 7 m. The face is vertical and the walls are composed of roughly squared mizzi blocks (Pl. 19: 2). The quality of the stonework is similar to the central section of the revetment on the west

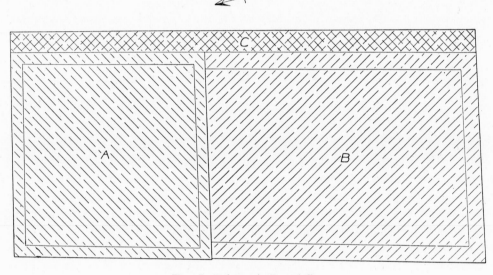

Fig. 5. Palaces A, B and C

side of the Bastion. It is distinctly superior in workmanship to the adjoining section of Palace B podium (Pl. 19: 3), as will be seen from a comparison of the left (A) and the right (B) sides of Pl. 19: 1. It will also be seen that though both sections were founded on town rubbish, the base of Palace B is a metre or so above the base of Palace A.

The core of this vast block of masonry was only partly investigated. It was found to consist of internal cross walls or casemates, artificially filled with hard earth and clay to form a solid basis for the upper structure, which has disappeared. The one wall which does not go down to the surface of the Ramesside mound is only half the depth of the other walls, and is probably contemporary with Palace B.

The filling of the casemates (Pl. 19: 4, 5) contained large quantities of LB sherds, fragments of alabaster and ostrich eggshell, besides a piece of a bowl inscribed in black ink which will be published in *Lachish IV*. The only sign of intermediate occupation was a series of grain pits cut down from the level on which the foundations of Palace A were placed. Some actually ran under the walls. The filling of one pit was sealed in by a thin layer of builders' rubbish, and had so obviously sunk after the building operations that it must have been in use very shortly before, but the contents did not provide any distinctive sherds.

Much of the material which had formed the cross walls had been removed by the post-exilic builders, and it was only the line of the filled-in trenches which revealed their position.

In the present incomplete state of excavation nothing more can be said about the construction of Palace A. However, a point of Biblical interest emerges from the evidence at hand.

Millo

Scholars have long been puzzled by occasional references to a "mysterious structure Millo",[1] mentioned in the history of the Kings (II Samuel V: 9; I Kings IX: 15, 24, XI: 27; II Kings XII: 20; I Chronicles XI: 8; II Chronicles XXXII: 5).

Taken together, the references suggest that David's Millo occupied a central position in the city, i.e. "built round about from Millo and inward". The root meaning of the word itself in Hebrew is "filling". Winckler has drawn attention in the Encyclopædia Biblica to the comparable Assyrian word, $mullû = tamlû$, meaning a terrace or artificial elevation, and from these indications it was supposed that David's Millo was founded on a raised platform. The great Assyrian palaces at Khorsabad and Nimrud were built on similar stone-faced structures, which illustrate the meaning of the word.

Summary of Pottery from the Surface Areas around the Citadel, presumably contemporary with Palace A–B[2]

North Wall	617, 625, 662
South Wall (including some forms from the trial cut at the south-east corner)	556, 588, 591, 595, 609, 620, 621, 622, 653, 661
East Wall	—
West Wall	156, 500, 524, 525, 536, 588, 592, 615, 617, 619, 621, 622, 625

Brick Walls associated with Level V, including the South Wall Trial Cut

Part of a wall built, perhaps, to enclose the palace precincts, occupied the western half of the tell. It was, in fact, covered for most of its remaining length of 80 m. by the south face of Palace B, and it is quite likely that it was cut down to make a sound foundation for that building. Its western end is shown by hatched lines in Grid Square G.14 on Pl. 115; it passed under Palace B to emerge at the south-east corner, from which it extended for a further 16 m. into Grid Square L.15.

Bonded into the main wall, which was nearly 2 m. thick, were four narrower brick walls extending from it at right angles to the south. The most westerly wall was covered by a stone wall of similar dimensions, but the brick part founded on stone is visible on Pl. 16: 4. The eastern wall of the building was not attached, but it may be incomplete owing to denudation. The remaining parts would give a plan divided into two halves, each 10 m. broad and of unknown length. The eastern half is subdivided into three by narrower partitions.

The main wall, founded at about 266 m., apparently cut down into the underlying Late Bronze Age rooms 2002–2003 to a depth of 88 cm., and was preserved at one point to a height of 1·40 m. The foundations of both the wall and those at right angles to it were at varying levels owing to the slope of the ground, but none were lower than 265·34 m., and the living level of the area was considered to be at 266·50 m., where most of the sherds were found which are described below.

In the present incomplete state of knowledge about this building and its relationship to other structures on the mound, it is included in Level V. Its affinity to the *hilani* type buildings is discussed in Chapter 1 under "The Fortifications and Buildings", but in preference to that architectural term it is referred to throughout this book as the government storehouse.

Level V. South Wall Trial Cut at the south-east corner of the Citadel

Fortunately the red, hand-burnished ware (Fig. 6), which was largely absent from the stratification on the west side, was recovered in some quantity from the trial cut at the south-east corner of the citadel (Grid Squares

[1] CAH III, p. 351, and APEF, 1923–1925, pp. 83 f.   [2] For complete Classified Summary, see Chapter 6, p. 140.

K.15/16). Pl. 16: 6 shows the brick walls of the Late Bronze Age rooms 2002–2003 in the middle of the picture, divided from the foundations of Palace C by about a metre of debris. A massive brick wall crossed the rooms at right angles at a higher level, and joined to it on the south were various narrower brick walls, visible on the extreme left of the photograph; see also the plan on Pl. 115. At 266·50 m. many sherds were found which can be confidently compared to sherds from Strata B_{2-3} at Tell Beit Mirsim (AASOR XII, Pls. 26–29), Tell el-Fûl I and II (AASOR IV, Pls. XXVI, XXVIII) and Stratum V at Megiddo (M. I, p. 7).

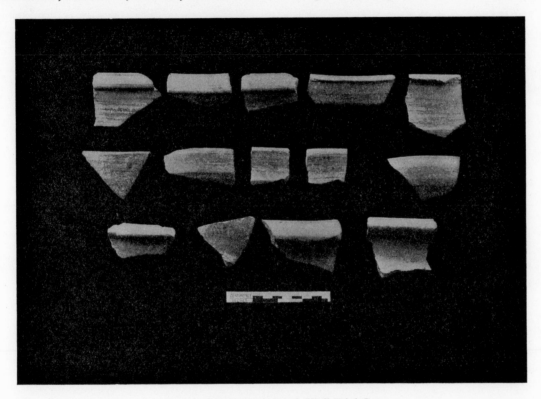

FIG. 6. Sherds from South Wall Trial Cut

Pits 2001: A–G, which partially destroyed the walls of rooms 2002–2003, did not contain the same highly decorated wares with painted chevrons, lattice pattern and animals, which distinguish Stratum C from Stratum B at Tell Beit Mirsim, and are characteristic of the Fosse Temple, Structure III at Tell ed-Duweir.[1] Only red painted bowls, with palmette and zigzags between lines, were found in pits A, E and G, and these also persisted into the Iron Age at Tell Beit Mirsim (AASOR XII, Pl. 29: 13 and XXI–XXII, Pl. 12: 1). Pits A and C included seven fragments of heavy bowl or krater rims, all horizontally hand burnished inside and out, which are prevalent in the occupation level at 266·50 m.

Comparison of the contents of the West Section at 258·34 m. and of the South Wall Trial Cut, south-east of the citadel at 266·50 m., emphasises the difference between them.

West Section at 258·34 m. (42 ft.)	*South Wall Trial Cut*
Scarcity of horizontal hand burnished wares; slip and burnish seldom extends to base of bowls	Preponderance of horizontal hand burnished wares; slip and burnish applied all over, with possible exception of base
Bowls, Classes B.1, B.4 absent	Bowls, Classes B.1, B.2 well represented
Bowls, Classes B.6, B.7, B.13 appear	

[1] *Lachish II*, Pls. XLVII–XLVIII.

Jugs, Class J.4, represented
Ware possibly more grey in tone

Storage jars, Classes S.4, S.5
Nothing similar at Tell el-Fûl

Jugs, Class J.4, represented
Ware possibly more orange in tone

Thick-walled large unburnished storage jars, common at Tell el-Fûl II (AASOR IV, pp. 12–13 and Pl. XXVIII: 17–24); Tell-en-Naṣbeh (TN II, p. 3, S.1–54)

List of Sherds from the South Wall Trial Cut in addition to those photographed and described on Pl. 105

Lower part of base-ring flask. Gy. H. fire, hand finished — cf. AASOR XII, Pl. 16: 17, Tell Beit Mirsim, Stra. C

Mycenean fragment. Bf. M. fire, cm. slip. Bk. paint in. and over rim. Part of bk. spiral — cf. AASOR XII, Pl. 15: 1, Tell Beit Mirsim, Stra. C

Fragment red painted ware. Pk., gy. core. M. fire, self bur. vertical strokes like Duweir Ewer — cf. L. II frontispiece

3 fragments bowl with red paint: zigzags between parallel lines, red border round rim. Pk., gy. core, traces self bur. — cf. AASOR XII, Pl. 25: 31, Tell Beit Mirsim, Stra. B

Fragment bowl, flared rim, red border inside. Pk., gy. core, M. fire — cf. hieratic inscription bowl, F. No. 6240 (to be published in *Lachish IV*)

Fragment goblet rim, horizontal red bands and part of palm-tree outside. Pk., gy. core, M. fire

Fragment goblet rim, painted red bands and black zigzags. Pk., gy. core, M. fire

Fragment goblet or chalice at base of bowl, with knob for insertion in stand. Coarse pk. M. or H. fire, heavily burnt.

Fragment bowl or small chalice, coarse pk., flint grits, M. fire, pk. slip

2 fragments storage jars. Pk., bk. core, large limestone grits, M. fire, self bur. out. Red painted lines

Fragment jar, pk., gy. core, M. fire, cm. slip, red painted lines

Handle storage jar, oval section. Pk., H. fire, painted red line down length of handle

Rim of storage jar. Pk., gy. core, M. fire, cm. slip fired pk. in parts — cf. AASOR XII, Pl. 21: 33, Tell Beit Mirsim, Stra. C

Base of storage jar. Pk., gy. core, coarse limestone grits, M. fire, cm. slip

4 jug handles. Coarse pk. or bf. with limestone grits, M. fire

Fragment thick-walled bowl rim, diam. 13 cm. Pk., gy. core, M. fire — cf. AASOR XII, Pl. 30: 39, Tell Beit Mirsim, Stra. B$_{2-3}$

2 rims large jars, rim diam. *c.* 16 cm., plain collar neck. Pk., M. fire, flint grits — AASOR IV, Pl. XXVIII: 17, Tel el-Fûl II; TN II, Pl. 1: 7

Fragment large jar rim, diam. *c.* 11 cm. Pk. M. fire, flint grits

Fragment storage jar rim diam. *c.* 8 cm. height of collar neck 3·5 cm. Pk. grits[3], M. fire

Fragment storage jar rim, diam. *c.* 8 cm., height of ridged collar neck, 4 cm. Pk., M. fire — cf. AASOR IV, Pl. XXVIII: 11, Tell el-Fûl II

8 fragments large bowls. All bn., S. or M. fire. Red slip in. and out., horizontal hand bur. in. and out. — cf. Kraters, type 621. AASOR XII, Pl. 31: 12, 13, 17, 19, 20, 23, 24; Tell Beit Mirsim, Stra. B$_3$–A$_1$

9 fragments bowls. Class B.3, plain or slightly carinate rims. All bn., gy. core, red slip. Horizontal hand bur. in. and out.

6 fragments bowl rims, Class B.3, plain rim, thin walled. All bn. M. fire, red slip in. and out. Horizontal hand bur. in. and out.

7 fragments bowls, class unknown. All bn., M. fire, red slip in. and out.

6 fragments jugs. Pk., M. fire, red slip, vertical bur. out.   cf. AASOR XII, Pl. 25: 9, 24, Tell Beit Mirsim, Stra. B

Fragment jug. Bn., M. fire, fine mica grits, red slip out., criss-cross bur.

4 fragments krater, inverted and everted rim. Pk., M. fire, pk. or bf. slip, unburnished

7 fragments bowls, class unknown, all bn. S.-M. fire, red slip in., horizontal or irregular bur. in.

Fragment bowl, pk., gy. core, M. fire, horizontal self bur. in.   cf. B.13, type 637?
Intrusive?

PALACE B

Even less is known about Palace B. Nothing has been seen of its floor level or superstructure, and the only evidence for its existence is the extension of the stone podium of Palace A to the south for an additional 46 m. It has already been noted that the foundations did not go as deep as those for Palace A, and the quality of stone used was inferior. The internal construction of the building was not examined, but the upper surface of the junction between the east wall of Palace B and the C extension was traced along almost its whole length (Pl. 19: 6).

Either the structure had been fully removed by the builders of Palace C, or a change in architectural plan before the completion of C necessitated the addition of a 3-m. strip along the east side.

In connexion with the same building phase, Rooms 1050, 1051 and 1052 should be considered. The stone foundation courses of this extension north of Palace A were narrower than those of the main building, but the brick superstructure was preserved on part of the dividing wall between Rooms 1050 and 1051. All three walls at the north-west corner were missing, but they seemed to be complete at the north-east end, as they finished in alinement with the main east wall. The doorways in 1051 and 1052 were almost as wide as the chambers themselves, which were possibly used as stables or chariot-houses. Two jar stamp handles found at floor level in Room 1052 suggest that the rooms continued in use during the period of Palace C. Two examples of a late type of storage jar (type 483) set in the floor of Room 1051, with patches of burning a few centimetres above the living level, may suggest that these three chariot-houses or store chambers were burnt out in the final destruction of Level II.

PALACE C

The podiums of Palace A and B, with the additional strip C, formed the foundations of a building referred to as Palace C, which underwent several phases of construction and repair.

The additional strip C is seen on Pls. 16: 5 and 17: 1, 2 where it adjoins Palace B at the south-east corner. Pl. 16: 6 shows the exposed foundation course of strip C at about 267·50 m., which is a metre or more above the foundation course of Palace B wall along the south face. The upper surfaces of both B and C walls were level along a considerable part of the east side (Pl. 19: 6). It was suggested in J. L. Starkey's field reports that they had been reduced to uniform height by the post-exilic builders of the Residency, but the possibility must also be considered that the complete stone section of the substructure remains, and that it is only the brick portion of the building which is missing.

The only internal traces of the structure were patches of plaster floor-surface, much blackened by fire (Pl. 23: 1). The plans on Pls. 118–119 demonstrate the lack of relationship between these floors and those of the Residency above them. In some cases the post-exilic walls had cut through the underlying floors, but where this did not occur—for example, patches H, I and L—some indication of room dimensions may be obtained. The average width of the walls would appear to have been somewhat broader than those of the Residency.

83

It is clear from the patches B, D and E that the pre-exilic building extended south of the outer wall of the Residency, and the small difference in level, of 10–20 cm., between these isolated patches and the nearest ones enclosed within the Residency, i.e. patches F and A, may uphold the connexion.

The sherds found below the Residency were nearly all small fragments, for they had been subjected to pounding during the preparation of the floors. As many as possible have been typed to shapes already drawn in the present volume, and occasionally comparisons have been made to pots published in the Corpus of Palestinian Pottery and Tell Beit Mirsim I and III (AASOR XII and XXI–XXII). They are omitted from the Plate Descriptions of Pottery.

The table which follows shows the levels of the remaining lime floors of Palace C, compared with the floors of the later Residency, some parts of which were directly superimposed.

Comparison between Palace and Residency Floor Levels, and List of Associated Pottery Fragments

PALACE C		POTTERY FRAGMENTS			RESIDENCY	
Floor	Metres above sea level	L. III types	TBM types	CPP types	Room	Metres above sea level
C	272·09	—	—	—	—	—
A	272·09	399, 484	III, Pl. 21: 8	—	D	272·24
F	272·10	—	—	—	—	—
H	271·73	442, 571	—	—	H	272·14
		68, 484, 488, 534, 570, 571, 574, 685	I, Pl. 65: 3, 6, 26	43 J 9; 48 Y	J	272·30
G	272·11	484, 510, 525, 568, 571, 694	I, Pl. 65: 3	42 G	K	272·28
I	271·90	—	—	—	—	—
		484 (groove round rim and plain), 574	—	—	N	272·49
J	272·15	695	—	—	—	—
K	272·23	—	—	—	—	—
L	272·19	442, 484, 488, 508, 525, 574, 699	I, Pl. 65: 3; III, Pl. 21: 10	$2 C^9$; 44 K	Q	272·43
		46, 568, 572	III, Pl. 20: 3, Pl. 21: 5	$2 C^9$; 7 E base	P	271·70–54
B	271·88	—	—	—	—	—
D	271·98	—	—	—	—	—
E	272·13	—	—	—	—	—
M	271·47	—	—	—	—	—
M	271·75	484, 488	I, Pl. 65: 3	—	U	271·93
Q	271·74	—	—	—	—	—
U, T	272·03–272·31	—	—	—	—	—
		488, 506, 568, 574	—	—	Z	—

It will be seen that patches J, K and L below the south portico of the Residency were laid at a slightly higher level than the floors at the north and south ends; the difference, in any case, is less than 40 cm., which would allow for a rise of two steps towards the main apartments. The raised level of the south portico floor in the Residency was therefore introduced to cover the underlying lime surface, and is now seen to be expedient, owing to the configuration of the previous building.

As C. H. Inge remarked in his second field report (February 1938), more was learned about the destroyed palace from the excavation of the open spaces surrounding it than from the clearance of the floors:

"The outer walls were built of stone in the foundations and of brick above. The unbaked bricks contained a good admixture

84

of chopped straw and measured about $20 \times 8 \times 5$ inches.[1] In between some of the courses, though probably not all, thick layers of reeds were laid in mud, the imprint of which we find in the burnt remains. [Pl. 42: 3.]

"The outer face of the walls was plastered with a coating of white plaster, probably crushed 'howr' about an inch thick, laid on an underlying layer of grey mud, both containing chopped straw. . . . The palace was burned from the inside, for we have found very few traces of burning on the surface of the white pavement, though many of the bricks are burnt red and hard. The outer wall was probably deliberately overthrown after the burning, by the extraction of stones from the highest course of stone-work. This would account for our finding large stones lying on the pavement buried by the fall of brick. In the ordinary way, the stones would have fallen last. . . ."

Cf. the similar treatment of the houses on each side of the gate street leading into the city, Pl. 114 and p. 103.

The Stairways of Palace C

The uppermost stairway is numbered L.13: 1063, and the adjoining part of the plastered court is L.12/14: 1066, with the curious pedestal and stone drum standing in the court. (See Pl. 18: 2–6, with plans and sections on Pls. 116, 117).

The stairway was well preserved, as it lay deeply buried by the fall of brick wall. North of the point to which the upper steps were intact there were no considerable traces of fallen brick. The debris consisted of chips of broken limestone which could easily be accounted for by the destruction of the upper part of the staircase and the platform to which it led. It would seem that the northern part of the palace-fort was possibly not built up to the same height as the rest of the building. It may well have been an open terrace raised high above the rest of the city, but at the same level as the floors of the palace rooms. The stairway and the porch would have led onto this terrace.

Inge described the steps in his field report for March 1938:

"There are ten steps in all, of which the five lowest are perfect. The staircase is about twelve feet in width, and the stones are exceptionally well laid and joined; but before lavishing our praise on this, we must remark that they are of the softest possible material and show signs of having been finished off in position. The 'howr' limestone, when wet at any rate, is so easily chipped and scratched that we have not yet attempted to clean the stairs. The surface can be rubbed smooth with a rag, but in spite of this the steps are only very slightly worn and so can hardly have been used at all. The view that they were just finished when the palace was destroyed is borne out by the heaps of rubble lying on the white floor. The space immediately at the bottom of the steps was clear—that is, covered by no debris except the fallen brickwork, but nearby are large heaps of chipped 'howr' limestone and apparently discarded stones.

"Where the upper part of the staircase is broken away, we can see what appears to be the remains of an earlier narrower staircase, which was built into the foundations of the structure which replaced it. Traces of the plastered retaining wall are visible, and one or two very worn steps of 'howr' limestone. . . .

"The extension of our work to the north-east corner of the palace-fort has shown that the staircase led to a porch built out from the east wall at its northern end. This is unfortunately broken down to below foundation level, and parts of it have completely disappeared. The platform between the staircase and the porch is also badly damaged, and the remains of a plastered face at the corner where the supporting wall of the platform joined the foundations of the porch, are so broken that we are unable to make out its original form or extent. The plaster is similar to that on the podium at the foot of the staircase [Pl. 18: 6]. Among the stones which formed the core of the foundations of the porch, we can trace a face of large stones, which seems likely to be the remains of an earlier porch belonging to palace A or B."

During the last month's work a further discovery was made:

"In the filling of the palace staircase two well-preserved steps have come to light, of a flight still earlier than the two previously noted. The steps are of soft 'howr' limestone, but of a darker and probably harder quality than that of which the latest staircase is constructed. On the vertical face of one of these steps is a crude drawing of an animal. . . ."

The animal—a lion of Judah?—is to be seen on Fig. 10, with other scribblings which include, near the outer corner of the step, the first five letters of the Hebrew alphabet. (See Pl. 48: 3 and pp. 118, 357, 358, 396).

---

[1] The measurements of three complete bricks were recorded: from K/L.14: 1061, $50 \cdot 50 \times 26 \times 14$ cm.; from L.13: 1063, $50 \times 25 \times 12$ cm.; from L.12/14: 1066, $54 \times 29 \times 13$ cm.

When the northern face of the earlier porch was exposed it was found that it did not conform to the line of the north end of the palace, like the later porch. It seems possible that when the earlier porch was built the store chambers at the north end were still standing and prevented a sight being taken along the face of the wall.

The remaining part of the Palace C wall, from the north-east corner to as far as it would have been covered by the porch and staircase, was of an entirely different character from the southern parts. It was badly built of smallish stones and was vertical. It was founded on the podium of the earlier porch, and therefore did not go as deep as the rest of the wall. There was a rough gap of half the thickness of the whole wall between the proper stone building and the face of Palace A wall. The gap was filled with burnt rubble, and particularly with burnt brick. It is possible that the wall was built in this way originally because its face would have been covered by the porch, and because it would not have to bear the weight of the great brick wall which existed farther south; but if this is so, the burnt bricks must have come from an earlier destruction, and hitherto the only bricks of their size known from this area were those which had fallen from the walls of Palace C, and which could not have been used in their burnt state in the construction of one of these walls. An alternative explanation is that this part of the wall was broken down to a lower level than elsewhere, and that an attempt to rebuild it was made after the great destruction.

For the contents of the chariot-houses or storerooms see Chapter 5, Rooms L.11: 1050–1052.

CHAPTER 4

THE FORTIFICATIONS, ROADS AND GATEWAYS

THE FORTIFICATIONS

BEFORE excavation began at Tell ed-Duweir certain features of the fortifications were already partly exposed. The position of the ascending road to the gates could be inferred both from the gentle slope of the ground and the projection of the south-west bastion, and at various points a few superimposed courses of stone indicated the presence of the revetment.

It was a simple matter to trace this revetment almost around the whole circuit of the mound, but its relationship to the meagre sections exposed of the upper city wall, and the comparative dates of various breaches and repairs, are much more complex and will be discussed at the end of the chapter.

The defences are as follows:

The Six-Metre Wall

A brick wall, 6 m. wide, based on one course of stone. The height of this wall, after it had been levelled to take the succeeding wall (described below), was 2·5 m. It was exposed in section north of the gateway (Pl. 109), and is known to continue as far as that point and for a short distance beyond. The top surface, as so far exposed, is shown on Pls. 111 and 114.

The foundation course of stones included some dressed blocks from earlier buildings. The bricks were laid in mud-mortar, and the outer face of the wall was only preserved for a short distance, but it showed a style of recessing similar to that of the revetment below. Against the base of the wall a mass of stone blocks set in mud-mortar had been piled to strengthen the foundations, where the slope of the mound would have made erosion likely.

The Rubble-Filled Wall

A stone wall, about 3·70 m. wide, founded on the preceding wall. It was traced for about 30 m. on either side of the gate but beyond it was lost through denudation as the ground level rose from the low gateway area. If this wall were complete around the edge of the escarpment, it would enclose 73,200 sq. m. or 18 acres. (Plan on Pl. 108, section on Pl. 109, photographs on Pls. 12: 2; 13: 9, 10). In this connexion see also Pl. 11: 2, which shows a small section of the upper city wall exposed at the north-east corner. It has not been planned.

The wall was little more than half the width of its predecessor and was built of medium-sized masonry, with a central filling of small stones and rubble. The outer face was vertical, and on the lower courses there were traces of white lime plaster. Along the remaining section of the wall recessed panels 14 m. in length alternated with salients measuring 4 m. These projections also afforded additional protection to the inner gate, both on the exterior and interior sides (Pl. 12: 1, 2). The gateway was 4·40 m. in width when the wall was constructed, and the threshold consisted of three nari blocks, carefully cut to accommodate a door opening inwards. The northern block was pierced to take a surface drain. The potsherds found under the southern pier of the inner gate were consistent with the pottery forms associated with Level III; therefore, on internal evidence, the stone wall can be no earlier than that period.

The Stone and Brick Revetment

A stone and brick revetment, approximately 4 m. wide, encircling the mound at a distance of about 16·5 m. from the top scarp. It was recessed in panels at equal distances along most of the west side, and both the recessed and the projecting sections measured 10 m. in length. Round the north, south and east sides an irregular series of recesses and salients took the place of panelling wherever a turn in the wall was required (Pl. 108).

The top four remaining courses of the revetment or lower defence wall were traced almost without a break around the whole circuit of the mound, but in default of a thorough clearance to bed-rock, on which it is assumed that the wall was founded, it cannot be said that each angle and buttress has been noted and planned.

The investigation was begun early in the programme of work in order to delimit the site. It was hoped to establish the date of the defence system and to locate the main gateway and any postern entrances. With these ends in view, work was begun in 1932 on the north-east side of the mound, at a point where some exposed courses of masonry protruded above a small plot of land enclosed by a cactus hedge (Pl. 108, Grid Square U.9, and Pls. 1: 3 and 11: 1). As excavation proceeded it became clear that the revetment was constructed of three superimposed sections, which are described below as Sections A, B and C.

Section A (Fig. 7 and Pl. 11: 1, 5, 6)

When the sloping accumulation of rubbish masking the face of the wall had been cleared, eleven courses of fine masonry were exposed, with an average height of 45–55 cm. for each course. Large untrimmed blocks of limestone had been set on bed-rock against a previously prepared face of tell debris, cut away at an angle to conform with the proposed batter of the wall, and as the building progressed the blocks were laid against it and were wedged in position by small stones at the angles and crevices. No mortar had been employed, and the size of the stones diminished in the upper courses.

The outer face of the section was inclined to an angle of 20 degrees, the total height of the eleven courses was 5·80 m., the length of the section preserved was 7·80 m. and it was terminated on the north side by a squared end 2 m. in width.

The wall was founded on the edge of the rock escarpment, which sloped steeply for about 9 m. and then dropped vertically towards the valley. According to local account, the missing part completing the circuit of the mound, south of the well at the north-east corner, fell into the valley some years ago (Pl. 1: 3).

The position was therefore suitable for a cross-cut into the stratification of the tell (to be fully described in *Lachish IV*; see also PEQ, October 1950), which showed that the wall rested against Early to Middle Bronze Age rubbish, and sherds of those periods came from the rock surface both inside and outside the line of the wall and filled the natural cavities. Subsequent excavation has, however, established the Iron Age origin of the wall.

The stratification outside the wall

The stratification of the soil outside the wall covering Section A was instructive.

Directly overlying the rock outcrop and the lowest courses of the stone revetment was a compact mass of marl with small pottery fragments, some dated as late as Iron Age II. This deposit would appear to be the remains of dumped ballast to protect the lower footing from the effects of continual drainage of rain-water down the great extent of both city and lower defence wall. The sherds within it are, therefore, no later than the foundation of the wall.

Above this compact mass and conforming to its angle of denudation was a white stratum, consisting in the main of partly burnt limestone, or else of the powdered disintegrated stone. This light scree contained much charcoal, which appeared to be derived from large-sized timber.

J. L. Starkey thought that the wood was burnt in a conflagration when stone buildings were destroyed by fire of sufficient intensity to calcinate the masonry. He suggested that the wood may have come from the projecting battlements shown on the Lachish Reliefs.

Over the white layer was an upper stratum of normal town rubbish, grey earth containing sherds of various periods, in which were many loose stones, mostly fallen from the upper courses of the defence wall and the upper city wall.

Though no more was done south of the cactus hedge in 1932, it will be convenient to describe the following season's work in the same direction in order to proceed from the low north-east corner of the wall to the highest point above the south-west angle.

Moving south along the massive Section A, a slight offset occurred eight courses above bed-rock, widening from a point to a ledge of about 46 cm., too narrow to be visible on Pl. 11: 6. The ledge marked the beginning of a bend in the line of defence, presumably in order to follow a deviation in the underlying rock foundation. It was also the first of the triangular recesses in the masonry; not only did it indicate a change of direction, but it marked a gradual change in the method of construction.

Section B (Pls. 11: 4, 7; 12: 5, 6)

Section A, inclined at an angle of 20 degrees, gradually gave way to an almost vertical section of the defence wall, built of small, untrimmed stones, roughly laid, which was the prevailing type of construction along the east side. The poor standard of building had resulted in collapse of the wall at various points, and the breaches had been enlarged by the insidious agency of small watercourses and by the pressure of earth from within.

Pl. 11: 7 shows a typical breach, and Pl. 11: 4 shows the wall approaching the south-east corner (Pl. 108, Grid Square T.15), with a poorly made constructional buttress exposed.

The south-east corner

Pl. 12: 5 illustrates the defence wall (Pl. 108, Grid Squares R.19/20) at the south-east corner. In view 5 the uppermost courses of Section A can be seen at the bottom of the picture, and above is part of Section B. This middle portion was also recessed vertically, forming a triangularly based panel, which was one of a consistent series of offsets designed to negotiate a turn in the rock whenever it occurred. To the left of the picture is another light constructional buttress, similar to one exposed in Grid Square T.15.

On Pl. 12: 5 and 6, the thick white coat of lime plaster, characteristic of all vertical sections of the wall, is particularly marked. Traces occur at all points, but in these angles, which were more deeply buried and less affected by damp, the surface was especially well preserved.

Section C

It was at first supposed that the various styles of construction to be seen in the lower defence wall were due to repairs and rebuilding at different periods. However, the section of the wall in Pl. 108, Grid Square O.21, seen on Pl. 12: 6, provided another explanation.

When first uncovered, an unbroken surface of white plaster covered the recess, but heavy rains soon afterwards exposed a join, where the crack can be seen in the photograph. It was then apparent that a brick and a stone section adjoined each other within the recess, both founded on the underlying Section A. An attempt to show the method of construction has been made in Fig. 7, extended from the evidence provided in Pl. 12: 6, which is indicated by a dotted line on the diagram:

"A" represents the section of massive masonry, similar in style and quality of stonework to that shown on Pl. 12: 5 and on Pl. 11: 5.

"B", above and to the south of "A", is the vertical section in inferior masonry.

"C", immediately above "A" in the foreground, is the brick section which originally continued along over "B", though the surface had fallen away when Pl. 12: 6 was taken. It was founded directly on "A", with no rubbish intervening.

The bricks were sun-baked, laid in mud-mortar. They were apparently made from the red alluvial soil accumulated at the foot of the mound, washed down from the Hebron hills—a deposit which is cut into annually by the winter floods of the Wadi Ghafr.

The strange junction made by these three sections, A, B and C, can only be explained by the fact that the limestone escarpment on the south end of the mound rises steeply to the south-west corner, and that the three sections noted separately represent three types of construction in the same wall.

For similar building methods at other sites, see Comparisons and Date of the Fortifications, pp. 99–102.

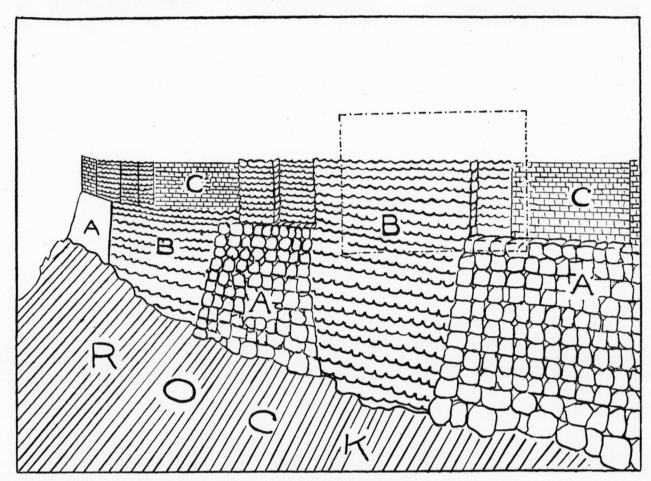

Fig. 7. Diagram of wall construction, south-east revetment.
See also Pl. 12: 6

The South-West Corner

The vertical stone section seen on Pl. 12: 6 was traced to within 6 m. of the highest point at the south-west corner, where it adjoined a brick section which projected to form the base of a tower and was the turning-point of the defences at the south-west corner (Pl. 2: 2). The wall then curved at right angles to its former line to meet the city gateway. Over the whole area there were abundant traces of burning, and the fuel for this destruction was still to be seen in the charred branches and blackened olive stones which were piled up against the walls. Stone slingshots (Pl. 40: 5) and innumerable arrowheads (Pls. 39: 4–6 and 60: 55–61, 71–77) testified to the war-like character of the assault.

If it is ever possible to examine the underlying strata at the south-west corner, it may be found that the extra height at this point was achieved by the use of dumped soil. J. L. Starkey considered the problem which must have faced those who made the Great Shaft, for they had to dispose of approximately 14,285 cubic metres (500,000 cubic feet) of debris from that cutting, but if the south-west corner were used for that purpose, some addition to the height of the pre-existing defence wall would have been necessary.

The circuit of the wall was interrupted at the south-west corner by the ascending roadway leading to the inner and outer city gates, set at right angles to each other within the Bastion. These features are discussed under the heading "Roads and Gateways", and the present account will proceed to describe the wall on the west side.

It is no longer possible to determine how the junction of the west wall with the north wall of the Bastion was originally planned. The problem is discussed more fully on p. 93 and here the wall is described as it now stands. It diverges at right angles from the Bastion, and the top four remaining courses dip more than 2 m. between Grid Squares E.17 and E.14, where the lowest reading of 248·84 m. above sea level was made on the west side (Pl. 12: 1). The line then rose again to the north-west corner.

Repairs on the west side

There were two main repairs on the west side. The first was close to the angle where the north wall of the Bastion met the western revetment. The repair consisted of stones laid in mud and chopped straw, and the work was much inferior to the original masonry. There were no traces of burning, and the position of the breach was such that it suggested a direct assault on the inner gate, avoiding the roadway and the necessity to force the two strong towers of the outer gate.

The second area of repair occurred near the middle of the west side, in Grid Square E.12, indicated by a dotted line on Pl. 108. The breach was caused by fire at this point, which is proved by the calcined blocks, charred earth and burnt brick fragments. A hurried repair had been made with any material available, and the surface had been hastily plastered, leaving thereon the imprints of a workman's hand. Apparently this attempt at patching up the wall was unsuccessful: the same weak point was attacked again, and a mass of fallen brick and masonry testified to its final collapse.

This evidence of two divergent methods of attack on the same wall suggests some difference in period.

Approaching the north-west corner, between the two most southerly buttresses, a section was cut at right angles to the wall face to test the stratification outside it (Pl. 12: 4). Eight stone courses from the top surface a smooth floor of white plaster was uncovered, which was presumed to be the overflow from the plastering of the two upper wall sections. Some 2 m. from the wall face it ceased abruptly, and similar floors were not recovered at other points.

The North-West Corner

The limestone escarpment at this corner was close to the surface, but it dropped 30 m. in a distance of 60 m., to the collapsed cavern 101 in Grid Square D.5 (Pl. 125 and Pl. 3: 1). On the small ledge of rock which projected beyond the ends of the buttresses of the defence wall, "cup" presses were found and the dark soil on the rock itself contained sherds of the Early and Middle Bronze Ages, consistent with those already noted on the north-east side. Beneath one buttress was a small cave which had been completely robbed.

The revetment turned the north-west corner in a bold sweeping curve, strengthened by at least eight buttresses founded on bed-rock (Pls. 1: 1 and 12: 4). They projected between 4 and 5 m. from the line of the wall and were each about 2 m. in width. They served to support the revetment at the turn, and though they were not bonded into the wall, they were contemporary with it. In one case the effect of a flying buttress had been obtained by leaning a large block against the wall and building out from it.

It is likely that there were buttresses at regular distances all round the tell, and that the spaces between them were filled with stone and lime plaster to form a solid matrix, thus burying much of the massive Section A. Where digging has been low enough at other points such buttresses have been found (Pls. 11: 4 and 12: 5), but they were rough constructions and obviously unfitted to be permanently exposed.

An examination of the limestone packing between the buttresses showed that the material was derived from the soft yellow howr limestone stratum, in which both the Middle Bronze Age Fosse and the Iron Age Great

Shaft were cut. Sherds and one whole flask (CPP type 74), belonging to the period of the Fosse, were found, possibly brought up in the rubbish from below.

Between the most northerly two buttresses, a white plastered ramp was found, descending towards the Fosse at an angle of 43 degrees; it is assumed to be part of that same system of defence (*Lachish II*, Pl. LXIX). A width of about 9 m. of the surface was uncovered, coated with white lime plaster; the face was preserved for some 14 m. downwards towards the Fosse, but, unfortunately, it came to an end before it reached that level.

However, there is clear evidence that where the ramp interfered with the proposed line of the stone wall and its buttresses it was cut away for their foundation trenches. It is therefore certain that it had no connexion with the Iron Age fortifications.

The North Side

To return to the line of the revetment: after it turned the north-west corner the character of the stone walling soon relapsed to the inferior workmanship and style visible on the south and east sides. Before excavation the north side of the tell presented a uniform and unbroken line, disturbed by small watercourses only. Thus it was expected that the top courses would be recovered at a uniform level along the whole length of the north side. At several points, however, between Grid Squares N, O, P, Q: 5 (Pl. 108), much work was needed before the face of the wall was traced, as both the upper sections of the wall had been destroyed and only the blocks of the underlying Section A remained. It was the greatest breach caused by fire now visible around the circuit of the mound. Lying with fallen stones and brickwork close to the wall was a large four-handled jar, type 487, similar to one from 'Ain Shems (AS IV, Pl. LXIX: 3) attributed to Stratum II c.

The North-East Corner

The junction of the north and east side of the mound was cut obliquely by a straight stretch of wall. The configuration of the ground on the corner, and the gentler slope of the outcropping limestone, suggested the possibility of a subsidiary gate at this point, for it would command the presumed line of approach from Jerusalem and Hebron.

Stone courses, which projected at right angles to the line of the wall some 20 m. beyond the north-east corner, suggested the presence of a bastion or other defensive structure between the corner and the original Section A above the cactus hedge, but a thorough examination was hampered by the fact that the intervening masonry had fallen into the valley. Defensive outworks may have contributed to the protection of the Bronze Age well in Grid Square S.6, which was incorporated in the Iron Age fortifications.

Pl. 11: 3 shows the south end of the revetment after the oblique turn at the north-east corner. The original revetment, founded on bed-rock and built almost vertically, was neatly finished off at this point, as if for an intentional gap in the line, and it corresponded in thickness to the similar end of Section A (Pl. 11: 5). There was, however, some inferior masonry, 10 m. in length, which was founded on about 10–20 cm. of rubbish topped by a layer of pebbles, which suggested the surface of a road (Pl. 11: 3). The presence of a blocked postern gate which was no longer in use at the time of the final destruction is a possibility which must await further investigation. The projecting T-shaped construction was less than a metre in height and could have been part of a retaining wall for the road.

The well

On the north-east corner, facing the modern village of Qubeibeh, was a circular hole in the masonry, flush with the top of the revetment, which proved to be a well-head, deliberately included in the system of defence now under discussion. The position of the well is seen where the men are working on Pl. 11: 1. The removal of the filling was an arduous task. At first buckets were used, pulled up by ropes, but as the depth increased this method was found to be impracticable, and a wooden frame was constructed from which a pulley block hoisted buckets and large iron drums to the surface. The circular well-head was 2·40 m. in diameter at the top. It was lined with blocks like those used in the revetment to a depth of 7·80 m., at which point the superstructure joined bed-rock.

At a depth of over 15 m. a large block of limestone was found jammed in the opening. Below the obstruction the well was free of debris and the water level stood at 203·60 m. above sea level, or 39 m. below the steyned well-head. Subsequently the water was pumped from the well, and digging continued in order to clear and remove all loose stones, and the bottom was reached at 198·60 m.

The sherds in the filling were all Iron Age, and near the bottom was a much corroded iron sword in its scabbard (NP). A metre or more of the lower filling was composed of a tenacious grey clay, full of small pieces of charcoal, possibly marking the layer of dirt deposited as a result of destruction by fire. Below this deposit the mud was more sandy and contained less charcoal.

The well is the only one so far exposed within the fortifications, and its importance to the city cannot be over-estimated. Though there is no positive evidence to confirm its attribution to the Bronze Age, it certainly predates the construction of the Iron Age wall, and continued in use probably until the final destruction of the city in 586 B.C.

The Bastion at the South-West Corner

The Bastion, measuring approximately 26×27·5 m., was built as a free-standing structure, which was later incorporated into the line of the revetment (Pls. 108, 111).

The length of the north wall to its junction with the revetment was 21 m. and it could be traced for another 5 m. within the thickness of that wall to the north-east angle. The length of the west wall was 27·5 m., but the difference is accounted for by the projection of the north-west corner which was not planned as a true right angle. Thus the approximate dimensions of the Bastion when it was an isolated building were 26×27·5 m. It is known that the south and east walls are under the guardrooms of Level II, and the south-east corner of the building was partly exposed. Two panels, each measuring 3 m. in length, were introduced in the north wall, and there was one panel 6·5 m. long in the west wall. The approximate width of the west wall was 7·5 m., but the constructional details of the other two sides are still obscured by the central filling of fallen masonry.

Good quality material was used throughout the construction and the standard of craftsmanship was generally high. The blocks of hard mizzi limestone at the corners were bonded and well cut (Pl. 13: 8), and the style of work was comparable to that of Palace A and to some parts of the revetment on the west side.

The foundations of the north and west walls of the Bastion were protected by great ramps of soil brought up from the valley below, and piled as a glacis against the lowest courses (Pl. 12: 3). Occasionally there were pockets of burnt brick deposited with the valley earth.

An overlying deposit of debris about 30 cm. thick against the west wall contained arrowheads (Pl. 60) and an iron lancehead (Pl. 63: 8), which can be compared with similar weapons lying in the burnt debris against the Stone and Brick Revetment. Some stamped jar handles came from rubbish close to the face of the revetment and should be considered in the same context.

THE ROADS AND GATEWAYS

The roads and gateways passing through the fortifications of the Iron Age city show various phases of construction which are difficult to distinguish in view of incomplete excavation. More than one phase was observed in each of the three areas listed below, which are described in detail in the following pages:

The roads and retaining walls from the base of the mound to the outer gate (Pl. 108, Grid Squares D/E: 18–22; Pls. 1: 2; 2: 3; 13; 14: 5, 6).

The roads and rooms within the Bastion, between the outer and inner gates (Pls. 108, 111–113, Grid Squares D–F.17/18; Pl. 14: 1–4; Fig. 8).

The roads and structures within the line of the upper city wall (Pl. 114, Grid Squares F–L.17/18; Pl. 113: 15 and 21).

The notes which follow will begin with the remains of Level III, for nothing of the earlier occupation levels has so far been exposed near the gate. However, the summary on p. 102 which attempts to relate road surfaces and structures, both inside and outside the city, to other phases of construction and destruction observed on the site is arranged in the order in which the levels were exposed.

Level III

On the evidence of the pottery found in the shops and houses flanking the road leading in from the gate, these appear to be contemporary with the rooms south of the palace. The contents of both areas are fully described in Chapter 5.

Within the confines of adjacent buildings, the roadway of Level III was well defined, both by the shops and houses on each side and by the cobbled threshold of the gate tower (Pls. 15: 1–4; 21: 1–6).

Towards the end of the last season it was obvious that this gateway in Grid Squares F/G.17/18 was too large and complicated a structure to be excavated in a limited time, and too important a monument to be left partly exposed. The structure was, therefore, reburied for protection, but the drain of Level II, running under the threshold of the contemporary inner gate, was left open to provide good drainage. It was primarily for this latter purpose that the limited programme of work in the area was undertaken late in the season of 1937–1938.

The gateway was apparently flanked on each side by brick piers on stone foundations, and the spaces between the piers were occupied by rooms or staircases leading to the upper structures. The walls were faced with white lime plaster. There may have been four piers on either side, if it is assumed that one pair of piers lies under the inner gateway of Level II (shown by dotted lines on Pl. 114 in Grid Squares F.17/18). The innermost pier on the north side was destroyed in the making of the Level II drain, where it turns north opposite the southern pier (Pl. 15: 4), which was partially uncovered in Grid Square G.18. On the southern side no attempt was made to expose the brick piers to their full depth, but their outline was traceable in the filling below the roads of Level II.

The relationship of the piers to the brick city wall, shown in section on Pl. 109, was not established. It is clearly the same wall which terminates in a re-entrant right angle on each side of the gate (see hatched lines on Pl. 114, Grid Squares F.17/18), leaving a gap of some 17 m. to be filled. Assuming that the actual gate was no wider than 4 m., the width of the road, some 6·6 m. would be left on each side. As the line of the outer face of the brick wall lies some 7 m. west of the supposed position of the most westerly piers, it is perhaps probable that there was a double re-entrant, as in the case of the later gateways.

At the raised threshold of cobblestones (Pl. 15: 2), the road, including the contemporary drain, was 4·60 m. wide, assuming that the missing pier was symmetrically placed. The threshold was bounded by two shallow grooves filled with ash, which possibly held wooden beams let into the road surface. There may have been a pair of gates to close this entrance, in which case the bolts would have been socketed into the wooden beams (cf. Nehemiah III: 3). C. H. Inge, however, thinks it more probable that they served merely as a curb to keep the cobblestones in position. If an *outer* gate of Level III is under the stone thresholds contemporary with Level II and the post-exilic period, there would be a total enclosure of 43 m. between the inner threshold and the outer gate during the occupation of Level III.

There is no doubt that the fortifications then in use were planned on a grand scale and constructed of brick on stone foundations, in keeping with the traces of other administrative and official structures partly exposed south of the citadel, but only further excavation can decide if the gate of Level III had survived in use from the city of Level IV.

The road surface of the period, G/H.17: 1087, was made of gravel. It was well marked from a level of 259·11 m. near the cobbled threshold of the gate to a point some 30 m. farther east, at level 260·73 m. Beyond, the rise of the ground prevented any clear definition, except at the eastern extremity of the excavated area, where an upper surface was distinguishable for about 25 m., rising from 263·60 to 265·72 m. This is numbered K.17:

1020 on Pl. 114, and as the surface was composed of chalk and gravel, it should be contemporary with G/H/J.17: 1087, for there were no "made" road surfaces above it. The sections on Pl. 113 show that the Level II surfaces (G/H.17: 1072) consisted merely of mud, hardened by usage. Objects from G/H/J.17: 1087 are listed on p. 12. Just north of K.17: 1020, a small section of road (unnumbered) protruded some 20 cm. below, and appeared to conform in direction to the line of the main easterly drain.

This drain flowed from the eastern extremity of the excavations, almost parallel to the road as far as the junction with an alley, J.17: 1044, which came from the north. It presumably passed underground at that point, and its further course lay under the northern unexcavated scarp. It should be noted that the levels at the easterly end, 265·12 m., 263·88 m. and 262·77 m. respectively, were taken on top of stones which covered the drain, and this cover was itself 10–20 cm. thick. The bottom of the drain was not exposed, but on the analogy of the later drains it may be about a metre in depth.

From the excavations on the north side of Road G.17: 1087 it was apparent that the surface drainage from the eastern and southern part of the city did not flow through the inner gate and across the Bastion area while that road was in use. The drain immediately north of the cobbled sill, which is contemporary, was only intended to take the water from the roof of the gate towers, and the main drainage flowed in a northerly direction, as indicated by the falling levels of the side road or alley G.17: 1095, where a deeper accumulation of rubbish had preserved the house walls to the height of 1·5 m. (Pl. 21: 3). The covered drain from the east in Grid Squares J/K.17 is earlier than, or contemporary with, the superimposed rooms J.17: 1040–1045. This is also true of the smaller drain from the north, and both should perhaps be attributed to Level III. The two drains may combine and swing round below Rooms 1079, 1088 and 1089, to emerge at some point under Road 1095.

No constructions or road surfaces which can be attributed to Level III have been uncovered in the area outside the upper city wall, with the exception of the top surfaces of the ruined brick wall on either side of the inner gate of Level II (see in relation to it on Pl. 111 and in relation to the roadway within the city on Pl. 114).

Level II, two phases

The next considerations are the two road surfaces of Level II, G/H.17: 1072, which were exposed inside the city. The sections on Pl. 113 will show that the upper and lower surfaces had coalesced near the top of the hump which was formed by the fallen brickwork of the towers flanking the cobbled threshold of Level III. East of the towers the two surfaces were visible, the upper surface continuing at an even level with the top of the hump, and a lower surface sloping down from it; they were divided from each other by fine earth wash or silt.

It is not possible to separate the two surfaces of Road 1072 from the underlying surface of Road 1087 beyond Grid Square H.17 eastward, but up to that point the Level III surface was defined by the flanking houses, the tops of which lay below Road 1072. In any case, the stratification would be unreliable, as the uppermost roads are close to the present ground surface from Grid Square J eastward, and are much disturbed by erosion and ploughing. The list of contents is given on p. 121, as far as possible in levels, but these should be viewed with caution, as most of the objects came from the burnt brickwork of the fallen gate towers, to be associated with the destruction of Level III. The section above the fallen gate towers of Level III is fairly clear; the lower surface of G: 1072 was described in C. H. Inge's field report for April 1938, as follows:

"It originally went downhill from the remains of the inner gateway into a kind of ditch between the mound formed by the collapse of the houses on either side. This ditch rapidly filled with mud, and three layers of water-laid deposit, probably attributable to three separate floodings, are visible. This deposit brought the road up to the level of the heaps of ruins and of the later gate level, and the surface was then metalled with a thin layer of broken burnt brick."

The higher surface of Road G: 1072 showed traces of cart or chariot ruts, which had cut into the burnt brick heaps formed by the collapse of the gate towers. This road level was associated with the squared nari doorsill of the last phase of Level II. Pl. 15: 5 shows the entry and northern door-jamb before the removal of the post-exilic blocking. The burnt layer visible on the road continued under the northern jamb to the earlier face of Level II. A heap of charcoal (marked "Burning" on Pl. 113) contained a red juglet, type 311, and a square-sectioned iron nail (F. No. 6153, NP), which may have belonged to the city gate.

View 5 was taken before the exposure of the stone-lined drain which was also covered by the layer of burning. Pl. 15: 6 shows the full width of the inner gateway after the removal of the blocking and after the excavation of the drain. These two views represent the late and early phases of city Level II. For the outer face of the inner gate blocking see Fig. 8.

The relationship of the drain from the north to the smaller drain from the east, exposed in Grid Square G.17, is shown on Pl. 15: 2, 3 and on Pl. 113. The eastern drain is attributed to Level III (see p. 95), and the

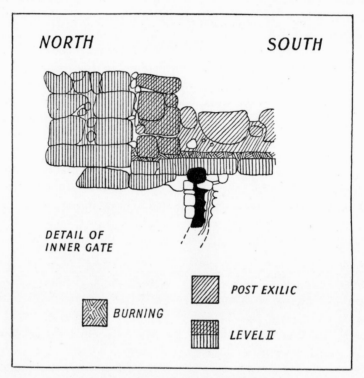

FIG. 8. Detail of Inner Gate Threshold

northern one is clearly somewhat later, though the layer of burning above it proves that it was involved in destruction by fire. Pl. 14: 1, 2 show the drain as it emerges from under the squared nari stone doorsill of Level II. In 1935 this drain was thought to be a post-exilic construction; however, it is now seen to be a continuation of the drain within the city, and it presumably continued in use at least until the final destruction of Level II.

The sides of the Level II drain within the city and Bastion area were lined with rough stones, and the covering of stones and mud had been supported by wooden branches placed across the drain and resting on the stone lining. The covered drain passed below the Level II threshold of the outer gate, which may have been re-used in post-exilic times (Pl. 14: 4) and was traced for some 9 m. along the ascending road, where it was lost through denudation.

Two phases of Level II were visible within the Bastion, E/F.17/18. A sectional sketch of the area may be seen on Pl. 113. For more detailed descriptions of the rooms and their contents, see pp. 128–130. The earlier road was only represented by a section of plastered floor, emerging from the guardroom E.18 C (formerly F.18 C), which was open to the north, and passing under the cobbled road marked on Pl. 111. It had not been exposed at any other point when the excavations ceased, and it showed no traces of burning. (Cf. the lime floors below paving stones in the Stratum III gate at Megiddo, M. I, p. 79.)

J. L. Starkey described the three rooms, F.18: A, B and E.18 C, constructed in the earlier period, on p. 11 of *Lachish I*:

"Only the lower and foundation courses of these chambers remain, and those to the west, flanking the outer gate, are damaged by fire. The external wall to the south has naturally suffered most and the roughly hewn blocks of both nari and mizzi limestone are split by thermal fractures or partly calcined. The mud mortar was reduced to a pinky-grey powder. . . .

"The first room to be examined was F.18 C [*now E.18 C*], underlying the foundation courses of a Persian [*now described as 'post-exilic'*] structure, possibly a tower, which had not been affected by fire, and it was not until the last course was removed that any burnt debris became visible. At first this consisted of limestone flakes in pinky-yellow earth, derived from mud brickwork. At this point the top of a stone bench was exposed against the south wall; just below this the colour changed to grey, and the lower levels were quite black. The soil contained much carbonised vegetable matter; in the upper zone of this deposit, close under the east wall, fragments of 16 of the Lachish Letters were found [Pl. 14: 3]. These inscribed potsherds are only a small proportion of hundreds of jar fragments found in this room. As so many had been affected by fire, it is impossible to know how much correspondence may have been destroyed in this way. The black ash lay on the flat stones which paved the floor; their upper surface was blackened by fire, though the heat was not sufficient to cause thermal fractures. The outer wall was 85 cms. thick, and the eastern jamb of the outer gates was built against it [Pl. 13: 4]; there was no north wall to the room. The masonry of this period is poor; where a stone wall is two courses thick, few, if any, headers are used to bond the two faces."

The unburnt plaster floor of the ostraca room continued under the stone bench built against the south wall of E.18 C, and therefore the bench must be somewhat later than the floor, though the difference in time may be very slight.[1] The top two courses of the south wall were rebuilt after the conflagration, as they showed no trace of fire. Starkey was convinced that the ostraca room was burnt from without, owing to the damage caused to the outer side of the south wall of the guardroom. If the fire had originated inside, it would have more seriously affected the plaster floor, which was uncharred below the stones. It is uncertain whether these stones were a deliberate paving or had fallen from the walls or ceiling. In the latter case, it would appear that the letters were kept in an upper chamber, as they were all found above the stones; alternatively there may have been two phases of destruction: one in which the walls collapsed without burning, and a second in which there was a great fire which may have marked the general sack of the town.[2]

It will be seen on Pl. 14: 4 that most of the west wall of the ostraca room is missing; in fact, only the foundation courses remain. Owing to the slope of the ground, it seems likely that the outer gate-sill in use in the post-exilic period (Pl. 13: 4) was originally a Level II construction; but, again, this cannot be verified without further excavation.

The ascending roadway from the base of the mound to the threshold of the outer gate was in use during the period of Level II. Here also two phases were apparent, as represented by two different road surfaces. The upper road was metalled with a layer of small limestone pebbles (cf. the chalk and gravel surface of Road K.17: 1020 within the city), and was everywhere covered with some centimetres of charcoal, ashes and burnt brick, which were in their turn covered by a mass of calcined scree fallen from the second and third walls (Pl. 14: 5).

The violent conflagration indicated by the debris (which contained large numbers of arrowheads) lying on this road suggests that it was contemporary with the final burning of the Level II city, which showed a comparable devastation inside the inner gate. An attempt to trace this road surface upwards towards the gate proved fruitless owing to denudation. The lower road was made of mud from burnt brickwork, which J. L. Starkey considered came from the burnt brick wall and towers of Levels IV–III (Pl. 114). It should therefore belong to the penultimate phase.

The plan on Pl. 108 shows four lines of walling parallel to the road:

(*a*) The lowest line was a retaining wall which joined the south-west corner of the Bastion in direct alinement

---

[1] Compare the skirting walls built into side chambers 503–504 in the Stratum III gate at Megiddo (M. I, Fig. 89 and p. 80), which also rested on the lime-plaster floors.

[2] Jeremiah LII: 6–15 states that in Jerusalem the houses were burned and the walls pulled down a full month after the fall of the city.

with its west side. Though the wall traced by excavation was largely post-exilic, it was founded within the line of an earlier wall, partly exposed and visible on Pl. 14: 6.

(*b*) The second wall delimited the roadway on its eastern side and helped to retain the vast mass of soil on the tell slopes above. The gradient rose from the south-west corner at 251·44 m. to the junction with the post-exilic breastwork in Grid Square E.19 at 253·24 m. The lowest courses of this retaining wall consisted of very large blocks of limestone, but in the upper section the stones used were progressively smaller in size (Pls. 13: 3, 7 and 14: 6). The whole wall was set at a pronounced batter. A breach, presumably made during the final attack on the city, revealed that native rock was immediately behind the retaining wall, and was undoubtedly an added safeguard against military assault. The breach can be seen above the four large stones in Pl. 14: 6.

Pl. 14: 6 also shows the expanse of roadway in use at the time of the burning, with the various retaining walls as excavated in 1936. The road surface was preserved under hardened and calcined scree (seen in the middle distance of Pl. 14: 5), and the same deposit, at an earlier stage of excavation, is shown on Pl. 13: 3. The lime was consolidated by the percolation of surface drainage, and the white mass seen behind the boy in the photograph was harder than native rock.

(*c*) The third wall was part of the Stone and Brick Revetment described earlier in this chapter. The few courses exposed were built of medium-sized masonry and were recessed in a similar manner to the revetment. Like the second wall, it was seriously damaged by fire. Starkey wrote in February, 1933:

"In clearing the base of the wall, we found buried in a mass of burnt debris a bronze crest mount in fragments and it was not until some time had been spent on it that we were able to recognise its significance. Preserved on its patinated surface are traces of cloth and leather fastening, and the rivets are still in position which fixed the mount to the casque. . . . For a contemporary picture . . . we have only to refer to the Lachish Reliefs, where such crests are shown on the helmets of spearmen, probably of second rank." [Pl. 39: 1, 3.]

"The presence of burnt olive stones found with charred wood against the destroyed revetment by the gateway gives a seasonal date for the burning of the city's defences so often referred to. The above is corroborated by other stones near the north-east corner of the tell, but the close proximity of the town rubbish made the lone evidence inconclusive, thus . . . the months of July and August are indicated."

(*d*) The fourth wall is the line of the upper city wall (seen against the skyline on Pl. 14: 6, and from the inner gate on Pl. 13: 9). It has not yet been exposed above the south-west corner, but it would not be surprising to find that the brick section in Grid Squares F.21/22, now incorporated in the third wall, was originally part of the brick Six Metre Wall, which follows the scarp along the west side.

Level I Road

The post-exilic road noted in section on Pl. 113 was well defined at the stone threshold of the inner gate, though the surface was lost for some 9 m., and was only recovered at a point farther east where it met the gradually rising road of Level II. Both roads passed over the heap formed by the fallen gate towers of the Level III city. The post-exilic surface continued at an even level with the top of the heap, and was soon lost through denudation at the ground surface.

Apart from the possible gatehouse in Grid Square G.18 (Pl. 23: 5), there were no post-exilic structures close to the road inside the city wall of this period. The whole area, therefore, seems to have been an open space, as it had been in the preceding phase. The road and open space were surfaced with mud and chalk, hardened by usage, on a rubble basis nearly a metre thick.

The drainage flowed naturally towards the inner gate, and in order to convey the water under the doorsill and to prevent flooding, an inlet, which presumably connected with the earlier Level II drain, had been constructed 8 m. east of the inner gate. The bottom of this inlet occurred at 260·77 m., which brought the top of the stone lining level with the post-exilic road surface at 261 m.

Level I Bastion

The plan on Pl. 112 and the photographs on Pl. 13 illustrate the remaining traces of the post-exilic defences and gateways, which were apparently reconstructed on a plan similar to that of the underlying structures of Level II.

Owing to the slope of the ground within the Bastion area, almost all the north and west walls were missing, and it was not possible to trace the relation of the post-exilic walls with the larger underlying Bastion.

The remaining walls were mostly built of small undressed stones or of material from other structures. For instance, some door-jambs were partially composed of small blocks of soft limestone, similar in size and dressing to the roofing blocks of the Residency (Pl. 22: 2). The normal style of masonry for the period consisted of large blocks of nari laid without mortar, and the crevices were filled with small stones (Pl. 13: 4, 7). Pl. 13: 4 also shows the threshold of the outer gate, which was apparently in use during the post-exilic period, though it may have belonged originally to the buildings of Level II.

The roadway ascending to the outer gate, which must have existed while the Residency was in use, was largely denuded, as were the second and third walls; indeed, it is unlikely that the latter were reconstructed. However, the lowest wall was rebuilt just within the line of the pre-exilic retaining wall, for there was a layer, some 2 m. deep, of fallen calcined masonry running under the wall, and this had spread over the charcoal and ash layer generally associated with the final catastrophe. The remaining portion of the wall belonging to the post-exilic reconstruction is shown on Pl. 112, in Grid Squares D.18/19.

The upper courses were built of roughly cut stones, carelessly laid and mortared with mud. Below the northern end of the wall, where it joined the Bastion, the lower courses had been constructed of larger blocks, but where the line of these foundations ceased, the last stones were thrown out of position.

The only other defensive structure which can be associated with this period is the breastwork in Grid Square E.19, Pl. 108, at right angles to the road. It measured 7.5×2.5 m. and was built of undressed stone, of which two courses were preserved. It blocked a direct approach at a point some 20 m. from the outer gate. It was founded on rubble above the burnt road and crossed the foundation course of the second wall (Pl. 13: 1, 2).

At the top of the sloping roadway to the left of the outer gate was another unexplained construction. The central part was over a metre square, and consisted of dressed blocks of howr of varying length, laid without mortar. Two further squares of undressed stone enclosed the central one, which may have been the pedestal for a statue or shrine. The whole was surrounded by a white plaster floor (Pl. 13: 5).

Near the apex of the eastern valley in Area 7000 (Pl. 130) part of a trackway was exposed, swinging towards the ascending road. There were cart or chariot ruts in the soft limestone, but it is impossible to assign the track to any particular period (Pl. 13: 6).

If a city wall was in use during the post-exilic period, it was apparently that of Level II. The upper courses had been rebuilt with inferior masonry, and the gateway partly blocked with stones, reducing the width from more than 4 m. to 3.60 m. A threshold of undressed stone replaced the carefully cut blocks of the previous period. The projections on either side of the gateway, facing west, were extended and broadened to form towers, and these upper structures were reached by steps, five of which remain on the south side (Pl. 112).

The rectangular tower on the right of the outer gate, like the few remaining traces of walls, showed no signs of burning. All these remains were clearly later than the final destruction of Level II.

Comparisons

In his excavations on the site of Gibeah, Tell el-Fûl, Professor Albright distinguished three fortresses, the first two of which are now attributed to the late eleventh and early tenth centuries (TN II, Appendix A, Introduction). Comparing the two periods of masonry illustrated in AASOR IV, Fig. 11 with the masonry of Palaces A and B at Tell ed-Duweir (Pl. 19: 1–3), it should be noted that mizzi and nari limestone were used in almost equal proportions in the masonry of the first fortress at Gibeah, while the inferior nari grade practically disappeared in the second building period, when the blocks used were nearly half the size and were hammered into rough oblong shape and laid in courses (AASOR IV, p. 9). The style of masonry and high percentage of good mizzi stone merits comparison between Palace A at Duweir and Fortress II at Gibeah (see The Archaeology of Palestine, p. 121, for a reconstruction of the plan).

Tell Beit Mirsim, where the city walls and houses, as exposed in their latest phase, are predominantly of the seventh century B.C., incorporates masonry at certain points which is comparable to earlier walls at Duweir. The two-metre wall, for instance, with its accompanying glacis (revetment) which Albright ascribes to the early ninth century, probably to the reign of Asa (AASOR XXI–XXII, p. 42 and Pl. 40b), is similar to the lower (outer) revetment at Duweir (Pl. 11: 6). The West Tower at Tell Beit Mirsim no doubt corresponded in functional duty to the Bastion at Tell ed-Duweir, and though it measures only 20×16 m., as against 27·5×26 m., it bears the same relation to the city wall, and incorporates the two-metre revetment. Compare the oblong blocks of masonry marked "δ" in AASOR XXI–XXII, Pl. 39B with the north-west corner of the Bastion at Tell ed-Duweir (Pl. 13: 8) for which a similar history is possible.

The plan of the East Gate at Tell Beit Mirsim is an illustration of a change in military defence planning which seems to have affected sites in Judah and elsewhere early in the seventh century B.C. Instead of the time-honoured plan of a gate or gates at right angles to the city wall, largely within that line of defence, an indirect means of access was provided, which extended beyond the enclosure of the city wall (AASOR XXI–XXII, Pl. 5). As Albright has remarked, this violent break with tradition is also to be observed in the contemporary gate at Tell ed-Duweir (AASOR XXI–XXII, p. 48, footnote).

Turning north from the site, the eye follows the ridge of low hills which overlook the coastal plain, where the spur of Tell eṣ-Ṣafi stands against the skyline. This natural site of great strength retains traces of a wall some 12 ft. (3·60 m.) wide, which was built of stone and brick faced with plaster (BM, p. 30 and Pl. 7). In style and method of construction it bears a close resemblance to the revetment wall at Duweir, and it is similarly recessed.

Nearly eight miles north-east of Tell eṣ-Ṣafi lies Tell er-Rumeileh ('Ain Shems), a site where excavations have yielded a most valuable index of pottery comparisons. The fortifications in use, however, during and after the Philistine domination, were those of the previous Bronze Age, patched and repaired. Grant and Wright have noted that such constructions were poor and at no time in the Iron Age was the city strongly defended (AS V, p. 25).

At the exclusively Iron Age fortress of Tell en-Naṣbeh, on the northern border of Judah, there does not appear to be so close a resemblance between the walls of that stronghold and Tell ed-Duweir as the similarity of the pottery would suggest. There is no evidence that any part of the structures were of brick, though the method of building in sections founded on bed-rock (TN I, p. 191) is one which may prove to be the normal procedure for community building schemes in Palestine.

The massive character of the masonry used for the construction of the isolated tower in Z, AA 12 (TN I, p. 189) appears more comparable to the stonework of Tell el-Fûl, Fortress I than to II, but it is interesting to note how closely the tower rested against the inner wall of the earlier construction at Tell en-Naṣbeh.

The Great Wall at Tell en-Naṣbeh (TN I, pp. 191–195), with its attached revetment, seems to represent an advance on the planned defence system of Level III, an impression which is enhanced by the provision of a gate or gates (TN I, Figs. 47 and 48) parallel to the city wall behind the protection of the East Tower. From that stage in military planning it would be a simple step to the system of indirect entry which was later achieved at other sites.

It is therefore difficult to make an architectural equation between the fortifications of Levels IV–III at Duweir and the Great Wall at Tell en-Naṣbeh, both of which have been tentatively attributed to the reign of Asa. The former is a descendant of Bronze Age tradition, and in the latter there are signs of experiment, both in the new angle of approach and in Wampler's proposed "earlier" gate (TN I, Fig. 48).

The problem of comparison between the fortifications at Duweir and the site of Megiddo is complicated by factors other than distance. There is, indeed, a substantial difference in the date assigned by the editors of

Megiddo I to Strata V–I, and those proposed by J. W. Crowfoot (PEQ, 1940, pp. 132–147) and W. F. Albright (AASOR XXI–XXII, p. 2, note 1; AJA, 1940, pp. 546–550).

R. S. Lamon and G. M. Shipton recognised a break of unknown duration before the construction of Stratum V, and they found no evidence of a city wall during that period, when private houses occupied the summit of the mound (M. I, pp. 3–7).

In Stratum IV the city was entirely replanned with buildings of administrative and monumental character, and the whole was enclosed by a wall of oblong stone blocks in alternating sections so that insets on the outer face corresponded with outsets on the inner side (M. I, pp. 28–29 and Fig. 38). It is unquestioned that the wall and associated buildings are comparable on architectural grounds to the structures of the first two periods at Samaria (M. I, pp. 58, 61 and PEQ, 1940, p. 146), which are characteristic of the shortlived proto-Phoenician style, which flourished from 880 to soon after 850 B.C. (SS I, pp. 5–9), but there is nothing of the kind at Tell ed-Duweir. It may be inferred either that relations were not sufficiently close to employ the services of Phoenician masons, or that public building works were not executed on a large scale during that time.

The city gate of Stratum IV at Megiddo lay almost at right angles to the wall, and was wholly within that line of defence (M. II, Fig. 389). With four evenly spaced doorways, it represents a development from the gateway of Levels IV–III at Duweir, inasmuch as the guardrooms or recesses are of equal size and there is no provision for a stairway. While it is not possible to say how the outer approaches were treated at Duweir, it is interesting to see that the system of indirect access was fully developed in the Stratum IV gate tower at Megiddo.

Having proved its use, the layout for the outer gate as constructed in Stratum IV was closely followed in the plan for Stratum III. As a logical result due to the diminished importance of the inner gate, the original plan only provided for three doorways, which were reduced to two before completion, leaving only a single guardroom on each side (M. I, Fig. 86).

Lamon and Shipton (M. I, p. 74) have remarked on the elements in common with the Assyrian gates at Khorsabad (cf. Victor Place, Ninive et l'Assyrie III (Paris, 1870), Pl. 12; Loud and Altman, Khorsabad II (OIP XL, 1938, Pls. 77–78)), and of even closer analogies with the south gate at Carchemish and the west gate of the outer town (Carchemish II, Pls. 12, 4). Nelson Glueck also makes a comparison between the three-doored gate of Ezion-Geber I (Tell Kheleifeh), a seaport on the Gulf of Aqabah, which, as he believes, was fortified in the reign of Solomon and possibly destroyed by Shishak. After a fire, a secondary main wall was built round the main wall of the previous city and the entrances to two pairs of guardrooms were blocked up (Other Side of the Jordan, pp. 100–105).

The inner town of Carchemish represents perhaps in plan and construction the closest parallel to the fortifications at Duweir. Along the bank of the River Euphrates the town was protected by a wall in which ashlar alternated with the coarsest rubble, and either might give place to mud brick. C. L. Woolley was "almost tempted to believe that the original work itself had been a patchwork" (Carchemish II, p. 45). On the landward side the town was defended by a moat and glacis. The west gate through this fortification (Carchemish II, Pl. 10c) projected beyond it, but otherwise it conformed closely in plan to the exposed southern portion of the city Level IV–III gate at Duweir, in the internal arrangements of the rooms and the provision of a stairway.[1]

Throughout this survey no certain evidence of date is obtainable from comparative material within the Iron Age, but it is possible to group the systems of fortifications named in a logical order of development, though the relationship of the series to history must remain uncertain. The problems of defence in Judah certainly became more urgent after the division of the monarchy; besides the initial schemes of Rehoboam and Asa, several of their successors executed building works in Judah, and the names of Jehoshaphat, Uzziah, Jotham and Hezekiah were also renowned. While the architects of Israel and Judah did not invent any sensational defence system, they may have evolved the gate plan with indirect entry from the bitter experience of the Assyrian campaigns, unless the improvement had already been made by the occupying force.

[1] In a lecture at the Institute of Archaeology in May, 1951, Sir C. L. Woolley proposed a date about 1750 B.C. for the fortification of the inner town at Carchemish.

Site	Doorways	Relation to wall	Access
Carchemish, West Gate of Inner Town	Four. Disposed in pairs flanking central room with stair and bench	Projects	Direct
Tell ed-Duweir, Inner Gate of Levels IV–III	,, ,, ,,	Internal	?
Megiddo, Stratum IV	Four. Evenly spaced	,,	Indirect
Carchemish, South Gate of Inner Town	Three. ,, ,,	,,	Direct
West Gate of Outer Town	Three. ,, ,,	,,	,,
Tell Kheleifeh, Ezion Geber I	Three. ,, ,,	,,	,,
Megiddo, Stratum III	Three. As planned	,,	Indirect
,, ,, ,,	Two. As constructed	,,	,,
Tell en-Naṣbeh, "Early" gate AA, AB 24, 25	Two and breastwork	Parallel	Behind East Tower
Gate R–S 23, 24	Two	,,	,, ,, ,,
Tell Beit Mirsim, East Gate	?	Projects	Indirect
Tell ed-Duweir, Level II	Two, with court between	,,	,,
Tell ed-Duweir, Level I	Two, with court between	,,	,,

Pictorial Summary of City Levels I–VI

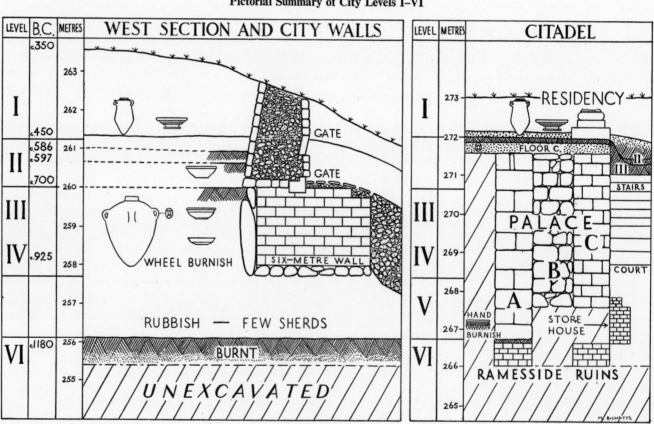

102

CHAPTER 5

HOUSES OF LEVELS V TO II AND GUARDROOMS WITHIN THE BASTION

THE descriptions which follow of each room or locus on the mound, with lists of their contents, provide the basis for a picture of living conditions among the people who dwelt in the houses around the citadel, which was the administrative centre of the district throughout the Iron Age. Soldiers and artisans, with their families, presumably occupied the poorly built hovels, and in assessing their standard of living it must be remembered that they comprised the poorest members of the community.

The plan on Pl. 114 shows the partially excavated rooms flanking the roadway 1087, which leads into the city from the gate. For convenience it will be called "the gate street". The floors of these two rows of shops and houses were flush with the surface of the 1087 road, so that there can be no doubt that the rooms were in use while the brick gate towers (shaded on the plan) were still standing. When the towers collapsed, the debris covered the road and the nearest rooms. A consolidated mass of burnt limestone and clay represented the fallen roofs, and the marks of wooden beams and brushwood which had supported them were clearly visible. After the fire it would appear that the stone lower courses of the walls were pulled out, in some cases down to floor level, to complete the destruction. (Cf. the east wall of Palace C, which was similarly treated, p. 85).

The contents of the rooms, however, remained comparatively undisturbed under the fallen mud roofs. Most objects were on or above floor levels, which were by no means easy to define, but whenever possible the find-spots are noted in the descriptions. Besides a large assortment of pottery, including many jars, there were loom weights and an unusual quantity of iron arrowheads, some of them fused into a mass.

Owing to only partial excavation, the town plan in this area has not yet been traced. Nevertheless, it is clear that at least three alleys led off from the gate street, one presumably rising to the south and the other two leading north. The road between Rooms 1089 and 1092, seen on Pl. 21: 3, sloped downhill towards the north, and the surface drainage from the gate street would also naturally flow in that direction. The house walls on either side of the alley were preserved to a height of almost 2 m., so that both indications suggest that a low-lying quarter exists under the unexcavated area, where there should be an alternative drainage system to carry surface water out of the town. It is not possible to say how the gate street houses were connected with those of the same period adjoining the south wall of the citadel, for the walls were denuded to ground level in both areas. Part of the intervening space may have been filled with small houses, and the road 1095 must have provided a means of communication between them.

The group of houses south of the citadel (Pl. 115) occupied a prominent position, as they were built over the sloping ramp constructed against the foundations of Palace B (Pl. 16: 2, 3).

Fig. 9 shows a section through the largest room, 1003, and illustrates the sloping nature of the floor and the denuded condition of the southern chamber. This section is typical of all the floor levels in the area.

Building methods for these crowded dwellings and for the houses in the gate street were similar. The lower parts of the walls were of stone, and the superstructure was largely of brick or mud. It was usual to cover the brick with mud containing chopped straw, and to finish the surface with a coat of white lime plaster.

Though the building methods do not show any change, there are a few points which permit some constructional order to be suggested for the main groups. In attempting a division it must be remembered that all the rooms were inhabited during the occupation of Level III or Level II, and that such poorly constructed buildings were not likely to have survived in use for much more than a century.

South of the Citadel (Pl. 115)

Group Rooms

1   1010   Level III or earlier.
        1032   The foundation courses of these three rooms have either cut down into the Late Bronze Age
        1039   city, or underlying walls of that period were re-used. The sherds were mostly Bronze Age, and a gold bead and a carnelian spacer (to be published in *Lachish IV*) seem more at home in that setting. Some rooms of Group 4 are partially superimposed.

2   1034   Level IV–III.
                 Remains of three or more long store chambers, built in alinement with the east wall of Palace B. The stone walls, 1 to 2 m. in width, were themselves founded on an earlier brick structure based on stone foundations, which should be attributed to Level V (Fig. 4).

                 These walls bear some relationship to the stone, clay and brick sections of the "enclosure" wall in close alinement with the south wall of the palace (Grid ref. G/H.14). Assuming that these great walls were built at the same time as part of a grandiose plan which cannot be interpreted without further excavation, they should precede the construction of such poor dwellings. In the case of 1002, at least, the stone section had been utilised as a north wall for that room, and there were signs that poor house walls had adjoined the massive west wall of 1034.

3   1030   It is uncertain whether these two small rooms, with the unnumbered chambers to the west, are con-
        1036   temporary with the brick or stone sections of the west wall of 1034. The walls were built of a row of single stones, which may serve to distinguish them from the building around the court 1015.

4   1035   Both these rooms were in use before the collapse of B–C palace wall. Pl. 20: 2 shows how the
        1073   fallen brick had covered the walls of 1035.

                 Compare the double row of stones used in the construction of Rooms 1010, 1032 and 1039. Possibly 1035 and 1073 are contemporary.

4   1001   This group lies outside the range of fallen brick from the south wall of the palace, and there is
        1002   no point of contact with Rooms 1035 or 1003. The double row of stones in the existing wall of
        1005   1002 does suggest an affinity with the earlier chamber. It is clear that the group succeeded all
        1006   three sections of the "enclosure" wall, as one corner of Room 1001 encroached on the clay and
        1007   brick, and the stone section had been used as the north wall of 1002.
        1008

4   1009   These deposits show that the clay and brick walls were broken down to their present level when
        1012   the houses were in use. 1009 is a pit cut into the south face of the "enclosure" wall, and contained eight jars of type 484. 1012 is a deposit of pottery lying on the clay section of the broken-down "enclosure" wall.

4   1013   This group is certainly later than 1010, 1032 and 1039, as it is partially superimposed on the
        1015   earlier walls. There is no point of contact between these rooms and 1003, though the north
        1016   walls are in alinement and the other walls are parallel to each other. The thicker walls of 1003
        1017   may justify a difference in date.
        1029

5   1003   Though the southern half of this cobbled room was missing through denudation, enough remained to show that it was the largest and most solidly built of all the dwellings. It was the only room south of the palace which retained a row of upright stone pillars; these occurred in the gate street houses, in the Level II rooms and in post-exilic buildings. The contents suggest that a weaver's industry was established in the room, where the trade may have continued during the occupation of Level II (Fig. 9).

5   1019   This isolated room is the only one south of the palace which is definitely founded on the fallen brick from B–C palace wall. Therefore it must be associated with the row of rooms east of the palace, attributed to Level II.

The order given here is suggested on constructional grounds and, of course, it does not follow that the contents are contemporary with the buildings. These represent, as a rule, the final occupation phase; the pottery from the rooms is homogeneous, and the same shapes recur frequently. The vessels were nearly all affected by fire; they were found embedded in a thick layer of ash.

Clear evidence of at least two layers of burning was established in the section C–D east of the citadel (Pl. 117). The wall of Palace C collapsed during or after the earlier destruction, and another thick burnt deposit covered the row of houses superimposed on debris and adjoining the masonry of the palace podium.

A problem exists with regard to the houses south of the palace: were they destroyed in the first burning and abandoned thereafter? Or were they partially destroyed and afterwards cleared out for re-use by the occupants of Level II?

An examination of the pottery does suggest that the first proposition is the more likely. The small area so far excavated on the mound does not provide a conclusive answer, but in order to examine the point in more detail it is necessary to note the conditions on the east side of the citadel.

Two sections of the stratification east of the citadel, above the plaster court, are shown on Pl. 117. Section A–B, close to the south-east corner, was dug in 1933, while section C–D was examined in 1938, when knowledge of conditions had developed (Pl. 116).

In both sections the fallen brick of Palace C wall was visible as it sloped down to the surface of the white plaster court (K.14/15: 1033, 1061). This brick debris had been cut into to provide a flat floor space for a row of rooms, which can therefore be placed, without doubt, after the collapse of the wall. The only room on the south side of the palace which was built on the fallen brick was 1019. Although 1003 was beyond that range, its structure and contents are not inconsistent with survival until the destruction of Level II.

East of the Citadel (Pls. 116, 117)

Rooms Level II (See Pls. 17: 6; 18: 1).

1059   The remains of ten poorly constructed rooms were recovered. In some cases the east walls were missing
1060   and the group may well have extended farther down the slope. With the exception of some square
1062   pillars, used in the walls of Rooms 1060 and 1064–5, which may have come from the burnt houses of
1064   Level III, the blocks were apparently re-used material from the palace platform, which was destroyed almost to the floor level of the rooms. Two floor levels were noted in Room 1060, suggesting that there
1065   was some break in the occupation of this room at least. A thick layer of burnt ash lay over the floors
1067   of all rooms except 1077. The conflagration left black scars on the masonry of the palace platform
1068   where the walls of these crude dwellings had been built. The roofs must have been some feet above
1071   the floor level of Palace C. The western part of this complex underlay the outer east wall of the post-
1075   exilic Residency, and the space between the structures had been packed with stone to provide a flat
1077   base for the later building.

ROOMS AND AREAS ON THE TELL AND THEIR CONTENTS

G.14: 1001 (Grid Reference, followed by Room or Area Number)   Level III

The walls consisted of two courses of small stones, and the upper parts were of mud. (See also Rooms 1005, 1006, 1007, 1008.) The floor was partly cobbled and there was intense burning throughout, affecting the pottery and sherds which were evenly distributed over the floor (Pls. 16: 3; 20: 7). The north wall ran over the brick and mud section of the "enclosure" wall, parallel to the south side of the palace; this room and those mentioned above must therefore be later in date.

Pottery: 45, 51, 75, 83, 86, 373, 450, 484

Objects:
Stamp, *zp*	F. No. 5416 NP
AE loop	Pl. 58: 29
Fe arrowheads	NP
Cowrie	NP
Pottery and bone disks	NP

H.14: 1002 Level III?

The east and west walls were built of small stones; the thick "enclosure" wall served as the north wall. A strip the width of the doorway was left uncobbled down the centre of the room. At the north end of the room was a saddle quern of brecciated flint set on a stone and mud pedestal at a convenient angle for use, and there was a second quern of the same material on the uncobbled central strip (Pl. 20: 3). Between the two lay a mass of clay loom weights. A burnt layer above the floor was uniformly covered with broken pots and sherds.

The use of the stone section of the "enclosure" wall as part of the structure of Room 1002 shows that the wall must be earlier. The presence of pottery (from G.14: 1012) farther to the west on the clay wall suggests that the stone section was either broken down or not completed at the time of the destruction of the rooms. It would seem, therefore, that the stone section is at least as early as Level III, and that the underlying clay and brick walls belong to an earlier context.

Pottery: 9(3), 13, 44, 51(2), 63, 73, 75(3), 77, 81, 82, 83, 84, 89, 120(2), 121, 122(2), 147, 148, 150, 168, 171, 176, 177, 220, 280, 284, 287, 292, 309(2), 310, 373(3), 442, 443(2), 449(3), 452,* 456, 462, 470, 472(2),* 484, 490(3)

    * See Pls. 77: 1, 78: 3

Objects:
Fe arrowheads	Pl. 60: 1
Fe chisel	Pl. 61: 8
Saddle querns	Pl. 20: 3
Quern, basalt	Pl. 65: 6
Stone ring	F. No. 5443 NP
Green serpentine hammer stone	F. No. 5444 NP
Chalk jar stopper	F. No. 5446 NP
Weights Nos. 18 and 23	Pl. 50: 6 and NP
Scaraboid	Pl. 44: 114
Bone spatula	Pl. 63: 25
Bone inlay	F. No. 5450 NP

H.15: 1003 Levels II, III

Part of this large room was lost through denudation; an alinement of stone pillars marked the southern limit, but the low connecting wall which presumably joined them was missing. See Fig. 9, which also shows the sloping floors which are typical of the rooms south of the palace.

A deep deposit of burnt mud and pounded chalk above floor level suggests that the roof was more substantial than the light mud and thatch roofs of the adjoining chambers. The presence of a heavy roller (Pl. 20: 5), found above the fallen brick and stones, would also indicate a solid roof. (Roof rollers are a feature of the "fellah" house today, and are used to smooth out cracks which are formed in the mud surface during the hot summer and which would let in the winter rain).

Some forty arrowheads (Pl. 60: 2–8) were found among the roof debris. They can be compared to similar

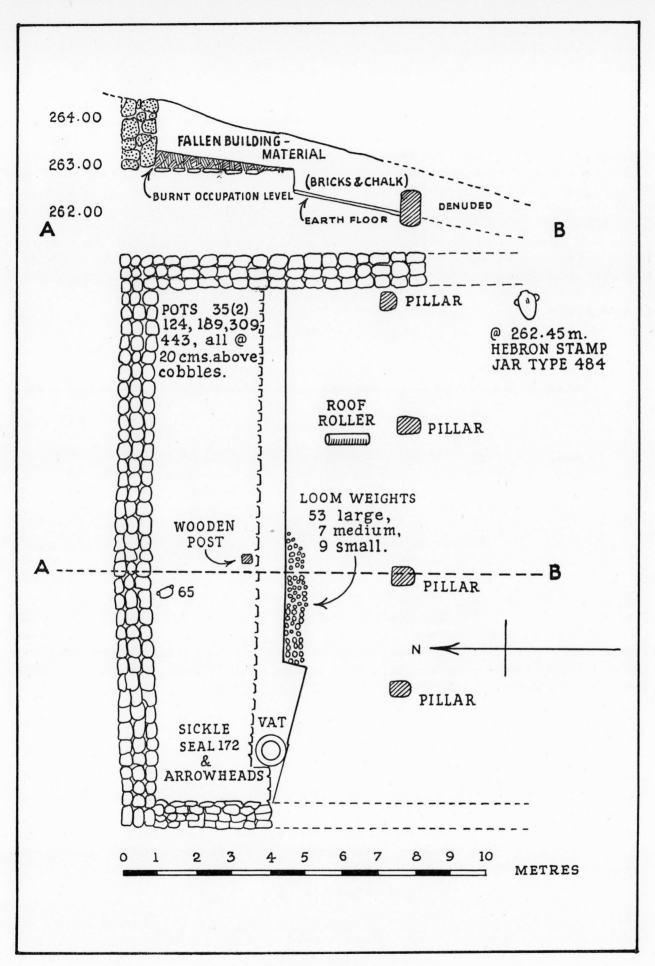

FIG. 9. Room H.15: 1003

caches in Room 1098 (Locus 1046, Pl. 60: 16–21) and Locus 1070. Iron spikes were characteristic of both the large groups (Pls. 60: 8; 61: 12). Presumably such deposits found within the city belonged to the defenders.

The same fallen mass contained a clay seal impression (Pl. 45: 172). On the reverse was the clear impression of the papyrus document to which it had been affixed, and marks of the binding thread.

There was a group of pottery in the north-east part of the room, lying about 20 cm. above the floor. It may have fallen from the roof or from an upper story, or it may represent a secondary occupation. It is therefore possible that the contents of the room date from Levels III and II. The north wall, or its upper part, is evidently later than 1035, q.v. The east wall could be contemporary with Room 1010.

A stone dyeing vat set in the floor at the junction of the cobbled surface with the mud floor adds to the other evidence that the room was part of a dyeing and weaving establishment. Note the many clay loom weights shown on Pl. 20: 5. There were fifty-three large, seven medium and nine small loom weights of the "doughnut" shape. The charred remains of a heavy wooden beam set upright at the end of the room suggests the presence of a vertical loom.

Pottery: 20 cm. above floor level in burnt filling: 35(2), 124, 189, 309(3), 443

floor level: 1(3), 9(4), 13, 37(2), 51, 73(2), 75(5), 81, 82, 91, 120, 121, 123, 150, 163, 180, 189, 273, 276(2), 282(2), 309(3), 396, 408, 417, 442(2), 443(2), 450, 452, 456(2), 475, 484(8),* 486

* Type 484 jar with *la-melekh hbrn* stamped on each handle, Pl. 78: 11; also PEQ, 1941, p. 91: 1.

Objects:				
Fe loop	Pl. 58: 30	Basalt weight?	F. No. 5490 NP	
Fe spike	Pl. 60: 8	Basalt dish	Pl. 65: 9	
Fe arrowheads	Pl. 60: 2–7	Roof roller	Pl. 20: 5	
Fe sickle	Pl. 59: 5	Chalk rubber	F. No. 5493 NP	
Fe knife	Pl. 59: 16	Bone frags.	F. No. 5494 NP	
Fe hoe	Pl. 61: 2	Loom weights	Pl. 65: 12	
AE hook	Pl. 58: 31	Bead	Pl. 66: 4	
Whetstone	F. No. 5488 NP	Seal impression	Pl. 45: 172 and p. 348; also PEQ 1941,	
Rubbers	F. No. 5489 NP		p. 102	

H.14: 1004 — Level II?

An undefined area immediately north of Room 1035. The number 1004 marks the position of an early "White Painted V" jug, type 350, lying in rubbish above the wall at 264·80 m. (Pl. 36: 66). It is unfortunate that the jug was not actually found in a room, so it cannot be used to establish the date of destruction of Level III, though its presence does confirm a terminal date for the use of Level II in accordance with other evidence. Gjerstad[1] has noted the occurrence of a similar jug found at Vroulia, Tomb 12, with Middle Corinthian pottery generally assigned to 600–575 B.C.

Pottery: 350
Objects: Arrowhead   NP
          Stamp, *hbrn* class ii

G.14: 1005 — Level III?

Part of the building containing Rooms 1001, 1006, 1007, 1008. The lower courses of the walls were of small stones, the superstructure was of brick. The walls running north and south were not bonded into the north wall, with the exception of the eastern wall, which was also the west wall of Room 1002. There were some remains of plaster on the narrow dividing wall. The burnt deposit over the floor contained two complete jugs, types 167, 171, and a dipper, type 309, besides numerous sherds.

---

[1] GSCE IV, Pt. 2, pp. 266 and 425.

Pottery: 39(4), 62, 66, 73(3), 81, 90(3), 167, 171, 180, 309, 448, 456, 484
Objects: Stone plummet   F. No. 5502 NP
        Clay jar stopper   F. No. 5501 NP
        Clay loom weight   Pl. 65: 1

G.14: 1006   Level III?

Part of the building containing Rooms 1001, 1005, 1007, 1008, constructed in a similar manner to those mentioned above. About twenty-five loom weights and hammer stones were piled in the north-east corner of the room, close to the doorway leading to Room 1001. The west walls were missing through denudation. The earth floor was covered with a burnt level containing much broken pottery.

Pottery: 75(2), 90, 392(2), 400, 484(3), 489,* 490
       * See Pl. 78: 10.
Objects: Hammer stones and rubbers   F. No. 5508 NP
        Loom weights, "doughnut" shape   F. No. 5509 NP

G.14: 1007   Level III?

Part of the building containing Rooms 1001, 1005, 1006, 1008. The floor level between Rooms 1006 and 1007 seemed to be continuous, and it may belong to the same large chamber. There was an irregular cobbled area and a layer of burning over the floor.

Pottery: 8(2), 40, 51(2), 63(2), 73(3), 75(2), 84, 443, 484(3)
Objects: Bone spatula   Pl. 63: 25

G.14: 1008   Level III?

Part of the building containing Rooms 1001, 1005, 1006, 1007. There was a stone-lined oven against the west wall, with fragments of a water jar upon it. The burnt floor was partly cobbled and a late intrusive grave (not numbered), oriented east and west, lay above it (Pl. 20: 4).

Pottery: 37, 40, 47, 73(2), 82, 84, 120(2), 122,* 168, 239, 280, 392(2), 437, 441, 478, 484(2),* 657
       * See Pls. 77: 2; 78: 5.
Objects: Fe arrowhead   Pl. 60: 9
        Pottery head   Pl. 31: 10
        Faience cowrie, for type see   Pl. 36: 53
        Clay spindlewhorls   Pl. 65: 2, 3
        Stamp, private, F. No. 5400, Pl. 47A: 9 and PEQ, 1941, p. 43
        Burnt fibres

G.14: 1009   Level III

Pit deposit marked by intense burning, and including about eight jars, type 484, some with stamped handles, all incomplete. The pit was cut down into the south face of the "enclosure" wall (Pl. 20: 1).
Pottery: 16, 151, 280, 484(8)
Objects: Stamped jar handles, *zp*, F. No. 5519, p. 342 and PEQ, 1941, p. 95

H.15: 1010   Level III

This room was part of a building including 1032 and 1034, built mainly of brick, which was at first thought to be contemporary with 1003 and the other burnt rooms to the west. It is, however, probably earlier, and it certainly precedes the complex 1013–1018, which is partially superimposed. The complete pots were piled in the north-east corner of the room, and there was a burnt layer over the floor (Pl. 20: 6).

Pottery: 183, 190, 439, 440, 484(3), 682
Objects: 2 glass beads   Pl. 66: 2

H.15: 1011

An open area, possibly a roadway, which was contemporary with building 1001, etc. The pots were some-what above the occupation level.

Pottery: 469,* 484(3)
　　　　　* See Pl. 78: 9.

G.14: 1012

A deposit of pottery lying on the clay section of the broken-down "enclosure" wall. (See 1001, 1002, 1009.)

Pottery: 67, 74, 75(2), 79, 238, 462, 603
Objects: Fe hook　　　　　Pl. 58: 33
　　　　　AE weight　　　　F. No. 5531 NP
　　　　　Stone weight, No. 44 in List of Weights, p. 354
　　　　　Stone bead　　　　Pl. 66: 7
　　　　　Tabular bead　　　Pl. 67: 120

J.15: 1013

Part of the stone building 1015, 1016, 1017, 1029. The floor level was indefinite, but the burnt layer, including the sherds, occurred at about 265·50 m. The water jar 484 and double juglet, type 368, had probably rolled from this deposit and were found lower down the slope.

Pottery: 311, 368,* 462, 466, 484, 490
　　　　　* See Pl. 36: 63.
Object: Pottery disk　　Pl. 35: 14

J.16/K.16: 1014

A white plastered surface, similar to that east of the palace. It was an extension of the adjoining area to the west, 1022. The hole-mouth jar, type 391, was set in the plaster floor and the other pots were lying on it.

Pottery: 311, 391,* 456, 484
　　　　　* See Pl. 78: 14.
Objects: 2 stamps, *hbrn*　　F. No. 6208 NP

J.15: 1015

Part of the stone building 1013, 1017, 1029. There was a rough stone bench in the north-east corner of this central room, with a stone and mud oven in the diagonal corner. Near the oven was a pile of some forty loom weights, and south of that line the earth floor level was lost through denudation. The burnt level over the sloping floor ranged from 265·60 to 265·20 m. Quern 6217 was set in the floor not far from the oven.

Pottery: 45, 46, 48, 73, 83, 120, 121, 192, 311, 402,* 442, 452, 484, 490
　　　　　* See Pl. 77: 35.
Objects: Stamps *hbrn* class ii　　　　　　　　　F. No. 6211, p. 342
　　　　　　　　1 *zp*, class iii　　　　　　　　　F. No. 6212, p. 342
　　　　　　　　2 private *Safan*　　　　　　　　F. No. 6213 NP
　　　　　Quern　　　　　　　　　　　　　　　　F. No. 6217 NP
　　　　　Stone frag.　　　　　　　　　　　　　　F. No. 6218 NP
　　　　　40 clay loom weights, "doughnut" shape　F. No. 6219 NP

J.15: 1016

Part of the stone building 1013, 1015, 1017, 1029. There was a low bench along the north side of the room. The mean level of the burnt layer was 28 cm. above the floor.

Pottery: 75, 148, 286, 309, 484, 490.

Objects: 4 clay loom weights, "doughnut" shape   F. No. 6221 NP

          Stone spindlewhorl   Pl. 65: 4

J.15: 1017   Level III

Part of the stone building 1013, 1015, 1016, 1029. The burnt level on the floor sloped down from 266·25 to 266 m.

Pottery: 45, 472, 484(2), 489, 572

Objects: Weight (frag.), No. 12 on List of Weights, p. 353

          Stamp, 1 *zp* class iii, p. 342 and PEQ, 1941, p. 95

J.15: 1018   Level III

An open area of passage-way between Rooms 1019 and building 1013. The mean level of the burnt floor was 266·20 m.

Pottery: 125*

        * See Pl. 77: 7.

J.15: 1019   Level II

An isolated room north of building 1013, etc. Only the stone foundations of the west wall remained, but the north wall was built of stone on 50 cm. of brick. It must be later than Room 1035, seen on Pl. 20: 2, because the fallen brickwork from the south wall of the palace covered that room, but ran on under Room 1019. There was a quern set on a pedestal against the east wall. The burnt deposit over the floor was exceptionally thick, and its average level was 266·05 m.

Pottery: 309

Objects: Fe arrowheads   Pl. 60: 10–12

          Fe armour   Pl. 58: 12, 14

K. 17: 1020   Levels II, III

Gravel and chalk road-surface or open space, flanked on the north side by a layer of loose stones, the covering of the underlying drain. As this road-surface reached the present ground level, it became increasingly difficult to follow it with any certainty. There were traces of a lower road-surface slightly to the north. The only objects found on the road were three iron arrowheads. (See Roads 1087, 1072.)

Objects: Fe arrowheads   Pl. 60: 13

K. 16: 1021   Level III?

A white plastered surface, similar to 1014, 1022.

J.16: 1022   Level III?

A white plastered surface similar to 1014, 1021. The few sherds found here may have come from deposit 1028.

Pottery: 83, 484

K.17: 1023   Level III

An open area which was possibly a rubbish heap.

K.16: 1024   ?

The north and west walls of a room, built of stone.

K.16: 1025   ?

Stone-lined pit. There were a few flints in it, and fragments of floor plaster containing shells.

K.16: 1026   ?

Stone-lined pit.

K.16: 1027   ?

The north and east walls of a room, largely denuded.

J.16: 1028   Level III?

A deposit of pottery, possibly connected with 1022.

Pottery: 484
Objects: Stamp, private, Pl. 47B: 2 and PEQ, 1941, p. 90, PM.38.717
         Fe spearhead   Pl. 61: 7
         Limestone stopper   Pl. 42: 1
         Bone inlay   F. No. 6237 NP, PM.38.718

J. 15: 1029   Level III

Part of building 1013, 1016, 1017. The sloping burnt floor level extends for about 75 cm. from the north wall. The rest was lost through denudation.

Pottery: 75, 82, 484

J.15: 1030   Level II

An alinement of single stones at right angles to the east wall of 1017. It was possibly connected with 1036.
Object: Scaraboid   Pl. 44: 86

K.16: 1031   Level VI?

Mostly Late Bronze Age debris, evidently thrown up from foundation digging in the Iron Age. Fragments from it will be published in *Lachish IV*.

Objects: 2 stamps, *hbrn* class ii, p. 342 and PEQ, 1941, p. 93
         Faience cowrie   Pl. 36: 53
         Bone pendant   Pl. 63: 21

J.15: 1032   Level III or earlier

Part of the complex 1010, 1039. The east and west walls of this room were built of brick, the north and south walls of stone. The stone west wall of Room 1013 ran across the centre of 1032. The sherds were chiefly Late Bronze Age.

Pottery: 682
Objects: Beads   Pl. 66: 4, 22

K.14/15: 1033   Levels II, III, VI

A part of the wide plastered court east of the palace (see also 1061, 1066), bounded on the east by a low stone retaining wall about 4 m. long and 45 cm. high. It was parallel to the east wall of the palace at a distance of 2 m. The court in this area sloped steeply to the east, and the space west of the low wall was filled up with grey silt to the top, which was covered with stones and brick from the main east wall, but it is uncertain whether this debris fell when Palace C was destroyed or when the podium was cleared for the building of the Residency.

Leaning against the main east wall were three large jars (Pl. 23: 3, types 483 (2 ex.) and 491) and it is possible that the low wall was built to provide a flatter surface for them. The vessels stood directly on the plaster floor at 269·20 m., and were also covered by fallen brick. Other pots and sherds were found with them at 270·70 m. The jars were comparable in ware to those from the guardroom of Level II, and to vessels set in the floor of

K/L: 1061 at 268·08 m., and it would seem that the whole deposit belongs to Level II. Jars, types 470 and 472, were found near by in 1934–1935.

A complication in the whole area is the number of circular pits (see Pl. 17: 2–4). Pit 57 illustrates how they were cut through the fallen brick extending for about 12 m. from the wall, and had in some cases penetrated the underlying plaster court beyond. Other pits, similarly cut, were Nos. 52, 53, 58, 59, 60 and 61. Pit 64 had been largely destroyed by an irregular area of cutting, which had also affected the circumference of pits 62 and 63. East and south of the cutting, pits 40, 46–51, 54–56, with 65–67 and 89–98, were cut directly through the plaster court. For contents of pits see Chapter 6.

The section on Pl. 117, line A–B, shows two layers of scree, both of burnt brick from the citadel, but separated by a layer of ordinary soil. The upper layer probably consisted of fallen brickwork thrown down the slope at the time of the necessary clearance which preceded the building of the Residency. The earlier building was certainly demolished down to floor level, so that there were only a few inches between the made-up floors of the Residency and the blackened plaster below. Most of the grain pits appeared to have been dug before the demolition of the Residency, but none of them seems to have been made before the burning of Palace C. The looseness of the fallen brick makes it difficult to be confident on this point.

Pottery: 60, 137, 152(2), 153, 274, 275, 277, 292, 425, 458, 470, 472, 478, 483(2), 491, 493, 568

Objects: Pottery head   Pl. 31: 16
        AE spear butt   Pls. 41: 7 and 58: 34
        AE scale armour   Pl. 58: 6(2)
        Scarabs   Pl. 43: 10, 57

K.15: 1034   Level IV?

The west wall of this stone building appears to be in alinement with the east wall of Palace B, with which it is probably contemporary. It projected southwards from the palace, and only parts of the north and east walls remain, with small sections of internal walls on the north side. Beneath it was a brick wall, 2 m. thick, with narrower walls projecting south which were denuded at their ends. The brick wall itself has stone foundations on which the boy in the photograph is standing (Pl. 16: 4, 5). The brick building is attributed to Level V. It is uncertain whether the massive stone wall above it is part of a building or whether it belonged to an embankment or enclosure wall.

The iron blade came from the foundation trench of the wall in alinement with Palace C wall. There were no sherds to assist dating.

Objects: Fe blade   Pl. 59: 7
        Bead   Pl. 66: 63

H.15: 1035   Level III

The stone walls of this room were destroyed and buried when the north wall of 1003, or at least its upper part, was built. This is clear from the different levels to which the walls of the two rooms are preserved. 1003 may belong to Levels II and III, but 1035 must belong to the earlier period. Together with a space to the west, 1023, it was covered by fallen brick from the south wall of the palace, and was therefore in use previous to that collapse. See also Room 1019 and Pl. 20: 2.

Objects: Stamp, *hbrn* class ii   F. No. 6253, p. 724
        Fe ploughshare(?)   Pls. 41: 11 and 61: 4
        Arrowhead   Pl. 60: 14
        Burnt grain   F. No. 6255 NP

J.16: 1036   Level III or earlier

This little room lies west of the wall running south from the palace. It should be earlier than the stone rebuilding of the wall K.15: 1034, and may be contemporary with the underlying brick wall on a stone foundation. See also Room 1030 and the two small chambers, unnumbered, lying immediately to the west.

Objects: AE helmet cheek piece Pl. 41: 5
    Beads   Pl. 66: 17, 52

J.15: 1037, 1038

These open areas were on the surface of the ramp which masked the foundations of Palace B, over which the north walls of Rooms 1013, 1016 and 1017 were founded. Like the wall running south from the palace (see Room 1036), the narrower wall dividing 1037 and 1038, and the smaller parallel wall farther east in the latter area, may have been constructed to retain the debris thrown up from the foundations of the palace.

The sherds from these areas were mostly decorated Late Bronze Age, and pieces of a bowl inscribed in hieratic, F. Nos. 6257 and 6259 (PM.38.723–4), to be published in *Lachish IV*.

Objects: AE arrowhead Pl. 60: 15
    Conical seal Pl. 45: 142
    Bead   Pl. 66: 33

J.15: 1039   Level III or earlier

Part of the complex 1010, 1032.

Objects: Fe armour   Pl. 58: 8
    Fe sickle   Pl. 59: 3
    Weight, No. 11 in List of Weights, p. 353.
    Faience amulet Pl. 35: 39
    AV bead   F. No. 6265⎫
    Carnelian spacer F. No. 6266⎭ to be published in *Lachish IV*
    Shell frag.   NP

J.17: 1040   Level III–II?

A room in a row of houses flanking the road running east of the city gate. The superstructure was of brick on stone foundations. There was a thick burnt deposit, apparently unstratified, for 75 cm. above floor level.

Pottery: 66, 73, 75, 78, 81,* 82, 83, 121, 150, 151, 282, 309, 311, 386,* 442, 470, 484
    * See Pl. 77: 4, 5.

Objects: Stamp, *hbrn*   NP
    Saddle quern and grinders F. No. 6273 NP
    Jar stopper   Pl. 64: 4
    Faience amulet   Pl. 36: 52

J.17: 1041   Level III–II?

A partially demolished room in complex 1040–1045, flanking the road running east from the city gate.

Pottery: 82, 177, 311, 355,* 440, 484, 490
    * See Pl. 77: 8.

J.17: 1042   Level III–II?

A partially demolished room in complex 1040–1045, flanking the road running east from the city gate.

Pottery: 64, 81, 148, 309, 456, 502, 560, 570, 573, 574, 575, 576, 584, 603, 605, 636
Objects: Weight, No. 50 in List of Weights Pl. 51: 15

J.17: 1043   Level III–II?

A partially demolished room in complex 1040–1045, flanking the road running east from the city gate.

Pottery: 75, 81, 83(2), 121, 168, 179,* 271(2), 282, 309(2), 442, 454, 484, 490.
   * See Pl. 77: 9.
Objects: Bone disk, pierced   Pls. 41: 10; 63: 15
   Burnt olive stones   F. No. 6284 NP

J.17: 1044   Level III–II?

A road or alley which joined the gate street from the north. A secondary drain runs below the surface into the main drain, where it goes underground towards the gate.

Pottery: 151, 171, 309, 311
Objects: Weight, No. 13 in List of Weights, p. 353
   Clay jar sealing, uninscribed, iike Pl. 52: 12
   Stamp, *hbrn* class ii, p. 342 and see PEQ, 1941, p. 43

J.17: 1045   Level III–II?

A partially demolished room in complex 1040–1045, flanking the road running east from the city gate.

Pottery: 59*
   * See Pl. 77: 14.

It will be seen that the complex of rooms, 1040–1045, was built over the city drains from the east and north. The incomplete nature of the rooms and the paucity of objects from them do not make it possible to establish definitely whether they are contemporary with Level III or Level II, though the latter period is more probable

H.17: 1046   Level III

Locus in Room 1098, marking position of a deposit of over fifty arrowheads, mostly fused into one mass. (See also Room H.15: 1003, Pl. 60: 2–8, and Locus 1070.)

Objects: Fe spike (2 or 3 ex.)   Pl. 61: 12
   Fe arrowheads   Pl. 60: 16–21
   AE strainer   Pl. 58: 38

L.14: 1047   Level III or earlier

A pit cut through a large heap of howr chips, east of the stairway platform. Both sides and bottom were faced with a mud or straw coating.

Pottery: 281, 465

L.14: 1048   Level II

A pit cut through the fallen brick from the east wall of the palace, underlying Room 1077. See section on Pl. 117 A–B.

H.18: 1049   Level III

A partially excavated room in the row of houses flanking the road running east from the city gate.

Objects: Stamp, *hbrn* class ii, p. 342
   2 stamps, illegible   NP

K/L.11: 1050 (Pl. 110)   Level III or earlier?

Storeroom, north of Palace A; see also 1051, 1052. The walls were of brick on stone foundations. The building was apparently contemporary in construction with Palace B–C, but it may have survived in use until the destruction of Palace C.

Plaster containing lumps of rock crystal was found thrown in between the south wall of 1050 and the north wall of the palace, and other bits were found in the robbed foundation trench of the palace north wall.

L.11: 1051   Level III or earlier?

Storeroom or chariot-house, north of Palace A; see also 1050, 1052. Note the wide doorway in this room and in 1052. The floor was made of crushed chalk, with burnt patches at 268·20 m. There were two water jars set in the floor, both type 483. Other sherds were found at various levels.

Pottery: 474, 477, 483(2)

L.11: 1052   Level III or earlier

Storeroom or chariot-house, north of Palace A; see also 1050, 1051. Note the wide doorway in this room and in 1051. The floor was probably at 268 m., which was the level at which the two jar handles were found (F. No. 6764) with fragments of jugs, types 189 and 220. There were sherds from all levels of the filling, and two bowls of LB form, types L.II 14 and 29, were found below the foundations of the south wall.

Pottery: 189, 220
Objects: Stamp, *shkwh*, class ii   F. No. 6764 (2), p. 342

K.11/12: 1053   Level V

Casemate foundations of Palace A. The walls were largely robbed by the builders of the Residency, leaving trenches filled with late debris. The original filling of the casemates contained much LB material and a few Iron Age burnished sherds at 269·55 m. There were pits underlying the casemates which must be earlier than the building. A scarab, F. No. 6769, will be published in *Lachish IV*.

Pottery: 590
Objects: Fe armour   Pl. 58: 13
           AE armour   Pl. 58: 9
           Frag. of diorite statue (?) in surface deposit   F. No. 6766 NP
           Beads   Pls. 66: 75; 67: 118

K.12: 1054   Level V

Casemate foundations of Palace A. The north, east and west walls were mostly robbed, except close under the north wall of the Residency. The south wall served as a foundation for the north outer wall of the Residency. The original filling between the walls, consisting of hard packed clay and debris containing mostly LB sherds, was intact. The trenches where the walls had been were filled with stone chips and building debris. The walls and filling lay on brick debris with a silo running under the west wall.

K.12: 1055   Level V

Casemate foundations of Palace A, partly excavated in 1937–38. See also 1054 for general remarks. There was, in this area, a thin layer of fine mizzi chippings between the filling and the underlying clay.

K.12: 1056   Level V

Casemate foundations of Palace A. See 1054 for general remarks. The walls were partly preserved on all four sides. The south wall was apparently based at a higher level than the others, and was leaning to the north. It was preserved because it lay partly under the north wall of the Residency.

Objects: Chalk stopper   F. No. 6771 NP

L.12: 1057   Level V

Casemate foundations of Palace A. See 1053–1056. An inscribed bowl fragment, F. No. 6773, from the LB debris, will be published in *Lachish IV*.

Objects: Bead   Pl. 66: 20

Casemate foundations of Palace A. See 1053–1057. Pit 38, containing Attic sherds, had been cut out in this area, and many sherds strewn around were associated with it; the bowl 558 should therefore belong to Level II or later.

Pottery: 558
Objects in filling of disturbed area: Fe armour   Pl. 58: 7
                                   Fe knife   Pl. 59: 15
                                   AE fibula   Pl. 58: 18

Below the disturbance there was a scarab and a scarab impression, F. Nos. 6778–6779, which will be published in *Lachish IV*.

One of a row of rooms built on the debris of the fallen east wall of Palace C (Pls. 17: 6 and 18: 1). Like the adjacent rooms 1060 and 1062, it was set in a deposit of burnt brick, and the floors were of mud.

Pottery: 469
Objects: Stamp, *hbrn* class ii (from the burnt brick under the room), F. No. 6781, p. 342 and PEQ, 1941, p. 93

One of a row of rooms built on the debris of the fallen east wall of Palace C (Pls. 17: 6 and 18: 1). Walls and floor were like those of 1059 and 1062, except that the outer face of the east wall had collapsed. Two square pillars were incorporated in it.

The floor level was destroyed at the north end of the room, where there was a substantial layer of ash containing sherds of Iron Age II.

An oven in the north-west corner of the room at 270·24 m. probably belonged to the floor level, though the line of burning passed over it at 270·30 m. There was apparently an intermediate living level running from 270·06 m. to 269·90 m. Under a second oven against the east wall of the palace (not marked on plan) there was a flat-based lamp, a broken rattle and some burnished sherds.

Pottery: 689, 691
Objects: Fe arrowheads   Pl. 60: 22
        Stamps, *hbrn*, class ii   F. No. 6783, p. 342
              shkwh, class ii   F. No. 6784, p. 342
              mmsht, class iii   F. No. 6785, p. 342

Part of the plastered area east of the palace. At a point on the line K/L.14 at 268·08 m. two large jars, types 479 and 492, were deeply set into the plastered court; the latter was covered by a bowl, type 78. Lying on the floor near by were three more jars, types 482, 484 and 491, somewhat comparable to the group against the main east wall at 1033. A similar low wall built over the plaster court was found slightly east of the group at 268·08 m., at a distance of 10 m. from the main east wall.

Pottery: 69(2), 78, 79, 479,* 482,* 484(3), 491, 492*
         * See Pl. 78: 4, 6, 8, 13.
Objects: Weight, No. 2 in List of Weights   Pl. 51: 2
        Brick, 50·5 × 26 × 14 cm. (see p. 81)   Pl. 42: 3
        2 stamps, *hbrn* class ii, from the fallen burnt brick, F. No. 6796, p. 342

L.13: 1062   Level II

One of a row of rooms built on the debris of the fallen east wall of Palace C; see also 1059, 1060. There was no floor level. The double bowl came from the burnt brick debris apparently belonging to Level III.

Pottery: 116*

    * See Pl. 77: 6.

L.13: 1063   Level III and earlier

Upper stairway of Palace C, underlying Rooms 1060 and 1064 (see Pls. 116, 117, 18: 2, 3, 4, 6). For detailed description see p. 85. There are two earlier flights of steps incorporated in the topmost set, which is contemporary with the plaster court around it. If this is correctly attributed to Level III, the underlying flights must belong to earlier phases in the history of the palace-fort. It should be noted that the soft limestone of the top flight

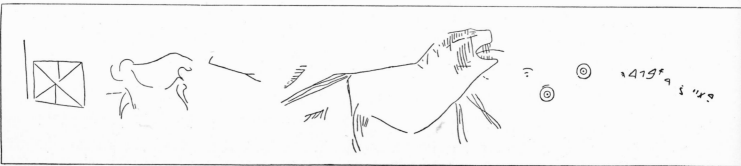

Scale 1:3

Fig. 10. Drawings scratched on the palace steps

showed little evidence of use, and the pile of howr chips close by suggest that they were only finished about the time of Level III destruction. The two steps of the intermediate flight which were exposed were, on the other hand, much worn, and the lowest flight, though made of a harder stone, was in good condition. On the vertical face of one of these steps was scratched a drawing of a lion, with some unintelligible scribbles and the lightly incised five letters of the Early Hebrew alphabet (Pl. 48B: 3 and Fig. 10). Both Professor Albright and Dr. Diringer agree that the letters may be assigned to the late ninth or early eighth century B.C. on palaeographic grounds (for detailed remarks see p. 357). It can therefore be said that the lowest flight is about a century older than the topmost one. As all three flights are associated with the additional strip C enlarging the east side of the palace, they can have no connexion with an earlier structure.

Pottery: 79

L.12/13: 1064   Level II

One of a row of rooms built on the debris of the fallen east wall of Palace C. See 1059, 1060 and 1062. The east wall was constructed of re-used stones. The floor was at the level of the highest step of 1063. An "annexe" at a slightly higher level had been cut out on top of the palace east wall, forming a small room or cupboard.

Pottery: 69, 79

Objects: Stamp, *hbrn* class ii, from the burnt brick under the room, p. 342

L.12: 1065   Level II

One of a row of rooms built on the burnt brick from the fallen east wall of Palace C (Pls. 17: 6; 18:1). It was covered and almost filled with a quantity of large stones on which the north-east corner of the Residency was founded. Against the east wall, constructed of stone robbed from the podium of the palace, was a saddle quern and rubber by the side of a plastered trough. A large selection of pottery was lying both on the cobbled and the mud areas of the floor at levels ranging between 269·50 m. and 269·90 m. There was a heavy deposit of burnt wood and brick over everything. The pottery forms a valuable group for contemporary dating, and includes jar 495, which was inscribed. The storage jar fragment, type 480, should belong to an earlier context.

While taking up the floor of Room 1065 to expose the palace stairway beneath, a fragment of an ostracon (Pl. 48A: 3) was discovered. It is therefore earlier by at least a few years than the inscribed jar 495 (Pl. 48A, B: 1).

Pottery: 37, 78(2), 149, 152, 246, 275, 276(3), 281, 292, 400, 442, 460,* 479, 480, 493, 494,* 495, 528, 552, 558
   * See Pls. 77: 3; 78: 15.

Objects:	Basalt dish	Pl. 65: 8
	Saddle quern	F. No. 6822 NP
	Bone spatulae	Pl. 63: 23, 24
	Ostracon XX	Pl. 48A, B: 1
	Ostracon XXI	Pl. 48A: 3

L.12/14: 1066 (not marked on Pl. 116)   Level III

A part of the wide plastered square east of the palace (Pl. 18: 2, 6) in the vicinity of the porch and steps 1063. See also 1033, 1061. It was in perfect condition, and was undamaged by late rubbish pits. The coating was 2·5 cm. in thickness and was mixed with straw. Above this surface were several heaps of howr chippings and small stones, possibly connected with the final dressing of the steps. The space immediately at the bottom of the steps was clear, and only covered by fallen burnt brick.

At a distance of 15 cm. from the palace wall and 1·70 m. from the foot of the stairway was a rough but massive drum of stone. The sides of the stone were slightly concave, and the upper surface was pitted with seven or eight small hollows, apparently formed by use. The deepest hollows were the most accessible, and showed signs of polishing. The stone stood about 30 cm. in height, and it measured nearly 1·50 m. across. The upper edge was worn and smooth from use (Pl. 18: 5).

Against the outer face of the stairway (1063) was a triple platform covered with hard grey plaster (Pl. 18: 3). It consisted of a central block, about a metre high, flanked on each side by similar blocks a few centimetres lower. It appeared to be made of stones and rubble, and little care had been taken to make it symmetrical. The plaster had many irregularities, and overlapped the stone steps, but it merged smoothly without a join into the plastered floor, showing that it was constructed at the same time as the last set of steps and the latest surface of the plaster court (Pl. 117). It may have been a mounting block or pedestal.

South of the stairway were some eight bone arrowheads (Pl. 63: 16, 17, 18) with one made of iron. In a similar deposit on the burnt roadway 1072, inside the city gate, a few more bone arrowheads were recovered, among many examples made of iron (Pls. 63: 19, 20; 60: 47–52, 62–65, 71). It is possible that the group near the stairway was not connected with the destruction of the city, for they were lying in a layer of mud which separated the fallen brickwork from the prepared surface at this point. Perhaps the bone arrowheads, at least, were used in more peaceful pursuits. A bronze arrowhead was found stuck in a crack between two stones of Palace C wall, 60 cm. above the floor.

Pottery: 64, 81, 82, 120, 128, 292, 309, 442, 497,* 630, 635, 644
   * See Pl. 78: 17.

Objects:	Fe arrowheads	Pl. 60: 23–24
	AE arrowhead	Pl. 60: 25
	Bone arrowheads	Pl. 63: 16–18
	Stamp, *zp*, class i in white deposit over floor	F. No. 6831, p. 342
	Stamp, *hbrn*	NP
	Brick, 54×29×13 cm.	NP

L.12: 1067   Level II

One of a row of rooms built on fallen brick from the east wall of Palace C. The walls on the west and south were constructed of poor stone, robbed from the palace podium. The east and north walls were missing. Part of the floor was cobbled at the south end, and on it were some seven pots, types 264, 479 and 558(5), at about 269·27 m. There were plentiful traces of burning.

Pottery: 78, 79, 264,* 281, 474, 479(3), 518, 528, 558(5), 566, 629, 636, 637, 648

      * See Pl. 78: 12.

Objects: Stamp, rosette   Pl. 53: 1

L.12: 1068   Level II

One of a row of rooms built on fallen brick from the east wall of Palace C. At this point there was a breach in the palace wall (not shown on plan), which was apparently not repaired, but merely filled in and masked by the Residency.

The eastern limits of Room 1068 were uncertain; the floor had been partially cobbled. Jar 484 was below the floor.

Pottery: 64, 95, 442, 456, 469, 484, 560

L.12: 1069   Level II

One of a row of rooms built on fallen brick from the east wall of Palace C. There was a good cobbled floor at 269 m. covered by a thick deposit of burning. The east wall was badly built of poor stone. Below the floor was a deposit of earth containing some burnt brick, and at 268·8 m. there was a hard surface sloping from south to north, up which the stones for building the steps were probably rolled. Lamp 152 was found below the floor, as were the bronze fibula and the jar stamp.

Pottery: 79, 152

Objects: AE fibula   Pl. 58: 20

         Stamp, *hbrn* class ii, p. 342

J.15: 1070   Level II

The number marks the burnt level west of Room 1019. About twelve iron arrowheads were found at this point, mostly fused into a mass. They lay on the brick, in a layer of ash which covers Room 1035 and runs under 1019. Thus it is more likely that they were dropped at the time of the final destruction, judging from the level of 265·90 m. at which they were found. The floor of Room 1073 was over a metre below this area. Cf. the arrowheads in Room 1003 and Locus 1046.

Objects: Fe arrowheads   Pl. 60: 26, 27

L.13: 1071   Level II

One of a row of rooms built on the fallen brick from the east wall of Palace C. See 1060 and 1062. A large part of the poorly constructed stone and mud walls was missing. There was a mud floor to the south, which was missing farther north where there was an oven in position, with mortaria fragments below it.

Pottery: 68

G/H/J.17: 1072 (see also 1020, 1087)   Level III–I

The latest road surfaces within the city gate are delimited on Pl. 114 and sections through them appear on Pl. 113. They consisted of rough stones and pebbles, many of which had been turned by the plough or had fallen from the post-exilic houses south of the gate. Despite the amorphous condition, the top layer of stones from the gate followed so closely the line of earlier roads that it should be included among them, though any trace of a prepared surface was lacking. It rose from a level at 262·29 m. within the gate to 263·03 m. at its easterly end, where it reached the present ground surface (Pl. 124).

It is not possible to say whether the bed of stones running in a southerly direction should be noted as a road; if so, it would be later than the houses in G.18, as it passed over them. Both these piles may therefore be associated with the occupation of the site in the fourth century A.D.

For a description of earlier phases of the road, see Chapter 4, The Roads and Gateways.

The objects from both phases of the Level II road are listed below; owing to denudation of the surface on the higher parts of the road towards the centre of the mound, no value can be attached to the positions in which the pottery and coins were found.

261·62 m.		Level of road surface at junction of grid squares. See section on Pl. 113
261·50 m.	*Object*:	Coin No. 15 on List of Coins, p. 412
261·30 m.	*Pottery*:	Lamp 150(2)
261·20 m.	*Pottery*:	Jug 281, dippers 282(2), potstand 400,* pilgrim flask 432.* (* See Pl. 77: 12, 33)
	Objects:	AE kohl stick F. No. 7054 NP
		Fe arrowheads Pl. 60: 62, 63
		Frag. of cloth F. No. 7069 NP
Over room 1079	*Object*:	Stamp, *hbrn* class i, p. 342 and PEQ, 1941, p. 41
260·85–80 m.	*Pottery*:	Attic bowl 30
	Objects:	AR ring F. No. 7062 NP
		Coin No. 5 on List of Coins, p. 412
260·78–74 m.	*Pottery*:	Funnel 374, lamp 151
	Object:	Stamp, F. No. 7068, PEQ, 1941, p. 99
260·67–63 m.	*Pottery*:	Bowl 82
	Objects:	Stamp, rosette, F. No. 7067
		Fe arrowheads Pl. 60: 47, 49–51
260·50 m.	*Pottery*:	Juglet 311
	Object:	Fe nail F. No. 7053 NP
260·40 m.	*Object*:	Fe arrowhead Pl. 60: 48, 64
260 m.	*Objects*:	Frit vase Pl. 36: 57
		Stamp, *mmsht*, class iii, F. No. 7071, p. 342 and PEQ, 1941, p. 97
		Stamp, private F. No. 7070, Pl. 47 A: 7 and PEQ, 1941, p. 41
259·90 m.	*Object*:	Fe chisel Pl. 61: 5

Sherds from tell surface (not included in Consolidated and Distribution Charts): 115,* 173, 280, 309, 459, 466, 530, 533, 551, 556, 561, 638, 642, 645, 674
                                 * See Pl. 77: 18.

J.17 above road

	Objects:	AE strainer Pl. 36: 55
		AE arrowhead Pl. 60: 52
		Fe spade or hoe Pl. 62: 1
		Fe knife Pl. 59: 1
		Bone arrowheads Pl. 63: 19, 20
		Stamp, *shkwh* class iii, p. 342

J.15: 1073   Level III

A burnt room or open space below the fallen brick from the south wall of Palace B–C; see 1035. Above it was a deposit of arrowheads from Room 1070, attributed to Level II. The objects from Room 1073 were found at an average level of 264·60 m., but this was not necessarily the floor level. The walls not in common with 1035 were missing.

Pottery: 452

Objects: Fe arrowhead   Pl. 60: 28
AE hook, broken   Pl. 58: 32
Faience sow amulet   F. No. 7083 NP
Bone calendar, frag.   F. No. 7084 NP
Stamp, *mmsht*, class iii   F. No. 7080, p. 342 and PEQ, 1941, p. 97 (F. No. 7081)
About 50 loom weights   NP

L.12: 1074   Level II

A pit cut through the fallen brick from the east wall of Palace C, underlying Room 1075; the bottom was of burnt brick. Sherds from the same pots were found in the pit and in the room.

Pottery: 281, 465

L.14: 1075   Level II

Partial remains of the most southerly room in the row built on fallen brick against the east wall of Palace C. There was no definite floor or limits to the south, but there were traces of burning at the north end, where a few "doughnut"-shaped loom weights were found. The underlying "gravelly" surface of burnt brick had been cut to provide a level space for the room. See also pit 1074, under the east wall, which contained fragments belonging to pots from the room floor. The jar, type 465, with incised drawings of ibex from this room is shown on Pl. 78: 16, and the drawing is reproduced at half scale on Pl. 50: 1. Also see section on Pl. 117 A-B.

Pottery: 269, 311, 442, 444, 465*

M.14: 1076   Post-exilic and later

An area or room, of which only part of the north wall remained. There were three floor levels discernible at 267·23 m., 267·60 m. and 267·64 m. They were of stamped mud, and an oven was apparently set in the lower floor. The floor at 267·23 m. corresponded to that of Rooms 41 and 42, which is a post-exilic structure, so the higher floors must belong to later squatters. The sherds came from the lowest floor, and six loom weights from the north wall.

Pottery: 400, 568, 637

L.14: 1077   Level II

Partial remains of a room adjoining 1075 to the east, in the row built against the east wall of Palace C. The underlying slope of burnt brick had been levelled to provide a flat floor surface. There was no trace of burning. The small section of wall remaining passed over a pit, 1048, and above the pit, at room floor level, was part of a two-handled jar, with the neck missing, similar to body type 479. See section on Pl. 117 A-B.

H.17: 1078   Level III

Partially excavated room, north of the road from the city gate. The walls were of brick, reinforced by three square stone pillars. There was a mud floor (Pl. 21: 1, 6).

Pottery: 147, 311, 400, 442, 469, 484(2), 501, 632, 671

Objects: Fe arrowheads   Pl. 60: 29, 30
Incised sherd, *bt lmlk* (above room)   Pl. 49: 1 and pp. 356, 357
Pottery head   Pl. 31: 6
Jar stopper   as Pl. 64: 4

H.17: 1079   Level III

A room, north of the road from the city gate, with the frontage to the road missing. The north wall was of brick and the floor of mud (Pl. 21: 1).

Pottery: 69, 75, 120, 150, 269, 279,* 294, 309, 313,* 399, 442, 469, 484, 490, 602, 629, 637, 652, 655, 694
        * See Pl. 77: 10, 11.

H.18: 1080   Level III

A room south of the road from the city gate. The frontage to the road was missing, and the floor partly plastered.

Pottery: 61, 81, 309(2), 400, 456, 484, 499, 501, 574, 627, 631, 632
Object: Pendant   Pl. 67: 135

H.18: 1081   Level III

A partially excavated room, south of the road from the city gate. The east and west walls were of stone, and the floor was of mud.

Pottery: 31, 144, 259, 397,* 400, 456, 484, 499, 550, 587, 603, 631, 650
        * See Pl. 77: 31.

Objects: Fe arrowheads   Pl. 60: 31, 32
          AE fibula   Pl. 58: 21
          2 stamps, *hbrn* class ii   F. Nos. 7104, 7104A, p. 342

H.18: 1082   Level III

A partially excavated room south of the road from the city gate. The east and west walls were of stone, and the floor of mud.

Pottery: 309
Objects: Fe sickle   Pl. 59: 4
          Fe arrowheads   Pl. 60: 33
          Fe point   Pl. 61: 10
          AE spear butt (?)   Pl. 58: 37
          Jar stopper   NP
          15 loom weights   NP

M.14: 1083   Post-exilic

A room or area, divided from 1076 by a south wall, the only one remaining. A bangle and Attic sherds lay on a floor at 267·45 m., over a burnt layer at 250·60 m., which may represent the destruction level of II or III.

Object: AE bangle   Pl. 63: 7

H.18: 1084   Level III

A room, south of the road from the city gate. There was a superstructure of brick on mud and stone walls, plastered. A plastered recess or bin inside the doorway contained olive stones. The main room was cobbled and there was more than a metre of plaster and brick debris above the floor.

Pottery: 35, 37, 41, 69, 81, 120, 282, 490
Objects: Fe ox-goad (?)   Pl. 61: 9
          Fe arrowheads   Pl. 60: 34
          Weight, No. 49 in Lists of Weights   Pl. 51: 10
          Weight, No. 30 in List of Weights, p. 353
          Stamp, *hbrn* class ii   F. No. 7119 (4 ex.), p. 342

H.17: 1085   Level III

A partially excavated room, north of the road from the city gate. It had brick walls, with two single square stone pillars set in the east wall. The floor was cobbled.

Pottery: 69, 73, 81, 121(2), 309, 399(2), 456, 484, 499
Objects: Fe knife   Pl. 59: 8
         Fe arrowheads   Pl. 60: 35

H.18: 1086   Level III

A room, south of the road from the city gate. There were brick walls and a plastered floor surface.

Pottery: 1, 39, 81, 177, 309(2), 484
Objects: Fe knife   Pl. 59: 14
         Fe arrowheads   Pl. 60: 36–38

G/H/J.17: 1087   Level III

Level of the road surface at the junction of grid squares H.17/G.17. See section on Pl. 113. For description, see Chapter 4, The Roads and Gateways.

Pottery: 81, 115, 167, 656, 680
         Sherds from tell surface (not included in Consolidated and Distribution Charts): 115, 280, 309, 459, 462, 466, 530, 533, 551, 556, 561, 642, 645, 656, 658, 674, 680
Objects: Fe arrowheads   Pl. 60: 39–42
         Fe knife   Pl. 59: 12
         Fe scale armour   Pl. 58: 11
         AE boss   Pl. 58: 36
         Pottery head   Pl. 31: 4
         Stamp, *hbrn* class ii   F. No. 7145, p. 342
         Stamp, *mmsht* class iii F. No. 7146, p. 342
         Stamp, *shwkh* class ii F. No. 7147, p. 342

H.17: 1088   Level III

A room north of the road from the city gate, with the frontage to the road missing. The remaining walls were of brick on stone foundations and the floor was cobbled. A stone vat stood against the west wall (Pl. 21: 3). Adjoining the road was a flight of three steps, presumably leading to an upper floor.

Pottery: 13, 85, 399, 431, 442, 484, 499, 576, 631
Objects: Fragments of Fe arrowheads   NP
         Seal impression   Pl. 45: 166

H/G.17: 1089   Level III

A room north of the road from the city gate. The walls were of brick on stone foundations. There was an oven against the north wall, and a stone-lined bin in the opposite corner. There was a mud floor, on which were numerous loom weights, much pottery and other objects.

Pottery: 82, 147, 187, 189, 261(2), 269, 282, 387, 399, 456, 476, 484, 633, 635, 649
Objects: Incised letter on sherd   Pl. 52: 9
         Fe ploughshare   Pl. 61: 1
         Fe oxgoad (?)   Pl. 61: 11
         Fe arrowheads   Pl. 60: 43, 44
         Fe link   Pl. 58: 35

Weight, No. 6 on List of Weights, p. 353
Bone fan handle (?)   Pls. 41: 13 and 63: 12
Bone fan handle (?)   Pl. 63: 13
Stamps, *hbrn* class iii   F. No. 7164, p. 342 and PEQ, 1941, p. 93
   hbrn class ii   F. No. 7163, p. 342 and PEQ, 1941, p. 92
   private   †F. No. 7166, Pl. 47A: 1, 2, PEQ, 1941, p. 38
   private   †F. No. 7167, Pl. 47A: 4–6, PEQ, 1941, p. 41
   private, square   F. No. 7168, Pl. 47A: 10, 11 (F. No. 7161), PEQ, 1941, p. 44
   shwkh class iii   F. No. 7165, p. 342 and PEQ, 1941, p. 97
   illegible   F. No. 7169 NP
Steatite scarab   †F. No. 7160 (to be published in *Lachish IV*)
Brick, 48 × 29 × 13 cm.   NP
† PM.39.824–5, 39.822.

H.17: 1090   Level III

A partially excavated room north of the road from the city gate. The doorway is visible on Pl. 21: 5.

Pottery: 402, 450, 484, 499, 501, 550, 599, 627, 635, 649, 682

G/H.17/18: 1091   Level III

A partially excavated room, south of the road from the city gate. The walls were brick on stone foundations, and the floor was cobbled. Some fragments of iron arrowheads and a slingshot were not kept.

Pottery: 121, 450, 484, 632, 638, 640

G.17: 1092   Level III

A room north of the road from the city gate. The walls were built of small stones and there was no trace of a brick superstructure. The room was partitioned down the centre, possibly to take the weight of a brick stairway leading to an upper floor, of which the lowest steps remained (Pl. 21: 2).

Pottery: 120, 462, 484
Objects: Fe knife   Pl. 59: 9
    Fe arrowhead Pl. 60: 45
    Fe balance beam Pl. 62: 2

H.17: 1093   Level III

A partially excavated room north of the road from the city gate. The walls were of brick and there was a mud floor.

Pottery: 467*
  * See Pl. 78: 2.

G.17: 1094   Level III

A partially excavated room, north of the road from the city gate. Some fragments of iron arrowheads were not kept.

Pottery: 6, 9(2), 16, 50,* 75, 122, 151, 309, 385,* 476, 499
  * See Pl. 77: 13, 16.

G.17: 1095   Level III

A partially excavated road leading north out of the main road eastwards from the city gate. It will be seen from the levels and from Pl. 21: 3 that the surface of this alley would collect the drainage from the main road and carry it downhill to a point in the unexcavated area. This suggests that there must be some alternative drainage system farther north.

Pottery: 109,* 115, 120, 122, 143, 452, 484, 509, 548, 549, 586, 632, 635, 638, 643
       * See Pl. 77: 17.
Objects: Clay jar sealing   Pl. 52:12

H.17: 1096   Level III

A room north of the road from the city gate. The walls were brick and the floor was cobbled. A square stone pillar was incorporated in the partition wall between Room 1096 and Room 1078 (Pl. 21: 6).
Pottery: 283

H.18: 1097   Level III

A partially excavated room south of the road from the city gate. The walls were brick and the floor was cobbled. An oven was set in the north-east angle of the room.
Pottery: 73, 121, 470, 544

Classified Summary of the Pottery in the Tell Rooms

LEVEL I

Bowls			Potstands	
Class	Type		Class	Type
B. 13	637		PS	400
B. 14	568			

LEVEL II

Bowls			Potstands	
Class	Type		Class	Type
B.6	95		PS	400
B.7	37			
B.8	558(7)			
B.11	64, 560		Cooking Pots	
B.13	69, 78(3), 79(3), 629, 636, 637, 648		CP	442(3), 444, 456, 460, 689, 691
B.14	68, 566			

Lamps			Storage Jars	
L.7–8	149		S.1	474
L.9–10	152(2)		S.2	469(3)
Jugs			S.4	479(4), 480, 493, 494, 495
J.7a	269		S.6a	528(2)
J.7b	246		S.6b	518
J.8	264, 275, 276(3), 281(3)		S.7a	484(4)
			S.7b	482
Dippers and Juglets			S.8	465
D.5b	292(2)		S.13	552
D.8	309		Miscellaneous	
			Misc.	116, 350

LEVELS II–III

Bowls			Bowls	
Class	Type		Class	Type
B.4b	13		B.8	1(3)
B.6	91		B.9	561
B.7	9(4), 37(2), 51, 605		B.10	35(2)

126

Bowls

Class	Type
B.11	59, 60, 64, 66, 560
B.12	570, 573, 574, 575, 576
B.13	69(2), 73(3), 75(7), 78(2), 79, 81(4), 82(4), 83(3), 120, 121(3), 123, 603, 636, 638, 642, 645
B.14	568

Chalices

Cha.	163

Lamps

L.4–6	148
L.7–8	150(3), 151(4)
L.9–10	152(2), 153
L.12	137

Jugs

J.4	168, 171(2), 177, 179, 180
J.5	173, 189(2)
J.7a	271(2)
J.8	273, 274, 275, 276(2), 277, 280, 281

Dippers and Juglets

D.5a	282(6)
D.8	309(10), (3115)

Potstands

PS	396, 400

Miniature Pithoi

Class	Type
MP	417, 425

Pilgrim Flasks

PF	408, 432, 674

Cooking Pots

CP	440, 442(4), 443(3), 450, 452, 454, 456(3), 458, 459

Storage Jars

S.1	475
S.2	472
S.3	530
S.4	470(2), 478, 479, 493
S.5	533
S.6a	486
S.7a	484(14)
S.7b	483(2)
S.9	491(2)
S.10	490(2), 492, 502
S.12	551
S.13	466

Miscellaneous

Misc.	30, 115, 355, 374, 386, 556, 584

LEVEL III

Bowls

Class	Type
B.1	85
B.3	128
B.4	8(2), 13(2), 6
B.5	41, 44, 586
B.6	89, 90(4)
B.7	9(5), 37(2), 39(5), 40(2), 46, 47, 48, 50, 51(5), 599, 602, 656(2)
B.8	1, 561
B.9	31
B.10	35, 61
B.11	62, 63(3), 64, 66, 67
B.12	16(2), 45(3), 572, 574, 576
B.13	69(3), 73(12), 74, 75(14), 77, 79(2), 81(8), 82(5), 83(4), 84(3), 86, 109, 120(10), 121(6), 122(5), 603(2), 627(2), 629, 630, 631(3), 632(4), 633, 635(4), 637, 638(2), 640, 642, 643, 644, 645, 649(2), 650, 652, 655, 657

Kraters

K	586

Lamps

L.1–3	143, 144, 147(3)
L.4–6	148(2)
L.7–8	150(2), 151(2)

Jugs

Class	Type
J.4	168(2), 171(2), 176, 177(2), 180, 183, 187
J.5	167(2), 189(2), 190, 192
J.6	220(2), 239, 259
J.7a	261(2), 269(2)
J.7b	238
J.8	279, 280(4), 281

Dippers and Juglets

D.2a	287
D.2b	671
D.4a	286, 294
D.4b	283
D.5a	282(2), 284
D.5b	292(2)
D.8	309(13), 310, 311(4), 313

Potstands

PS	397, 399(5), 400(5), 402(2)

Pilgrim Flasks

PF	431, 437, 439, 674

Cooking Pots

CP	440, 441, 442(6), 443(3), 448, 449(3), 450(3), 452(4), 456(7), 459, 462(4), 694

127

Storage Jars			*Storage Jars*	
Class	Type		Class	Type
S.1	474, 476(2), 477		S.12	392(4), 549, 550, 551
S.2	469(2), 472(3), 509		S.13	466(2)
S.3	489(2), 530			
S.4	467, 470(2), 478			*Jugs or Jars with Spouts*
S.5	533		JS	373(5)
S.7a	484(47)			
S.7b	483(2)			*Miscellaneous*
S.8	465, 544		Misc.	10, 84(3), 115(3), 125, 350, 368, 385, 387,
S.10	490(9), 499(6), 501(4)			497, 587, 658(2), 680(2), 682
S.11	391, 548			

LEVEL V?

Bowls	
Class	Type
B.2	590
B.9	558

THE ROOMS AND AREAS WITHIN THE BASTION AND THEIR CONTENTS

For a general account of the Bastion area, see Chapter 4, The Roads and Gateways (pp. 93 f.).

Note

The plan on Pl. 111 was also published in *Lachish I*, p. 223, but it should be noted that an error occurred in the numbering of the grid squares which has been corrected in the present plan. In the list below, therefore, the revised grid reference is followed by the original one, in brackets.

The plan on Pl. 112 records the arrangement of the gate rooms during the post-exilic occupation of the tell (Level I). The sherds associated with the period are to be found in the list below under the following references: F.18: E, F, G, L; F.17: O; and E.18: Q. The pottery showed no trace of burning.

E.17: B (late F.17: N)

Part of the central area between the gates.

Pottery: 274, 275, 626, 680

F.18: A (late G.18: A)

A small room south-west of the inner gate within the Bastion. There was a circular stone-lined pit in the room, which was empty, with two square pits on the south side; the south-east pit contained a post-exilic juglet, type 292, and the south-west pit contained a bowl, type 61, at 258·50 m. It is likely that both pits had penetrated from the post-exilic level above.

Pottery: 61, 292, 494, 680

F.18: B (late G.18: B)

A room immediately south of the inner gate, filled with burnt brick rubbish.

Pottery: Sherd only, 528

E/F.17/18: N (late F.18: B)

The letter N applies to the central area between the two gates, above the cobbled road surface. Pl. 113 shows the depth of constructional filling between the cobbled road and the post-exilic road surface, and most of the sherds not found in the drain came from this packing. They may therefore belong to either of the last two phases of occupation.

Types 152, 264, 442, 539, 542, 568(2), 648 came from the "upper" (easterly end?) of the drain, with a bone spatula illustrated on Pl. 63: 27, a fragment of a calcite vase, F. No. 5241 NP, and an iron arrowhead, F. No. 5243 NP.

Pottery: E/F.18: N: 115, 151, 152, 234, 238, 264, 442, 508, 539, 541, 542, 543, 546, 550, 568(2), 648, 696
F.17/18: N: 283, 499, 538, 543, 546, 648(2)
Inscribed sherd: Lachish ostracon XVI came from the constructional filling under the post-exilic road

Objects:

Fe arrowheads	Pl. 60: 55–61, 72–77, F. No. 5243 NP
Fe balance beam (?)	Pl. 62: 3
Fe fork	Pl. 62: 4
Fe lancehead	Pl. 63: 8
AE fibula	Pl. 58: 17
Bone spatula	Pl. 63: 27
Calcite vase	F. No. 5241 NP

E.18: A (late F.18: A)

Space south of the outer gate.

Pottery: Sherd incised with letter Pl. 52: 10 and p. 357
Object: Fe ploughshare Pl. 61: 3

E.18: C (late F.18: C)

A small room, walled on three sides, but opening on the north to the enclosed road within the Bastion. It was referred to throughout *Lachish I* as "the guardroom", and its position between the two gates strongly supports the attribution.

The general condition of this important room, and its two fellows, F.18: A and B, is described on p. 11 of *Lachish I*, and the text is reproduced in this volume on p. 97.

There was little variety in form among the hundreds of blackened jar fragments piled close to the east wall of the guardroom. It was impossible to estimate the number of jars of type 498 which were originally present. It is not clear why several ostraca were written on parts of the same jar (L. I, p. 220). Either they were all sent from the same source, or they were file copies of correspondence received or forwarded to another destination.

Pottery: 79, 153, 274, 498, 509, 537(2), 538, 539, 541, 542, 543, 544, 547, 568, 606, 635, 639, 666, 691
Objects: Lachish ostraca I–XV
Lachish ostracon XVIII, recovered from dump heap

E/F.18: D (late F/G.18: D)

This rectangular block of masonry, filled with rubble in the same style as the upper city wall, seems to be one of a pair of piers or towers flanking the inner gate within the Bastion. Its fellow is preserved at the eastern and narrower end, and both would have been at an equal distance from the inner gate threshold when it was exposed to its full width. The remaining height of the tower was less than a metre. The pottery found above the pier consisted largely of jar fragments, none of which showed any trace of burning, suggesting that they had been deposited in the post-exilic period. An interesting piece was the footbath, type 680, but it most probably belongs to an earlier period, as straw was used in tempering the clay.

Pottery: 79, 518, 538, 543, 676, 680

F.18: E, F, G, L (late G.18: E, F, G, L) not marked on plan

Adjoining areas within the Bastion, south of the inner gate. The pottery showed no trace of burning and is probably post-exilic in date.

Pottery: E: 513, 539, 543, 647
F: 538, 543, 546
G: 537, 543, 546, 680
L: 442, 494, 504, 509, 543, 610, 654

F.17/18: J–K (late G.17/18: J–K)

The letters J–K were allocated to the material from the foundations of the inner gate, including the adjoining area southwards. The sherds included folded-rim bowls, characteristic of Levels III–II, two high-footed lamp bases, type 153, and other forms which were in keeping with a date no earlier than Level II for the foundation of the stone upper city wall (Pl. 111).

Pottery: 61, 70, 71, 79, 153(2), 442, 460, 550, 624, 634, 637(2)

F.17: O (late G.17: O), not marked on plan

Pottery: 68, 79, 151, 499, 510, 513

F.17: P (late G.17: P), not marked on plan

Pottery: 275, 292

E.18: Q (late F.18: Q), not marked on plan

Pottery: 488,* 510, 550, 610, 680
* See Pl. 78: 7.

Classified Summary of the Pottery within the Bastion Area

Bowls		Cooking Pots	
Class	Type	Class	Type
B.1	606, 624, 654	CP	442(3), 460(2), 462, 691
B.10	61(2)		
B.11	64		
B.13	70, 71, 72, 79(4), 626(2), 634, 635, 637(2), 639, 647, 648(3), 657		Storage Jars
		S.2	509(2), 510(2)
B.14	68, 568(3)	S.3	488
		S.4	494(2), 513(2)
		S.6a	528
Lamps		S.6b	518
L.7–8	151(2)	S.8	498, 537(3), 538(4), 539(3), 541(2), 542, 543(8), 544
L.9–10	152, 153(3)		
		S.9	547
Jugs		S.10	499(2)
J.6	234	S.11	546(4), 550(3)
J.7b	238, 666	S.13	504, 508, 696
J.8	264, 274(2), 275(2), 676		
Dippers and Juglets		Miscellaneous	
D.4b	283	Misc.	115, 610(2), 680(5)
D.5b	292(2)		

130

CHAPTER VI

POST-EXILIC REMAINS

RESIDENCY, HOUSES AND PITS OF LEVEL I

Residency (Grid Squares J, K, L/12, 13, 14: Rooms A–O, Q, R, T–AF. Courts P, S. Area AG)

THE most prominent feature of the mound at Tell ed-Duweir is the rectangular block of masonry covering 2,630 square metres, towards the north-west corner (Pl. 16: 1, 2). On superficial examination it was evident that buildings of several periods were superimposed, and the spacious layout of the topmost structure suggested the presence of an administrative centre.

A clearance on the east, west and south sides of the block showed that the outer walls of the uppermost building were not in alinement with the massive masonry below (Pls. 118–119). The main east wall, for half its width, was founded on rubbish dumped beyond the edge of the earlier building, and as the late complex only covered four-fifths of the lower ruin, the latter was always exposed at the south, and possibly the north, end. It is not clear how the terraces which resulted from the construction of the smaller building were approached from the town.

The tops of the walls of the last building were merely covered by some 20 cm. of humus, which was normally under cultivation. The walls had been denuded to a common height of just over a metre, down to the level of the stones which filled all the rooms with the exception of Court P. The blocks were of soft, light howr limestone, and many of them had been cut to a definite curve, unlike any stones used in the construction of external or internal walls. Their position on the floor clearly indicated barrel vaulting (Pl. 22: 1, 2), with masonry courses spanning the long walls obliquely, and not at right angles. The preservation of the curve as the blocks lay on the ground may suggest that the vault was constructed with leaning courses, a method which had become common in late Roman architecture throughout the Near East (see suggested elevation on Pl. 120). The average size of the roofing blocks was $50 \times 25 \times 15$ cm., with a larger and less common type of $70 \times 35 \times 15$ cm.

In the atrium (Court P), masonry was only found in the four corners adjoining the vaulted rooms, and it was merely a shallow accumulation in the centre, over which a deep mud deposit had collected, filling up to the general level of the ruin.

The roof of the apartments around the court was probably covered with packed mud, which filled the interstices between the stones as a matrix of consistent quality and had penetrated through water action to the floors beneath the fallen roof. This condition was observed in all chambers throughout the building.

The walls were built of small, roughly cut nari stones, set in mud mortar. The floor was laid on a base of pounded chalk, and both walls and floor were then covered with a hard lime plaster. Apparently the stone doorsills, columns and column bases were similarly coated, as they had been comb-dressed.

As the floor surface in the atrium was exposed to the weather, it was uneven and coarse and less well preserved than the floors elsewhere. Pl. 22: 3, 4 shows part of the atrium, with a column base from the south portico fallen from position into a pit possibly caused by subsidence of a chamber or vault below.

The ground plan of the Residency (Pl. 119) was almost intact on the south and east sides. The west wall was completely missing, and all that remained of the north end was an incomplete wall at the north-west corner (Pl. 22: 8). The plan conformed to the usual Oriental conception of a large open court surrounded by rooms. These are lettered A to AF on the plan, while AG designates the platform or terrace outside the south wall where most of the jar handles were found, though these actually belong to the underlying building.

It is uncertain whether the only entry was at the north-east corner, where a socket for the doorpost was still in position. The doorway was 2 m. across, and led through a small hall and lobby to the atrium; but owing to the denudation of the north end, it is impossible to say whether there may have been another doorway and a series of rooms beyond.

The atrium was bounded on the south and west sides by steps leading to various apartments. Across the court to the west were two columns or stepped plinths (Pl. 22: 4, 6). Both plinths on the west side were in position (Fig. 11), and the southerly one retained the rounded base of its column. A short distance away, prone

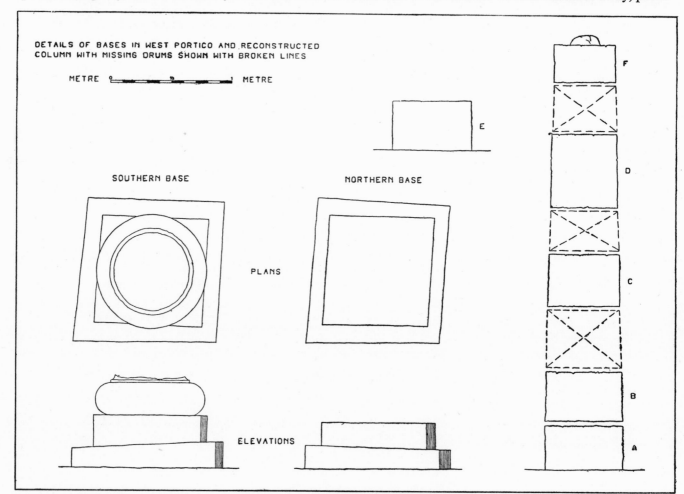

FIG. 11. Column bases in west portico

on the ground, was one of the central sections of the shaft, together with the uppermost drum, topped by a circular tenon, on which the capital had presumably rested. Three drums from the Residency had been re-erected in Room AE at a later period (Pl. 22: 7).

Beyond the western portico were two rooms which were three times as long as they were broad, with small chambers or alcoves leading from them. As the whole length of the west wall is missing, it is possible that a main entrance may have existed on the west side, leading through Rooms T and U to the courtyard. Perhaps the small alcove S may have been the substructure of a stairway to the roof.

Three steps led from Court P to the southern half of the building, divided along the east and west axis into three main apartments, flanked by private rooms and domestic offices. The detail of the doorway from the south portico to these rooms is shown on Fig. 12. Room B was apparently the bathroom, and adjoining it was a water-closet in Room A (Pl. 22: 5). The bathroom floor was plastered and sloped towards a drain which took the waste water through a pottery pipe within the partition wall: the water apparently then flowed across the water-closet floor and was carried off through an outlet in the east wall (Pl. 23: 1). It is possible that parts of the fitment are missing, for the system as it remained seems somewhat impracticable.

It was noted in the description of Palace A (p. 84) that the plaster floor of the southern apartments of the Residency had been laid to conform with the rise in the floor level of the southern half of the earlier building.

During the demolition of the Residency it was found that a segment of a palm capital had been incorporated in a partition wall. Starkey did not think at the time that it belonged to the post-exilic building, as the diameter of the drum was too great for the western portico and the quality of stone did not conform to that used for the existing column bases. The fragment, F. No. 7234, is in the Palestine Museum (PM. 38.776).

Another transitional occupation of the Residency was recognised. After the building was partly ruined (Pls. 22: 7 and 23: 2), some rooms were reoccupied at a higher level, about 40 cm. above the plastered floor. In others, where the roof presumably remained intact, the original plaster floor was exposed, though ovens had been cut through its surface.

At the time of excavation Starkey was of the opinion that the temporary resettlement of the ruined Residency took place in the middle of the fifth century B.C., on the evidence of the Black Glazed and Black Figured Attic sherds, which J. H. Iliffe dated to 475–425 B.C. Further investigation of the position of sherds in relation to the Residency floor levels, however, does not preclude the possibility that the good quality Attic imports were used by the original inhabitants of the building, for there were Attic sherds lying on or close to the original floor surfaces in several rooms.

As the Attic wares and orange-paste amphorae are accepted in this publication as being part of the contents of the penultimate occupational phase of the Residency, there is nothing beyond some mortars, querns and stone troughs to indicate when the building was re-used by settlers.

Contents and Comparisons

The objects from the Residency were few and uninteresting: the fibula on Pl. 58: 19, the alabaster dishes on Pl. 64: 2, 3, and the small altar on Pl. 64: 1 may have some value for comparative purposes (Pl. 64: 2, cf. AAA, Vol. VII, Pl. XXVI: 5, Deve Huyuk, Persian period, 550–330 B.C.).

Nearly all the pottery fragments found in or near the Residency floors had been pounded during the construction and were too small to be identified. Where possible they were compared to forms drawn in the present volume, and occasionally the Corpus of Palestinian Pottery and the publications of Tell Beit Mirsim (AASOR XII, XXI–XXII) were used. The comparisons are noted in the accompanying list, but are omitted from the descriptions opposite Plates 79–104.

The dominant pottery forms on the Residency floors were fragments of the soft orange-paste jar 488 (12 examples), and the heavy greenish mortarium 568 (6 examples), which are characteristic of Stratum II at Tell Abu Hawam, late sixth to early fourth century B.C.

Taking into consideration Sir J. D. Beazley's remarks on the Red Figured sherds, Miss du Plat Taylor noted an equal proportion of fifth- and fourth-century types, which limits the time range more closely to the last half of the fifth century, continuing into the fourth century B.C.

Architectural Comparisons

An open court surrounded by a single series of covered rooms is the common plan of buildings in the Near East. In the case of the Residency, however, the disposition of the rooms, doorways and columns is precise and orderly, and there are a few buildings at other sites where these features are so similar that more than common tradition may be inferred.

As Lamon and Shipton have themselves observed, the parallel between buildings 1369 and 1052 at Megiddo

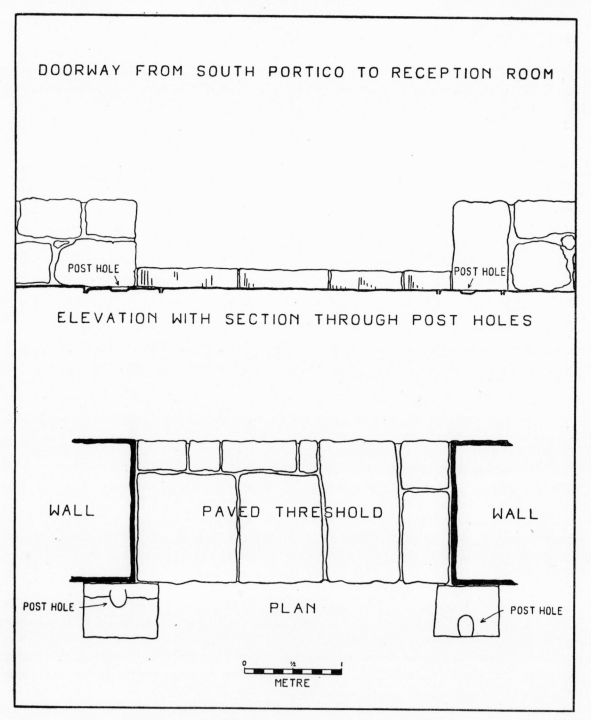

DOORWAY FROM SOUTH PORTICO TO RECEPTION ROOM

POST HOLE

POST HOLE

ELEVATION WITH SECTION THROUGH POST HOLES

WALL

PAVED THRESHOLD

WALL

POST HOLE

PLAN

POST HOLE

0   ½   1
METRE

FIG. 12. Doorway in the Residency

134

(M. I, pp. 69–72 and Fig. 89) and the Residency is very striking. The length of the first building at Megiddo is oriented north and south, like the Residency, while the other lies east and west. The sloping buttress walls around both can also be matched by the fallen deposits at Tell ed-Duweir, which raised the Residency floors well above surrounding ground level.

The excavators remark that the pottery was of little value as dating material as the buildings were overlaid by nothing but surface soil, except for a few remains of Stratum I. They consider that both buildings came into use during the occupation of Stratum III (780–650 B.C.). In default of closer evidence, the buildings at Megiddo are therefore the earliest comparisons, and the only ones which are probably pre-exilic, though another structure on the same plan is attributed to Stratum I (M. I, Fig. 98: 736).

There is a close parallel at Gerar in Building A at 198–197 ft. (Gerar, Pl. XI). Only the western end of this massive brick structure remains, as all the rest has been denuded through the action of the flood waters of the Wadi Jemmeh. The width of the building is 125 ft. or about 37 m., which is also the width of the Residency, and though the disposition of the rooms within differs in detail, both buildings have rooms which are abnormally long in proportion to their width. Sherds of orange-paste amphorae, type 488, were found in the foundation levels, and Attic sherds, including a Red Figured lekythos, were used by Petrie to establish the date of the Persian level at about 457 B.C. (Gerar, p. 4). He also noted a resemblance to the fortresses at Daphnae and Naukratis.

Some features of the building units at Tell Sandaḥannah (BM, Pl. 16) are reminiscent of the Residency, and a limestone column base moved from its original position at that site (BM, Pl. 19: 11) is comparable; in any case, it is very natural to find resemblances at the site which supplanted Tell ed-Duweir as the centre of the district.

The closest parallel to the plan is undoubtedly to be found in Syria: it is the central block of the topmost building at Arslan Tash (cf. Arslan Tash par F. Thureau-Dangin, A. Barrois, G. Dossin et Maurice Dunand, Paris, 1931), which is itself similar to the earlier "House of Ivories" on the same site. Apart from general resemblances to Parthian and Sasanide style (op. cit., p. 19), the excavators searched in vain for outside parallels (op. cit., p. 54) and were unable to date the later building precisely.

The basalt pillar base found in the "House of Ivories" between the court and antechamber resembles that made of limestone from the same position in the Residency.

E. Gjerstad considered that the mid-sixth century B.C. Palace of Vouni was comparable (GSCE IV, Pt. 2, p. 232), but it is by no means as close as the buildings at Arslan Tash.

There is in any case no similarity of plan between the great palaces at Pasargadae and Persepolis, built in the sixth and fifth centuries B.C., and there is nothing in the architecture or contents of the Residency to suggest strong Persian influence. Indeed, as C. Watzinger suggests, the plan of the building is "Syrian-Hittite rather than Persian".[1]

Date

The builders of the Residency cleared away the ruins of the palace-fort on the summit of Tell ed-Duweir in order to provide a level site for their construction. In doing this, they appear to have removed any debris which had accumulated between the destruction of the earlier building and the construction of the Residency. Nothing was found in or under the foundations which could be used to establish the length of time between the two events, and all the sherds and jar stamps were typical of Level III.

The contents of the floors and filling of the Residency rooms were consistent. Characteristic Attic sherds provided the best comparisons to dated pottery from other sites, ranging from the mid-fifth to mid-fourth century B.C.

A date for the occupation of the Residency from about 450–350 B.C. is in close agreement with the historical evidence, for Lachish is mentioned as one of the villages in which the children of Judah dwelt after Nehemiah's return about 445 B.C. (Nehemiah XI: 30).

[1] C. Watzinger, Denkmäler Palästinas, 1935, Vol. II, p. 5.

Contents of the Residency Rooms

Plan on Pl. 119, photographs on Pls. 22, 23.

N.B. Nearly all the pottery forms referred to in the following account are represented by small fragments only.

Room	Approx. floor level (metres)	
A	272·39	Water-closet at extreme south-east corner of the Residency, communicating with Room B (Pls. 22: 5; 23: 1). Cf. closet at Arslan Tash.
		Pottery: Fragment of potstand, type 440
		Small sherds of bowls, type 20
		Sherds cf. CPP 21B, 21V, intrusive
		2 sections of overlapping drainpipe, type 390, under foundations of west wall to convey water from Room B through Room A to outlet in east wall
B	272·45–27	Bathroom with sloping plastered floor, leading into Room A (Pls. 22: 5; 23: 1).
		Pottery: Frags. of an exceptionally thin-walled jar, type 496, covered with cream slip (cf. frag. of similar rim from house in G.12/13: 7)
		Bowl types cf. CPP 16 K, 22 C2, 28 H possibly represented
		2 frags. widely spaced bur.
		1 frag. "Minyan" ware
		1 frag. Bichrome "bird and fish" (cf. L. II, Pl. LVIIIA)
		Object: Jar handle at 272·20 m. (below floor), Pl. 47B: 10 and PEQ, 1941, p. 53 (19)
C	272·29	Easterly recess of large chamber D, E, communicating with Room AF.
		Object: Dolerite weight No. 17, in filling at 273 m., see p. 353
D	272·24	Easterly part of large chamber D–E opposite door threshold.
		Pottery: Frag. orange ware jar, type 488
		Base of jar, type 700 (cf. CPP, type 46D)
		Bowl frag. similar to CPP, 16 J2 with burnish inside
		Below floor: 271·60 m. *Object*: Stamp, *hbrn* F. No. 5269 NP
		272·10 m. *Object*: Inscribed sherd (on floor of Palace C) F. No. 5270 NP
E	272·15	*Pottery*: Mortaria 68
		Ribbed mortaria 567, 568
		Potstand 399
		Orange ware jar 488
		Storage jar 528 (5th cent. B.C.)
		Baking plate 682
		Attic sherds (2 at 273 m.), 1 decorated, F. No. 1487, at 272·10 m.
		Lamp at 272·70 m.
		Objects: Fe arrowhead at 272·70 m.
		Sickle flint at 272·60 m.
		Stone bead at 272·80 m.
F	271·98	*Pottery*: Frag. orange ware jar 488
H	272·14	
J	272·30	*Objects*: Jar handles at 271·88 m.: 2 *hbrn*, 2 square, 2 illegible

Room	Approx. floor level (metres)	

K 272·28   *Pottery*: Rim of Black Glazed cup, buff body, poor iridescent glaze, flaked and worn out. Two shallow grooves outside rim, cf. TCHP, C7, mid 3rd–2nd cent.

Frag. orange ware jar 488

Cooking pot 695

EB, MB sherds, many frags.

LB milk bowl, Base-ring, etc.

Bowl 604

Objects: Jar handles at 272 m.:   1 *shwkh*, F. No. 5271, NP

6 *hbrn*, F. No. 5272, NP

at 272·15 m.: 8 *hbrn*, F. No. 5273, NP

4 *hbrn*, class ii, F. No. 5274, p. 342 and PEQ, 1941, p. 93

11 illegible

Carnelian bead, F. No. 1477, at 272·30 m. (Colt)

Scarab, very worn, Pl. 43: 38 at 272·30 m. (Colt)

Sickle flints at 272·60 and 273·20 m.

Fe nail at 272·80 m.

L 272·35   *Pottery*: Decorated sherd at 272·60 m.

Objects: Fe nail, Pl. 63: 10, at 272·80 m.

Sickle flints at 272·80–50 m.

Carnelian bead at 272·80 m. (Colt)

M 272·39

N 272·49   *Pottery*: Ribbed mortaria 568 at 272·10 m.

Potstand 401 (Pl. 77: 34) at 272·10 m.

Lamp, type 137

Jar base 699

Objects: AE fibula, Pl. 58: 19 at 272·10 m.

Footbath (?) 680 at 272·10 m.

NB. All this group appears to be below the floor.

O 271·55   *Pottery*: Unguentarium 672, 4th cent.

Object: Sickle flint at 272·80 m.

P 271·70–54   *Pottery*: Handle of Kylix krater (?), reddish-buff ware, iridescent black glaze on one side only. Late 5th cent.

Handle of lamp (?), at 272 m. Poor buff ware, iridescent black glaze, Broneer type VI, (Corinth IV, Pt. 2), *c.* 475–425 B.C.

Flaring rim of column krater at 272 m. Hard reddish ware, poor wash of black glaze on surface of rim; border of hearts between lines below rim on red surface. (Cf. larger frag. from Room X, F. No. 1483 (PM. 34.132) at 273·40.) Late 5th cent. (Fig. 13)

Handle of Black Glazed skyphos, K.13: P at 272 m. Reddish-buff ware, good black glaze, thin walls and plain rim

Handle of amphora, reddish-buff ware, softer than bowls, very iridescent black glaze on outside of handle and inside of vase. Late 5th cent.

Orange ware jar 488	Flask 664
Handle 506, cf. CPP 47 Y	Storage jars 466, 528, 534
Mortaria 568 (cf. CPP 8 K), 567	Unguentarium 672 (4th cent.)
Lamp, spout only, 137	Bowl 577
Cooking pot 690	

Objects: Alabaster dish, Pl. 64: 2, at 272·30 m.
Part of altar, Pl. 64: 1
Sickle flint at 272·30 m.
Fe knife, Pl. 59: 18 at 272·60 m.

Attributed to Palace C:

Pottery: Oil flask, type 209 at 271·30 m.

Objects: Jar handles: 6 *hbrn* (5 NK), F. No. 5275, at 271·60 m.
7 *hbrn* (5 NK), F. No. 5276, at 271·70 m.
9 *hbrn* (6 NK), F. No. 5277, at 271·58 m.
4 *hbrn* (8 NK), F. No. 5278, at 271·60 m.
2 *hbrn* F. No. 5279, at 272·20 m.

Q 272·43

R 272·07 *Pottery*: Bowl 612

S 272·01–91

T 271·85–93 *Pottery*: Orange ware jar 488
Bowl 620
Mycenean sherd at 271·35 m.

U 271·93 *Pottery*: Frag. of foot of Black Glazed dish at 272 m. Hard reddish ware, good black glaze
preserved at junction of foot and plate, and on flat base of foot
Frag. of foot, as above, at 272 m. Buff ware and similar glaze. Foot has angular
edge glazed all over
Mortaria 567, 568
Bowls 579, 580, 585, 620
Storage jars 484, 528
Orange ware jar 488
Potstand 399
Cooking pots 684, 688, 695

V 272·02 *Pottery*: Attic sherd at 272 m.

W *Pottery*: Storage jar 528
Bases 696, 698
Cooking pot 695
Objects: Bone spatula, Pl. 63: 22, at 271·80 m.
AE nail, Pl. 63: 11, at 272 m.

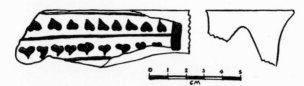

FIG. 13. Decorated Krater Fragment

Room	Approx. floor level (metres)		

X   272·05   *Pottery*: Flaring rim of column krater, F. No. 1483 (PM. 34.132) at 273.40 m. (Fig. 13). Decanted border of hearts between lines below rim and on surface. Cf. smaller frag. from Court P
Jar 394
Orange ware jar 488
Cooking pot 695
Object: AE handle, Pl. 41: 4, at 272 m.

Y   *Pottery*: Base of lamp (?) at 271·90 m. Thick soft buff ware, reddish-brown lustrous glaze on outside only
Mortaria 567, 568
Cooking pot 688
Storage jar, orange ware, 488
Potstand 402
Object: AE bangle, Pl. 63: 4

AA   271·90   *Pottery*: Attic sherds at 271·80, 272·50 and 273 m.

AB   *Pottery*: Frag. of base of Black Glazed bowl showing 4th-cent. groove. Hard red ware, good black glaze all over, except on edge of foot
Coarse roulette on floor at 272·70 m.
Objects: AE pin, F. No. 1488 NP, at 271·80 m.
Spacer bead at 272·30 m.

AC   *Pottery*: Attic sherd at 272·80 m.

AD   272·35   *Pottery*: Storage jar, orange ware, 488
Mortaria 568
Cooking pot 695
Object: Jar handle, *shwkh* class ii, p. 342 and PEQ, 1941, p. 96

AE   272·19   *Pottery*: Rim of Black Glazed carinated cup at 272·30 m. Thin, hard brick-red ware, glossy black glaze. ? late 5th cent.
Storage jar, orange ware, 488
Objects: Alabaster dish, Pl. 64: 3
Pottery handle, NP

AF   *Pottery*: Potstand 399

Classified Summary of the Pottery in the Residency Rooms

Class	Type
Bowls	
B.1	620(2)
B.2	604
B.4	20, 577
B.14	68, 567(4), 568(6)
Kraters	
K.	612
Lamps	
L.12	137(2)
Jugs	
J.2	209
Dippers and Juglets	
D.9	664

Class	Type
Potstands	
PS	399(2), 400, 401, 402
Cooking Pots	
CP	684, 688(2), 695(5), 690
Storage Jars	
S.2	698
S.3	488(11)
S.4	699, 700
S.5	534
S.6a	528(4)
S.6b	496
S.7a	484
S.13	466, 506, 696
Miscellaneous	
Misc.	390, 394, 579, 580, 585, 672(2), 682

Classified Summary of the Pottery from the Surface Areas around the Citadel

Area AG Class	Type	Level	North Wall Class	Type	Level	South Wall* Class	Type	Level	East Wall Class	Type	Level	West Wall Class	Type	Level	H.14: 23 Class	Type
B.1	598	V–IV	B.1	617	V–IV	B.1	620	V–IV	B.11	62	I	B.1	617	V–IV	B.7	581
B.1	617	V–IV	B.1	625	V–IV	B.1	621	V–IV	B.13	69	II	B.1	621	V–IV		
B.2	593	V–IV	B.8	559(2)	II	B.1	622	V–IV				B.1	622	V–IV		
B.10	35	III	B.12	569	III–II	B.1	623	V–IV				B 1	625	V–IV		
B.10	61	III	B.13	634	III–II	B.1	653	V–IV				B.2	588	IV–III		
B.12	571	III–II	B.13	639	III–II	B.2	588	IV–III				B.2	592	V–IV		
B.12	575	III–II				B.2	591	V–IV				B.3	615	V–IV		
B.14	68	I				B.2	595	V–IV				B.12	574	III		
						B.5	609	V–IV								
						B.7	600	III								
						B.12	608	III								
			Cha.	662	IV–III							Cha.	156	IV–III		
									K.	613	I				K.	403
						L.12	137	III–II	L.11	659	I				L.11	660
J.7a	257	III			III–II											
D.6a	337	III													D.9	348
PS	399	III													D.9	351
			PF	679	I										PF	436
															PF	678
						CP	694	III–II							CP	461
S.5	520	III	S.3	488	I	S.4	512	II	S.3	488	I	S.3	488	I		
S.5	523	III	S.5	516	IV–I				S.5	516	IV–I	S.5	524	IV–I		
S.7a	484	III	S.5	531	IV–I				S.6a	529	II	S.5	525	IV–I		
			S.6a	507	II				S.9	547	II–I	S.5	536	IV–I		
			S.6a	528	II				S.13	508	I	S.6a	528	II		
			S.6a	535	II							S.8	540	II		
			S.6b	519	II–I							S.8	543	II		
			S.9	547	II–I							S.13	557	III–I		
			S.9	553	II–I											
			S.11	545	III							Misc.	500	III		
			S.13	508	I							Misc.	610	II		
				667		Misc.	556	IV–III				Misc.	619	V–IV		
			Misc.			Misc.	661	V–IV				Misc.	682	III–II		

* For details of other fragments from the South Wall trial cut, see Chapter 3, pp. 81 f. and Pl. 105

BLACK GLAZED WARES FROM THE RESIDENCY AREA

Black Glazed bowl with flaring wall and out-turned lip. Hard buff body, good black glaze inside and out. Cf. TCHP, A.9, Fig. 117. Fourth to third century.

Black Glazed bowl, similar to above. Very thin hard red body, good brownish glaze. Approx. diameter, 16 cm.

Fragment of Red Figured vase. Thick, reddish-buff ware, thin iridescent black glaze, traces of fine painted lines near edge.

Shallow Black Glazed bowl with incurving rim and wide round base ring without groove. Hard reddish ware with poor brownish-black glaze all over and under foot. Glaze flaked and worn from outside rim. Kiln ring visible. Decoration of stamped palmettes joined by interlacing circles and surrounded by a line of rouletting. Diameter 14 cm. Probably fourth century B.C.

The Solar Shrine (Grid Squares P/Q/R.12/13: 101–106)

North-east of the Residency a much smaller building measuring 27×17 m. was exposed in 1935. The materials used and the method of construction were similar, and the walls were equally thick, and carefully plastered with a hard lime plaster, on which there were some faint traces of a coloured surface. Fallen chalk blocks indicated that the roof was vaulted.

The main axis of the building lay east and west. Presumably it had very little substructure, as each level was constructed on and against sharply rising ground; thus the west wall was standing to a height of 2 m., while the storerooms at the east end were denuded to half a metre. These were poorly constructed in comparison with the sanctuary walls (Pl. 24: 2).

The ground plan (Pl. 121) consisted of a square courtyard, occupying half the total area of the building, flanked on the east by a row of five small rooms, and on the west by the main apartments. The entrance to the court was towards the east end of the north wall. A flight of five steps, possibly extending across the width of the court, led to a rectangular antechamber at a higher level (Pl. 24: 1), and beyond it was an inner sanctuary approached by three steps (Pl. 24: 4). The floor of the inner room was at a higher level than that of the subsidiary chambers on each side.

Exposure of the ground plan made it seem probable that the building had served a religious purpose. Points which led Starkey to this opinion were:

(*a*) The east–west axis of the building.

(*b*) The difference in level (2 m.) between the sanctuary and the court, which would be sufficient to allow a clear view of the rising sun over the roofs of the storerooms at the east end of the court.

(*c*) The presence of a square limestone altar (Pl. 42: 8, 9), bearing the traces of a large hand and a standing male figure with upraised arms in relief on two of the four sides. The symbols on the remaining faces were chipped and unrecognisable. The altar appeared to have fallen from the antechamber into the court, where it was lying on its side.

(*d*) The asymmetrical arrangement of the highest treads of both flights of steps, with extended space to the north, though it is possible that the flight was no longer intact at the time of excavation.

(*e*) The construction of a drain in the centre of the entrance to the inner sanctuary, suggesting that this central point was marked by a libation altar. There was a second drain in the floor, below a carefully plastered niche in the south wall of the inner sanctuary.

In a lecture to the Palestine Exploration Fund in 1935 (PEQ, Oct. 1935, p. 203), Starkey said:

"It seems certain that this room was the sanctuary of a building dedicated to one of the later intrusive cults introduced during the Persian regime. The eastern orientation of the building and the position of the libation altar on the open axis line suggest a solar cult."

The chambers north and south of the inner sanctuary had apparently been re-used at a later time (Pl. 24: 3); the original plastered floors had been taken up and there was a second floor a few centimetres above. The large antechamber 105, running across the main axis of the building, was in better condition, and the plaster was preserved almost to the height of the walls (Pl. 24: 2). A large area of the floor in the centre of the room, between the two doorways, was blackened by fire, and two wooden beams, probably fallen from the roof, lay at the foot of the steps leading to the inner sanctuary (Pl. 24: 4).

Until the foundations of the Solar Shrine are exposed, there is no means of establishing the date of construction, and even then the evidence may not be forthcoming. It seems that the foundation courses were not dug deeply into underlying city deposits, which would be, in any case, contemporary with the burnt Levels III or II. It remains uncertain whether the building was constructed, as Starkey suggested, under Persian influence.

In the opinion of Miss du Plat Taylor, the few pots and sherds from the building are to be dated to the latter half of the second century B.C. Though the date of the coins associated with the shrine is consistent, their position, between 50 and 100 cm. above floor level, suggests that both pottery and coins should belong to the final phase of occupation in the building.

Among a miscellaneous collection of other objects, the most striking is a bronze lamp like one from Deve Huyuk, now in the British Museum. There is another from Idalion in Cyprus (GSCE II, Pl. CLXXIX: 18). Both comparisons are datable to the fifth century, and it may be that the lamp in the later shrine survived in the service of the cult. Crude chalk altars, and the broken figure of a pottery horseman, provide a link with post-exilic deposits such as 506, 515, 522 and 534.

The large agate beads 119, 120, one of which came from the drain in the sanctuary, are distinctive.

Contents of the Solar Shrine

P.12: 101   Square room at southern corner of building, communicating with Room 105 (Pl. 24: 2, 3). No plaster remained on walls or floor except at the doorsill. There appeared to be a later floor level in which the amphora 465 was set at 262·12 m. It contained bowls 67 and 111 and was covered by another example of bowl 111. A bronze coin, F. No. 4112, at the same level, has not been found in the London collection.

Pottery: 67,* 111(2), 465
     * Pl. 77: 19.
        67: Mat glazed fish plate. Grey body, very worn brown glaze, adhering only in parts. Restored. Diameter 16·5 cm. Cf. Samaria Group A types, and unpublished dishes from the Agora, both dated to the late second century B.C.; TCHP, grey ware of Group E, first century B.C.
      111: Red mat glazed bowl with folded handles. Fine red-buff ware with mat red slip. Restored. Diameter, 16·5 cm. Another, more roughly made, tool grooves on outside. Buff ware with white grits. Base and part of rim. Cf. Tomb 217.

Q.12: 102   Inner sanctuary of Solar Shrine, approached by steps from Room 105. All four walls and the floor were covered by at least two thick coats of plaster. The broken bowl 130 was just above floor level. In the centre of the doorway was a small circular hole in the plaster to act as a drain, but as the rooms were left intact it is not known how the outlet connects, if at all, with another drain near the recess or cupboard to the left of the doorway.

Pottery: 130*
     * Pl. 77: 22.
     Mat glazed bowl with incurving rim. Base dented before firing. Reddish-buff ware, finger smoothed, and dipped in coarse reddish slip which has run down outside. Diameter, 14 cm.
Objects in recess at 263·24 m.:
     AE strainer   F. No. 4114 NP
     Marble palette   Pl. 64: 9

Objects in drain at 262·41 m.:

        AE coin, No. 39 on List of Coins, p. 413
        Lead hook   NP
        Agate bead   Pl. 67: 119
        Agate bead   Pl. 66: 26
        Pottery figure frag.   F. No. 4117a NP

Objects on or above floor at 262·80 m. approx.:

        Schist hawk   Pl. 36: 56
        Calcite lid   Pl. 65: 11
        Bead   Pl. 67: 120

Q.12: 103   Room north of inner sanctuary communicating with Room 104. There were no traces of plaster on the floor or walls, and blocks from the fallen vaulted roof were in the filling. The lamp 138 was only 4 cm. above floor level at 262·30 m. A loom weight, fragments of alabaster and glass were too high in the filling of the room to be significant. A sherd of a Black Glazed carinated bowl was at 262·50 cm. It was of thin buff ware with some mica and a poor black glaze, flaked off outside.

Pottery: 138

Objects: Loom weight   F. No. 4101 NP
         Alabaster frags.   F. No. 4100 NP
         Glass frags.   NP

Q.12: 104   The chamber along the north wall of the building was twice the size of any preceding one, and it could be entered from Room 103 and from the antechamber 105. There were some traces of plaster on the south wall. Six blocks of a fallen arch lay in alinement on the apparent floor level at 262·53 m. and there was a bench made of roughly dressed stone against the south wall. On it were nine crude altars without incisions or designs, cut in pillar form, about 8 cm. square and averaging about 20 cm. in height. All the objects from this room were found between 10 and 20 cm. below the measured floor level. The iron sickle at 261·96 m. might belong to the underlying city.

Pottery: 376(2)

        Fusiform unguentarium. Coarse reddish-buff clay, poorly made. Finger-smoothed surface. Height, 16·5 cm.

Objects: AE lamp   Pls. 42: 2 and 63:1
         FE sickle   Pl. 59: 6
         Marble palette   Pl. 64: 10
         Chalk altars (9 ex.) F. No. 4098 NP

Q.12: 105   Steps from the east led to the antechamber which gave access by three more steps in the west side to the inner sanctuary. The antechamber extended across the building for three-quarters of its total width and it was the only chamber to conform in proportion to the main apartments of the Residency. Doorways at the north and south ends led to Rooms 104 and 101 respectively.

All the walls were covered by at least two coats of plaster and there were flagstones under the plaster floor at 262·19 m.

The principal object was a limestone altar lying on its side on a level with the third step leading to the court. It had apparently been thrown out of the antechamber. At the south-east corner of the room at 262·20 m. was a small trachyte altar. Some iron fragments, including nails, were just over 30 cm. above floor level, and belonged perhaps to the charred fragments of two wooden beams which lay before the steps.

The agate and carnelian beads were both close to the floor. The broken pottery figure of a horseman was 50 cm. above the floor and does not necessarily belong to the period of occupation.

Objects:
Pottery figure, bkn., as Pl. 33: 4	F. No. 4104 NP
Fe nails and ring fragments	F. No. 4103 NP
Limestone altar	Pl. 42: 8, 9
Trachyte altar	Pl. 64: 7
Agate bead	Pl. 66: 76
Carnelian bead	Pl. 66: 55
Onyx bead	Pl. 67: 117

Q.12: 106   The only entrance to the building was apparently in the north wall of the court 106, marked only at the time of excavation by a gap in the wall. The court occupied half the whole area of the building and as it was open to the sky most of the floor surface has worn away. At the base of the steps the level was at 260·92 m., and it was some 16 cm. lower in the centre of the court, so it is by no means certain which objects can be definitely associated with the occupation of the building.

Both coins were found just north of the steps: No. 43 at 261·75 m. and No. 36 at 261·40 m.; and both are unreliable for dating evidence. The pottery listed in the court was all found close to floor level, though deposits from the earlier city were visible in places where the surface was missing.

The inscribed weight, No. 5 on the List of Weights, p. 353, was found with a spindle whorl and a polished stone at 260·80–60 cm., and is likely to be *in situ*. The rosette jar stamp is also probably in position. The beads were found in surface rubbish.

Pottery: 60, 78, 153, 276, 292(3), 399*
   * Pl. 77: 32.
  60: Shallow dish with hard buff body fired grey at centre, large white grits. Fine surface finish obtained by wheel burnishing on orange-red slip. Restored from two-thirds of bowl. Diameter, 25 cm.
  78: Dish of coarse brick-red vesiculated ware. Grooves on outside wall and ring burnished inside. Traces of blotchy white slip. Section only, approx. diameter, 26 cm.

Objects:
Head of pottery figurine	F. No. 5255 NP
Fe arrowhead	Pl. 60: 70
AE needle	Pl. 63: 9
Stone quern	Pl. 64: 6
Basalt dish	Pl. 65: 7
Weight, No. 5 on List of Weights	Pl. 51: 4
Stone spindlewhorl	F. No. 5262 NP
Stone rubber	F. No. 5263 NP
Clay loom weights (2 ex.)	Pl. 65: 10
Jar stamp, rosette	as Pl. 53: 3
Beads	Pls. 66: 49, 65; 67: 122
Coin, No. 36 on List of Coins, p. 413	
Coin, No. 43 on List of Coins, p. 413	

Q.13: 107, 108   Nothing was found in any of the four small rooms to the east of the main court, and the walls

R.12: 109, 110   were denuded to less than a metre in height. Structurally the rooms were square and simple in plan, with various poorly constructed partition walls and rough benches.

A sherd of "West Slope" ware and part of an incised amphora neck in Mat Glazed ware are not, in Miss du Plat Taylor's opinion, earlier than the third century, and may well continue into the second century B.C.

Object: Coin, No. 6 on List of Coins, p. 412

Classified Summary of the Pottery in the Solar Shrine

Bowls		*Dippers and Juglets*	
B.11	60, 67	D.5b	292(3)
B.13	78		
		Potstands	
Lamps		PS	399
L.9–10	153		
L.12	138	*Storage Jars*	
		S.8	465
Jugs			
J.8	276	*Miscellaneous*	
		Misc.	111(2), 130, 376(2)

House in Grid Square G.12/13: 1–8

The house was situated some 40 m. due west of the Residency, on the edge of the tell escarpment. The walls were badly built of small undressed stone; only the foundation courses remained and around most of the building they consisted merely of a single or double alinement of stones (Pl. 23: 6).

The plan (Pl. 122) appeared to be more or less intact, except at the north-west and south-east corners. The long axis of the building was oriented roughly north and south and was not in exact alinement with the Residency, though accuracy of detail is not to be expected in a building where the walls were poorly planned and built at all angles to one another. Unlike the plan of the Residency, the small rooms were grouped at the north and south ends of the court, and there were no subsidiary chambers on the east and west sides.

Contents and Comparisons

Some Attic fragments (F. No. 6297) were found in Room 4 and the base of a Black Glazed vessel, possibly a jug, lying in the courtyard, was made of hard reddish-buff ware with poor iridescent black glaze outside and under the base, flaked and worn.

Nearly all the fragments of undecorated domestic wares are comparable to those found in the Residency and its associated rubbish pits, but it is perhaps worth mentioning that fragments of the soft orange-paste storage jars 488 are not recorded as present in the house. The upper part of a jar 405, with a chevron pattern incised at the base of the neck (Pl. 78: 18), is interesting for its connexion with similar wares illustrated by Sellin and Watzinger at Jericho (SW, p. 147).

The neck of a flask 255 can be matched in Graves 183 and 184, where the only funerary offerings provided were single complete examples of this form.

Date of the House

At Megiddo (M. I, Pl. 1: 6 and p. 167), flasks similar to type 255 were exclusive to Stratum I and were noted as common in fifth- to fourth-century graves at 'Athlit (QDAP II, p. 51 and Fig. 4h), and at Tell Abu Hawam (QDAP III, Pl. XXIII). The absence of fragments of the soft orange-paste storage jar 488 agrees with Lamon and Shipton's observation that the late form of "sausage" jar was missing from Stratum I at Megiddo, indicating, in their opinion, that the phase of occupation in the Greco-Persian period was slightly earlier than at either

'Athlit or Tell Abu Hawam. The house G.12/13: 1–8 may well be contemporary with Stratum I at Megiddo, and may precede by a few years the occupation of the Residency.

The recovery of an Aramaic ostracon from the soil above the house, written in script which is close to that of the Elephantine papyri (fifth century B.C.), supports the conclusion that the main period of occupation took place late in the sixth or early in the fifth century B.C. The Gatehouse G.18: 25–33 is of similar date.

Contents of the Rooms

Pottery:

G.12: 1	395
G.12: 5	568
G.12/13: 7	255, 399, 405,* 459,*¹ 496, 501, 517, 567, 568, 679
	* Pls. 77: 30 and 78: 18.

Objects:

G.12: 5	Fe knife	Pl. 59: 17
	Ostracon	Pl. 49: 2

Classified Summary of the Pottery in the House

	Bowls			Pilgrim Flasks	
B.14	567, 568(2)			PF	679
	Kraters			*Cooking Pots*	
K.	405			CP	459
	Jugs			*Storage Jars*	
J.8	255			S.5	517
				S.6b	496
	Potstands			S.10	501
PS	395, 399				

Medieval Graves (Grid Squares G.12/13/14: 9 and J/H/G.15/16: 36)

The depression within the city immediately north of the gate was thickly pitted with shallow single graves (Pl. 122 shows the northern end of the group). They did not cut into the underlying city, and became rare and isolated towards the east. One grave was superimposed on H.14: 1008, but had not disturbed the contents.

The graves were mostly oriented east and west, though there was a tendency to shift the axis to the northeast in the southern section, 36. With two exceptions, the bodies were found with heads to the west, feet to the east, and faces to the south. The bodies in two graves were lying with heads to the east and faces to the north. The only object recovered was a bronze ring. In some cases the graves were covered with two or three flat stone slabs.

Date of the Graves

The evidence for the date of these graves is inconclusive. There were altogether nearly a hundred (as shown on Pl. 122, with another cluster in Grid Squares J/H/G.15/16). Local tradition retained no knowledge of their presence and no objection was made to their removal.

Building in Grid Squares R/Q/S.15/16: 10–21

A hundred and ten metres east of the Residency there were indications of a building slightly smaller than the Solar Shrine and separated from it by some 40 m. The overall dimensions of the building after excavation were 25×16 m., but it appeared that most of the southern side was missing, possibly owing to its collapse due to

¹ Cooking pot, brown to grey sandy ware, much mica. Shaved smooth surface. Height 12 cm., one handle and most of rim and base missing.

146

subsidence in the filling of the adjoining cavity of the Great Shaft (Fig. 14 and Pl. 23: 4). After this occurrence the wall south of the courtyard was strengthened and made twice the thickness of any other in the building. All the walls of the structure were built of undressed stone laid in mud mortar.

The only entrance to the building was in the north wall, leading through a lobby, Room 16, into the central Court 10. The stone doorsill with a square socket for the doorpost was in position at the outer threshold. The chief apartment was approached from the court through a central doorway with a similar doorsill. It was a rectangular chamber (Rooms 11 and 12), divided into two unequal parts by a row of eight square nari pillars 1·25 m. in height and 0·35 m. in diameter which were joined by a roughly built stylobate of small stones (Pl. 24: 5, 6). The floor within the smaller portion was paved with flat stone slabs and the width of the paved portion (marked CF on Pl. 123) was 2 m. The remainder of the chamber had a plastered floor surface.

The presence of howr stones in the upper levels of the filling suggest that, as in the case of the Residency and Solar Shrine, some chambers at least were vaulted.

Contents and Comparisons

Nearly all the pottery fragments were found on or in the floor levels of the building and can be associated with it. Some doubt may exist about the fragments in Court 10, where there was no proper floor level which may account for the presence of some of the storage jar rims in Classes S.1: 468, 474; S.2: 511 and S.4: 514.

Of the types which occur more than once, the Mat Glazed bowl 10 is an imported third-century form, and bowls 130 and 562 are comparable to Seleucid wares from the Shephelah (BM, Pls. 60: 30 and 61: 26). Fragments of the mortaria 568 belong to the latest, ribbed type, and compare with examples from "A" building at Tell Jemmeh and Strata III–I at Megiddo, and are dated at Tell en-Naṣbeh between 600 and 400 B.C.

The unguentarium 376 is also found locally in the Shephelah (BM, Pl. 60: 6).

The cooking pot 692 may prove to be a typical third- to second-century variety (BM, Pl. 54: 6). The closed lamp 138 is a shape commonly found at Seleucia, extending from the second century B.C. to the second century A.D.

Architectural Comparisons

The construction and plan of the building is similar to certain incomplete houses in Stratum II at Tell Abu Hawam (QDAP IV, Pl. I, Grid C.5: 1 and E.2–5), which R. W. Hamilton attributed to the early phase of Stratum II (late sixth to early fourth century B.C.). He suggested that the use of monoliths to strengthen a rubble wall was a survival from the Early Iron Age, and he distinguished another building technique involving the use of ashlar pillars as characteristic of Stratum II (QDAP III, pp. 78–79).

There are no buildings with standing monoliths between rubble walls to be seen at Megiddo in Stratum I (c. 600–350 B.C.), but the proximity of the incomplete houses to the surface may account for the absence of upright stone pillars which are always valuable as building material. The peak period for the use of stone pillars is to be found in the buildings of Stratum IV at Megiddo (M. I, Figs. 34, 49), and their use is less common in Stratum III. W. F. Albright observed that they were less frequently used before the end of Stratum A at Tell Beit Mirsim (AASOR XXI–XXII, §§ 33–35).

It can be said, therefore, that the building at Tell ed-Duweir is a late example of a technique which flourished more particularly in the eighth to seventh centuries B.C. and is exclusive to sites in Palestine. The use of pillars is widely spread. Besides the sites already alluded to, see Gezer I, p. 193 and Tell en-Naṣbeh I, p. 185 and Fig. 43, and p. 214, where the excavators would date the style to 700–589 B.C. or later.

Date of the Building

It is clear that the building was still in use when the Great Shaft was filling up in the third century B.C., and that the Shaft existed prior to the building. The date of construction cannot be definitely established, but it would appear to be after the destruction in 588 B.C.

It would seem, therefore, that the structure was of some antiquity when it was finally abandoned, for there are enough fourth- to third-century forms in the rooms to show that the house was in use at that time.

The coin of Antiochus IV comes from the filling of R.15: 14 and can perhaps be taken as an indication of the period of abandonment. The coins from the Ascalon Mint are not significant as dating evidence, for they were found in S.16: 19, on the east corner, where much had been denuded.

At the Seleucid site of Tell Sandaḥannah, near by, which succeeded Tell ed-Duweir as the local district centre, no buildings with pillars are recorded, suggesting that the style had died out by the second century B.C.

Contents of the Building

Pottery:

R.16: 10 (on floor)
67, 75, 130, 138, 376, 391, 395, 468, 474, 501, 511, 514, 527, 535, 551, 679

Q/R.16: 11
10, 136,* 376, 539, 583, 670
* Pl. 36: 61.
10: Mat Glazed bowl with incurving sides. Thin buff ware, with reddish-black mat slip all over. Diameter, 10·5 cm. 3rd century B.C.

Q.16: 12
139,* 658, 692*
* Pl. 77: 25.
658: Broneer lamp type VII (Corinth IV, Pt. 2). 5th–4th century B.C.

R.15: 13
127, 349,* 407
* Pl. 77: 28.
407: Neck and shoulder of amphora. Fine soft buff ware with white grits. Finger smooth surface. Traces of mat reddish-buff paint.

R.15: 14
10, 59, 130, 138, 376, 501, 521, 568, 602, 635

R.16: 15
79, 152, 376, 401,* 501, 534, 665
* Pl. 77: 34.

R.16: 16
486 (on floor): Jar shoulder and neck only. Hard red ware with grey core; white grits and some mica. Thin white slip on outside. Rim diameter, 12·5 cm.

R.16: 17
540

R.16: 18
60, 138, 175,* 510, 562, 568
* Pl. 77: 20.
175: Cooking pot. Reddish-buff ware with white grits. Shaved and smoothed surface. Height, 8 cm.
NP: Mat Glazed bowl rim with folded handle, cf. 111.

S.16: 19
67, 130, 501, 515, 532, 555, 568, 692
NP: Neck of jar, rim missing. Hard buff ware with white grits and some mica. Creamy white slip inside and out. Pendant stripes of mat red paint hanging from band encircling neck. Diameter, 10·5 cm.
Shoulder and neck of jug. Well silted greyish-buff ware with large lime grits. Upper par and inside covered with reddish-brown wash. Approx. diameter, 13 cm., neck diameter 8 cm. Cf. BM, Pl. 60: 15.

R.15: 20
67

R.16: 21
—

Objects:

Q.16: 11	AE arrowhead	Pl. 60: 68
	Chalk altar	Pls. 42: 6 and 64: 11
	2 stone rubbers	F. No. 6314 NP
R.15: 13	Scarab	Pls. 44 and 45: 156
R.15: 14	AE coin, No. 40a on List of Coins, p. 413	
R.16: 18	AE arrowhead	Pl. 60: 53
	Bead	Pl. 67: 93
S.16: 19	AE coin, No. 56a in List of Coins, p. 413	
	AE coin, No. 56b in List of Coins, p. 413	
	Stamp, *hbrn* class ii	

Classified Summary of the Pottery in the Building

Bowls

B.7	602
B.11	59, 60, 67(3), 562
B.13	75, 79, 635
B.14	568(3)

Lamps

L.9–10	152
L.12	136, 138(3), 139

Jugs

J.4	175
J.8	665

Dippers and Juglets

D.9	349

Potstands

PS	395, 401

Pilgrim Flasks

PF	679

Cooking Pots

CP	692(2)

Storage Jars

S.1	468, 474
S.2	510, 511
S.4	514
S.5	515, 521, 527, 532, 534
S.6a	535
S.8	539, 540
S.9	555
S.10	501(4)
S.11	391
S.12	551

Miscellaneous

Misc.	10(2), 127, 130(3), 376(4), 407, 583, 658, 670

Earth ramp on west side of citadel (Grid Square H.14: 22)

The number 22 in Grid Square H.14 designates the surface of the earth ramp at the south-west corner of the citadel, between the building and a stone retaining wall, of which only a few blocks of masonry remained. The area is bounded on the south by the "enclosure" wall seen on Pl. 16: 3 and on Pl. 115. Some alabaster fragments were found, with the handle of a Cypriote milk bowl, and sherds showing irregular hand burnish both inside and out. The area number is not marked on Pl. 115, as the sherds were mostly associated with the Late Bronze Age city, the debris of which was disturbed by the construction of a ramp round the citadel, early in the Iron Age. The area remained open until post-exilic times.

Area west of stone retaining wall (Grid Square H.14: 23)

The number 23 designates the adjoining area west of the stone "enclosure" wall, between H.14: 22 and a broken-down stone wall on the south. The pottery mostly came from the ruin of the wall, and it appears to be a contemporary group, deposited perhaps in the sixth century B.C. The "blob" style scaraboid on Pl. 44: 71 may survive from an earlier context.

Pottery: 348, 351,* 403, 436, 461, 581, 660, 678
           * Pl. 77: 27.
Object: Bone scaraboid   Pl. 44: 71

Area adjoining G.14: 24

This area lies between H.14: 23 and the tell escarpment. It belongs to the same stratum (sixth century B.C.) and may be connected with the mud or clay wall in G.14: 1012. The area remained open till post-exilic times.

Gatehouse (Grid Square G.18: 25–33)

From the position of the structure just inside the inner gate of Level I, south of the roadway in use at about the same time (Pl. 108), it is permissible to assume that it represented the gatehouse and guardroom.

The plan of the building was no longer intact, for all the walls on the south side were missing. Part of the walls on the west side adjoined the upper city wall, south of the inner gate, and that main wall may have been used as a support for the west wall of the house (Pls. 124 and 23: 5).

It seems that entry to the building was obtained from the north, through a partially blocked doorway leading into an open area or Court 27, around which a series of rooms were placed, though only five of them were reasonably intact in plan. The foundation courses of the remaining rooms consisted, for the most part, of a double alinement of poorly dressed stone, and some structural alterations were made during a late phase of occupation, notably the partitions or bins 29 and 30 in Room 28. Floor levels of beaten earth were hard to distinguish, owing to erosion and proximity to the surface. There were remains of a floor in Room 28, sloping from north to south at 262·60 m. approximately, and a pit had been cut in it and used at a time before the construction of bins 29 and 30.

It was noted that a scree of stones had fallen from the city wall, covering burnt brick debris which probably represented part of the superstructure of the defences and covered part of the open area 27. Pits A, B and C had been cut in the burnt debris and should therefore be later than the destruction of both the walls and Gatehouse.

Contents and Comparisons

The building was so close to the present ground surface that sherds in the filling and on the undefined floor levels were not in a reliable context, and they were undoubtedly disturbed by ploughing and erosion, for nothing of any size or note was recovered.

No Attic sherds were noted in the rooms or the filling, which would be in keeping with the utilitarian purpose of the Gatehouse, and fragments of the orange-paste jar 488 were also missing, though both plain and ribbed mortaria were common.

Date of the Gatehouse

The comparison of pottery fragments would suggest that the Gatehouse was in use at about the same time as the house in Grid Square G.12/13: 1–8, and the similarity also extends to the style of wall building in double and single alinements of stones. The presence in the filling of a Rhodian jar stamp (Pl. 52: 7 and 53: 12) dated by Miss Virginia Grace to the third quarter of the third century B.C. suggests that the place was falling into disuse at that time.

Contents of the Gatehouse

Pottery (sherds only):

G.18: 26   517 (in filling)
G.18: 27   351, 563, 567 (in pits A, B, C)
G.18: 28   525(2), 539, 568(2), 607, 648, 682, 695, 696

G.18: 29 578 (in filling)
G.18: 31 137 (on floor), 469, 486, 535, 567, 568, 578, 580, 644, 679, 695, 696 (in filling)
G.18: 32 255, 525, 565

Objects:
G.18: 27 Pottery bust of figurine Pl. 32: 2
      Faience *ushabti*, broken Pl. 35: 40
G.18: 28 Rhodian jar handle Pls. 52: 7 and 53: 12
G.18: 32 Weight, No. 21 in List of Weights, p. 353

Classified Summary of the Pottery in the Gatehouse

Bowls		Pilgrim Flasks	
B.7	607	PF	679
B.13	644, 648		
B.14	563, 565, 567(2), 568(3)	*Cooking Pots*	
		CP	695(2)
Lamps			
L.12	137	*Storage Jars*	
		S.2	469
		S.5	517, 525(3)
Jugs		S.6a	486, 535
J.10	255	S.8	539
		S.13	696(2)
Dippers and Juglets			
D.9	351	*Miscellaneous*	
		Misc.	578(2), 580, 682

Road in G.18: 34, 35

The open area immediately north of the Gatehouse in G.18. It is mostly the post-exilic road surface within the city gate. See G/H/J.17: 1072.

Pottery (sherds only):
G.18: 34 567, 679
Object:
G.18: 34 Marble palette Pl. 64: 8

Circular pits and late structures associated with the Residency

K.14: 59; K.15: 89–99	L.14/15: 66, 67	M.12: 86, 88
L.11: 38; L.13: 79	L/M.14: 41–43, 60, 83, 84	M.14: 44
L.14: 57, 61, 62, 65, 78, 85, 87	L/M.14/15: 52, 53, 58, 63, 64, 68	M.14/15: 69
L.15: 39, 40, 45–51, 55, 56	L/M.15: 54	M.15: 70–77

Concentrated near the south-east corner of the citadel and Residency, and extending along the east side, were more than fifty circular pits which had been dug through the fallen brick from the collapsed walls of Palace C; beyond the range of that collapse the pits had often penetrated the plastered court associated with Palace C (Pls. 16: 5; 17: 2–4; 108; 115–116).

C. H. Inge noted in a field report dated February, 1938, that most of the grain pits appeared to have been dug before the builders of the Residency undertook the demolition of Palace C—"but it does not seem that many of them were made before the burning of the palace, and the looseness of the fallen brickwork makes it difficult to be confident on this point".

A survey of the contents will show that though the pottery is mixed in date, the forms represented in the Residency are quite common. It is logical to conclude, therefore, that the pits were dug one after the other as the need arose during the occupation of the Residency in the fifth and fourth centuries B.C. Some may have remained open to a later date.

Contents and Comparisons

The pottery fragments from the pits were nearly all very small and many of them obviously belonged to the underlying Bronze Age city, which was frequently disturbed by the construction of the pits.

Objects of interest which may find parallels elsewhere are the bronze fluted terminal for furniture (Pls. 41: 2 and 63: 2); the mould-cast figure of a man in Hellenistic style (Pl. 32: 6); agate and crumb beads (Pls. 66: 23, 77, and 67: 120); and three fibulae (Pl. 58: 22, 24 (2 ex.)).

L.11: 38

The pit had been cut into the post-exilic debris overlying Palace A at the north end. It was filled with black ash and stones. It contained some Attic sherds, F. No. 7186 (PM. 39.826), among other late fragments.

Pottery: 517, 522, 632, 697
Objects: AE furniture fitting   Pls. 41: 2 and 63: 2

L.15: 39

Not used.

L.15: 40

Pit in plaster court east of Palace B–C.

Pottery (sherds): Iron Age burnish, one fragment Mycenean

L/M.14: 41, 42, 43

A series of three adjoining rooms. The walls were built of a single thickness of large oblong stones. Only the ground course remained, except at the south-west corner, where there was a second course. The floor was roughly paved. The sherds included late mortaria and part of a potstand, type 400.

Pottery: 400, 679

M.14: 44

Area east of Rooms 41–43. The upper plaster court contemporary with the rooms had been cut by an irregular pit, exposing a lower plastered floor at 267·11 m., on which the pottery lay.

Pottery: 30, 68, 137, 375
Object: AE fibula as Pl. 58: 24

L.15: 45

The pit was broken on three sides.

Pottery: 30, 469, 517, 567, 646
Objects: Fe arrowhead   F. No. 6363 NP
             Flints   F. No. 6364 NP
             Stamp, *shwkh* class ii, p. 342

L.15: 46

A partly stone-lined pit, filled with fine earth and stones.

Pottery: 27, 150, 461, 506, 695

> 27: Half section of shallow dish with low ring foot. Thick buff to grey ware with large white grits, light finger-smoothed surface. Much pitted inside.

Objects: Stamp, private   F. No. 6366 Pl. 47A: 3 and PEQ, 1941, p. 40

L.15: 47

This pit cuts into pit 48, and had brick walls below. It was filled with fine earth and ash.

Pottery: 567, 568, 660

Objects:			
Fe knife	Pl. 59: 10	Agate bead	as Pl. 66: 23
AE bangle	Pl. 63: 3	Crumb bead	Pl. 66: 77
Pottery figure	Pl. 32: 6	Snail shells	NP

L.15: 48

A double silo, cutting into pit 47, with brick walls below and filled with fine earth and ash.

Pottery: 68,* 79, 150(2), 391, 442, 460, 564, 567, 660, 679, 686

>   * Pl. 77: 23
>
> 68: Ring-footed mortar. Reddish ware with black grits and mica, greenish-white slip. Diameter, 31·5 cm. See Bowls, Class B. 14, p. 279

Objects: AE arrowhead   Pl. 60: 69
         Fe knife   Pl. 59: 19
         Pendant   Pl. 67: 133
         Stamp, *hbrn*, class ii, p. 342

L.15: 49

A shallow depression cut into the filling of yellow marl chips below the surface of the plastered court.

L.15: 50

This pit cut into pit 54 and was filled with fine earth and stones. It had not disturbed the plaster court, which formed the bottom of the pit.

Pottery: 79, 617, 4 Attic sherds
Object: Scarab   Pl. 43: 28

L.15: 51

The filling of this pit was fine earth with traces of straw.

Pottery: Sherds only, including mortaria
Object: Stamp, *zp*, class i, p. 342 and PEQ, 1941, p. 96

L/M. 14/15: 52

The filling of the pit was gravel and fine earth; the bottom was of mud.

Object: Bone handle   Pl. 63: 14

L/M.14/15: 53

This pit was cut into fallen brick, and the sides had collapsed. The filling was earth and the bottom was mud.

Pottery: (L. II: 65, 91, 364, 389), 442

L/M.15: 54

The pit cuts into 50, and was filled with fine earth and ash. The bottom was clay.

Pottery: 97, 525, 568

L.15: 55

Double silo filled with earth and ash, with brick walls below.

Pottery: (L. II: 325, 367), 484, 524, 526, 660, 679, 695, 697
Objects: Fe arrowhead   F. No. 6386 NP
         AE fibula   Pl. 58: 22
         Limestone animal   Pl. 41: 3
         Stamp, *hbrn*, class ii, p. 342

L.15: 56

This pit was filled with fine earth and ash, with an earth bottom.

Pottery: 695
Object: Ostrich egg fragments

L.14: 57

The pit was cut into the fallen brick (see section on Pl. 117).

Pottery: 68, 484, 488, 508, 550

L/M.14/15: 58

Pottery: (L. II: 379), 153, 399, 528, 568
Object: Ostrich egg fragments

K.14: 59

The pit penetrated the fallen brick and two plaster courts, and was filled with earth and sherds.

Pottery: 399, 499, 506, 568, 668

L/M.14: 60

The pit was filled with ash and the bottom was of burnt brick.

L.14: 61

The filling was of earth and the bottom of burnt brick, below which there was another large pit.

Pottery: Sherds, EB and LB

L.14: 62

The pit was cut through and below the fallen brick into the plaster court below. The filling was of earth and ash, and the bottom of mud (Pl. 17: 4).

Pottery: 79, 276, 442, 488, 643, 666
Objects: Fe arrow   F. N. 6394 NP
         Bone inlay   Pl. 63: 28

L/M.14/15: 63

The pit cut through the burnt brickwork, with one side built up, possibly for use as an oven. There was an earlier pit with a mud bottom below.

L/M.14/15: 64

The pit was in the edge of the fallen brick, with a filling of earth and stones, and mud sides and bottom (Pl. 17: 4).

Pottery: Sherds, not typable

L.14: 65

A shallow pit cut in the plaster court.

Pottery: Sherds, not typable
Object: Weight, No. 52 on List of Weights   Pl. 50: 11

L.14/15: 66

A pit slightly deeper than pit 65, filled with earth, stones and some ash. It was cut through a white plaster floor which may be an extension of the plaster court east of Palace B–C. It contained three LB sherds and one Attic fragment.

L.14/15: 67

A double pit with a mud bottom. It was filled with fine earth, and contained sherds which were not typable.

L/M.14/15: 68

A pit cut in the hard earth surface and filled with fine earth.

M.14/15: 69

A double pit cut in the hard earth surface and filled with fine earth.

Pottery: (L. II: 80), 399, 469, 517, 527, 567, 695
        NP: Fragment of Red Figured amphora, showing bottom border and part of feet of figures; additional design in white paint. Rather poor glaze.
        Two fragments of another Red Figured amphora, with better paste and glaze.
        Rim of Red Glazed cup. Thick red glaze on fine buff clay, traces of vertical burnishing.
        Fragment of Mat Glazed bowl.
        Lamp. Fine purplish-grey ware, unpainted. Broneer type VII. (Corinth IV, Pt. 2: Nos. 115, 136). 5th–4th century B.C.
Object: Worked stone   F. No. 6400 NP

M.15: 70

A pit cut in the lower plaster court. It contained no sherds or objects.

M.15: 71

A stone-lined pit, filled with fine earth. The bottom was of mud with traces of straw.

Pottery: Sherds, including EB and LB
Objects: Land snail shells (*Helix cincta* Müller)

M.15: 72

A pit with a mud bottom, cut in the upper plaster court.

Pottery: Burnishing sherd
Object: Glass slag

M.15: 73

An irregular pit or pits, cut on three sides into the upper plaster court, and on the fourth side into the hard earth surface.

Pottery: Sherds

M.15: 74

A pit cut in the upper plaster floor on three sides and into the hard earth surface on the fourth. There were traces of a wall beneath.

Pottery: Sherds, including mortaria
Object: Glass slag

M.15: 75

A pit cut in the hard earth surface, with a mud bottom.

Pottery: 382, 568, 679
Objects: AE fibula   Pl. 58: 24
       Stamp, class ii (doubtful)

M.15: 76

A pit cut in the lower plaster court. The bottom was of stones.

Pottery: LB sherds (including L. II, types 51, 163)

M.15: 77

A pit cut in the upper plaster court on three sides, and into the hard earth surface on the fourth. The lower plaster court was visible on the west side. There were no sherds or objects.

L.14: 78

This pit was cut through the fallen brick of Palace C. It penetrated into the LB stratum; brick walls were visible in the side and under the pit, embedded in a heavily carbonised layer containing many bones (cf. 83, 84).

Pottery: LB sherds and mortaria

L.13: 79

A pit cut in the fallen brick, probably within Room 1002. The bottom was of mud on a plaster surface.

L/M.13: 80

A double pit cut through the plaster court, and divided by a line of small stones. The filling was of heavily burnt earth and the bottom was of mud.

Pottery: (L. II: 7, 135, 162, 163, 386), 79, 249, 409,* 679, 695
        * Pl. 77: 29.
    409: Amphora neck. Brick-red ware, brownish core, sandy with large white grits. Finger-smoothed inside. Greenish-white slip outside. Groove at junction of shoulder and neck. Band of mat red paint and smear strokes on either side of neck. Neck diameter, 10·2 cm.

L/M.13: 81

A pit cut in three sides through the fallen brick, with the fourth side broken. The plaster court was visible in section, with burnt brick and LB sherds below.

L/M.13: 82

A pit cut on three sides through the fallen brick, with the fourth side missing.

Pottery: 51, 249,* 488
        * Pl. 77: 26.
    249: Jug. Good crimson body with large white grits, making pitted surface. Wheel made, rough finger-smoothed surface, vertical burnish on neck and upper part of body. Poorly fired, giving

cream to dark red surface. Handle, from rim to shoulder, missing. Height, 17 cm. Mid-sec
century B.C. Cf. TCHP: D.62. See Jugs, Class J. 7b, p. 292.

Object: Bead   Pl. 66: 4

L/M.14: 83

A pit cut through the loose earth at the base of a slope of fallen brick, penetrating the plaster court. The
filling was of heavily burnt earth and ash.

Pottery: 568

L/M.14: 84

A pit cut in the hard surface east of the plaster court penetrating Room 1083. The filling was of stones with
fine earth below, reaching to the LB stratum. Cf. pits 78, 83.

Pottery: 568, Greek sherd F. N. 7197 (PM. 39.828) NP
Objects: Fe knife   Pl. 59: 2
            AE nail and Fe point Pl. 63: 5, 6
            Stamp, *hbrn*, class ii, p. 342

L.14: 85

A pit cut through the fallen brick between the walls of Rooms 1075 and 1077. The bottom was of fallen
brick.

Pottery: 27, 488
            27: Bowl, as L.15: 46. Red ware, well-burnished inner surface.

M.12: 86

A regular pit cut through the plaster court. The bottom was of hard mud.

Pottery: 114, 510
            114: Krater. Soft pinkish-buff vesiculated body, much black and pink grit, some mica. Finger-
                  smoothed outside. Base, part of rim and one handle. Diameter approximately 28 cm., height
                  17·5 cm.

L.14: 87

A pit cut through the plaster court and filled with burnt brick debris. The bottom was made of mud and
some large stones, possibly part of an underlying building.

Pottery: 488, miscellaneous sherds
Object: Stamp, *hbrn*, class ii, p. 342

M.12: 88

A small pit full of heavily carbonised earth, cut through the plaster court and penetrating the hard mud floor
about 15 cm. below. The bottom and sides were of mud.

Pottery: LB and miscellaneous sherds
Object: Agate bead   Pl. 67: 120

K.15: 89–92

Pits cut through the plaster court. There were no contents.

K.15: 93

A pit cut through the plaster court. It contained sherds only.

K.15: 94

A pit cut through the plaster court.

Objects: Bone spatula (2 ex.) Pl. 63: 26

Weight, No. 20 in List of Weights, p. 353

K.15: 95–99

Pits cut through the plaster court. There were no contents.

Classified Summary of the Pottery in the Pits

	Bowls			Pilgrim Flasks	
Class	Type		Class		Type
B.1	617		PF		679(5)
B.6	97				
B.7	51			Cooking Pots	
B.13	79(3), 632, 643, 646		CP		442(3), 460, 461, 695(5)
B.14	68(3), 564, 567(4), 568(7)				
				Storage Jars	
	Kraters		S.2		469(2), 510
K	686		S.3		488(5)
			S.5		517(3), 522, 524, 525, 526, 527
	Lamps		S.6a		528
L.7–8	150(3)		S.7a		484(2)
L.9–10	153		S.10		499
L.11	660(3)		S.11		391
L.12	137		S.12		550
			S.13		506(2), 508, 697(2)
	Jugs				
J.7b	249(2), 666			Miscellaneous	
J.8	276		Misc.		27(2), 30(2), 114, 375, 382, 409, 668
	Potstands				
PS	399(3), 400				

THE GREAT SHAFT

The contour map of the tell (Pl. 106) shows a semicircular depression on the south-east side of the mound. Its diameter at the tell edge was about 90 m., and its radius from the edge to the periphery of the circle was some 75 m., rising nearly 7 m. in that distance. From the first inspection of the site, J. L. Starkey was greatly interested in this feature (Grid Ref. PQR: 16–18 and Fig. 14), but he realised that its excavation would be a formidable task and work was not begun there until March, 1935. From that time until his death the Great Shaft, as it came to be called, was always a subject of speculation, experiment, achievement—and disappointment.

In brief, the story and the method of the excavation is as follows: An area some 18 m. by 16 m. was laid out in the lowest part of the depression, and removal of the top surface, consisting of 60 cm. of black soil, revealed no trace of walls. Three companies then began to sink a trench (A) running north-west and south-east across the axis of the depression. At a point 2·50 m. below the surface in the western half of the trench the men reached the face of a sloping scree of earth and stones. This was followed down until it crossed the width of the cutting at a depth of about 3·60 m. on the eastern section. Starkey wrote as follows in April, 1935:

"The most surprising feature of this excavation was the consistent nature of the soil through which we had sunk our trench. The stratification was perfectly horizontal down the axis of the trench, with a light tilt downwards from north-west to south-east. This deposit consists of small fragments of pottery and small stones, all water laid; the fact that 'mortaria' fragments of the late Persian period were found almost at the bottom of our trench, immediately told us that we were dealing with an area which had remained open for drainage until that date. It was now clear that our next course would be to sink a further trench at right angles to this one, south-eastwards, in the hope of finding what it was that the revetment was rising from. At 12 ft. (3·60 m.) at the southern side of this cutting, we struck native rock, which showed signs of having been quarried, as large blocks had been removed. We followed the face of this escarpment down for another 12 ft., where we found the rock had been cut vertically, forming what we think is the corner of a large square shaft. We have dug down into this corner another 6 ft. (2 m.)." (Pl. 26: 2.)

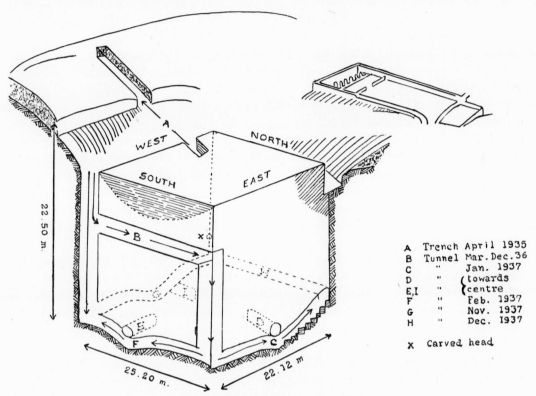

FIG. 14. Diagram of the Great Shaft

At 12·60 m. from the surface the soil became increasingly fine, and was largely composed of small particles of powdered brickwork, water-laid, presumably the result of surface wash from the late burnt city levels. At the end of the season the pit at the south-west corner of the Great Shaft had reached a depth of 16 m. (Pl. 26: 1).

When the new season opened in November, 1935, Starkey wrote:

"Before beginning the clearance of the Great Shaft, it seemed advisable to test the extent of the late accumulation filling the hollow. We cut a four-foot trench up through the water-laid deposits overlying the earth glacis, which we found running upwards from the western side of the shaft seen in our sounding last year. The debris runs up in a series of steps over yellow mud, which marks the original sloping tell surface. In fact, I visualise the tell levels north, south and west, as a great funnel sloping down to the neck of the shaft. One must presume that one function of the shaft was to collect water. . . ." (Pl. 26: 3.)

In March, 1936, men were concentrated on the western area in order to discover the north-west corner of the shaft, which should establish its square and the position of the other corners. This data was necessary before full-scale excavation could be planned; already the removal of soil was hard work, with a dead lift of over 9 m., and the construction of a suitable ramp was essential.

Meanwhile a small tunnel (B) was driven along the rock face of the south side of the shaft for 11 m. beyond the corner (Pl. 25: 1, 2, 4, 5), and the pottery fragments which were buried throughout the water-laid mass of filling confirmed previous observations that the upper levels were not filled in until post-exilic or early Hellenistic times.

159

By April, 1936, surface excavations had laid bare the western edge of the shaft, and a tunnel (not shown in the diagram) driven northwards soon struck the north-west angle. Thus the length of the western side was over 20 m., while the length of the south side was even greater, as the tunnel along the face had passed that point without any sign of a corner.

The first task, when work was resumed in 1936, was to clean and widen the tunnel (B) and remove projecting blocks of stone in the filling. The tunnel was, at this stage, 1·40 m. in height and a metre wide at floor level, which allowed basket boys to pass each other easily.

The rock cutting at the south-east corner, when reached by means of this tunnel, showed a clean angle with vertical sides (Pl. 25: 1). It was then decided to sink a shaft here to ascertain the depth of the pit, and pulleys and winches were set up underground on a wooden scaffold to hoist the soil to the level of tunnel B.

The filling of the shaft 19 m. below the surface was still water-laid, though the soil showed practically no clay, which had apparently been carried away by free drainage; in fact, the filling was not nearly so damp as that of most ancient wells. There was a large number of big stones, with some boulders weighing over a hundredweight. These were broken up *in situ* below ground, and the residue brought to the surface in buckets with the soil.

Simultaneously with the work below ground, the eastern and northern sides of the rock and earth slope leading to the shaft were being exposed (Pl. 25: 6). A steep scree of stones lined the slope on the north side, which was certainly open during the post-exilic period. From the water-laid deposits above came a steatite plaque of Aa-kheperu-Ra, Amenhetep II, 1449–1423 B.C. (F. No. 6147), one of the many fragments of all periods from the city levels above.

FIG. 15.
Gold Ear-ring

When the head of the shaft was completely cleared, it was evident that the continuous scree of large and small roughly hewn stones which sloped down into it from the post-exilic city level could never have been a lining to the funnel of the shaft (Pl. 25: 6). A gold ear-ring was found under the stones which compares with one from Deve Huyuk of about the fifth century (AAA VII, Pl. XXIII). Inscribed Rhodian jar handles, dated by Miss Virginia Grace to *c.* 275–250 B.C. (Pls. 52–53), came from the same place, with tall necked flasks of types 376 and 382. Pl. 25: 3 shows the earth slope forming the neck of the shaft below the scree of stones, with the post-exilic building against the skyline.

Returning to the work below ground, two tunnels (C and F) were driven northwards and westwards respectively from the base of the vertical examination shaft at the south-east corner. At a depth of 22·50 m. in tunnel C the length of the east side was established at 22·12 m., and at this low level the tool marks of the original cuttings were well preserved. The rock base of the tunnel proved to be much lower in the centre, reaching a depth of 25 m. from the ground surface.

Starkey wrote in January, 1937:

"From this new sounding, we see that the bottom of the shaft, or at least the lowest point, does not represent the full depth of the ancient excavation, for the stones and soil are lightly packed and drainage is still passing down to a lower level, which we presume is more central. . . . The potsherds from the lowest point are all of the last phase of the Jewish city, and a characteristic feature is the presence of large lumps of charcoal and burnt stones."

Starkey then decided to drive two further tunnels (D and E) from the centres of the east and south sides respectively, towards the middle of the shaft. The task was much hampered by numbers of big stones, closely packed together with very little soil. All these had to be broken in the confined space of the tunnels before they were lifted to the surface through the shaft and upper tunnel.

The tunnel (D) from the centre of the base of the east side was projected at right angles to the pit face for a length of 3·50 m., but the rock floor maintained the same level throughout. There was therefore no indication that the tunnel along the east face had followed a narrow ledge. Starkey felt sure, in view of the softness of the stone, that, if a central pit had existed, any surrounding ledge would have been denuded by weathering to a gentle slope. At this stage it was considered advisable to abandon further examination of the central area in this tunnel in order to concentrate on work along the south face.

At 20 m. from the south-east corner the floor of the tunnel (F) began to drop rapidly, and the soil filling the cavities between the huge blocks of stone was all fine water-laid deposit, much of it pure mud, which was extremely wet but easy to dig. Starkey wrote in February, 1937:

"It appears possible that we may be within a short distance of the lowest point of the base of the Great Shaft, where the drainage has been escaping. This is certainly indicated by the heavy deposits of mud. Here also we continue to find quantities of calcined stones and charcoal, with a fair sprinkling of small potsherds, which confirm our theory that the shaft was out of use directly after the firing of the city in 588 B.C."

When the south-west corner at the base of the shaft was reached it was found to be full of hard mizzi boulders, embedded in a matrix of mason's chips. The walls at this point oozed water at many places, and it was therefore necessary to deepen the original shaft which led from the surface at the south-west corner in order to open up the roof of the tunnel and secure better ventilation. The soil at the bottom of the new shaft was fortunately free from stones, in contradistinction to the filling of the east side, where the stone city wall had probably collapsed and fallen in at the time of the final destruction.

At the point where the rocky floor dipped in the base of the tunnel, following the south face of the shaft, the floor had been undercut to form a small low cave, on the bottom of which was a large deposit of olive stones in a layer of carbonised soil.

At the close of the season the base of the shaft had been followed along two sides, and only the north and west sides, with the north-west corner, remained to be examined.

A surface clearance along it had established that there was no stairway descending from the north on the north–south axis of the pit, which at one time seemed probable.

Starkey summarised his conclusions in April, 1937:

"As to the date, the evidence is by no means definite as yet, but three pieces of circumstantial evidence may point to a late one: (1) The sharp freshness of the tool marks round the lower part of the pit, despite the fact that the bottom of the shaft was open to the weather. (2) The large areas of chalk pavements seen in the region of the palace-fort, extending southwards even beyond the limit of the roadway, all of which must be dated to the final restoration of the city's defences under the Jewish kingdom. (3) The fact that a short-handled pick seems to have been used to dress the sides, which would most probably preclude a date before the Iron Age. . . . To be more precise, it does not seem to me possible to date it earlier than Josiah (638–609 B.C.) but further evidence could turn the scales in favour of a later date.

"As to the purpose of such a shaft, it seems clear that the ancient engineers were endeavouring to get a new way down to the water level; the need, however, for a shaft of such large dimensions remains a complete mystery. We must remember that until we reach a central point in the bottom of the shaft, and prove that the rock floor is continuous, a doubt exists as to the possibility that the walls of our shaft belong to the enlargement of an earlier original scheme.

"We have, with this problem in view, made two unsuccessful attempts to tunnel to the centre, but both have been frustrated by the dangerous condition of the loose stones in the filling. We have seen for twenty feet along the base of the west side, and the filling here is almost devoid of stones. Good, hard, compact mud deposits show that the fallen masonry (on the east side) fell in from the line of the city wall, and I still have hope, therefore, that an effort to work in from the west side may be successful.

"I have often referred to the low entrance with the tower over it which is shown in the Lachish reliefs. From the foregoing remarks, it is obvious that our shaft can have no direct connection with this construction, which must have been in existence as early as 701 B.C. Further enquiries are necessary before we can set aside our problem, and the explanation for the smaller depression at the north-east corner of the tell, below the lote tree, must be forthcoming." (See Pl. 1: 3.)

Finally, in November, 1937, work was resumed on the tunnel (G) along the western side of the base of the Great Shaft. The soil proved to be comparatively free of large boulders, and at the lowest point, which occurred a little over half-way to the north-west corner, the rock was cut in steps upwards, showing that blocks of stone about 90 cm. in depth had been quarried. There is no doubt that this corner was never finished. In 1·75 m. there was a rise of 3·66 m., which made it awkward for the workmen, as they had to dig above their heads.

Just above the floor level at the north-west corner a large boulder of crystalline limestone had been left projecting by the masons, as its complete removal would have meant damaging the well-cut angle of the corner above and below. It had been trimmed back, but an oddly shaped projection had struck the imagination of a worker and he proceeded to increase its resemblance to a human head adorned with a beard (Fig. 16). As Starkey wrote at the time: "It reminds us of the human qualities of those who strove at a gigantic task." It is estimated that 14,285 cubic m. (500,000 cubic feet) of solid rock were quarried from a shaft measuring

FIG. 16. Carved Head at base of Great Shaft

$22 \times 25 \cdot 20 \times 25 \cdot 50$ m. ($74 \times 84 \times 85$ ft.), and it should be remembered that this prodigious task was begun during a period of difficulty and stress in Judah. Starkey finally reached the conclusion that the cutting of the Great Shaft took place during the later Judaean period, and that it was never completed. The latter fact was proved during the final attempt to reach the centre of the shaft, described in Starkey's last field report, written in December, 1937:

"I am pleased to say that our effort to reach the centre of the shaft has been successful, and despite the loose state of the stone boulders encountered in the tunnelling, we were able to reach our objective without shoring up. On the north side of our tunnel, as the central point was approached, we found we were working towards a vertical rock face—most gratifying evidence that the quarrying operations at the centre were abandoned before it had been cut down to a common level. It now seems clear that the quarrying was being done in a series of levels from south to north, the more advanced work being against the south face, some twenty feet below the operations on the north side. The large hard mizzi limestone blocks were removed from their matrix of softer limestone by undercutting with short-handled iron picks, and this accounts for the curious pockets cut down into the rock floor over which our tunnel has passed. . . . In a few days we shall have cleaned out the floor of our tunnel on the three sides, and all that will remain will be the levelling for the final survey."

C. H. Inge has contributed the following note on the Great Shaft:

"I am satisfied that the Shaft was intended to be a water reservoir, filled by rain water draining from the eastern parts of the city, and especially from the plastered open space east of the palace. Examination of the floor of the cutting showed that the work was left unfinished. The porosity of the rock would have required that the reservoir should be plastered before use.

"It is unlikely that the excavation was intended primarily as a quarry for building stone. It is too regular in design and in the finish of the vertical sides. Moreover, the rock extracted would have been mainly soft howr, which was not commonly used as a building stone in the Iron Age until the post-exilic period. The hard mizzi rock, which occurs in the walls of the Shaft in isolated concretions, was not generally used by masons of the late Jewish monarchy, who preferred the inferior nari rock, which occurs only on the surface where howr has been long exposed to the atmosphere."

Date of the Great Shaft

From the foregoing accounts there is little evidence to establish the date of the construction of the Great Shaft. It apparently belongs to a late phase in the history of the city, for there is some indication that the great areas of plastered court surrounding the citadel were constructed from small rock chips overlaid with crushed chalk, which may well have come from the cutting of the Great Shaft. The plastered areas are largely associated with Level III, which was terminated, according to the present view, by Sennacherib's destruction in 700 B.C. Wherever the plaster surface was undisturbed by the cutting of later pits, it remained in good condition and showed little signs of wear. Therefore it does not appear likely that it was in use for long before its destruction.

It is not unreasonable to suppose that Hezekiah took action to secure the water supply for Lachish in the same way as he did for Jerusalem (II Chronicles XXXII: 2–4, 30 and II Kings XX: 20), and if this were so, it would account for the short period of use of the plastered courts.

When Starkey summarised his conclusions in April, 1937, and decided that the Shaft could not be earlier than the reign of Josiah, he was proceeding on the assumption that Level III was destroyed in 597 B.C. (PEQ, 1937, July–Oct.). Nevertheless, the sherds found at the lowest point are more consistent with that date. There were parts of a plain mortarium, class B.14, type 68; a flask, type 673; two pieces of decanters in class J.8 and a bowl rim with handle, class B.13, type 649.

If the first assumption that the Shaft was abandoned in 700 B.C. were correct, it would have filled up too rapidly to admit such late forms. At 7 m. from the surface three coins were found in the filling with mint dates between 336 and 187 B.C. (Appendix B, Nos. 8, 27, 35). It was noted that the south wall of the building RQS. 15/16: 10–21 had been strengthened against collapse into the depression, which is consistent with the presence of third-century pottery in the upper filling of the Shaft.

Summary of the Contents of the Great Shaft

Metres above sea level	Sherds		Stamped Handles	Metal	Stone	Miscellaneous
	Types	Remarks				
258 surface	—	—	Rhodian, Pls. 52: 7, 53: 12	—	—	—
257	568	All periods — EB to Roman	—	AE hook, NP	Basalt weight (?) NP Alabaster jug frag. NP Sickle flints, NP	Frag. faience bowl, NP Pottery animal head, NP Pottery wand, NP
256	544	,,	—	—	—	Bead, Pl. 66: 35
255	593†	,,	shwkh, class iii Private, 'Abdi	—	—	—
254	376, 382, 399, 501, 623,† 673	,,	hbrn ii, zp i, ii, shwkh ii Incised name, lbnh, Pl. 52: 8 Rhodian, Pls. 52: 3, 53: 8	—	Sickle flints, NP Stone celt frag., NP	Frag. Arab glaze, NP Scarab impression on clay, F. No. 7246*
253	138	All periods, including Attic and mat glaze	Rhodian, Pls. 52: 5, 53: 10	Ear-ring, Fig. 15	Weight No. 9	Pottery head, Pl. 31: 8
252	501	All periods, including Arab bucchero, mat glaze	hbrn ii, broken ii, doubtful ii Rosette, as Pl. 53: 2	AE arrowhead, Pl. 61: 14	Weight No. 48	—
251	137, 138(2), 399, 499, 506, 575, 582, 672	—	Private, Karmi Yofiyahu, Pl. 47B: 7	Scale armour, Pl. 58: 10 AE fibulae, Pl. 58: 25–27 Coins Nos. 8, 27, 35	LB scarabs, F. Nos. 7243–7244* LB seal, F. No. 7245* Weight No. 32	Beads, Pl. 66: 3, 14, 17, 32 Loom weights, NP
250	138, 560, 562	—	2 doubtful ii	AE arrowhead, Pl. 61: 13 AE ring, fibula, NP	Alabaster dish frag., NP	2 pottery animal heads, NP
249	506, 644, 672, 691	Attic, Cypro-Geometric, LB	Rhodian, Pls. 52: 4, 53: 9	—	—	—
248	649	—	—	—	—	—
247	617†	—	—	—	—	—
235·50 bottom of shaft	68, 254, 280, 649, 673	—	—	—	—	—

* To be published in *Lachish IV*.   † Levels V–IV?

Classified Summary of the Pottery in the Great Shaft

Bowls

Class	Type
B.1	617, 623
B.2	593
B.11	560, 562
B.12	575
B.13	644, 649(2)
B.14	68, 568

Lamps

L.12	137, 138(4)

Jugs

J.8	254, 280

Potstands

Class	Type
PS	399(2)

Cooking Pots

CP	691

Storage Jars

S.8	544
S.10	499, 501(2)
S.13	506(2)

Miscellaneous

Misc.	376, 382, 672, 673(2)

THE ROMAN ROAD

AREA 700

In January, 1937, ten gangs started work in the valley north of the tell, moving south-west from the banks of the Wadi Ghafr in line with the modern track which leads via Tell el-Ḥesi to Gaza from Beit Jibrin (Pl. 10: 5). A tomb of the xviiith dynasty had been found in the region during a previous season, but early caves were often re-used by Roman and Byzantine farmers guarding the crops in the valley. Resting on mizzi limestone, which also occurs at the north-west corner of the tell, the soil washed down by the wadi formed a thick and fertile layer.

However, as soon as the higher ground was reached (210–215 m. above sea level) a line of large stones indicated the position of an exceptionally broad wall, which, when uncovered, seemed to be the foundations of an aqueduct (Pl. 10: 4). Adjoining it to the west was a cambered road, 4 m. wide, which had been surfaced with small pebbles, and a path for pedestrians was marked by a curb of stones on the eastern side of the aqueduct.

J. L. Starkey wrote:

"The Roman road with its parallel water channel or aqueduct, appears to run on south-westward, rising up to the south-west head of the western valley. Here the remains of a large dam are to be seen, known locally as 'the pool of the prophet'. The reservoir above the dam is now completely filled with silt, but one of the oldest inhabitants of Qubeibeh told me before he died, three years ago, that there was a flight of steps leading down to it. This road may well be the main road to the south from the Roman Lachish, referred to by Eusebius in the Onomasticon, as the only other Roman road in our district goes eastward to Duweimah . . . the final stretch of Roman road exposed is shown on the photograph (Pl. 10: 6). At this point it appears to continue on moderately well-preserved for at least 200 yards, or at any rate, large stones which form the basis of the aqueduct, can be seen for this distance. It would seem that the central drainage channel of this valley, as it runs north-east, follows the side of the roadway for some distance, and this is quite consistent with the usual method of Roman road construction, the roads being on the upper levels of a drainage bed, running parallel to it. The same photograph shows the increasing depth of alluvial deposit since Roman times, largely due to the complete deforestation of the surrounding hills."

From the "pool of the prophet" (Birket en-Nebi), where travellers no doubt paused on their way, the Roman and Byzantine settlement of Khirbet Duweir stands on an adjoining spur, 1,100 m. to the south-east. The expedition did not excavate there, but ample evidence of its occupation in that period was obtained from the potsherds.

The position of Khirbet Duweir, therefore, some five English miles as the crow flies from Beit Jibrin, would be in general agreement with the statement made by Eusebius, quoted on p. 39, allowing for the deviations of the road.[1]

The road was no doubt constructed some time after A.D. 200, when Septimus Severus refounded Beit Jibrin under the name of Eleutheropolis, which became the centre of the Shephelah. The coins on its surface show that it was most in use during the fourth century A.D., and the last dated coin extends its existence into the fifth century.

Objects: AE coins, Nos. 2, 34, 41, 45, 51, 54, 55, 57, 63, 66, 76, 78, 80, 83–85, 90, 91, 96, 115, 121, 122 on List of Coins, pp. 412–415.

  AE fibula Pl. 58: 23
  AE bell   Pl. 58: 28

COINS

Mr. J. S. Kirkman was responsible for the cleaning and classification of the coins in the field, and has since prepared the following note and the list given in Appendix B:

"The coins found during the excavations at Tell ed-Duweir, mostly on or near the surface and unassociated with structural remains, show that the site was not completely deserted when it ceased to be the administrative centre. Their interest lies in that

---

[1] Six English miles are equivalent, approximately, to six and a half Roman miles.

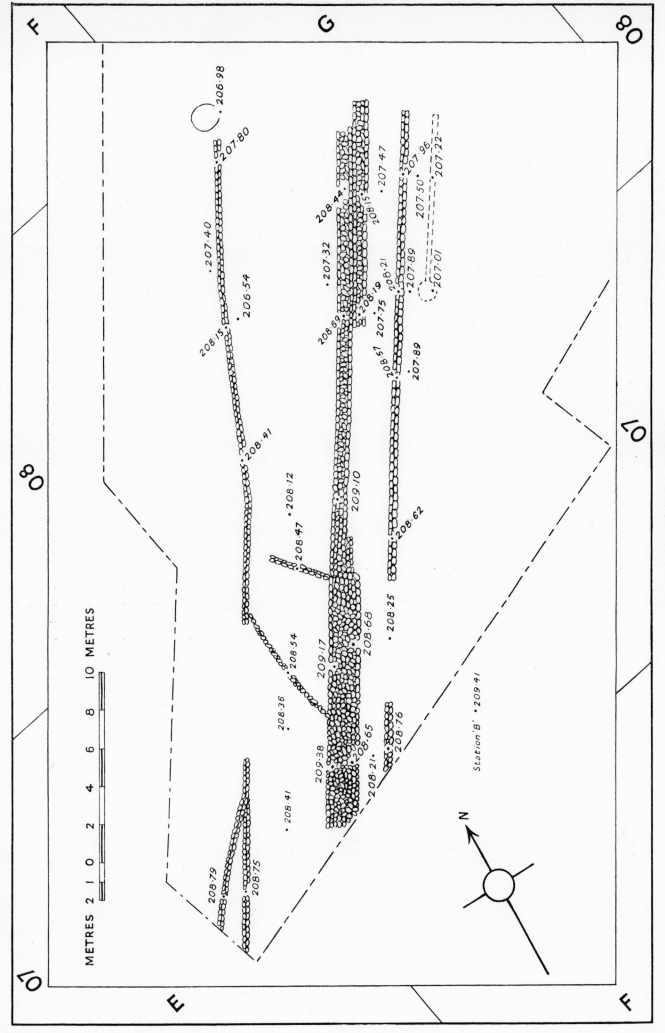

Fig. 17. Plan of the Roman Road

they are a sample of the coins in circulation amongst the cultivators and herdsmen in a southern area of Palestine off the main trade routes.

"The appearance of coins of Macedonia and Side, a small town in Pamphylia, is surprising. They could only have been accepted as currency if any coin, whatever stamp it bore, was accepted, but there is no record that this was a normal trade practice of the Hellenistic world. Their presence is more likely to be due to the passage of soldiers than the passage of commerce, and their acceptance would depend on the degree of persuasion exercised by the individual soldier. No doubt, if there were a large enough supply, some enterprising merchant in Gaza would buy in bulk to sell to the mints in Syria and Egypt. In this connection, it is interesting to note that both Pamphylia and Macedonia were recruiting grounds for the armies of the Seleucids and it is possible that Tell ed-Duweir may have served at times as a camp for soldiers watching the marches against Ptolemy."

In and about the region of the Roman road, Area 700, the majority of the coins were of the fourth century A.D., which gives some additional weight to the identification of the road with that which Eusebius used, at a time when the country enjoyed a fair measure of peace and prosperity, as is also witnessed by the number of fourth century coins in Palestine.

The analysis which follows tells its own story.

Analysis of Coins found on and near the Tell

Fourth century B.C.

B.C.
c. 400	Athenian tetradrachms	3
c. 370	Abdashart of Sidon	2
336–323	Alexander the Great	4
c. 300	City, Side in Pamphylia	1
		10

Third century B.C.–second century B.C.

B.C.	*Ptolemaic*		*Seleucidan*	
285	Ptolemy I, II, III	16	Seleucus I	3
			Antiochus I	1
221	Ptolemy IV	1	Antiochus III	6
175–163			Antiochus IV	2
			Seleucid	1
		17		13

Second century B.C.–first century B.C.

B.C.
166–103	Early Maccabean kings not represented.	
103–76	Alexander Janneaus (expansion of the kingdom) .	2
		2
76–31	Later Maccabean kings and Roman provincial control not represented.	

First century B.C.–first century A.D.

B.C.
63	Palestine under Rome.

	Roman			Herodian	

		Roman				Herodian	

31 B.C.–A.D. 14 Augustus 1

14–37 Tiberius . . . . . 2 Herod Agrippa I 3

41–54 Claudius 1

Tyre

c. 47 Tetradrachm 1

54–68 Nero . . . . . $\frac{3}{7}$ $\overline{4}$

68–138 Revolt against Rome. Capture of Jerusalem in A.D. 70, followed by a century of unrest.

Second century A.D.–third century A.D.

Roman

A.D.

138–161 Antoninus Pius 2

161 Lucius Verus 1

169–181 Titus, Ascalon 1

211–212 Geta, Ascalon 1

222–235 Alexander Severus 1

Roman provincial . . . . . . $\frac{2}{8}$

235–306 Period of unrest and disorder.

Fourth century and fifth century A..

Roman

A.D.

311–325 Licinius I 1

Byzantine

306–337 Constantine I 3

337–340 Constantine II 1

337–361 Constantius II 9

364–375 Valens or Valentian I . . . . . $\frac{5}{19}$

375–395 Period of unrest in the Eastern Empire, see Cambridge Medieval History, Vol. I, p. 263.

Late fourth and early fifth century A.D.

Illegible . . . . $\frac{28}{28}$

Byzantine

A.D.

395–408 Arcadius 2

Barbarous 1

425–455 Valentinian III 1

457–474 Leo I . . . . $\frac{1}{5}$

475–518 Period of unrest. See CMH I, p. 429.

Sixth century A.D.

Byzantine

A.D.

518–527	Justin I	1
533	Belisarius' attack on the Vandals, see CMH I, p. 315.	
578–582	Tiberius II	1
582–602	Maurice Tiberius	2
		4

Seventh century A.D.

Byzantine

A.D.

610–641	Heraclius	1
	Heraclius or Constans II	1
641–668	Constans II	3
	Illegible	1
		6

641   Arab conquest of Egypt.

Ummayad

670	Raqqah	1
	Illegible	1
		2

Eighth century–thirteenth century A.D.

A.D.

750–1258 Period of Abbasid rule in Baghdad.

Fourteenth century A.D.

Mameluk

A.D.

1363	al-Ashraf Shaaban	1
	Illegible	1
		2

Fifteenth century A.D.

Islamic

A.D.

1421	Murad II	1
	Illegible	11
		12

PART III
THE CEMETERIES

GENERAL NOTES

IT is intended to describe in Part III the graves and tombs, pits and caves, cisterns and quarries, houses and other structures containing Iron Age objects which are in the close vicinity of Tell ed-Duweir.

Bronze Age pits re-used

In a district which has been inhabited for so long it is inevitable to find that cuttings made in one period have often been re-used, and the contents are not necessarily contemporary with the construction. The Early Bronze Age people occupied the mound and had some cave dwellings in the north-west suburb beyond the western valley, but they also seem to have used several natural caves at the north-east corner of the mound, and no doubt many others of those to be described were likewise inhabited in that populous period.

Several cuttings show signs of being made in the Middle Bronze Age, but most material of that period is to be found in the north-west suburb, as easily accessible tombs near the mound were soon cleared and re-used for later burials.

Pits and caves made during the Middle and Late Bronze Ages, with a few which were altered later, are as follows:

MB bilobate chambers	MB circular chambers with recesses
107	⌠4002
108, plastered later (?)	⌡4003
117 (?)	4005 (?) (Fig. 29)
218, altered (Fig. 25)	4010
224 (?), entry in 228	4016
230, new entry cut in Iron I	4017
	4031

LB or earlier pits and caves

120, plastered	⌠4002, plastered (Fig. 28)
221	⌡4003, entry
223, altered (Fig. 27)	4012
520	4019, plastered
523	4023, plastered
530, plastered	⌠4024, plastered
553, plastered	⌡4030, entry
569	7005, plastered

Single graves oriented north and south

During the occupation of the Fosse Temple in the fifteenth to thirteenth centuries there were no contemporary tombs within 90 m. of its walls, but after it became a ruin, about 1200 B.C., the area began to be used for burials, and a group of graves were crowded together in the narrow space between the slope of the mound and the east wall of the building. There were also graves to the south of the Fosse Temple, and some later ones encroached within its walls.

The burials divide into two groups: there were twenty-six single oval graves oriented north and south, which subdivide according to the position of the body:

	Head north		Head south			
Face up	Face west	Face ?	Face up	Face west	Unknown	Total
6	3	3	3	1	10	26

Owing to proximity to the surface, the skeletons were broken and friable, and in some cases had disappeared.

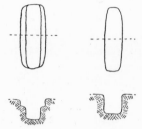

Those which did not conform to the standard position do not contribute much to the question of chronology, for only two graves among them contained pottery. On the whole, the bodies with heads to the south appear to have a slightly earlier trend, but the contents are too meagre to be conclusive.

The classes found in the series range as follows: B.2–7, L.1–3, D.1, 3, 4, 6, 7, 8, J.2, 5, 8 and S.1, 4. Eliminating J.8 and D.8, classes which occur in Graves 160 and 132 only, and appear to fall at the end of the series, contemporary with the central and upper layers of Tomb 1002, the remaining classes appear to belong early in the period represented by the large groups from 218 to 1004, i.e. in the late tenth to early ninth centuries, before the introduction of wheel burnish.

FIG. 18. Typical grave sections, N.–S. series

Single Graves, oriented N–S, near the Fosse Temple

Grave No.	Metres above sea level	Relation to Fosse Temple	Position of Head	Position of Face	Pottery: classes and types			Remarks
110	215·91	93 m. NW.	N.	up	B.3 128 D.6a 329(2)	B.4 20 MA 414 416(2)	D.3 296(2) S.1 476	AE anklets, Pl. 54: 68 AE bangle, NP Plaque, Pl. 45: 135 Seal, Pl. 45: 153 Beads, Pl. 65: 6, 23
132	230·15	20 m. N.	N.	up	B.5 41(2) MP 425	L.1–3 144 S.1 473	D.8 309(3)	View, Pl. 5: 1
137	232·13	25 m. N.	N.	W.		—		—
138	232·25	25·5 m. N.	S.	up		—		—
139	233·90	22·5 m. N.	N.	up		—		260 cm. from surface
147	230·35	above	N.	—	B.4 8 S.4 470	D.6 337 338	D.7 322	View, Pl. 5: 2 AE anklets, Pls. 55: 30 and 36: 58–60
152	230·18	above	N.	—	D.3 285 S.1 476	D.6 337	D.7 322	
154	231·68	above	N.	—	B.4 12 D.1 302	B.6 93 D.7 322		—
159	226·90	20 m. SW.	—	—	B.6 93	J.2 203	D.7 322(2)	—

172

Grave No.	Metres above sea level	Relation to Fosse Temple	Position of Head	Face	Pottery: classes and types			Remarks
160	226·85	25 m. SW.	—	—	B.5 41	B.7 37 48	J.8 281	*Tyt-ymn* scaraboid, dyn. xxii? Pl. 44: 110 2 skeletons
					D.6 337	D.7 322(2) 318	D.8 309	
167	230·57	above	N.	up	J.2 203	D.4 286	D.6 337	—
					D.7 322	S.4 478		
169	233·90	22·5 m. N.	—	—	B.6 91	D.1 298		—
182	230·45	above	—	—	B.7 9	D.1 288 301	S.1 473	View, Pl. 5: 4
189	229·44	12·5 m. S.	N.	up	L.4–6 148	J.2 197	CP 444	AE bracelet, Pl. 55: 31 Spindlewhorl, Pl. 55: 32 Bead, Pl. 66: 14 View, Pl. 5: 6
191	231·94	9 m. E.	—	—	B.2 132	D.3 296	S.1 476	Plaque, Pl. 45: 130, dyn. xxi?
192	232·74	10 m. E.	S.	up	B.4 8			—
193	232·26	9 m. E.	—	—		—		AE bracelets, Pl. 55: 33 Bead, Pl. 67: 129
194	232·21	17 m. SE.	S.	up	J.5 192	D.1 289		Fish back seal, Pl. 45: 132 Fe bracelet, NP View, Pl. 5: 7
195	231·30	20 m. SE.	—	—		—		—
196	232·16	15 m. SE.	N.	up	B.2 104	Misc. 334		—
197	232·08	12·5 m. E.	N.	up	B.4 14			—
198	232·10	10 m. E.	—	—		—		—
222	217·48	92 m. NW.	S.	W.		—		—
229	216·30	92·5 m. NW.	—	—	B.4 20	J.2 203(2)	D.3 296	—

Single Graves, oriented N-S, near the Fosse Temple (*cont.*)

Grave No.	Metres above sea level	Relation to Fosse Temple	Position of Head	Face	Pottery: classes and types	Remarks
231	233·80	12·5 m. E.	—	—	D.7 315	—
236	232·98	12·5 m. E.	N.	W.	—	AE bracelet, Pl. 56: 17
239	232·98	12·5 m. E.	N.	W.	D.1 302	—

An isolated grave, 518, close to the city gate, is also oriented north and south.

Comparisons may be made with Megiddo, Tomb 37 B (MT, p. 77), Tomb 62 (op. cit., p. 119) and Tomb 950 (op. cit., p. 134).

Single graves oriented east and west

The second group near the Fosse Temple consists of five graves which are consistently oriented east and west (Pl. 5: 3–5):

Grave No.	Metres above sea level	Relation to Fosse Temple	Position of Head	Face	Pottery: Classes and types	Remarks
180	230·67	3 m. S.	W.	up	—	Over 182 at 230·45 m.
183	230·83	6 m. S.	W.	—	J.8 255	—
184	230·45	10 m. S.	W.	S.	J.8 255	Over 189 at 229·44 m.
185	230·39	15 m. S.	—	—	—	—
186	230·75	16·5 m. S.	—	—	—	—

Isolated graves oriented east and west in other areas which may be comparable are 525, 4007 and 4027, with the loci 4026 and 4015. Grave 519 was oriented north-west to south-east.

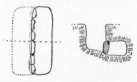

FIG. 20. Typical grave section E.–W. series

Comparisons may be made with Megiddo, Tomb 37 C.1 (MT, p. 77), Tomb 37 D (MT, p. 79), Tomb 17 (MT, p. 117), Tomb 232 (MT, p. 132), Tomb 236 (MT, p. 133) and Tomb 857 (MT, p. 134).

Iron Age tomb chambers

Only nine tombs were apparently cut during the Iron Age without any later alterations. In suggested order of development, they are Tombs 521, 6006 (Fig. 31), 116, 219 (Fig. 26), 105 and 106 (Fig. 21), 109 (Fig. 22) and 114, and 217 (Fig. 23).

Caves or pits cut in earlier times, to which structural alterations were made during the Iron Age, were Tombs 120, 218 and 223; they will be considered with the series.

The shape of Tomb 1002, which contained the largest deposit of pottery, was so much denuded that only a pit with no trace of a dromos remained. If it were an original Iron Age construction, it may have been similar to Tomb 1 at 'Ain Shems, where the main room and two subsidiary alcoves were circular, with a ventilation shaft in the roof (APEF II, Pl. IV). Assuming that neither of these tombs was cut before the Iron Age, they would seem to represent the earliest phase of development.

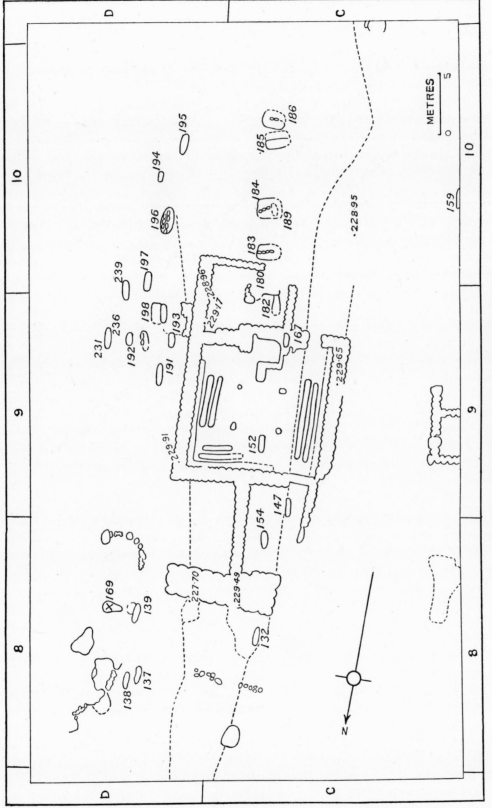

FIG. 19. Single graves around site of the Fosse Temple

175

The first approach to a rectangular tomb shape is to be found in Tomb 521. Cut on the edge of the isthmus which joins the site of the city to the southern plain, Tomb 521 was approached by a small shaft or pit to the east. The doorway leading to the chamber was just large enough to admit a recumbent body through a circular aperture. Inside, a rectangular chamber, 5×3 m. square, had been hewn from the rock, leaving a bench along the north side and a narrower ledge opposite. The cutting of the roof and walls was extremely casual, leaving jagged blocks and unfinished angles everywhere (Pl. 8: 1–3).

In contrast, Tomb 6006 (Fig. 31) was very well and accurately made, showing a marked improvement in construction. Five steps led to a doorway a metre high, and inside was a chamber about 3 m. square, with benches on the north and west sides.

Tombs 6006 and 521 were the only ones in the series which were entered from the east, but it is not possible to say whether the east–west axis was merely due to the exigencies of the ground or whether it was a deliberate choice.

Tomb 116 also consisted of a single chamber about 3 m. square, and the entrance to it had been cut in the south wall of a pit of much earlier construction. As in all the tombs in the 100–200 cemeteries, access was obtained from the north-west or west.

Adapted for re-use during the Iron Age, Tombs 223, 218 and 120 are much larger and less regular in cutting. Tomb 223 measures 5 m. across, and Tombs 218 and 120 are more than 6 m. Moreover, with the increase in size, there was an attempt to divide the space into three chambers, contrived partly by cutting into the rock, and partly by building rough stone walls.

A notable addition to the plan in each case was the provision on the east side of a circular repository which was no deeper than the floor of the adjoining chamber.

Tomb 219 conforms to the same plan of three rooms, but later quarrying may have removed some features, including the repository.

Tombs 105 and 106 were constructed side by side at the same time, and are the most elaborate and well-made burial-places at the site. Each had three rooms divided from one another by doorways of normal height, though entry was obtained through a passage and open court which led to a square-blocked aperture large enough to admit a body. Around the sides of each room, which averaged between 2 and 3 m. square, there were benches, and four circular repositories were associated with the group (marked "Well" on Fig. 21).

Tombs 109 and 114 formed part of a similar unit to the north, but their plans were largely destroyed by quarries and denudation.

Tomb 217 (Fig. 23) adheres to the principle of three rooms and an eastern repository, though the rooms are not much more than 2 m. square, and the construction of the walls and benches is poor and irregular.

The series divides, therefore, into two groups: single rectangular chambers without additions, and triple-chambered tombs with repositories on the east side.

Comparisons

The reasons which have reduced the list of true Iron Age tombs at the site contribute to the scarcity of comparisons elsewhere.

The tomb at Ez-Zahiriyye (QDAP IV, p. 109) consists of three interconnecting rectangular chambers, but has no repository.

Tomb 5 at Tell en-Naṣbeh (TN I, Fig. 8) consists of two rooms approached from a court, all on the same axis, and there is no repository. The contents are contemporary with the upper layers of Tomb 1002, and a "beehive" jar (TN II, Pl. 76: 1753) is matched by fragments of a similar vessel from Level III (type 408). Tomb 3 at the same site (TN I, Fig. 11) consisted of a single rectangular chamber, 4×3 m. square, with two small recesses—possibly the prototype of a repository. The contents of the tomb included two fully developed decanters, which would place the group very close in date to Tomb 106.

The closest parallels are to be found at 'Ain Shems, Tombs 2 and 3 (APEF II, Pls. V–VI). Both tombs are approximately 3·5 m. square with a pit or repository at the south-west corner and benches around three sides. The earliest pottery from the pit includes an archaic type of decanter (op. cit., Pl. XXXIII) and lamps with a high foot, indicating a date in the seventh century. See also Tomb 14, dated to the sixth century (AS I, p. 10, AS V, p. 77).

Tombs 5–9 at 'Ain Shems, disposed around a central court (op. cit., Pl. VII), conform individually to the same plan and dimensions. Here again the contents are similar to those of Tomb 106.

A characteristic of all the comparisons named is the square entry at the base of a vertical hewn façade, approached from a forecourt open to the sky.

In conclusion it may be inferred that a single chamber, longer than it was broad, gave place to rooms between 3 and 4 m. square, which were later made in groups of three. The pit repository seems to have been a seventh-century addition.

Industrial and domestic constructions

Rooms and areas	Cisterns	
118 in B.8	215 in B.5	558 in AA.25/26
169 in D.8	225 in A.6	1009 in C.27
227 in AA.6	509 in C.24	1010 in C.27
505 in D.25	562 in C.26	4021 in U.4
506 deposit in B.25	1001 in G.14	4029 in U.3
511 in E.26	7007 well, unfinished in J.28	6003 in U.4
522 deposit in B.25	7008 in J.28	6004 in U.4
534 in A.24		6010 in U.4
535 in AB.22/23	*Pits and caves*	6011 in U.4
540 in C.22	102 in B.5	6015 in U.4
544 furnace in AA.23	104 in B.5	6020 not marked on plan
545 trough in A.24	126 in C.7	7010 in J.25
546 in AA.24	503 in B.22	
560 in C.25	504 in C/D.24/25	
566 furnace in B.26	507 in C.23	*Quarries*
4028 troughs in V.3	513 in B.21	220 in A.4
6012 in U.4	515 in AA.23	4006 in T.2
6022 in U.5	517 in A.24	4025 in S.3
6023 in U.4	520 in AA.22	4032 in T.3
6024 in U.5	526 in A.24	4035 in T.1
7002 in F.26	529 in A.24	6021 in P.4
7013 in K.26	531 in AB.23	7001 in E.25

CHAPTER 7

AREAS 100, 200

(PLS. 1: 1, 108, 125)

EXCAVATION areas 200 and 100 were contiguous and extended from the north-west corner of the mound in a southerly direction. They were bounded on the east by the line of the lower stone revetment more than half-way up the tell slope. The northern limit included the collapsed cavern 101 at the north-west corner (Grid Square D.5, Pl. 125) and the southern boundary merged into the adjoining areas 300 and 400, which led towards the crest of the isthmus joining the tell to the plateau where Cemetery 500 was situated. The western confine followed an arbitrary boundary (shown by a dotted line on Pl. 125) along the valley bed, where the basic rock was Eocene limestone covered by only a shallow deposit of alluvial soil.

As the rock rose towards the tell, in the 100 and 200 areas, the soft howr limestone was found to be honey-combed with tomb chambers of the Middle and Late Bronze Ages, and this stratum continued until the harder nari capping of the plateau and tell promontory was reached. The southern end of Area 100, with the adjoining sections 300 and 400, were curiously devoid of tombs, despite the fact that the rock was of the type usually preferred by tomb diggers.

Throughout the excavation of the western slopes, which was continued at intervals during the entire campaign, the system of digging was to proceed forward and up towards the mound, throwing the soil behind and using the loose stones removed to build retaining walls at suitable intervals, following the contours of the slope. In this way four terraces were made, and the soil between them was left clear for cultivation by the landowners.

101 Collapsed cavern in Grid Square D.5 (Pl. 3: 1)

The entrance to this large cave was partly open when the site was visited by J. L. Starkey and members of the Expedition in 1932. Its position at the base of the slope on the north-west corner was both inconvenient and interesting, for it was necessary to explore it before the area could be used as a dumping ground, and speculation as to its purpose was varied.

Starkey thought it might mark the site of the isolated tower drawn on the lower part of the Lachish Reliefs (see Frontispiece), guarding, perhaps, a secret way into the city, but he soon discarded this theory owing to the position of the cave. He then began to test a second possibility that the cave was part of the valley drainage system, serving as a reservoir for water collected from the Middle Bronze Age fosse.

The apparently large dimensions of the cave made it impracticable to remove the whole filling until some indication of its purpose had been obtained, and it was decided to drive a 15-m. trench along the central axis towards the far wall and to dig down in search of the rock floor. Before this could be done it was necessary to remove the collapsed roof, which consisted of a mizzi stratum which outcropped at the north-west corner. Mizzi is a hard-quality limestone much sought after in early Christian times to make grindstones for mills and presses, and the illustration on Pl. 3: 1 shows a circular block for the purpose partially detached. As a result of extensive quarrying, the roof of the cavern had been weakened, and once the hard covering was removed, the softer under-lying howr was ready to fall. Roman potsherds of the fourth to fifth centuries A.D., found beneath the large blocks of mizzi which had formed the façade and roof of the cave, show that the roof survived intact until that date.

Once the fallen blocks had been removed by blasting, a trench was driven through to the back of the cave and the filling was dug out to a depth of 8·5 m. A shaft was then sunk through the remaining deposit, and floor level was established after a descent of nearly 18 m.

A second examination shaft was driven down against the back wall of the cavern which sloped inwards towards the tell and where clear traces of Roman quarrying were seen. It appeared, from indications at the base

178

of the shaft, that the rock piers originally supporting the roof had been cut away after the lower levels of the central area of the cavern had been partly filled up with limestone debris.

Starkey found it difficult to explain the need for a large quarry in so late a period, owing to the scarcity of Byzantine remains in the locality. The soft howr is never used for making lime in modern times, but it is very suitable for barrel vaulting, owing to its lightness, and it was used for that purpose both in the Residency and in the modern "fellah" houses of Qubeibeh. In any case, the cave was cut or enlarged at an earlier period and remained in use for varying purposes for many centuries. The possibility that it formed part of the Bronze Age drainage system will be discussed in *Lachish IV*, and the presence of Late Bronze Age potsherds covered by some tons of fallen roof suggest that it is at least as old as that period. At a later time it was in use as a dwelling or stable, for the remains of partition walls were found at approximately the present ground level.

102 Pit in Grid Square B.5 — c. 1500–1200 B.C. Re-used c. 925–900 B.C.

Contents disturbed and robbed. Pilgrim flask 430 was found high in the filling, and bowl form 594 was drawn from a sherd. See Grave 110, cut in the filling of this pit.

Pottery: PF   B.2
      430, 594

103 Tomb in Grid Square B.5 — Cut c. 700–600 B.C. Re-used.

The original chamber type was no doubt similar to Tombs 105 and 106, but the roof had collapsed, and the chamber was cleared and enlarged for conversion to a dwelling in the second century A.D. (as indicated by ribbed water jar 505). The roof at that time was supported on limestone pilasters, the lower courses of which are visible on Pl. 3: 2. Note the mastaba in right foreground and the entrance to an inner chamber, part of the original tomb, before excavation. There was no trace of an outer entrance.

Pottery: S.13
      505

104 Lime kiln in Grid Square B.5 — ?

Contained sherds of mixed periods, chiefly Roman.

105 Tomb in Grid Square B.6 — 700–600 B.C.

A triple-chambered complex parallel and similar to Tomb 106. The contents had been removed anciently, and from the congestion in Tomb 106 it may be suggested that the contents had been placed there.

106 Tomb in Grid Square B.6 (Fig. 21) — c. 670–580 B.C. Fourth century A.D. intrusions.

A triple-chambered tomb parallel and similar to Tomb 105. The outer court was open to the sky and one course of limestone blocks bisected the courtyard (Pl. 3: 3). The low rectangular entrance was partially blocked with a sealing of mud and stones, but the bottom courses had been removed to introduce the latest burials. On clearance of the sealing, the upper layer of the contents of the outer chamber became visible, as the tomb was not completely filled with debris.

Inside the entrance to the north-west were two rock-cut steps and to the north of the door was a bench cut in the rock (Pl. 3: 5). Access to the inner chamber was gained by a well-cut doorway of normal height (Pl. 3: 4) and the inner room was also provided with benches on three sides. In the north-east corner there was a circular repository some 60 cm. in depth (Pl. 3: 6).

The third room was approached through a doorway in the south wall of the outer chamber; it was similar in plan to the inner chamber and was provided with a repository on the east side.

The mass of human remains in the three rooms had been turned over many times, but some twenty-five skulls were noted, though it was not possible to preserve them.

Date and Comparisons

Burials in Tomb 106 were made in two periods, the seventh to sixth centuries B.C., possibly extending into the fifth century, and the third to fourth centuries A.D.

The main occupation, however, is the earlier one, which falls between those of Houses III and II. The tomb may have come into use before the destruction of Level III and the closure of Tomb 1002, but there is no pottery which suggests that burials other than those of the Byzantine period were made in Tomb 106 after the destruction of Level II.

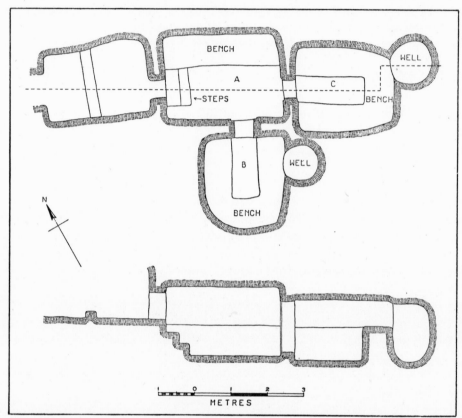

FIG. 21. Tomb 106

The orderly plan and careful cutting of the tomb compares closely with the series at 'Ain Shems, described in the General Notes at the beginning of this Part. The method of sealing was presumably analogous to that of Tomb 14 at 'Ain Shems, where there was a stone slab near by and a cylindrical stone to block the square rebated entry. In Tomb 106 these were no doubt removed when the Byzantine burials were inserted, and the entry was re-blocked with mud and stones.

Pottery types in common with those in the series at 'Ain Shems are numerous and close, though references are only tentative as there are photographs, but no drawings, in Mackenzie's publication (APEF II). Contact with Tomb 14 is not so near, and it is clear that it contained burials of a later phase in the sixth century. The lamps published in AS IV, Pl. XLVIII: 7, 8, 12 belong to Classes L.4–6 and L.9 in the Duweir classification, and there are also comparisons among the dippers (AS IV, Pl. XLVIII: 5, 11). The later tendency of that group is seen in the fragments in AS IV, Pl. LXVIII, which includes jar rims in Class S.6 and a cooking pot with flared neck (AS IV, Pl. LXVIII: 23) which occurs also in Houses II and I at Tell ed-Duweir.

Two bottles, types 383 and 384, classified under Miscellaneous, were found in the innermost Room C, and are decorated with rings of brownish-red paint. The late Mrs. E. Henschel-Simon referred to them in her Note

180

on the Pottery of the 'Amman Tombs (QDAP XI, p. 76) and classed them with the bulky forms of Iron Age II. Both the Duweir bottles appear to be later in form and decoration than those from 'Amman, an observation in accordance with the earlier trend of that group, where there are no disk-based or footed lamps, and where the collection of jugs is comparable to those in Tomb 1002.

Bottles like those from 'Amman are more common from the Iron Age tomb at Sahab (QDAP XIII, p. 98: 31–37, 42, 43) where six disk-based lamps and one footed lamp occur with round-based lamps, which are still in the majority. The series from the Adoni Nur Tomb (APEF VI, in preparation) confirms Mrs. Henschel-Simon's deductions which place the debased bottles with little decoration and no burnish at Tell ed-Duweir toward the end of the seventh century.

Further support for a date *c.* 600 B.C. is afforded by the decanters (QDAP XI, p. 71: 28, 29; XIII, p. 100: 56–58). There is a total of five in both these groups, whereas in Tomb 106 there are five times that number.

In establishing the range of Tomb 106, the largest proportion of heavy-based lamps in Classes L.9–10 would seem to place the main phase of burial after the homogeneous Adoni Nur group at 'Amman, dated to the middle of the seventh century, where nearly all the lamps had a low disk base. No specimens with a heavy foot were found.

The pottery figurines are mostly from the innermost Room C, where there is one pillar-base figurine with a woman's head, poorly moulded, and two with beak faces. They may be attributed to the early half of the seventh century from their position in Room C, which would agree with a date before Josiah's reforms in 640 B.C., from which time the manufacture of human figurines was officially discouraged.

The contemporary scarabs and scaraboids are poorly cut and degraded in design, and they are, on the average, smaller than those in any other group except the ossuary 120. At least two appear to be survivals from the Middle Bronze Age (Pl. 43: 21 and Pl. 45: 157), while a seal and a cylinder are close to Late Bronze Age models (Pl. 45: 138, 155). The only scarab which might contain a royal name of a Delta kinglet ruling in the xxvth dynasty is on Pl. 43: 36.

Of the metal work which may be attributed to the main period of burial in the seventh to sixth centuries, bronze and silver ear-rings with ball drops (Pl. 54: 1, 5) are comparable to one found at Megiddo, Stratum III (M. I, Pl. 86: 21), and similar ear-rings are common in Tomb 1 at 'Ain Shems, and are placed at level GA 185 ft. at Tell Jemmeh (Gerar, Pl. I: 4). Pl. 54: 6 is a variety duplicated at Gerar, at level AW 200 ft., and in the graves at 'Athlit (QDAP II, Pl. XXIV: 617). In that same Tomb 21 B at 'Athlit there is a fibula (QDAP II, Pl. XXIV: 613), which is like those shown on Pl. 54: 40, and in Grave L 12 (QDAP II, p. 65, Fig. 23) there is a bronze buckle which compares with the iron ones on Pl. 54: 17, 18.[1] In Déchelette's Manuel IV, Fig. 540, similar annular fibulae are shown as characteristic of the second Iron Age in Iberia, from 500 B.C. to the Christian era, which would place the Palestinian examples in reasonable context. It may, however, be preferable to allow for a time-lag, and to place the iron fibulae from Duweir with the later phase of burial.

The pottery and objects of the third to fourth centuries A.D. have been divided from the contents of the earlier burials whenever possible; they are presented in a separate schedule.

Most of these objects which can definitely be attributed to the later period came from the topmost layers of Rooms A and B, and Room A, at least, was filled with earth and objects to within a metre of the roof.

The glass unguentarium was the only object in Room C which does not appear to belong to the earlier phase of burial; its nearest neighbours in the deposit were the decorated bottles, types 383 and 384. D. B. Harden considers the unguentarium typical of the third to fourth century A.D.; for his notes and the comparisons, see p. 399.

Pottery

Owing to the disturbed condition of the burials, the record of stratification is not entirely reliable, but an analysis of the frequency of common forms found in the three rooms and the repositories does suggest that the inner deposits are the earliest.

---

[1] C. N. Johns would attribute the buckle from 'Athlit to the medieval period.

The earlier tendency of the contents of Room C is well illustrated by the figures for lamp types 148 and 152, where the number of round bases equals the total found in Rooms A and B, while the number of flat bases in Room C is a quarter of the combined totals for the two later rooms.

The same trend is seen in the decanters, where examples of earlier forms 279, 280, 281 occur in Rooms B and C, while the late type 275 is represented by eighteen examples in Rooms A and B as against two in Room C.

The forms are, on the whole, mass-produced, and more uniform in size and finish than in previous groups. Quality and variety give place to quantity.

The ware is very different in colour and consistency. It is hard buff or pink, unevenly fired, so that the surface varies in colour from cream to deep red. The grits used are large and uneven in size. Slip, when it has been applied, is rather thick and creamy in colour and consistency. These remarks apply to the bowls and jugs, especially the decanters in Class J.8 and the majority of the dippers in Classes D.4 and D.5.

Bowls

Class	Types	Total
B.4	17	1
B.6	89, 95(6)	7
B.7	37(3), 39(2), 48(3), 49, 51(5)	14
B.9	5, 31, 33(2), 34, 106, 107	7
B.10	35, 36	2
B.11	63, 64(10), 65, 66, 80	14
B.12	16, 45(5)	6
B.13	69(2), 70(9), 71, 72, 73(5), 75(2)	20
		71

Analysis of Burnish

HAND BURNISHED				WHEEL BURNISH		PLAIN		WORN AND UNDEFINED	
In. and to keel out.		*In. only and transitional*		*Spiral on red slip or self*					
Class	Type	Class	Type	Class	Type	Class	Type	Class	Type
								B.4	17*
						B.6	89	B.6	95(5)*
							95		
				B.7	37			B.7	37(2)
					39				39
					48(2)				48
					49				
									51(5)
B.9	5			B.9	33	B.9	106	B.9	31
					34		107		33
				B.10	36	B.10	35		
				B.11	64(3)				
					65			B.11	63*
									64(7)*
									66
									80
						B.12	45(2)	B.12	16*
									45(3)
		B.13	73	B.13	69(2)	B.13	72	B.13	70(5)
					70(4)				73(3)
					71				75(2)
					73				
TOTALS	1		1		20		8		41

* Pink, buff. Red slip in., no bur.

Bowl classes 7, 11 and 13 are the most common in the group. The bowls tend to be larger than those in earlier tombs and classes; some range from 22 to 26 cm. in diameter, and 12 to 14 cm. is an average size. The proportion of disk to ring bases is approximately 2:1.

Lamps

Class	Types	Total
L.1–3	144(10)	10
L.4–6	148(18)	18
L.7–8	149(2), 150(10), 151(33)	45
L.9–10	152(62), 153(28)	90
		163

The four main classes of Iron Age lamps are all represented in Tomb 106, though it is instructive to note how the proportions of later groups increase. The semi-disk-based lamps are only half as numerous as the footed lamps, and it is these which are characteristic of the tomb. The ware is also distinctive, a soft paste, almost orange in tone, with a powdery surface and some uneven-sized grits. The thick solid base was rapidly cut from the wheel while still in motion, leaving a whirl, and no attempt was made to trim or finish it. (See Chapter 9, p. 283).

Jugs

Class	Types	Total	Class	Types	Total
J.2	201, 205, 206, 207	4	J.7a	261(2), 269(4)	6
J.3	210, 211, 218(4)	6	J.7b	243, 248, 353	3
J.4	178, 180, 187(13)	15	J.8	275(20), 279, 280(2), 281(2)	25
J.5	190, 191	2	J.9	193(2), 194(4), 198, 199(2)	9
J.6	230, 235, 242	3			73

Jugs classes 2, 3 and 5 are only sparsely represented in Tomb 106. Round-bottomed jugs with plain rims (J.4) are more numerous than jugs with moulded rims (J.5), and the ridge-necked jugs (J.7a or b) have passed their zenith both in quantity and quality. Jugs in classes 4 and 5 tend to be slightly larger than those in Tomb 1002.

It is in Tomb 106 that "decanters" (J.8) became popular, ranging from the archaic forms 280 and 281 to the more developed angular-shaped 275. Kelso and Thorley have already noted the apparent use of standard sizes in decanters at Tell Beit Mirsim (AASOR XXI–XXII, § 124), but there are not enough examples from Tomb 106 available in London to provide more detailed estimates of size and capacity. Those examined range from 17 to 21 cm. in height.

The ware is described under the general notes above; except for the archaic type 280, the surface was usually burnished, either with or without a slip. The lines were usually vertical on the neck and horizontal round the body, and rather closely spaced. Though 280 usually had an oval or ridged handle, the ribbon variety was more common on later types.

Red jugs (Class J.9) confined to Tomb 106 were found in all chambers, but the distribution suggests that they were less popular in its final phase.

Dippers and Juglets

Class	Types	Total
D.2b	305	1
D.4a	286(3)	3
D.4b	283(37)	37
D.5b	292(10)	10
D.6b	331, 410, 411	3
D.8	309(47), 310(9), 311(14), 312(2), 313, 320(8), 321(4)	85
		139

D.4 and D.5 are the best represented classes of elongated dippers. The ware is described above in the general notes (see also Chapter 9, p. 296). Nearly all the examples examined in London are vertically burnished either on the plain surface or on a creamy buff slip. The dippers range from 11·5 to 14·5 cm. in height.

There are no true Cypriote wares in Tomb 106, but there are certain derived forms which attempt to imitate them (see Chapter 9, Class D.6b, pp. 300, 301).

Black burnished juglets, Class D.7, are missing from the tomb, and Class D.8, with handle joining the rim has replaced them. The average height is 6·5 to 7·5 cm., and occasionally there is a pinkish example. The surface seldom shows signs of slip or burnish, but in most cases it is worn, friable and pocked.

Miniature Pithoi

Class	Types	Total
MP	424, 425, 426	3

Pilgrim Flasks

Class	Type	Total
PF	430	1

Cooking Pots

Class	Types	Total
CP	443, 445(2), 449(4), 452, 458(3), 462(3)	14

Few cooking pots were found in proportion to the total amount of pottery in the tomb. The deep pot was more common than the shallow variety, and the ridged neck was usual.

Storage Jars

Class	Type	Total
S.6a	485	1

Jugs or Jars with Spouts

Class	Type	Total
JS	360	1

Miscellaneous

Class	Types	Total
Misc.	127, 366, 383, 384, 388	5

Distribution of Pottery in Tomb 106

Type	Class	Room A	Room B	Room C	Total
5*	B.9	—	1	—	1
16*	B.12	1	—	—	1
17*	B.4	—	—	1	1
31	B.9	—	1	—	1
33*	B.9	1	—	—	1
34	B.9	—	1	—	1
35	B.10	1	—	—	1
36	B.10	1	—	—	1
37*	B.7	1	1	1	3
39	B.7	1	—	1	2
45	B.12	4	1	—	5
48*	B.7	1	2	—	3
49*	B.7	—	1	—	1
51	B.7	2	1	2	5
63	B.11	—	—	1	1

Type	Class	Room A	Room B	Room C	Total
64	B.11	2	4	4	10
65	B.11	—	1	—	1
66	B.11	—	—	1	1
69	B.13	—	—	2	2
70	B.13	7	1	1	9
71*	B.13	—	1	—	1
72*	B.13	—	—	1	1
73*	B.13	1	3	1	5
75	B.13	—	2	—	2
80*	B.11	1	—	—	1
89	B.6	1	—	—	1
95	B.6	2	1	3	6
106*	B.9	1	—	—	1
107	B.9	—	1	—	1
127*	Misc.	—	1	—	1
144*	L.1–3	3	2	5	10
148*	L.4–6	6	3	9	18
149*	L.7–8	—	2	—	2
150*	L.7–8	—	3	7	10
151*	L.7–8	15	7	11	33
152*	L.9–10	24	26	12	62
153	L.9–10	8	10	10	28
178*	J.4	—	—	1	1
180*	J.4	1	—	—	1
187*	J.4	4	6	3	13
190*	J.5	—	1	—	1
191*	J.5	1	—	—	1
193*	J.9	1	—	1	2
194*	J.9	1	2	1	4
198	J.9	—	—	1	1
199	J.9	—	1	1	2
201	J.2	1	—	—	1
205	J.2	—	1	—	1
206*	J.2	1	—	—	1
207*	J.2	1	—	—	1
210	J.3	—	—	1	1
211	J.3	—	1	—	1
218*	J.3	—	4	—	4
230	J.6	—	1	—	1
235	J.6	—	1	—	1
242	J.6	—	—	1	1
243*	J.7b	—	1	—	1
248*	J.7b	1	—	—	1
261*	J.7a	1	1	—	2
269*	J.7a	1	2	1	4
275*	J.8	6	12	2	20
279	J.8	—	1	—	1
280	J.8	—	1	1	2
281	J.8	—	1	1	2
283	D.4b	17	8	12	37
286*	D.4a	2	1	—	3
292	D.5b	—	10	—	10

Distribution of Pottery in Tomb 106 (*cont.*)

Type	Class	Room A	Room B	Room C	Total
305	D.2b	—	—	1	1
309	D.8	19	26	2	47
310*	D.8	—	—	9	9
311	D.8	5	3	6	14
312*	D.8	1	1	—	2
313	D.8	1	—	—	1
320	D.8	6	1	1	8
321	D.8	4	—	—	4
331*	D.6b	—	1	—	1
353	J.7b	1	—	—	1
360	JS	—	—	1	1
366	Misc.	—	—	1	1
383	Misc.	—	—	1	1
384	Misc.	—	—	1	1
388	Misc.	—	—	1	1
410*	D.6b	1	—	—	1
411	D.6b	—	—	1	1
424	MP	—	—	1	1
425*	MP	—	—	1	1
426*	MP	—	1	—	1
430	PF	—	1	—	1
443	CP	1	—	—	1
445*	CP	—	1	1	2
449*	CP	1	1	2	4
452*	CP	—	1	—	1
458*	CP	2	—	1	3
462	CP	—	3	—	3
485	S.6a	—	1	—	1

* See Pl. 75.

Distribution of Objects in Tomb 106

	Room A	Room B	Room C
Pottery figurines	Pl. 27: 2, 6 F. No. 114 NP, cf. Pl. 29: 20	—	Pl. 27: 1, 3, 4, 5, 7
Amulets	Pl. 34: 1 F. No. 321, head of Mut, NP	Pl. 34: 2	F. No. 345 NP, cf. Pl. 36: 51
Scarabs, scaraboids and seals	Pl. 44: 109 Pl. 45: 137, 158 (and Pl. 54: 43) F. Nos. 324, 373, 375, all paste, illegible, NP F. No. 375, carnelian, plain, (Colt) NP	Pl. 43: 58 Pl. 45: 157, 171	Pl. 43: 21
Metal	Fe tweezers Pl. 54: 27 Fe nail Pl. 54: 33 Fe chisel Pl. 54: 34 Fe knives Pl. 54: 30, 45 Fe arrowheads Pl. 54: 47–52	AE fibula (2 ex.) Pl. 54: 40	Fe knives Pl. 54: 29, 31, 44 Fe arrowheads Pl. 54: 46, 53
Stone	Spindlewhorl Pl. 54: 42		

The following objects were found in the tomb filling:

Scarabs, scaraboids and seals: Pl. 43: 19, 36
　　　　　　　　　　　　　　　Pl. 44: 78
　　　　　　　　　　　　　　　Pl. 45: 129, 138, 139, 145, 154, 155, 168
　　　　　　　　　　　　　　　Pl. 54: 15, 43

Metal: AE, AR ear-rings　Pl. 54: 1, 5, 6, 8, 9
　　　　AE rings　　　　　Pl. 54: 11, 12
　　　　Fe arrowheads　　Pl. 54: 51

Beads: Pl. 66: 1, 2, 6, 8, 13, 14, 17, 21, 22, 47, 48, 51–54, 58, 60, 62, 63, 75, 78, 80, 82, 85, 86
　　　　Pl. 67: 98, 99, 100, 101, 103, 104, 118, 140, 141

Pottery and Objects attributed to Intrusive Burials

	Room A		*Room B*		*Room C*	
Pottery	Base of ribbed water jar, F. No. 3 NP Lamp 135		—		—	
Metal	AR, AE ear-rings	Pl. 54: 2, 3, 7	AE ear-ring Gs bead on	Pl. 54: 4	—	
	Fe ring bezel	Pl. 54: 14	Fe chain	Pl. 54: 10		
	AE bell	Pl. 54: 19	Fe buckle	Pl. 54: 18		
	AE bangles	Pl. 54: 16, 21–26	AE ring	Pl. 54: 20		
			AE pin	Pl. 54: 32		
	AE sheath	Pl. 54: 35	Fe bird	Pl. 54: 41		
			Fe knife	Pl. 54: 28		
Bone	Plaque	Pl. 54: 55	Inlays	Pl. 54: 36, 37, 39	—	
	Fish hook	Pl. 54: 38	Plaque	Pl. 54: 56		
Glass	—		Vase	Pl. 54: 54	Unguentarium	Pl. 40: 2

The following objects from the tomb filling are also attributed to the intrusive burials:

Metal: AR ring bezel　Pl. 54: 13
　　　　Fe buckle　　　Pl. 54: 17

Beads: Pl. 66: 87

　　　　Pl. 67: 94

Coins: 3 AE pierced coins, F. Nos. 352–354, NP

107 Tomb in Grid Square A.6, re-used as an ossuary, adjoining and above Tomb 120	MB bilobate chamber. Burials c. 900 B.C. (?) Bone deposits, 700–600 B.C.

The roof of this chamber, like that of Tomb 120, had collapsed, and entry to it was obtained through the hole. Inside was a mass of charred animal bones, mostly pig (see Appendix A), overlaying a quantity of human remains (Risdon, Nos. 148–172, 477–498, 646–654, 676, 686, 689, 691, 692, 704–706, 730, 731). These had all been thrown in through the hole in the roof and no order was observable; juglet 171 was actually inside a skull. The apex of the pile of bones was about 1 m. above the floor level, and the height of the roof was 2 m. from the floor.

The pottery is similar in character to that of the main ossuary group 120, and as in that group, there seem to be two phases of use. The earlier phase, probably associated with normal burials in the cave, is represented by the dippers in Classes D.1 and D.2, the scarabs, faience amulets and some of the metal ornaments, all of which are typical of Tomb 218. That such objects cannot extend to the period of the ossuary deposit seems clear from the absence of Sekhmet and scarcity of Isis amulets from the intervening Tomb 1002.

Pottery: B.7 B.11 J.4   J.6 D.4b D.2a D.1b D.8 D.7a   D.7b   Misc.
       37, 64,* 171,* 245, 283, 287,* 300, 309, 317(3), 322(5), 357*

        * See Pl. 76: 1, 6, 10, 14.

Objects:	Pottery animal vase	F. No. 383 (Colt) NP	AE and AR ear-rings	Pl. 54: 58
	Amulets	Pl. 34: 3–6	AR ring	Pl. 54: 59
	Amulet, Bes	F. No. 418 (Colt) NP	Fe bezel	Pl. 54: 60
	Amulets, Uzat	F. Nos. 419–422 NP	Fe anklet	Pl. 54: 61
	Amulets, Sekhmet	F. Nos. 425–427, 429	Bone spacer	Pl. 54: 63
		(Colt) NP	Bone pendants	Pl. 54: 64–67
	Amulet, Isis	F. No. 423 NP (as Pl. 36: 51)	Beads	Pl. 66: 1, 3, 5, 13–15, 25, 34, 37, 38, 41, 44, 48, 55, 62, 65, 68, 69, 70, 74
	Amulets, Bast	F. Nos. 430, 431 NP		
	Scarabs	Pl. 43: 3, 16, 30, 43		Pl. 67: 102, 106, 114, 124, 126, 139
	Scaraboids	Pl. 44: 73, 75, 116, 119		
	Scarab	Pl. 54: 62	Rattle	F. No. 393, NP
	AE bangle	Pl. 54: 57		

108 Tomb in Grid Square A.6, re-used as an ossuary, adjoining and interconnected with Tombs 107 and 120   MB bilobate chamber. LB deposits. Bone deposits, 700–600 B.C.

The roof had partly collapsed. The two halves of the pit were divided by a stepped pilaster of original rock left uncut in the middle of the east wall (Pl. 4: 1). A thick coat of lime plaster covered the wall surfaces. From the numerous fragments of alabaster and stone vases found on the floor (their position is marked by a pile of stones in Pl. 4: 2), it appears that some use was made of the pit during the xviiith dynasty, though the bilobate chamber suggests an earlier date for the construction. The original entry, which no longer exists, was probably from the west, as it is usual to find it opposite the pilaster in this type of tomb.

Pl. 4: 1 shows an attempt to excavate an Iron Age tomb in the back wall of the north-east side, but a trial in the opposite recess was more successful, and led to Tomb 116. Pl. 4: 2 shows the small square entry in the south-east wall. Owing to the presence of Tomb 117 below Tomb 108, the masons had refrained from cutting a level floor surface in order to avoid breaking through to the lower chamber.

In the shallower part of Tomb 108 the deposit of bones reached roof level (2·2 m. above the floor). The upper layer of animal bones was thick, but the human remains were more scattered than in the deposits 107, 117 and 120 (Risdon, Nos. 186–190, 517–519, 708).

Pottery: B.13 J.4 J.3 D.1b D.7a
       76,* 180, 218, 300, 327
         * See Pl. 76: 2.

Objects: Loom weight and pounder   NP
         Stone vase frags.   F. Nos. 441, 442 (to be published in *Lachish IV*).

109 Tomb in Grid Square B.5 (Fig. 22)   600–550 B.C.

The plans of the adjoining Tombs 109 and 114 are incomplete owing to denudation and the removal of stone for building purposes. If an entrance passage like that of Tomb 105 existed for Tomb 109, it has disappeared with part of the north wall of the outer room. Beyond it on the same north–south axis was a smaller room, and both chambers were provided with benches on the east and west sides.

The contents of Tomb 109 were disturbed; bones and pottery had been piled in a heap over and close to the entrance step in the south chamber, as if it had been intended to remove them.

One example of each of the pottery types 32, 69, 152, 274, 292, 312 and 353 came from the base of a circular depression in the floor, which suggests an attempt at making a repository. No small objects were found, emphasising the thorough nature of the clearance.

Pottery: B.9   B.13   Misc.   L.9–10   J.6   J.7b   J.8   J.8   D.5b   D.8   D.7a   D.7a   J.7b
         32,   69(3)*,   129,   152(8),   233,   246,*   274(4),   276*   292(4),   312,   318,   326,*   353.   See Pl. 76.

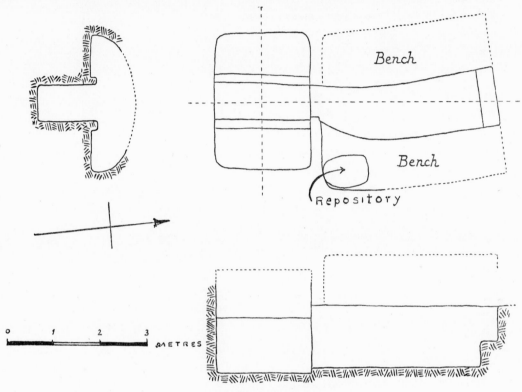

FIG. 22. Tomb 109

110 Grave in Grid Square B.5   *c.* 925–900 B.C.

The burial had been made in the filling of pit 102. The skull was unfit for preservation, and the long bones had disappeared. The pottery was grouped round the head, and the anklets were in the position where the feet should have been in relation to the skull, which suggests a north–south orientation for the body, with the head to the north, face up. This would accord with other graves of this cemetery and period.

The group is interesting for two reasons: firstly, it is homogeneous, and secondly, it proves that single burials were put in disused pits or caves in the earlier part of the Iron Age—a procedure suspected from the occurrence of classes of pottery and small objects in the ossuary groups which were inconsistent with the period of the bone deposits.

On the pottery evidence, the burial should be contemporary with Tomb 218, which would also agree with the presence of cowrie shells in both groups. The plaque and seal both appear to be heirlooms. The beads were of good quality carnelian, crystal, serpentine and coral, with some of paste or glaze and limestone; they are much superior to the beads in later groups.

Pottery: B.4   B.3   D.3   D.6a   MA   MA   S.1
         20,   128,   296(2),   329(2),   414,   416(2),   476

189

<table>
<tr><td>*Objects*: Plaque</td><td>Pl. 45: 135</td></tr>
<tr><td>Seal</td><td>Pl. 45: 153</td></tr>
<tr><td>4 AE anklets</td><td>Pl. 54: 68</td></tr>
<tr><td>AE bangle</td><td>NP</td></tr>
<tr><td>Beads</td><td>Pl. 66: 1, 2, 6, 15, 23, 29, 31, 32, 46 (Colt)</td></tr>
<tr><td>Cowrie shells</td><td>Pl. 66: 116</td></tr>
</table>

112 Cutting in Grid Square B.8

Date unknown

Trial cutting for a tomb shaft, abandoned before completion.

113 Dwelling in Grid Square B.5

Post-exilic

Cut after the construction of Tomb 114. There were no contents.

114 Tomb in Grid Square B.5

600–550 B.C.

The plan was incomplete and uncertain; the main axis of the tomb was at right angles to the adjoining chambers of Tomb 109, and parallel to Tombs 105 and 106 at a distance of 5 m. north.

There were two rooms, with benches along the walls, and the inner apartment was provided with a repository in the east wall. The human remains and pottery were much disturbed.

The pottery is similar to that of Tomb 109, but may represent a shorter period.

Pottery:
B.5	B.13	L.4–6	J.8	J.8	J.8	D.4b	D.5b	D.8	JS
44,	69,	148(5),	276(2),	277,	278,	283,	292,	319(3),*	367*

* See Pl. 76: 27, 28.

Objects:
Ivory kohl-pot	Pl. 54: 70
Beads	Pl. 67: 146 (Colt)
	F. No. 493 NP

116 Tomb in Grid Square A.6, re-used as an ossuary

c. 875 B.C. Re-used, 700–600 B.C.

The square entrance to this single rectangular chamber was cut in the south wall of pit 108 (Pl. 4: 2), at a time when the earlier internments had been cleared away, and before the pit was used as an ossuary. Inside a chamber about 3 m. square there was one step leading to the floor, and benches of rock were provided along the west, south and east sides. The roof was 1·60 m. above floor level. Formal burials had been laid out on the benches, but they were covered and mixed with other bones which had been piled on from the ossuary (Risdon, Nos. 173–185, 499–516, 655–662, 707). With the possible exception of bowl 45 and the dippers 308 and 310, the contents belong to the early interments.

Date and Comparisons

The pottery of Tomb 116 represents a short range of time which falls within the occupation period of Tomb 218. The small objects are also consistent with that equation, and they include two scarabs of *Mn-ḫpr-Rˁ* and two naming the god *Ymn-Rˁ*, both of which are most common in Tomb 218.

Pottery

Bowls

Class	Types	Total
B.3	26	1
B.4	6, 21, 100	3
B.5	55, 57(2)	3
B.6	95	1
B.12	45	1

190

Analysis of Burnish

HAND-BURNISHED RED SLIP				PLAIN	
In. and to keel out.		In. only			
Class	Type	Class	Type	Class	Type
				B.3	26
		B.4	6		
			21		
			100		
B.5	57(2)	B.5	55		
B.6	95				
				B.12	45
TOTALS	3		4		2

It should be noted that in the case of types 95 and 100, an irregular hand burnish is continued over the unslipped surface of the exterior. Cf. bowl F. No. 5007 in Tomb 224.

Lamps

Class	Types	Total
L.1–3	141, 144(3)	4
L.4–6	146, 148	2
		6

Jugs

Class	Types	Total
J.2	197, 200, 203, 208(3)	6
J.4	165(3), 187	4
J.5	195	1
J.6	240	1
		12

Straight-necked jugs in Class J.2 predominate over those with curved necks in Class J.4. Classes J.5 and J.6 are only represented by single examples of types 195 and 240 respectively, but the latter may rate early in the series, as it is covered with vertical hand burnish all over.

Dippers and Juglets

Class	Types	Total
D.1	290, 300(3)	4
D.2	299	1
D.3	285, 296(3)	4
D.7	317, 318, 322(4), 324	7
D.8	310	1
		17

Classes D.1, 2, 3. The unburnished dippers in the group contain a high proportion of limestone grits. Vertical hand burnish over red slip on types 299 and 300 covers the original ware, except for a few patches of the buff surface which can be seen near the handle and grooved rim of 299.

Class D.7. Two juglets in the group, types 317 and 318, have button bases, but the surface is so worn that it is impossible to distinguish the burnish. Examples of type 322 are well and smoothly polished with only faint traces of the vertical strokes. As it was incomplete, it was uncertain whether type 310 (Class D.8) should be included in the group.

Chalices

Class	Types	Total
Cha.	160, 161	2

Typologically, type 161 is somewhat earlier than 160, but both are well placed towards the end of the series.

Miniature Pithoi

Class	Type	Total
MP	419	1

The pithos can be compared for ware and decoration to jug 335 in Tomb 521, and the vessels decorated with red and white lines in Tomb 223.

Storage Jars

Class	Types	Total
S.1	473, 476*	2
	* See Pl. 78: 19.	

Jugs or Jars with Spouts

Class	Type	Total
JS	356*	1
	* See Pl. 78: 20.	

Miscellaneous

Class	Types	Total
Misc.	308, 357	2

Objects:
Scarabs	Pl. 43: 2, 5, 15, 17, 20, 29, 56
Scaraboids	Pl. 44: 72, 122
Seals	Pl. 45: 131, 140, 147, 152, 161
Amulet	Pl. 34: 7
Amulet, Sekhmet	F. No. 560 (Colt) NP
Fe knife	Pl. 54: 69
AV, AR, AE ear-rings	Pl. 54: 71–74
AE bangles	Pl. 54: 75, 79
AE anklets	Pl. 55: 1, 2
AE bangles	Pl. 55: 3
Bone pendants	Pl. 54: 76, 77, 78
Beads	Pl. 66: 13, 17, 18, 33, 41, 48, 63, 78, 86, 100

117 Cave in Grid Square A.6   MB–LB. Re-used, 700–600 B.C.

The cave is situated directly below pit 108, but is not marked on Pl. 125. Its presence was known to those who cut the upper chamber, as the masons had stepped up the floor level to avoid cutting through the roof (Pl. 4: 2). Thus the original cutting of Cave 117 can be no later than the Late Bronze Age, and is more likely to belong to an earlier period.

The human remains and most of the pottery seemed to belong to the ossuary deposit 120, and the contents were in the same disorder, though it is probable that the cave had previously contained normal Iron Age burials. Cf. Tombs 107 and 108.

Pottery:
B.12	L.1–3	L.4–6	L.9–10	D.1b	D.8	D.8	D.7b	Misc.
16,	144,	148,	153(2),	300,	309(5),	311,	322(3),	366

118 Dwelling in Grid Square B.8   10th century B.C.

Rectangular cutting for house foundations, more than half denuded to the west. A small paved area remained to the east of the cutting, laid directly on the rock.

The lamp and jar are both early types which would be expected to occur in the tenth century or earlier.

Pottery: L.1–3 S.1
      140,   474

| 120 Tomb in Grid Square A.6, re-used as an ossuary, interconnecting with Tombs 107 and 108 | LB chamber. Cleared and re-used for dwelling or burial purposes, *c.* 900 B.C. Bone deposits, 700–600 B.C. |

The original entrance was from the west, down a narrow sloping shaft, and the door sealing of irregular blocks of stone was still in position and undisturbed. Owing to the collapse of the roof in ancient times, the rectangular chamber was easily accessible, and human and animal remains had been piled in through the hole (Pl. 4: 3), and had overflowed into the adjoining pits 107 and 108, where the roofs were also missing.

The top layer consisted of many animal bones, mostly pig (see Appendix A), while the lower or main deposit was almost a solid mass of human bones, the remains of at least 1,500 bodies.[1] As they were thrown in, the skulls rolled down from the apex of the pile to the sides of the chamber (Pl. 4: 3, 4). Some bones and skulls were partially calcined, but careful supervision of the clearance failed to establish that any crania were in articulation with vertebrae, and the lower jaws were rarely in place: in fact, no order was to be seen in the jumbled mass.

The presence of sherds such as L. II: 176, 280, 283 and 301, with some Mycenean fragments in the filling, suggests that the original occupation of the cave was at least as early as the Late Bronze Age. In addition, parts of the walls retained a facing of white plaster, which is so far unknown in Iron Age tombs at Tell ed-Duweir.

Before the collapse of the roof some attempt had been made to alter the cave to meet Iron Age requirements, and the walls were dressed with a pronounced inward slant to produce a more rectangular chamber. At the same time, perhaps, a repository was provided at the north-east corner, and a much smaller recess was made near the doorway opposite (Pl. 4: 3, 5, 6).

Pl. 4: 3 shows a ledge of rock left uncut along the main axis of the chamber which served as a foundation for a wall of stones, possibly intended to support the roof. At the west end one course of these blocks was still in position on the ledge. A square sump or depression was cut in the floor parallel to the rock ledge, which was itself cut through to floor level half-way along its length (Pl. 4: 6).

Date and Comparisons

The foregoing description of the tomb and its contents demonstrates that it was no ordinary burial-place in its later period of use; it is clear that most of the human remains were deposited when the flesh had already disintegrated from the bones and skulls, some of which showed signs of burning. For similar indications see Tomb 1002, which is in part contemporary.

It does seem, however, that the tomb contained normal burials during a previous phase of use which would appear to be contemporary with that of Tomb 218.

An attempt has been made in the Distribution Charts given at the end of Chapter 9 to divide the pottery accompanying Tomb 120 (Ossuary) from that which may be associated with Tomb 120 (Burials), but in the Consolidated Chart the contents have been considered as a whole and placed in an intermediate position. The impression obtained from a study of the position of Tomb 120 (Ossuary) in the Distribution Charts would not preclude a shift to a position midway between Houses III and Houses II, which would favour a date after 700 B.C. rather than before. In this case the positions of the associated deposits 107, 108 and 117 would also be affected.

J. L. Starkey suggested that the deposit might represent a clearance of city rooms after the destruction of

---

[1] For a full account, see 'A Study of the Cranial and Other Human Remains from Palestine, excavated at Tell Duweir (Lachish) by the Wellcome-Marston Archaeological Research Expedition' by D. L. Risdon (Biometrika, Vol. XXXI, Parts I and II, July, 1939).

Level III. Alternatively it might have been caused by a wholesale clearance of idolatrous burials during the religious reformation of Josiah (see Chapter 1: Religion and Burial).

Analysis of the pottery shows an abnormal proportion of sherds, as opposed to complete vessels, of which the small dippers and juglets are in the majority. The presence of fragments of cooking pots, and of large bowls with handles from Class B.13, rarely found in normal burials, and which are ubiquitous in Houses III, supports the first suggestion.

The reason for the division of the group into two periods is based on various small points. Firstly, faience amulets and bone pendants, which are characteristic of tenth- to ninth-century groups such as Tomb 218, become uncommon by the eighth century. In the large Tomb 1002 of that date there were no amulets of Sekhmet and only one of Isis, though it contained figures of Bes, and Uzat eyes, which are known to have a later range. Secondly, the average size of the scarabs—15·50 mm.—is greater than that for those from Tomb 1002, which averaged 13·50 mm., while the motifs and the workmanship indicate an earlier trend. Thirdly, the presence of the so-called Cypriote wares in Tomb 120, which are indistinguishable from those in Tomb 218, would be out of place in any context later than the earlier levels of Tomb 1002.

The conclusion is, therefore, that the ossuary deposit, with the overlying layer of animal bones, was made during the seventh century. The female figurine (Pl. 27: 8) and the rattle (Pl. 27: 9) would belong to that period. The amulets, pendants and scarabs were presumably associated with burials of the tenth to ninth centuries.

Pottery

As a large part of the group is in the Palestine Museum, Jerusalem, the pottery cannot be described in full detail. A classified summary is given below.

Classified Summary of the Pottery in Tomb 120

Bowls

Class	Types	Total
B.4	4, 53	2
B.7	47, 48, 51, 52, 601, 602	6
B.8	1	1
B.11	60, 62	2
B.13	86, 120, 123, 647, 648, 651	6
		17

Lamps

Class	Types	Total
L.4–6	145	1
L.7–8	150	1
		2

Jugs

Class	Types	Total
J.4	168, 170, 171, 172(2), 176(3), 181, 183	10
J.5	190, 196	2
		—
		12

Dippers and Juglets

Class	Types	Total
D.1a, b	289, 300	2
D.2b	304	1
D.3	285(3)	3
D.4a	286(2), 293, 295, 297	5
D.4b	283(5)	5
D.5a	282(2)	2
D.6a	330, 336(2), 337	4
D.7a, b	318, 322(6)	7
D.8	309(2), 310(2)	4
		33

Miniature Amphorae

Class	Types	Total
MA	415	1

Pilgrim Flasks

Class	Types	Total
PF	429, 677	2

Cooking Pots

Class	Types	Total
CP	445, 450, 456, 462, 684, 685, 687, 693	8

Storage Jars

Class	Types	Total
S.2	472	1
S.4	514	1
S.5	521	1
S.10	503, 499	2
		5

Jugs or Jars with Spouts

Class	Types	Total
JS	364	1

Miscellaneous

Class	Types	Total
Misc.	117, 358, 380, 611, 669	5

Distribution of Pottery in Tomb 120

Type	Class	Top layers	Bottom layers	Sherds	Total
1	B.8	—	—	1	1
4	B.4	—	1	—	1
47	B.7	—	—	1	1
48	B.7	—	—	1	1
51	B.7	1	—	—	1
52	B.7	—	—	1	1
53	B.4	—	—	1	1
60	B.11	—	—	1	1
62	B.11	—	—	1	1
86*	B.13	—	1	—	1
117*	Misc.	1	—	—	1
120	B.13	—	1	—	1
123	B.13	—	1	—	1
145	L.4–6	—	1	—	1
150	L.7–8	1	—	—	1
168	J.4	—	1	—	1
170	J.4	1	—	—	1
171	J.4	1	—	—	1
172*	J.4	2	—	—	2
176*	J.4	2	—	1	3
181	J.4	—	1	—	1
183	J.4	—	1	—	1
190	J.5	—	1	—	1
196	J.5	1	—	—	1
282*	D.5a	2	—	—	2
283	D.4b	1	—	4	5
285	D.3	3	—	—	3
286	D.4a	—	2	—	2
289	D.1a	—	—	1	1
293	D.4a	1	—	1	2
295*	D.4a	—	1	—	1
297*	D.4a	—	1	—	1
300	D.1b	1	—	—	1
304*	D.2b	1	—	—	1
309	D.8	—	2	—	2
310	D.8	2	—	—	2
318	D.7a	—	—	1	1
322	D.7b	5	1	—	6
330	D.6a	—	1	—	1
336	D.6a	—	1	1	2
337	D.6a	—	—	1	1
358*	Misc.	1	—	—	1
364	JS	—	—	1	1
380*	Misc.	—	1	—	1
415	MA	—	1	—	1
429*	PF	—	1	—	1
445	CP	—	—	1	1
450	CP	—	—	1	1
456	CP	—	—	1	1
462	CP	—	—	1	1
472	S.2	—	—	1	1

* See Pl. 76: 3–5, 7–9, 11–13, 15, 16.

195

Distribution of Pottery in Tomb 120 (*cont.*)

Type	Class	Top layers	Bottom layers	Sherds	Total
499	S.10	—	—	1	1
503	S.10	—	—	1	1
514	S.4	—	—	1	1
521	S.5	—	—	1	1
601	B.7	—	—	1	1
602	B.7	—	—	1	1
611	Misc.	—	—	1	1
647	B.13	—	—	1	1
648	B.13	—	—	1	1
651	B.13	—	—	1	1
669	Misc.	—	—	1	1
677	PF	—	—	1	1
684	CP	—	—	1	1
685	CP	—	—	1	1
687	CP	—	—	1	1
693	CP	—	—	1	1

Objects:

Pottery figurine	Pl. 27: 8
Rattle	Pl. 27: 9
Zoomorphic vase	Pl. 30: 28
Amulets	Pl. 34: 8–17
Amulets, Bast and Sekhmet	F. Nos. 5181, 5182 (PM. 36.1590) NP
Scarabs	Pl. 43: 4, 9, 22, 23, 35, 59, 61
Scaraboids	Pl. 44: 76, 77, 90
AE ring	Pl. 55: 5
Fe, AE bangles	Pl. 55: 4, 6–10
Fe arrowhead	Pl. 55: 12
AR ear-ring	Pl. 55: 15
Bone pendants and gavels	Pl. 55: 17–29
Bone pendants and gavels	Pl. 37: 6–15, 17
Bone spindlewhorl	Pl. 55: 14
Bone pendant	F. No. 5145 NP
Stone spindlewhorl	Pl. 55: 11
Gypsum flask	Pl. 55: 16
Neck of glass jug	Pl. 55: 13 and Pl. 40: 3
Beads	Pl. 38: 2
	Pl. 66: 2, 4, 12, 13, 14, 15, 17, 22, 28, 37, 41, 44, 53, 55, 57, 63, 65, 74
	Pl. 67: 99, 127, 137, 139

126 Lime kiln in Grid Square C.7   ?

Sherds only, mostly Roman.

132 Single grave in Grid Square C.8   *c.* 750 B.C.

The grave was cut in the filling of the Bronze Age fosse. The burial was undisturbed and the body was oriented with head to the north, face up, attitude extended. The bones were friable and incomplete, and the top of the storage jar placed at the feet was broken owing to its proximity to the surface. The juglets 309 were in the bowl 41 close to the head, with a two-handled vase, type 425 (Pl. 5: 1).

Pottery: B.5   L.1–3   D.8   MP   S.1
        41(2),* 144, 309(3), 425,* 473
        * See Pl. 73: 21, 22.

137 Single grave in Grid Square D.8 950–700 B.C.

The grave was cut in the earth, and the body was undisturbed. It was oriented with the head to the north and face to the west, attitude extended. A few Late Bronze sherds near the body were not necessarily associated with it.

138 Single grave in Grid Square D.8 950–700 B.C.

The grave was cut in the earth, only some 260 cm. from the surface, beside Grave 137. The body was undisturbed, but the bones were friable and incomplete. Contrary to custom in this series of single burials, though the grave was oriented north and south, the skeleton lay with head to the south, face up, in an extended position. No objects were found.

139 Single grave in Grid Square D.8 950–700 B.C.

The grave was cut in the earth, some 260 cm. from the surface. The body was undisturbed, but the bones had largely disintegrated. It was oriented with head to the north, face up, attitude extended. A water jar had been placed at the feet, but only the base remained.

147 Single grave in Grid Square C.8 *c.* 850 B.C.

The grave was cut in the earth filling above the Fosse Temple. The head had been placed to the north, but only the lower part of the skeleton remained. Two bronze anklets were still in position on each leg, and storage jar 470 was set close to the feet. The juglets 322, 337 and 338 had been placed in a bowl similar to type 8 (Pl 5: 2).

Pottery: B.4   D.7b   D.6a   D.6a   S.4
        8,   322,* 337,* 338,* 470*
        * See Pl. 73: 4–7.

Objects: AE anklets   Pls. 55: 30 and 36: 58–60

152 Single grave in Grid Square C.9 *c.* 850 B.C.

The grave was cut in the earth filling above the Fosse Temple. The body was oriented north and south with the head to the north, attitude extended. The burial was disturbed.

Pottery: D.3   D.7b   D.6a   Misc.   S.1
        285,* 322(2), 337, 371,* 476
        * See Pl. 73: 8, 9.

154 Single grave in Grid Square C.8 *c.* 850 B.C.

The grave was cut in the earth filling above the Fosse Temple. It was oriented north and south. The bones were very friable; the skull, placed to the north, was in fragments, and the attitude was extended, with the hands up to the face. The juglets had been placed near the head.

Pottery: B.4   B.6   D.1b   D.7b
        12,* 93,* 302, 322*
        * See Pl. 73: 10–12.

159 Single grave in Grid Square C.10 *c.* 850 B.C.

The grave was cut in the earth and oriented north and south. The burial was disturbed and the bones disintegrated.

Pottery: B.6 J.2 D.7b
    93, 203, 322(2)

160 Double burial in Grid Square B.10 *c.* 850–750 B.C.

The grave was cut in the earth and oriented roughly north and south. It had originally contained two skeletons, but only fragments of bone remained, and the pottery was much broken. It is possible that the burials were made at different times, in which case the presence of dippers in Classes D.7 and D.8 is not significant.

Pottery: B.7 B.5 B.7 J.8 D.8 D.7a D.7b D.6a
    37, 41, 48, 281, 309, 318, 322(2), 337

Object: Scaraboid Pl. 44: 110

164 Oven in Grid Square B.10 ?

167 Single grave in Grid Square C.9 *c.* 850 B.C.

The grave was cut in the earth, directly over a wall of the Fosse Temple. The level of the bottom of the grave was 230·57 m., about half a metre above the wall. The body was oriented north and south, with the head to the north, face upwards and attitude extended. Only part of the skull and some long bones remained. Water jar 478 was close to the head.

Pottery: J.2 D.4a D.7b D.6a S.4
    203, 286, 322, 337, 478

169 Locus in Grid Square D.8 *c.* 850 B.C.

The number 169 marks the position of a burnished bowl 91 and a juglet 298, found in the earth at this point.

Pottery: B.6 D.1a
    91, 298

180 Single grave in Grid Square C.9 *c.* 550–450 B.C.

The grave was cut in the earth filling of the Fosse Temple, on a level with the north wall, with its floor level at 230·67 m. It was oriented west and east. The body was placed with the head to the west, face upwards, attitude extended. No objects were found.

See Pl. 5: 3 for the relationship of the grave and the Fosse Temple. Note also that the water jar 473 from Grave 182, which was oriented north and south, is visible at a lower level than Grave 180.

182 Single grave in Grid Square C.9 *c.* 850 B.C.

The grave was cut in the earth filling above the Fosse Temple, with its floor level at 230·45 m. It was oriented north and south. The skull was crushed at the north end of the grave and the body was supine, with hands on the pelvis.

Storage jar 473 was close to the head, with bowl 9 above the right arm. Juglet 288 was close to the left shoulder and 301 lay to the left of the body (Pl. 5: 4).

Pottery: B.7 D.1a D.1b S.1
     9,* 288,* 301,* 473
         * See Pl. 73: 1–3.

183 Single grave in Grid Square C.10   *c.* 550–450 B.C.

The grave was cut in the earth and was oriented west and east. It was approached by a vertical shaft sealed by stones, four of which were in position. The body lay with head to the west, attitude extended and hands on pelvis (Pl. 5: 5). The bones were in better condition than is usual in the case of graves oriented north and south.

Jug 255 lay close to the left side of the pelvis and was the only object found.

Pottery: J.8
     255

184 Single grave in Grid Square C.10 (see Fig. 20)   *c.* 550–450 B.C.

The grave was cut in the earth 1 m. above Grave 189, at 230·45 m., and was oriented west and east. It was approached by a vertical shaft divided from the grave by blocks of stone.

The body lay south of the stone partition with the head to the west, face to the south, and attitude extended, with hands on pelvis. The only object found was another example of jug 255, as seen in Grave 183.

Pottery: J.8
     255

185 Single grave in Grid Square C.10   *c.* 550–450 B.C.

The grave was cut in the earth and was oriented west and east, adjoining and nearly parallel to Grave 186. It was approached by a vertical shaft similar to that of Graves 183 and 184, but in this case the stone blocking was not in position. The body was missing and no objects were found. The loculus for the body was to the south of the shaft.

186 Single grave in Grid Square C.10   *c.* 550–450 B.C.

The grave was cut in the earth and oriented west and east. It was adjoining and nearly parallel to Grave 185, at the same level. It was approached by a vertical shaft similar to those of Graves 183 and 184, and three of the stones blocking the loculus for the body were still in position. The loculus was to the south of the shaft. The body was missing and no objects were found.

189 Single grave in Grid Square C.10   *c.* 900 B.C.

The grave was cut in the earth, one metre below Grave 184, at 229·44 m. It was oriented north and south. The body lay with the head to the north, face upwards and attitude extended. The skull was crushed and the bones were in a friable condition. The burial was undisturbed. A jug, type 197, was placed to the left of the head, with a lamp 148 and a cooking pot 444 at the feet (Pl. 5: 6).

Pottery: L.4–6 J.2 CP
     148, 197, 444

Objects: AE bracelet   Pl. 55: 31
         Bone spindlewhorl   Pl. 55: 32
         Carnelian bead   Pl. 66: 14

191 Single grave in Grid Square B.9   *c.* 825 B.C.

The grave was cut in the earth at 231·94 m., a metre and a half above a pit associated with Structure II of the Fosse Temple (L. II, Pl. LXVII). The body was placed with the head to the north, face upwards and attitude extended, with hands on pelvis. The burial was undisturbed, but the skull was crushed and the bones were friable. Storage jar 476 was at the head, with bowl 132 inverted over it. Juglet 296 was found in the jar.

Pottery: B.2 D.3 S.1
132, 296, 476

Object: Steatite plaque   Pl. 45: 130

192 Single grave in Grid Square B.9 *c.* 900 B.C.

The grave was cut in the earth, and was oriented north and south. The body was placed with the head due south, face upwards, attitude extended, with hands on pelvis. The bones were friable. Two stones remained of the original sealing.

Bowl 8 was to the right of the head and was the only object found.

Pottery: B.4
8

193 Single grave in Grid Square B.9 *c.* 900 B.C.

The grave was cut in the earth at 232·26 m. and was oriented north and south. The loculus was partly sealed by some small stones. The body was missing.

Objects: AE bracelets   Pl. 55: 33
Bone pendant   Pl. 67: 129
Shells

194 Single grave in Grid Square B.10 *c.* 900 B.C.

The grave was cut in the earth, and was oriented north and south. The body was placed with the head to the south, face upwards. It appeared that the knees had been flexed at the time of burial, as they had fallen apart. The arms were flung out. The skull was crushed and the bones were friable. A jug 192, and a dipper 289, were placed to the right of the body (Pl. 5: 7).

Pottery: J.5 D.1a
192, 289

Objects: Fe bracelet   NP
Scaraboid   Pl. 45: 132
Carnelian bead   NP

195 Single grave in Grid Square B.10 950–700 B.C.

The grave was cut in the earth and oriented north and south. It rested almost directly on the scarp of the Hyksos fosse, but was not cut into it. The body was placed with the head to the south, face to the west, and attitude extended, with hands on pelvis. The skeleton was well preserved, but no objects were found.

196 Single grave in Grid Square B.10 *c.* 900 B.C.

The grave was cut in the earth, and was oriented north and south. Its northern end rested against the edge of the scarp of the Hyksos fosse. The body was placed with the head to the north, face upwards, and attitude extended, with hands on pelvis. The skeleton and contents were crushed under the stones used to seal the grave. A bowl with spatulate handle, type 104, and jug 334 were placed close to the left shoulder.

Pottery: B.2 Misc.
104, 334

197 Single grave in Grid Square B.9   950–700 B.C.

The grave was cut in the earth, and was oriented north and south. The body was placed with the head to the north, face upwards, attitude extended, and hands on the pelvis, holding bowl 14. The skull was crushed and the bones friable.

Pottery: B.4
14

198 Single grave in Grid Square B.9   950–700 B.C.

The grave was cut in the earth and oriented north and south. The body was missing, and no objects were found.

215 Cistern in Grid Square B.5   300–200 B.C.

The cistern was cut in the rock, and had been plastered. The top was narrow and roughly circular and widened to a bell shape towards the bottom. In the centre was a square hole which was possibly intended as a drain for the silt.

Pottery: Misc. D.9
306   347

Objects: Stone quern   F. No. 4430 NP
Stone pounder   F. No. 4431 NP

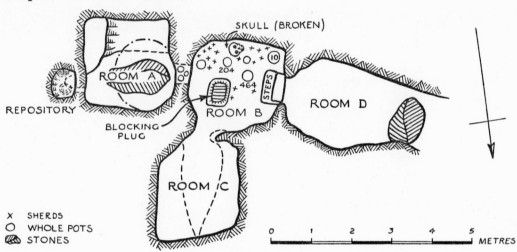

FIG. 23. Tomb 217

217 Tomb in Grid Square A.5 (Fig. 23)   Triple-chambered tomb, *c*. 150–100 B.C.

Tomb 217 is similar in plan and orientation to Tombs 105 and 106, and 114, though it does not form part of that group. It lies about 20 m. north-west, and is entered down a sloping passage (Room D), which leads to three chambers: B and A on the same axis, with C opening off B on the north side.

On the floor of Room B was a large cut stone which had been used as a blocking for the entrance to Room A. The irregularity of cutting, which lacks the precision used in the construction of Tomb 106, and the presence of a repository, would suggest a date late in the history of the site for the original construction.

The pottery (Fig. 24) was mostly found in Room B, and there were no bones except a broken skull, lying on the south side of that room.

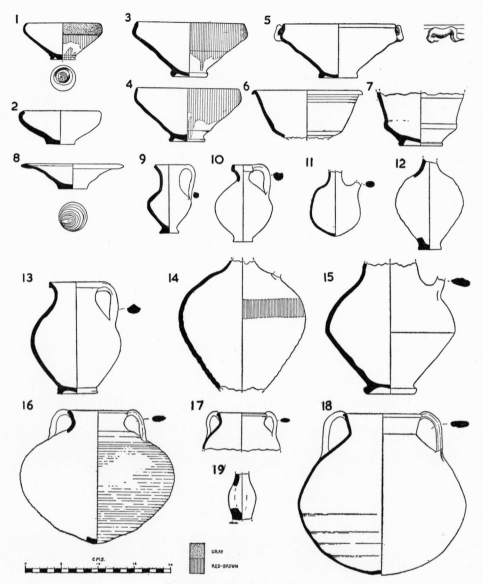

GRAY

RED-BROWN

FIG. 24. Pottery in Tomb 217

FIG. 24

1. Mat glazed bowl. Hard brownish-buff, with mica and grits[1]. Wet-smoothed in., rough out. Dipped in red-brown slip. Band of grey slip on outside. Diam. 11 cm. Type 10. Cf. BM, Pl. 60: 31, 33.

2. Another, brown, grits[1]. S. Surface fired red inside, cream slip out. Disk base, whorl finish. Type 10.

3. Mat glazed bowl, well silted red-brown, grits[1]. H. Dipped in reddish-brown slip, fired dark grey in patches, and partly covering exterior. Semi-ring base, well turned. Diam. 15 cm. Restored from sherds.

4. Mat glazed bowl. Reddish-brown, large uneven grits[2]. H. Dipped in reddish-brown slip. Diam. 14 cm. Restored from sherds.

5. Mat glazed bowl. Fine red clay, grits[1]. H. Fired grey in parts. Dipped in red slip, surface imperfectly covered. Flattened ring base. Folded handles. Diam. 16 cm. Type 111. Cf. SS III, C.5, *c.* 150 B.C.; Soli, Fig. 63: 9, 1st cent. B.C.; BM, Pl. 61: 28.

Another, not illustrated. Well silted red clay, grits[1]. H. Surface shaved and finger-smoothed. Dipped in red slip, surface imperfectly covered. Ring base, well turned. Type 111. Cf. as above.

202

Another, not illustrated. Well silted red-brown, grits[1] and mica. H. Tool and finger-smoothed. Red-brown slip, worn or wiped off outside rim. Diam. 20 cm. approx. Type 111. Cf. Ay Philon, Level III, 1st cent. B.C., unpublished.

6. Mat glazed bowl. Well silted, reddish-brown, grits[1]. H. Dipped in reddish-brown slip, fired grey in parts outside. Base missing. Diam. 15 cm. Partly restored from sherds.

7. Mat glazed beaker. Yellow-brown, grits[2] and straw. M. Dipped in reddish-brown slip, fired grey in parts inside. Flattened ring base. Rim and sides missing. Restored from sherds.

8. Dish. Yellow-brown, grits[1], pitted surface. M. Wet-smoothed in. and out. Disk base, whorl finish. Diam. 14·4 cm. Restored from sherds.

9. Juglet. Handmade. Brown, grits blown. M. Rough surface, fired buff to red. Round section handle, poorly attached. Ht. 9 cm. Type 343.

10. Juglet. Brown, large grits[3], mostly blown. S. Thin greenish-white slip. Ridged section handle, poorly attached. Ht. 10 cm. Type 344.

11. Juglet. Thin buff-brown. S. Surface worn. Neck and handle missing. Restored from sherds.

12. Juglet. Yellowish-brown, grits[1]. S. Traces cream slip, surface worn. Neck and handle missing.

13. Jug. Fine brown, grits[2]. M. Surface buff and wet-smoothed. Ridged handle poorly applied. Well-turned flattened ring base. Ht. 14·5 cm. Type 204. Cf. Dura-Europos II, Pl. XLII, Tomb 17, 305–281 B.C.

14. Jug. Fine yellow-brown. M. Traces cream slip. Band of red slip painted round body. Neck, handle and base missing. Partly restored from sherds.

15. Jug. Fine brown, large grits[2]. M. Surface buff and wet-smoothed. Neck and handle missing. Semi-ring base. Partly restored from sherds.

16. Cooking pot. Thin red, large grits[1]. H. Wet-smoothed inside rim, slightly ribbed surface out., black to grey. Two ribbon handles, poorly attached. Ht. 17·5 cm. Type 464.

17. Cooking pot. Fine red, grey core, grits[1]. H. Two ribbon handles, poorly attached. Base missing.

18. Cooking pot. Thin red. H. Incipient ribs on body. Two ribbon handles poorly attached. Ht. 21 cm. Type 464.

19. Unguentarium. Reddish-brown. H. Rough surface. Neck and base missing. Type 376.

As the above notes make clear, the pottery in the group is fairly consistent, and the comparisons from other sites range from the beginning of the second century to the first century B.C. Some pieces in Tomb 217 are comparable to fragments from the Solar Shrine, which was not abandoned until the end of the second century B.C.

Pottery: Misc. Misc. Misc. D.9 D.9 Misc. K. CP CP
10,* 111(3),* 204, 343, 344, 376, 403,* 446, 464(2)
* Pl. 76: 24–26.

Objects: AE kohl stick, corroded   F. No. 4690 NP
Stone spindlewhorl   F. No. 4692 NP
Beads   Pl. 66: 1, 14, 20, 53, 89

218 Tomb in Grid Square A.5 (Fig. 25)   MB bilobate chamber. Altered and re-used c. 900 B.C.

The main axis of the tomb was roughly west–east, with the entrance shaft on the west side still blocked by stones. In the doorway were three dozen pots, together with a mass of human remains, lying in disorder. The roof at that point had collapsed, but the roofs of Rooms A and C, beyond, were in better condition. Most of the human and animal bones had been piled in Room A, where there was also a group of eight bracelets. To the east of Room A there was a circular repository containing Middle and Late Bronze Age sherds, which had presumably been cleared from the rooms to make way for later interments. Room C contained a deposit of scarabs lying together (Pl. 43: 14, 18, 44; Pl. 44: 111, 112; Pl. 45: 150).

The contents had been much disturbed, and only two skulls, some long bones and a few animal bones were worth preserving out of the many skeletons which had been buried originally.

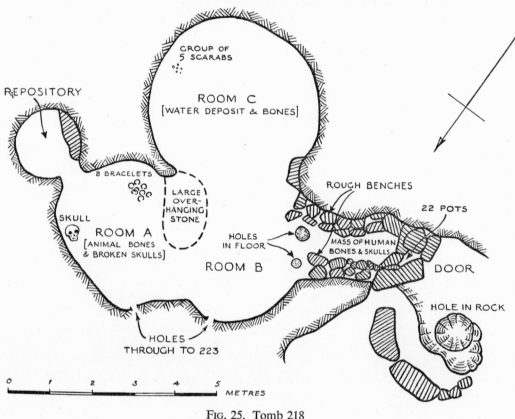

FIG. 25. Tomb 218

Date and Comparisons

Tomb 218 was used as a burial-place before the occupation of Tombs 521 or 223, but bodies were deposited in it for a much longer period so that its main phase is somewhat later. In contrast to other tombs at the site, its contents are more varied and less poor.

The pottery exhibits a consistent and continuous range; three-quarters of the bowls were hand burnished, and showed almost equal numbers of each kind of finish. So-called Cypriote wares, which appear in this group, are described in detail in Chapter 9. They are components of a period which Gjerstad has named Cypro-Geometric III, though, in his opinion, the wares were foreign to the island, and mark an immigration of Syrian tribes into Cyprus about 850 B.C. There is no doubt that these decorated wares are in no way related to the ceramics of Judah or of Egypt, and for that reason their point of diffusion must be sought elsewhere, possibly in Syria or Cilicia.

Renewed relations with the south reached a climax in Tomb 218, for at no other time in the Iron Age were the products of Egyptian culture so common. Despite the introduction of scaraboids made of limestone and steatite, scarabs predominated, exhibiting various hieroglyphic designs which included two of *Mn-ḫpr-Rʿ*, one of *Ḫpr-Rʿ* and various combinations of the god *Ymn*.

It is uncertain whether the two royal names can be attributed to any particular Pharaohs. Pl. 43: 44 could belong to Osorkon III (PSC, Pl. LI: 1–14), who, according to the dating proposed in the Cambridge Ancient

History, reigned from 804 to 750 B.C. (CAH III, p. 265). There is a duplicate of this scarab from Tomb 1 at 'Ain Shems.

The well-cut scarab on Pl. 43: 6 is comparable to those of Men-Kheper-Ra Khmeny (PSC, Pl. LIII: 22, 23), a king of the xxist or xxvth dynasty, whose reign is obscure. There is a very similar scarab from Tomb 32 at Tell en-Naṣbeh, which is attributed to the xxvth dynasty by some authorities.

For comparable material from Egypt, see Lahun II, Pl. L, Tombs 602, 603, where several elements common to Tomb 218, Tomb 1 at 'Ain Shems and Tomb 32 at Tell en-Naṣbeh (TN I, Pl. 54: 3, 10, 15, 16) are present. Besides the scarabs, there are, among the smaller objects, amulets, iron lanceheads or arrowheads, and a profusion of shells and cowries; it should be noted, however, that scaraboids with animal designs, and bone pendants and gavels, are missing from the Egyptian groups.

Though the pottery from Lahun is not otherwise comparable, two sherds are illustrated (Lahun II, Pl. L) which can be matched on Palestinian sites: the neck of Cypro-Phoenician ware (cf. Class D.6) and that of a black burnished juglet (cf. Class D.7).

There are also traces of a third influence in this tomb, and the direction from whence it came may be indicated by the sphinx amulet with negroid head and hair style (Pl. 35: 30).

Moreover, Tomb 218 was rich in metal ornaments. There were gold, silver and bronze ear-rings, and nearly fifty bangles of varying thickness and weight. Though there were also many iron bangles among them, these were too broken and corroded to be counted.

The bone pendants and gavels illustrated on Pl. 55 are so far unknown from sites outside Palestine, although similar objects have been found in use today in primitive African societies. The profusion of shells and cowries from southern seas adds some weight to the suggestion that the contents of Tomb 218 were influenced by the settlement of Libyan or Nubian troops in the vicinity at the time of Shishak's invasion.

Pottery

Bowls

Class	Type	Total
B.2	22, 24, 28, 592, 596	5
B.3	126	1
B.4	4, 8(2), 13, 19(2), 29(2), 53	9
B.5	41, 42, 43, 55, 57(2)	6
B.6	88(2), 89, 96, 97	5
B.7	48(2)	2
B.13	73, 81	2
		30

Class B.4 attained its peak during the occupation of the tomb, followed by Classes B.5 and B.6: these three classes together should cover the main phase of burial. In addition, there are many sherds burnished all over which should fall in Classes B.2 and B.3. Owing to their fragmentary nature they have not been classified. Two sherds can be compared with Class B.7, forming a link with the subsequent Tombs 224, 1004 and 1002, where Class B.7 is prevalent. One fragment is highly burnished with close strokes, presenting a very smooth finish all over, but it is too small to include in the Analysis of Burnish; the other is only burnished inside. Both have slightly everted profiles and flat rims. For comparisons in the same class, see a sherd from the West Section at 258·34 m., Tell el-Fûl (AASOR IV, Pl. XXXII: 15) and Tell Beit Mirsim (AASOR XII, Fig. 1). Two sherds in B.13, types 73 and 81, seem out of place, but it is perhaps significant that the burnish was applied by hand. Furthermore, it should be noted that fragments belonging to B.13 also appear for the first time in the West Section at 258·34 m.

The distinctive finish of bowls in Tomb 218 was an irregular hand burnish inside and to the keel out, conforming to the method of application observed in Tombs 521 and 223. Burnished bowls were more common than plain ones in the group, and both the earlier system of a complete burnish all over, and the later restriction of burnish to the interior only, are well represented.

Analysis of Burnish

HAND BURNISHED						PLAIN	
All over		*In. and to keel out.*		*In. only*			
Class	Type	Class	Type	Class	Type	Class	Type
B.2	28	B.2	22				
	592		24				
			596				
				B.3	126		
B.4	4	B.4	8	B.4	13	B.4	19(2)
	8		53				29(2)
B.5	57	B.5	43	B.5	41	B.5	42
			55				57
B.6	89			B.6	88(2)	B.6	96
							97
				B.7	48(2)		
				B.13	73		
					81		
TOTALS	6		7		9		8

The conclusion to be drawn from a study of the bowls and the method of burnish is that continuity is maintained with the earlier groups 521 and 223, while there is an extension of range towards the subsequent Tomb 224 (q.v.).

Lamps

Class	Types	Total
L.1–3	143(2), 147	3
L.4–6	148(2)	2
		5

Apart from a few sherds, only five lamps were found in Tomb 218—a remarkably small proportion in so large a group. It will be noted that all are more or less flanged, a development from the earlier Tombs 223 and 521, where an occasional lamp with a plain rim profile occurred.

Jugs

Class	Types	Total
J.1	222	1
J.2	201, 203(2)	3
J.3	215	1
J.4	171(2), 172(2), 174, 176, 178, 180(3), 184	11
J.5	192	1
J.6	244	1
		18

Classes J.1, J.2 and J.3 are only represented by one or two specimens each; J.4 is very common, containing jugs with an average height of 9–10 cm. The ware is a coarse grey or red, with a high proportion of limestone grits. The jugs are rather heavy in relation to their size; a straight collar neck is typical, and the mouth of the vessel is always round.

There are only single examples of jugs which can be allocated to Classes J.5 and J.6.

Dippers and Juglets

Class	Types	Total
D.1a, b	289(2), 300, 301, 302(5)	9
D.2a	287(3), 299	4
D.3	285, 296	2
D.4b	283(7)	7
D.6a	332, 336, 337(2), 338, 339A	6
D.7a, b	326, 327(2), 322(10), 324(3)	16
		44

Classes D.1–4. The dippers are chiefly divided between Class D.1 and Class D.4. Those in the first group are mostly unburnished, while those in Class D.4 are nearly all covered with red slip, vertically hand burnished all over. The trend towards a longer bag-shaped body, observed in type 283 in Tomb 223, is very marked. The form, allied to a deep red slip and vertical burnish, is missing from Tomb 224, but it reappears in Tomb 1002 in conjunction with a smooth light burnish, firing buff to pink. The spouted dipper, Misc. type 357, is comparable to others from Group 107 and Tomb 116.

Class D.6: Cypro-Phoenician wares. The jugs or juglets in this class were all incomplete, with necks and/or handles missing. Types 336, 337 and 338 can all be placed in Gjerstad's classification of Cypriote forms as Black-on-Red I (III) (GSCE IV, Pt. 2, pp. 186–194). A bag-shaped juglet 339A, of which the base is missing, can be compared to a vessel illustrated in the same volume and classed as Black-on-Red II (IV) ware (op. cit., Fig. XXXVIII: *21*). The body and handle of a juglet—not classified in the Duweir series—is probably White Painted III (op. cit., Fig. XXV: 3a); a barrel-shaped juglet, type 332, is Black or Grey Polished ware. There are also some fragments of the body of a larger barrel-shaped jug, which can be classified as Bichrome I ware in Cyprus (op. cit., Fig. VIII: *10*).

The incomplete nature of all the specimens, in a tomb which contained a large proportion of complete vessels, suggests that the so-called Cypriote wares, like the highly burnished bowl fragments of Classes D.2 and D.3, do not belong to the latest burials.

For a full discussion of the chronological implications of these forms, see Chapter 9.

Class D.7. Type 324 is comparable to an example from Tomb 223. All three examples from Tomb 218 are incomplete; the ware is brown, soft or medium fired, and covered with a brown slip.

Less than a dozen black burnished juglets, type 322, were recovered. They were fired soft to medium; the surface was often worn, but whenever burnish was distinguishable it was either applied in close vertical strokes, or smoothly, so that the lines were barely visible. They ranged in size from 11 cm. to 7 cm., with one example less than 6 cm. in height, with a squat body, but as the neck was missing it cannot be definitely attributed to type 309. There were a few transitional forms leading towards that later development, but in no case did the handle join the rim.

Miniature Amphorae

Class	Types	Total
MA	412, 415, 416	3

Two out of three examples were black burnished, fired soft to medium; the third was of brown ware, much worn, with traces of red slip. It had a small ring base, but neck and handle were missing. The lug handles of types 412 and 416 were pierced vertically.

Cooking Pots

Class	Type	Total
CP	444	1

The only vessel of its kind in Tomb 218 was made of dark brown ware, fired or burnt hard, for the base was very black. It does not appear to contain the quantities of grit which were usual in later cooking pots.

Storage Jars

Class	Types	Total
S.1	473, 476	2

Only two storage jars were associated with the group; one was found in the doorway and the other in Room B. Compare a vessel from Tell Abu Hawam, Stratum III, 1100–925 B.C.

Miscellaneous

Class	Types	Total
Misc.	119, 357, 370, 669	4

Animal Vase

The head and forepart of a quadruped (Pl. 30: 27) was made of soft brown ware with faint traces of slip and burnish. The cylindrical body was wheelmade, and the neck and spouts inserted into the back were hand finished. The neck and mouth were pierced.

Distribution of Pottery in Tomb 218

Type	Class	Room A	Room B	Room C	Door sealing	Sherds	Total
4	B.4	—	1	—	—	—	1
8	B.4	—	1	1	—	—	2
13	B.4	—	—	—	1	—	1
19	B.4	—	—	—	1	1	2
22	B.2	—	1	—	—	—	1
24	B.2	—	—	—	1	—	1
28	B.2	—	—	—	1	—	1
29	B.4	1	1	—	—	—	2
41	B.5	—	—	—	1	—	1
42	B.5	—	—	—	—	1	1
43	B.5	—	1	—	—	—	1
48	B.7	—	—	—	—	2	2
53	B.4	—	—	—	—	1	1
55	B.5	—	1	—	—	—	1
57	B.5	—	—	—	—	2	2
73	B.13	—	—	—	—	1	1
81	B.13	—	—	—	—	1	1
88	B.6	1	1	—	—	—	2
89	B.6	—	—	—	1	—	1
96	B.6	—	—	—	1	—	1
119	Misc.	—	1	—	—	—	1
126	B.3	—	1	—	—	—	1
143	L.1–3	—	1	—	1	—	2
147	L.1–3	—	1	—	—	—	1
148	L.4–6	—	2	—	—	—	2
162	Cha.	—	—	—	—	1	1
171	J.4	—	—	—	2	—	2
172	J.4	—	—	—	2	—	2
174	J.4	—	—	1	—	—	1
176	J.4	—	1	—	—	—	1
178	J.4	—	—	—	—	1	1
180	J.4	—	1	—	2	—	3
184	J.4	—	—	—	1	—	1
192	J.5	1	—	—	—	—	1

Distribution of Pottery in Tomb 218 (*cont.*)

Type	Class	Room A	Room B	Room C	Door sealing	Sherds	Total
201	J.2	—	1	—	—	—	1
203	J.2	2	—	—	—	—	2
215	J.3	—	1	—	—	—	1
222	J.1	—	—	—	1	—	1
244	J.6	1	—	—	—	—	1
283	D.4b	1	3	—	3	—	7
285	D.3	—	—	—	1	—	1
287	D.2a	—	2	—	1	—	3
289	D.1a	—	1	—	—	1	2
296	D.3	—	1	—	—	—	1
299	D.2a	—	—	—	1	—	1
300	D.1b	—	—	—	1	—	1
301	D.1b	—	1	—	—	—	1
302	D.1b	—	3	—	2	—	5
322	D.7b	—	9	1	—	—	10
324	D.7b	—	—	—	3	—	3
326	D.7a	—	—	1	—	—	1
327	D.7a	—	1	1	—	—	2
332	D.6a	—	—	—	1	—	1
336	D.6a	—	1	—	—	—	1
337	D.6a	—	2	—	—	—	2
338	D.6a	—	1	—	—	—	1
339A*	D.6a	—	—	—	1	—	1
357	Misc.	—	—	—	1	—	1
370	Misc.	—	—	—	1	—	1
412	MA	—	1	—	—	—	1
415	MA	—	1	—	—	—	1
416	MA	—	—	—	1	—	1
444	CP	—	—	—	1	—	1
473	S.1	—	—	—	1	—	1
476	S.1	—	1	—	—	—	1
592	B.2	—	—	—	—	1	1
596	B.2	—	—	—	—	1	1
669	Misc.	—	—	—	—	1	1

* See Pl. 36: 62.

Distribution of Objects in Tomb 218

	Room A	Room B	Room C	Door
Pottery animal vase	Pl. 30: 27	—	—	—
Jar handle, incised	—	—	—	Pl. 52: 11
Amulets	Pl. 34: 20, 27 Pl. 35: 34, 35 F. No. 4820, NP	Pl. 34: 22, 23, 29 Pl. 35: 31, 32	Pl. 34: 18, 19, 21, 26	Pl. 34: 24, 25, 28 Pl. 35: 30, 33
Scarabs, scaraboids and seals	Pl. 43: 27 Pl. 45: 126	Pl. 43: 6, 40 Pl. 45: 125, 136, 143 F. No. 4825, haematite seal, NP	Pl. 43: 14, 18, 44 Pl. 44: 79, 84, 85, 88, 111, 112 Pl. 45: 150, 151	Pl. 43: 1, 12, 13, 52 Pl. 44: 121

	Room A	*Room B*	*Room C*	*Door*
Metal	AE anklets and bracelets, Pl. 55: 34–39	—	—	AV, AR, AE ear-rings and ring, Pl. 55: 40–43 Electrum ear-rings, F. No. 4810a NP
Bone	—	Pendants, Pl. 55: 44–47 (also Pl. 37: 19–23)	—	Gavel, Pl. 55: 48 and Pl. 37: 24 Gavel, Pl. 55: 49 Gavel, Pl. 55: 50 and Pl. 37: 25 Pendant, Pl. 55: 51 and Pl. 37: 18
Stone	—	Hone, Pl. 55: 52	—	—

The following objects were found when the tomb filling was sieved:

Scarabs, scaraboids and seals: Pl. 43: 11, 50
Pl. 45: 128, 159, 162
F. Nos. 4863, limestone, illegible, NP

Beads: Pl. 66: 4, 5, 11, 14, 16, 18, 21, 22, 27, 28, 33, 34, 38, 39, 41, 42, 43, 44, 48, 49, 55, 57, 58, 62–66, 69, 71, 73, 74, 77, 79, 84, 86
Pl. 67: 91, 100, 103, 107–110, 112, 113, 116, 128, 130, 136, 137, 143

219 Tomb in Grid Square A.4 (Fig. 26)   Chamber tomb 850–750 B.C.?

The tomb was entered by a narrow sloping passage to the west; it had consisted of at least three chambers, with a further blocked door to the north, isolating the tomb from a quarried area. The cutting of the doorways was square and regular, and there were sharp angles at the floor level of Room A. The roof had collapsed anciently and there were no traces of burials (Pl. 6: 2).

Pottery: L.4–6 J.2 Misc. Misc.
148, 209, 307, 377

Objects: Bone pin   Pl. 56: 1
Faience playing piece   Pl. 56: 2
Beads   Pl. 66: 13, 38
Stone weight, No. 39 on List of Weights, p. 354

220 Quarry (?) in Grid Square A.4   Roman. 3rd–4th cent. A.D.

The cutting adjoined the Late Bronze Age Tomb 221 on the west, but it had not quite broken through to the earlier chamber. The five steps were deeper than is usually required for a stairway, and they appear to have been removed for building purposes. No human bones were found, though an ox-skull lay on the bottom step. The broken juglet, type 309, belongs to the period of the Jewish monarchy.

Pottery: Misc. D.8 CP
272, 309, 464

Objects: AE ear-ring   NP
Frag. Fe nail   NP

221 Tomb in Grid Square A.5   LB cutting

Most of the objects from this tomb were Late Bronze in date, but there were some Iron Age sherds.

222 Single grave in Grid Square AA.6   950–700 B.C.

The grave was oriented north–south, and cut in the rock. The skeleton lay with head to the south, face to the west, and attitude extended. The stone paving of building 227 was laid over the lower part of the skeleton,

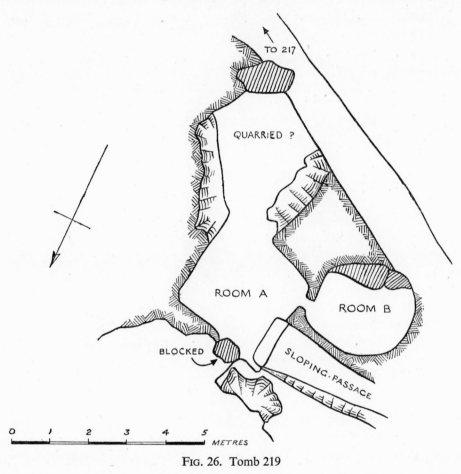

FIG. 26. Tomb 219

and it is therefore certain that the grave pre-dates the building. It probably formed one of the series of single graves, many of which are grouped round the Fosse Temple.

Sherds included fragments of a storage jar.

223 Tomb in Grid Square A.5 (Fig. 27)   LB cave adapted as triple-chambered
tomb, under Tomb 218, over Tomb
230. Burials *c.* 900 B.C.

In the floor of Tomb 218 cavities were found which proved to be due to the collapse of the ceiling of the chambers below. The blocked entrance passage of this lower tomb was provided with seven steps flanked by retaining walls, and led to three rooms or recesses. The innermost room had a circular repository on the east side.

Room C, nearest the entrance, had been completely cleared, and was divided from the inner rooms, A and B, by a rough wall of stones extending across the width of the tomb. Apparently the skeletons and objects in Rooms

A and B were collected there and sealed off from the entry when a square shaft was cut in the floor of Room C to give access to another chamber at a lower level, Tomb 230 (Pl. 6: 3–5).

All three tombs, 218, 223 and 230, had been driven into the escarpment rising towards the tell from the west. It would appear that Tombs 218 and 230 were both originally bilobate and contained some Middle Bronze Age sherds. Tomb 223, however, where Late Bronze Age sherds and Base-ring ware similar to L. II, type 280, were collected in Room A, was the later cutting. The offerings and bones in the inner rooms were roughly contemporary with those in Tomb 218, though they did not cover such a long range.

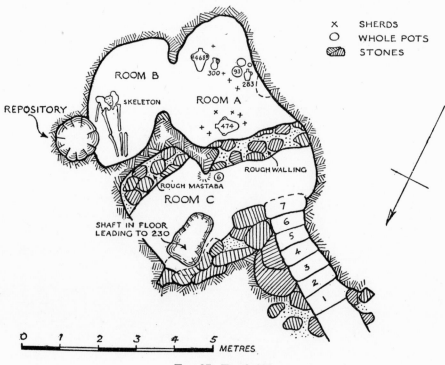

FIG. 27. Tomb 223

Date and Comparisons

The pottery and objects in Tomb 223 form a sealed group which was deposited before the partition wall was built. While there is nothing in the contents which could not equally have come from Tomb 218, it is clear that Tomb 223 had a much shorter history.

The first sign of renewed Egyptian contact is seen in the presence of a faience amulet of Sekhmet, and though there are no scarabs, two plaques with designs on both sides record an interest in Egyptian motifs.

Bronze, silver and iron were used for personal ornaments; among them, the plain, semicircular arc fibula is extremely rare in Palestine, though it is not unknown in Circassian sites. Beads were common. They were coarse descendants of LB types and more than half were disks of bone or composition.

Pottery
Bowls

Class	Types	Total
B.4	6(2), 8(3), 11, 13, 20, 53	9
B.5	41, 57	2
B.6	93	1
		12

212

Two-thirds of the bowls in the group were plain, without slip or burnish, made of a pink to buff ware which had contained many limestone grits. The usual base is a low ring, which shows an interesting development in type 6, where the middle is lower than the surrounding wall—a peculiarity which also occurs in some jugs in the group and in Tomb 218.

The four burnished bowls, types 11, 20, 53 and 93, are all covered with red slip inside, extending half-way down the exterior. The method of application is similar to that of bowls in Tomb 521 in three cases—the strokes follow the rim and are then applied irregularly across the centre—but type 20 shows a bold technique of widely spaced strokes so as to form a rough square.

Lamps

Class	Types	Total
L.1–3	140, 144, 147	3
L.7–8	151(2)	2
		5

Five lamps are listed, but two examples attributed to Class L.7–8 have not been traced; they would, indeed, be incongruous in the present context. The three remaining lamps belong to Class L.1–3. An example of type 140 is comparable to a lamp from Tomb 521, but the carinated exterior of others in that early group is not represented.

Jugs

Class	Types	Total
J.1	221	1
J.2	203	1
J.3	226	1
J.4	180	1
		4

Each class is represented by a single jug. Jug 221 is conspicuous for its dark red, almost plum-coloured slip, carefully burnished in close vertical strokes over the neck, body and base. There is a slight groove below the rim, and black and white bands are painted around the body. For ware and technique, compare the small pithos 418, and dippers 296 and 283, from the present group, and jug 220 from Tomb 218.

Dippers and Juglets

Class	Types	Total
D.1b	300, 302(3)	4
D.3	296(3)	3
D.4b	283	1
D.7b	324(2)	2
		10

Types 300 and 302 are two varieties of pinched-mouth juglets characteristic of all groups prior to Tomb 1002. They do not differ greatly from those in Tomb 521, except that they are fired to a lighter red.

Type 296 is represented by two juglets, both covered all over with a burnished red slip; in one case the strokes are applied vertically over the neck and body, and in the other they tend to be irregular below the neck.

Type 283 is the earliest example of a shape and style common in Tomb 218. It retains a plum-coloured vertical burnish, but has acquired a drop-shaped body and an oblong rather than a pinched mouth.

Type 324 was originally covered with red slip and burnish, but nearly all the surface has worn away. The lower part is missing and it is therefore uncertain whether it had a button base. Typologically it is early in the development of the class.

Chalices

Class	Type	Total
Cha.	164	1

Miniature Pithoi

Class	Type	Total
MP	418	1

Storage Jars

Class	Types	Total
S.1	468, 473, 474(4), 476	7
S.4	470	1
		8

Distribution of Pottery in Tomb 223

Type	Class	Room A	Room B	Sherds	Total
6	B.4	2	—	—	2
8	B.4	2	1	—	3
11	B.4	1	—	—	1
13	B.4	1	—	—	1
20	B.4	—	1	—	1
29	B.4	—	1	—	1
41	B.5	—	1	—	1
53*	B.4	—	1	—	1
57	B.5	—	1	—	1
93	B.6	1	—	—	1
143	L.1–3	—	1	—	1
144	L.1–3	1	—	—	1
147	L.1–3	1	—	—	1
151	L.7–8	1	1	—	2
164*	Cha.	1	—	—	1
180	J.4	1	—	—	1
203	J.2	1	—	—	1
221	J.1	1	—	—	1
226*	J.3	1	—	—	1
283	D.4b	1	—	—	1
296*	D.3	2	1	—	3
300	D.1b	1	—	—	1
302	D.1b	1	2	—	3
324	D.7b	—	2	—	2
418*	MP	1	—	—	1
468	S.1	1	—	—	1
470	S.4	1	—	—	1
473	S.1	1	—	—	1
474	S.1	4	—	—	4
476	S.1	1	—	—	1

* Pl. 73: 13–18.

Objects:

Pottery bird vessel	Pl. 30: 25	AR ear-rings	Pl. 56: 6
Amulet	Pl. 35: 36	Fe fibula	Pl. 56: 7
Plaques	Pl. 45: 133, 134	AE ring	Pl. 56: 8
Bone lid	Pl. 56: 3	AE awl (?)	F. No. 4945 NP
AE bangles, anklets	Pl. 56: 4, 9	Beads	Pl. 66: 5, 13–15, 17, 33, 38, 55, 65, 86
AE handle	Pl. 56: 5		Pl. 67: 116

All the objects came from Room A.

224 Tomb in Grid Square A.5

Oval chamber. MB bilobate?
Burials *c.* 860–820 B.C.

The shaft numbered 228 which led to Tomb 224 from the west was blocked by large and small stones. The roof of the chamber within was intact and had been supported at one time by a rough stone wall which bisected the chamber along the main axis, from east to west. Unlike Tomb 218, which adjoined 224 to the north at the same level, no repository had been added.

Only eight skulls out of many burials were moderately intact, and the pottery and small objects had been much disturbed.

Date and Comparisons

Though the bulk of the pottery found in Tomb 224 was comparable in many ways to that of Tombs 218 and 116, a distinct retrogression in the use of burnish is very noticeable. Bowls were no longer covered all over with slip and burnish. The former was only applied on half the exterior face, and in a further phase it was only used on the interior of the bowls.

The first examples of wheel burnish appear in this tomb: two are round-based bowls in Class B.6.

No ornaments made of iron were recovered; an iron knife and two armour scales suggest that the metal was reserved solely for practical purposes. Bangles, rings and ear-rings of bronze were much less common than in other tombs.

The three scarabs were very poor in workmanship and design, but in compensation, there were two striking scaraboids of shaggy-necked beasts, besides another of inferior execution. There were fewer faience amulets of Sekhmet, but the first examples of the Sacred Eye appear.

Beads were present in quantity, but the quality was indifferent.

Pottery

Bowls

Class	Types	Total	Class	Types	Total
B.4	7(2), 8, 13	4	B.7	9(10), 39(2), 40(2), 48	15
B.5	42, 56	2	B.10	35(2), 102	3
B.6	89, 90(3), 91(2), 93(2), 94(4), 96	13			37

Plain bowls without slip or burnish are prominent in the group. They mostly belong to Class B.7, which is only represented by sherds in Tomb 218, but there are almost as many bowls with irregular hand burnish inside and to the keel out, which can be divided between Classes B.4–7.

The figures given below should be compared with those for Tomb 218.

Analysis of Burnish

HAND BURNISHED				WHEEL		PLAIN	
In. and to keel out.		In. only and transitional					
Class	Type	Class	Type	Class	Type	Class	Type
B.4	8	B.4	7(2)			B.4	13
B.5	42					B.5	56
B.6	90(2)	B.6	91(2)	B.6	89		
	94(4)		93(2)		90		
	96						
B.7	40(2)			B.7	39	B.7	9(10)
	48						39
B.10	35(2)	B.10	102				
TOTALS	14		7		3		13

One bowl, F. No. 5007, not included in the list, had a red slip and irregular hand burnish inside and to the keel out, with the burnish continued over the base on a plain surface. Otherwise it will be noted that bowls burnished all over were no longer made.

Lamps

Class	Types	Total
L.1–3	144, 147(26)	27
L.4–6	145(2), 146, 148(3)	6
		33

The predominant form is type 147. The type specimen is drawn without a flange inside, but many examples have a rounded rim which is closely approaching the flat internal rim of type 148. The ware is nearly always brown or light brown, medium fired.

Jugs

Class	Types	Total
J.2	200, 203(4), 207, 208	7
J.3	215, 217	2
J.4	165, 168(5), 176(2), 177(2), 180(3), 183(6), 184, 187(2)	22
J.5	189, 190(2), 196	4
J.6	241	1
		36

The jugs are larger than those in Tomb 218, ranging from 12 to 18 cm. in height, and the necks are curved rather than straight as in the previous groups. The ware is red or light brown, well levigated without many grits, in contrast to the jugs in Tomb 218, and made of coarser clay without much limestone temper. The mouths of the jugs in Tomb 224 are round, with the exception of types 215 and 217.

Outstanding forms include type 241, for which there are parallels in Phoenician colony sites of the eighth and seventh centuries. In Cyprus, such jugs were imported during Cypro-Geometric III B, *c.* 775–700 B.C. (GSCE IV, pt. 2, pp. 296 and 438).

Dippers and Juglets

Class	Types	Total	Class	Types	Total
D.1b	300(2), 301(7), 302(5)	14	D.6a	329, 337(5)	6
D.3	296	1	D.7a, b	317, 322(25)	26
D.4	286(3)	3			50

Classes D.1, 3, 4. Dippers are less numerous than in Tomb 218, and only one example, type 296, is covered with dark red slip and vertically burnished, while two specimens of type 286 introduce a light vertical self burnish on a brown surface, destined to become popular in later groups.

Class D.6: Cypro-Phoenician wares. The five specimens of Black-on-Red I (III) juglets do not show any typological advance on those from Tomb 218. Tomb 224 also contained a fragment of a barrel-shaped juglet made of buff ware, fired medium and decorated with fine black matt lines encircling a red centre. It is comparable to Bichrome III ware. For a full discussion of the chronological implications of these forms, see Chapter 9.

Class D.7. Twenty-six black burnished juglets were recovered, twice the number found in Tomb 218. The surface of the juglets is better preserved than in the previous group, due to harder firing, and the slip and burnish had been carefully applied in vertical strokes all'over. The average height ranges from 10·5 to 7·5 cm.; two examples have a small squat body, approaching type 309, but in no case does the handle join the rim.

Chalices

Class	Types	Total
Cha.	158, 159, 162(2)	4

All these forms have an angular keel and a wide flanged rim, like the fragment in Tomb 218. The ware is pink or buff, fired soft to medium, and there are occasional traces of paint.

Potstands

Class	Type	Total
PS	395	1

Ring potstands were not usually placed in tombs, and this is the only example found with burials at Tell ed-Duweir.

Miniature Amphorae

Class	Type	Total
MA	415	1

This single example is close to the end of the series of amphorae. It was made of black ware, fired medium and had some traces of burnish on a worn surface. The lug handles were pierced vertically.

Storage Jars

Class	Types	Total
S.1	468(2), 474, 475	4

Two examples of type 468 were so badly broken that they were not preserved. Types 474 and 475 belong to the same class.

Jugs or Jars with Spouts

Class	Type	Total
JS	363	1

The strainer spout jug, type 363, is less evenly burnished than type 364 from Tomb 521, and has a handle with a plain oval section and an unridged neck. Both these features are typologically early.

Objects:	Fe knife	Pl. 56: 10
	Fe armour	Pl. 56: 11, 12
	AE anklets	Pl. 56: 15
	AE ear-ring	Pl. 56: 16
	AE armour	F. No. 5047A NP
	Bone ferrule	Pl. 56: 13
	Bone pendants	Pl. 56: 14 and
		Pl. 37: 26, 27
	Scaraboids	Pl. 44: 83, 100, 101, 117
	Scarabs	Pl. 43: 45, 60
	Scarab, amethyst, plain	F. No. 5057 NP
	Amulets	Pl. 35: 37, 38
	Amulet, Sekhmet	F. No. 5061 NP (as Pl. 34: 29)
	Knuckle bones	F. No. 5064 NP
	Beads	Pl. 66: 2, 4, 13, 15, 17, 21, 22, 33, 34, 38, 41, 44, 49, 66, 69, 72, 81
		Pl. 67: 90, 92, 97, 98, 116, 143, 145

225 Well or cistern in Grid Square A.6   *c.* 2000–700 B.C.

The well head was partially stone-lined, and there was a circular annexe to the north-east. Sherds of Middle Bronze, Late Bronze and Iron Age date came from the filling, but the well was not excavated to its full depth.

227 Room in Grid Square AA.6   *c.* 450 B.C.

Part of a building constructed over the original Bronze Age entrance to ossuary 120, the blocking of which had never been disturbed. The two chalices marked as from 227 were probably associated with the funerary offerings made at the entrance to Tomb 120.

There were several paved floors in the building, which probably continued under the unexcavated area to the west. Below the floors there were two single graves, 222 and 229, both oriented north–south, and probably part of the series which was mainly grouped round the Fosse Temple. The building must therefore be later than the graves: the style of stone work suggests a sixth- to fourth-century date.

Pottery: Cha. Cha.
         157, 160

228 Outer part of Tomb 224 in Grid Square A.5
See Tomb 224.

229 Single grave in Grid Square A.6   950–700 B.C.

The grave was cut in the earth and was oriented north and south. It was approached by a shallow shaft, and there was a space for the burial alongside. The body was missing, but four pots were grouped together at one end of the grave. Although it was not actually covered by the walls or floor of building 227, the grave appeared to be within the limits of the structure, which is presumably later.

Pottery: B.4   J.2   D.3
         20, 203(2), 296

230 Tomb in Grid Square A.4/5   Oval chamber. Burials *c.* 850 B.C.

The chamber, somewhat larger than Tomb 224 to the south, was cut in the escarpment rising towards the tell, and was the lowest of three superimposed tombs. During the Iron Age it was re-entered from a small shaft cut in the floor of Tomb 223 above (Pl. 6: 5), for the original entry to the west, with two steps, was still blocked by stones.

Nine pots, equipment for one or two burials at most, would fall within the range of Tombs 116 and 224. No bones were found, but large blocks of stone had fallen from the ceiling (Pl. 6: 6).

Pottery: B.5 L.1–3 L.4–6 D.3 D.1a D.7b Misc. S.4 S.1
         42, 141, 145, 296, 298, 314, 354, 471, 473

231 Single grave in Grid Square D.9   950–700 B.C.

The grave was cut in the earth and was oriented north and south. The head had been placed to the north, but was missing, and the attitude of the skeleton was extended. A burnished flask, similar to form 315, was close to the place where the head had been. Grave 231 overlay Grave 236.

236 Single grave in Grid Square D.9   950–700 B.C.

A shallow grave under Grave 231 was oriented north and south; it contained a skeleton with the head to the north, face to the west, and attitude extended. A bracelet was in position on the left arm, but nothing else remained of the funerary equipment, beyond a few sherds.

Object: AE bracelet   Pl. 56: 17

239 Single grave in Grid Square D.9   950–700 B.C.

The grave was cut into the earth and was oriented north and south. The body was placed with head to the north, face to the west, and attitude extended. The skull was kept for examination (see Appendix A, No. 807). There were some sherds, mostly of Late Bronze Age origin.

Pottery: D.1b
         302

CHAPTER 8
AREAS 500, 1000, 4000, 6000, 7000

Area 500 (Pls. 7: 1–2; 126)

THE exposed rock surface of Area 500 consisted of nari limestone, the whole extent of which had been tunnelled and undercut by the excavation of large chambers in the softer underlying howr stratum; eventually the upper layer weakened and collapsed, and the contents of the cave chambers were buried in a matrix of water-laid red mud from the alluvium of the plateau, which stretches as far as the eye can see to the south-west of the mound.

Very naturally, the isthmus of land providing an easy means of access to the city was normally occupied in ancient times by shacks and booths, so that the camphouse of the Wellcome Expedition was constructed on a site which had been lived on from the earliest times (Pl. 7: 1, 2). Except where caves had subsided and filled up, the rock was either exposed or covered with such a thin layer of soil that sectional observations were untrustworthy.

On both sides of the line of approach from the Wadi Ghafr there were traces of rubble and stone house foundations, and on the lower terrace, which formed the courtyard of the camphouse, there were some more substantial remains of buildings, with rough cobbled floors and an alinement of upright pillars in the style of Levels III–II. Like similar houses on the mound, they had been destroyed by fire.

On the way up from the south-western valley the nari cap breaks off suddenly, leaving a jagged, uneven edge along the scarp (Pl. 2: 3). Except for the unique Tomb 521, excavation of that area was unproductive, owing to constant denudation and regular use of the path. Close to the summit of the isthmus were traces of a cutting which may represent the exterior edge of the Middle Bronze Age Fosse. In the broken side two large chambers had been cut and faced with plaster, but they were much damaged by quarrying in mid-Jewish times. Inside and outside the chambers, and probably in the Fosse, which was not excavated to its full depth, there were many fragments of anthropoid coffins, with pottery and objects which should date from the last phase of the Bronze Age with a possible extension into the Early Iron Age. As the pottery of these tombs, 570 and 571, is more closely allied to the ware and decorative motifs of the Bronze Age, the contents will be published in *Lachish IV*. The pits formed by the subsidence of the two caves had been filled and levelled during the Jewish period, and the approach road to the city passed over them.

Though there are few structural remains which can be attributed with confidence to the post-exilic period, there are scattered deposits of pottery, crude altars, and figurines (Groups 506, 515, 522 and 534), which show that people still congregated near the gate of the city.

503 Pit in Grid Square B.22   c. 1300 B.C.–c. A.D. 100

The pit contained Late Bronze, Iron Age and Roman sherds. High in the filling was the ribbed cooking pot, type 463. Below it were the Iron Age fragments, and at the bottom were some Bronze Age forms, to be published in *Lachish IV*.

Pottery: D.2a D.6b CP
    287, 325, 463*
    * Pl. 76: 33.

504 Cave in Grid Squares C/D.24/25   c. 2000 B.C., in frequent use until c. A.D. 400

The roof of this large irregularly shaped cavern had partly collapsed. Though it was originally made during the Early Bronze Age, it had frequently been used as a dwelling and quarry. During the Iron Age it seems to have been a dyeing establishment. A stone vat was set below floor level, and the surrounding area drained into it. In the centre of the chamber was a shaft Grave 525, cut in the rock (Pl. 7: 4). The fine seal (Pl. 45: 141) found in the cave filling possibly belonged to the burials. The lamps 134 and 135 are forms of the fourth century A.D.

Pottery: L.12 L.12
134, 135(2)*
* Pl. 76: 29.

Objects: Conical seal   Pl. 45: 141
AE bangle   Pl. 56: 18
Frags. pottery and glass   F. No. 3438, NP

505 Buildings in Grid Square D.25   Built after 700 B.C., burnt in 588–586 B.C.

The plans were incomplete in all directions, and there was seldom more than one course of the remaining walls in position. There may have been two houses, side by side, for on the analogy of similar constructions the alinement of upright stone pillars normally divides the narrow width of the building. The relationship of the large room, or Court A, to the smaller apartments (B, C and D), adjoining it on the south, is therefore uncertain. Some burnt brickwork found on the floor of A suggests that the walls were made of brick, founded on one or two courses of rough stones. There were six standing pillars of nari limestone, somewhat square in section: the spaces between them were filled, in some cases, with rubble and small stones. Four or five pillars had fallen on their sides, and parts of the roughly paved floors were still in position (Pl. 7: 5). The building was destroyed by fire, and both iron and bronze arrowheads were found in the vicinity. There were no complete pots, but the sherds are comparable to those from Level II, so that it is reasonably certain that the building, which was perhaps used as a stable, was destroyed in 588–586 B.C.

Pottery: B.7 B.7 B.13 B.13 B.13 B.13 B.13 J.8   PS   S.2 S.7b S.9 S.12 B.11 B.13 CP   CP
48, 54, 73, 81, 84, 120, 122, 280, 396, 472, 483, 491, 550, 560, 640, 684, 693
(all from Court A).

506 Deposit in Grid Square B.25   550–450 B.C.

The number 506 denotes a deposit of limestone altars, found in the soil only a few centimetres below the present ground surface. Similar undecorated forms were found in the deposits 515 and 522 (Pls. 68: 2 and 71: 18, 24) and the group 534 should also be considered in the same context.

Objects: 13 altars, F. No. 3440, NP

507 Pit in Grid Square C.23   *c.* 850 B.C.

The irregularly cut pit may have contained one or more burials, but only two skull fragments were found under bowl 89, and it was obvious that the group had been much disturbed. The four pots have some value as a contemporary deposit. The bowl is hand burnished inside and to the keel outside, so that the group should be contemporary with the early occupation of Tomb 224, before the introduction of wheel burnish.

Pottery: B.6   J.4   D.6b S.1
89, 165, 325, 474

Objects: Sandstone hone   Pl. 56: 19

509 Cistern in Grid Square C.24   ?

No contents.

511 Stones in Grid Square E.26 ?

Two lines of stones parallel to the edge of the slope down to the Wadi Ghafr, and consisting of a single course only, should perhaps be considered as the remains of a retaining wall rather than as part of a building. Five scarabs found in the vicinity all show characteristics of the Middle Bronze Age and will be published in *Lachish IV*.

Objects: AE, Fe arrowheads   F. No. 3465 NP
         Beads   Pl. 66: 16, 61

513 Domestic rubbish pit in Grid Square B.21 *c.* 700–586 B.C.

An irregularly shaped pit containing some sherds, mostly of cooking pots, which are typical of Levels III and II.

Pottery: CP CP CP
        443, 450, 458

515 Cave in Grid Square AA.23 *c.* 2000 B.C., in frequent use until *c.* 100 B.C.

An irregularly shaped cavern constructed as a dwelling in the Early Bronze Age. The entrance to the west was still sealed with stones and earth, though the roof had partially collapsed. It contained human remains and thirty limestone altars, which were similar to those in the deposits 506, 522 and 534. With the altars was part of a pottery horse and rider, and this association is also to be observed in the Solar Shrine. The scarab was crude enough to fit into this late context, and the flat beaten ear-ring almost certainly belongs. For a general view of the deposit during clearance, see Pl. 7: 6.

Pottery: L.12 D.9 D.9
        138, 340, 341

Objects: Pottery figurines   Pl. 33: 4
         Scarab   Pl. 43: 48
         AE ear-ring   Pl. 56: 20
         30 crude altars, some decorated F. No. 3481 NP and Pl. 71: 19

517 Domestic rubbish pit in Grid Square A.24 ?

The pit was small and irregularly shaped; it contained sherds only.

518 Single grave in Grid Square A.24 *c.* 950 B.C.

A single oval grave, oriented north and south, cut in the soil. The skeleton lay in an extended position, with the head to the north. The only offering was a small irregularly hand-burnished flask.

Contemporary with the burials near the Fosse Temple, Grave 518 appears to be the only one of the kind so near the city gate. It is surprising that it remained undisturbed.

Pottery: Misc.
        316

519 Single grave in Grid Square A.24 950–700 B.C.

A single grave, probably oval in shape, cut in the surface soil. The head of the skeleton was placed to the south.

Pottery: J.6
        230

520 Pit in Grid Square AA.22

An irregularly shaped hole cut in the rock, in which there were no traces of human remains. The only contents were some Late Bronze and Iron Age sherds.

521 Tomb in Grid Square AA.22 Rectangular chamber, shaft entry, *c.* 1000 B.C.

Cut close to the scarp which dips to the western valley, Tomb 521 was entered through a shaft or pit on the east and narrow side of the rectangular chamber. When the shaft was cleared of earth the entry was found to be still blocked with stones. Their removal exposed a door some 60 cm. in diameter, and beyond, in the dark interior which was free of the usual filling of fine infiltrated soil, the skeletons and offerings were laid out, undisturbed except by the action of water.

Along the north wall of the tomb there was a metre-wide bench composed of natural rock and boulders, and lying on it with heads to the west were two skeletons, which had originally been placed one above the other. The uppermost was that of an adult male (Appendix A, No. 800), and the body had shifted so close to the edge of the bench that a leg hung down. The smaller skeleton, which was in less good condition, was not preserved (Pl. 8: 1, 2).

Though there was nothing on the very narrow ledge along the south wall, there were the remains of two more interments lying slightly above floor level at the far end of the tomb (Pl. 8: 1). If they were displaced to make room for the bodies on the bench, the removal must have been carefully done while the bones were still in articulation, for the skeletons were not disturbed, though they were crushed by a fall of rock from the roof.

The smaller vessels in the tomb were grouped close to the heads on the bench, while the storage jars were lying on the floor. On the rock near the entrance was the iron trident (Pl. 8: 3).

Date and Comparisons

The contents of Tomb 521 are exceptional; they represent the funerary equipment of the earliest large tomb exclusively belonging to the Iron Age which has been so far recovered from the site. Moreover, it appears that the tomb was never re-entered after the last bodies were interred, so that the group is consistent and contemporary.

There are points of contact between the group and Tombs 223 and 218, but its earlier position is established by a higher percentage of burnished bowls. Other burnished forms are the jugs with strainer spouts which are mainly grouped in the tenth to ninth centuries at Gerar, and the jug 202 which imitates the metal prototype. Of the four storage jars, types 477 and 480 are uncommon, finding their best parallels with fragments from Tell el-Fûl dated to the eleventh to tenth centuries, and 'Ain Shems, Stratum II respectively.

The trident and one of three iron knives are comparable to products of the Early Iron Age in Europe. The habit of placing tridents or bidents in tombs was common at Sialk Necropolis at about the same time; a close adherence of pottery to metal prototypes here, and the use of gaming boards are other links which should not be ignored.

On the single scarab, which is very worn, it is perhaps possible to recognise a kneeling Nile figure introduced on the scarabs of Painozem I of Thebes, who reigned *c.* 1070–1030 B.C. (CAH III, p. 254).

The ivory (bone?) gaming board or calendar, of which a better example was found by Petrie at Tell el-Fara, seems to be the Palestinian variety of a widespread class.

In conclusion, the few comparisons available suggest a date in the vicinity of 1000 B.C. for the tomb, which seems to have been used by a family of four people, two of whom may have been of an older generation, or of inferior rank.

Pottery

The group contained over twenty vessels—bowls, lamps, jugs, dippers and jars—comprising the usual stock of the Iron Age potter. There is a striking similarity of ware and burnish throughout the group, and the outstanding characteristics are described below, and under the appropriate numbers opposite the pottery plates.

Bowls

Class	Types	Total
B.4	8, 99(2),* 105*	4
B.5	55*	1
		5

Types 8 and 55 show traces of a red slip inside, though the surface has suffered so much through damp that the variety of stroke remains uncertain.

Type 99(2): Each bowl was covered with a slip and burnish all over, including the flat base. Inside, the strokes conformed to the rim line for about 3 cm., and were then applied irregularly across the centre. The effect on the exterior was irregular or criss-cross. The larger bowl (diameter 21·5 cm.) had an exceptionally wide base (12 cm.) marked with two concentric grooves. The second example measured 18 cm. in rim diameter. Both had unpierced lugs attached to the rim and originally each had a bar between the lugs, marking a degraded stage of the spatulate handle.

Type 105 was 13·5 cm. in diameter, and two small lugs were attached close to the rim, with a bar between them. Irregularly burnished slip covered the interior of the bowl and reached half-way down the exterior.

Lamps

Class	Types	Total
L.1–3	140, 142,* 143(2)	4

The shapes are still close to some Late Bronze Age forms; in three out of four examples the distinctive feature is an exterior carination, marked in the interior by a definite flange. All are carefully finished, and there are indications of a sunk centre in two examples.

Jugs

Class	Types	Total
J.2	202*	1
J.4	184	1
		2

Type 202 is an exceptional piece: like the bowls in the group, it shows how closely the potter followed the metal prototype in reproducing knobs to represent the rivets for the handle of the metal original, both inside and outside the rim and at the base of the handle.

Type 184 is the earliest representative of the most common form in the Middle Iron Age; there is little to distinguish it from later examples, though the ware is possibly a deeper shade of red. The unburnished surface has been affected by damp.

Dippers and Juglets

Class	Types	Total
D.1b	302(2)	2
D.7a	328	1
		3

Both examples of type 302 are similar in ware and finish; they measure 12 cm. and 10 cm. in height respectively. The soft brown ware is covered with a deep red slip, in rather striking contrast to the similar juglets in the later groups 223, 218 and 224, which are more often plain, with a harder surface.

Type 328 is the earliest black burnished juglet, indicated by the elegant form with a button base and the low attachment of the handle.

Storage Jars

Class	Types	Total
S.1	468, 476, 477	3
S.4	480*	1
		4

The jars vary in the shape of the body and the height of the plain neck, but they all show a marked angle at the turn of the shoulder.

Type 480 is uncommon at Tell ed-Duweir. The ovoid body is normal, but the ridged neck (diameter 11 cm.) can be compared with fragments from Tell el-Fûl (AASOR IV, Pl. XXVIII: 1, 2, 9–11), which Albright dates to the late eleventh and early tenth centuries.

Type 477 is also rare and may find affinity with a jar from 'Ain Shems (AS IV, Pl. LXV: 41) which came from Stratum II, b–c. The surface of both 480 and 477 is well smoothed, in contrast to types 468 and 476, which are somewhat coarse and gritty. They seem to belong to an earlier tradition, while 468 and 476 became common during the occupation of the later tombs.

Jugs or Jars with Spouts

Class	Type	Total
JS	364*	1

Type 364, with a strainer spout, is a well-made specimen burnished all over with close vertical strokes. The thick red slip flakes off easily to expose a soft brown ware. The neck is only slightly ridged by the addition to the exterior of a narrow strip of clay, but the handle is deeply grooved, like those of the decanters in Class J.8 (cf. type 363 from Tomb 224, where the section of the handle is oval and the neck is plain).

Miscellaneous

Class	Types	Total
Misc.	118, 335*	2

Type 118, a bowl with three loop feet, is covered with slip; the interior (diameter 9 cm.) is irregularly hand burnished, and the exterior is similarly treated as far as the loop attachments.

Type 335 can be compared to the only other round-based jug form with a narrow ridged neck which was found on the site, but ware and finish are very different. The plain surface without slip or burnish was originally ornamented on the neck, handle and body with red and white painted bands, but all the details are not clear, as much of the surface has perished.

* Pl. 72: 1–10.

Objects:

Fe knives	Pl. 56: 22, 26, 27
Fe trident	Pls. 56: 38 and 40: 7
Haematite pendant	Pl. 56: 21
Scarab	Pl. 43: 51
Scaraboid	Pl. 44: 96
Bone seals	Pls. 56: 24 and 37: 4; Pls. 56: 25 and 37: 1
Bone calendar?	Pls. 56: 23 and 37: 3
Bone spindlewhorl	Pl. 37: 2, 5

522 Area in Grid Square A.22

A number of pottery figurines were found scattered over the ground only a few centimetres below the present surface. They were associated with miscellaneous sherds, some dating to the Roman and Arab periods. The figurines were cast hollow in double moulds, and are illustrated and described on Pl. 33.

Objects: Pottery figurines   Pl. 33: 3, 5–14, 16–20

         Pottery figurines   F. Nos. 3488, 3489, 3491, 3492, 3494, 3498, 3504, 3505, 3507, 3508, 3510–3513, 3515, 3516, 3518–3522, 3524–3528 NP

523 Cave in Grid Square B.23

Date of construction unknown.
In use *c.* 1300–1000 B.C.

An artificial cavern of irregular shape, entered from the west. Various depressions in the floor suggest that at one time it was used for domestic or industrial purposes. Of the pottery forms recorded, all but two were typical of Structure III in the Fosse Temple. The Iron Age bowls were both burnished, and type 28 is the finest example from the site and must be dated very early in the period. Some fragments of iron were found, too corroded for identification.

Pottery: B.2   B.10

      28,   102

Object: Pottery figurine, worn and broken   F. No. 3539 NP

525 Grave in Grid Square C.25

c. 550–350 B.C.

Towards the southern end of the large cave and quarry 504, a grave had been cut deep into the rock floor. It was oriented east and west, and the main shaft had semicircular recesses to the south and west, which were not necessarily cut at the same time as the grave, though it seems probable that they were needed to lower the four large slabs of stone, which, with smaller stones in the crevices, still sealed the aperture of the shaft.

When the slabs were removed, two skeletons were found; that of an adult male lying above a disturbed body, presumably that of a female. The male skeleton lay extended with head to the east and the hands on the pelvis, and the lower body was similarly oriented. Nothing was found with the burials, but the bowl or footbath was in fragments on the stone sealing above.

A fine conical seal (Pl. 45: 141) found in the filling of the cave may have belonged originally to the burials. For views of the cave and the grave within, see Pl. 7: 3, 4.

Comparisons for the type of grave with east–west orientation are to be found in the "Philistine" graves at Gezer (Gezer I, pp. 289–300) and at 'Athlit (QDAP II, p. 41). Both groups are now dated to the 5th and 4th centuries B.C. (QDAP IV, p. 185).

Pottery: Misc.

      87*

       * Pl. 76: 17.

526 Cave or pit in Grid Square A.24

c. 700 B.C.

The pit was only partially excavated. From the pottery available it would appear to have been in use about the same time as the upper levels of Tomb 1002.

Pottery: B.4   B.4   B.10   D.8

      13,   20,   108,   309(2)

529 Cave in Grid Square A.24

?

The cave adjoined the partially excavated pit 526, and was divided from it by a streak of mizzi embedded in the softer howr limestone. The roof had consisted of the nari stratum, which was uppermost at Tell ed-Duweir, but it had partially collapsed. There were no human remains. The presence of a late lamp, and of a storage jar type which had an earlier history, is explained by a distinction of two levels in the cave.

Pottery: L.9–10   S.4

      153,   470

530 Pit in Grid Square AA.22   *c.* 1400–900 B.C.

    The oval pit was divided into two by a stone partition wall, and its sides had been plastered. The only fairly complete bowl was irregularly hand burnished inside and outside, which suggests that the pit was open until the tenth century at least.

Pottery: B.2
        597

531 Pit in Grid Square AB.23   ?

    The pit had been cut between two Late Bronze Age caves, 539 and 541. It was empty except for a juglet and some iron fragments.

Pottery: D.7a
        326

534 Cave in Grid Square A.24   *c.* 450–350 B.C.

    The number 534 marks the position of a deposit of limestone altars which had been thrown in disorder into a cavity made by the collapse of the cave (Pl. 8: 5, 6). The plastered trough 545, seen on Pl. 8: 6, is not necessarily contemporary. The pottery forms, which are exclusively associated with post-exilic buildings and pits, place this group and the similar ones 506, 515 and 522 in the fifth century B.C.

    The mortarium, type 568, is the distinctive vessel in the group, so common on the Residency floors. The storage jar rims are all consistent and belong to Class S.5. The fibula belongs to a class well established by the seventh century B.C. Professor Dupont-Sommer dates the Aramaic inscription on the altar (Pls. 49: 3 and 68: 1) to the fifth to fourth centuries B.C.

Pottery: S.5   S.5   S.5   S.5   S.5   B.14   B.12 Misc. PF
          517, 522, 525, 526, 527, 568,   575,   580,   675

Objects: AE fibula   Pl. 56: 29
          Altars   Pls. 68, 69, 70; Pl. 71: 17, 20–27; Pl. 42: 4, 5
          Inscribed altar   Pl. 49: 3
          Crude limestone carving of a locust   F. No. 3671 NP

    There were over 150 crude altars, nearly all in fragments; besides those published, there are 19 examples in the Palestine Museum (PM. 35.2960–2978) and at least 135 other examples.

535 Pit in Grid Square AB.22/23   ?
    Sherd only, NP.

540 Locus in Grid Square C.22   ?

    The number 540 marks the position of three cooking pots, two bronze bracelets and the fragments of an oil flask typed to a Middle Bronze Age form. The type of cooking pot is equally represented in Tombs 106 and 1002, but there is not enough evidence to establish a close date for the group.

Pottery: CP
        458(3) and an MB II oil flask
Objects: 2 AE bangles   Pl. 56: 28

544 Furnace in Grid Square AA.23   ?

    An industrial construction, probably a furnace, of which the plan only was preserved. It was oriented east and west and shaped like a cross, 3·5 m. in length, with two interconnected transverse limbs of 2 m. each.

545 Trough in Grid Square AA.24   ?

The trough was an oblong plastered construction founded directly on the howr rock, for the nari stratum had been quarried away in this area. It was placed centrally within a rectangle of single stones, which seems to have formed one side of a series of rooms 546, surrounding an open court. From the style of the building, it should belong to the post-exilic period. Hole-mouth jars found in the trough support this attribution. (Note trough in the background of Pl. 8: 6.)

Pottery: S.8
     537(3)

546 Building in Grid Square AA.24   ?

The building, already referred to in connexion with the plastered trough 545, was originally a construction covering about 20 square metres. Only one course of the stone foundations remained on the west and south sides, based directly on the rock.

The presence of two Late Bronze Age Tombs 543 and 556 beneath the walls has resulted in an admixture of sherds which range from that period onwards, and they are therefore no help in providing a date.

Pottery: L.7–8
     151

553 Pit in Grid Square A.25   *c.* 1400–1200 B.C. Re-used later.

The sides of the pit had originally been plastered. It had been largely cleared of its contents and was filled with masons' debris, possibly from the construction of the building 546 close by. An iron spike and some charcoal were the only objects found.

Object: Fe spike   F. No. 3765 NP

558 Pit in Grid Squares AA.25/26   ?

Details of the condition of the pit are not available. There is no record of the discovery of any human remains.

Pottery: L.7–8   D.8
     150,   311

Objects: Fe spearhead   Pl. 56: 30
          Fe arrowhead   Pl. 56: 31
          Faience flask   Pl. 56: 32
          Bone spindlewhorl   Pl. 56: 33

560 Building in Grid Square C.25   ?

The single course of small undressed stones set in double alinement which formed the foundations of the building was based on or close to the howr rock, underlying the uppermost stratum of nari which had been largely removed. Part of the building passed over a Bronze Age Cave 561, and the plan stopped short where the walls reached the nari outcrop. It would appear that the traces which remain belong to the substructure only. The walls on the higher plane, which completed the plan of the building, may have been cleared away for re-use elsewhere, and in late times a column base, very similar in style to those in the Residency, was partially detached from the nari stratum (marked on Pl. 126 at 248·84 m.).

A juglet, which is only paralleled by a form in Grave 182, *c.* 850 B.C., was the only whole type recovered, and any sherds found were uninformative. The "knee" type fibula probably belongs to the seventh-century period of occupation.

Pottery: D.1a
  288
Object: AE fibula   Pl. 56: 36

562 Cistern in Grid Square C.26

c. 750–450 B.C.

The cistern was approached by a small shaft from the south, and its sides were plastered. The flask, type 376, associated exclusively with post-exilic groups at Tell ed-Duweir, was found high in the filling. The five examples of jugs were well represented in the large Tombs 106 and 1002. Two rope-marked stones gave further confirmation that the pit was used for water storage, and it may have also served the adjoining building 560. The jar stamp classified as *hbrn* i (see Chapter 10) may date from about 700 B.C. or just before, and the "knee" type fibula belongs to a class which was well established by the seventh century B.C.

Pottery: J.4   J.4   J.5   Misc.
       169, 187(3), 189(2),   376
Objects: AE fibula   Pl. 56: 37
        Rope-marked lumps of limestone   F. No. 4384 NP

566 Oblong oven or furnace in Grid Square B.26

?

The oven was partly covered by a wall which ran over it, and a small area west of the construction was cobbled, suggesting that it was originally placed in an angle of the room, of which nearly all traces have disappeared. The sherds associated with it were of mixed date, from Middle Bronze Age II onwards.

569 Cave in Grid Square B.25

c. 1400–1200 B.C. In use to 8th century or later.

The cave was probably used as a tomb chamber in the Late Bronze Age, and part of the original funerary equipment remained. Sherds similar to those in Structure III of the Fosse Temple were found (L. II, types 125 and 250). Use of the cave continued in the early part of the Iron Age, as was indicated by the presence of bowl fragments, irregularly hand burnished inside and out; on the evidence of a decanter fragment, type 254, it was not abandoned until about the end of the eighth century.

Pottery: B.4 B.7 B.7 J.8
       18, 40, 48, 254
Objects: Fe knife   Pl. 56: 34
        AE spike   Pl. 56: 35

Area 600

Number not allocated.

Area 700 in Grid Squares E/F.07/08 (See Fig. 17)

For description of the Roman Road, see pp. 164.

Areas 800, 900

Numbers not allocated.

Area 1000 (Pls. 7: 1; 106)

The number 1000 designates the upper terrace of nari limestone, the eastern limits of which are represented by contour line 249 on the map (Pl. 106). This plateau extends for a considerable distance towards the south, and the level surface of alluvial soil is regularly ploughed. It is doubtful whether there are cuttings beyond the edge of the escarpment, where the softer limestone is not so easily accessible (Pl. 7: 1).

Construction of the camp premises led to an examination of the broken rock edge along the upper terrace where several caves were found which had been used at different times.

1001 Cistern in Grid Square D.29 4th century A.D.

A circular hole about a metre in diameter gave access to a deep bell-shaped cistern. The walls had been carefully plastered and the base, about 3 m. in diameter, was cut in the rock. Within a metre of the bottom, quantities of sherds of small spouted jugs were found, with some friable glass beads and bronze finger rings (NP).

Objects: Bone dagger top (?)   Pl. 57: 1
            Serpentine cylinder   Pl. 57: 2

1002 Cave in Grid Square E.30 Irregularly shaped pit, *c*. 810–710 B.C.

All that remained of the most productive burial-place at the site was an irregular pit cut in soft limestone underlying the nari stratum which had long since collapsed. Many boulders from that roof of nari blocked and hindered the clearance of the cave. There was no sign of an entrance passage, and it is possible that entry was gained through a hole in the roof, which was a means of access in the case of Tomb 1 at 'Ain Shems (APEF II, Pl. IV) which contains deposits of the same date.

The position of the cave (Pl. 8: 4) makes it a natural channel for the drainage of water towards the valley, and this, together with the collapse of the roof, had seriously affected the condition of the perishable contents.

However, neither cause is sufficient to account for the extreme disorder and fragmentary nature of the bones and there is reason to believe that part of the contents of the tomb were burned. Three skulls, at least, were blackened and partially destroyed by fire, and burnt patches were observed on the surface of many vessels. There is nothing to indicate that a burnt layer was observed during the excavation, and the filling throughout consisted of reddish waterlaid soil washed down from the plateau above.

The inference is that, like the ossuaries 107, 108, 116, 117 and 120, the deposit consists of secondary burials, and that the contents in all these groups were affected by fire before they were reburied.

Over 600 pottery vessels were recovered in good preservation, mixed with human remains and many small objects. For purposes of comparison the contents are presented in three divisions: layers 1–5 came from the upper part of the deposit, layers 6–10 represent the middle part, while layers 11–13 contain those vessels which were on or near the floor. Objects marked "Unstratified" are mostly associated with the lowest levels.

Date and Comparisons

Despite the disorder in the tomb the change between the contents of the bottom and topmost layers leaves no doubt that the contents were deposited over a considerable period of time. On the evidence of pottery form the floor of the tomb came into use shortly after the occupation of Tombs 224 and 1004, when wheel burnish was rapidly displacing a hand-finished surface. The final deposits may coincide with the middle years of Level III, though the evidence of bowl classes 12 and 13 seems to suggest that few burials were made as late as the date of its destruction.

On the whole, objects of Egyptian affinity show a decline in quality. The scarabs, for instance, are extremely poor; the designs are haphazard, the hieroglyphs are meaningless, and some motifs are introduced, such as the bird on Pl. 43: 41, which could never have been made by an Egyptian. On comparison with Tomb 218 the average size of the scarabs is seen to have decreased. There are fewer faience amulets, and the god Bes and the Sacred Eye replace Sekhmet and Isis in popularity, though there is one fine inscribed figure of Isis and Horus which may have been valued for some years.

Designs on the scaraboids have changed and are reduced to two: a man or men, and an antelope with conventional floral motifs. Whereas in Tomb 218 the scaraboids are all made of limestone or steatite, in Tomb 1002 there are only two of that material, with seven of bone and four of paste.

In relation to the size of the tomb, there is only a moderate amount of metal. The silver ear-rings include some formed to represent a female head and bust, which are rare, and bronze ear-rings are comparatively plentiful. Bangles, on the other hand, are less common than in Tomb 218, and are no longer so thick and heavy. Fragments of iron bangles are exclusive to the lowest layers. A plain iron fibula from the same horizon provides a close link with the deposit in Tomb 223, and a further development in the history of the safety-pin is illustrated by the insertion of an iron pin in a bronze semicircular arc. Bone pendants of all kinds are out of fashion, and are virtually extinct.

Pottery models make their chief appearance in Tomb 1002. In the lower layers there are three zoomorphic vessels of a kind which occur sporadically at various periods, a model of a bare-back horseman riding well forward on his steed, and a miniature bed. Concentrated in the upper part of the tomb are the pillar-base figurines, the birds on a stand, other model furniture, and the rattles. They closely resemble the pottery models from Tomb 1 at 'Ain Shems (APEF II, Pl. XXIII).

It is not easy to judge the span of years represented by the contents of Tomb 1002. In any case, it came into use when wheel burnish had gained the ascendancy over hand finish, when Egyptian contacts were less close, and when iron was less freely used for ornaments.

Following the decline in popularity of bone pendants and faience amulets, the pillar figurines and other pottery models introduced a new element into the funerary equipment of the time, which also penetrated independently into the Greek world, from a common unknown source, by the middle of the eighth century.

The division of the tomb contents into three parts represents an even division of time, judging from the numbers of bowls, lamps, jugs and dippers which are fairly balanced. If the tomb did not come into use until wheel burnish had become general, about 800 B.C., the final deposits should have been made nearly a hundred years later, though the scarcity of bowls in Class B.13 seems to rule out a date as late as 700 B.C. When it is recollected that the folded rim bowls were newly introduced to Samaria after the historic destruction of 720 B.C., the last deposits in Tomb 1002 should belong to the following decade.

Pottery

Bowls

Class	Layers 1–5			Layers 6–10			Layers 11–13		
	Types	Total		Types	Total		Types	Total	
B.3							26	1	
B.4	4, 11, 23(2)	4		13	1		7, 11, 13(4), 25	7	
B.5	41	1		43	1		56	1	
B.6	89(3), 92, 98	5		89(2), 90, 95(2)	5		89(3), 91, 95(2)	6	
B.7	9(4), 38, 40(3), 48(3), 52	12		9(3), 37, 39(2), 40(2), 46, 48(2), 49(3)	14		37(2), 40(3), 47, 48(4)	10	
B.8	1, 2	2		3(2)	2		3	1	
B.9	31(2)	2					5	1	
B.10	36, 102	2		36(2)	2				
B.11	62	1		60, 62, 63	3				
B.13	75(2)	2							
TOTALS		31			28			27	

230

It is unfortunate that not all the bowls from the group are available for final study. Of those in London, there are twelve hand-burnished bowls, thirty wheel-burnished specimens, and seven which are plain. The predominant finish is wheel burnish, either applied on a red slip, as found on hand-burnished bowls, or on a plain, unslipped surface. Two bowls from layers 11–13 had slip inside and to the keel outside, without burnish (B.4, type 11 and B.6, type 89).

Class B.3 is only found in the bottom of the tomb, and Classes B.10–13 are missing from those layers. Class B.6 is evenly represented throughout the group, but Class B.7 contains most examples in each layer. It is perhaps worth noting that the semispherical bowl type 8, so typical of earlier groups, is lacking, and its successor, type 13 in Class B.4, is only found in the lower part of the deposit. On the other hand, type 9 in Class B.7, which belongs to the second main group of common bowls, is confined to layers 1–10.

The proportion of ring to disk bases on the bowls is about equal.

Analysis of Burnish

HAND BURNISHED				WHEEL		PLAIN		WORN AND UNDEFINED	
In. and to keel out.		*In. only and transitional*		*Spiral on red slip or self*					
Class	*Type*	*Class*	*Type*	*Class*	*Type*	*Class*	*Type*	*Class*	*Type*
Layers 1–5								B.4	23
B.4	11			B.4	23				4
								B.5	41
						B.6	98	B.6	89(3)
									92
		B.7	38	B.7	48	B.7	9(2)	B.7	48
			40	(self)	48		40		9(2)
					52				40
				B.8	1				
					2				
				B.9	31			B.9	31
B.10	102	B.10	36					B.11	62
								B.13	75(2)
TOTALS	2		3		7		4		15
Layers 6–10									
				B.4	13				
B.5	43								
B.6	95			B.6	90			B.6	89(2)
					95				
B.7	46			B.7	39	B.7	40	B.7	9(3)
	48			(self)	40				37
				(self)	48				39
					49				49(2)
				B.8 (self)	3			B.8	3
		B.10	36	B.10	36				
				B.11 (self)	60			B.11	63
					62				
TOTALS	4		1		11		1		11

HAND BURNISHED				WHEEL		PLAIN		WORN AND UNDEFINED	
In. and to keel out.		*In. only and transitional*		*Spiral on red slip or self*					
Class	*Type*	*Class*	*Type*	*Class*	*Type*	*Class*	*Type*	*Class*	*Type*
Layers 11–13									
								B.3	26
B.4	25	B.4	7	B.4 (self)	13(2)	B.4	13	B.4	11*
								B.4	13
						B.5	56		
				B.6	89			B.6	89
					91				89*
									95(2)
				B.7	37			B.7	37
					40				40(2)
					47				48(2)
					48(2)				
				B.8 (self)	3				
				B.9	5				
TOTALS	1		1		11		2		12

* Red slip in. and to keel out., no burnish.

Lamps

	Layers 1–5		Layers 6–10		Layers 11–13	
Class	*Types*	*Total*	*Types*	*Total*	*Types*	*Total*
L.1–3	144(15), 147	16	—	—	147	1
L.4–6	146(3), 148(9)	12	148(23)	23	146(7), 148(30)	37
L.7–8	150(3), 151(2)	5	—	—	150(2)	2
L.9–10	153(4)	4	153	1	—	—
TOTALS		37		24		40

All classes are present in the group, though the emphasis is strong on Class L.4–6, containing varieties with round bases and flat flanged rims. Disk-based and high-footed lamps are missing from the lowest layers, and do not become significant until layers 1–5.

Jugs

	Layers 1–5		Layers 6–10		Layers 11–13	
Class	*Types*	*Total*	*Types*	*Total*	*Types*	*Total*
J.2	203, 206, 207	3	203(5), 207(3), 213	9	200, 201(2), 203(2), 206, 207, 208(2)	9
J.3	210(2), 218(2), 219	5	227(3), 228	4	214, 215(2), 224, 225, 227(2), 228	8
J.4	168, 171(7), 174, 176(4), 177, 178(6), 180(2), 182(2), 187(6)	30	165, 166, 169(4), 170(2), 171, 172, 176(8), 177, 178(5), 180(3), 182, 184(3), 187(6), 188	38	165, 168(5), 169(3), 170(2), 172, 176(5), 178(10), 180(3), 181, 184(3), 187(11)	45
J.5	185(3), 189(4), 190(3), 191(2), 195(2), 196(2)	16	186, 189, 190(10), 196(4)	16	167(3), 173, 186, 189(5), 190(17), 191, 196	29
J.6	220, 230, 247(2)	4	229, 230, 232, 236, 237	5	231(2), 247, 259	4
J.7	250, 252(4), 260, 261(3), 267, 269(2), 271	13	250(4), 252, 253, 258, 261, 262, 265(2), 267, 270, 271(3)	16	252(2), 256, 257, 258, 263, 265(3), 266, 268, 271(4)	15
J.8	—	—	—	—	254	1
TOTALS		71		88		111

Plain unburnished jugs were the most common vessel in Tomb 1002, and the incidence was very equally divided between the layers. Broadly speaking, it can be said that the forms with straight necks are typologically earlier than those with curved profiles, while a moulded rim is an even later development which is extremely rare before the occupation of this tomb.

Though more than a score of jugs in Class J.2 are recorded, the proportion is small in comparison with earlier groups. The ware is coarse red to brown or light brown, and originally contained a large amount of limestone; it is comparable to the ware of many jugs from Tombs 223, 218, 116 and 224 in Classes J.2 and J.4, which have a straight collar neck. The characteristic placing Class J.2 apart from J.4 is the provision of a small ring base, between 3·5 and 4·5 cm. in diameter. Otherwise there is often nothing to distinguish some jugs in Class J.2 from those in Class J.4.

Only five jugs in Class J.3 came from groups prior to Tomb 1002, and though trefoil-mouthed jugs with a flat base were never common, they are best represented in Tomb 1002. They are usually made of a light brown or pinkish ware with some grits, well fired and carefully finished, and no burnished examples are recorded.

In Class J.4 round-bottomed jugs are predominant, and the neck profiles vary from straight to curved. The ware of many examples is orange in tone, soft-fired, and where the surface is preserved traces of a buff slip are sometimes visible. At least four examples of type 176 were vertically hand burnished, over a red slip in one case, and over the plain surface of the pot on the other three vessels.

The jugs with a moulded rim in Class J.5 become prominent for the first time in the lower layers of the tomb, and continue throughout. Such jugs are nearly always plain, made of red or light brown ware, and singularly free from grits. One example of type 196 was recorded as burnished.

The narrow-necked jugs in Class J.6, which are only represented by single examples in Groups 6024, 218, 116 and 224, muster more than a dozen in Tomb 1002, but they are varied in detail and finish. They do not appear to be of local manufacture.

The ridge-necked jugs of Class J.7 are a speciality of Tomb 1002, Houses III and Tomb 106. Several examples from Tomb 1002 are burnished over a red or brown slip. The finest piece is the unique type 256 from the lowest layers, which is still remarkably close to a metal prototype. Types 259 and 271 in this class retained faint traces of painted black, white and red bands around the body.

A single example of type 254 introduces Class J.8, in which the well-known water decanters are placed, but the specimen from Tomb 1002 is distinctly archaic, covered with a thick red slip and vertically hand burnished. Its position in the bottom layers is further evidence of its antiquity.

Dippers and Juglets

| Class | Layers 1–5 | | Layers 6–10 | | Layers 11–13 | |
	Types	Total	Types	Total	Types	Total
D.1	—	—	300	1	300	1
D.2	303, 305	2	287(3), 299	4	305	1
D.3	—	—	—	—	296(3)	3
D.4	283(8), 294	9	283(2), 286(12), 293(3), 294	18	283, 286(8)	9
D.5	291	1	282(8)	8	282(2)	2
D.6	—	—	—	—	336(2), 339	3
D.7	322(4)	4	315, 322(13)	14	322(14), 326	15
D.8	309(18), 311, 313, 320(2)	22	309(2), 321	3	309(3), 311, 320, 321, 323	7
TOTALS		38		48		41

Dippers in Classes D.1 and D.3 become extinct before the end of the occupation of Tomb 1002, while Class D.2, which is transitional between pinched and round-mouthed juglets, achieves its zenith in the central layers.

Classes D.4 and D.5 are best represented in layers 6–10, and D.6, containing Cypriote wares, is no longer found at the top of the tomb.

The evolution from Class D.7 to D.8, which occurs in Tomb 1002, is clear and instructive. The burnish of dippers in Class D.7 is superior, retaining—owing to better firing—marks of vertical strokes over neck and shoulder, which become irregular over the base.

Chalices

	Layers 11–13	
Class	*Types*	*Total*
Cha.	160(2), 161(4)	6

Both forms of chalice appear to belong to a late phase of development, and all six examples were found in the lowest levels of the tomb.

Miniature Amphorae

	Layers 1–5	
Class	*Types*	*Total*
MA	413, 415	2

The two examples in this class seem to represent the final phase of manufacture: type 413 is especially poor, and type 415, though better in form, has unpierced handles.

Miniature Pithoi

	Layers 1–5	*Layers 6–10*	*Layers 11–13*	
Class	*Type*	*Types*	*Types*	*Total*
MP	420	421, 422, 423	424, 425	6

The variety of shapes among a few examples does not permit recognition of the chronological development, though it is instructive to find the contemporary use of wide and narrow necks, and round, pointed and knob bases.

Pilgrim Flasks

	Layers 1–5	*Layers 11–13*	
Class	*Types*	*Types*	*Total*
PF	434, 435	431, 434	4

The common feature of the four pilgrim flasks is a pronounced ridge on the neck. While the ridged neck and the ware of types 434 and 435 are reminiscent of the earlier decanters in Class J.8, the buff or grey-green ware of type 431, with its incised decoration and applied knobs, is close to jug type 237 in Class J.7, illustrating once more the continuous progression of ceramic development.

Cooking Pots

	Layers 1–5	*Layers 6–10*	*Layers 11–13*	
Class	*Types*	*Types*	*Types*	*Total*
CP	448, 451, 454(4), 457, 458(2), 462	442, 450, 452, 453(2), 455, 462(3)	447, 450(2), 454(3), 455, 458	27

Two-handled vessels with deep or wide and shallow bodies are described as cooking pots in this volume. The coarse brown ware with heavy limestone content and frequent burnt patches is typical alike of the handleless Late Bronze and Early Iron Age cooking pots and of some one-handled jugs in Class J.2 and J.4, which may well have been used for the same purpose.

Two-handled cooking pots with deep bodies, ranging between 12 cm. and 20 cm. in height, make their first appearance in quantity in the lowest layers of Tomb 1002, but relatively few are made of the ware so commonly associated with cooking vessels. They are more often made of an orange paste, fired soft, or, in later examples, the firing appears to be much harder, producing a darker red-brown surface. The clay is well levigated and the walls of the pots are thin, but in both varieties limestone temper is negligible. Two examples of type 455 and one of type 462 have an incised cross on the handle.

An incomplete specimen of type 442 is the only shallow, wide cooking pot from Tomb 1002—a form destined to enjoy a revival of popularity during the occupation of the houses of Level III.

Grant and Wright (AS V, p. 138), writing of two-handled, deep-bodied cooking pots found at 'Ain Shems, place them "not much before the eighth century", a date which agrees with their appearance in Tomb 1002.

Storage Jars

Class	Layers 6–10 Type	Layers 11–13 Type	Total
S.1, S.4	476	470	2

Only two complete storage jars were found in the tomb, indicating how far the habit of including such vessels in the normal tomb equipment had declined.

Jugs or Jars with Spouts

Class	Layers 1–5 Types	Layers 6–10 Types	Total
JS	361, 364	359, 362	4

Three of the four spouted jugs have ridged necks with handles attached at that point. The fourth example has a closed-in sprinkler top. Only type 364 is burnished all over on a dark red slip, in a style which was archaic before the occupation of the tomb. As the neck was missing the vessel may have come from the deposit in which burials were previously placed.

Miscellaneous

Class	Layers 1–5 Types	Layers 6–10 Type	Layers 11–13 Types	Total
Misc.	223, 372, 378, 379	333	112, 369, 381	8

The jug type 223 would be comparable to Class J.7, were it not for the especially wide neck. For other comparisons, see notes on Miscellaneous forms, Chapter 9.

Distribution of Objects in Tomb 1002

	Layers 1–5	Layers 6–10	Layers 11–13	Unstratified
Pottery figurines and rattles	Pl. 28: 11, 12, 14–16 Pl. 29: 18–20 F. No. 1254, Female (Colt) NP F. No. 1270, animal, NP F. No. 1271, head of vase, as Pl. 27: 7	Pl. 28: 10, 13 Pl. 29: 22 F. No. 1290, bird on stand, NP F. Nos. 1291, 1299, 1300, rattles (Colt) NP F. No. 1301, bkn., NP	Pl. 29: 17, 21 Pl. 30: 23, 24, 26	—
Amulets	Pl. 36: 49, 50 F. No. 1263, (Colt) NP F. No. 1275 (Bes) NP F. No. 1282 (2)(Uzat) NP	Pl. 36: 48, 51 F. No. 1286, Uzat, NP	F. No. 1337, Uzat, NP F. No. 1343, cat, NP	F. Nos. 1447, 1448, Bes, NP F. No. 1594, Uzat, NP F. No. 1595, unidentified, NP F. No. 1596, cat, NP

	Layers 1–5	*Layers 6–10*	*Layers 11–13*	*Unstratified*
Scarabs, scaraboids and seals	Pl. 43: 47, 53 Pl. 44: 66	Pl. 43: 34, 37, 55 Pl. 44: 62, 63, 67, 89, 103	Pl. 43: 7, 31, 41, 42, 49 Pl. 44: 65, 95 Pl. 57: 14	Pl. 43: 26, 32, 33, 39, 46, 54 Pl. 44: 64, 68, 87, 92, 93, 94, 107, 108, 118
Metal	AR ear-rings Pl. 57: 5, 9, 11 AE ear-rings Pl. 57: 6, 13 AE armour Pl. 57: 17 AE ring Pl. 57: 21 F. No. 1257, AE bangle, NP	AR ear-ring Pl. 57: 3 AE ear-rings Pl. 57: 8, 12 Fe knife Pl. 57: 15 AE bangles Pl. 57: 18, 20, 24 AE fibula Pl. 57: 26 F. No. 1305, AE ear-rings, NP	AR ear-rings Pl. 57: 4, 7, 10 AE armour Pl. 57: 16 AE and Fe bangles Pl. 57: 19 AE rings Pl. 57: 22, 23 F. No. 1339, Fe bangles, NP	Fe blade Pl. 57: 25 Fe fibula Pl. 57: 27 F. No. 1587, AE bangles, NP F. No. 1591, AE ear-ring, NP F. No. 1592, AR ear-rings, NP
Bone	Pendant Pl. 57: 30	Finial(?) Pl. 57: 32	Pendant Pl. 57: 31	Calendar Pl. 57: 28 Pendant Pl. 57: 29 and Pl. 37: 16 F. No. 1589, pendant (PM. 33. 2119) NP
Stone	—	F. No. 1304, hone, NP	—	—

The following beads were found when the filling of the tomb was sieved:

    Pl. 66: 1–5, 10, 13–17, 19, 21, 22, 24, 26, 30, 31, 33, 34, 37–39, 41, 45, 46, 48–50, 52, 53, 55, 56, 63, 65, 66, 69, 76, 78, 83, 89

    Pl. 67: 91, 98, 105, 112, 116, 126, 127, 131, 132, 135, 136, 139, 140, 145, 146

1004 Tomb in Grid Square E.30   Irregularly shaped pit. Burials *c.* 820–810 B.C. Re-used?

The burial pit was only divided from another of equal size to the south-west by a boulder of mizzi limestone and a few stones. The two pits may have been part of one earlier construction, possibly a large chamber of the usual bilobate Middle Bronze tomb type. On the other hand, those who were cutting Tomb 1004 may have broken through into the Late Bronze Age deposit 1003, and then sealed the breach with stones. At some time an attempt was made to cut through the lower corner of the mizzi block. One skull (Appendix A, No. 834) and a few bones remained of the much disturbed burials.

The following pottery forms came from a depression in the floor of the tomb to the north:

    B.7   J.4   J.5   D.1b   D.7b   MP
    9(2 ex.), 177, 190, 301, 322(7 ex.), 428

Date and Comparisons

Tomb 1004 ends at the same time as Tomb 224, though it does not begin so early. On the evidence of the burnished bowls, it is closer in time to Tomb 224 than to Tomb 1002; though there is a sharp fall in hand burnish the corresponding rise in wheel-finished bowls is less marked.

No metal of any kind was found. The scaraboid, Pl. 44: 102, demonstrates the degradation of a design of shaggy-necked beasts otherwise exclusive to Tomb 224 (Pl. 44: 100, 101), while Pl. 44: 120 is a very poor rendering of ring-and-dot circles.

Pottery

Bowls

Class	Types	Total
B.4	13, 15, 18	3
B.6	89, 90	2
B.7	9(3), 39	4
B.10	61	1
		10

Only two bowls show signs of burnish. Type 39 has faint traces across the centre of the inside and across the base outside, but the intention may have been to fill in a crack caused by bad firing. Type 90 is a very well-made bowl, with fine walls and a spirally finished ring base; the slip inside is spiral wheel burnished in wide strokes. Though type 18 is covered with red slip inside and over most of the exterior, the surface is so worn that the use of burnish is uncertain.

Lamps

Class	Types	Total
L.1–3	144, 147(3)	4

The lamps are insignificant in quantity and quality. Two are flanged both inside and out, though the inner lip is still rounded. The plain profile of a much worn specimen of type 144 retains the older tradition.

Jugs

Class	Types	Total
J.4	168(2), 177	3
J.5	189, 190	2
		5 .

Three jugs out of five have a moulded rim and the necks are all curved, suggesting an advance in development over Tomb 116.

Dippers and Juglets

Class	Types	Total
D.1b	300, 301(6), 302	8
D.4a	286	1
D.7b	322(7)	7
		16

Classes D.1–4. All three varieties of pinched-mouth dippers were originally represented in the group. The specimens of types 300 and 301 are made of rather coarsely levigated clay with some grits. The bodies are elongated and baggy, and the sizes range from 11·5 to 14 cm. An example of type 286, with vertical hand burnish all over on a brown slip, is comparable to another from Tomb 224.

Class D.7. The set of six juglets now preserved at the Institute of Archaeology in London ranges in height from 11 to 8 cm., each example diminishing by an average of 5 mm. Like other local pottery forms, it is possible that they were made to standard sizes. All show traces of vertical hand burnish, and in no case does the handle join the rim.

Miniature Pithoi

Class	Type	Total
MP	428	1

The surface, though damaged and worn, shows traces of vertical hand burnish on a pinkish slip, under painted red and white bands.

Storage Jars

	Class	Type	Total
	S.1	476	1

Objects: Scaraboids   Pl. 44: 102, 120

1007 Tomb in Grid Square D.29

Irregularly shaped pit. Burials *c.* 550–350 B.C.

The pit was directly under the escarpment of the upper terrace, and the roof was part of the edge of the nari stratum. The contents had been disturbed and plundered anciently. There was a jar of a type comparable to one from Tell Sandaḥannah which is dated to the Seleucidan period by Macalister (BM, Pl. 58: 12). For comparable groups, see the "Philistine" graves from Gezer (Gezer I, Tomb 4, Figs. 154–155), also 'Athlit (QDAP II, Tomb L.21: 551) and Deve Huyuk (AAA VII, Pl. XXII).

Pottery: Misc.
    404

Objects: AE mirror   Pl. 57: 33
    AE ring   Pl. 57: 34
    AE kohl stick   Pl. 57: 35
    Calcite tripod   Pls. 42: 7 and 57: 36
    Calcite dish frag.   NP

1009 Natural cave in Grid Square C.27

Iron Age dwelling, destroyed by fire. Burials *c.* 450 B.C.

The nari roof of this cave, adjoining Cave 1010 on the upper terrace behind the camphouse, had fallen in. The cavern was irregular in shape and had apparently been used as a dwelling or for industrial purposes. At the south end of the cave a bag-shaped vat with an opening 22 cm. in diameter had been cut; the vat and the slopes leading to it had been plastered, and to the north was a shallower and unplastered depression in the cave floor.

There was a layer of burning on the west side of the cave, which was in its turn covered by a stone bench or mastaba. The level was associated with some disturbed burials above the burnt layer, and the pottery and other objects formed part of the funerary equipment.

Pottery: Misc. Misc. D.9
    376(3), 382(3),* 664*
    * Pl. 76: 31, 32.

Objects: AE kohl stick   Pl. 57: 37
    AE and Fe frags.   NP

1010 Natural cave in Grid Square C.27

750–550 B.C.

The nari roof of this cave adjoining Cave 1009 on the upper terrace behind the camphouse had collapsed. The cavern was irregular in shape and had been used as a dwelling in the late Judaean period, contemporary with Level III. There were two jar handles and a cache of seeds at a high level in the cave, and also some fragments of pottery figurines.

Pottery: J.9 CP CP
    194, 452, 462

Area 4000, at the north-east corner of the mound (Pl. 128)

The area was excavated in 1936–1937, in order to clear the base of the tell slope. Work proceeded from the Wadi Ghafr towards the mound, and it was thought that the trench of the Middle Bronze Age Fosse would be intercepted, as it dipped and rose again to the glacis at the north-east corner (Pl. 1: 3). The trench may pass between the excavated area and the city wall, at a distance of about 20 to 40 m. from the fortifications, for the only trace of the fosse was found in Grid Square R.4, where it had been much quarried, and nothing could be

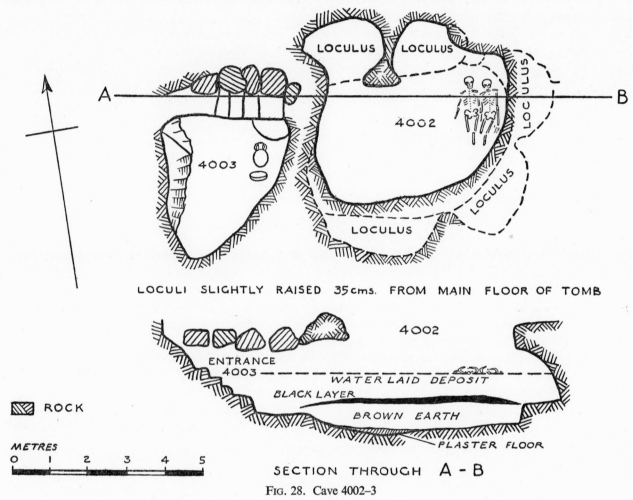

FIG. 28. Cave 4002–3

seen of the limestone packing of the glacis, nor of its plastered face which had been visible at the north-west corner. The rock rose steeply from the valley to the mound, and was cut into by tombs, quarries and buildings of all periods. As these were normally driven into the rock face, the steps or passages leading to them were usually on the north side. Tomb 4002 is an exception, with the entry to the north-east, but this cave, like most of the others in the vicinity, was not an Iron Age construction.

4002 Cave, artificially enlarged, in Grid Square S.1 (Fig. 28) Circular chamber with five loculi
c. 2000–900 B.C.

It is possible that the original adaptation of the cave for burials was made in the Middle Bronze Age (Pl. 9: 1), as circular tombs surrounded by low recesses are a feature of the horse burials at Tell el-Ajjul (AG I, Pl. LVII). In support of the comparison, an equine mandible was found with the contents.

There were traces of a plaster floor; on it was a layer of brown earth containing most of the pottery, which included Mycenean sherds (to be published in *Lachish IV*). Above, on a level with the loculi, was a layer of black earth. Gradually the tomb filled with a water-laid deposit containing fragments of at least three bowls, hand burnished inside and out, and part of some spatulate and knob handles. On the water-laid layer were two skeletons with heads to the north, facing west (not facing upwards as drawn on Fig. 28), and with attitude extended, like the bodies in the graves near the Fosse Temple. For remarks on one of the skulls, see Appendix A, No. 829. The pottery is also comparable to that of the Fosse Temple graves.

Pottery: B.5 L.1–3 L.4–6 D.3 Misc. S.7b
   57,* 141, 148, 296, 406,* 482
    * Pl. 73: 19, 20.

Objects: Fe knife Pl. 57: 38
    Beads   Pl. 66: 5, 13, 17, 35, 45, 49, 61, 62, 64
         Pl. 67: 110, 113, 144
    Clay loom weights NP ⎫
            ⎬ in passage
    Equine mandible NP ⎭

4003 Dromos in Grid Square S.1, leading to 4002

4005 Cave, artificially enlarged, in Grid Square T.1 (Fig. 29)   Rectangular chamber with loculi, *c.* 2000 B.C. Burials *c.* 900 B.C. and after 600 B.C.

It is possible that the cave, like Tombs 4002, 4016 and 4017, was first used for burials in the Middle Bronze Age, to judge from the plan (Fig. 29 and Pl. 9: 2), but no contents of that period were found. Over fifty burials had been made during the Iron Age, and each one had been pushed aside to make room for later interments, but this was an orderly process, rather different from the chaos left by plunderers. Many skeletons were still partly articulated, and some anklets and bracelets were in position on the bones (Pl. 9: 3). For remarks on the skulls, see Appendix A, Nos. 801–803, 813–815, 817–820, 827 and 843.

In comparison to the number of bodies there was very little pottery. Most of it is compatible with a date in the tenth century, especially the strainer-spouted jug 364 and the bowl with vestigial handle, type 110. The bowl 84 is somewhat later, leading on, perhaps, towards those in Class B.13. All the small objects, with the possible exception of the bangles, seem to belong to an interment of the post-exilic period, with which the dipper, type 345, and possibly the bowl, type 58, should be associated, although the classification of the latter favours an earlier date and some known parallels from Tepe Hissar for the onyx eye beads and pendants occur in the second millenium.

The bronze fibula, the ear-rings and the glass scaraboid should be dated no earlier than 650 B.C.

Pottery: B.5 Misc. Misc. D.3 D.1b D.7a D.9 JS MP PF S.1 S.1
   58,* 84,* 110,* 296, 301, 318(2), 345,* 364, 427,* 436,* 468, 473
    * Pl. 73: 23–26, 28, 29.

Objects: AE fibula   Pl. 57: 39
    AE ear-rings Pl. 57: 40–42
    Fe ring   Pl. 57: 44
    AE anklets   Pl. 57: 45, 46
    Scaraboid   Pl. 44: 123
    Shell ring   Pl. 57: 43
    Beads   Pl. 66: 9, 12, 66
         Pl. 67: 115, 142
    Stone rubber and polisher F. Nos. 5845, 5846 NP

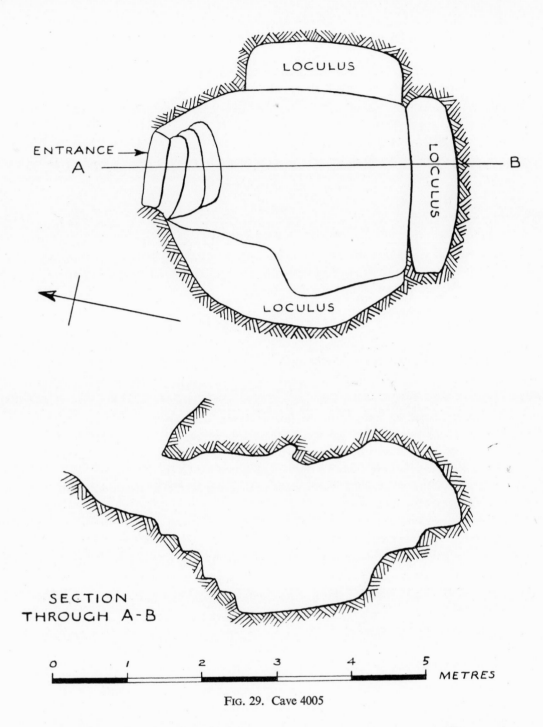

ENTRANCE
A
B

LOCULUS

LOCULUS

LOCULUS

LOCULUS

SECTION
THROUGH A-B

0   1   2   3   4   5
METRES

FIG. 29. Cave 4005

4006 Dwelling (?) and quarry in Grid Square T.2

Irregular quarry, *c*. 1200 B.C.
Re-used from *c*. 750 B.C.
onwards

This large area lay between a Late Bronze Age Tomb 4019 and the tomb chamber 4016. Three steps in the south-west corner gave access to the floor, on which there were many detached and partly detached blocks of stone, varying in size from 60 to 100 cm. long, 30 to 40 cm. wide, and 15 to 20 cm. in depth. From the style of dressing on the blocks it would seem that the tool used was a small narrow-bladed pick (cf. dwelling 6024 and quarry 4022).

Some Late Bronze Age sherds were recorded, similar to forms published in *Lachish II* (L. II, type 125, 165 and 279), which may have fallen from the tell slopes above, or may have belonged to the original chamber on the site.

Pottery: B.13   Misc.   J.2   D.9
         123(2),   130,   203(2),   342

Objects: Hammerstone, grinders and polishers   F. Nos. 5861, 5862, 5864, 5865 NP
          Fabricator flint   F. No. 5863 NP

4007 Single Grave in Grid Square U.7   *c.* 750–550 B.C.

The grave was cut in the rock, to the west of a Middle Bronze Age group, 4008. Like Grave 4027, it was oriented east and west and contained one skeleton, lying in an extended position, with head to the east and facing south. The bones were in a poor state of preservation, but were undisturbed. A pilgrim flask and some arrowheads were the only objects associated with the burial.

Pottery: PF
       438*
         * Pl. 73: 27.

Objects: Fe arrowheads (4 ex.) NP

4010 Tomb chamber in Grid Square U.2   *c.* 2000–1200 B.C. Re-used *c.* 900–600 B.C.

The tomb was entered by three steps from the north. It was cut during the Bronze Age, but the original shape was much altered and enlarged. There were irregular benches, raised some 50 cm. above the floor, on each side except the north. A rock partition opposite the entrance may be part of the original bilobate chamber. There were two further entrances on the south side, one of which led to the Cave 4009.

The burials had been disturbed and the bones were so disintegrated that they could not be preserved; the remains of at least five skeletons were noted.

The Iron Age dippers and bowls came from high in the filling, and were fairly complete. Many Late Bronze Age forms were recorded, similar to those published in *Lachish II* (L. II, types 100, 123, 135, 149, 177, 268, 279, 284, 301, 309, 344, 351), but they were represented by sherds only.

Pottery: B.4   J.4   J.4   D.5a   D.1a   D.3   D.8   D.7a   S.8   B.2   B.1
        101,*   176,   180,   282,   289,   296(4),   320,   326,   537,   596,   621
         * Pl. 73: 30.

Object: AE arrowhead   F. No. 5898 NP

4012 Cave, recut for industrial use, in Grid Square T.1   ?

The original cave or tomb had been recut and enlarged, probably in Roman times, to form a deep oblong chamber with vertical sides, carefully finished with hammer dressing. There was a rectangular trough, 2×1 m. square, in the centre, with a shallow groove or channel leading towards it at each corner. A drain and sump (Pl. 9: 5), only a few centimetres deeper than the main trough, were located on the east side. Various other depressions cut in the floor can be seen on Pl. 9: 4. It is clear that the area was used for some industrial purpose, possibly as a wine or olive press, but the few sherds recovered were not informative.

4015 Double grave in Grid Square V.3   ?

The southern part of the grave cut in the rock had been removed by quarrying. There were originally two burials, lying side by side. The skull and torso of one body were undisturbed, lying supine with the head to the south and the arms folded on the chest, while only the skull of the second body was found.

A few glass beads and some fish (?) bones were all that remained of the funerary equipment.

Objects: Glass beads (6 ex.)   NP

4016 Tomb chamber in Grid Square T.2   Circular chamber with loculi, *c.* 2000 B.C.

The tomb was entered by five steps from the north. There were loculi on the south and west sides of the chamber; one of these was nearly level with the floor, the other was raised about 15 cm. above it. The roof had collapsed, and the tomb had been plundered anciently. All traces of the burials had been removed, and only some sherds were found.

4017 Tomb in Grid Square T.2   Circular chamber with loculi, *c.* 2000 B.C.

A rectangular chamber, similar in size and plan to Tombs 4005 and 4016, approached by four steps from the north. Only a lamp (NP) and some sherds were found.

4019 Tomb in Grid Square T.2   Circular chamber with loculi. Re-used *c.* 900–600 B.C.

A circular plastered tomb, containing pottery and objects of the Late Bronze Age, to be published in *Lachish IV*. There were some Iron Age sherds in the northern part of the tomb.

4021 Pit in Grid Square U.4   ? Burials *c.* A.D. 240–300

The pit was roughly circular, with a rectangular depression sunk in the centre of the floor. There were four burials, which had been disturbed: they were apparently associated with the small objects in the group, though the lamp and alabaster dish are earlier and inconsistent with the date of the coin in the third century A.D.

Pottery: L.7–8   D.9   CP
        149,   346,*   463
          * Pl. 76: 30.

Objects: AV ear-ring   Pl. 57: 47
        AE bell   Pl. 57: 48
        AE coin, No. 60 on List of Coins, p. 413
        Alabaster dish   Pl. 57: 49
        Fe nails   F. No. 6045 NP

4023 Pit in Grid Square T.3   *c.* 1500–1200 B.C.   Re-used 900–600 B.C.

A circular plastered pit approached by five steps (not shown on Pl. 128) on the south side; opposite the entrance was a bench raised some 75 cm. from the ground. There were no human remains, and only a few sherds besides the miniature amphora.

Pottery: MA
        414

4024 Pit in Grid Square T.3   *c.* 1500–1200 B.C.   Re-used later

A round plastered pit rather smaller than 4023, adjoining the quarry 4032. There were no traces of burials, and the only contents were some sherds of mixed date.

4025 Quarry in Grid Square S.3   *c.* 900–600 B.C.

An open triangular area used as a quarry. A few Iron Age sherds were found.

4026 Locus in Grid Square R.3

The objects found at this point may have been part of the adjoining burial 4027, as there were no other graves of the period in the vicinity. They were lying in the earth, 30 cm. below the present ground surface.

Pottery: MA
　　　　415

Objects: AE bracelets (4 ex.)　　Pl. 57: 50
　　　　Beads　　　　　　　　Pl. 66: 13, 62

4027 Single grave in Grid Square R.3　　　　　　　　　　　　　　　　　　　　*c.* 900–700 B.C.

The grave was cut in the earth about 1·25 m. below the present ground surface, and oriented east and west. The burial was undisturbed, and the body was placed supine with the head to the west and the arms crossed over the chest. The objects in group 4026 may have belonged to this grave, but it is strange that there are no others of the same period in the vicinity. Its nearest neighbours are Graves 4007 and 4015, and all these have affinities with the closely packed single graves which surround and cover the site of the Fosse Temple. It is unusual to find a single grave with east–west orientation containing dippers in Class D.7, which does not persist in the large groups beyond 700 B.C.

Pottery: D.7b　D.7a
　　　　315,　326

Objects: AE pins　　　　　NP
　　　　Flint sickle blade　NP

4028 Plastered troughs in Grid Square V.3 (Fig. 30)　　　　　　　　　　　　　*c.* 900–600 B.C.

Two plastered troughs were connected with a pit at a lower level by narrow drainage channels. The system was partly cut in the rock, though the south-west side, at least, was founded on the filling of a rectangular pit 4029, and was divided from it by a row of stones. The area was not fully cleared, owing to the presence of a modern building, and it is not certain whether the system continued underneath the walls. There was no roof.

A similar trough has been recorded at Tell en-Naṣbeh (TN I, p. 257; Fig. 68) as a wine press, but its date is uncertain.

4029 Pit in Grid Square U.3　　　　　　　　　　　　　　　　　　　　　　　*c.* 900–600 B.C.

It is not clear how the deep pit 4029 was connected with the plastered troughs 4028 lying over it. The drainage flow from them led to a pit marked on Fig. 30, which may have been part of this underlying chamber. The excavated section of 4029 showed that the bottom was filled with large stones covered by a layer of yellow earth.

Remains of at least five skeletons, with some animal bones, were found in the yellow earth, but they were much disturbed; three skulls were retained for examination (see Appendix A, Nos. 822, 823 and 828).

Pottery: D.7b
　　　　322

4030 Entrance to Cave 4034 in Grid Square R.4　　　　　　　　　　　　　　*c.* 1200 B.C. and later?

The number 4030 was allocated to the dromos leading to a large natural Cave 4034, partly cut in the drainage ditch of the Hyksos fosse. The cave will be described in detail with its contents in *Lachish IV*. Most of the pottery was typical of the material found in the Fosse Temple, but there are indications that the cave-workshop continued in use after the temple was destroyed, though it was not necessarily maintained as a potter's establishment.

244

The narrow entrance way to the west was lined with stones, and the light earth filling of the passage contained some Iron Age sherds, besides many Late Bronze Age fragments. It is possible that the builders of House 4033, above, used the cavern as an underground stable. A small square space enclosed by a low stone wall

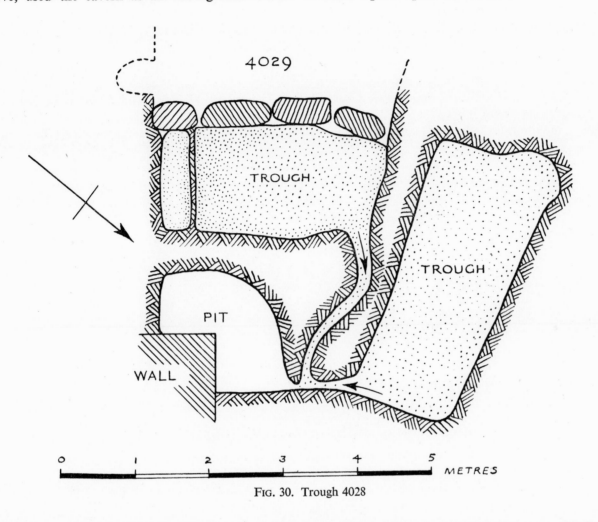

FIG. 30. Trough 4028

adjoining a double row of rough stones was recognised by the workers as a stall and manger still quite fit for use.

Pottery: D.3   PF
            296, 436

4031 Pit in Grid Square U.3   ?

The irregular, roofless pit was entered from a shaft on the west side. On the left of the entrance was a rock-cut recess. Near the middle of the floor was an oblong depression about a metre across. There were no burials, and among the contents were some sherds of mixed date. It should be noted that the floor level of chamber 4031 was 2 m. above pit 4029 and was in no way connected with it.

Objects: AE hook   Pl. 57: 51
           AE anklets (2 ex.)   cf. Pl. 57: 45

4032 Quarry in Grid Square T.3 c. 900–600 B.C.

This oval area was the largest ancient cutting in the cemetery. As it was undoubtedly a quarry, it was only cleared to a depth of 4·5 m. The rock face was exposed and weathered for some 3 m., but below that point the marks of cutting with a narrow-bladed pick were fresh and clear. Many stone blocks had been partly excavated; they varied in size from 70 to 100 cm. long, and 30 to 50 cm. wide, with an average depth of 15–20 cm. For similar cutting marks, compare quarry 4006 and dwelling 6024. Only a few Iron Age sherds were found.

4035 Quarry in Grid Square T.1 c. A.D. 300–450

When discovered in 1937, the quarry was thought to be a cistern, but further investigation in the following year proved its similarity in shape to the "bell" or "bottle"-shaped quarries of Tell Sandaḥannah, at nearby Beit Jibrin, though it was somewhat smaller in size. The soft howr walls showed the diagonal pick dressing of later times.

The pit contained water-laid earth and stone resting on grey mud; partly quarried blocks were in position at the bottom, including an unfinished stone water trough. In the filling were several complete Byzantine pots, and a number of coins were lying on the rock floor. The earliest coin among them was No. 62 on the List of Coins, c. A.D. 311, while the thirteen examples of No. 95 carry the use of the quarry into the fifth century. With the exception of the strainer 371, the bowl 633 in Class B.13, and the chalice 663, the pottery appears to be contemporary.

Pottery: Misc. Misc. Misc. Misc. PF S.13 B.13 Cha.
212,* 216(8),* 352(2),* 371, 433,* 505, 633, 663
* Pl. 76: 34–37.

Objects: Fe fragments F. No. 7007 NP
AE rings (2 ex.) Pl. 57: 52
AE coins, Nos. 62, 95 (13 ex.) on List of Coins, pp. 413, 414
Glass fragments F. No. 7006 NP
Stone trough NP

Area 6000, at the north-east corner of the mound (Pl. 129)

The area was situated south-east of Cemetery 4000, and was excavated in 1937–1938 (Pl. 1: 3) in continuation of the clearance of the lower tell slopes, where the soil was deepest close to the mound.

The tombs of various periods were even more thickly crowded than usual and cut in the soft howr limestone. A notable feature of both areas was a black, sooty deposit, seen on the exposed rock and soil, which had also penetrated into any open spaces in the tomb chambers. Samples were submitted to the Soil Science Laboratory, Hebrew University, Jerusalem, for analysis. In a letter dated March, 1938, A. Reifenburg reported as follows:

'Microscopic observation shows that with all probability the black stuff does not represent a burnt layer, but consists of decayed organic material. The colour, under the microscope, is brown, and not black as the colour of coal; furthermore generally speaking, burnt matter would show traces of the original structure.

'The decayed organic matter owes its origin to decayed animal-matter, since all reactions for lignin were negative. (Lignin is most resistent against decomposition, and can, for example, always be detected in peat). On the other hand, a qualitative test showed a relatively high content of phosphoric acid. This phosphoric acid content speaks likewise for animal (or human) origin, since animal-matter, especially bones, always contains a high amount of this substance.'

The sooty layer was not observed elsewhere on the lower slopes, but the possibility cannot be excluded that some striations noted as burnt layers in the north-east section high on the slopes were of a similar nature. It was not until the caves in this vicinity were excavated that a doubt arose as to whether the sooty deposits in them had been caused by fire, for they were tenacious and sticky and had penetrated to parts where the lack of air space would discourage burning. Only further excavation can decide whether the "burnt" layer which brings the Bronze Age Level VI to a close is in any way comparable. In this connexion, the "beds of ashes" noted by Petrie at Tell el-Ḥesi (Lachish, p. 16) from 298 to 308 ft., or dating from *c.* 1300 to 1100 B.C. should be considered. For F. J. Bliss's opinion, see A Mound of Many Cities, pp. 64–65, but both authorities are agreed that it was no ordinary destruction layer.

6003 Cave in Grid Square U.4   Cut before 2000 B.C. Intermittent use thereafter

The northern half of a cave, divided from the southern half, 6004, by a stone wall. The roof of the latter collapsed somewhat earlier than that of 6003, leaving only a part of the cave open for use as a dwelling. There was a small rubbish pit in the floor. Sherds of storage jar type 484 (and a fragment from Cave 6004) were the only parts of such vessels found outside the tell rooms of Level III; other sherds included a bowl, typed to L. II: 45, common to Structures II–III of the Fosse Temple, and one with irregular hand burnish, type 641, which should belong to the ninth to eighth centuries B.C. The cave was probably in use intermittently throughout the occupation of the tell.

Pottery: Cha. MA S.7a S.11 B.13
       156, 416, 484, 554, 641

6004 Cave in Grid Square U.4   Cut before 2000 B.C. Intermittent use thereafter

The southern half of a cave divided from Cave 6003 by a stone wall. The sherds suggest the same range of occupation as 6003, though fragments of a Roman jar found in the central pit 6009 indicate that it was still open at that period.

A sherd of jar type 484 was of heavier make than those from 6003. There were no complete pots. Some fragments of Late Bronze Age Base-ring ware and Iron Age sherds with irregular hand burnish were found.

Pottery: B.7 B.4 J.7b S.7a
       9, 13, 238, 484

6006 Tomb and Enclosure 6017 in Grid Square U.3 (Fig. 31)   *c.* 875 B.C.

The dromos to the east was sealed with neatly packed stones (Pl. 10: 1). When they were removed a small doorway was exposed, approached by three steps (Pl. 10: 2). Inside the rectangular tomb chamber two more steps led to the floor. On the west and north sides were rock benches raised some 25 cm. from the floor. A female skeleton lay on the western bench with head to the north, face up and attitude extended. Flask types 315, 324 (3 ex.) and 329 were by the head. The scarab on Pl. 43: 25 lay close to the left hand. For details of the skull, see Appendix A, No. 804.

The male skeleton was much disturbed. The skull had been washed on to the floor, owing to water seepage from a crack in the rock above the bench. With the skull was an iron knife, Pl. 58: 1, and a storage jar, type 476. A bowl, type 15, and a chalice, type 154, remained on the bench where the male skeleton had been. In a niche above the bench to the right of the entrance was a lamp, type 148.

A sooty deposit similar to that referred to on p. 246 was very noticeable in this tomb, which was not completely filled with earth. It seemed to have penetrated through the cracks in the rock, and to have spread over the contents after the chamber had been sealed. The pottery forms a homogeneous group associated with two burials only, and it therefore follows that the sooty layer was deposited after the occupation of the tomb in the ninth century B.C.

Pottery: B.4 L.4–6 Cha.   D.3   D.1a   D.7b   D.7b   D.6a   S.1
       15, 148, 154,* 285(2), 289, 315,* 324(3), 329, 476(2)
       * Pl. 73: 31, 32.

Objects: Fe knife   Pl. 58: 1
       Scarab   Pl. 43: 25

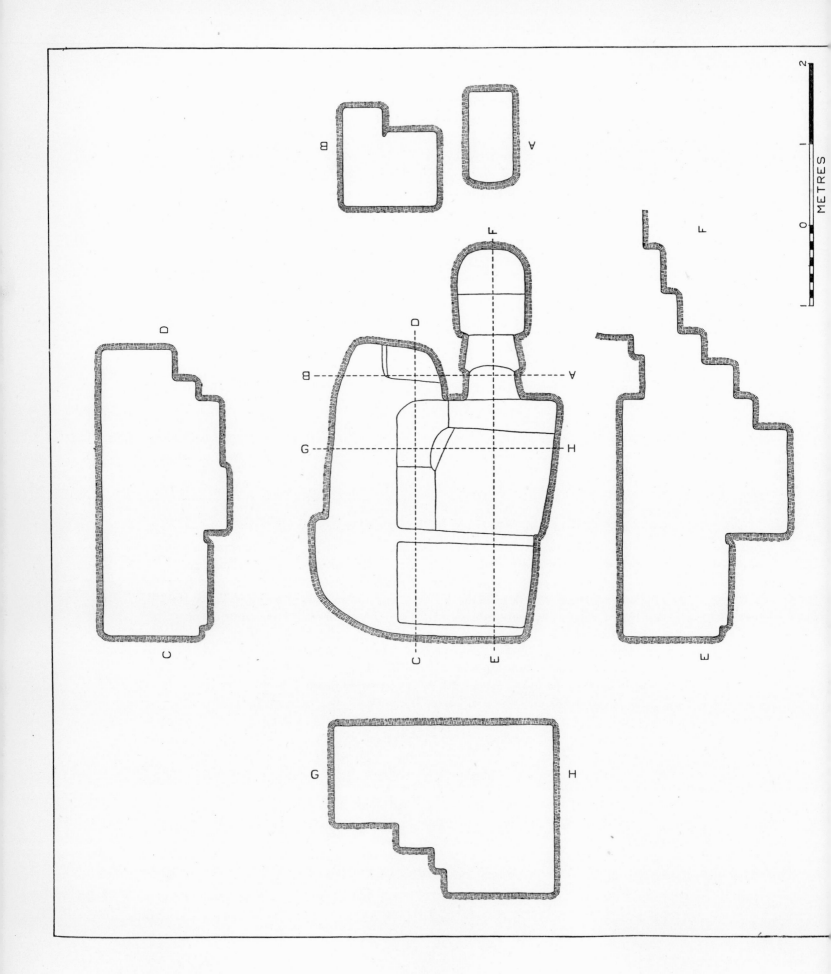

6010 Cave in Grid Square U.4   Cut before 2000 B.C. In continuous use as a dwelling

The roof and upper part of the cave had been removed through quarrying operations. The floor was covered by loose, grey earth and stones to a depth of over a metre, and the filling contained an Early Bronze Age jug (to be published in *Lachish IV*) besides sherds of the same period. Above the earth and stones a plaster floor had been made, which no doubt belonged to the stone building 6023 which was constructed over the underlying caves. Sherds of all periods were found in the vicinity.

6011 Cave in Grid Square U.4   Cut before 2000 B.C. Intermittent use thereafter. Burials *c.* 950 B.C.

A large irregular cave originally cut or enlarged in the Early Bronze Age, when it was used as a dwelling. The entrance was from the north. Subsequently the cave filled with debris, and during the Iron Age some burials were put in the south-east corner. No attempt was made to clear away the earlier debris or to recut the rock, and the entrance was only roughly sealed by stones. Comparatively soon afterwards the roof collapsed, damaging the contents considerably. There were traces of two burials, but the remains and the pottery apparently associated with them had been disturbed by the fall from the roof.

Pottery: L.1–3 S.1   S.1   S.4
144, 468, 475(8), 481

6012 Area in Grid Square U.4   Cut before 2000 B.C. Intermittent use thereafter

An open ledge to the east of an Early Bronze Age Cave 6013. The Iron Age inhabitants of the cave had re-used the area, and left some sherds and one bowl lying there.

Pottery: B.7
54

6015 Pit in Grid Square U.4   ?
An oval pit or depression, divided by a row of single stones. There were no contents.

6017 Enclosure in Grid Square U.3
See Tomb 6006.

6020 Cave, not marked on Pl. 129   *c.* 825 B.C.

A cave situated east of the path leading up to the tell, which marks the eastern limit of the excavations. It was not completely cleared of its filling, as part of it lay under the path. The roof had collapsed. There were no traces of burials, but fragments of cooking pot ware indicate that the cave was used for domestic purposes.

Pottery: B.7 Cha. J.2
52, 156, 197

6021 Quarry in Grid Square T.4   *c.* 900 B.C.

An area lying to the west of Cemetery 6000, where the rock rises sharply towards the tell. It had been used as a source of building stone. Large numbers of cut and partially detached blocks approximately $100 \times 60 \times 15$ cm. lay about on the rock; they were similar in size to those cut from the adjoining quarry, 4032.

There were traces of a white puddled clay floor about 20 cm. above the surface of the rock. The whole quarry was covered by a black layer some 15 cm. thick. Whether this was burnt debris or organic matter is uncertain.

Pottery: Sherds only

6022 Court in Grid Square U.5

A square court or platform leading through a narrow passage to the dwelling and workshop 6024. Note the holes at roof level to take wooden beams and the marks of the narrow-bladed pick (Pl. 10: 3). The court, the passage and the Cave 6024 showed the same type of pick marks, and were apparently cut at much the same time (cf. quarries 4006, 4032). Under the court was a Cave 6005, occupied mainly in the Early Bronze Age. A tabular flint scraper, F. No. 6570 (to be published in *Lachish IV*), may be associated with this earlier period.

6023 Building in Grid Square U.4   900–600 B.C.

The west wall of a building which may continue under the unexcavated area. It was built over an Early Bronze Age dwelling 6010 and a Cave 6031, which had filled with debris after the roofs had fallen in. Only two or three courses of the foundations remained, rising from a level of 216·89 m. at the northern end to 217·39 m. at the southern extremity.

Pottery: D.1b
           301

6024 Dwelling and workshop in Grid Square U.5 (Fig. 32)   Cut before 2000 B.C. Altered and
                                                           re-used *c.* 1020 B.C.

A large, partly denuded cave, with irregular chambers or recesses, used as a dwelling in the Early Bronze Age. The Iron Age inhabitants drove a passage through the rock from the square court 6022 to gain entry, as part of the roof had collapsed. The marks of the narrow-bladed pick used in the Iron Age to enlarge the cave can be clearly distinguished from those of the wide-bladed Bronze Age adze (see also 6022 and quarry 4006).

The cave appears to have been used as a weavers' dwelling and workshop; seven clay loom weights were found together in a recess, where the loom may have been set up, and there were six pottery disks or plaque fragments which may have been used in the industry. At some time after the chamber was deserted, water had flooded it, and the lighter objects had risen from their original positions to the top of the mud deposit.

Date and Comparisons

The group as a whole is undoubtedly the earliest in the Iron Age series at Tell ed-Duweir, both for reasons of form and of burnish. Hand-burnished sherds were common, but comparisons for most of the vessels are altogether lacking. The reddish-grey matt unburnished slip, streakily applied, is a feature of the group which is rarely found elsewhere, and for this reason the possibility that the pots were awaiting completion may be considered. The absence of lamps and the varied nature of the contents suggest a dwelling or a workshop rather than a tomb. The clay head is spirited enough to be a caricature (Pl. 31: 17).

Pottery

Bowls

Class	Types	Total
B.1	85	1
B.2	103,* 133,* 589	3
B.3	614	1
B.4	8*	1
		6

All the bowls were made of brown or light brown ware containing grits and/or straw, and were soft or medium fired. Types 8, 133, 589 and 614 were covered with red slip and irregularly hand-burnished all over; types 85 and 103 were covered with a matt red unburnished slip, very streakily applied, which extended halfway down the exterior. They are unusual, and it remains uncertain whether they were unfinished pieces awaiting burnish.

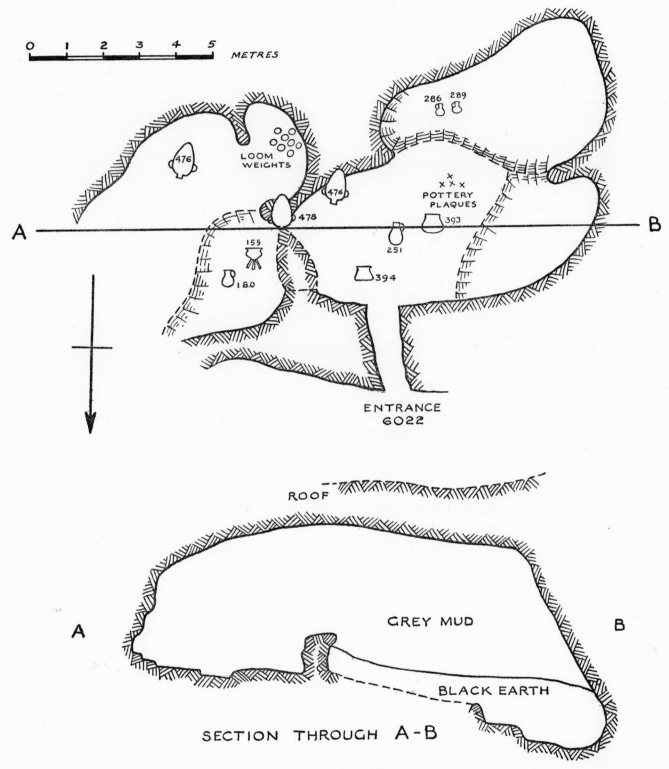

0 1 2 3 4 5 METRES

286 289

476

LOOM
WEIGHTS

476

x x x
POTTERY
PLAQUES

A ⌐ 478 393 B

251

155

180

394

ENTRANCE
6022

ROOF

A B

GREY MUD

BLACK EARTH

SECTION THROUGH A-B

FIG. 32. Cave 6024

Jugs

Class	Types	Total
J.3	217	1
J.4	180	1
J.6	251*	1
		3

The jugs are of brown or buff ware, variously fired. Type 251 is unique, and larger than the average jug in its class.

Dippers and Juglets

Class	Types	Total
D.1a, b	289,* 302*(2)	3
D.4a	286(10)	10
D.6a	337	1
D.7b	322(2), 324(3)*	5
		19

Vertical hand burnish on a dark red slip was found on some dippers in Classes D.1 and D.4. The burnish on dippers in Class D.7 was also vertical and regular.

Chalices

Class	Type	Total
Cha.	155*	1

Besides the example drawn there were several fragments of tripod bases belonging to other similar vessels. The three supports were attached to an open ring about 10 cm. in diameter and 2·5 cm. in depth. Both supports and ring were partly covered with a red or grey matt unburnished slip.

Potstands

Class	Type	Total
PS	398	1

Storage Jars

Class	Types	Total
S.1	476(2)	2
S.4	478*	1
		3

Miscellaneous

Class	Types	Total
Misc.	358, 389,* 393,* 394,* 398,* 668	6

Type 358 is comparable to type 357 from Tomb 107, which was used later as an ossuary. The unusual vessels, types 389, 393 and 394, were made of pink ware containing grits. They were hard fired and often covered with a buff slip. Type 668, which was reminiscent of the earliest kinds of decanter, contained grits and straw temper in the soft brown clay, and the surface was finished with a dark red slip.

* Pl. 72: 6, 11–22.

Objects:	Clay head	Pl. 31: 17
	Pottery disks	Pl. 41: 12 and Pl. 58: 2; Pl. 41: 14
	Flint knife frag.	F. No. 6593 (PM. 38.751) NP

Area 7000, at the head of the southern valley (Pl. 130)

The excavated area was triangular, rising to an apex where the southern and western valleys meet. It was bounded on the north by the lower slopes of the mound, and the southern limit was marked by the line of the modern road leading to the camp. A general view (Pl. 2: 2), taken in 1935, shows an old burnt road surface in section, sloping from about 2 m. to less than a metre below the present ground level. The thick layer of charcoal and ash makes this surface contemporary with one of the periods of destruction by fire, but the evidence does not permit a closer attribution. Pl. 7: 1 shows a view from the south-west corner of the mound, taken later in the same season, when the upper part of the area had been used as a dump. Pl. 13: 6 was taken from the apex of the area, looking down the valley. It shows the thin earth deposit over the rock, scored with chariot or cart ruts. At the eastern side of the triangle the debris had accumulated to a depth of about 2 m.

Owing to the proximity of the surface, and to the use of the whole region as a quarry for stone and clay, it is impossible to reconstruct a detailed picture of the various roads leading to the gate of the city. There must have been frequent repairs, as the main thoroughfare was always kept open for use. It is significant that no tombs have been found in the vicinity.

The plan on Pl. 130 suggests the presence of three road surfaces, besides the one seen on Pl. 2: 2:

(*a*) North of the track marked "Road" is a line of small stones, extending for 16 m. Starkey considered that the row delimited the post-exilic road, which is still hidden under the tell slope. A similar line of stones can be seen round the corner leading up to the road (Pl. 126).

(*b*) The cart ruts on the rock (Pl. 13: 6) follow the natural rise to the city gate. Both chariots and wagons are depicted on the Lachish Reliefs, and chariots, at least, were in use many centuries earlier. The bare rock at this high level may have been frequently or permanently exposed.

(*c*) A paved road marked "S.P." on Pl. 130, edged by undressed stone blocks, and intersected at intervals by courses of stone to hold the gradient and provide a gutter for drainage, does not strictly come into this survey, as it is almost certainly of the second millenium. It should be noted that the paving blocks are square and worn, and much larger than the cobbles which are characteristic of the tell rooms.

7001 Quarry in Grid Square E.25

c. 900–600 B.C.

An irregular quarry, whose outline followed the existence of clay and yellow howr pockets, and which was probably used for pottery or plaster making. The limestone conglomerate here consisted of masses of soft rock held in yellow clay. In some cases the quarrymen had followed the seams of clay for a considerable distance. The quarry was apparently open during the Iron Age, as it contained some pockets of burnt material from the destruction of the city.

7002 Building (?) in Grid Square F.26

c. 700–600 B.C.

Part of a rectangular structure composed of single, undressed blocks of stone. Only one course remained, founded on a metre of debris. The southern end presumably continued under the surface of the road leading to the camp. The structure adjoined a similar row of stones at a lower level, which seemed to edge the line of the cart track scored in the rock.

Pottery: L.4–6 J.5 D.5 CP S.10
148, 190, 282, 442, 490

7005 Pit (not marked on Pl. 130)

c. 1500–1200 B.C. Re-used for burials

The contents were mostly of the Late Bronze Age, but the upper layers of water-laid deposit had been disturbed. It is uncertain whether the bronze armour scales and ring are contemporary with the pottery, which will be described in *Lachish IV*.

Objects: AE ring   Pl. 58: 3
          AE scale armour   Pl. 58: 4 and Pl. 39: 7
          AE scale armour   Pl. 58: 5

7006 Number not used

7007 Well (excavation unfinished) in Grid Square J.28   ?
   The well was filled with water-laid deposit and contained some pottery.

Pottery: B.13 L.4–6 CP
        120,   146,   442

7008 Cistern in Grid Square J.28   *c.* 1500–1200 B.C. Re-used

   A roughly hewn cistern, plaster-lined and straight-sided. It was probably a construction of the second millenium, which remained in use throughout the Iron Age. Some long pipes with handles for drainage, F. No. 6614, and a bowl, F. No. 6685, will be published in *Lachish IV*.

Pottery: L.1–3
        140

7010 Pit (excavation unfinished) in Grid Square J.28   ?

7013 Area in Grid Square K.26   *c.* 1500–600 B.C.

   An open area on the rock where many sherds were found, including part of a burnished jar with a moulded face, F. No. 6697 (PM. 39.795), which will be published in *Lachish IV*. The burnished bowl, type 592, and the hole-mouth fragment, type 542, are contemporary with the guardroom of Level II, and were among many fragments which had been thrown away here at different periods.

Pottery: S.8 B.2
        542,   592

PART IV
THE OBJECTS

The smith also sitting by the anvil, and considering the iron work, the vapour of the fire wasteth his flesh, and he fighteth with the heat of the furnace: the noise of the hammer and the anvil is ever in his ears, and his eyes look still upon the pattern of the thing that he maketh; he setteth his mind to finish his work, and watcheth to polish it perfectly:

So doth the potter sitting at his work, and turning the wheel about with his feet, who is alway carefully set at his work, and maketh all his work by number;

He fashioneth the clay with his arm, and boweth down his strength before his feet; he applieth himself to lead it over; and he is diligent to make clean the furnace:

All these trust to their hands: and every one is wise in his work.

Without these cannot a city be inhabited: and they shall not dwell where they will, nor go up and down:

Ecclesiasticus XXXVIII: 28–32.

CHAPTER 9

THE POTTERY

THE common and uninspiring vessels of the Iron Age in Palestine have long been familiar objects in public and private collections, but apart from a few recent outstanding studies, little attempt has been made to set the material in order, and considerations of date have always been treated with the utmost reserve.

Sources

The pottery recovered from Tell ed-Duweir came from two sources:

1. Accumulated city rubbish on the mound, divided into three distinct superimposed building levels or strata, referred to throughout as Levels (or Houses) III, II and I. Level I is uppermost, close to the present ground surface. Levels (or Houses) IV, and possibly V, also belong to the Iron Age, but they were not excavated.
2. Burial caves, tombs, single graves and other funerary and domestic deposits on the surrounding slopes and in the valleys north, west and south of the mound.

The two divisions supplement each other in many respects. When fragments in the three city levels were large enough to be identified as part of a well-known shape, their distribution and frequency in each layer were often instructive, while there were many other vessels which could only be drawn and described when better preserved examples were found in the tombs. However, most of the pottery was broken or incomplete, and it was rare indeed to find an absolutely perfect specimen.

No doubt it would have been ideal to keep the whole collection intact, but practical considerations of transport and storage made it impossible, and much was discarded on the site after special scrutiny.

Owing to the existence at the same place of superimposed building levels and large caves used for burial over a long period, it has been possible to arrange the pottery from both sources in a chronological series. Few, if any, sites in Judah have provided and published sufficient material of both kinds for the purpose, and the present study must await the discovery of dated inscriptions to confirm or deny the conclusions which are offered in the following pages.

System of Numbering

Tell, Tomb, Group and Field Numbers. Each pot and significant sherd was entered on the appropriate tell or tomb card by the field assistant in charge. The pots were marked at the same time with the tomb group or room number, prefixed by the letter "D" for "Tell ed-Duweir". Small letters after the tomb number denoted the position of a pot in a group, as recorded on the card and field sketch.

At the end of each day the pottery was brought to the storeroom for cleaning and preliminary repair. Later, drawings to the scale of 1 : 4 were made on squared paper, and each drawing was given a "Field Number", used to identify one or more pots in the same group. The Field Numbers followed on consecutively throughout the six seasons, and were used in the Division Lists prepared annually for the statutory division of finds with the Government of Palestine (British Mandate) Department of Antiquities. The Field Numbers are printed on the right-hand margin of the descriptions facing the pottery plates 79–104.

Type Numbers. As the material from the site increased, the Field Numbers came to serve a double purpose. When a pot was found which closely resembled another which had already been drawn, it was compared or "typed" to the first drawing of the kind in the Division List. In this way many pots acquired two numbers in addition to the Tell room or Tomb group number, i.e. a Field Number and a Type Number, referring back to a pot of a similar shape found in another locality. All the occurrences of a similar form are noted in the descriptions facing the pottery plates 79–104, in the column headed "Remarks".

Plate Numbers. When the preparation of the present volume was begun before World War II, it was intended to defer the publication of the material from the tell building levels until more work had been done. However, by 1946 it was clear that prospects of further field excavations in Palestine were slight, and it was decided to include all Iron Age pottery and objects in *Lachish III*. Pottery plates 79–95 were already prepared and numbered from 1 to 492 consecutively, according to a system in which all vessels of one kind were grouped together. Plates 79–95, therefore, contain the majority of nearly complete vessels found in cemeteries, while Plates 96–104, Nos. 493–700, are mostly incomplete pieces from the mound. In the second part, it appeared more practical to present the sections in a solid block, for the sake of clarity, though the plates in the first part conform to the precedent of *Lachish II*, and the sections are presented as dotted lines.

Classification of the Pottery Forms

In the present study the collection of pottery drawings, Nos. 1–700, has been sorted and arranged in classes and subdivisions, according to the function and shape of the vessel. Method of manufacture and decorative finish have also been considered as subsidiary aids to classification. The characteristics of the subdivisions are described in detail in the following pages, and comparisons with similar vessels from other sites are noted. The order of presentation adopted in *Lachish II* (p. 78) is followed, with some modifications and additions. It is repeated below with the necessary alterations and explanations. Notes on vessels which do not fit into the adopted scheme are to be found at the end of the chapter under the heading "Miscellaneous".

Bowls	*Pls. 79–82, 98–102*
	Types
A. Bowls without flare; in the case of carinates the width at the rim is equal to that at the keel	1–30, 117–119, 558–568, 591–598, 614–616, 617, 619–621, 623, 649, 650, 653–655, 657
B. Flared bowls	31–112, 569–576, 578–581, 599–603, 605–608, 626–648, 651–652, 656
C. In-curving bowls, i.e. in which the diameter at the rim is less than the diameter at the sides	124–133, 582, 583, 588–590, 604, 609, 610, 618, 622, 624–625

The diameter of the rim is taken from the outer edge of the lip in all cases. The three classes of bowls are divided as follows:

	Classes
i. Straight-sided bowls without any moulding to the rim. (Bowls with curved sides, where the rim neither flares nor turns in, are considered as straight-sided. They are referred to, in this volume, as "plain" bowls)	B.4, 8
ii. Bowls with slight keel and plain rims	B.9, 10, 12
iii. Bowls with internally flanged rims	B.7
iv. Bowls with externally flanged rims	B.11, 13, 14
v. Bowls with straight sides from rim to keel, either vertical or sloping	B.3

258

	Classes
vi. Bowls with flared sides from rim to keel: the diameter at both points in Class B being greater at the rim than at the keel; and in Class C, less at the rim than at the keel. They are sometimes called "cyma" profile bowls	B.5
vii. Round-bottomed bowls	B.6
viii. Bowls with handles or lugs of any kind	see pp. 265, 266
ix. Bowls on feet	Types 117–119
x. Grooved bowls	B.2
xi. Bowls with external and internal flange	B.1

	Classes	Plates
Development of bowls: Double bowl		81
Lamps	L.1–11	82, 83, 103
Chalices	CHA.	83, 103
Kraters	K.	91, 100, 104
Jugs	J.1–9	84–87, 103
Dippers and Juglets	D.1–9	88, 89
Potstands	PS	90
Miniature Amphorae	MA	91
Miniature Pithoi	MP	91
Pilgrim Flasks	PF	91, 92, 103
Cooking Pots	CP	93, 104
Storage Jars:	S.1–10	94–96
Cylindrical	S.11–12	95, 97
Miscellaneous	S.13	94–97
Jugs or Jars with Spouts and/or Strainers	JS	89

Distribution Charts

The five charts at the end of the chapter, of Bowls, Lamps, Jugs, Dippers and Juglets, and Storage Jars, concentrate the commonest classes of vessel from individual tell and tomb groups in the same progressive order on each page. The groups have been so arranged as to keep the subdivisions of each class as close together as possible in the vertical columns. The subdivisions throughout have been placed from left to right in a suggested chronological order of development. It will be appreciated that most of the small groups are contemporary with one or more of the large cave burials (p. 172), therefore the order of arrangement is only approximate, and a general idea of the nature of the series and its progressive overlap is to be gained from a study of the Consolidated Chart on p. 330. It appears that from the occupation of Tomb 223 onwards, the last burials in each cave were contemporary with the first ones in the tomb which comes next in date. The domestic pottery of the building Levels III and II on the mound fits neatly into the tomb series, and is contemporary with the upper layers of Tomb 1002, the ossuary deposit 120, etc., and the rock-cut Tomb 106.

The desertion of the site after the destruction of Level II is reflected in the lack of material to fill the gap between the end of Level II and the contents of the administrative buildings of Level I.

Methods of Manufacture

The task of archaeologists, who are rarely experts in the manufacture of pottery, has been greatly lightened by an excellent study on "The Potter's Technique at Tell Beit Mirsim, particularly in Stratum A" by J. L. Kelso and J. Palin Thorley, published in AASOR XXI–XXII. The descriptions could equally well apply to the pottery from Tell ed-Duweir during the latter part of the Iron Age, and throughout this volume the authors' conclusions are freely used and gratefully acknowledged. If an expert were prepared to spend many months applying the same tests to the comparable material from Tell ed-Duweir, a valuable control check would no doubt be achieved, but unfortunately further research, by the Expedition is impossible. However, much of the pottery will remain in London, at the Institute of Archaeology, for anyone who cares to undertake the task, or who wishes to check any particular detail.

Clays, Colours and Contents. The red clays used for the ordinary domestic wheel-made pottery at Tell ed-Duweir and Tell Beit Mirsim (op. cit., § 66), were subject to many possible colour combinations, and it is not easy to provide an adequate description of the colour within the narrow range of red, brown and buff. The gradations are so fine and vary so much, even on different parts of the same pot, that individual descriptions are unsatisfactory, but certain forms can be associated with certain wares, and it is hoped that the general aspect is made clear in the notes which follow.

The brief descriptions of colour, grits, temper and firing opposite the pottery plates apply to the type specimen or to the duplicate which replaces the type. Other examples may not be exactly similar, but the variations are slight and cannot be adequately described in words or photography. The original appearance of the surface is often destroyed by the accretion of lime deposits and exposure to humidity. Crushed limestone was purposely added to the natural clays in most of the pottery made locally in Judah. The amount of temper and the size of the grits varied according to the purpose of the vessel and its place in the chronological development. A standard for the approximate density of grits is given in L. II, Pl. XXXI: 45–47, and the same examples were used for the pottery of the Iron Age. It should be remembered, however, that sometimes all the grits are concentrated on one side of the pot, or they are hidden beneath a surface slip or burnish. The word "grits" almost invariably means crushed limestone, except in the case of cooking pots and the mortaria, where a mica or silicate temper is sometimes used.

Kiln Firing. In the descriptions opposite Plates 79–104, under the column headed "Firing", there is a somewhat arbitrary assessment of the kiln temperature applied to the type specimen. The abbreviations, H = hard, M = medium, S = soft, indicate the extremes within the low firing capacity of Iron Age kilns, as studied by Kelso and Thorley (AASOR XXI–XXII, § 62), i.e. between 900 and 1,050 degrees Centigrade. The surface of the "soft" pots is powdery and easily scratched; that of "hard" examples gives a good metallic ring.

Slip, Wash and Burnish. Kelso and Thorley give a clear definition of "slip" as opposed to "wash" (AASOR XXI–XXII, § 100), which is adhered to as much as possible in the present volume. "Both slip and wash", they write, "are basically liquid clay at about the consistency of cream, but a wash usually contains a considerable admixture of lime, ochre or some other pigment. *A wash, however, is never fired; a slip is always fired.*"

Application of a slip increases resistance to porosity and improves the appearance of the ware. It was the usual preliminary before the surface was burnished and polished by means of a smooth pebble applied by hand in varying strokes. As Kelso and Thorley remark, it was one of the first decorations to appear on pottery (AASOR XXI–XXII, § 98); after an initial popularity in the Early Bronze Age, it became less fashionable during the second millennium B.C., though there are signs that the technique was generally known.

Soon after the beginning of the Iron Age, however, application of a reddish-brown slip, hand-burnished, became the distinctive and decorative style of the period. That slip and burnish were first applied in an attempt to imitate metal vessels is well known, but it is rare to find such a close reproduction as the jug 202 in Class J.2, which is irregularly hand-burnished all over, and reproduces the technical details of the metal prototype. The pottery of the tomb in which the jug was found was mostly red burnished, and iron was more common than in later groups.

The necessary supplies of red ochre may well have emanated from the same source as the iron ores, nuggets and seals of haematite which are characteristic of the first phase of the Iron Age. As the source of supplies was exhausted or became inaccessible to pottery-makers in south Palestine, the amount of slip applied to individual vessels was reduced, and gradually this finished surface became confined to the interior of bowls only. In the later wheel-burnished wares the last phase is marked by wheel burnish applied on the unslipped surface of the pot.

The value of the gradual transition from pebble burnish applied by hand in a variety of ways, to burnish applied while the vessel was spinning on the wheel, cannot be underestimated as a guide to chronological development, and it is hoped to show in the following pages that the development is in harmony with the progression of form which is the basis for the suggested order of the series at Tell ed-Duweir. An analysis of the varying styles of burnish seen in bowls, made as far as the available material permits, is given below. Bowls were examined for this purpose as they were the form to which slip and burnish were most frequently applied. It should be emphasised that the examination of slip and burnish was conducted independently from that of form, and both investigations have resulted in a similar progression.

Analysis of Burnish in Bowls*

| Tomb or group | Irregular hand burnish | | | | | Wheel burnish | | Plain | | Worn or undefined | | Total examined |
	All over	In. and to keel out.	In. only, transitional	Total	%	Total	%	Total	%	Total	%	
Bastion	—	—	—	—	—	5	35	4	30	5	35	14
Houses II	—	—	1	1	4	10	36	13	46	4	14	28
Tomb 106	—	1	1	2	3	20	28	8	11	41	58	71
Houses III	—	—	2	2	5	14	37	18	48	4	10	38
Ossuary 120	—	—	1	1	7	1	7	10	66	3	20	15
Tomb 1002	—											
layers 1–5	—	2	3	5	16	7	23	4	13	15	48	31
layers 6–10	—	4	1	5	17	11	40	1	3	11	40	28
layers 11–13	—	1	1	2	8	11	40	2	8	12	44	27
Tomb 1004	—	—	1	1	10	1	10	6	60	2	20	10
Tomb 224		14	7	21	57	3	8	13	35	—	—	37
Tomb 116		3	4	7	77	—	—	2	23	—	—	9
Tomb 218	6	7	9	22	73	—	—	8	27	—	—	30
Tomb 223	—	4	—	4	33	—	—	8	67	—	—	12
Tomb 521	2	3	—	5	83	—	—	—	—	1	17	6
Cave 6024	4	2	—	6	100	—	—	—	—	—	—	6
TOTAL	12	41	31	84		83		97		98		362

The percentages for all layers of Tomb 1002 are: Hand burnish, 14%; Wheel burnish, 34%; Plain, 8%; and Worn and undefined, 44%.

* Prepared from a study of the bowls available at the Institute of Archaeology, London.

It is known that Level V of the city deposits—represented by the trial pit sunk at the south-east corner of Palace B–C (Palace South Wall, Chapter 3, pp. 80 f.)—contained a preponderance of hand-burnished wares, and fragments of bowls have also been found in the casemate filling of Palace A (K.15: 1053), which is structurally of much the same period. The only group in the tomb series which equates with the period on considerations of slip and burnish is Tomb 521. The contents of Cave 6024, which was apparently in use as a workshop, may cover part of the same period, but the group contains many unusual features, including some vessels covered with a mat red unburnished slip, which is occasionally referred to in this and other publications as a "grain wash"—a term which is neither descriptive nor precise.

261

In and under the brick wall excavated in section on the west side of the mound, the proportion of hand-burnished wares is small, and the style and amount of the surface covered with slip suggests a later phase in development (Chapter 3, p. 73). Probably contemporary, therefore, with Level IV—unexcavated elsewhere on the mound—are Tombs 223, 218 and 116, in which hand burnish of various styles is common, and it is in the next large group, 224, that the first examples of wheel-burnished bowls appear, as they do at 258·04 m. in the West Section.

According to the indications in the Analysis of Burnish, the introduction of wheel burnish was a rapid development, increasing from 8 and 10 per cent. of the total number of bowls in Tombs 224 and 1004 respectively, where it first appears, to an average of 34 per cent. in all layers of Tomb 1002, and it is matched in these groups by a corresponding decrease in hand burnish. On the evidence of burnish alone, a steady decline in the use of hand-finished wares is apparent, reaching virtual extinction at the end of the period under review. Wheel burnish continued throughout the remaining groups examined, though there is reason to believe that the decline had set in.

The initial date for the occupation of Houses III on the evidence of pottery form is not much later than the occupation of Tomb 116 and the lower layers of Tomb 1002, though the small amount of hand burnish observed in the examples from the mound which were examined does suggest a later trend.

It is perhaps significant that the bowls in two particular classes are chiefly affected by the change from hand to wheel burnish, and this is best appreciated by isolating the types concerned, as shown below:

| Tomb | Irregular hand burnish | | Wheel burnish | |
	In. and to keel out.	In. only, transitional	Spiral on red slip	Self
1002, all layers	*Type* B.7 48 B.6 95	*Type* B.7 38 40	*Type* B.7 39 40 48(4) B.6 90 95	*Type* B.7 40 48(2)
	2	2	8	3
1004		B.7 39	B.6 90	
		1	1	
224	B.7 40(2) 48 B.6 90(2) 94(4) 96	B.6 91(2) 93(2)	B.7 39 B.6 89 90	
	10	4	3	

Fig. 33 illustrates typical examples of round-bottomed bowls, showing the change from hand to wheel burnish in the three successive tombs 223, 224 and 1002.

With regard to Class B.13, types 73 and 81, the most common class in tell Level III, two sherds of that class were found in Tomb 218, covered with red slip inside and to keel outside and irregularly hand burnished over all the remaining part. At the other end of the scale, two sherds, types 631 and 643, of Class B.13, similarly hand burnished, were found in rooms of Level III, by which time wheel burnish was normally predominant.

To turn to comparisons from other sites, the excavations at Samaria have established the fact that wheel burnish is not found among the few sherds attributed to the first period in and under the foundation levels of Ahab's buildings (880 B.C.), and Miss K. M. Kenyon considers that wheel burnish did not come into general use until Period IV, *circa* 800 B.C.

At Megiddo (M. I, p. 164), wheel burnish became common in Stratum IV, which the excavators would date from 1000 to 800 B.C., and here again the Samaria evidence, which was not available to them at the time, would point towards a later date for that stratum.

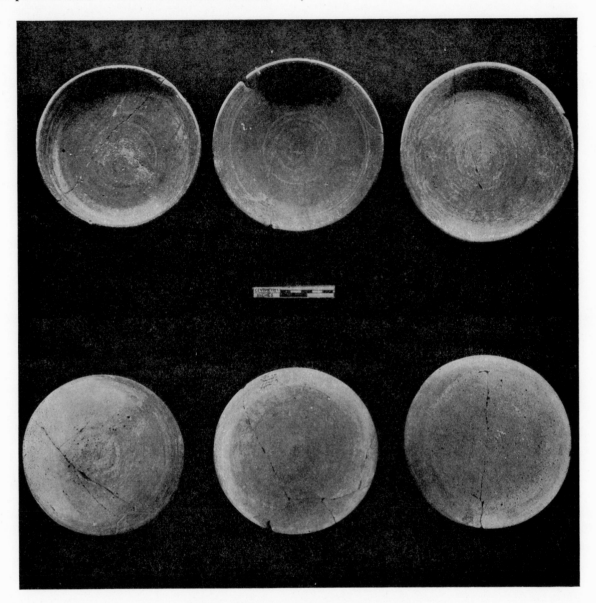

FIG. 33. Hand and wheel burnish on bowls

Tomb 1 at 'Ain Shems (APEF II, pp. 53–54) contained bowls and saucers burnished by hand both inside and over the rim as far as the keel. Mackenzie does not note any wheel burnish on them, but this would not be easily recognisable owing to their worn condition. Grant and Wright state that the most characteristic pottery of Stratum IIb is the burnished ware (AS V, p. 136). They found both hand and wheel burnish in that stratum, and the characteristic feature of the sherds is burnishing over the exterior from the rim down to about the middle of the side. References to bowls from 'Ain Shems comparable to Classes B.1, B.2 and B.3 are noted under those headings in the section on bowls.

Tomb 32 at Tell en-Naṣbeh (TN I, pp. 93–94) contained bowls with criss-cross or chordal hand burnishing, but there was a preponderance of ring burnish, covering the interior and exterior down to a point below the carination.

Albright has contributed to the discussion on burnished wares from Gibeah (AASOR IV, pp. 21 ff.) and from Tell Beit Mirsim (AASOR XII, §§ 86, 87 and 117; XXI–XXII, §§ 98, 132 and 160), where the technique is also admirably described. Other references are from Jericho (SW, pp. 141–143) and from Ascalon (PEQ, 1923, pp. 72 ff.).

Type specimens, other than bowls, which show hand burnish, are:

Chalices	Jugs		Jugs or Jars with Spouts
Cha. 161	J.1	221, 222	JS 362, 363, 364
	J.2	202, 209	
	J.3	225	
	J.4	181, 185	
	J.5	195	
	J.6	230, 236, 239, 240, 241, 244, 667	
	J.7	246, 248, 249, 253, 256, 266, 270	
	J.8	254, 273, 274, 275, 276, 277, 281, 665	

Many juglets in Classes D.1–3 are hand burnished, and some in Classes D.4–5, while all in Class D.6 are smooth polished. The majority in Classes D.7 and D.8 are vertically hand burnished on the body, with horizontal strokes round the neck.

Forms which show traces of wheel burnish are type 292 in Class D.8, and the fully developed decanters in Class J.8.

Decoration. Paint: After the variety and exuberance of Late Bronze Age painted design, and the elaborate motifs on the Philistine pottery, it is strange to find how completely the tradition had perished by the second part of the Iron Age. Bowl 66, with the centre painted red, and bordered with a wide outer band of red, limited by black lines, is the only painted bowl.[1]

The chalice 159, the miniature amphorae and pithoi, types 411, 418, 419, 422 and 428, and the pilgrim flask 430, owe their rudimentary decoration of red and black lines to a survival of Late Bronze Age tradition.

The jugs 221, 262, 263 may be locally made, but types 259, 334 and 335, with the juglet 325, seem strange to that tradition. The elaborate finish of the so-called "Cypriote" wares, decorated with black lines and concentric circles—types 329, 330, 331, 336–339, and the jug 350—places them far above the simple local standards of the period. Flasks 383 and 384, decorated with bands of brown paint, have close affinities with the numerous bottles found in seventh-century tombs in Jordan.

Jar fragment 508 was decorated with a pink band under the rim, and a black circle.

Incisions: Wheel-made incisions or grooves round the outer rim are characteristic of bowls in Class B.2, surviving from the first part of the Iron Age.

Jugs 237, 244 in Class J.6, and 270 in Class J.7a, have non-local affinities, and the tiny debased flask 366 with an incised spiral certainly derives from "Cypriote" wares.

Wheel-made incised circles or spirals round both sides of pilgrim flasks 429, 431, 432, 438, 678 follow in the Late Bronze Age tradition of painted circles.

---

[1] Red lines or bands are shown in this publication by fine vertical strokes, and black is filled in solid.

Cooking pots 451–456 have one or more incisions round the neck, and examples of type 455 sometimes have a cross incised on the handle.

Incisions around the body at the base of the spout are also a feature of the spouted jug 373. Incised marks occurred on storage vessels 472 and 487.

In contrast to the lack of decorative effort characteristic of the Jewish monarchy, there is one curious and attractive reminiscence of a popular Late Bronze Age motif. It is a well-balanced design of two ibexes eating a drooping lotus plant, jar 465 (Pls. 50: 1 and 78: 16), incised while the jar was "leather" hard before firing, as it stood upside down. The vessel came from a room attributed to Level II occupation, and the sketch is an expression of artistic merit, very different from the childish incisions illustrated on Pl. 50: 2, which are themselves comparable to the scratched drawings on the palace steps (Fig. 10), buried under the row of houses in which the jar was found.

Handles

On Bowls

The handles attached to bowls may be divided into four classes and a Miscellaneous section.

Spatulate, knob and bar: Class B.2   Types 103 (Pl. 72: 12), 104, 604
                Class B.4   Types 99 (Pl. 72: 2), 100, 105 (Pl. 72: 3)

The spatulate or bar handle is only found on bowls in Class B.2, and it will be seen that no complete examples came from the main tomb groups. Two fragments came from the South Wall trial cut (Pl. 105: 13, 14). A bar attachment between round knobs, which is found on a few bowls in Class B.4, appears to be a degraded form of the bar handle, and is confined to Tombs 521 and 116, which are among the earliest of the series. A rather similar handle on a bowl like type 99 is dated at Samaria to Period I, 880–850 B.C.

Rudimentary bar handles on bowls are not unknown in the Fosse Temple, Structure II–III (L. II, Pl. XLII f.: 142, 158, 164) and continue into the Iron Age at Tell Beit Mirsim (AASOR XII, Pl. 28: 12) from Stratum B_2, 1150–1100 B.C., but they are small and simple compared with those on burnished bowls which seem to be derived more closely from the metal prototype.

J. C. Wampler (TN II, p. 38, § 45) does not consider that the bar (spatulate) handle is a reliable indication of an early date. It is possible that the position of the handle in relation to the rim is a better guide. At Tell en-Naṣbeh (TN II, Pl. 60: 1378–1391) and at Megiddo (M. I, Pl. 24: 36–39), where they occur in Strata IV–II, the bars are attached low on the side, in contrast to those few from Tell ed-Duweir where the bar rises up to the rim line (cf. those from Tell Beit Mirsim (AASOR XII, Pl. 25: 1, 7, 16) from Stratum B).

At both Tell en-Naṣbeh and Megiddo the bars are attached to burnished bowls, and at Megiddo they are all listed as wheel burnished, which should establish their continuation into the eighth century at least. It is, however, surprising that the two examples attributed to Stratum V are considered to be intrusive (M. I, p. 169, § 56). If that opinion is based on the fact that they are wheel burnished, it would add to the argument for the reduction of the date of Stratum V.

Button: Class B.2   Types 132, 589, 592, 593, 596
        Class B.3   Type 615

The plain round button imitates the head of a metal rivet. It is found singly or in groups on bowls in Classes B.2 and B.3. The circumferences of those forms drawn from fragments on Pl. 99 are often too inadequately preserved to establish the existence or number of button attachments. For close parallels to type 615, see AASOR XII, Pl. 24: 7–8, Stratum B, and Tell el-Fara, Level BA 389 (Collection at the Institute of Archaeology, London).

Pinched knob:	Class B.1	Type 606
	Class B.4	Type 101 (Pl. 73: 30)
	Class B.6	Type 98
	Class B.7	Type 607
	Class B.9	Types 106 (Pl. 75: 12), 107

Apart from one example of a pinched knob on a bowl grouped with Class B.1—on form, but not on provenance, which was uncertain—it would appear that one or more pinched knobs was a late though not a common development to be found on bowls from Tombs 224 and 1002, layers 1–5, ending with two miniature bowls in Class B.9 from Tomb 106.[1]

Loop:	Class B.1	Types 653, 654
	Class B.7	Type 656
	Class B.10	Type 108
	Class B.13	Types 109 (Pl. 77: 17), 120, 121, 122 (Pl. 77: 2), 123, 647–652, 655, 657

No recollection of the Bronze Age tradition of horizontal loop handles, such as the wishbone handle and its derivatives, remains in the present series, and when loop handles are found on some bowls in Classes B.1 and B.10, and more commonly in B.13, the handles are always attached vertically as a practical adjunct to the larger mixing bowls.

Lack of such vessels in the tombs indicates their primary domestic purpose, for they were found in Houses III and II, dwelling 505, and ossuary 120, with fragments on open spaces and in rubbish pits. No doubt domestic vessels of Level IV were similarly provided with handles, and both types in Class B.1 would seem to come from that horizon.

Where the handles are preserved, and not merely represented by a stump, they are usually plain oval in section, but a few show a ridged surface (e.g. types 655, 657) reminiscent of the stamped jar handles of Class S.7a.

Miscellaneous: Types 110 (Pl. 73: 26), 111 (Pl. 76: 25), 112 (Pl. 74: 6), 113–115 (Pl. 77: 18), 124

Another indication of the early limit of the series, or, alternatively, its isolation from Philistine or coastal influence, is to be seen in the scarcity of bowls with tilted horizontal handles. Only type 110 carries a vestigial reminiscence of those handles on Late Helladic III kraters, which were imitated in Palestine during the thirteenth and twelfth centuries (W. F. Albright, Haverford Symposium, p. 46).

On Jugs

The characteristic handle section of jugs up to and including the prototypes in Class J.8 is a plain oval, carefully attached to the rim or neck, and well rounded where it joins the shoulder.

The spouted jug type 364 (Pl. 72: 9), of which the type specimen comes from Tomb 521, has a grooved ribbon handle and the ridged neck which seem to be early manifestations of late features. The ridges on the three handles of the spouted jug type 373 are similar to those on stamped jar handles in Class S.7a. Use of the ribbon handle is largely confined to the fully developed decanters in Class J.8.

A sure indication of post-exilic date is the careless method of attaching the handle to the body, without any attempt to round off the angle at the join. Examples among the jugs are on Pl. 84: 175, 204, Pl. 85: 212, 216 and Pl. 87: 255, 272. The same observation has been made by Wampler at Tell en-Naṣbeh (TN II, p. 26, § 64).

---

[1] At 'Ain Shems, button and knob handles on bowls are ubiquitous in Stratum IIa and probably the early part of IIb, 1000–825 B.C., so it is not surprising that they are poorly represented in the Duweir series, which is mainly later (AS IV, description of item 14 on Pl. LXIII).

On Dippers

Dippers and juglets in Classes D.1–8 have round or oval-shaped handles when seen in section. The point of attachment to the rim is a chronological consideration of importance which is discussed in the section on Dippers and Juglets, Classes D.7 and D.8.

The post-exilic character of the dippers in Class D.9 is seen in the careless attachment of the handles, leaving an elliptical space (see also Pl. 88: 306).

Basket handles are associated with the spouted dippers on Pl. 89: 355, 358, and the fragment 365.

On Cooking Pots

Good stout handles with plain oval section are provided on the cooking pots, and some are incised with a cross. Late forms are on Pl. 93: 446, 463 and 464, with ribbon rather than oval handle sections.

On Storage Jars

On storage jars provided with two handles the normal section is a plain oval. Where there are four handles one or two ridges are more common, but the occurrences are by no means always consistent. For a fuller discussion, see under Storage Jars, p. 312 and Jar Handle Stamps, p. 340.

Estimated totals of vessels

A total of 3,136 vessels has been examined and classified, but it is a minimum number. It consists of the following:

Bowls	731	Miniature Amphorae	13
Lamps: Saucer	396	Miniature Pithoi	16
Closed	24	Pilgrim Flasks	31
Chalices	25	Cooking Pots	163
Kraters	6	Storage Jars	379
Jugs	548	Jugs or Jars with Spouts and/or Strainers	15
Dippers and Juglets	591	Miscellaneous	163
Potstands	35		

BOWLS

General Notes

Bowls are undoubtedly the simplest as well as the commonest of all ceramic forms, and it is perhaps for these reasons that they are particularly difficult to classify. A true progression of form and sequence can only be seen on those rare and valuable occasions when a stratified site is examined, and the comparative and statistical methods now in use can then establish securely the range and development of form within the period at any particular place.

For instance, the development of bowl forms can be followed in detail throughout the Late Bronze Age at Tell ed-Duweir. A glance at Pls. XXXVII–XLII of *Lachish II* will show how the wide open bowl characteristic of MB II (1650–1550 B.C.) persisted throughout the occupation of all three structures of the Fosse Temple. It also illustrates how other forms, such as the carinate bowls (Pls. XLI, XLII) still prominent in Structures I and II, had softened in outline and lost a sharp keel before the destruction of Structure III. Other shapes, with a functional or ritual purpose only, may be confined to one Structure (see, for example, bowl 66 on Pl. XXXIX).

Unfortunately there is at present no similar clear story of the succeeding Iron Age at Tell ed-Duweir. There is little which can be definitely assigned to Iron Age I (1200–900 B.C.). When the threads are picked up there is no question of a closely stratified site, because the material that exists for the earlier part of Iron II is contained in less than a dozen large tomb groups, all but one of which had been disturbed and pillaged, though the later part is more securely founded on the pottery forms from tell Levels III, II and I.

Although there are many dangers in all statistical methods, the system has been used in default of a better one, and the resulting Distribution Chart of bowl forms on p. 325 is based on the frequency of type in each group and the relation of groups to one another. The scheme for the classification of bowls adopted in *Lachish II* (described on p. 78 of that volume) has been followed as far as possible.

The Distribution Chart shows that there are three common types of bowl within the period under review: the bowls with plain rims in Class B.4, the bowls with slight keel and internally flanged rims in Class B.7, and the folded rim bowls in Class B.13. All three types overlap in part, but there is a clear progression: the plain bowls are fewest in number because they had passed their zenith, though they are found in all groups until Tomb 106, where there is only one example. The internally flanged bowls are represented in Tomb 218 by two examples, and continue in subsequent groups until Level I.

Folded rim bowls are represented by two examples only in Tomb 1002 and Tomb 218, and they became the outstanding form in the subsequent tell levels. As the period under review covers a span of three hundred years, it may be permissible to suggest that the bowls in Class B.4 are characteristic of the tenth–ninth century, those in Class B.7 of the ninth–eighth century, and those in Class B.13, of the eighth–seventh century, a conclusion which the present writer finds is in agreement with J. C. Wampler's opinion expressed in TN II, p. 37, § 40. Moreover, the chart demonstrates very clearly the theory that the date of any given form should be established at the point of maximum frequency, for isolated occurrences may anticipate or succeed the zenith by a century or more (TN II, p. 34, § 27).

At the beginning of the period under review are the bowls with external and internal flange in Class B.1, which belong to Levels V–IV, so far unexcavated, and at the end of the scale are the plain and ribbed mortaria, characteristic of Level I, which are assembled in Class B.14.

The intervening classes are devoted to smaller groups which could be distinguished by one or more characteristics, and it is hoped that these divisions will provide a basis for a closer analysis of bowls belonging to Iron Age II (900–600 B.C.) than has hitherto been possible.

Classification in suggested chronological order	Types	Classification according to form
B.1	85, 598, 606, 617, 620–625, 653–654	xi
		Bowls with internal and external flange

This small but important group contains most of the few bowl types so far recovered from areas which may prove to belong to Levels V–IV. The sherds were chiefly found in and on the earth ramp which surrounded the podium of the palace. Those marked "South Wall" come from the trial pit sunk at the south-east corner of the palace, which penetrated through Levels IV and possibly V to a Late Bronze Age brick building.

Two sherds of this form and ware are recorded from the floors of the Residency, and one was found in the contemporary pits; three sherds came from the Bastion area, but their presence, so far removed from their true horizon, accentuates the lack of intervening debris as already observed between the Residency rooms and the floors of Palace B–C, which are all that remain of the building in use until the destruction of Level III.

The fragments of types 500 and 618, classified under Miscellaneous, from the area beyond the palace walls would also seem to belong to the Levels V–IV occupation.

The ware of the bowls, which are mostly incomplete, is very consistent. The body is usually brown with an admixture of grits[2], and occasionally some straw has been added. The firing is medium or soft.

A red slip or wash frequently covers the interior of the bowl, and extends over the rim, and in nearly every case the inside surface has been irregularly hand-burnished, while the exterior often shows a brown self burnish, extending beyond the portion covered by the slip down to the base.

The characteristic feature of these large deep bowls is the external and internal flange to the thick flat rim. Two or more handles are a common addition on similar bowls at other sites, and it is no doubt owing to the fragmentary nature of the Tell ed-Duweir examples that so few specimens are certainly provided with them. Type 617, for instance, is comparable to forms from Megiddo and Tell en-Naṣbeh, which have handles preserved (see also fragment 653).

At 'Ain Shems the class is well represented by the rims of wide-mouthed bowls illustrated in AS IV, Pl. XXXVIII: 15–19 and Pl. LX: 26, described by Grant and Wright. Most are finished with a burnished red slip which was more common in Stratum II, after 1000 B.C.; in Stratum III and the early part of II the burnishing was done by hand "just as it was in Stratum B of Tell Beit Mirsim where, next to Philistine pottery, burnish was a very distinctive characteristic" (AS V, p. 131).

Related bowls which first appeared in Stratum IV at 'Ain Shems (AS IV, Pl. XXXII: 1–5) carried on into Stratum III (AS IV, Pl. LXI: 10–16) but were apparently no longer made in the period of Stratum II. The bowls with internal and external flange were "more common in IIb than in any other period" (AS IV, Pl. LXIV: 1–7 and AS V, p. 137). Comparisons for two of these bowls are found in types 621 and 625.

Then, referring to deep bowls, classified as kraters, Wampler writes: "At Tell en-Naṣbeh, it seems that the more complete the form is, the more certainly it is EI" (TN II, p. 40). The outstanding point about the distribution of fragments at Tell ed-Duweir is that they are not found in the large groups; indeed, the only piece from a tomb came from Tomb 4010, which was in use during the Bronze Age and extended into the following period. Including those fragments marked as coming from the Residency floors and pits, the Bastion and the Great Shaft, which all actually belong to Levels V–IV, the material suggests that the bowls in this class should be dated prior to 900 B.C. There is nothing at Tell ed-Duweir to show that they survived into the following century, though Wampler admits the possibility at Tell en-Naṣbeh and draws attention to the longevity of the form at Megiddo (TN II, p. 40). Alternatively, his observation may be used to support an altered date for Strata V–II at Megiddo.

			B.C.
617	Tell el-Muteselim (M. II, Pl. 147: 10) Stratum V–I		1050–350
617	„ „ (M. I, Pl. 27: 86) „ III		1000–800
617	Tell en-Naṣbeh (TN II, Pl. 65: 1479) AB 25, 26, Sub.R. 221, I, x8		"EI with LB connexions"
621	'Ain Shems (AS IV, Pl. LXI: 12) Rm. 445 (1933), Stratum III		1200–1000
625	„ „ (AS IV, Pl. LXI: 15) Rm. 430 (1933), Stratum III		1200–1000
653	Tell en-Naṣbeh (TN II, Pl. 65: 1479) AB 25, 26, Sub.R. 221, I, x8		"EI with LB connexions"

Classification in suggested chronological order	Types	Classification according to form
B.2	22, 24, 28, 103 (Pl. 72: 12), 104, 132, 133 (Pl. 72: 14), 588–597, 604	x Grooved bowls

The earlier bowls in this group, five of which came from the open area south and west of the palace walls, all show a rounded internal flange to the rim profile, which seems to be a characteristic of bowls in Levels V–IV. This profile is also to be seen on a large bowl fragment 103 from Cave 6024, covered inside and over the rim by a "grain wash".[1] Type 133 from the same deposit has only a slight thickening of the rim, and is irregularly hand burnished all over.

Types 22, 24 and 28 from Tomb 218 belong to a possible later phase in the development, where the rim is no thicker than the rest of the bowl. It should be noted, however, that sherds of types 592 and 596 were found among the burnished fragments from this tomb, so that an alternative suggestion that the stronger, thicker rim was only applied to the bigger bowls must be considered.

---

[1] See p. 261.

The evidence is still too slight to determine if a diminution in the number of grooves indicates a later date, but sherd 590, which has a single groove and a plain, unthickened rim and came from Level III, may favour the suggestion.

The majority of the grooved bowls are made of a brown ware, containing grits[1] or sometimes grits[2], and no admixture of straw was observed. The firing is usually medium, but some of the later examples tend towards a pinker and harder body (i.e. types 24, 103, 104, 133). Only type 28 is classified as a soft pink ware.

The earlier examples in the class, including those from the south and west walls of the palace (types 104, 133, 589, 591, 592, 593, 597, 598), are covered with a red slip and are irregularly hand burnished all over, but in the case of the last grooved bowls in the series from Tomb 218 (types 22, 24, 28, 596), the burnish only extends as far as the keel in all but one example (i.e. one specimen of type 28, which is soft fired). Sherd 588 from the west wall of the palace is one of the few to show an even red burnish inside and out. The indications of ware and burnish in the class are consistent with the suggested development of the bowl rims noted above.

Grooved bowls are rather uncommon at other sites. The best selection of fragments, with two or more grooves below the rim and an occasional knob on the exterior, is found in Stratum IIb at 'Ain Shems (AS IV, Pl. LXIII: 13, 15, 17 and Pl. XLIII: 9–11, 16–19). Some of those shown on Pl. XLIII seem to have the rounded internal flange characteristic of the bowls attributed to Level IV at Tell ed-Duweir (Nos. 591–598).

There are a few examples from Tell en-Naṣbeh (cf. TN II, Pl. 60: 1394), but they seem to be missing from Megiddo.

Small grooved bowls with straight sides from Gerar (CPP, 18 E3, 4) come from levels 183–188, and should belong to the early tenth century; the nearest comparison is type 132, but it has a knob instead of a vestigial handle. Vestigial handles only appear on bowl type 110 (see Handles on Bowls, p. 266).

Type 133 can be compared to the form of a bowl at Samaria (SS III, Fig. 1: 1), though it is unburnished.

While the origin of the grooved bowls should be placed in Level IV or earlier, prior to 900 B.C., the later varieties with unthickened rim and less slip and burnish seem to continue into the ninth century.

597 Tell ej-Judeideh (BM, Pls. 55: 3 and 21: 4) Stratum II
                         Jewish

Classification in suggested chronological order B.3	Types 26, 126, 128, 614–616	Classification according to form A.v Bowls with straight sides from rim to keel, either vertical or sloping

The few bowls in Class B.3 all have a sharp angle at the keel, and the profile down to that point is almost straight; except for type 126, there is no flare or thickening of the rim.

The ware is pink or brown, more often soft than medium fired, and all examples except type 26 were covered with a red slip. Types 128 and 616 were not burnished, but the other fragments show irregular hand strokes, applied horizontally round the bowl, while in the case of type 615 a very fine, even surface has been achieved (see Handles on Bowls, p. 265).

These plain, well-made bowls are largely survivals from Iron I and comparisons for them are found in Stratum III at 'Ain Shems and at Tell el-Fûl, Strata I–II (AASOR IV, Pl. XXVI), late eleventh and early tenth centuries B.C.

		B.C.
26	'Ain Shems (AS IV, Pl. LXII: 14) Below foundations of Rm. 387, Stratum III	1200–1000
126	„ „ (AS IV, Pl. LXII: 12) Rm. 441, Stratum III	
615	Tell el-Fara (Level BA 389, Institute of Archaeology Collection)	„ „ 900–800

Classification in suggested chronological order	Types	Classification according to form
B.4	4, 6, 7 (Pl. 74: 2), 8 (Pl. 72: 11), 11, 12, 13–15, 17–21, 23, 25, 29, 53, 99 (Pl. 72: 2), 100, 101 (Pl. 73: 30), 105 (Pl. 72: 3), 577	i Plain bowls

The common forms in this category are types 8 and 13. The ware is usually pink, and rather badly levigated, producing an uneven surface, and contains some grits. The firing is usually medium, though variations do occur. Some examples have a pink slip which is irregularly hand burnished inside and to keel out, but the majority are plain.

Forerunners of the whole group may be found in Structures II and III of the Fosse Temple (L. II, Pl. XXXVIII: 47, 48, 50), at 'Ain Shems (AS V, p. 135) in the common bowls of Stratum III, 1200–1000 B.C. (AS IV, Pl. XXXVII: 19–21, 24 and Pl. LXII: 18–20, 22–25), and of Stratum IIa (AS IV, Pl. XLII: 19–24, 26–29 and Pl. LXIII: 1–10), 1000–950 B.C. Some forms included in Wampler's first group of small bowls with plain rim "predominant in EI until about the ninth century" also occur (TN II, p. 34, §§ 27 ff. and Pl. 54: 1219–1221). This agrees with the indications of the Distribution Chart, for examples of type 8 are confined to the earlier tombs, while type 13, with a tendency towards a slight keel, survives in Tomb 1002. Type 9 is typologically later and is included with the fully developed bowls in Class B.7 of the chart.

The use of bowls like type 8 had passed its zenith of popularity before the occupation of the tomb series had begun, but the form merged gradually by way of type 13 during the ninth century towards the common bowl, represented by type 9 of the following century.

		B.C.
8	Tell el-Muteselim (M. I, Pl. 30: 123) Stratum V	1050–1000
15	Tell en-Naṣbeh (TN II, Pl. 54: 1219) Ts. 32, 54	EI–early MI

Classification in suggested chronological order	Types	Classification according to form
B.5	41 (Pl. 73: 21), 42–44, 55 (Pl. 72: 1), 56, 57 (Pl. 73: 19), 58 (Pl. 73: 24), 131, 586, 609. 103–104, see B.2; 124 not classified according to form	A. ii Bowls with "cyma" profile, some internally flanged.

On the basis of form, the twenty-two examples included in this group must be divided from the other bowls with internally flanged rims assembled in Classes B.7 and B.10 of the chart, but they do not in themselves make a very compact section.

The shape of types 41–44 is reminiscent of some plain Late Bronze bowls (L. II, Pl. XL: 75–77) from Structure I. Types 55 and 57 can be compared to one of the most typical forms of Stratum III at 'Ain Shems (AS IV, Pl. LIX: 13, 14, 20 and AS V, p. 130), which places the major phase of these bowls between 1200 and 1000 B.C.

Though Class B.4 was typical of Stratum IIa at 'Ain Shems (AS IV, Pl. LXIII: 1–10), the cyma profile reappeared as a common form in Stratum IIb (950–825 B.C.), with one fairly close parallel from Tell ed-Duweir, type 609, which is similarly burnished. The fragment came from the trial pit at the south-east corner of the palace, and is consequently from Levels V–IV prior to 900 B.C. The steadily diminishing occurrence of these bowls in the tomb groups does show, however, that they did not disappear completely until about 700 B.C.

The prevailing ware at Tell ed-Duweir is a pink paste containing grits[1]; the firing can be soft, medium or hard. Four examples have a dark red slip inside and to the keel outside, irregularly hand burnished, but in no case does slip or burnish extend to the base.

		B.C.
41	Sahab (QDAP XIII, p. 97, No. 8)	700–600
55	Tell en-Naṣbeh (TN II, Pl. 54: 1192) R. 658, AB 18, I, x12	common phase
		1100–800
55	Tell en-Naṣbeh (STTN, Pl. XXIII: X 189) Tomb 5	c. 900–700
55	Samaria (SS III, Fig. 1: 1) Period I	880–850
609	'Ain Shems (AS IV, Pl. LXIII: 11) Stratum IIb	950–825

*Classification in suggested
chronological order
B.6*

*Classification according
to form
vii*

Round-bottomed bowls

Locus	Types											Total
	88	89	90	91	92	93*	94	95	96	97	98	
106	—	1	—	—	—	—	—	6	—	—	—	7
Houses III	—	1	4	—	—	—	—	1	—	—	—	6
1002												
layers 1–5	—	3	—	—	1	—	—	—	—	—	1	5
layers 6–10	—	2	1	—	—	—	—	1	—	—	—	4
layers 11–13	—	2	—	1	—	1	—	3	—	—	—	7
507	—	1	—	—	—	—	—	—	—	—	—	1
116 late	—	—	—	—	—	—	—	1	—	—	—	1
159	—	—	—	—	—	1	—	—	—	—	—	1
1004	—	1	1	—	—	—	—	—	—	—	—	2
154	—	—	—	—	—	1	—	—	—	—	—	1
169	—	—	—	1	—	—	—	—	—	—	—	1
224	—	1	2	2	—	2	4	—	1	—	—	12
218	2	1	—	—	—	—	—	—	1	1	—	5
223	—	—	1	—	—	1	—	—	—	—	—	2
TOTAL	2	13	9	4	1	6	4	12	2	1	1	55

* Pl. 73: 11.

It may be considered unnecessary to make a separate class for bowls with a round base, for they occur throughout the Iron Age. However, there are more than double the number of round-bottomed bowls in Tomb 224 than in Tomb 218, and in relation to the amount of pottery they are rare in Tomb 1002.

On the basis of distribution, it will be seen that the major phase took place half-way through the period under review. The section on burnished wares also shows that these forms had both hand and wheel finish, and sometimes both techniques are visible on the same bowl, confirming the transitional nature of the form.

Types 88, 91 and 93, with a countersunk base, seem to be early, types 89 and 90 enjoy a long range, while type 95, which is less carefully formed, appears to be typical of the last phase.

This conclusion is supported at Megiddo (M. I, p. 169, § 57), where the forms equivalent to types 90 and 93 have most examples in Stratum V and die out in Stratum IV, while the shape similar to type 95 is largely concentrated in Stratum III (M. I, Pl. 24: 55). J. W. Crowfoot's dates for Stratum V (c. 960–870), Stratum IV (c. 870–840) and Stratum III (c. 800–) would best suit the observation from Tell ed-Duweir.

There is a good variety of round-bottomed bowls from Tell Beit Mirsim (AASOR XII, Pl. 64; XXI–XXII, Pl. 25: 1–12), all belonging to Stratum A. At Tell en-Naṣbeh (TN II, Pl. 53: 1173–1179). C. C. McCown remarks on the EI context of such forms as S.1177 and S.1173 (TN I, p. 93), which have no close parallels at Duweir, and he notes the MI connexions for S.1175 and S.1176.

There are apparently some round-bottomed bowls in Tomb 1 at 'Ain Shems (APEF II, Pl. XXII: 2(?), 4(?), 5(?)), but the photographs do not show the bases clearly; they are missing from the city levels at this site.

The ware of the examples at Tell ed-Duweir is pink, brown or buff, usually without grits. The firing is medium with an ocasional soft or hard-fired specimen. Almost all are covered with a dark red slip inside, and in the case of the bowls from Tomb 224 they are irregularly hand burnished inside and to the keel outside. Where the same forms occur in Tomb 1004 and 1002, they show a ring or spiral wheel finish inside.

Though round-bottomed bowls occur between 900–600 B.C., types 88, 91 and 93 appear to belong to the ninth century, while type 95 can be placed in the eighth and seventh centuries.

		B.C.
89	Tell Beit Mirsim (AASOR XXI–XXII, Pl. 25: 3) Stratum A	9th–7th cent.
89	Tell en-Naṣbeh (TN II, Pl. 53: 1175) Tomb 5	major phase 1050–700
89	Tell en-Naṣbeh (STTN, Pl. XXI: 1369) Tomb 5	900–700
89	Tell Jemmeh (Gerar, Pl. XLIX: 12w, 16u) HV 185, CW 192, Level VI, Level XIV	10th–8th cent.
90	Tell el-Muteselim (M. I, Pl. 28: 93A and p. 169) Strata V–IV	1050–800
93	„ „ (M. I, Pl. 28: 93B and p. 169) „ „	„
93	Tell en-Naṣbeh (STTN, Pl. XXIII: X191) Tomb 5	900–700
93	Tell Jemmeh (Gerar, Pl. XLIX: 13h, 13k) EM 190, Level XI	c. 800
94	„ „ (Gerar, Pl. XLIX: 13t) DH 193, Level XV	c. 700
95	Tell el-Muteselim (M. I, Pl. 24: 55) Strata IV–III	1000–650

Classification in suggested chronological order B.7	Types	Classification according to form B.iii
	9 (Pl. 73: 1; Pl. 74: 3), 37 (Pl. 75: 4), 38–40, 46, 47, 48 (Pl. 75: 6), 49 (Pl. 75: 7), 50 (Pl. 77: 16), 51, 52, 54, 581, 599–602, 605, 607, 656	Bowls with internally flanged rims

The bowl types which make up this group are among the most characteristic at Tell ed-Duweir, and are second in number only to the folded rim bowls in B.14. They are also very closely confined within certain limits; they do not appear at all before Tomb 218, and there are only two sherds in that large group. The class is represented in Tombs 224, 1004 and the ossuary 120, and is prevalent in Tomb 1002 and tell Level III; it wanes in Tomb 106 and is missing from Level II. The sherds recorded as from G.18: 25–33, a post-exilic gatehouse, are not necessarily in their true context.

Most of the bowls are made of brown or pink paste, with a varying admixture of grits. The proportion of hard to medium fired examples is about the same, which is in keeping with the later range of the form. A red or pink slip inside the bowl is common, though it seldom extends beyond the rim. Irregular hand burnish is quite usual, especially in Tomb 224, but a spiral burnish inside supersedes it in the later Tomb 1002.

J. C. Wampler has placed similar bowls from Tell en-Naṣbeh (TN II, Pl. 55–57: 1245–1307) in his second main group of small bowls (TN II, p. 35, §§ 34 ff.), with a common phase in the ninth–eighth centuries B.C. At Megiddo (M. I, Pl. 24: 29–31, 34, 35) analogous types are largely concentrated in Stratum III (780–650 B.C.). Grant and Wright (AS V, p. 137) state that the forms illustrated in AS IV, Pl. LXVI: 4, 5, 7–16 "are typical of the last phase of Stratum II" (825–586 B.C.), but not all are to be classed with the B.7 bowls.

Available comparisons therefore present a consistent picture, which is also in keeping with the internal evidence.

Though type 9 is always unburnished, more fully developed forms like types 39, 40 and 48 are sometimes burnished inside, and an equal number exhibit both irregular hand and spiral wheel techniques (see Analysis of Burnish for Tombs 224 and 1002).

As in B.6 and B.13, the use of both methods of burnishing marks the traditional nature of the three classes.

In the writer's opinion the bowls in B.7 are rare before 800 B.C. Type 9 is confined between the occupation of Tombs 224 and the destruction of Level III, possibly in 700 B.C.

		B.C.
9	Tell en-Naṣbeh (TN II, Pl. 55: 1241) T.5, x 186	900–700
9	'Ain Shems (AS IV, Pl. LXVI: 10) Rm. 391, Stratum IIc	825–586
11	„ „ (AS IV, Pl. LXVI: 40) North of Rm. 306, Stratum II	825–586
37	Tell en-Naṣbeh (TN II, Pl. 55: 1250) Ci.163 AJ21	c. 1000–500
37	„ „ (STTN, Pl. XXI: 1356) Tomb 5	900–700
37	'Amman, Adoni Nur Tomb (APEF VI, in prep.) type 67	c. 650
46	Tell Jemmeh (Gerar, Pl. XLVIII: 3d)	
47	'Ain Shems (AS IV, Pl. LXVI: 16) Rm. 350, Stratum IIc	825–586
48	Tell en-Naṣbeh (TN II, Pl. 55: 1257) T.5, x 173	900–700
48	„ „ (STTN, Pl. XIV: 1164) Tomb 3	? 700–600
48	'Amman, Adoni Nur Tomb (APEF VI) type 64	c. 650
51	Tell en-Naṣbeh (STTN, Pl. XIV: 1162) Tomb 3	? 700–600
52	'Ain Shems (AS IV, Pl. LXVI: 4) Area R.31, Rm. 252. Probably belongs to Stratum IIb	950–825
602	'Ain Shems (AS IV, Pl. LXVI: 15) Rm. 386, Stratum IIc	825–586
602	Tell en-Naṣbeh (TN II, Pl. 55: 1255) T.5, x 197	900–700

Classification in suggested chronological order	Types	Classification according to form
B.8	1 (Pl. 74: 1), 2, 3, 558, 559, 561	i
		Straight-sided bowls

Typologically this group is not very satisfactory, though it certainly does not assimilate into another class. The dishes, types 1–3, are unusually flat and open for the period, and are mostly to be found in Tomb 1002 and tell Level III. A single example comes from the ossuary 120. The ware is pink, buff or brown, with a small admixture of grits. The firing is medium to hard. The type specimens of dishes 1–3 have a spiral burnish on a red slip inside.

The miniature dishes 558, 559, 561, made of pink, buff or brown ware, are unburnished. They are of better quality than the cups 5, 31–34, 106 and 107 in Class B.9, and seem to take their place in the rooms and areas ascribed to Level II.

Some comparisons are to be found in TN II, Pl. 68, discussed on p. 41, § 70 of that work, but they are not very close. Tell Beit Mirsim (AASOR XII, Pl. 65: 13–19; XXI–XXII, Pl. 15: 15, 16) shows other varieties, all from Stratum A. The material from Tell ed-Duweir would suggest that these miniature dishes are typically seventh century and did not survive the destruction of tell Level II.

561 Tell Jemmeh (CPP 12 G4)

Classification in suggested chronological order	Types	Classification according to form
B.9	5 (Pl. 75: 1), 31, 32, 33 (Pl. 75: 3), 34, 106, 107	A.ii

The coarsely made cups or dishes 5, 31–34, 106 and 107 appear to be confined to Tomb 1002, tell Level III and Tomb 106. All but two specimens are made of pink paste, with little or no grit admixture; the firing is more often hard than medium, and there is an occasional red slip. Only the type specimen for 5 shows an irregular hand burnish inside and to the keel outside.

The range of these utility products covers the end of the eighth and most of the seventh century.

Classification in suggested chronological order	*Types*	*Classification according to form*
B.10	35, 36, 61 (Pl. 77: 15), 102, 108	B.ii
		Flared bowls with a slight keel and plain rim

These forms are thinly distributed from Tomb 224 onwards. Possibly types 35, 36 and 61 may be leading towards the plates with thickened rims in the next class, but they did not achieve any popularity.

The ware is pink, usually without grits, and is covered by a buff, pink or red slip. The firing is soft to medium. An irregular hand burnish inside the bowl is found on at least three examples.

		B.C.
35	Tell en-Naṣbeh (TN II, Pl. 55: 1252) R.337, Z23, I, x 29	"Apparently LB to LI"
36	„ „ (TN II, Pl. 55: 1248) R.301. W12, I, x 15	9th–8th cent.
102	„ „ (TN II, Pl. 60: 1393) T.5 x 165	"Major phase, possibly EI–MI"

Classification in suggested chronological order	*Classification according to form*
B.11	iv
	Plates with externally flanged rims

Locus	Types											Total
	60	62*	63	66	64*	65	80*	560	59*	67*	562	
Solar Shrine	—	—	—	—	—	—	—	—	—	1	—	1
Houses I	1	—	—	—	—	—	—	—	1	3	1	6
Houses II	—	—	—	1	4	—	—	2	1	—	—	8
120	—	—	1	—	1	—	—	—	—	—	—	2
106	1	1	—	1	10	1	1	—	—	—	—	15
Houses III	1	2	3	1	—	—	—	—	—	1	—	8
1002	1	2	1	—	—	—	—	—	—	—	—	4
	4	5	5	3	15	1	1	2	2	5	1	44

* Pl. 74: 5; Pl. 76: 1; Pl. 75: 11; Pl. 77: 14; Pl. 77: 19.

The common form in this group of flat bowls or plates is type 64; it appears in all three chambers of Tomb 106 and continues into tell Level II. The very shallow plates 60, 62, 63, with narrow rims, are apparently somewhat earlier.[1] The later types are distinguished by a pronounced rim. Type 80 is a smoothly burnished bowl, for which no parallels have been found in Palestine; it is possibly more akin to Assyrian ware of the seventh century.

Most of the plates are made of pink ware, occasionally containing grits. The firing can be soft, medium or hard. A red slip inside is common, with a few examples which tend to be pink or buff. A widely spaced spiral burnish is a characteristic feature.

Possibly relatives for these plates are types 35, 36 and 61 in Class B.10, but the varieties grouped in Class B.11 first appear in the ossuary deposits and the topmost levels of Tomb 1002, and cannot therefore be more than a decade or so earlier than the seventh century B.C. That they continued well into the following centuries is shown by the presence of the later types in a post-exilic house.

---

[1] A close comparison for type 62 comes from Hielite Jericho, destroyed in 700 B.C.

External evidence is in agreement with this conclusion. Wampler notes the importance of plates during Middle Iron (TN II, p. 41, § 70), but though fairly common at his site and at Samaria, they seem to be rare at Megiddo, and in the city levels at 'Ain Shems.

		B.C.
62	Jericho (SW, Pl. 38: D, 12)	c. 870–700
64	Tell Beit Mirsim (AASOR XXI–XXII, Pl. 21: 4; Pl. 71: 2) Stratum A	900–600
65	Samaria (SS III, Fig. 4: 17) Period III	850–800
65	Tell en-Naṣbeh (TN II, Pl. 68: 1551) R.498, AE16, I, x 18	MI–LI
65	'Ain Shems (APEF II, Pl. XXXIII: 24 (?)) rep. of T.2	
65	„ „ (APEF II, Pl. LVII: 1 (?)) T.8	7th–early 6th cent.
65	„ „ (APEF II, Pl. LIV: 8 (?)) rep. of T.8	
67	Tell Sandaḥannah (BM, Pl. 61: 26)	Seleucidan
560	Tell Beit Mirsim (AASOR XXI–XXII, Pl. 21: 4) Stratum A	900–600
562	Samaria (S, Pl. 174: 10)	?
562	'Amman, Adoni Nur Tomb (APEF VI) type 68	c. 650 B.C.

Classification in suggested chronological order	Types	Classification according to form
B.12	16 (Pl. 75: 2), 45, 569–576, 608	C.ii

These straight-sided, thin-walled bowls with plain rims are typical of Levels III and II. They do occur in the ossuary periods of Tombs 116 and 117, but are missing from the large Tomb 1002, and from all previous groups. On the mound, it will be seen that out of thirteen examples, eight are certainly or probably from Level III, while the remaining five all come from Room J.17: 1042, which it is proposed to date to Level II. Sherds of types 569, 574 and 608 came from the north, west and south walls of the palace respectively, and there were two sherds of types 571 and 575 from the podium AG south of the palace. The presence of type 575 with the chalk altars in Group 534, and in the filling of the Great Shaft, are further pointers to a late date.

Comparative material is valuable. Wampler (TN II, p. 35, § 31 and Pl. 54: 1213–1217) places the common phase of these bowls between 700 and 500 B.C. Grant and Wright (AS V, p. 137 and AS IV, Pl. XLIII: 21–25 and Pl. LXIII: 23–27) found them especially common in Stratum IIb, extending possibly as late as the ninth or eighth century (see description for No. 23). Albright (AASOR XI–XXII, pp. 152 ff., § 160) discusses them with the ring-burnished bowls, saucers and plates, but leaves a closer division for further study.

The bowls from Tell ed-Duweir are made of pink, brown or grey ware with a fair proportion of grits. The firing is soft to hard, and there is only an occasional red or brown slip or wash. Only type 608 from the south wall of the palace, where a trial pit penetrated to Levels V–IV, shows an even red burnish inside and out. At Tell Beit Mirsim, however, burnished examples are more common than plain.

The absence of these bowls from all tomb groups prior to tell Level III would place them only a decade or so earlier than 700 B.C., and their presence in Level II and in post-exilic deposits substantially confirms Wampler's conclusion.

		B.C.
16	Ez-Zahiriyye (QDAP IV, Pl. LXI: 1) Atrium	
16	Tell en-Naṣbeh (TN II, Pl. 54: 1217) Ca193, Si C, AG28	c. 700–500
16	„ „ (STTN, Pl. XIV: 1166) Tomb 3	? 700–600
45	„ „ (TN II, Pl. 54: 1214) Ci.370, AF19	c. 700–500
570	Tell Beit Mirsim (AASOR XII, Pl. 65: 8) Stratum A	9th–7th cent.
571	„ „ (AASOR XII, Pl. 64: 16) Stratum A	„ „
572	'Ain Shems (AS IV, Pl. LXIII: 26) Strip 8 west	9th–8th cent.
572	Tell Beit Mirsim (AASOR XXI–XXII, Pl. 24: 16) Stratum A	9th–7th cent.
573	'Ain Shems (AS IV, Pl. LXIII: 23) Surface debris, strip 8 west	9th–8th cent.
573	Tell Beit Mirsim (AASOR XII, Pl. 67: 2) Stratum A	9th–7th cent.
574	„ „ (AASOR XII, Pl. 64: 9) „	„ „
576	Tell en-Naṣbeh (TN II, Pl. 54: 1215) Ci.370, AF19	c. 700–500

Classification in suggested chronological order	Types	Classification according to form
B.13	69 (Pl. 76: 23), 70, 71 (Pl. 75: 8), 72 (Pl. 75: 9), 73 (Pl. 75: 10), 74, 75, 76 (Pl. 76: 2), 77–79, 81, 82, 83, 85, 86 (Pl. 76: 3), 603, 626–646	B.iv Bowls with externally flanged rims
	With handles: 109 (Pl. 77: 17), 120–123, 647–652, 655, 657	

As Levels I, II and III are the only ones so far excavated at Tell ed-Duweir, it is natural to find a predominance of "folded rim" bowls. The term is adopted from Wampler's classification in TN II, p. 35, § 34, though it cannot always be established without breaking the bowls that the thickening of the rim was in fact achieved by folding the clay over at the rim. "Moulded" or "thickened" rims might provide an alternative name.

The smaller shapes without handles are well represented in Tomb 106, and it is therefore all the more remarkable that there were only two examples of type 75 from the topmost layers of Tomb 1002. There were sherds of types 73 and 81 from Tomb 218, otherwise folded rim bowls were missing from the earlier tomb groups.

Bowls with curved sides predominated over those with a definite angle at the keel in Tomb 106, where there were fourteen examples of the first variant and only three of the second, but it is not yet clear whether the distinction is an indication of date. There were two specimens of type 69 in Tomb 109 and one in Tomb 114, and both these groups appear to be contemporary with Level II or later. Altogether there were twenty-six examples of small folded rim bowls from the ossuaries 120 and 108 and Tombs 106, 109 and 114. Single sherds of types 73, 81 and 640 came from the dwelling 505 outside the gate at the south-west corner.

The Distribution Chart shows that the majority of these bowls were found in Level III, but the proportion remains high in Level II in comparison with the amount of pottery found. It seems clear that folded rim bowls were characteristic of both phases and were represented in post-exilic times by types 78 and 79. There are six examples of the slightly ribbed bowl 78 (of which half are from certain Level II contexts), with fifteen examples of the finely turned shape 79, seven of which were found in the rooms of Level II, and the associated Bastion area.

There is naturally some variety of ware in the very large class of folded rim bowls. The greater number are pink, often with a grey or black core, and there are a few buff and brown examples. Grits are rather rare. The firing is evenly divided between hard and medium specimens, with an occasional soft one. A red, pink or brown slip is often found, but perhaps a greenish-buff surface is most common. The characteristic finish to many examples is a close spiral burnish inside.

Despite a strong family resemblance, much variety in detail makes it difficult to provide close comparisons for folded rim bowls, except from Tell Beit Mirsim, where many parallels exist, all from Stratum A (900–600 B.C.).

But a closer limit is achieved at Samaria, where comparable small bowls of hard metallic ware only appeared in Period VII after the historic destruction of 720 B.C. (verbal information supplied by Miss K. M. Kenyon, to be published in SS III).

For the first time in this survey it is therefore possible to suggest a *terminus post quem* for the introduction of a particular shape, which becomes all the more important when it is established that the folded rim bowl is common to sites in Israel and Judah, for there are usually many regional differences between shapes and wares of the northern and southern kingdoms. At this point it will be best to examine comparative materials and reserve for later discussion the complex historical problems which arise. The incidence of the form is compared here with the same class at Megiddo.

Tell ed-Duweir	Tombs 218, 1002	Level III 800–700 B.C.	Level II 700–588 B.C.	Level I
Bowls as above	4	119	37	5
Megiddo I	Stratum IV and filling	Stratum III 800–733 780–650	Stratum II 733–600 650–600	Stratum I
Bowls 5–9, 61–66	3	33	7	7

Lamon and Shipton have already compared the bowls from Megiddo with examples from Tell Beit Mirsim (cf. M I, p. 169 and AASOR XII, Pls. 61–63).

At 'Ain Shems the small bowls without handles are rare, see fragments from Stratum IIb–c (AS IV, Pl. LXVI: 13–14). At Tell en-Naṣbeh they are "predominant during the 7th–6th centuries B.C." (TN II, p. 35, §§ 34, 38, 39, 40), and, as Wampler has already recognised, they belong to the third main group of bowls in the Iron Age, in which S.1314 is the most common type at Tell en-Naṣbeh.

The Samaria bowls will help to fix the later limits of Tombs 218 and 1002, which must have been closed before the folded rim bowls became common.

The stratified deposits at Tell Jemmeh are not helpful in this connexion, for only two fragments are recorded (Gerar, Pl. L: 21v and 24b) and both seem to be out of context. Evidently these bowls were not in common use so far south.

The analogous large bowls with two or four handles, types 120–123 and 647–652, 655 and 657, occur freely in tell Level III (twenty-eight examples), and there were nine sherds of various forms from Level II and the contemporary Bastion. Owing to the size of the vessels and their probable use for culinary purposes, they do not occur in tombs at Tell ed-Duweir. The presence of three fragments in the ossuary 120 only adds to the evidence that it was no ordinary burial-place (compare the '*aggan* illustrated in PEQ 1939, Pl. XVIII (1)).

Grant and Wright have noted (AS V, p. 137 and AS IV, Pl. LXIV) that the types represented by 12–16 and 18 continue throughout IIc, though they were larger and heavier when they first appeared in IIb. Only Nos. 15, 16 and 18 at 'Ain Shems are to be classed with B.13. Wampler (TN II, Pl. 62) describes his type S.1427 (L. III: 122(?)) as "one of the most numerous types at TN, and 1428, 1429 and 1439 are also very common" (TN II, p. 39, § 49). He also notes on p. 40 the scarcity of the large bowls at Megiddo.

Though comparisons have been established with the main sites of Israel and Judah, the problem of an absolute date is by no means solved. The following list gives the dates of the relevant strata as proposed by the excavators and others.

Maximum occurrence of folded rim bowls

		B.C.
Samaria	Period VII	720–
Megiddo	Stratum III, *c.* 800–? (Crowfoot), *c.* 780–733 (Albright), *c.* 750–? (Kenyon)	*c.* 780–650
Tell en-Naṣbeh	Third group of small and medium bowls. TN II, pp. 36, 39 f.	*c.* 700–500
Tell el-Fûl	Period III	*c.* 750–589
Gezer[1]	No comparisons. Site almost unoccupied 900–500 B.C.	
'Ain Shems	Stratum IIc. Comparisons uncommon from city	*c.* 825–586
Tell ed-Duweir	Level III, typical	*c.* 720–700
	Also occurs in Level II	*c.* 700–586
Tell Beit Mirsim	City A. Typical	*c.* 900–600

As the pottery recovered from all city deposits belongs largely to the final phase of occupation before destruction, the terminal dates in the list above are of most value.

---

[1] See Albright, Archaeology of Palestine, pp. 30–31, and his remarks in AASOR, IV, p. 22.

		B.C.
73	Tell en-Naṣbeh (TN II, Pl. 58: 1324) Ci.119, AK22, x 1	c. 700–500
73	„ „ (STTN, Pl. XIV: 1160) Tomb 3	c. 900
73	Tell el-Fûl (AASOR IV, pp. 22 f., Pl. 29: 19)	c. 750–589
84	Tell Jemmeh (Gerar, Pl. L: 21v) EU 189, Level X	9th cent.?
86	Jericho (SW, Pl. 37: A, 51)	871–700
643	Tell en-Naṣbeh (TN II, Pl. 57: 1311) Ci.165, AH20, x 24	c. 700–500
643	Samaria (SS III, Fig. 11: 2) Period VII	post-720
643	'Ain Shems (AS IV, Pl. LXVII: 11) Ci.25, Stratum IIc	8th–early 6th cent.
643	Tell Jemmeh (Gerar, Pl. L: 24b) GQ 185, Level VIII	Intrusive
603	Tell Beit Mirsim (AASOR XII, Pl. 65: 20 A) City A	900–600
626	„ „ „ (AASOR XXI–XXII, Pl. 21: 9) City A	„
628	„ „ „ (AASOR XXI–XXII, Pl. 20: 1) „	„
628	'Ain Shems (APEF II, Pl. 44 A: 4(?)) Tomb 6	„
631	Tell Beit Mirsim (AASOR XII, Pl. 62: 1) City A	„
634	„ „ „ (AASOR XXI–XXII, Pl. 23: 10) City A	„
636	„ „ „ (AASOR XXI–XXII, Pl. 23: 1) „	„
636	Samaria (SS III, cf. Fig. 11: 1–6) Period VII	post-720
638	„ (do. exact parallels unpublished) Period VII	„
640	Tell Beit Mirsim (AASOR XII, Pl. 63: 4) City A	900–600
644	„ „ „ (AASOR XII, Pl. 61: 15) „	„
647	„ „ „ (AASOR XXI–XXII, Pl. 20: 16) City A	„
648	„ „ „ (AASOR XXI–XXII, Pl. 20: 12) „	„
649	„ „ „ (AASOR XII, Pl. 60: 7) „	„
649	„ „ „ (AASOR XXI–XXII, Pl. 20: 11) „	„

Classification in suggested chronological order	Types	Classification according to form
B.14	Plain: 68 (Pl. 77: 23), 563, 565, 566	A.iv
	Ribbed: 564, 567, 568	Bowls with externally flanged rims

Sherds of both the plain and ribbed mortaria were found in the Residency and in the pits on its east side, but the proportion of ribbed sherds was four times greater than the number of plain ones. Nearly all the fragments were very small, and the only fairly complete specimen of a ribbed mortarium came from the group 534 which contained the altars (Pl. 8: 5).

Of the two plain fragments of mortaria ascribed to Level II, the first, from L. 18: 1071, may be associated with a late squatter's oven found in the room, and the second, in L. 12: 1067, is not necessarily in its proper context.

The ware of these heavy bowls is very distinctive. Those without ribs are either pink or brown, with a high proportion of crystalline grits (mica?). The firing is medium, and the surface is frequently covered with a greenish slip inside and out. The ribbed examples tend towards a green or pink body, with many grits, medium fired, but they do not seem to have a slip.

The evidence from Tell ed-Duweir would place both ribbed and plain mortaria in the post-exilic period, but as the majority of fragments came from the Residency floors and pits, which were probably constructed after 500 B.C., it must be assumed that the ribbed mortaria, which predominate, are more typical of the fifth century than of the sixth century B.C. The plain mortaria would, on typological grounds, appear to be more characteristic of the sixth century, a period which is poorly represented at Tell ed-Duweir, though a somewhat deeper version of type 566 persists in the fifth century in Cyprus and elsewhere.

The best comparative material is obtained from Stratum II at Tell Abu Hawam, late sixth to early fourth century. Wampler (TN II, p. 37, § 43) considers that the major history of the mortaria falls between 600 and

400 B.C. Lamon and Shipton (M. I, p. 168, § 53) would admit a date before 600 B.C., but they are quoting from Gerar evidence, which is much obscured by the presence of many pits.

B.C.

68	Tell en-Naṣbeh (TN II, Pl. 29: 500) AA26X, x 14	c. 600–400
68	Tell Abu Hawam (QDAP 4 (1934), p. 4, Fig. 4) Stratum II	late 6th–early 4th cent.
68	Samaria (SS III, Fig. 12: 13) Period VIII	6th cent.
68	Tell el-Muteselim (M. I, Pl. 23: 17) Stratum II	650–600
68	Tell Jemmeh (Gerar, Pl. XLVIII: 7°) CM 193, Level ?	6th cent.
566	Tell Jemmeh (Gerar, Pl. XLVIII: 7ᶜ) EY 187 in pit, Level X	Intrusive?
566	Tell en-Naṣbeh (TN II, Pl. 59: 1357) Ci.325, AA14, II, x 28	c. 600–400
566	Tsambres (TA, Fig. 42: 11) Tomb 23: 4	5th cent.
566	Mersin (AAA XXVI, p. 107, Pl. LII: 1) Level IV	8th–4th cent.
567	Gezer (Gezer III, Pl. CLXXXVII: 13) Ci. in IV 11	Hellenistic
567	Samaria (S, Pl. 292: 15a)	Babyloneo-Grecian
568	Tell Jemmeh (Gerar, Pl. XLVIII: 8ᵏ) AO 198, "A" building, Level ?	6th cent.
568	Tell el-Muteselim (M. I, Pl. 23: 16) Strata III–I	780–350
568	Tell en-Naṣbeh (TN II, Pl. 29: 499) AD13X, x 14	c. 600–400
566	Tell Sheykh Zuweyyid (Anthedon, Pl. XXXII, 8R3) Town H	c. 824–630
566	Naukratis (Naukratis I, Pl. IV: 2)	before 520
566	Vroulia (Vroulia, Pl. 23: 8)	7th–6th cent.
566	Gezer (Gezer III, Pl. 174: 5) "Fourth Semitic"	revised to 4th–1st cent.
566	Al Mina (British Museum collection) Level IV	520–430
566	Ajia Irini (GSCE II, Pl. CLXXXVII: 2747) Period 5	600–475

CHALICES

(Abbrev. Cha.)

	Types													
Locus	154*	155*	164*	156	157	158	159	160	161	162	163	662	663	Total
4035	—	—	—	—	—	—	—	—	—	—	—	—	1	1
Pal. walls	—	—	—	1	—	—	—	—	—	—	—	1	—	2
Houses III	—	—	—	—	—	—	—	—	—	—	1	—	—	1
6003–4	—	—	—	1	—	—	—	—	—	—	—	—	—	1
6020	—	—	—	1	—	—	—	—	—	—	—	—	—	1
1002, layers 11–13	—	—	—	—	—	—	—	2	4	—	—	—	—	6
224	—	—	—	—	—	1	1	—	—	2	—	—	—	4
116	—	—	—	—	—	—	—	1	1	—	—	—	—	2
218	—	—	—	—	—	—	—	—	—	1	—	—	—	1
227 (entrance to 120)	—	—	—	—	1	—	—	1	—	—	—	—	—	2
6006	1	—	—	—	—	—	—	—	—	—	—	—	—	1
223	—	—	1	—	—	—	—	—	—	—	—	—	—	1
6024	—	2	—	—	—	—	—	—	—	—	—	—	—	2
TOTAL	1	2	1	3	1	1	1	4	5	3	1	1	1	25

* Pl. 73: 31; Pl. 72: 13; Pl. 73: 15.

The great range and variety of decorated chalices and goblets which contribute elegance and interest to the pottery of the Late Bronze Age (L. II, Pl. XLVII), and which had maintained popularity at other sites throughout Iron I, were almost exhausted by the beginning of Iron II.

Twenty-five examples, not all of them complete, were found at Tell ed-Duweir, and in view of the small number concerned, it is not possible to reach a definite conclusion as to their range within Iron II. They do not occur in Tomb 521 or in the single graves, but a few examples were found in each subsequent large group, including Houses III. Type 163, the only example from a room, has a folded rim, which is the hall-mark of the period (cf. Class B.13).

Typologically it seems possible to group 154, 155 and 164 as being earlier in the sequence than 157–162, 662 and 663, which have a flatter rim and more angular bowl, while type 156, with a pronounced keel, may represent a later phase. 663 from the quarry 4035 appears to belong to the series, though its presence in a late context is not easy to explain.

Only type 159 retained the Bronze Age tradition of decoration, and showed red paint on the base. Traces of the Iron I practice of applying a thick red burnish were visible on one example of type 161, but the usual attempt at a finish during Iron II was a red or buff slip, sometimes covering the bowl only. The tripod on a ring stand (type 155), like other pieces in the cave 6024, was covered with a mat red slip. The ware was usually pink, containing a fair proportion of grits, the firing varying from soft to hard.

Observations at 'Ain Shems showed that no chalice at that site seemed to be later than Stratum IIb (950–825 B.C.), and the conclusion is drawn that "it seems probable they were no longer made after the eighth century" (AS V, p. 142).

There is no reason to contest this statement on the evidence from Duweir, as the chalices which appear on the list to be in a later context were not from large well-stratified groups. Type 163, with its distinctive rim, is the exception which may prove the rule as far as Judaean sites are concerned.

However, it should be remembered that decorated chalices continued to develop at Megiddo in Strata III to I, but are poorly represented and doubtfully placed in Stratum IV, 1000–800 B.C. (M. I, p. 170, § 69 and chalices 9, 11 on Pl. 33), and all forms comparable to types 157–162, 662, 663 are missing from that site. Exclusive to Stratum V (M. I, Pl. 33: 18, 20), two forms occur with a curved bowl and less pronounced rim, very close to type 154 at Duweir, which, with types 155 and 164, should perhaps be placed at the beginning of the series, though this would be at variance with Wampler's opinion (TN II, p. 44, § 8) that the more flaring bowls with a somewhat shorter stand are the best candidates for a late date (op. cit., Pl. 69: 1576–1577). That these curved forms belong to a period before the division of the monarchy is indicated by their presence at Megiddo, for all the ceramic evidence goes to show that many cultural links were broken between Israel and Judah after that time.

No chalices were found in the earlier periods at Samaria, and nearly all those illustrated in SS III, Fig. 25 came from Site 207, which may be equated with Period VI, and these are comparable to chalices at Megiddo from Stratum III.

The only example of an Iron Age chalice traced from Tell Beit Mirsim (AASOR, XII, p. 67 and Pl. 27: 4) is "part of the wide flat lip of a chalice" from a room-group restricted to Stratum B₃, which is placed by Albright in the second half of the tenth century B.C.

That chalices with a curved bowl take precedence over those with a deeper, more angular profile is indicated in Room 316 at 'Ain Shems (AS IV, Pl. LXII: 48–50, 53), dated to IIa, while the forms in Room 317 and 313 (AS IV, Pl. LXIV: 33, 34, 38) extend into IIb.

		B.C.
154	Jericho (SW, Pl. 36: A47d)	Jewish period
154	'Ain Shems (AS IV, Pl. LXII: 50) Rm. 316, Stratum IIa	1000–950
154	Tell el-Muteselim (M. I, Pl. 33: 18) Stratum V	1050–1000
154	Tell Abu Hawam (QDAP IV, p. 23, Fig. 88) Stratum III	1100–925
154	Tell el-Fara (CPP 17 E4) T.542, 615, Tell 373·10 m.	c. 1200
156	'Ain Shems (AS IV, Pl. LXIV: 34) Rm. 317, Stratum IIa, b	1000–825
159	Ez-Zahiriyye (QDAP IV, Pl. LXI: 1)	c. 1000
	(cf. AS V, p. 137, note 9, in which Grant and Wright suggest a later date for the first burials in the tomb)	
159	Jericho (SW, Pl. 36: A47b)	Jewish period

KRATERS

(Abbrev. K.)

Locus	403*	405*	612	613	686	Total
217	1	—	—	—	—	1
G.12: 1–8	—	1	—	—	—	1
H.14: 23	1	—	—	—	—	1
Residency Pits	—	—	—	—	1	1
Residency and Walls	—	—	1	1	—	2
TOTAL	2	1	1	1	1	6

The header row "Types" spans columns 403*, 405*, 612, 613, 686.

* Pl. 76: 24; Pl. 78: 18.

Few of the deep bowls classed as "kraters" in the publication of Tell en-Naṣbeh (TN II, S. 1471–1539) were recovered from Tell ed-Duweir. Comparisons for some in the earlier part of Wampler's series are to be found under Bowls, Class B.1, and a Tell ed-Duweir parallel for a later form placed by him in a "period subsequent to 600 B.C." (op. cit., p. 40, § 62), S.1580–1525, is recorded below.

Wampler's attribution of these forms to Late Iron and Hellenistic dates, though based on somewhat limited parallel material (§ 62), is therefore supported by the evidence from Tell ed-Duweir. The later shapes renew the impression, by their scarcity, that Tell ed-Duweir was almost deserted during the sixth century B.C.

405   Jericho (SW, p. 147, for decoration)
612   Tell Jemmeh (Gerar, Pl. LI: 27q) GD 184
686   Tell en-Naṣbeh (TN II, Pl. 67: 1525) R.273, T.23, I, x 5   Possibly mainly LI

LAMPS

(Abbrev. L.)

The history of lamps during the Middle and Late Bronze Ages is well established, and the progression of form from a shallow saucer, only slightly pinched, to a deeper bowl with a pronounced spout and flange had already taken place before the destruction of the Fosse Temple at Tell ed-Duweir (L. II, Pl. XLV).

Nearly four hundred saucer lamps found in Iron Age groups at the same site provide an unparalleled opportunity to clarify their development during the last few centuries of their use, and a Distribution Chart in suggested chronological order, in which the classes are grouped in four main categories, appears on p. 326.

Comparison of the drawings will show that some lamps with a round base and simple rim are very close to types found in the Fosse Temple (e.g. L. III, Pl. 83: 140 and L. II, Pl. XLV B: 195), but only types L. II: 203 and 204 from Structure III have the everted flange which is characteristic of the majority of lamps illustrated in this volume. The simple rim with little or no exterior flange ends in the present series before the occupation of Tomb 224.

A decisive change from round to disk-based lamps took place between the occupation of Tombs 1002 and 106, and the trend is well illustrated by the relevant percentages tabulated on p. 283.

The long sequence of round-based lamps (Classes L. 1–6) ends in Tomb 106, while those with a small disk base (L. 7–8), which were introduced no earlier than Tomb 1002, lingered on until the desertion of the site.[1] The characteristic form, however, of Tomb 106, is the coarse and heavy-based lamp (Classes L. 9–10) of which examples are also found in the buildings of Level II.

---

[1] The use of disk-based lamps occurred very much earlier in Syria (see Claude F. A. Schaeffer, Ugaritica II, Fig. 114).

The history of the flat-based lamp (Class L.11) cannot be followed at Tell ed-Duweir, but Grant and Wright (AS V, p. 142) state that they were not displaced by the closed lamp (Class L.12) until the third century B.C.

Lamps are scarce and number less than a score in the earlier large groups until Tomb 224, where they suddenly appear in quantity. In Tomb 1002 they form an important item, but they are poorly represented in tell Levels III and II, in contrast to the situation at Megiddo, where 60 per cent. of the total number from Strata I to V came from Stratum III.

Tomb	Classes 1–3 Types 140–144, 147, 661	Classes 4–6 Types 145, 146, 148	Classes 7–8 Types 149–151	Classes 9–10 Types 152, 153
	%	%	%	%
106	6	11	28	55
1002				
layers 1–5	15	16	4	3
layers 6–10	—	23	—	—
layers 11–13	1	36	2	—
224	85	15	—	—

Nearly all the lamps have spouts which are blackened from use. Those with round bases are commonly pink or buff, with an occasional admixture of grits. The firing is medium to hard, and it is rare to find any evidence of a slip.

The disk-based lamps are more inclined to be pink or red, with some coarse limestone grits added. The firing of types 149–152 is medium to hard. The solid base in all cases was simply detached from the wheel without finish, and the appearance of the lamps is coarse and uncouth. For examples of a similar method of removal from the wheel while in motion, see jug types 277 and 278 in Class J.8, and types 376 and 382 in Miscellaneous. The final degradation is achieved in the examples of type 153, made of soft paste, almost orange in colour, with a powdery surface, which is allied to the ware of the storage jar type 488, typical of Level I.

Lamps are found in every Judaean site, but detailed analysis is altogether lacking. Mackenzie's series of tombs from 'Ain Shems would be especially valuable if full statistics were available (APEF II, Pl. XXV and pp. 58 f.), though he was among the first to recognise the chronological significance of the form. He stated that out of seventy-four lamps in Tomb 1 at 'Ain Shems, only one had a disk base (op. cit., Pl. XXV: 8, possibly the same as L. III type 150?). The reverse was the case in the repository of Tomb 2 (op. cit., p. 65) where there was only one round-based lamp, and at least two examples of the high-based variety. It can be said, therefore, that the period represented at Tell ed-Duweir by the upper layers of Tomb 1002 and the occupation of Houses III is missing from the 'Ain Shems tomb series. Grant and Wright consider that the "small semi-disk base" (L. III, type 150) was not added before the ninth century, a date which may, perhaps, be reduced on the Duweir evidence by nearly a hundred years (AS V, p. 141 and AS IV, Pls. XLV: 21, 23; LXVII: 20, 23).

At Tell Beit Mirsim most of the lamps from Stratum A can be equated with Classes L. 7–8, with a pronounced flange and a small disk base (AASOR XII, Pl. 70 and § 119 f.; AASOR XXI–XXII, Pl. 15 and § 161). At Tell en-Naṣbeh it is significant that few disk or heavy-based lamps were found in the tombs, while round-based lamps are rare on the mound (TN I, p. 92 and TN II, pp. 44 f.).

The common type of lamp at Samaria was of a soft, pinkish-buff ware, and unburnished, and was nearly always broken. For this reason few drawings of the lamps are recorded in SS III, and the closest parallel is, perhaps, Fig. 27: 1 (L. III, type 148), though there is a slight difference in the turn of the spout.

At Megiddo there was one disk-based lamp in Stratum V, none in Stratum IV, and they are still rare in Stratum III (fifty-six round-based lamps and two with a disk base, all with flanged rims). The heavy-based lamp (M. I, Pl. 37: 6, and p. 171) is not so pronounced as the Duweir examples. W. F. Albright considers that the latter are typical of Stratum III, but the figures do not confirm his suggestion (AASOR XXI–XXII, p. 58).

Two groups from Jordan show that similar lamp shapes were in common use and were apparently subject to the same development:

	Classes 1–3 Types	Classes 4–6 Types	Classes 7–8 Types	Classes 9–10 Types
Sahab Tomb (QDAP XIII, p. 101)	75, 76 (4 ex.)	77–81 (12 ex.)	73, 74, 82–86 (16 ex.)	72 (1 ex.)
Adoni Nur Tomb, Amman	87 (1 ex.)	—	82–86 (5 ex.)	—

The Adoni Nur deposit is dated by a seal of that functionary to about 650 B.C., and if ceramic development in Moab did not lag behind that of Palestine, the absence of the heavy-based lamps would suggest that they were a speciality of the latter part of the seventh century.

Class	Types
L.1	140, 141, 142, 143

Lamps with a plain or carinated profile, round base

As noted above, types 140 and 141 are close in shape and outline to lamps from the Fosse Temple. With types 142 and 143, the characteristic factor is an exterior carination, the first sign of an everted flange which appears in subsequent types. In type 142 the carination is so marked that the line is reproduced on the interior. Except for one example of type 143, which should belong to Level IV rather than Houses III where it was found, no lamps in the class occur later than Tomb 116; their main phase should occur, therefore, in the tenth century B.C.

140   Judaean sites (BM, Pl. 66: 1)

Class	Type
L.2	147

Lamps with a thickened rim, round base

Examples came chiefly from Tomb 224, where lamps first become a common item of funerary equipment. The exterior carination has disappeared and given place to a thickened rim, though its edge is not visible in the interior of the lamp. This class is typical of the ninth century B.C.

	B.C.
147 'Ain Shems (APEF II, Pl. XXV: 1?, 2?, 3?) Tomb 1 earliest forms	c. 900

Class	Type
L.3	144 (Pl. 75: 14)

Lamps with a thickened rim and slight flange, round base

The type is represented in most of the large groups. Though the exterior flange is everted, it is more rounded and less marked in the interior of the lamp. In common with the lamps in Classes L.1 and L.2, the spout is not as pinched as in later types.

Class	Type
L.4	146

Lamps with everted flange and marked rim inside, round base

With the lamps in Class L.5, these lamps are transitional, having acquired a marked rim inside, though the spout is not so emphatically pinched as it is to become in the last of the round-based lamps.

284

Class
L.5

Lamps with everted flange and marked rim inside, round base

    See Class L.4.

Type
145

B.C.

145 Judaean sites (BM, Pl. 66: 2)   Jewish period

Class
L.6

Lamps with wide, everted flange and marked rim inside, round base

Type
148 (Pl. 75: 15)

    Type 148 is characteristic of Tomb 1002, though it is found in most of the big groups from Tomb 218 onwards. Its major phase occurs in the eighth century B.C.

B.C.

148 Sahab (QDAP XIII, p. 102, types 77–81)   6th–7th cent.
148 Samaria (SS III, Fig. 27: 1) E.207, Period VI   *c.* 720

Class
L.7

Lamps with everted rim and slight disk base

Types
149 (Pl. 75: 18),
150 (Pl. 75: 19)

    Though there are a few examples of a disk base in Tomb 1002 and Houses III, more are found in Tomb 106; on analogy with the Adoni Nur deposit, the class should belong to the early seventh century B.C. The small version, type 149, with a rather heavier base, comes appropriately enough from Tomb 106 and Houses II.

B.C.

150 Amman, Adoni Nur Tomb (APEF VI) Lamps 82–86   *c.* 650
150 Sahab (QDAP XIII, p. 101, type 74)   6th–7th cent.
150 Tell el-Fara (BP I, Pl. XL) T. 201   10th cent.
150 'Ain Shems (AS IV, Pl. LXVII: 20, 23) Stratum II   825–586

Class
L.8

Lamps with everted rim and disk base

Type
151 (Pl. 75: 16)

    Type 151 is a coarser, heavier and larger version of type 150. Most examples were found in Tomb 106, and its main phase is confined to the seventh century B.C.

B.C.

151 Sahab (QDAP XIII, p. 101, type 72)   6th–7th cent.

Class
L.9

Lamps with a wide flanged rim and footed base

Type
152 (Pl. 75: 17)

    There are 62 examples of this class, as against 33 of Class L.8 and 28 of Class L.10 in Tomb 106, so it should represent the period of maximum occupation of the tomb.

B.C.

152 'Ain Shems (AS IV, Pl. XLVIII: 8, 12) Tomb 14   6th cent.
152 Tell Beit Mirsim (AASOR XII, Pl. 70: 8) Stratum A   9th–7th cent.
152 Tell Muteselim (M. I, Pl. 37: 6, 7) Stratum III   780–650

Class
L.10

Lamps with wide flanged rim and heavy-based foot

Type
153

    Besides the high, solid foot of lamps in this class, the careless finish and soft, powdery orange ware are characteristic. Typologically, lamps in Class L.10 represent a late phase in the evolution of saucer lamps characteristic of the seventh century B.C.

		B.C.
153	Judaean sites (BM, Pl. 66: 4, 5)	Jewish period
153	Samaria (SS III, Fig. 27: 4) Dj unique; red ware	? period
153	'Ain Shems (AS II, Pl. XLV: 40, 42) Stratum II	1000–586

Class	Types
L.11	659, 660

Lamps with a flat base

The final development of saucer lamps exhibits a marked reaction from the coarse, high-based varieties of the seventh century.

Only two incomplete forms were found at Tell ed-Duweir, which is in keeping with the almost complete desertion of the site in the sixth century, but the fragments which remain are closely matched at those sites which have a post-exilic history.

Both types were made with a flat base across the whole diameter, turning at a sharp angle towards the rim, which is incompletely preserved.

		B.C.
659	Judaean sites (CPP 91 M3 and BM, Pl. 66: 2)	Jewish period
660	'Ain Shems (AS IV, Pl. XLVIII: 9; AS II, Pl. XLV: 43) Stratum IIc	6th cent.
660	Tell Jezer (Gezer III, Pl. 187: 12) Ci. in IV 11	4th cent.
660	Kountoura Trachonie (GSCE I, Pls. 73 ff.)	3rd cent.
660	Tell Abu Hawam (QDAP IV, p. 4, Fig. 5) Stratum II	late 6th–early 4th cent.
660	'Athlit (QDAP VI, Fig. 6) Burial IVb	7th–6th cent.
660	Samaria (SS III, Fig. 27: 3) Zd	Post-Israelite

Class L.12

Closed Lamps

	Types							
Locus	137*	658	138	135*	136*	139*	134	Total
504	—	—	—	2	—	—	1	3
106 (late)	—	—	—	1	—	—	—	1
Solar Shrine	—	1	1	—	—	—	—	2
R/Q/S.15/16: 10–21	—	1	3	—	1	1	—	6
G.18: 25–33	1	—	—	—	—	—	—	1
Great Shaft	1	—	4	—	—	—	—	5
H.17: 1087 (tell surface)	—	1	—	—	—	—	—	1
515	—	—	1	—	—	—	—	1
Residency Pits	1	—	—	—	—	—	—	1
Residency and Walls	2	—	—	—	—	—	—	2
K.13: 1033	1	—	—	—	—	—	—	1
TOTAL	6	3	9	3	1	1	1	24

* Pl. 77: 24; Pl. 76: 29; Pl. 36: 61; Pl. 77: 25.

Few closed lamps have been discovered at Tell ed-Duweir, and the commonest forms are considered to be imports. Attic influence is represented by types 137 and 658 (Corinth IV, Part 2, Class VIII), forms which appeared in the Greek world during the fifth century B.C., and continued through the fourth, surviving in use in adjoining lands as late as the third century B.C.

On the other hand, Type 138 is common in Mesopotamia, and Grant and Wright have compared an example

286

from Tomb 14 at 'Ain Shems with lamps found at Kish (AS V, p. 145, note 47) dated to the "Neo-Babylon' period. Similar shapes with the high rim are found at Seleucia (PPS, Fig. 374), where they extend from the latter part of the second century B.C. to the second century A.D.

Type 135 is comparable to lamps in a tomb dated by its coins to about A.D. 396, excavated at El Bassa (QDAP III, pp. 81–91), and the form is found elsewhere in Palestine, while types like 136 and 139 are illustrated as typical of the Seleucidan period in Bliss and Macalister's volume on Excavations in Palestine.

These local wares are usually pink, fired soft to hard; the lamps are cast in two parts and the upper decorated surface is sometimes covered by a thick red slip (cf. type 139).

135	El Bassa (QDAP III, p. 86, Fig. 12)	c. A.D. 396
135	Nablus Rd., Jerusalem (QDAP IV, Pl. LXXXVI: 10)	4th cent. A.D.
135	Palestinian types (BM, Pl. 66: 6)	Seleucidan
136	„ „ (BM, Pl. 62: 2)	„
138	„ „ (BM, Pl. 62: 1)	„
138	Beth-zur (BZ, p. 51, Fig. 42)	Hellenistic
138	'Ain Shems (AS IV, Pl. XLVIII: 10) Tomb 14	6th cent. B.C.
138	Marissa (Painted Tombs, Pl. XXI) Tomb 1	c. 200–100 B.C.
139	Palestinian types (BM, Pl. 62: 20)	Seleucidan c. 300 B.C.

JUGS

(Abbrev. J)

Over five hundred jugs were recorded from the tombs and houses at Tell ed-Duweir. They have been divided on the basis of shape alone into nine categories, covering most of the tenth to the sixth centuries B.C., and though the chronological progression is not always apparent, and some classes are contemporary, certain useful facts do emerge.

Class J.1, for instance, has no real place in Iron II, and is represented by two survivals from the earlier period. Classes J.2 and J.3 differ in the shape of the mouth, but both have flat bases and a comparable history. Classes J.4 and J.5, with round bases and a plain or moulded rim, are the most popular varieties, with the balance strongly in favour of Class J.4, which has greater numbers and a longer range.

The jugs in Class J.6 mostly owe their inspiration to non-local models, and are segregated for that reason. With Class J.7 a further subdivision is profitable, for it will be seen that J.7a is largely confined to Tomb 1002, Houses III and Tomb 106, while J.7b follows that tradition from the occupation of Tomb 106 onwards. Class J.8, the well-known "water decanter", is represented by only one early form in Tomb 1002 and does not become popular until after the destruction of Houses III. Class J.9 is small and distinctive and is confined to Tomb 106 and Cave 1010, used as a dwelling.

Nearly half the total number of jugs came from Tomb 1002, far outnumbering the bowls from the same deposit, which comprised about 11 per cent. of the total number recorded. A Distribution Chart of jugs in suggested chronological order will be found on p. 327.

Class	Types
J.1	221, 222

Jugs with ridged body

Both these forms are easily distinguishable from the majority of Iron II jugs, which all have a globular body. If they were not actually made during Iron I, they are clearly a relic of that tradition. Both are burnished all over; the body of type 221 is covered with even vertical strokes, and is decorated with horizontal bands of black and white paint. The ware is buff to pink and the firing in each specimen is medium.

222	Tell en-Naṣbeh (TN II, Pl. 33: 578) T.54, x 42	Late EI–early MI

Class	Types
J.2	197, 200, 201, 202 (Pl. 72: 7),
Jugs with flat base and round mouth	203, 205, 206 (Pl. 75: 27), 207
	(Pl. 75: 28), 208, 209, 213
	Post-exilic 204

Jugs made with a flat base, round mouth and a globular body are well represented in the earlier tomb groups. The series begins with a beautifully made specimen of the potter's art, type 202; it is irregularly hand-burnished outside, including the base, and knobs represent the rivets for the handle of the metal prototype, both inside and outside the jug. Type 209 is the only other example in this class which is irregularly hand-burnished outside; the neck is very straight and the body is inclined to be angular, so that it is closely related to the preceding class of jugs with a ridged body.

The class runs concurrently with pinched mouth jugs (J.3), up to and including Tomb 106. A single example of type 204 occurs in a post-exilic context, but the ware is typical of its period, like the method of applying the handle.

The body in most cases is pink or buff, with a corresponding slip, and the firing is usually medium. The characteristic feature, beside the straight collar neck, is the heavy thick ware of specimens from the earlier groups.

B.C.

207   Ez-Zahiriyye (QDAP IV, Pl. LXII: 1, 2) Chambers A, B (cf. AS V, p. 137, note 9: revised date, c. 900 B.C.)   c. 1000

Class	Types
J.3	210–211, 214 (Pl. 74:
Jugs with flat based and pinched mouth	15), 215, 217, 218 (Pl.
	75: 29), 219, 224, 225,
	226 (Pl. 73: 16), 227
	(Pl. 74: 16), 228

This class runs concurrently with Class J.2, though it does not appear to begin quite so soon, and is not so popular in the earlier tomb groups; however, during the use of Tombs 1002 and 106 the pinched mouths nearly maintained equality with the preceding class. Only type 225 showed some traces of burnish; a few others had a buff or pink slip, but the majority were pink, buff or brown ware, fired medium to hard.

Jugs of this shape were said to be common in Stratum III at 'Ain Shems (AS V, p. 131) and at Tell en-Naṣbeh in Middle Iron (TN II, p. 16, § 4), and their history may therefore extend over four centuries.

B.C.

217	Tell en-Naṣbeh (STTN, Pl. XVII: 1387) T.5 (cf. TN I, p. 99)	900–700
218	„ „ (TN II, Pl. 32: 566) Ci.285, P22, baskets 75–87, x 96	750–586
225	'Ain Shems (AS IV, Pl. LX: 2) Ci.14 in Area S.28 (1929) Stratum III	1200–1000
227	Tell en-Naṣbeh (TN II, Pl. 31: 544) Ci.285, P22, baskets 60–74, x 76	750–586
227	Jericho (SW, Pl. 34: A, 20d)	c. 870–700

Class	Types
J.4	165–166, 168, 169, 170 (Pl. 74: 8),
Jugs with a round base and a plain-rimmed neck	171 (Pl. 76: 6), 172 (Pl. 76: 7), 174,
	175 (Pl. 77: 20), 176 (Pls. 74: 9;
	76: 8), 177, 178 (Pl. 75: 20), 179
	(Pl. 77: 9), 180 (Pls. 74: 10; 75:
	21), 181–184, 187 (Pl. 75: 22), 188

These jugs are the simplest as well as the most common form at Tell ed-Duweir. On the whole, it can be said that the shape evolves from a straight-sided neck (i.e. types 165, 180, 184) towards a flared neck (i.e. types 187, 183 and 181) which reaches its final expression in the flared jugs grouped in Class J.9.

The great majority have a pink body, medium fired, without slip or burnish; the two exceptions are type 181, which is very close to Class J.9, and type 188. The former shows vertical burnish on the neck and horizontal strokes on the body, while the latter is irregularly hand-burnished all over.

Type 175 is correctly placed in its post-exilic content, as it has the elliptical handle which is typical of the sixth century B.C. onwards.

The smaller pots are classed as "cups" by Wampler (TN II, p. 27, § 76) and are described as smaller versions of the one-handled pot by Albright (AASOR XII, p. 84), and both varieties are acknowledged to have a wide range. Wampler suggests a major phase for them in the tenth century. The evidence from Tell ed-Duweir indicates that the popularity of these jugs, both large and small, remained paramount during the ninth to eighth centuries, and was only challenged by the decanters in Class J.8 towards the end of the seventh century B.C.

168	Tell Beit Mirsim (AASOR XII, Pl. 57: 5) Stratum A	9th–7th cent.
168	'Ain Shems (AS IV, Pl. LXVII: 15) Area T28, drain (1929)	1000–586
170	Ez-Zahiriyye (QDAP IV, Pl. LXIII) Chamber B (cf. AS V, p. 137, note 9, revised date c. 900)	c. 1000
171	Tell en-Naṣbeh (TN II, Pl. 44: 933) T.32, E strip, x 283 M 1981, major range	1000–586
177	'Ain Shems (AS IV, Pl. LXVII: 13) Area Z31 (1930) Stratum II	1000–586
178	Ez-Zahiriyye (QDAP IV, Pl. LXI: 2)	c. 1000
180	Tell en-Naṣbeh (TN II, Pl. 44: 932) T.29, x 37 M 1770 major range	1000–586
181	„ „ „ (TN II, Pl. 44: 934) T.5, x 243 M. 1404 major range	1000–586
181	'Ain Shems (APEF II, p. 57, Pl. XXIV: 4?) T.1, see AS V, p. 136	late 10th–early 9th cent.
183	Tell en-Naṣbeh (STTN, Pl. XVIII: 1403) T.5	900–700
184	Tell Beit Mirsim (AASOR XII, Pl. 57: 17) Stratum A	9th–7th cent.
184	Jericho (SW, Pl. 34: A, 25a)	871–700
187	Tell en-Naṣbeh (TN II, Pl. 45: 961) Ci.119, AK22 x 10 M 158	c. 1050–550
187	'Ain Shems (AS IV, Pl. LXVII: 2) Ci.25, Stratum IIc	c. 825–586

Class	Types
J.5	167, 173, 185, 186 (Pl. 74: 12), 189,
Jugs with a round base and a moulded rim	190 (Pl. 74: 13; Pl. 75: 23), 191 (Pl. 75: 24), 192, 195, 196 (Pl. 74: 14)

Jugs with a thickened moulded rim, externally or internally flanged, appear to be contemporary with similar jugs having a plain rim, though they are less than half as numerous. If more examples were available it might be possible to achieve a finer distinction among the varieties, and to establish a later beginning for the moulded rim.

The type specimen for 195 came from the early Tomb 116, and was burnished all over, otherwise the jugs in this class do not normally show traces of burnish or slip.

The medium-fired ware is apt to retain a redder hue, which becomes more noticeable in specimens from the later tomb group 1002. Some grits are present, but they are crushed very fine, so that they seldom show unless the pot has been broken. A few examples of type 190 were soft-fired, but may possibly have come from the same batch in the kiln.

Comparative material admits a long history for jugs with moulded rims, but it is not easy to decide whether the internal flange—see types 167, 173, 185—precedes those with moulding on the exterior—types 189–192. The prominence of the former in Stratum V at Megiddo (M. I, Pl. 5: 119) is in favour of the suggestion, with the type surviving into Stratum III, as it does into Level III at Tell ed-Duweir.

It may be suggested that the external flange is a later development which did not become common until Tomb 1002 was in use. Its major phase, therefore, should fall in the eighth to seventh century, a conclusion which would conform with Albright's attribution of jugs with both plain and moulded rims from Tell Beit Mirsim to late A$_2$, eighth to seventh centuries (AASOR XXI–XXII, p. 149 and Pl. 17: 7–15).

Class	Types
J.6	220, 229–236 (Pl. 74: 17), 237, 239,
Jugs with a flat base and narrow neck, plain or trefoil mouth	240, 241 (Pl. 36: 65), 242, 244, 245, 247, 251 (Pl. 72: 15), 259 (Pl. 74: 21)

The narrow-necked jugs are a small class, but they show considerable variety in the detail of the neck, and a high degree of finish. They are good-quality products in marked contrast to the jugs in common use.

Types 240, 241 and 244 are exceptionally elegant, and show traces of a smooth burnish on a red or brown slip; they come from Tombs 218, 116 and 224, and are therefore the earliest forms in the series. Type 239, on the other hand, is a clumsy shape, befitting its appearance in a room of the eighth-century Houses III, though it retains an irregular hand burnish.

D. B. Harden, writing on "Punic Urns from the precinct of Tanit" (AJA XXXI, p. 309, Fig. 20), describes "pear-shaped" jugs similar to the Tell ed-Duweir types 240 and 241 as "typical early Punic", which can be as early as the eighth century, and are certainly from the seventh century. There is no doubt that an affinity exists between these jugs and many others found in Phoenician colonies overseas, and both are probably derived from a common source on the Syrian littoral.

Types 229, 230, 233, 234, 236, 237 have certain elements in common with the preceding forms, but they have rounded, rather than pear-shaped, bodies and tall graceful necks, with the handles reaching to the rim.

Types 229 and 237 are provided with strainers in the mouth, while types 232 and 237 have double-strand handles and applied knobs below to represent rivets. The paste in most cases has fired medium pink, but there is a tendency to introduce red, grey, cream or buff slip. All these jugs were found in the central layers of Tomb 1002.

Despite individual differences, the late Mrs. E. Henschel-Simon considered that similar jugs from the Amman tombs were variations of the same species (QDAP XI, p. 79). She drew attention to comparisons at Megiddo (M. I, Pl. 3: 83–86) found in Strata IV–II, though the greater number were recovered from Stratum III (780–650 B.C.); from Samaria (C.502) and from Tell en-Naṣbeh (TN II, Pl. 35: 624 is a better parallel than Pl. 36: 633 which she quotes).

C. N. Johns (QDAP VI, pp. 129 ff.), in discussing the parallels for an oenochoe illustrated on p. 142, Fig. 6 of his article, recognises the foreign origin of the jugs, rejects Cyprus as a possible source, and proposes the Phoenician colonies as exporters of these distinctive jugs. While agreeing with him that jugs with pear-shaped bodies, tapering necks and small trefoil mouths are due to the same inspiration, the present writer submits that the prototypes, at least, were possibly derived from Phoenicia.

With regard to the second variety, types 229, 230, 232, 236 and 237, which are found at Tell ed-Duweir in a later context than types 240, 241 and 244, another point of origin may be considered.

So far, the greatest number of these jugs have been recovered from tombs in Jordan, notably Amman A, Nos. 30–36, Amman B, Nos. 51–52, 54 (QDAP XI, pp. 67–74), Sahab, Nos. 48–51, 53 (QDAP XIII, pp. 92–102), and the Adoni Nur Tomb, Amman, Nos. 109–112 (APEF VI, in preparation). L. Harding suggests in his account of the last-named tomb that trefoil-mouthed jugs are copies of metal originals, and he thinks that the consistent quality of ware establishes them as local products. However, in view of the many Assyrian connexions of this valuable tomb, dated to the middle of the seventh century, "the matter must remain in doubt until we know more of Assyrian pottery of the period".

The common jugs at Samaria in Periods V and VI are illustrated on Figs. 22: 7 and 10: 15, 16 in SS III (in preparation) and are made of buff ware, with a thick red slip, and are unburnished.

		B.C.
230	Tell en-Naṣbeh (TN II, Pl. 31: 550 and p. 16, § 4) Ci.176	Latter half of MI
233	'Amman Tomb A (QDAP XI, No. 30) The late Mrs. Henschel-Simon (op. cit., p. 79) equates these two forms as exactly parallel, but it will be seen that the point of attachment of handle to neck is different.	
235	'Ain Shems (APEF II, Pl. XXII: 15) T.1, Stratum IIb	late 10th–early 9th cent.
239	Tell Beit Mirsim (AASOR XII, Pl. 38: 14) Stratum A	9th–7th cent.
241	Amathus (GSCE II, Pl. XIX and pp. 82–83) T.13, No. 38 Red Slip I (III) ware	900–650
242	Jericho (SW, Pl. 34: A, 21)	870–700
251	Tell Sheykh Zuweyid (Anthedon, Pl. XXXVII: 58J) LE 296	c. 1100

Class
J.7
Jugs with a flat base and a ridged neck

The Distribution Chart shows that jugs with a flat disk or ring base and a ridged neck do not normally occur before the period of Tomb 1002. Exceptions are type 668, classified under Miscellaneous, and type 364 classified under Jugs or Jars with Spouts. Within the class, two further subdivisions can be made which seem to show some chronological progression.

Class	Types
J.7a	250(5), 252(7) (Pl. 74: 18), 253,
Jugs with round mouth, handle to ridge	256, 257, 258(2) (Pl. 74: 19), 260, 261(8) (Pl. 74: 20; Pl. 75: 31), 262, 263, 265(5) (Pl. 74: 22), 266, 267(2), 268, 269(9) (Pl. 75: 32), 270, 271(7) (Pl. 74: 23)

Most of the forms appear to be exclusive to Tomb 1002, but types 261 and 269 carry on in use through tell Level III and Tomb 106. The ware is always pink, with some grits, fired medium to hard. A red or pink slip is very usual; the proportion of disk to ring bases is four to one. Type 262 is decorated with red bands, and 263 has white and red lines round the body; type 270 has two bands of incised lines.

J. C. Wampler has suggested a progression of form from the vessels illustrated from Tell en-Naṣbeh (TN II, Pl. 32: 553–555 and p. 16) through intermediate shapes shown by W. F. Albright from Tell Beit Mirsim (AASOR XII, Pls. 58: 2; 59: 7, 8), which are equivalent to Class J.7a at Tell ed-Duweir. Wampler ends the series with a more slender variety, S.672–674, of which a later phase is seen, perhaps, in the decanters, J.8, types 277–278.

		B.C.
250	Ez-Zahiriyye (QDAP IV, Pl. LXIII) cf. AS V, p. 137, note 9	c. 1000
250	Tell Beit Mirsim (AASOR XII, Pl. 59: 7) Stratum A	9th–7th cent.
250	Tell en-Naṣbeh (TN II, Pl. 32: 555) Ci.285, P.22, x 113	c. 750–586

Class	Types
J.7b	238, 243, 246(2) (Pl. 76: 21), 248
Jugs with slightly pinched or round mouth, handle to rim	(Pl. 75: 30), 249 (Pl. 77: 26), 353(3)
	(Pl. 75: 37), 666

Types 243, 246 and 248 display similar characteristics and come from Tombs 106 and 109. Types 249 and 353 have round mouths and are found in a Level I context. The ware is pink with some grits, the later specimens are thin and metallic. There are more disk than ring bases in the group.

B.C.

238   Tell en-Naṣbeh (TN II, p. 17, § 10 and Pl. 33: 584–588)   700–500

249[1]   Tell Sandaḥannah (BM, Pl. 58: 13) found in Seleucid stratum, said to be survival from lower
     Jewish stratum, see p. 125

249   Zakariya (BM, Pl. 49: 11)

Class	Types
J.8	254, 255, 264 (Pl. 78: 12), 273, 274,
Jugs with narrow neck, handle to ridge, round or drop-shaped body	275 (Pl. 75: 33), 276 (Pl. 76: 20),
	277, 278, 279 (Pl. 77: 10), 280, 281,
	665, 676

The class of jug under discussion has commonly been described as a "water decanter", and was probably manufactured in bulk to standard sizes (cf. AASOR XXI–XXII, §§ 123–4, 132). At Tell ed-Duweir the decanter did not become common until after the destruction of Level III, but there are prototypes which occur in an earlier context: type 254, for instance, was found in the lowest layers of Tomb 1002 and in pit 569. The ware was pink or brown, medium fired, with a dark red or brown slip, vertically hand burnished. The next development is represented by types 279, 280 and 281. Five examples of the three forms were found in Level III rooms. Only type 279 was irregularly hand burnished: type 280 was of pink ware with grits and harder firing, and in type 281 the first red ring burnish appeared, though none of these forms displayed the typical wide-spaced rings associated with the fully developed decanter. The handles were oval in section, without ridges.

An example of the developed form 273 and two of 276 were recovered from Room H.15: 1003, which probably continued in use into Level II, and there is therefore no clear evidence that the development was complete before the end of the seventh century. Decanters were used during the occupation of Level II and were in greatest demand when Tombs 106, 109 and 114 were being filled; a few examples were found in Level I contexts.

Types 264, 273–278 were nearly all made of hard pink paste containing some grits, very unevenly fired, so that the surface varied in colour from cream to deep red. The body was horizontally wheel burnished, with or without a slip, and the neck usually finished with vertical strokes. The ribbon handle displayed marked ridges. One example of type 276, found in the courtyard of the Solar Shrine (Q.12: 106), was made of hard pink ware with a thick cream slip, unburnished. From its position about 50 cm. below the floor it should belong to the underlying stratum, which has still to be equated with Levels III or II.

The small decanters 277 and 278 seem to end the series at Tell ed-Duweir. They are made of a very coarse pink paste, medium fired, and they were carelessly finished and hurriedly removed from the wheel in the same way as the thick lamp bases of type 153. (For examples of a similar method of removal from the wheel in motion, see Miscellaneous, types 376, 382.)

J. C. Wampler (TN II, pp. 21–22) agrees with Grant and Wright that the decanter is rare before the eighth century. The stereotyped forms are especially common in Tombs 2–8 at 'Ain Shems, and those from the repository of Tomb 2, comparable to Duweir types 280, 281, "probably represent the earliest types" (AS V, p. 140).

---

[1] For a full description of type 249, see under Pit L.13: 82 in Chapter 5. It compares with Hellenistic jugs of the mid-second century B.C. (TCHP, D.62).

At Megiddo decanters exhibit early characteristics (M. I, Pl. 4: 95–110), and do not compare with the fully developed decanter, Class J.8, which Albright (AASOR XII, pp. 82 f.) and Wampler (TN II, p. 21, note 37) consider to be largely confined to southern Palestine. At the northern site the earlier forms were found in profusion in Stratum III (780–650 B.C.), and no further development took place.

On the other hand, Miss K. M. Kenyon's forthcoming report on the pottery at Samaria (SS III) will show that some early types are common in Strata V–VI, but not before c. 750 B.C. and the fully developed types do not appear. In Jordan decanters of the normal shape are found in Tomb A at Amman (QDAP XI, p. 71, Nos. 28, 29), but slight variations in the rim do not allow comparison with specific Tell ed-Duweir examples. At Sahab (QDAP XIII, p. 100) Nos. 56–57 are normal, with No. 57 a close parallel to Duweir type 276, but they are not present in great quantity.

Neither the variants found in the Adoni Nur tomb (APEF VI, in preparation, Nos. 102–104)—wider at the shoulder than at the base—nor those from Tomb 14 at 'Ain Shems (AS IV, Pls. XLVIII: 15 and LXVIII: 2, 6)—with pear-shaped rounded bases—also occurring at Tell Jemmeh (Gerar, Pl. LVIII: 65 l, m), were found at Tell ed-Duweir.

R. A. S. Macalister noted the resemblance of decanters from southern sites (BM, p. 102 and Pls. 49: 6; 50: 4; 52: 6) to an example found by Petrie at Defenneh (Tanis II, Pl. XXXV: 44), which was a fort in use between 665 and 565 B.C. The type was also said to be common at Naukratis (op. cit., p. 64).

The distribution of decanters in Class J.8, among the latest groups at Tell ed-Duweir, seems to constrict their range to the last years of the seventh and the first decades of the sixth centuries B.C.

Though small, and displaying the marks of advanced degradation, it is perhaps permissible to see in type 255 a lingering tradition of the decanters. Complete examples came from Graves 183 and 184, two of the east–west series near the Fosse Temple, and are the only vessels associated with them. Fragments were found in Houses I.

At Megiddo they are among forms of Stratum I, 600–350 B.C. (M. I, p. 167, § 45), and rather similar shapes occur in Stratum II at Tell Abu Hawam (QDAP III, Pl. XXIII: 8–9), 550–350 B.C. The variety associated with the fifth- to fourth-century tombs at 'Athlit is less close (QDAP II, p. 51 and Fig. 4h) and may be a slightly later.

		B.C.
254	Tell el-Muteselim (M. I, Pl. 7: 174) Stratum V	1050–1000
255	„ „ (M. I, Pl. 1: 6) Stratum I	late 6th–early 4th cent.
255	Tell Jemmeh (Gerar, Pl. LX: 83r) EH, FH 190, Level ?	
274	Tell en-Naṣbeh (TN II, Pl. 39: 735) T.3, x 69, M 1153	major phase 800–586
274	'Ain Shems (APEF II, Pls. XXXVII: 14?; XLI: 14; XLIV: 10; XLVII: 13; LVI: 13) Tombs 2–8 (for revised date, see AS V, p. 136)	c. 700–600
275	'Ain Shems (APEF II, Pl. XLI: 18; LIV: 21; LVII: 13, 16) T.5, 8	see 274
275	Tell en-Naṣbeh (TN II, Pl. 39: 737) Ci.171, Q6	major phase 800–586
275	Tell el-Ḥeṣi (BM, Pl. 49: 6)	Jewish period
275	Defenneh (Tanis II, Pl. XXXV: 44)	665–565
276	Sahab (QDAP XIII, p. 100: 57)	8th–7th cent.
279	Tell Beit Mirsim (AASOR XII, Pl. 59: 5) Stratum A	9th–7th cent.
280	'Ain Shems (AS IV, Pl. LXV: 42) Rm. 395 (1933) Probably IIb	950–825
281	„ „ (AS IV, Pl. LXVII: 7, 8) Ci.25 (1933) Stratum IIc	825–586
281	Tell Beit Mirsim (AASOR XII, Pl. 59: 1) Stratum A	9th–7th cent.
281	Jericho (SW, Pl. 33: A, 15c)	870–700

Class	Types
J.9	193 (Pl. 75: 25), 194, 198, 199 (Pl. 75: 26)
Jugs with convex base and flared neck	

Nine out of ten examples belonging to the class were found in Tomb 106, the tenth fragment being from Cave 1010, contemporary with the final phase of Level III.

The ware was pink or brown with some grits, and soft, medium or hard fired. The surface had been covered in all cases with a thick mat red slip, which was sometimes well smoothed.

Wampler has placed similar jugs from Tell en-Naṣbeh under the heading "Red Jugs" (TN II, Pls. 34–35: 606–614) and he has noted that they are apparently confined to the southern kingdom (op. cit., p. 17). Taking all the material into account, he considers that their main range extends from 700 to 500 B.C.

At 'Ain Shems examples of the red jugs occur in Tombs 2 and 6 (APEF II, Pls. XXXVII: 13; XLIV: 9), in company with the fully developed decanter of normal type and the high-footed lamp. The same three forms are found together at Tell ed-Duweir, and reach a peak period during the occupation of Tomb 106.

DIPPERS AND JUGLETS

(Abbrev. D)

The juglets are divided into nine classes. Classes D. 1–5 contain the numerous varieties of dipper juglets; Class D.6 is devoted to the so-called "Cypriote" Black-on-Red juglets, with their imitations; and Classes D.7–8 include the oil or perfume flasks, which are frequently black burnished. Class D.9 consists of post-exilic shapes. The primary criterion of form indicates a chronological progression in the classes, and within them certain variations occur, which also seem to have some value in the sequence. A Distribution Chart of dippers and juglets in suggested chronological order will be found on p. 328.

Class	Types
D.1a and b	(a) 288 (Pl. 73: 2), 289 (Pl. 72: 16),
Dippers with pinched mouth, handle to rim	290, 298
	(b) 300, 301 (Pl. 73: 3), 302 (Pl. 72: 17)

Dipper juglets were introduced during the second millennium, and early forms had a pinched mouth, which was also characteristic of the juglets found in the Fosse Temple Structures I and II (L. II, Pl. LII). In Structure III the bodies of these juglets lose the pointed base and become more globular, with an increasing tendency to sag at the base; while in the still later forms the necks become wider and shorter in proportion to the body, and the tops of the handles are invariably affixed at rim level. Types 302 and 301 seem to be the most aesthetically successful of these forms, while 300 is a clumsy development.

There is little to choose between the colour and firing of the wares in this class, which are pink, brown, or buff, with black examples of types 288 and 300. Most of them are fired medium to hard. Some examples from the earlier groups such as Tomb 521, Cave 6024 and Tomb 223, are soft-fired, but in many the juglets show traces of a dark red slip and burnish. Type 289 is soft-fired, with a buff or brown slip. There is, however, a distinct increase in the number of grits mixed in with the clay in the later groups.

Lamon and Shipton (M. I, p. 165, § 27) have noted that their "jug type 142"—with a pinched mouth—"is obviously a Stratum V carry-over from Stratum VI and LB traditions" and the same can be said of their jugs 140–141, all of which are from Stratum V (1050–1000 B.C.).

Albright states that at Tell Beit Mirsim (AASOR XII, p. 83) "pinched spouts . . . are restricted exclusively to EI I juglets, though a survival into the ninth century is entirely possible". Wampler (TN II, p. 23) endorses the essential importance of Albright's observation, subject to the modifications imposed by the evidence from 'Ain Shems (AS V, pp. 135, 138). Wampler places pinched and round-mouthed juglets in his class 2 (S. 758–797) and considers that the change over from pinched to round-mouthed forms took place in the tenth century B.C. (TN I, p. 89 and TN II, p. 23, §§ 52–53). Grant and Wright (AS V, p. 139, note 20) prefer the ninth century, a date which would conform more happily to the evidence from Tell ed-Duweir, where the true pinched mouth persists in a late form (type 300) into the central layers of Tomb 1002, and is retained in a transitional stage in types 287, 299, which occur as late as Tomb 106. The pinched mouth, therefore, changed and in decreasing numbers, does survive into the seventh century B.C.

		B.C.
300	Jericho (SW, Pl. 35: A, 31)	870–700
300	'Ain Shems (AS IV, Pl. LXIV: 42) Rm. 315 (1933) "A typical IIa form"	1000–950
301	„ „ (AS IV, Pl. LXVI: 37) Area U 27, Rm. 97 (1929) Stratum IIb	950–825
302	Samaria (SS III, Fig. 1: 7) Period I	880–850
302	Tell Abu Hawam (QDAP IV, p. 20: 58) Stratum III (or IV)	1100–925
302	Tell en-Naṣbeh (TN II, Pl. 40: 762) Tomb 54	10th cent.
302	Jericho (SW, Pl. 34: A, 26b)	870–700

Class	Types
D.2a and b	
(a) Round mouth, slightly pinched	287 (Pl. 76: 10), 299
(b) Round or pinched mouth, handle curving above rim	304 (Pl. 76: 12), 303, 305, 671

Class D.2 contains two varieties which appear to be transitional between the pinched and round-mouthed juglets. The distribution of Class D.2a places it before Class D.5b, which contains the final phase of the round-mouthed juglets, and the occurrences of juglets in Class D.2b follow on very clearly from the juglets in Class D.1b.

D.2a

The tendency to replace an ovoid pinched mouth with a round one, finished on the wheel, is well illustrated in types 299 and 287, confined to groups 107, 116, 218, 503 and 1002 and to tell Level III. The type specimen for 287 has a soft black body with a black slip, but the other examples cover the usual range of buff to pink ware with a slip of the same tone, and few grits. They are fired soft to medium, and are usually irregularly hand burnished.

D.2b

Types 303–305, represented by six examples only, show a round or pinched mouth, and have a big handle rising well above the rim. The ware is pink or brown, medium to hard fired, with no grits visible. Two out of six examples are burnished, but further details of these are not available.

		B.C.
303	Tell Beit Mirsim (AASOR XII, Pl. 68: 34) Stratum A	9th–7th cent.
671	Tell Sandaḥannah (BM, Pl. 32: 1, CPP 51 W)	Jewish period

Class	Types
D.3	285 (Pl. 73: 8), 296 (Pl. 73: 17, 18)

Dippers with round mouth, often with a moulded rim

Contemporary with Class D.1, there is a group of juglets with a round or oblong mouth, which appear to have inherited the tradition of Iron I juglets, if they do not actually date to that period. The form is only sparsely represented in the large tomb groups, and does not occur after the lowest layers of Tomb 1002.

The characteristic juglet is type 296. The ware is consistently brown, medium fired with a red slip, carefully burnished with vertical strokes over neck and body. The mouth is often distorted, for it was pulled away from the handle to produce an oblong shape with a slight lip. Type 285 is a less pronounced version with much the same characteristics.

The major phase of these dippers had no doubt been passed before the tombs at Tell ed-Duweir came into use, but they lingered on to the end of the ninth century B.C.

		B.C.
296	'Ain Shems (APEF II, Pl. XXII: 24, Pl. XXIV: 11) Tomb 1, Stratum IIb	late 10th–early 9th cent.
296	Tell el-Muteselim (M. I, Pl. 5: 120 and p. 163, § 25) Stratum V	1050–1000

Class	Types
D.4a and b	(a) 286 (Pl. 75: 34), 294 (Pl. 74: 25), 295 (Pl. 76: 5), 297 (Pl. 76: 11), 293
Dippers with round mouth, some moulded rims	(b) 283

The later trend is marked by the varieties in Classes D.4a and b. All the type specimens, except 294, which is late in the series, show traces of irregular hand burnish. The wares are pink, buff or brown, usually medium fired, with red, pink or brown slip. The body is less globular than in the previous class, and the rim is carefully finished.

Some examples typed to 283 from Tomb 223 and 218 retain a style of burnish similar to type 296 in Class 3. Others from Tomb 218 and Tomb 1002 only retain traces of burnish, and are less angular at the neck. Similar juglets in Level III and Tomb 106, where they are especially common, have acquired a cream instead of a red slip.

Class D.4 is represented in the main groups, but there is a marked development in form and a clear transition from hand to wheel burnish between type 296, a tenth-century form surviving into the ninth century, and its eighth- to seventh-century descendants.

					B.C.
283	Tell Muteselim (M. I, Pl. 2: 65 and p. 162, § 11) Stratum IV (1 ex.)				1000–800
	” ” ” ” Stratum III (10 ex.)				780–650

Class	Types
D.5a and b	(a) 282 (Pls. 74: 24; 76: 9), 284, 291
Dippers with long cylindrical body	(b) 292

Another late peculiarity is expressed by Class D.5a, where the body is as wide at the shoulder as it is at the base. The type specimen 282 has a pinched mouth, similar to the transitional juglets 287 and 299 in Class D.2, but most of the other examples have round mouths.

The final development is expressed in type 292, which first appears in tell Level III. It becomes prominent in Tomb 106 and the contemporary groups 109 and 114. Two other specimens came from the Bastion, and are, no doubt, in their true context. Two out of three examples from the courtyard of the Solar Shrine (Q.12: 106) were found below the floor level, and would appear to belong to the underlying stratum, like the decanter 276 in Class J.8, though it is not established whether that occupation level should be equated with Houses III or II.

The juglets of type 292 have a round mouth with an everted moulded rim. The ware is a hard pink, containing some very large grits; the surface is covered by traces of a smoothly burnished buff slip, which often merges into deep pink, owing to uneven firing temperature.

The Distribution Chart shows that juglet 292 first occurs in Houses III, is typical of the tombs associated with Houses II, and possibly continues into Houses I. Wampler is in a position to trace a longer history for them, and he considers that the juglets represented by S.788 at Tell en-Naṣbeh were common in the sixth to fifth centuries, and might be somewhat later. Grant and Wright (AS V, p. 139, note 21) compare an example from Tomb 14 at 'Ain Shems to another from Samaria found in a group with a Greek lekythus, "which can be dated in the first half of the fifth century". The common juglet at Samaria in Periods V–VI is cylindrical and has a pinched, or more often, round mouth (SS III, Fig. 10: 22–23; Fig. 23: 10–12).

		B.C.
292	'Ain Shems (AS IV, Pls. XLVIII: 5 and LXVIII: 3) Tomb 14, Stratum IIc	6th cent.
292	Samaria (S, p. 285 I 6A) S3–314	5th cent.
292	Tell Abu Hawam (QDAP IV, p. 15: 9) Stratum II	late 6th–early 4th cent.
292	Tell en-Naṣbeh (TN II, Pl. 41: 788) T.53, x 3 M 2394	6th–5th cent.

Class	Types
D.6a	329, 330, 332, 336 (Pl. 36: 64), 337
Cypriote or Cypro-Phoenician Wares	(Pl. 73: 6), 338 (Pl. 73: 5), 339, 339A (Pl. 36: 62)

The class includes six varieties of decorated wares, superficially similar in shape and ornament to jugs and juglets found in Cyprus, which have been ably classified by E. Gjerstad in the publications of the Swedish Cyprus Expedition and summarised in GSCE IV, pt. 2.

In that work (p. 270, note 1) he distinguishes between foreign (Syrian) wares imported into the island from c. 1050 B.C., and local imitations and modifications of Syrian prototypes which were not made by Cypriote potters until about 850 B.C., when the local products were manufactured in quantity.

The chronology of Iron Age ceramics in Cyprus, like that of Tell ed-Duweir, is still based on sequence and frequency of form, analysed from tomb groups, owing to the absence of securely dated epigraphic matter of historic importance; therefore while relative comparisons of form and ware may be very valuable, attempts to achieve an absolute date can easily lead to a vicious circle.

As far as published detail will permit, Gjerstad has examined with minute care all the so-called Cypriote pottery found in Syria and Palestine (op. cit., pp. 242–257), and in his opinion it is mostly of non-Cypriote origin. Of the common Black-on-Red I (III) ware found at Tell el-Fara he writes: "I have not seen one specimen among those examined by me which I would call Cypriote", and of the same ware at Tell Jemmeh, "the bulk of which was found in Strata G and H at levels 183–185 is altogether of the non-Cypriote class" (op. cit., p. 243).

Gjerstad considers that the form of the handle-ridge juglets with funnel-shaped mouth was of Syrian derivation, and he describes the characteristic features of the non-Cypriote ware:[1]

"1. there is often a grey core in the walls of the vases; 2. a bright orange, burnished surface, with the decoration applied after the burnish; 3. the surface flakes off very often. . . . The Cypriote ware of the corresponding class is never characterised by (1) and (3), but the technique of applying the decoration after the burnish occurs in Cyprus, parallel with the opposite technique of burnishing after the decoration has been painted."

Not all the examples listed under types 336, 337 and 338 are now available for study in London, but those examined show that two out of the three features of non-Cypriote ware are present in the majority of cases. Where it is possible to see the section, no grey core is visible in the walls of these juglets, but a pocked surface is very common and the mat black paint is usually applied after the burnish.

Thirteen examples of type 337 are decorated with four or more bands around the body and one or more concentric circles above the shoulder. The top of the handle is parallel to the ridge on the neck. The eight examples of type 336 have more bands on the body, on the neck and on the handle. The top of the handle curves down somewhat to join the ridge on the neck. Type 338 is represented by two specimens; they are juglets with flared neck, pinched rim, handle from rim to shoulder, and decorated with groups of concentric circles. One specimen was found in Tomb 218 and exhibits characteristics 2 and 3 of the non-Cypriote ware; the other came from Grave 147 and is now in the Palestine Museum, where Gjerstad examined it. In the same small grave there was an example of type 337, and Gjerstad considers that both juglets are of Cypriote origin (op. cit., p. 244). Dr. Ben-Dor dates the group to about 800 B.C. (op. cit., p. 423, note 1); in the writer's opinion it could be half a century earlier.

All the juglets from Tomb 218 and all those from Tomb 224, with one exception, are incomplete, and it is not possible to give full dimensions. The diameter of the base ranges from 2·5 to 3 cm., in sharp distinction to the Black-on-Red II (IV) juglets, which have a base averaging 5 cm. in diameter. The exception from Tomb 224 is covered with an orange slip, fired grey in patches, burnished vertically over neck and shoulder and horizontally round the body, with a well bevelled neck ridge. It is 8 cm. in height, with a base diameter of 2·5 cm.

---

[1] GSCE IV, pt. 2, p. 270, note 1.

The paint was applied after burnish (Pl. 36: 64). The only other example which approaches the smooth "soapy" texture and "smoky" shade of this juglet is one measuring 7 cm. in height with a proportionately wide base diameter of 3 cm. It was found in Grave 167 with specimens of the black burnished juglet 322 (cf. a very similar juglet, identical in size and decoration, from Tomb 227 at Tell el-Fara (CPP, type 82 G4)).

Two examples of type 336 were found in layers 6–13 of Tomb 1002, but they are not available for study in London. The incomplete juglet type 330 (PM. 36. 1523) from the bottom layers of the ossuary deposit 120 may "possibly" be of Cypriote origin, according to Gjerstad (op. cit., p. 244). These pear-shaped handle-ridge juglets were newly introduced into the Cypriote repertory with Black-on-Red II (IV) ware (op. cit., p. 70 and Fig. XXXVIII: 4a, 4b), and the later classification of the form in Cyprus would be in keeping with its presence in the ossuary deposit, though it must be remembered that the pit had been used for earlier single burials. The preponderance of sherds of type 336—four times as many as of type 337—also argues for the later date.

It will be seen that the bulk of Black-on-Red I (III) ware is divided between Tombs 218 and 224 which, with the lower layers of Tomb 1002, possibly cover the period of the tenth to ninth centuries B.C. on Palestinian evidence. The period of Tomb 120 is too uncertain for use in this connexion, though the fragments presumably belong to the ordinary burials.

Other varieties of wares, classified as "foreign" by Gjerstad, and no less alien to the traditions of south Palestine, are listed below in the chronological order of the tombs in which they were found.

Cave 6024

On considerations of form and burnish, the varied contents of the cave are placed first in the series at Duweir and dated at about 1000 B.C. The sherd 337 may not belong to the earliest phase of use, and would not be out of place in the first half of the tenth century.

Grave 110

This small group is placed early in the series of tombs at Tell ed-Duweir, and is certainly earlier than Tomb 218, in which the so-called Cypriote wares were found. It is therefore significant that two complete juglets, type 329, are identical with an example found at Tell el-Fara in Tomb 223 (CPP 86 H) which can be classed as Bichrome III. Tomb 223 at Tell el-Fara also contained a White Painted I pilgrim flask.

The two barrel-shaped juglets, type 329, are made of powdery ware, almost orange in tone. They are ornamented on the neck and body with fine mat lines, and the rims are covered with red ochre, apparently applied after firing. One example is in H. D. Colt's collection, and the other is at the Institute of Archaeology, London.

Tomb 218

Type 332, found at the door sealing, is a barrel-shaped juglet with neck and handle missing, black ware, hard fire, with grey slip smoothly polished all over. The form is not represented in the repertory of Black and Grey Polished wares in Cyprus (GSCE IV, pt. 2, pp. 82 f.), but it is known on the island from White Painted I onwards.

Type 339A (Pl. 36: 62) is inadvertently omitted from the line drawings. The ware is apparently pink, medium fired, covered with a red slip and smoothly burnished in vertical strokes. The painted black bands and concentric circles were possibly applied before burnish. The base is reconstructed as seen in the photograph, but it was probably flat like those of its fellows from Cyprus. The vessel is the first of its kind to be recovered from Palestine. In Cyprus the form is not of local derivation; introduced with Black-on-Red I (III) ware (op. cit., p. 69 and Fig. XXV: 9), it continued into Black-on-Red II (IV), and Fig. XXXVIII: 10 is a very close parallel to the example from Tell ed-Duweir.

There are also some fragments of the body of a large barrel-shaped jug, comparable to Bichrome I ware (GSCE IV, pt. 2, Fig. VIII: 1). The body and handle of a juglet in White Painted ware is comparable to the shape of III period (op. cit., Fig. XXV: 3a). It is not classified in the Duweir series as neck and handle are missing, but it is identical in form and ware with an example from Tomb 229 at Tell el-Fara (CPP type 82 L2).

Tomb 6006

Type 329, as described for Grave 110, Bichrome I, II, III.

Tomb 224

Besides five examples of Black-on-Red I (III) handle-ridge juglets, the tomb contained a small fragment of a barrel-shaped juglet made of buff ware, medium fired, decorated with fine black mat lines encircling a red centre. It is comparable to Bichrome III ware (GSCE IV, pt. 2, Fig. XXII: Jug 1).

Tomb 1002

The supply of so-called Cypriote ware was almost exhausted when Tomb 1002 came into use, for only three vessels were recovered from that large group. There were two examples of type 336 from layers 6 and 11 respectively, and an incomplete miniature amphora—described as a bottle in Gjerstad's work—which can be compared to Fig. XXXIX: 12, Black-on-Red II (IV) ware. The example from Tell ed-Duweir is 10·5 cm. in height to the handle-ridge, with a small base measuring only 3 cm. The ware is pink, with exceptionally thin walls, which tend to be grey in section. The burnished slip is worn, and flakes off easily, but the surface is not pocked. Mat black paint was apparently applied after burnish. A thick band of fine lines encircle the body and there are small concentric circles on the shoulder.

Summary

Gjerstad has noted that a new combination of pottery types, with the intrusion of new wares—Black-on-Red, Grey Polished and Red Slip—characterise the period of Cypro-Geometric III (GSCE IV, pt. 2, p. 191) and he considers that their appearance indicates an immigration of Syrian tribes to Cyprus at about 850 B.C. From that date onwards "the Black-on-Red and Red Slip wares are Cypriote and represent in shape and decoration a combination of Cypriote and Syrian elements" (op. cit., pp. 314–315).

It will be seen that Black-on-Red I (III) and Grey Polished are both present in Tomb 218 together with fragments of Bichrome I and White Painted III, which are, in Cyprus, components of Cypro-Geometric IIIA. Moreover, the form of the vessel illustrated on Pl. 36: 62 is non-Cypriote, though the nearest comparison from that island would extend the range of the Tomb 218 into Black-on-Red II (IV), i.e. Cypro-Archaic IA after 700 B.C. There is, however, no reason why the vessel in question should not have found its way down the coast from its place of origin somewhat earlier.

Red Slip I ware, the third new element in Cypro-Geometric IIIA, is present in the next group, Tomb 224 at Tell ed-Duweir (cf. type 241 and GSCE IV, pt. II, Fig. XXVII: 4), so that in the two groups there are the main features of a new influx radiating from an unknown place of origin, with Cyprus close to the centre of influence and Tell ed-Duweir far out on the periphery.

The incontestable evidence that pottery comparable to Cypriote Iron Age types (White Painted III, Bichrome III and Black-on-Red) was made at Tarsus in Cilicia (AJA XXXIX, 1935, p. 535 and XLII, 1938, p. 41) suggests a very likely source for the analogous wares at Tell ed-Duweir. The kilns at Tarsus were no longer working after the destruction of the city by Sennacherib in 696 B.C., and it would appear that trade facilities with south Palestine had diminished considerably before that date, because only two ridge-handled juglets and a bottle came from the large tomb 1002, which was apparently closed before 700 B.C. The eagerly awaited publication of Dr. Hetty Goldman's excavations at Tarsus, on behalf of the Bryn Mawr College Archaeological Institute of America and Harvard University, arouses great expectations among those who seek a solution for the origins of these distinctive decorated wares.

As a contribution to the problem, the results at Tell ed-Duweir suggest that the new influence which reached Cyprus so suddenly about 850 B.C. had also its effect on the imports of an inland city of Judah, off the main trade route, at about the same time, though there is no indication that any attempt was made to reproduce or imitate the imported pottery in bulk. Gjerstad's suggestion that direct trade facilities with Cyprus are evident in the presence of two juglets of true Cypriote make in Grave 147 is a conclusion which must depend solely on comparative methods of manufacture, of which he is no doubt the best judge.

J. C. Wampler sums up the present inconclusive state of knowledge concerning Cypriote wares and their relationships in TN II, p. 25, § 63, and he provides a comprehensive list of parallels under numbers 873–877, to which the reader is referred. In the present volume, parallels are confined to stratified sites, and to individual juglets, where they are available, for comparison of ware and decoration.

The Distribution Chart shows that Black-on-Red III ware is equally divided between Tombs 218 and 224, continuing to the central layers of Tomb 1002, but it is uncertain whether the four juglets from Tomb 120 should be attributed to the earlier burials or to the period of the ossuary deposit. The ware in Palestine appears to centre in the ninth century, with a possible extension into the eighth century B.C.

Bichrome III (GSCE IV, pt. 2, Fig. XXII: Jug 1)

		B.C.
	Cypro-Geometric IIIA–Cypro-Archaic IIA	*c.* 850–600
329	'Ain Shems (AS IV, Pl. XXXVIII: 3) Below foundations of Rm. 301, Stratum III	1200–1000
329	Tell el-Fara (CPP, 86 H) Tomb 223, xx–xxiind dyn.	11th–9th cent.
	(Cf. example from Tomb 110, which is identical)	

White Painted III (GSCE IV, pt. 2, Fig. XIX: 2)

	Cypro-Geometric IIB–Cypro-Archaic IIA	900–650
329	Tell el-Fara (BP I, Pl. XXXIX: 86 D) Tomb 229, xx–xxiind dyn.	11th–9th cent.

Black-on-Red I (III) (GSCE IV, pt. 2, Fig. XXV)

	Cypro-Geometric IIB–Cypro-Archaic IB		*c.* 900–600
336	Tell el-Fara (BP I, Pl. XXXIX: 82 G³) Tomb 229 xx–xxiind dyn.		11th–9th cent.
336	Tell el-Muteselim (M. I, Pl. 5: 123) Strata V (6 ex.), IV (2 ex.), III (4 ex.)		1050–650
337	'Ain Shems (AS IV, Pl. LXI: 39) Stratum III		1200–1000
337	Tell Jemmeh (Petrie Collection, Inst. of Arch.) Ep 183, Level V		*c.* 1000
337	„ „ (Gerar, Pl. LX: 82e) GV 185, GP 183		
	„ „ („ Pl. LX: 82g) GL 183	Level V	*c.* 1000
	„ „ („ Pl. LX: 82k) GB 184		
337	Tell el-Ajjul (AG II, Pl. XXXV: 82 K³) Tomb 1074		xxist dyn.
337	Tell Beit Mirsim (AASOR XII, Pl. 51: 9) SE 22 B–4 Stratum B₂		1150–1000
339	Tell Jemmeh (Gerar, Pl. LX: 82f) GK 183 HV 183 (HL on sherd), Level V–VI		*c.* 1000
339	Tell Muteselim (M. I, Pl. 17: 87) Strata V–III		1050–650
339	„ „ (M. II, Pl. 89: 6) Stratum Va		1050–1000

Black-on-Red II (IV)
(GSCE IV, pt. 2, Fig. XXXVIII)

	Cypro-Archaic IA–IIB	700–475
330	Tell Abu Hawam (QDAP IV, Pl. XIII: 87) Stratum III	? 1100–925
330	Tell en-Naṣbeh (TN II, Pl. 43: 875) T.32, E strip, x 294a. M2025	Mainly EI
330	Tell Muteselim (M. II, Pl. 88: 18) Stratum Va	1050–1000

Class	Types
D.6b	325, 331 (Pl. 75: 40),
Juglets or miniature amphorae of Cypro-Phoenician manufacture or affinity	410 (Pl. 75: 41), 411

The miniature amphora 339 in Class D.6a is no doubt the original model which is so poorly imitated by types 410 and 411 (cf. CPP, class 71). Type 331 is also a local version of the common Black-on-Red juglets

336 and 337. The ware of the imitations is hard pink or brown, and 411 has traces of burnish besides some painted black bands. All three examples were found in Tomb 106, and can be little earlier than the seventh century. Type 325, like the other forms in this class, may have more in common with Phoenician than with Cypriote wares, and exhibits a similar style of burnish and decoration to the large jug 334.

A fragment of a heavy brown burnished base, with a countersunk bottom, belongs to a class which is not otherwise represented at Tell ed-Duweir. It came from H.18: 1084, a room on the tell, and had been ground down for a secondary use and should be earlier than the context in which it was found. For comparisons, see Tomb 201, types 83 K2, K3 from Tell Fara (BP I, Pl. XL); 'Ain Shems (AS IV, Pl. XLIV: 24–25), Stratum II; and Tell Beit Mirsim (AASOR XXI–XXII, Pl. 68: 10), Stratum A.

These heavy brown-burnished juglets or amphorae, which Grant and Wright suggest were imported in the tenth to ninth centuries (AS V, p. 140) displacing Black-on-Red III about 900 B.C., were missing from the tombs at Duweir.

They should not be confused with smaller and lighter copies of imitations, sometimes painted with crude bands (i.e. Types 410, 411 from Tomb 106), for which parallels may be found from Tell Jemmeh (Gerar types 71–72, 82–83) and from Stratum A at Tell Beit Mirsim (AASOR XII, § 116, revised in AASOR XXI–XXII, § 157).

The writer would therefore prefer to relegate the original imports to the tenth century, before the main tomb series at Duweir began, and to place the imitations quite late in the seventh century B.C.

		B.C.
410	Tell Beit Mirsim (AASOR XII, Fig. 14: 16) Stratum A	7th cent.
410	Tell Jemmeh (Gerar, Pl. LIX: 71 1) 15 ex. at levels E, F 192–188, Levels XIV–X	9th–7th cent.
410	Tell Muteselim (M. I, Pl. 9: 2, 3) Stratum II	650–600

Classes
D.7–8
Juglets (Oil or Perfume Flasks)

The division of Classes D.7–8 is difficult; not only is there much variety in ware, firing and finish, but the present condition of the examples does not always allow these details to be accurately assessed.

The indication of form is also unsatisfactory; the somewhat uncommon juglets, for instance, with long necks and button or pointed bases, seem to run concurrently with the round-based varieties, and they continue as late as Tomb 109; nor does the shape of the body appear to be a reliable guide. They are to be found on the Distribution Chart under Class D.7a.

Two distinct classes in the commonest black juglets, types 322 and 309, have long been recognised. D. Mackenzie showed that the earlier kind with long neck and handle joining it some way below the rim, was common in Tomb 1 at 'Ain Shems (APEF II) now dated by Grant and Wright to about 900 B.C. (AS V, p. 8), and continued in use down to the period of Tomb 2 repository. W. F. Albright (AASOR XII, §§ 94 and 113) showed that the later class with handle affixed to the rim continued at Tell Beit Mirsim to the end of the seventh century.

The black juglets from Tell Jemmeh are too fragmentary for a clear picture of the transition, but types similar to 322 (Gerar, Pl. LIX: 73b, 73o) appear at levels 183–187, tenth century B.C., while types like 309 (Gerar, Pl. LIX; 73e, 73w) are most common at 190 feet, and single examples extend to 193 feet, ninth to seventh centuries. Thus the change should take place shortly after 900 B.C., according to the revision of dating (AJA, 1939, p. 460).

Wampler (TN II, p. 24, § 59) also considers that the black (or brown) juglets, with graceful bodies and long necks (TN II, Pl. 41: 798–807), began to give way to the common MI types 846–871 in the tenth century.

Adhering to the classification of form, and ignoring details of ware, colour or burnish, the Distribution Chart of examples from Tell ed-Duweir will tell its own story. If the date of the destruction of Level III is accepted at 700 B.C., and if half a century is allowed for the topmost levels of Tomb 1002, where Class D.8 became predominant, it does not seem possible to date the change from D.7 to D.8 much earlier than 750 B.C.

It is in any case a natural typological development, for the tendency to affix jug or juglet handles nearer to the rim in later types is very marked. There is no need, therefore, to attribute the change from D.7 to D.8 to foreign influence.

Class	Types
D.7a	328, 317, 318, 326 (Pl. 76: 19), 327

Handles to centre neck, rising to rim, ovoid body, button base

There can be no doubt that the elegant little juglet 328 from the intact Tomb 521 begins the series at Tell ed-Duweir. It is not clear whether type 317 with a similar body and handle should be equated with the original burials or the intrusive ossuary deposit in Tomb 116. Type 318 is sometimes made in pink or grey ware, and its presence in Tomb 109 does suggest a late date for the form, despite its low handle attachment. Type 326 is only found in the smaller groups, but it is associated with a pinched spout juglet 289, four examples of the burnished juglet 296 and a cylindrical juglet type 282 of Class D.5, all from Tomb 4010. Type 327, where the handle almost meets the rim, is an early example from Tomb 218 of the later tendency.

J. C. Wampler suggests that the types with disk bases and long neck (TN II, Pl. 41: S.798–802) are earlier in EI than those with a pointed or button base, such as types S.803–807 and 842–845 "which possibly belong to the last half of EI and extend into the earlier part of MI" (TN II, p. 24, § 57). The material from Duweir does not provide a decision in this matter, for the types of each kind (318, 326, 327, disk, and 317, 321, 328, pointed) are evenly distributed throughout the series.

Grant and Wright consider that the ancestor of the small black juglet is to be found in Stratum III at 'Ain Shems; it is seldom black, and almost always has a small flat base (AS V, p. 131; AS IV, Pls. XXXVII: 22, 23, 27).

		B.C.
317	Tell en-Naṣbeh (TN II, p. 24, § 56 and Pl. 41: 802) T.54, x 116	Mainly EI
317	Tell Muteselim (M. I, Pl. 5: 126) Stratum V–IV	1050–800
318	'Ain Shems (APEF II, Pl. XXIV: 15) Tomb I, Stratum IIb	10th–9th cent.
326	Ez-Zahiriyye (QDAP IV, Pl. LXIII, 2 ex.) Chamber B	c. 1000
326	Jericho (SW, Pl. 38: C, 1)	871–700

Class	Types
D.7b	314, 315 (Pl. 73: 32), 322 (Pl. 73: 4, 12), 324 (Pl. 72: 6)

Handles nearing rim, inclined to drop body

Types 314, 315 and 324 are variants of type 322, which was the common form during the early part of the period under review. It was unchallenged during the occupation of Tomb 224, and in layers 6–13 of Tomb 1002 it remained predominant. However, in the topmost layers of the latter tomb there were only four examples of type 322, as against eighteen of the later type 309, which suddenly took the lead, and no specimens of type 322 were found in a later context.

The great majority of juglets in the class were made of grey or black paste, medium fired, covered with a black slip and hand burnished; the strokes on the body were applied vertically or had been subsequently polished, and the class as a whole showed evidence of careful workmanship.

Similar dippers from other sites suggest that the type was well established in the tenth century; at Duweir it is still characteristic of the ninth century and continues apparently into the eighth century.

		B.C.
322	Tell Beit Mirsim (AASOR XII, Pl. 51: 2, 3, 8) Strata B₃ or A₁	1000–800
322	'Ain Shems (APEF II, Pl. XXIV: 14, 16, 17, 18) Tomb 1	10th–9th cent.
322	„ „ (AS IV, Pl. LXVI: 30; AS V, p. 139) Stratum IIa–b	1000–825
322	Tell Muteselim (M. I, Pl. 2: 52) Stratum III	c. 780–650
322	Ez-Zahiriyye (QDAP IV, Pl. LXII) Chamber B	c. 900
324	Tell en-Naṣbeh (TN II, Pl. 42: 847) T.54, x 122 Major phase	EI

302

Class	Types
D.8	309, 310 (Pl. 75: 35), 311, 312 (Pl.
Handles affixed to neck, squat or slightly drop-shaped body	75: 36), 313 (Pl. 77: 11), 319 (Pl.
	76: 27), 320, 321, 323

The squat black burnished juglet 309 shares with its typological forerunner 322 the distinction of being the most common form of juglet at Tell ed-Duweir, for over a hundred examples of each are recorded.

The type is lacking from all the big tomb groups prior to Tomb 1002, in which it only achieves ascendancy over type 322 in the topmost layers. In the rooms of tell Level III, Tomb 106 and tell Level II, juglet 309 has completely displaced type 322.

There was, however, a short period when both types were to be found together, well illustrated in the double burial 160, which contained two examples of 322 and one of 309, besides single examples of 318 and the Black-on-Red juglet 337. (Note: this transitional phase is also seen at Ez-Zahiriyye (QDAP IV, pp. 99 ff.) where the tomb excavated by Baramki contained black burnished juglets of both Duweir types 322 and 309 in a proportion of about two to one).

The majority are made of grey to black paste, soft fired, and many of them have lost their surface, exposing a few large grits, but others retain traces of a vertical burnish on a black slip. The examples found in tell Level III differ somewhat from those found in the tombs, for they have lost all trace of burnish, if any existed, and some are pinkish-buff in colour, possibly due to the effects of burning in the general destruction of the city.

The standard of workmanship has deteriorated, the bases are carelessly finished, with the handles large in proportion to the body and clumsily applied. The admirable study of the comparable squat black perfume juglets from Tell Beit Mirsim prepared by Thorley and Kelso (AASOR XXI–XXII, § 125) could equally well describe the Tell ed-Duweir examples. The authors note that the colour is organic, and that the few buff examples made in the same way had been insufficiently fired to produce a rich red. Occasional buff or red examples found at Duweir are therefore included in the class of black burnished juglets. All the juglets from Tell Beit Mirsim, Stratum A (AASOR XII, Pl. 68: 1–32, discussion on pp. 69, 71, 83 and XXI–XXII, Pl. 18: 1–9), are comparable to Class D.8, and should therefore be typical of the eighth to seventh centuries. At Megiddo the range appears to extend from Strata IV–I, but the majority of examples come from Stratum III (780–650 B.C.).

		B.C.
309	'Ain Shems (APEF II, Pl. XXIV: 13) Tomb 1	10th–9th cent.
309	„ „ (AS IV, Pl. LXVIII: 4) Tomb 14, Stratum IIc	6th cent.
309	Ez-Zahiriyye (QDAP IV, Pl. LXI: 2, 6) Chamber B (cf. AS V, p. 137, note 9)	c. 1000
309	Tell ej-Judeideh (BM, Pl. 53: 20) Burnt layer, Stratum II	Jewish
309	Tell Muteselim (M. I, Pl. 2: 49–56, except 52) Strata IV–I	1000–350
309	Tell en-Naṣbeh (STTN, Pl. XVII: 1245) Tomb 5 (cf. TN I, p. 99)	1000–700
309	„ „ (STTN, Pl. XV: 1149, 1152) Tomb 3	c. 900
309	Jericho (SW, Pl. 38: C, 3)	870–700
311	Samaria (SS III, Fig. 10: 24) Period VI	c. 720 or earlier
313	Jericho (SW, Pl. 38: D, 5)	870–700
319	Tell en-Naṣbeh (TN II, Pl. 42: 826 and p. 25, § 61) R.467, AD21, I x 13. M. 2485	700–500

Class	Types
D.9	340, 341, 342 (Pl. 77: 21), 343, 344,
Miscellaneous	345 (Pl. 73: 29), 346 (Pl. 76: 30),
	347, 348, 349 (Pl. 77: 28), 351 (Pl.
	77: 27), 664

The miscellaneous forms included in Class D.9 vary in the shape of the body, which tends to be pear- or drop-shaped on a flat disk base; all but one have a carelessly attached handle, which places them without doubt in the post-exilic period. The ware is red, pink or buff, containing some large grits, and the surface is rather rough. On the whole, the pottery is well fired.

Type 351, which has the only handle rounded at the inner point of attachment, came from two open areas (G. 18: 27 and H.14: 23) on the mound which are included in Level I, and are certainly later than the 586 B.C. destruction. Type 348 was associated with the second of the two examples of type 351. Type 345 from Tomb 4005 may be contemporary with them.

Type 347 from cistern 215, and type 349 from building R.15: 13 are attributed to the fourth to third centuries B.C.

Types 340 and 341 from Cave 515, and types 343 and 344 from Tomb 217 are second-century forms, judging from the associated pottery.

Type 346, with its ribbed body, came from pit 4021, and belongs apparently to the third century A.D.

		B.C.
340	Tell Sheykh Zuweyid (Anthedon, Pl. XXXVII: 53 Y2) Gl.463	630–447
342	Tell Sandaḥannah (BM, Pl. 60: 14)	Seleucidan
344	Tell en-Naṣbeh (TN II, Pl. 42: 835) and p. 25, §§ 62, 64	Hellenistic–Roman
345	Tell Abu Hawam (QDAP III, Pl. XXIII: 3) Stratum II	late 6th–early 4th cent.
349	Tell Sandaḥannah (BM, Pl. 60: 16)	Seleucidan
664	Samaria (CPP 56 R3)	

POTSTANDS

(Abbrev. PS)

	Types								
Locus	395	396	397*	398*	399*	400*	401*	402*	Total
Solar Shrine	—	—	—	—	1	—	—	—	1
G.12/13: 1–8	1	—	—	—	1	—	—	—	2
R/Q/S.15/16: 10–21	1	—	—	—	—	—	1	—	2
Residency Pits	—	—	—	—	3	1	—	—	4
Residency and Walls	—	—	—	—	3	—	1	1	5
Great Shaft	—	—	—	—	2	—	—	—	2
Houses II	—	—	—	—	—	1	—	—	1
505	—	1	—	—	—	—	—	—	1
Houses III	—	1	1	—	5	6	—	2	15
224	1	—	—	—	—	—	—	—	1
6024	—	—	—	1	—	—	—	—	1
TOTAL	3	2	1	1	15	8	2	3	35

* Pl. 77: 31; Pl. 72: 20; Pl. 77: 32–35.

The ring potstand was made for domestic and industrial use and was not normally placed in tombs. The only exception at Tell ed-Duweir is the small ring stand 395, on which a bowl could have been placed, though it seems rather too shallow to take the base of a storage jar.

Potstands were fairly common during the occupation of Level III, and fragments have been found in each of the subsequent periods. That they were only found twice in older contexts is no doubt due to lack of excavation in the earlier Iron Age town deposits. Potstands were not infrequent in the Fosse Temple (L. II, Pl. LIII), but the forms were taller in proportion to their width and the sides were less thick. The firing was softer in many cases, which produced a black core to the pink body of the potstand.

The ware of the larger Iron Age potstands was grey, pink or brown, containing a good proportion of grits, the firing usually being hard. The two small specimens 396 and 397 were buff and pink respectively, fired medium and soft, and brown and pink slips had been applied.

At Megiddo the Late Bronze Age forms seem to persist into Stratum III, but Lamon and Shipton have noted the appearance of forms in Strata IV and III which "on account of their unusual squatness may eventually prove of some importance" (M. I, p. 170). Grant and Wright state that potstands are common in Stratum II at 'Ain Shems, but there are no close parallels.

		B.C.
395	Tell Muteselim (M. I, Pl. 34: 10) Stratum IV–III	1000–650
398	Samaria (SS III, Fig. 28: 1–2) E.207, Period VI	*c.* 750
401	Tell Beit Mirsim (AASOR XII, Pl. 71: 11) Stratum A	9th–7th cent.

MINIATURE AMPHORAE

(Abbrev. MA)

	Types					
Locus	412	413	414	415	416	*Total*
6003	—	—	—	—	1	1
1002						
layers 1–5	—	1	—	—	—	1
Unstratified	—	—	—	1	—	1
224	—	—	—	1	—	1
218	1	—	—	1	1	3
120 (Burials)	—	—	—	1	—	1
4023	—	—	1	—	—	1
4026	—	—	—	1	—	1
110	—	—	1	—	2	3
TOTAL	1	1	2	5	4	13

Even though there are only five forms in this category, it appears that they belong to the early part of the three hundred years under review. The table shows that ten out of thirteen examples came from groups placed early in the chronological sequence of the tombs, and of the three exceptions, type 416 is a fragment from Cave 6003, while one example of type 415 came from the unstratified debris of Tomb 1002. Type 413, from the top layers of the same tomb, was a childish production, possibly more akin to the pithoi in the following section, which supports the general indication that the form had almost died out before Tomb 1002 came into use.

The ware was usually soft black or hard pink, with a slip which had fired black or dark red. Where the surface remained, it was either smooth or irregularly hand-burnished. A high proportion of grits was visible in those specimens where the burnish had worn off. The handles were all applied lugs, pierced vertically.

Wampler (TN, pp. 47 f.) has made a good case for his suggestion that the "common phase had been passed by the early part of the tenth century" (§ 31). The scarcity of miniature amphorae at Tell ed-Duweir strongly supports his conclusion; the fact that few examples came from the large groups, Tomb 218 at Duweir and Tomb 1 at 'Ain Shems (APEF II, Pl. XXII: 27), is also encouraging. In addition, there is Grant and Wright's statement that a black burnished form at 'Ain Shems, comparable to type 415, represents a decadent type (AS V, p. 130) and two out of five among the Duweir examples are similarly fired and finished. Two black burnished specimens from Megiddo were found in Strata IV, III. For Albright's remarks on examples from Tell Beit Mirsim, see AASOR XXI–XXII, p. 5, § 3.

Not many close comparisons occur, for there is some variety in the modelling of the neck and rim which may eventually prove to be of dating value. The best group is to be seen in Tomb 32 at Tell en-Naṣbeh, where twenty-three examples were found, more than the total number from Duweir, and it may therefore be correct to say that the miniature amphorae under discussion, which developed in LB II from a Mycenaean prototype (cf. L. II, Pl. LIV: 344, 345; MT, Pl. 34: 23 and p. 157), were still being made after 950 B.C. and that black burnished and some buff varieties lingered on for over a century.

		B.C.
415	'Ain Shems (AS IV, Pl. LX: 17) Rm. 429 (1933) Stratum III	1200–1000
415	Tell Beit Mirsim (AASOR XII, Pl. 51: 4) SE 23B–8, Stratum B	950–900
415	Tell Muteselim (M. I, Pl. 9: 35) Stratum III	780–650
415	Tell el-Fara (CPP 55 Q 2–3) Tomb 231, xxi–xxiind dyn.	c. 900

MINIATURE PITHOI

(Abbrev. MP)

Locus	Types												Total
	417	418	419	420	421	422	423	424	425	426	427	428	
106	—	—	—	—	—	—	—	1	1	1	—	—	3
Houses III	1	—	—	—	—	—	—	—	1	—	—	—	2
1002													
layers 1–5	—	—	—	1	—	—	—	—	—	—	—	—	1
132	—	—	—	—	—	—	—	—	1	—	—	—	1
1002													
layers 6–10	—	—	—	—	1	1	1	—	—	—	—	—	3
layers 11–13	—	—	—	—	—	—	—	1	1	—	—	—	2
1004	—	—	—	—	—	—	—	—	—	—	—	1	1
4005	—	—	—	—	—	—	—	—	—	—	1	—	1
116	—	—	1	—	—	—	—	—	—	—	—	—	1
223	—	1	—	—	—	—	—	—	—	—	—	—	1
TOTAL	1	1	1	1	1	1	1	2	4	1	1	1	16

In contrast to the miniature amphorae, the pithoi are largely concentrated in the last third of Iron II. They are lacking from the large groups 521, 218 and 224, and it is clear that the single examples of types 418 and 419, from Tombs 223 and 116 respectively, are distinct in ware and decoration. These two forms are closer to the thirteenth-century prototype from which they are derived (see Albright in AASOR XII, p. 80, § 108; AASOR XIII, p. 90, § 55), but it seems that no examples were found in the groups noted above—another timely warning, perhaps, of the dangers of negative evidence.

Lamon and Shipton note the same peculiarity at Megiddo: "Jar type 24 (Stratum III, 780–650 B.C.) certainly seems to be a derivative of types 113–114 from Stratum V, though there is no intermediate type in Stratum IV" (M. I, p. 165, § 34).

A nearly complete example and some fragments came from Samaria (SS III, Pl. 23: 1), painted, and found exclusively in S Tombs and E.207.

The miniature pithoi are pink, buff or brown, with some grits, fired soft to medium. A pink or red slip is usual, and is sometimes finished with a vertical burnish. Traces of painted bands of black, red or white are also seen.

The material from Duweir is not enough to permit any chronological distinction in form. Tomb 1002 contains both round and pointed (or knob-based) forms in layers 1–13, type 417 from Houses III has a knob base. Tomb 106 has two knobs to one rounded base. On the whole, there seems to be a trend from round to pointed or knob bases. Wampler has observed that a type from Tell en-Naṣbeh similar to 417 is "limited to the latter part (of Iron II)" (TN II, p. 13, §§ 62, 63). Grant and Wright note that "amphorae" with pointed or knob bases are very common in Iron II (AS V, p. 141). The example illustrated in AS IV, Pl. LXVII: 1 comes from Cistern 25, which is dated to 700–586 B.C. and contains other forms which are comparable to those from the burnt houses of Level III. The parallel for type 428 from Tell Judeideh is especially interesting, as it comes from a burnt layer in that mound, containing other types (e.g. 309, 373, 451, 454, 472) which are associated with Houses III and contemporary groups.

		B.C.
417	Tell en-Naṣbeh (TN II, p. 13 and Pl. 27: 443)	1000–600
418	Ez-Zahiriyye (QDAP IV, Pl. LXII: 3) Chamber B	c. 1000
418	Tell Muteselim (M. I, Pl. 19: 101) Stratum V	1050–1000
419	Tell Jemmeh (Gerar, Pl. LVII 55e) DX 193, Disturbed area	c. 700
423	'Ain Shems (APEF II, Pl. XXII: 20) Tomb 1, Stratum IIb	10th–8th cent.
427	Jericho (SW, Pl. 39: E, 1a)	870–700
428	Tell Judeideh (BM, p. 102 and Pl. 49: 7) Burnt layer, Stratum II	Jewish

PILGRIM FLASKS

(Abbrev. PF)

Locus	Types																	Total
	408	429*	430	431	432*	433*	434*	435	436*	437	438*	439	674	675	677	678	679	
4035	—	—	—	—	—	1	—	—	—	—	—	—	—	—	—	—	—	1
G.12/13: 1–8	—	—	—	—	—	—	—	—	—	—	—	—	—	—	—	—	1	1
R/Q/S.15/16: 10–21	—	—	—	—	—	—	—	—	—	—	—	—	—	—	—	—	1	1
G.18: 25–33	—	—	—	—	—	—	—	—	—	—	—	—	—	—	—	—	2	2
Residency Pits	—	—	—	—	—	—	—	—	—	—	—	—	—	—	—	—	5	5
Palace Walls	—	—	—	—	—	—	—	—	—	—	—	—	—	—	—	—	1	1
534	—	—	—	—	—	—	—	—	—	—	—	—	—	1	—	—	—	1
Houses II	—	—	—	—	1	—	—	—	—	—	—	—	—	—	—	—	—	1
106	—	—	1	—	—	—	—	—	—	—	—	—	—	—	—	—	—	1
102	—	—	1	—	—	—	—	—	—	—	—	—	—	—	—	—	—	1
Houses III	1	—	—	1	—	—	—	—	—	1	—	1	1	—	—	—	—	5
1002 layers 1–5	—	—	—	—	—	—	1	1	—	—	—	—	—	—	—	—	—	2
120 (Ossuary)	—	1	—	—	—	—	—	—	—	—	—	—	—	—	1	—	—	2
1002 layers 11–13	—	—	—	1	—	—	—	—	—	—	—	—	—	—	—	—	—	1
Unstratified	—	—	—	—	—	—	1	—	—	—	—	—	—	—	—	—	—	1
4005	—	—	—	—	—	—	—	—	1	—	—	—	—	—	—	—	—	1
4007	—	—	—	—	—	—	—	—	—	—	1	—	—	—	—	—	—	1
4030	—	—	—	—	—	—	—	—	1	—	—	—	—	—	—	—	—	1
H.14: 23	—	—	—	—	—	—	—	—	1	—	—	—	—	—	—	1	—	2
Total	1	1	2	2	1	1	2	1	3	1	1	1	1	1	1	1	10	31

* Pl. 76: 13; Pl. 77: 12; Pl. 76: 37; Pl. 74: 29; Pl. 73: 23; Pl. 73: 27

No pilgrim flasks were found in the earlier large tomb groups. Apart from examples of type 430 from the filling of pit 102 and from Tomb 106, which are reminiscent of Late Bronze Age prototypes (cf. L. II, 349), they first appear in three localities in cemetery 4000, represented by types 436 and 438. The bodies of both types were made in two parts of unequal depth, joined by a straight band. The clay was pink or brown, covered with a buff or brown slip, and type 436 had been ring (or spiral?) burnished. Contrary to the usual practice, the handles of 438 were affixed to the body and were not joined to the neck. An analogous form (neck missing) was type 678, which came from the open area west of the citadel and may be contemporary. The ware was a medium-fired greenish paste with grits. Few good parallels have been noted for these flasks, but on the Duweir evidence, if they are not of eighth-century date, they should have a post-exilic history (see CPP 87 S).

The forms 429 and 431 came from the ossuary 120 and layer 12 of Tomb 1002, with an incomplete example in tell Level III. They were made of buff or grey-green ware, only medium fired, and one example had a buff slip. The decoration in each case consisted of applied knobs below the handles and incised lines round the body, and both features (with the double-strand handles of type 429) are reminiscent of the jug 237, Class J.7, from layer 9 of Tomb 1002, which is made of similar pottery. The occurrence of flasks 429 and 431, in association with forms dated to the eighth to seventh centuries over a wide area (see Jugs, Class J.7) in three groups which are in close proximity in the Duweir sequence, is instructive. It is very possible that a common source in some non-local pottery workshop should be sought for this distinctive ware. Comparisons are available for flask 431 from 'Ain Shems, Tell Beit Mirsim and Megiddo; though Albright considers the "white clay, knife finished to imitate alabaster" as foreign to his site, Lamon and Shipton would accept the "green-brown ware with many light grits" as local at Megiddo. In this connexion, see also the Megiddo jug types 83, 85, 86, 87, and p. 162, § 19 of Megiddo I. Both flasks and jugs should prove to be reliable indications of eighth to seventh-century date.

Types 434 and 435 came from the top layers of Tomb 1002, the ridged neck being reminiscent of the earlier decanters (cf. Jugs, Class J.8, types 280, 281) and the hard pink or brown ware is similar.

Types 437 and 439 are contemporary with the flasks 429 and 431, but they may be local products, following in the Late Bronze Age tradition. The body in each case bulges more on one side than on the other, but is less angular at the join. The rim is not so pronounced as on the earlier flasks. The ware is pink or buff, medium fired, with a pink or buff slip; two examples were originally burnished. Similar flasks from Tell Beit Mirsim were also found in an eighth- to seventh-century context, and as the examples from both sites were reasonably intact, it may be assumed that they were still in use when the houses were destroyed by fire.

The fragment 408, with a spiral groove on the body and apparently made without handles, came from room H.15: 1003, the contents of which may cover the occupation of city Levels III–II. Wampler suggests that the handleless variety preceded the flasks with loop handles, which first appeared in the seventh to sixth centuries (TN II, p. 50, § 46).

Nine fragments of form 679 were exclusive to the post-exilic houses and the Residency pits, while a tenth example came from the open area near the palace walls. The ware was red to brown, often with an orange tinge, the firing was soft to medium, and a wash or slip was not common. At 'Ain Shems flasks in this ware are dated to the sixth century; they also occur at Tell en-Naṣbeh from the latter half of MI, extending through LI, perhaps to Hellenistic (TN II, p. 50, § 44). They are apparently typical of the sixth and following centuries, and should cover the same range as the soft orange clay storage jars in Class S.3, type 488. We need to know the place of manufacture of this poor but distinctive ware.

		B.C.
408	Tell Jemmeh (Gerar, Pl. LX: 87f) AJ 190. Between C and A building levels	
408	Tell en-Naṣbeh (TN II, Pl. 76: 1753) T.5, x 117; see TN I, p. 99 for date	10th–8th cent.
408	Tell Muteselim (M. I, Pl. 36: 1, 2) Strata III–I	780–350
408	Samaria (SS III, Fig. 24: 1–6) E.207, Period VI	c. 750
431	'Ain Shems (AS IV, Pl. XLV: 17) Silo of Stratum II in Rm. 390	1000–586
431	Tell Beit Mirsim (AASOR XII, Pl. 71: 5 and p. 87, § 120) Stratum A₂	8th–7th cent.
431	Samaria (SS III, Fig. 24: 8) E.207, Period VI	c. 750
437	Tell Beit Mirsim (AASOR XII, Pl. 70: 15; 71: 6 and p. 87, § 120) Stratum A₂	8th–7th cent.
437	„ „ „ (AASOR XXI–XXII, Pl. 16: 12 and p. 152, § 159) Stratum A₂	8th–7th cent.
674	Tell Jemmeh (Gerar, Pl. LX: 85t) EP 190, ER 190	9th–8th cent.
679	„ „ (Gerar, Pl. LX: 87n) BN 200	c. 600
679	'Ain Shems (AS IV, Pl. LXVIII: 1 and AS V, p. 143) Tomb 14	6th cent.
679	Tell en-Naṣbeh (TN II, Pl. 76: 1749 and p. 50, § 44)	9th–7th cent.

COOKING POTS
(Abbrev. CP)

Locus	SHALLOW Collared rim Types 440, 445, 684, 685, 693, 694	SHALLOW Ridged and grooved rim Types 441–444, 687	Total	DEEP Plain, rilled or ridged necks Types 447–450, 457; 451–456; 458, 462	DEEP Flared necks Types 446, 460, 689, 691, 692	DEEP Straight necks Types 459, 461, 463, 464, 688, 690, 695	Total
220	—	—	—	—	—	1	1
4021	—	—	—	—	—	1	1
503	—	—	—	—	—	1	1
217	—	—	—	—	1	2	3
Houses I							
R/Q/S.15/16: 10–21	—	—	—	—	2	—	2
G.12/13: 1–8	—	—	—	1	—	—	1
G.18: 25–33	—	—	—	—	—	2	2
H.14: 23	—	—	—	—	—	1	1
Residency Pits	—	3	3	—	1	6	7
Residency Rooms	1	—	1	—	—	8	8
Residency Walls	1	—	1	—	—	—	—
Great Shaft	—	—	—	—	1	—	1
Bastion	—	3	3	1	3	—	4
Houses II	—	4	4	1	3	—	4
106	2	1	3	11	—	—	11
505	2	—	2	—	—	—	—
513	—	1	1	2	—	—	2
540	—	—	—	3	—	—	3
1010	—	—	—	2	—	—	2
Houses III	3	17	20	30	—	2	32
7002	—	1	1	—	—	—	—
7007	—	1	1	—	—	—	—
120	4	1	5	3	—	—	3
1002							
layers 1–5	—	—	—	10	—	—	10
layers 6–10	—	1	1	8	—	—	8
layers 11–13	—	—	—	8	—	—	8
189	—	1	1	—	—	—	—
218	—	1	1	—	—	—	—
TOTALS	13	35	48	80	11	24	115

Cooking pots are easily identifiable owing to the characteristic ware and frequent signs of burning (for a technical description, see Kelso and Thorley, AASOR XXI–XXII, § 137). Two main groups are distinguishable: the wide-necked shallow pots, without handles, which are common from the fourteenth century B.C. onwards (L. II, Pl. LVIB: 362–371), persisting with only slight modifications well into the Iron Age, when they acquired handles; and deeper pots with narrower necks and a variety of rims, and invariably provided with handles, which are characteristic of Tomb 1002 and Level III.

The series will remain incomplete at Tell ed-Duweir unless Level IV is excavated, for the earlier tombs seldom contain these two-handled vessels (but see Pl. 5: 6 for an example of type 444 in position). From the number of one-handled jugs which are discoloured by fire in the earlier tomb groups, it may be inferred that many of them had been used for culinary purposes.

Though comparative material is abundant on all sites, excavation reports contain very few drawings of complete forms, for such exclusively domestic vessels were only discarded after breakage. Any discussion, therefore, is largely based on rim fragments, from which the diameter, but not the depth of the pot, can be assessed.

W. F. Albright noted a standard diameter of 23–26 cm. for cooking pots from Tell el-Fûl (AASOR IV, p. 10 and Pl. XXV), and placed the shallow vessels with a variety of moulded profiles chiefly in the eleventh century B.C., a date which he has more recently revised to the late eleventh and early tenth centuries (TN II, Appendix A, p. 69). He modified a statement that the deep-bodied and narrow-necked type completely displaced the shallow vessels in the ninth century, owing to the existence of the latter form at Samaria, which was founded in 880 B.C. (AASOR XII, p. 68, § 88).

The publication of Megiddo I enlarged the range of shallow cooking pots still farther, for it appears that they retained predominance there from Strata V–I (M. I, Pls. 39–40 and p. 172, § 76), and only two deeper forms are illustrated (M. I, Pl. 40: 14, 17). At Tell en-Naṣbeh, Wampler (TN II, pp. 30–31) has distinguished three major groups, which correspond to the main divisions suggested in the present volume. O. R. Sellers (Beth-zur, p. 40) shows a variety of shallow, handleless cooking pots from the EI I stratum at Beth-zur, north of the fortress.

Despite the accumulation of evidence which places the major phase of shallow vessels early in the series, the chart at the head of the section shows that they were also associated with Level III and that single examples were found in later contexts.

	Types
Shallow vessel, collared rim, with or without handles	440, 445 (Pl. 75: 42), 684, 685, 693, 694

Of the six types, all but one have handles. The ware is coarse pink, brown or buff, with large grits, and fired medium to hard. The distribution of examples from late contexts, which are nearly all disturbed groups or open areas, does not necessarily establish their position in Levels III–I. It seems more likely that their true horizon is to be found in Levels VI–IV.

The best comparisons are to be found at 'Ain Shems (AS IV, Pl. LXII: 45, 46; Pl. LXIII: 29–32) from Stratum IIa, b, 1000–825 B.C.; at Tell en-Naṣbeh (TN II, Pl. 46: 983–984, 997–998); and from Tell el-Fûl (AASOR IV, Pl. XXV) in the late eleventh and early tenth centuries B.C.

	B.C.
684 Tell Beit Mirsim (AASOR XII, Pl. 55: 9) Stratum A	9th–7th cent.
694 Tell Jemmeh (Gerar, Pl. LII: 32e) EF 185	10th cent.

	Types
Shallow vessels with two handles, ridged and grooved rims	441, 442 (Pl. 74: 30), 443, 444, 687

Vessels of both kinds were largely concentrated in Level III, but pots with the grooved rim, type 442, may have a longer history, extending possibly into Level II.

W. F. Albright dates comparable pots at Tell Beit Mirsim "after the end of the seventh century" (AASOR XII, p. 81, § 109 and Pl. 55: 2, 4, 5, 7, 9). A similar cooking pot was found in Tomb A at 'Amman (QDAP XI, pp. 78 f. and No. 27) which the late Mrs. E. Henschel-Simon placed at the end of the seventh century (op. cit., p. 80).

Good comparisons from Tell en-Naṣbeh are to be found in TN II, Pls. 47–48, of which S.1002, 1007, 1013–1015 have a similar tendency for the handle to rise above the rim.

	B.C.
442 Tell Beit Mirsim (AASOR XII, Pl. 56: 2 and pp. 81 f.) Stratum A₂	c. 600
442 Sahab (QDAP XIII, p. 101: 67)	8th cent.
442 Tell Sheykh Zuweyid (Anthedon, Pl. XXXIV: 32D³/) HS 414, JE 380	910–630
442 'Ain Shems (AS II, Pl. XXXVII: 90) T.28, II 93	900–600
442 Tell Muteselim (M. I, Pl. 39: 4) Strata IV–I	1000–c. 350
442 Samaria (S, p. 284, Fig. 160: 7)	900–700
442 Jericho (SW, Pl. 32: A, 10a)	870–700

Deep vessels with two handles and		Types
(a) Plain necks		(a) 447, 448, 449 (Pl. 75: 43), 450, 457;
(b) Rilled necks		(b) 451, 452 (Pls. 75: 44; 77: 1), 453, 454, 455 (Pl. 74: 31), 456;
(c) Ridged necks		(c) 458 (Pl. 75: 45), 462

The three varieties of neck on a deep body are to be found in the main groups from Tomb 1002 onwards, and no difference in date is distinguishable at Tell ed-Duweir. As noted in the description of Tomb 1002 (Chapter 8), the ware of these vessels is made of soft orange paste which, when fired harder, tends to acquire a darker, red-brown surface. While deep-bodied cooking pots do not appear in any tomb prior to Tomb 1002, their absence may be due to the fact that such domestic vessels were not normally included among tomb offerings before that date. However, their sudden appearance in Tomb 1002 does support the view expressed by Grant and Wright (AS V, p. 138) that they did not develop much before the eighth century B.C. Very naturally, most examples were found in the rooms of Level III, and pots with plain necks were missing from Houses II. The later history of these forms is best studied at Tell en-Naṣbeh (TN II, Pl. 49: 1035, 1039, 1050 (plain necks); Pl. 50: 1063–1069 (rilled necks); Pl. 48: 1010 (ridged necks). At ʻAin Shems, rilled neck fragments (AS IV, Pl. LXIV: 28–31) and a ridged fragment (AS IV, Pl. LXIV: 27) occur in Stratum IIb–c.

		B.C.
452	Tell ej-Judeideh (BM, pp. 105, 76 and Pls. 54: 5; 21: 5) Burnt layer	750–c. 350
453	Jericho (SW, Pl. 32: A, 10c)	870–700
456	Tell Beit Mirsim (AASOR XII, Pl. 55: 3, 6, 11, 12) Stratum A₂	c. 600
456	„ „ „ (AASOR XXI–XXII, Pl. 19: 6–11) Stratum A₂	„
456	Tell ej-Judeideh (BM, pp. 105, 76, Pls. 54: 1; 21: 13) Burnt layer	750–c. 350

Deep-bodied vessels, flared necks	Types
	446, 460 (Pl. 77: 3), 689, 691, 692

Among the few cooking pots associated with rooms and areas attributed to Level II–I are eleven examples with a neck profile which slopes out. The pots are made of thin red ware, with some grits, and fired hard. Two examples of type 692 came from the fourth- to second-century building, R/Q/S. 15/16: 10–21, and ribbing is introduced on the body, reaching up to the neck.

Comparable forms from Tell en-Naṣbeh are to be found in TN II, Pl. 49: 1034 and Pl. 50: 1053, 1055.

Deep-bodied vessels, straight necks	Types
	459 (Pl. 77: 30), 461, 688, 690, 695, 463 (Pl. 76: 33), 464 (ribbed bodies)

The fragments of pots with straight necks and plain bodies are exclusively associated with the Residency, its pits, and buildings G.12/13: 1–8 and G.18: 25–33. The wares are red, brown or buff, often with a grey core, and contain some mica grits. The firing is usually hard. Type 688 has a cream wash outside. The imported sherds of Black Glazed and Red Figured Attic ware, which are dated from the last half of the fifth century to the fourth century B.C., are common in the Residency, and would suggest that the cooking pots belong to the same period.

Examples of ribbed cooking pots, types 463 and 464, came from pit 503, Tomb 217, Quarry 220 and a burial in pit 4021; the last group may belong in part to the third century A.D.

The example from pit 4021 is made of hard brick-red ware, with a few white grits and some mica, and was finger-smoothed. The ribbing was rather undercut by a tool, and the height was 13 cm.

463	ʻAin Yabrud (QDAP VI, Pl. IV: 19)	4th cent. A.D.
464	ʻAin Shems (AS IV, Pl. LXIX: 8) Area R.23–24.	„ „
688	Tell Muteselim (M. I, Pl. 9: 33) Strata II–I	650–350 B.C.
688	Tell Abu Hawam (QDAP IV, p. 4, n. 1 and Fig. 6)	6th–4th cent.
688	Samaria (CPP 32 S4) 176.2g	650–330

STORAGE JARS

(Abbrev. S)

Lack of space in the cave tombs was no doubt the main reason why so few large jars were found in them, but it would also appear that they were more common in the earlier groups, Tomb 521 (4 examples), Tomb 223 (8 examples) and Cave 6011 (10 examples) than in the later ones, for Tombs 218, 1002 and 106, containing the largest amount of pottery, provided only a few jars apiece. However, in the single graves above the Fosse Temple they seem to have been a normal item of funerary equipment, and jars were placed by the head or feet in burials 132, 147, 152, 167, 182 and 191. (For the jars in position, see Pl. 5: 2, 4, and Class S.1 for further details).

In tell Level III it is very natural to find a preponderance of jars, for they were essential containers for oil and wine, and comestibles such as lentils and pressed figs (AS V, p. 130). By that time the common type 476 of the earlier phase of Iron II had given place to the most characteristic four-handled jar, type 484, with the royal stamp on each handle. Fragments of these jars covered the southern end of the palace podium, while smashed jars were recovered from almost every room in the vicinity (see Class S.7).

Some varieties of form are to be noted in tell Level II and the Bastion area, where the jars show a high standard of craftsmanship, which is in very marked contrast to the deplorable mass-produced vessels so common in the period of post-exilic reoccupation. The many fragments of jar 488 in Class S.3 seem to represent the lowest degradation of the potter's art, but it need not be inferred that the local industry had declined to that extent, for this type of jar has been found on other sites, in Palestine and elsewhere, of the same period.

With regard to the development of form, the writer agrees with Wampler's observation (TN II, p. 9, § 42) that high rims gradually gave place to low ones. At the same time, handles were attached closer to the neck and they protruded farther from the side of the vessel. Little was noted at Tell en-Naṣbeh (TN II, p. 11, § 52) respecting the careless attachment of handles, a characteristic, as Wampler remarks, of sufficient commonness in LI and Hellenistic periods to be mentioned elsewhere (QDAP IV, 1934, p. 7). This feature is very marked in the post-exilic period at Tell ed-Duweir.

C. C. McCown discussed the cross-sections of jar handles at some length in TN I, Chapter 14, and the subject is also referred to in Chapter 10 of the present work. The oval handle is characteristic of the storage jars in Class S.1. With the advent of Class S.7, single and double ridges on the cross-sections were marked, though the development was by no means consistent, and oval sections sometimes recurred.

A Distribution Chart of storage jars in suggested chronological order will be found on p. 329.

Storage Jars with Two Handles

Class	Types
S.1	468, 473–475, 476 (Pl. 78: 19), 477

Plain neck, angular shoulder, ovoid body

The most common form of storage jar during the earlier part of Iron II was type 476, made of coarse pink ware, fired medium to hard. A distinctive feature of the class was the angular turn at the shoulder. The top of the handles were invariably set on a level with this angle, leaving a proportion of about a quarter to a sixth of the total height of the jar above the line. The handles were in all cases plain and unridged with an oval profile.

The class was already established in the earliest tomb groups found at Tell ed-Duweir, but it had almost disappeared before the occupation of tell Level III, and only sherds were recovered from that and the subsequent levels.

In an earlier phase of development the type was common in Stratum III at 'Ain Shems (cf. AS IV, Pls. XXXVIII: 24, XL, 9–11; LXI: 9) and a body with an angular shoulder is quoted as typical of Stratum IIa in the description of No. 43 on Pl. LXV.

At Tell en-Naṣbeh Wampler suggests that a jar somewhat like type 476 was introduced in the tenth to ninth centuries (TN II, p. 9, § 42). Parallels from Tell Abu Hawam and Samaria are equally consistent with the evidence from Tell ed-Duweir. The nearest comparison from Megiddo for jars in Class S.1 (M. I, Pl. 13: 69) is not a very common form, but occurs in Strata IV–II (1000–600 B.C.).

The scarcity of comparisons for S.1 at Tell Beit Mirsim (AASOR XII, Pls. 52–53; XXI–XXII, Pl. 13) agrees with its disappearance early in the seventh century B.C., if not before.

		B.C.
468	Samaria (SS III, Fig. 1: 18) Period I	880–850
468	Ez-Zahiriyye (QDAP IV, Pl. LXIV: 2). (Cf. AS V, p. 137, note 9)	*c.* 1000
473	Tell Abu Hawam (QDAP IV, Pl. XXXVI: 99) Stratum III	1100–925
476	Tell el-Fara (BP I, Pl. XL: 43K² and CPP 43 K4) Tomb 201	xxiind dyn. *c.* 900
476	Tell en-Naṣbeh (TN II, Pl. 16: 281) T.29, xl M.1748	10th–7th cent.

Class S.2 Plain neck, angular shoulder, pear-shaped body	Types 469 (Pl. 78: 9), 472 (Pl. 78: 3), 509– 511, 698?

The storage jars in Class S.2 had acquired a more pointed base, producing a pear-shaped rather than an ovoid body. There was less space between the rim and the angle of the shoulder, which was almost flat, and the handles were more circular in outline and projected farther from the body. Type 472 seemed to be confined to tell Level III and associated loci, but type 469 survived into tell Level II and presumably led to the development of Class S.3. The ware is pink to red, medium to hard fire, with a fair proportion of grits.

A similar form at Tell Judeideh in the burnt layer of Stratum II, and others from Tell Beit Mirsim, Stratum A, also destroyed by fire, suggest that type 472 is very characteristic of the eighth to seventh centuries. Albright has observed (AASOR XII, p. 79, § 104) that the form is common at Tell Jemmeh (CPP 46: P1–2) during the ninth to seventh centuries, but the initial date cannot be established on the material from Duweir, as Tomb 1002, which was predominantly eighth century, contained few storage jars, and Level IV is unexcavated. There are no good parallels from ʿAin Shems, Tell en-Naṣbeh or Megiddo.

		B.C.
472	Tell Judeideh (BM, p. 102 and Pl. 49: 1) Burnt layer, Stratum II	Jewish
472	Tell Beit Mirsim (AASOR XII, Pls. 52: 14; 53: 2, 5) Stratum A	9th–7th cent.
472	Tell Jemmeh (CPP 46 P2) levels 190–194 and AQ 200	7th cent.

Class S.3 Moulded rim, angular shoulder, waisted body	Types 488 (Pl. 78: 7), 489 (Pl. 78: 10), 530

Developing from Class S.2, jars 489 and fragment 530 came respectively from tell Levels III and II. Both forms had acquired a narrow waist and moulded rim, and in the case of type 489 the handles were not carefully applied.

The "sausage" jars of Megiddo provide some comparisons which show a similar development, for the variety equal to 530 was not found below Stratum III. Lamon and Shipton observe that a slightly later development of "sausage" jar, which is missing at Megiddo, is characteristic of Tell Abu Hawam, late sixth to early fourth century, and of the tombs at ʿAthlit, fifth to fourth century B.C. (M. I, p. 167, §§ 43–45).

It is the equivalent shape at Duweir, type 488, which was so common in the rooms of the Residency and pits of Level I. Though no complete examples were found, the soft and powdery orange ware was unmistakable.

Wampler remarks that low rim jars were not especially numerous at Tell en-Naṣbeh (TN II, p. 10, § 51) and they were not recorded at ʿAin Shems. They were, however, common in the A building level at Tell Jemmeh.

Jars of similar form and ware came from the Swedish Cyprus Expedition's work at Marion and Vouni, and from various tombs excavated by Miss du Plat Taylor at Tsambres and Aphendrika, but they are not common there or elsewhere on the island. In Cyprus the jars are apparently no later than mid-fourth century B.C., but the ware appears to be of better quality.

		B.C.
488	Marion (GSCE II, Pl. XLIII) Tomb 20, No. 2	475–400
488	„ (GSCE II, Pl. LXIX) Tomb 62, Nos. 48, 49	600–475
488	„ (GSCE II, Pl. CXXXIII: 3) Tomb 82, No. 32	475–400
488	Vouni (GSCE III, Pl. CII) Tomb 6, No. 3	400–325
488	„ (GSCE III, Pl. CVI) Tomb 11, No. 7	400–325
488	Aphendrika (TA, Tomb 38: 1, 4)	4th cent.
488	'Athlit (QDAP II, Pl. XIX: 384 and p. 44) Tomb L.16	5th–4th cent.
488	Tell Abu Hawam (QDAP IV, p. 4, Fig. 3) Stratum II	Late 6th–early 4th cent.
488	Tell Jemmeh (Gerar, Pl. LVI, type 47h) AJ, AQ 200, AM 195, B.196	c. 600
488	Tell el-Fara (BP I, Pl. XLIV) Tomb 650 (For revised date see QDAP IV, pp. 182–186)	c. 850
488	Tell en-Naṣbeh (TN II, Pl. 19: 331)	5th–4th cent.
489	Tell Muteselim (M. I, Pl. 16: 81) Stratum IV–I	1000–350
489	Tell Jemmeh (CPP 47v) EW 191	8th cent.
530	Tell Muteselim (M. I, Pl. 16: 79) Stratum III–I	780–350

Class	Types
S.4	467 (Pl. 78: 2), 470 (Pl. 73: 7), 471
Plain collar neck, curved shoulder, ovoid body	478 (Pl. 72: 22), 479 (Pl. 78: 6), 480 (Pl. 72: 10), 481, 493, 494 (Pl. 78: 15), 495, 512, 513, 514 (frags.), 699? 700?

Isolated examples of the class, made of the usual coarse pink ware, came from the earliest tombs and some single graves, but they are less than a dozen in all.[1] The form appears to have enjoyed its best period during tell Level II, when the vessels were made of a fine pink paste, tempered with grits, fired medium to hard; contrary to the general rule, the surface was covered with a cream or buff slip. The fragments 512–514 may belong to the series.

Many rims from Tell en-Naṣbeh seem to belong to the latter phase of these jars (cf. TN II, Pls. 15–16), but in default of more complete examples the comparison cannot be pursued. They may belong to the distinctive jar shape S.240, of good quality ware and finish with a plain rim, described by Wampler as not earlier than c. 500 B.C. (TN II, p. 9, § 40). Such fragments reflect a high standard of pottery manufacture in Judah about the time of the return from exile.

		B.C.
481	Tell en-Naṣbeh (TN II, Pl. 18: 303) Ci.285, P22, M 1711	c. 750–586
699	Tell Jemmeh (Gerar, Pl. LV: 46p) Common in A building level	
700	Tell el-Fara (CPP 46 D) Tombs 221, 266	

Class	Types
S.5	515, 516, 517, 520–527, 531–534,
Moulded rim on collar neck, shape of shoulder and body unknown	536

There is little to say about the rim fragments in the class, except that they were mostly found in association with the north, east or west walls of the Residency, or in pits to the east of that building. Some fragments came from the deposit 534, which contained the altar stands (see Chapter 12) and others were recorded from the post-exilic buildings. A few fragments came from the West Section at 42–38 feet, which would associate

---

[1] Type 480 from Tomb 521 has a ridged rim comparable perhaps to fragments illustrated from Tell el-Fûl (AASOR IV, Pl. XXVIII) dated by Albright to the second period (late eleventh to early tenth centuries B.C.).

them with Level IV. The pieces are, in any case, so small that it is impossible to make a firm decision in the matter. The best comparisons are found at Tell en-Naṣbeh, Cistern 285, c. 750–586 B.C., and Cistern 370, c. 700–586 B.C. (see TN I, Chapter XII), but the former at least has earlier and later elements among its contents.

The ware was consistently pink, brown or buff with a high proportion of grits, fired soft to medium, with a few harder examples.

533   Tell el-Fara (CPP 43 K8) UN 377

Class	Types
S.6	(a) 485, 486, 507, 528, 529, 535
Moulded rim, tall neck and narrow body	(b) 496, 518, 519

All but three of the nine forms included in the class have an unusually tall neck with a moulded rim. The exceptions, 496, 518 and 519, are included because the rim profile seems to fit best into the class, though there is some difference in ware and firing. Where the handles are preserved, they begin on a level with the shoulder angle. The only complete type is 485, but the remaining parts of the others suggest that the body is narrow in proportion to the height.

The ware is usually pink, medium fired, but 507 is an exception, being made of brown paste with grits, covered with a green slip, and burnished horizontally to the keel and then vertically. For a full description of one example of type 486, see under Building R/Q/S.15/16: 10–21 in Chapter 5.

Both variations appear to have a major phase during the occupation period of Houses II, with an extension to Houses I, covering the seventh century and possibly part of the sixth century B.C.

Storage Jars with Four Handles

Class	Type
S.7a	484 (Pl. 78: 1, 5, 11)
Plain sloping neck, ovoid body	

Type 484 is aesthetically the most successful form of storage jar found at Tell ed-Duweir. It was made to a standard size (Chapter 10 and PEQ, 1941, pp. 37–109), of a hard, metallic, greyish-red ware containing grits, and the walls and rims of the vessel were exceptionally thin and even. The handles were carefully applied at the greatest diameter of the body, and a double ridge ribbing was usual (Pl. 78: 1, 5, 11).

It was exclusively this type of jar which was impressed with the royal jar stamp on each handle (Chapter 10, Jar Handle Stamps) and for the first time repairable examples of the form were recovered and restored.

Nearly all the rooms attributed to city Level III contained at least one example of this vessel, and they were virtually confined to it, for three of those examples recorded as from Level II are from the plastered area K/L.14: 1061, part of which was in use in both periods. The same applies to two fragments from Rooms J.17: 1041 and 1043, and the other specimen was found below the floor of Room L.12: 1068.

Rim fragments of type 484 were found below the Residency floors, and on the space AG beyond the building to the south, but no fragments of jars typical of Level II rooms were recovered from those places, which supports the theory advanced on other evidence that the site of the citadel remained deserted after the burning of city Level III until the construction of the Residency.

In comparing the pottery forms from other sites an erroneous impression is obtained, for drawings of similar four-handled jars are only to be found in the publications of Tell Beit Mirsim and Tell en-Naṣbeh. However, the quantities of handles with royal stamp impressions, now known to be exclusively associated with jars in Class S.7, prove that the form was common on the chief Judaean sites in the eighth century, and is so far unknown elsewhere (see Chapter 10, Jar Handle Stamps).

W. F. Albright has discussed the jars in AASOR XII, §§ 104–5, AASOR XXI–XXII, § 36, notes 7 and 146, and the technical method in § 138; Wampler refers to them in TN II, p. 10, § 49. It will be seen from their remarks and from the few comparisons published by Grant and Wright in AS IV that the excellent form of the jars is not the only distinguishing feature, for the ware itself is hard and well fired, and produces a metallic sound when struck, and is very different from the storage jars of the preceding centuries. There are contemporary bowls (equal to Class B.13) from Samaria in the collection at the Institute of Archaeology, London, which are very similar in ware. Could it be that the jars were made by potters trained in a northern school who moved south after the fall of Samaria in 720 B.C.?

The rim and shoulder of a storage jar on which the letters *b-t l-m-l-k* were inscribed presumably belongs to Class S.7, but it is very early in the development of the form. The ware is much softer than the average example of type 484, and it is lighter in colour. Albright (AASOR XXI–XXII, p. 59) agrees with Diringer that on palaeographic grounds the inscription should be earlier than the Late Jewish period. From the position of the find, over Room 1078 (destroyed, according to present evidence, in 700 B.C.), the sherd may belong to the late eighth century or earlier.

		B.C.
484	'Ain Shems (AS IV, Pl. XLVI: 21–23, 25) Jar handles with and without royal stamps, Stratum IIc	825–586
484	'Ain Shems (AS IV, Pl. LXV: 1, 2, 3) Jar rims in Rms. 486, 444 (intrusive) and 387	1000–586
484	Tell el-Fûl (AASOR IV, p. 23, Pl. 30: 12–14) Fortress III	750–589
484	Tell Beit Mirsim (AASOR XII, Pl. 52: 10, 11; XXI–XXII, Pl. 13: 3) Stratum A	900–600
484	Tell en-Naṣbeh (TN II, Pl. 22: 357) R.74, AH20, x 4, M.396	*c.* 1000–586

Class
S.7b
Moulded rim on collar neck, ovoid body

Types
482 (Pl. 78: 4, 8), 483

Nearly complete examples of the two forms were found on or set in the plastered court, east of the palace. Two of type 483 were leaning against the wall, with an example of Class S.9 of type 491, while jar type 482 had been set in the plastered court farther down the slope (see Pls. 17: 5 and 23: 3). Sherds of similar jars occur in dwelling 505 and in Houses II.

Comparative material is rare, but some of the large jar rims published in TN II, Pls. 14–15 (e.g. S.246 and 258) may well belong to the class, which would seem to be typical of Stratum II, late seventh century B.C. to early sixth century B.C.

Storage Jars with Two Handles

Class
S.8
Hole-mouth jars with two handles and a round base

Types
465 (Pl. 78: 16), 498, 537–544

Type 465, the only one with a drop-shaped body (Pl. 78: 16), which had had a drawing incised on it before baking (Pl. 50: 1), is securely established as a Level II form by its presence in Room L.14: 1075, and in the contemporary rubbish pit. Another example is a fragment from a post-exilic house, G.12/13: 1–8, but it is not necessarily in context.

Type 498 is of special importance as five of the Lachish ostraca, Nos. II, VI, VII, VIII and XVIII, were written on its fragments. The jar was among more than a score of broken vessels found in the guardroom; their rims showed some variety, and it was not clear whether, like type 498, they all had handles. The ware is pink, buff or grey with a fair proportion of grits, it is fired medium to hard, and is similar to that of jars in Class S.7.

Class S.8 was predominant in the guardroom of Level II, and such vessels may therefore be assigned to the first decades of the sixth century B.C.

Comparable forms are published from Tell en-Naṣbeh (TN II, Pl. 26: 427–429, and Megiddo (M. I, Pl. 11: 54), Strata IV–I, but they are not numerous.

Storage Jars with Two or Four Handles

Class	Types
S.9	491, 547, 553, 555

Hole-mouth jars with high domed shoulder, flat ribbed rim, extremely small
flat ring base

Only the type specimen 491 was complete, so that the classification of the other forms was made on the strength of the rim alone, which is in itself distinctive. The complete jar came from the bench against the east palace wall, and another example belonged to the contemporary group on the plastered court 1061 (Pls. 17: 5 and 23: 3). The remaining fragment came from the dwelling 505.

The incomplete forms agree in the matter of ware, for all in the class are buff, brown or red, often with a grey core and some grits. Only one fragment is in a certain Level II context, and others come from the surface area close to the north and west walls of the palace.

No close comparisons have been traced, but the distribution does show that Classes S.8 and S.9 are contemporary and should belong to the early sixth century B.C.

Class	Types
S.10	490, 492 (Pl. 78: 13), 499, 501, 502, 503

Hole-mouth jars, with handles attached on or just below a plain or ribbed
flanged rim. Flat ring base

The large jars with two or four handles set on or just below a wide flanged mouth seem to begin with types 490 and 499 in tell Level III. Their main characteristics are a diminutive flat ring base, a plain rim, which becomes ribbed later, with two or more slight ridges on the upper part of the body between the handles. There is sometimes a double ridge ribbing on the handles.

A few fragments were found in Level II, the Bastion area, the Residency pits and the Great Shaft. Other fragments of types 501–503 would seem to belong to Level III.

The ware is pink or brown with some grits, fired hard, and on a few examples there is a buff or greenish slip.

Possible parallels were found at Tell en-Naṣbeh (TN II, Pl. 19: 323–325) and three intact examples came from Tell Beit Mirsim, Stratum A. The form appears to be mainly seventh century extending into the sixth century B.C. Wampler suggests that "ring bases for zirs . . . do not begin before 600 B.C." (TN II, p. 4, § 12, cf. S. 95 and 122). The occurrence of nearly complete jars in tell Level III, destroyed in 700 B.C., would therefore be very early in the series.

	B.C.
499 Tell Beit Mirsim (AASOR XXI–XXII, Pl. 13: 1, 2, 4) Stratum A	9th–7th cent.

Cylindrical Jars

The term "cylindrical jar" is adopted from J. C. Wampler's classification in TN II, pp. 11–12.

The writer distinguishes two varieties in the class, the first with a plain flanged rim protruding beyond the sides of the jar, the second with a corrugated rim. Wampler places both varieties, which are far more common at Tell en-Naṣbeh than at Tell ed-Duweir, in the seventh century or slightly earlier; at his site they were of frequent occurrence in the sixth century, but are a rarity by the end of the fifth century B.C.

Though the evidence at Duweir would not support a date any earlier than the eighth century for the introduction of these forms, it does suggest that Class S.12 continued in use into the sixth century, while S.11 did not survive the burning of city Level III.

Lamon and Shipton (M. I, p. 166, § 40) find prototypes for the form in Stratum V (1050–1000 B.C.), but examples of the jars in later levels are not numerous (see jars 53–57), for the commonest form in Stratum III, type 55, should perhaps be compared to the *zirs* in Class S.13.

Albright discusses the jars in AASOR XII, § 103, and quotes evidence from Tell Jemmeh (Gerar, Pl. LII: 31g and 31k), placing them in the ninth to seventh centuries, but some of the examples of type 31g, at least, are known to be in unreliable context (Gerar, p. 5 and Pl. LXX).

Grant and Wright (AS V, p. 143) state that almost every house at 'Ain Shems contained "hole-mouth" jars during the occupation of Stratum IIc, but the form was not common before that period, though it does occur. The shape was, no doubt, for domestic or industrial use, and Albright found two examples with the dyeing-plant at Tell Beit Mirsim (AASOR XII, Pl. 33: 3 and Pl. 52: 8), which he dates to the end of the eighth century B.C.

O. R. Sellers (Beth-zur, p. 39) reports that fragments of about a hundred hole-mouth jars were found around locus 151, his EI II stratum, with a layer of burning between it and the Hellenistic debris above. From the associated forms shown in Fig. 32, the period should be contemporary with city Level III at Duweir.

As cylindrical jars are rarely found in tombs, and as Level IV is unexcavated, they may predate the occupation of city Level III, but they continued into Level II and therefore appear to cover the eighth to seventh centuries at least. One cylindrical vessel without handles was found in the Adoni Nur tomb at 'Amman (APEF VI, type 93), which is dated *c.* 650 B.C., and the rim best compares with those of jars in Class S.8.

Class	Types
S.11	391 (Pl. 78: 14), 545, 548, 554

Jars with plain flanged rim and rounded base

The complete cylindrical jar 391 was set in the floor of a white plastered area, J.10: 1014; as fragments of type 484 and two stamped handles were found with it, the group should be attributed to Level III. The fragment of a similar jar type 548 came from the street in use during the occupation of Level III. Type 554, part of a much larger vessel, was found in the cave 6003–4, which has been equated with Level III on other evidence. The only fragment from a locality of uncertain date is type 545 from the north wall of the palace.

The ware is coarse pink, brown or buff, with a good proportion of grits, medium fired. Type 391 seems to have had a buff slip. The walls and rims of the jars are thick and heavy, in marked contrast to the jars in Class S.8.

For the reasons stated in the general note on cylindrical jars, the jars in Class S.11 are confined to Level III, *c.* 700 B.C., at Tell ed-Duweir, but comparisons from other sites would admit a longer history.

		B.C.
391	Tell en-Naṣbeh (TN II, Pl. 26: 421) Ci.363, AB16, I, x 25	700–500
391	'Ain Shems (AS IV, Pl. LXV: 27) Rm. 208, Stratum IIc	825–586
391	Tell Beit Mirsim (AASOR XII, Pls. 33: 3 and 52:8) Stratum A	9th–7th cent.
554	Samaria (SS III, Fig. 6: 20) Period IV	800–

Class	Types
S.12	392, 546, 549, 649, 550, 551

Jars with flanged and ribbed rim, and round base

Like Class S.11 these jars mostly occur in city Levels III and II. They broadly resemble the previous class in form and ware, and the chief difference is in the corrugation of the upper surface of the rim.

Besides the comparisons listed below, a form illustrated in Megiddo I (Pl. 11: 57) belonged to Strata IV–I (1000–350 B.C.).

		B.C.
546	'Ain Shems (AS IV, Pl. LXV: 31) Rm. 300 (1933), Stratum IIc	825–586
546	Tell en-Naṣbeh (TN II, Pl. 23: 384) X12X, x 42	7th–6th cent.

318

		B.C.
549	Tell Beit Mirsim (AASOR XII, Pl. 52: 1) Stratum A	9th–7th cent.
549	„ „ „ („ „ Pl. 52: 6) „	„ „
550	Tell en-Naṣbeh (TN II, Pl. 66: 1492 and p. 40, § 60) Dump from AF19X, x 2, "information limited"	

Miscellaneous Storage Jars

Class	Types
S.13	487, 466, 552, 557, 506, 505, 508, 504, 696(?), 697(?)

The only jar recovered from Tell ed-Duweir, comparable to Wampler's first main division of *zirs*, belongs to the last group of bent-up rims on high necks, with handles attached (TN II, p. 4, § 9) ascribed mainly to the period 700–500 B.C. Broken, but eventually repaired, type 487 lay in the debris of burning and destruction close against the outer face of the northern revetment.

One complete form (type 466), two fragments with the same rim section, and the analogous type 557, can be compared to Wampler's second main class of *zirs*, which were "numerous and characteristic" between 750 and 450 B.C. (TN II, p. 4, § 10). Three out of four examples from Duweir were apparently in a post-exilic context.

Grant and Wright note the development of similar jars in Stratum IIc at 'Ain Shems (AS V, p. 144). A fragment of rim from Megiddo Strata IV–I was especially common in Stratum III (M. I, Pl. 11: 55).

The jars provided with two heavy loop handles rising vertically from the shoulder are rarely found complete. Exclusive to Stratum I at Megiddo (M. I, p. 167, § 44), associated with Stratum II at Tell Abu Hawam (QDAP II, p. 50), and recovered from pits of A building level at Tell Jemmeh, these forms appear to be missing from Tell en-Naṣbeh and 'Ain Shems. Type 506 is a characteristic handle, of which there were a few examples in surface areas.

Types 504, and possibly 508, are similar neck and rim profiles to those jars which are impressed with the so-called "Rhodian" stamps on the handles.[1] For drawings of the profiles of handles on which stamps are found, see Pl. 52; the impressions are photographed on Pl. 53.

		B.C.
466	'Ain Shems (AS IV, Pl. LXV: 5) Ci.25, Stratum IIc	825–586
466	Tell en-Naṣbeh (TN II, Pl. 5: 71) X13, E. of R.347, x 20	750–450
504	Tell el-Fara (CPP 48 O) 387 ft.	
505	Tell en-Naṣbeh (TN II, p. 10, Pl. 21: 352) T. 15, x 1	2nd cent.-?
506	Tell Muteselim (M. I, Pl. 12: 63, 64) Stratum I	600–350
506	'Athlit (QDAP II, p. 50 and Fig. 4f)	LI–Hellenistic
506	Tell Abu Hawam (QDAP III, Pl. XXIII: 12–13) Stratum II	6th–4th cent.
506	Tell Jemmeh (Gerar, Pl. LIV: 43$^{r, s, t}$) CV 194, BCC 197, Level XVIa, BO 201, BN 202, "A" building	c. 650–500
508	Tell el-Fara (CPP 48 N) 382, 385, 390 ft.	
552	Tell en-Naṣbeh (TN II, Pl. 26: 435 and p. 12, § 60) X12X, x 5	700–500
552	Samaria (SS III, Fig. 6: 24) Period IV	800–
696	Tell Jemmeh (Gerar, Pl. LVI: 47k) ABB 200	c. 600
697	Tell el-Fara (CPP 47 Q)	

---

[1] See "Standard Pottery Containers of the Ancient Greek World" by V. G. Grace, in *Hesperia* Supplement VIII, American School of Classical Studies at Athens, 1949.

JUGS OR JARS WITH SPOUTS AND/OR STRAINERS

(Abbrev. JS)

Locus	Types									Total
	356	359*	360	361	362	363*	364*	367*	373	
114	—	—	—	—	—	—	—	1	—	1
106	—	—	1	—	—	—	—	—	—	1
Houses III	—	—	—	—	—	—	—	—	4	4
1002										
layers 1–5	—	—	—	1	—	—	1	—	—	2
layers 6–10	—	1	—	—	1	—	—	—	—	2
224	—	—	—	—	—	1	—	—	—	1
4005 (early)	—	—	—	—	—	—	1	—	—	1
116	1	—	—	—	—	—	—	—	—	1
120 (Burials)	—	—	—	—	—	—	1	—	—	1
521	—	—	—	—	—	—	1	—	—	1
TOTAL	1	1	1	1	1	1	4	1	4	15

* Pl. 74: 26; Pl. 36: 67; Pl. 72: 9 and Pl. 74: 27; Pl. 76: 28

Jugs or jars with spouts and/or strainers have a functional use which has not yet been clearly explained. The earliest kind represented at Tell ed-Duweir seems to be the burnished jugs 362, 363 and 364, derived from the side-spouted strainer jugs, often decorated with painted designs, which became popular at the time of the Philistine invasion, soon after 1200 B.C. That the jugs were filled through the spout affixed to the side is indicated by type 362, for the perforated top could not be used for the purpose, though a thin liquid could be sprinkled from it. The spout was apparently left open so that some kind of sediment could be removed easily, for it would hardly be practical (assuming that the strainer were necessary) to pour the concoction through the narrow neck and clean out the vessel afterwards. Alternatively these jars were well adapted to serve as water sprinklers.

Fragments of strainer-spouted jugs from Tell Jemmeh (Gerar, Pl. LVIII, class 67, and p. 22) are found between levels 182–189, with a later example at 194 feet. They follow on from the cessation of Philistine painted sherds, and are mainly grouped in the tenth and first part of the ninth century B.C. (see AJA, 1939, p. 460). The examples from the tombs at Duweir therefore represent the end of the series. Types 359 and 361 (with 364) have ridged necks characteristic of Class J.8, which are largely confined to the central layers of Tomb 1002 and to Tomb 106. Albright has remarked on the Stratum A₂ context of a strainer jug, which is like type 361 (AASOR XII, p. 87, § 120).

Lamon and Shipton (M. I, p. 162, § 16) have noted a country-wide distribution of strainer jugs, though the writer would suggest that the form was possibly more popular in coastal and southern sites, due to Philistine affinities, than in Judah. At 'Ain Shems, for instance, one incomplete example was found in a Stratum II context, 1000–586 B.C. (AS IV, Pl. LXV: 36). At Tell en-Naṣbeh four vessels were found in Tombs 54, 32 and 5, groups which are said to cover the tenth to seventh centuries. At Megiddo the major phase of jug types 75–77 falls in Stratum III, an argument which might be used to support an earlier date than that proposed by Lamon and Shipton for the destruction of Stratum III; alternatively, such jugs may have a longer history in the north.

Other discussions on strainer spouts are to be found in APEF II, pp. 56 f.; AASOR XII, pp. 67, 73, 87; MT, p. 159 and TN II, p. 18, § 21. Owing to the incomplete nature of these forms, which often lack neck, rim and handle, only two close comparisons are offered.

		B.C.
361	Tell Beit Mirsim (AASOR XII, Pl. 70: 13) SN 913 SE 13A–6 Stratum A₂	8th–7th cent.
363	Tell en-Naṣbeh (TN II, Pl. 35: 621) T.32, S. strip, x 150	10th–9th cent.

Jars with two or three handles from the body to the neck, and a pierced funnel spout joined to the rim, are represented at Tell ed-Duweir by types 356, 360 and 373.

An early development of the form would seem to be type 356, made of somewhat heavy pink ware. Two possible parallels from Tell Jemmeh (Gerar, Pl. LV: 44 f. from EF 185, and 44g from GK 183), and a rather similar vessel from Tell Ḥesi (TH, Pl. IX: 190 at 314 ft., NE. City VI) have smooth unribbed handles, like type 356.

Comparing the jars from Megiddo (M. I, Pl. 12: 61–62 and Pl. 50) with those from Tell Beit Mirsim, Albright has noted that the jars from his site are typologically later. Early tendencies include the unpierced spout which is lower than the rim and the unridged handles (AASOR XII, p. 80, § 106; XXI–XXII, p. 146, § 148), and these features are characteristic of the specimens assigned to Strata III–II at Megiddo (780–600 B.C.).

On the other hand, the vessels from Duweir, 'Ain Shems and Judeideh—like those from Tell Beit Mirsim—are later in development, and are associated with a period of destruction. The four vessels of type 373 came from two rooms south of the citadel, one of which is only tentatively attributed to Level III.

G. A. Honeyman (PEQ 1939, p. 79) identifies the jars illustrated in AASOR XII, Pl. 54: 1–3 with the Biblical term 'asuk (II Kings IV: 2), but the form does not seem very suitable as an oil container. The type example from Duweir was evidently suspended, on occasion, for marks of thin string webbing are visible. A practical use for these jars would be as water sprinklers, to keep down the dust on the mud floors of the houses.

		B.C.
373	Tell Beit Mirsim (AASOR XII, Pl. 54: 1; XXI–XXII, Pl. 15: 17) Stratum A	900–587
373	Tell Judeideh (BM, Pl. 49: 3 and p. 102) Stratum II	Jewish period
373	'Ain Shems (AS IV, Pl. LXVII: 12 and AS V, p. 144) Ci.25, Stratum IIc	825–586
373	Tell en-Naṣbeh (TN II, Pl. 30: 527 and p. 14, §§ 73–77) Latter half of main period	1000–600
373	Jericho (SW, p. 137. Fig. 144)	c. 870–700

MISCELLANEOUS

(Abbrev. Misc.)

The types listed below are not classified in the foregoing pages; for further descriptions see Pls. 79-105 and Parts II and III.

Type No.	Locus	Remarks	Plate No.
10	217	Bowl. Other examples in Q.16: 11, R.15: 14	76: 26
27	L.15: 46	Bowl	
30	H.17: 1072	Bowl. Other examples in M.14: 44, L. 14: 45	
87	525	Footbath? Cf. types 585, 680	76: 17
110	4005	Bowl. See Handles, p. 266	73: 26
111	P.12: 101(2)	Bowl. See Handles, p. 266. Other examples in 217(3)	76: 25
112	1002 layers 11–13	Bowl. See Handles, p. 266	74: 6
113	100	Bowl. See Handles, p. 266	
114	M.12: 86	Bowl. See Handles, p. 266	
115	G.17: 1072	Round-bottomed bowl, cf. L. II, Pl. XXXIX: 66, from which the form is possibly derived. Other examples in H.17: 1087, G.17: 1095 and E/F.18: N. See also Handles, p. 266	77: 18
116	L.13: 1062	"Double" bowl. Cf. L. II, Pl. XLIV: 179-183. Common in the Fosse Temple, Structure III, c. 1200 B.C. Occasional Iron Age examples in use during the occupation of Level III	77: 6
117	120	Bowl without flare, three stump feet. See type 119	76: 4
118	521	Irregularly hand-burnished bowl (or lid?) with three loop feet. Cf. Hama, p. 76, Fig. 118, Period II (1075–925?) G VIII 264	72: 4

Type No.	Locus	Remarks	Plate No.
119	218	Bowl without flare. Three stump feet. Types 117 and 119 are uncommon, but they imitate stone prototypes	
124	H.15: 1003	Great incurving bowl with eight loop handles, from burnt filling of room. See Handles, p. 266	
125	J.15: 1018	Incurving bowl	77: 7
127	106	Bowl. Another example in R.15: 13	75: 13
129	109	Incurving bowl	76: 18
130	Q.12: 102	Bowl. Other examples in 4006, R.16: 10, R.15: 14, S.16: 19	77: 22
204	217	Jug. See Handles, p. 266	
212	4035(8)	Jug, slight ribbing. See Handles, p. 266	76: 34
216	4035	Jug, slight ribbing. See Handles, p. 266	76: 35
223	1002 layers 1–5	Jug with ridged neck, close to Class J.7	
272	220	Jug. See Handles, p. 266	
306	215	Dipper with ribbed body. See Handles, p. 267	
307	219	Dipper	
308	116	Dipper with perforations in base	
316	518	Dipper with roll rim and loop handle to neck	
333	1002 layers 6–10	Jug with round base	
334	196	Jug with round base. See type 325 in Class D.6b	
335	521	Jug with round base and ridged neck	72: 8
350	H.14: 1004	White Painted V jug (GSCE IV, Pt. 2, p. 425) c. 600 B.C.	36: 66
352	4035(2)	Jug, ribbed body, handle missing	76: 36
354	230	Jug	
355	J.17: 1041	Dipper with basket handle and spout, see type 358. Cf. APEF II, Pl. XXIV: 7, Stratum IIB, 10th–8th cent.	77: 8
357	107	Juglet with pinched mouth, loop handle and spout. Other examples in 116, 218	76: 14
358	120	Juglet with basket handle and spout, see type 355. Another example in 6024	76: 15
365	100	Dipper with basket handle	
366	106	Miniature flask. Another example in 117	
368	J.15: 1013	Twin dippers	36: 63
369	1002 layers 11–13	Vessel with four lug handles pierced horizontally	
370	218	Flask with pinched mouth	
371	152	Strainer with loop handle. Cf. AS IV, Pl. LXIV: 39, Stratum IIa? Another example in 4035	73: 9
372	1002 layers 1–5	Strainer, handmade	
374	G.17: 1072	Funnel	
375	M.14: 44	Funnel, loop handle missing	
376	Q.12: 104(2)	Unguentarium. Cf. bases of Class L.9–10, and Class J.8, types 277 and 278. Other examples in 217, 562, 1009(3), Q.16: 11, R.16: 10, R.15: 14, R.16: 15, 17, PQR.17	
377	219	Pot	
378	1002 layers 1–5	Pot, see type 584	
379	1002	Lamp with multiple spouts. Cf. AS II, Pl. XLV: 18, 19 (for Albright's discussion see AASOR XXI–XXII, p. 8, § 4); BM, Pl. 66: 7, AASOR XII, Pl. 23: 3; AS V, p. 142	
380	120	Brazier or censer. See PEQ, Oct. 1940, Pl. X, Fig. 1. Cf. SW, Pl. 38: D, 7	76: 16
381	1002 layers 11–13	Brazier or censer, see type 380	

Type No.	Locus	Remarks	Plate No.
382	1009(3)	Unguentarium. Cf. bases of Class L.9–10 and Class J.8, types 277–278. Other examples in M.15: 74 and PQR.17: 254m.	76: 31
383	106	Bottle, pointed base. Cf. QDAP XI, p. 75; QDAP XIII, p. 98: 31–37	
384	106	Bottle, pointed base, see type 383	
385	G.17: 1094	Flask	77: 13
386	J.17: 1040	Pot	77: 5
387	H.17: 1089	Flared cup	
388	106	Pot	
389	6024	Brazier	72: 21
390	K.14: Res. Rm. A–B	Drainpipe	23: 1
393	6024	Pot	72: 19
394	6024	Pot. Another example in L.12: Res. Rm. X	72: 18
404	1007	Jar with loop handles. Cf. BM, Pl. 58: 12	
406	4002	Pot with two handles missing	73: 20
407	R.15: 13	Pot with two handles	
409	L.13: 80	Pot with two handles	77: 29
497	L.13: 1066	Jar with two handles. Base and one handle missing. Cf. CPP 47 W	78: 17
500	J.12/13: Pal. W. wall	Jar neck. See Class B.1.	
556	H.17: 1072	Jar fragment. Another example in J. 14: Pal. S. wall	
578	G.18: 29, 31	Two fragments of the same vessel	
579	K.12: Res. U	Bowl fragment	
580	534	Bowl. Other examples in G.18: 31, K.12: Res. U	
582	P.17: 251 m.	Incurving bowl. Traces black glaze	
583	Q.16: 11	Incurving bowl	
584	J.17: 1042	Pot fragment, see type 378. Cf. AASOR XII, Pl. 67: 20–26	
585	K.12: Res. U	Footbath? See types 87 and 680	
587	H.18: 1081	Jar fragment	
610	F.18: L	Bowl. Another fragment of the same bowl in E.18: Q; another example in J.12/13: Pal. W. wall	
611	120	Bowl fragment	
618	J.16	Bowl fragment	
619	J.12/13: Pal. W. wall	Bowl fragment	
658	H.17: 1087	Lamp. Traces mat glaze. Cf. CPP 91 W. Other examples in Q.12 and Q.16: 12	
661	J.14: Pal. S. wall	Lamp, incomplete. Cf. CPP 91 Fo	
667	L.12: Pal. N. wall	Jug	
668	6024	Jug. Another example in L.14: 59	
669	218	Dipper with ridged neck, round base. Another example in 120	
670	Q.16: 11	Lagynos. Cf. QDAP XI, p. 72: 39A and p. 77	
672	K.12: Res. O	Unguentarium. Other examples in K.13: Res. P, and PQR. 17: 251m., 249 m.	
673	Q.17: 254–253 m.	Unguentarium, decorated with red bands. Another example in PQR.17: 235 m.	
680	E.17: B	Footbath? Cf. types 87, 585. Other examples in H.17: 1087, E/F.18: D, F.18: A: G, E.18: Q	
681	K.15	Lid with ventilation holes, one loop handle	
682	H.17: 1090	Baking plate. Cf. TN II, Pl. 68: 1540–1546; M. I, Pls. 24: 26, 28: 104, 31: 152 and p. 168, 55; AS IV, Pl. XXXIX: 14–16; AS V, pp. 124, 132; SW, Pl. 36: A, 49. Other examples in H.15: 1010, J.15: 1032, G.18: 28, J.14: Res. E, J.12/13: Pal. W. wall. Fragments of these plates are uncommon at Tell ed-Duweir and are confined to tell rooms of Level III and later. The form as preserved is closest to M. I, Pl. 24: 26, which comes from Stratum III, 780–650 B.C. The occurrence of baking plates at Hielite Jericho (SW, Pl. 36: A, 49), destroyed in 700 B.C., confirms an eighth- to seventh-century date	
683	G.12	Stand or jar neck, incomplete	

NOTES ON THE DISTRIBUTION CHARTS

In the five charts which follow, forms which occur in rooms which may have been used during more than one level of occupation have been assigned to the earliest level in which they were found.

"Palace Walls" is a term which denotes the exposed open spaces around the citadel, and sherds under this heading are allocated to the appropriate level according to form, when stratigraphical evidence is lacking.

Sherds found on and near the roads G/H/J.17: 1072 and 1087 are not included in the Charts.

Bowls in Classes B.1–8 which are marked as from the Residency should find their true horizon in the underlying buildings of Levels V–IV.

In the Charts of Bowls and Lamps, the most common form has been drawn to represent each class, and its type number is underlined.

BOWLS

The following table records the distribution of bowl types (classes B.1–B.12 and additional type groups) by locus. Owing to the density of the original chart, only the clearly legible entries and the marginal totals are reproduced with certainty.

Locus	B.1 (85, 598, 606, 617, 620–625, 653, 654)	B.2 (22, 24, 28, 103, 104, 132, 133, 588–597, 604)	B.3 (26, 126, 128, 614–616)	B.4 (4, 6–8, 11–13, 14, 15, 17–21, 23, 25, 29, 53, 99–101, 105, 577)	B.5 (41–44, 55–58, 131, 586, 609)	B.6 (88, 89, 90–98)	B.7 (9, 37–40, 46–52, 54, 581, 599–602, 605, 607, 656)	B.8 (1–3, 558, 559, 561)	B.9 (5, 31–34, 106, 107, 167)	B.10 (35, 36, 61, 102, 108)	B.11 (59, 60, 62–64, 65–67, 80, 560, 562)	B.12 (16, 45, 569–576, 608)	69–74, 75–79, 81–84, 86, 603, 626–646	109, 120–123, 647, 652, 655, 657	68, 563, 565, 566	564, 567, 568	Totals
Solar Shrine													1		1		3
I — Houses I																	
G.12/13: 1–8															3		3
R/Q/S.15/16: 10–21													3	1	3	2	13
H.14: 23																	1
G.18: 25–33															5	1	10
M.14: 1076															1		2
Residency Pits															12	3	24
Residency and Walls													1	2	10	2	20
534															1	1	2
Great Shaft													1	2	1	1	11
II — Bastion	3												14	4	3	1	28
Houses II							1	7			2		7	1		2	21
109																	4
114																	2
Tomb 106					1	7	14		7	2	14	6	20				71
569														2			3
505							2				2	1	4	2	1	1	9
4006													1		1		2
III — Houses III	1		1	6	3	6	34	5	1	4	12	13	110	33	1		230
6003–4							1			1			1				3
526													1				3
7007										2			3				1
Palace Walls							1	1			2		1	5			12
Tomb 120 (Ossuary)							6						1				17
108													1				1
107							1	1			1	1	1	1	2	1	2
117												1		1		1	1
116												1					1
Tomb 1002																	
layers 1–5				4	1	5	12	2	2	2	1		2				31
layers 6–10				1	1	5	14	2	1	2	3	1		1			28
layers 11–13	1		1	7		6	10	1				1					27
6012							1										1
6020					1	2	4			1							10
IV? — Tomb 1004		1		3	2	13	15			3							37
Tomb 224				4						1							2
523				1	1	1	1										1
507				1													1
4005 (early)					3	1					1			1			9
Tomb 116		5		3		1	2						2				30
Tomb 218				9	6	5						1		1			12
Tomb 223	1			9	2	1											3
4010		1		1													3
4002	1				1												1
230			1														1
6006	1			1	1												5
V? — Tomb 521		3		4													6
Cave 6024		1	1	1	1						3		5				1
530		1									1		6				1
102		1									1		1				1
7013												1	1				
Palace Walls	13	6	2										21				21
TOTALS	24	21	7	62	24	54	125	21	12	20	48	29	182	51	40	11	731

325

DISTRIBUTION CHART OF COMMON POTTERY FORMS IN SUGGESTED CHRONOLOGICAL ORDER

SAUCER LAMPS

Classes	L.1-3 Types 140–144, 147	L.4-6 Types 145, 146, 148	L.7-8 Types 149, 150, 151	L.9-10 Types 152, 153	L.11 Types 659, 660	Totals
Locus						
Solar Shrine	—	—	—	1	—	1
I Houses I						
R/Q/S.15/16: 10–21	—	—	—	1	—	1
H.14:23	—	—	—	—	1	1
Residency Pits	—	—	3	1	3	7
Residency Walls	—	—	—	—	1	1
Bastion	—	—	2	4	—	6
II Houses II						
109	—	—	1	2	—	3
114	—	5	—	8	—	13
Tomb 106	10	18	45	90	—	163
7002	—	1	—	—	—	1
Houses III	5	3	11	3	—	22
546	—	—	1	—	—	1
558	—	—	1	—	—	1
529	—	—	—	1	—	1
7007	—	1	—	—	—	1
III Tomb 120 (Ossuary)	—	—	1	—	—	1
117 (")	—	—	—	2	—	2
Tomb 1002						
layers 1–5	16	12	5	4	—	37
layers 6–10	—	23	—	1	—	24
layers 11–13	1	37	2	—	—	40
6011	1	—	—	—	—	1
IV? Tomb 1004	4	—	—	—	—	4
Tomb 224	27	6	—	—	—	33
Tomb 116	4	2	—	—	—	6
Tomb 218	3	2	—	—	—	5
Tomb 120 (Burials)	—	1	—	—	—	1
117 (")	1	1	—	—	—	2
219	—	1	—	—	—	1
Tomb 223	3	—	2	—	—	5
4002	1	1	—	—	—	2
230	1	1	—	—	—	2
6006	—	1	—	—	—	1
V? Tomb 521	4	—	—	—	—	4
118	1	—	—	—	—	1
7008	1	—	—	—	—	1

DISTRIBUTION CHART OF COMMON POTTERY FORMS IN SUGGESTED CHRONOLOGICAL ORDER

CLASSES	J.1 Ridged body, Types 221, 222	J.2 Flat base, round mouth, Types 197, 200–203, 205–209, 213	J.3 Flat base, pinched mouth, Types 210, 211, 214, 215, 217–219, 224–228	J.4 Round base, plain neck, Types 165, 166, 168–172, 174–184, 187, 188	J.5 Round base, moulded rim, Types 167, 173, 185, 186, 189–192, 195, 196	J.6 Flat base, narrow neck, Types 220, 229–237, 239–242, 244, 245, 247, 251, 259	J.7 a Flat base, handle to ridged neck, Types 250, 252, 253, 256–258, 260–263, 265–271	J.7 b Flat base, handle to rim, Types 238, 243, 246, 248, 249, 353, 666	J.8 Decanters, handle to ridged neck, Types 254, 255, 264, 273–281, 665, 676	J.9 Convex base, flared neck, Types 193, 194, 198, 199	TOTALS
JUGS — Locus											
I											
Solar Shrine	—	—	—	—	—	—	—	—	1	—	1
Houses I											
G.12/13:1–8	—	—	—	—	—	—	—	—	1	—	1
R/Q/S.15/16:10–21	—	—	—	1	—	—	—	—	1	—	2
G.18:25–33	—	—	—	—	—	—	—	—	1	—	1
Residency Pits	—	—	—	—	—	—	—	3	1	—	4
Great Shaft	—	—	—	—	—	—	—	—	2	—	2
II											
Bastion	—	—	—	—	—	—	1	1	6	—	8
Houses II	—	—	—	—	—	—	—	2	8	—	10
109	—	—	—	—	—	1	—	2	5	—	8
114	—	—	—	—	—	—	—	—	4	—	4
Tomb 106	—	4	6	15	2	3	6	3	25	9	73
569	—	—	—	—	—	—	—	—	1	—	1
505	—	—	—	—	—	—	—	—	1	—	1
4006	—	2	—	—	—	—	—	—	—	—	2
7002	—	—	—	—	—	—	—	—	—	1	1
1010	—	—	—	—	—	—	—	—	—	—	—
III											
Houses III	—	—	—	16	9	4	6	—	14	—	49
Palace Walls	—	—	—	—	—	—	1	—	—	—	1
Tomb 120 (Ossuary)	—	—	—	10	2	—	—	—	—	—	12
108	—	—	1	1	—	—	—	—	—	—	2
107	—	—	—	1	—	1	—	—	—	—	2
Tomb 1002 layers 1–5	—	3	5	30	16	4	13	—	—	—	71
layers 6–10	—	9	4	38	16	5	16	—	—	—	88
layers 11–13	—	9	8	45	29	4	15	—	—	—	111
519	—	—	—	—	1	—	—	—	—	—	1
6020	—	—	—	3	1	—	—	—	1	—	5
IV?											
Tomb 1004	—	7	2	22	4	1	—	—	—	—	36
Tomb 224	—	—	—	—	—	1	—	—	—	—	1
507	—	2	—	4	—	—	—	—	—	—	6
562	—	6	—	4	1	1	—	—	—	—	12
Tomb 116	1	3	—	11	1	1	—	—	—	—	18
Tomb 218	—	—	—	1	—	—	—	—	—	—	1
219	—	1	—	2	—	1	—	—	—	—	4
Tomb 223	1	1	1	—	—	—	—	—	—	—	2
4010	—	—	—	1	—	1	—	—	—	—	2
V?											
Tomb 521	—	1	1	1	—	—	—	—	—	—	2
Cave 6024	—	—	—	3	—	—	—	—	—	—	3
TOTALS	2	47	29	207	85	28	58	10	72	10	548

DISTRIBUTION CHART OF COMMON POTTERY FORMS IN SUGGESTED CHRONOLOGICAL ORDER

CLASSES	D.1 a (288–290, 298)	D.1 b (300, 302)	D.2 a (287, 289, 299)	D.2 b (303, 305, 671)	D.3 (296, 285)	D.4 a (286, 293–295, 297)	D.4 b (283)	D.5 a (282, 284, 291)	D.5 b (292)	TOTALS	D.6a Grey Polished (332)	D.6a Bichrome III (329)	D.6a Black-on-Red III (330, 336–339, 339A)	D.6b Imitation (325, 331, 410, 411)	TOTALS	D.7 a (328, 317, 318, 326, 327, 328)	D.7 b (314, 315, 324)	D.7 (322)	D.8 (309)	D.8 (310–313, 319–321, 323)	TOTALS	D.9 Miscellaneous (340–349, 351, 664)
Locus																						
4005 (late)																						1
Solar Shrine									3	3												
I Houses I																						
R/Q/S.15/16: 10–21																						1
H.14: 23																						2
G.18: 25–33																						1
Residency																						1
Bastion																						
II Houses II							1		2	3									1		1	
109									2	2						2				1	3	
114									4	4										3	3	
Tomb 106				1		3	37	1	10	51				3	3				47	38	85	
7002								1		1												
III Houses III / 526			1	1		2	1	9	2	16									23	11	34	
558																			2		2	
503					3					3			3	1	4					1	1	
Tomb 120 (Ossuary)			1			1	5	2		9									1	2	3	
107																						
117																						
Tomb 1002 layers 1–5			4	2		1	8	1		12								4	18	4	26	
layers 6–10		1		1		16	2	8		31							1	13	2	1	17	
layers 11–13		8				8	1	2		16						1		14	3	4	22	
IV? Tomb 1004			1		1	1				9						1		7			7	
Tomb 224		14		1		3				18		1	5		6	1		25			26	
531					1																1	
507		1			1											1					1	
4005 (early)			1		1					2				1	1	2					2	
Tomb 116	1	3	1		4					9						2		4			8	
Tomb 218	2	7	4		2		7			22	1		5		6	3	3	10			16	
Tomb 120 (Burials)		1			3					9			4		4	1	1	6			7	
108	1	1								1						1		1			1	
107	1	1								3								5			8	
117		1								1						3		3			4	
Tomb 223		4			3					8							2				2	
4010					4		1			6												
4002					1					1						1						
4027																						
4029					1					1							2					
4030					1					2												
230										3		1			1	1					1	
6006		2			1					3							4				4	
V? Tomb 521	1	2								2											1	
Cave 6024	1	2				10				13			1		1			2			5	
6023	1	1								1							2					
560	1									1							3				5	
TOTALS	9	48	12	6	26	49	65	24	24	263	1	2	18	5	26	20	16	94	104	68	302	6

CLASSES	STORAGE JARS	S.1 Plain neck, ovoid body *Types* 468, 473–477	S.2 Plain neck, pear-shaped body *Types* 469, 472, 509–511, 698?	S.3 Moulded rim, wasp-shaped body *Types* 488, 489, 530	S.4 Two Handles, Curved Shoulder, Ovoid Body *Types* 467, 470, 471, 478–481, 493–495, 512–514, 699? 700?	S.5 Collar neck *Types* 515–517, 520–527, 531–534, 536	S.6a Tall neck *Types* 485, 486, 507, 528, 529, 535	S.6b Short neck *Types* 496, 518, 519	S.7a Plain neck *Type* 484	S.7b Moulded rim *Types* 482, 483	S.8 Rounded base *Types* 465, 498, 537–544	S.9 Ribbed rim, ring base *Types* 491, 547, 553, 555	S.10 Plain or flanged rim, ring base *Types* 490, 492, 499; Rims only *Types* 501–503	S.11 Plain flanged rim *Types* 391, 545, 548, 554	S.12 Ribbed flanged rim *Types* 392, 546, 549, 550, 551	S.13 Miscellaneous *Types* 466, 487, 504–506, 508, 552, 557, 696? 697?	TOTALS
Locus Solar Shrine											1						1
I Houses I — G.12/13: 1–8						1	1						1				3
R/Q/S.15/16: 10–21			2		1	5	1	1			2	1	4	1	1		20
G.18: 25–33			1			4	2				1					2	10
Residency Pits			3	5		8	1		2		2		1			5	27
Residency and Walls			1	14	3	2	9	2	2		2	2			1	4	42
534						5											5
Great Shaft											1		3			2	6
II Bastion			4	1	4				4		22		2		7	3	47
Houses II		1	3		8		2	1		1	1	1				1	22
Tomb 106										1							1
505			1					1				1			1		4
7002													1				1
III Houses III		5	7	2	9		1		61	4	2	2	23	2	8	1	127
6003–4					1				2								3
529														1			1
Palace Walls						6								1		1	8
Tomb 120 (Ossuary)			1			1							2	1			5
Tomb 1002 — layers 1–5					1												1
layers 6–10		1															1
layers 11–13																	—
6011		9			1												10
IV? Tomb 1004		1															1
Tomb 224		4															4
507		1															1
4005		2															2
Tomb 116		2															2
Tomb 218		2															2
Tomb 223		7			1												8
4010		1															1
4002		1															1
230		1			1												2
6006		2															2
V? Tomb 521		3			1												4
Cave 6024		2			1												3
7013											1						1
TOTAL		45	23	22	33	32	18	5	71	7	35	8	37	6	18	19	379

B 2424

329

T t

CONSOLIDATED CHART OF COMMON POTTERY FORMS

LOCUS	Type	1	2	3	4	5	6	7	8	9	10	11	12	13	14
Houses I	Bowls	5	2		2		1	4	2			11	2	16	44
	Lamps							3		1	2	5			
	Jugs				1			3	7						
	Dippers					3				5					
Bastion	Bowls	3										2	1	18	4
	Lamps								2	1		3			
	Jugs						1	1	6						
	Dippers				1	2									
Houses II	Bowls						1	1	7			2		8	2
	Lamps							1		2					
	Jugs							2	8						
	Dippers					2			1						
Tomb 106	Bowls				1			7	14		7	2	14	6	20
	Lamps			10				18	12	33	62	28			
	Jugs		4	6	15	2		3	9	25	9				
	Dippers		1		40	10		3	85						
Houses III	Bowls	1		1	6	3	6	34	5	1	4	12	13	143	1
	Lamps	2	3				3	5	6	3					
	Jugs		2		16	9	4	6	14						
	Dippers				3	11			34						
Tomb 120	Bowls				2			6	1			2		6	
	Lamps				1	1		1							
	Jugs				10	2									
	Dippers	2	1	3	10	2	4	4							
Tomb 1002 Layers 1-5	Bowls				4	1	5	12	2	2	2	1		2	
	Lamps		1	15	3		9	3			4				
	Jugs		3	5	30	16	4	13							
	Dippers		2		9	1		4	22						
Tomb 1002 Layers 6-10	Bowls						1	1	5	14	2	2	3		
	Lamps							23							
	Jugs		9	4	38	16	5	16							
	Dippers	1	4		18	8		14	3						
Tomb 1002 Layers 11-13	Bowls				1		7	1	6	10	1	1			
	Lamps							7	30	2	15				
	Jugs		9	8	45	29	4	15	1						
	Dippers	1	1	3	9	2	3	15	7						
Tomb 1004	Bowls						3		2	4		1			
	Lamps		3	1											
	Jugs				3	2									
	Dippers	8			1				7						
Tomb 224	Bowls				4	2	13	15				3			
	Lamps		26	1	1	2	3								
	Jugs		7	2	22	4	1								
	Dippers	14		1	3		6	26							
Tomb 116	Bowls				1	3	3	1							
	Lamps	1		3	3	1	1								
	Jugs		6		4	1	1								
	Dippers	4		4				7	1						
Tomb 218	Bowls		5	1	9	6	5	2						2	
	Lamps	2	1				2								
	Jugs	1	3	1	11	1	1								
	Dippers	9	4	2	7		6	16							
Tomb 223	Bowls					9	2	1							
	Lamps	1	1	1				2							
	Jugs	1			1	1									
	Dippers	4		3	1		2								
Tomb 521	Bowls				4	1									
	Lamps	4													
	Jugs		1		1										
	Dippers	2				1									
Cave 6024	Bowls	1	3	1	1										
	Jugs			1	1		1	1							
	Dippers	3			10		1	1	5						

KEY: Bowls (black), Lamps (horizontal lines), Jugs (diagonal hatch), Dippers (dotted)

CHAPTER 10

EARLY HEBREW INSCRIPTIONS

By DAVID DIRINGER, D.LITT.

OSTRACA

ALL clear signs on the ostraca are transcribed in modern Hebrew letters and the text is translated into English when the readings are generally agreed. Less distinct letters, inferred from existing traces, are marked above by one or two lines, to denote a decreasing degree of probability in the reading of the sign.

Effaced, illegible or otherwise doubtful letters which can be inferred from the context are put in brackets when agreement has been reached. In other instances the missing signs, when few, are indicated by dashes corresponding to the probable number of letters. Controversial cases are generally omitted, except in a few instances which are discussed in the footnotes.

Ostraca XIX–XXI, found in 1938, could not be included in *Lachish I*. They were mentioned by C. H. Inge in PEQ, 1938, p. 254, and by W. F. Albright in BASOR 73, p. 16. H. Torczyner included them in his Hebrew edition of the Lachish ostraca. Owing to war-time conditions, neither the members of the Wellcome-Marston Expedition nor the present writer knew of the publication of these three documents, or of the references in BASOR 80 and 82. The article in PEQ, 1943, pp. 89–99, on the Ostraca XIX–XXI, is therefore written quite independently, and with a few exceptions its readings agree with those of Professors Torczyner, Ginsberg and Albright. See particularly D. Winton Thomas, in Essays and Studies.

The ink of the ostraca seems to be slowly fading away: as far as the present writer remembers, when he first examined the originals at the British Museum in March, 1939, some sherds appeared clearer, but this may only be his personal impression. However, there is no doubt that the photographs which have been published are much clearer than the originals, although the originals will always be useful to check the reading of particular signs.

Finally, it must be emphasised that the last word rests with philologists: nothing more can be done from the epigraphic standpoint, except perhaps, as mentioned, in the examination of such details as the *beth* in Ostracon II, line 5. The quintessence of expert opinion based on lively discussion over more than a decade is therefore presented as the standard reading in the following pages, which should be read in conjunction with the Bibliography on pp. 21–24.

LETTER I (OSTRACON)

Field No. 4022—B.M. 125701

TRANSLATION	TRANSLITERATION
1. **Gemaryáhū son of Hiṣṣilyáhū**	1. גמריהו . בן הצליהו ,
2. **Ya'azanyáhū son of Ṭobshillēm**	2. יאזניהו . בן טבשלם .
3. **Ḥagab son of Ya'azanyáhū**	3. חגב . בן . יאזניהו
4. **Mibṭaḥyáhū son of Yirmeyáhū**	4. מבטחיהו בן ירמיהו
5. **Mattanyáhū son of Neriyáhū**	5. מתניהו . בן . נריהו

LETTER II

Field No. 4023—B.M. 125702

TRANSLATION

1. To my lord Ya'ôsh: May *YHWH* let hear
2. my lord tidings of peace (well-being)
3. this very day, this very day! Who is thy servant
4. (but) a dog, that my lord remembered
5. his [s]ervant? May *YHWH* . . . .*
6. my [saying] something what thou dost not know!

TRANSLITERATION

1. אל אדני . יאוש ישמֹעֹ .
2. יהוה , את אדני . שֻׁמֹעֹת של
3. ם . עתֿ . כים עת כיםֿ מי . עבדֿ
4. ך . כלב . כי . זכרֿ . אדני . את .
5. וﬠ﬒בדה . יﬕבכר . יהוה . את . א
6. ﬖ ?]ﬗ דבר . אשר לא . ידעתה

LETTER III

Field No. 4024—PM 38.127

TRANSLATION

Obverse

1. Thy servant Hōsha'yáhū hath sent to
2. tell my lord Ya'ôsh: May
3. *YHWH* let hear my lord tidings of peace!
4. [And now:] [[*A.*: thou hast sent a letter]] . . open-eyed(?)
5. . . . . thy servant to the letter which
6. my lord hath sent to thy servant yesterday (and hath said) that
7. thy servant's heart is sick, since thou hast sent to thy serva-
8. nt and that my lord hath said: Thou dost not know it
9. read (a) letter. As *YHWH* liveth, no one has
10. ever tried to read to me a letter! And also
11. whatever letter may have come to me, I
12. have not read it and even . . . .
13. anything. And to thy servant it hath been told
14. saying: Down went the commander of the army
15. Kōniyáhū son of Elnathan to go
16. into Egypt. And

TRANSLITERATION

1. עﬓבדך . הושעיהו . שﬔלח . ל
2. הﬕגד .] ל﬒אדﬓﬔ י﬒אוש﬘ . ישמע .
3. יהוה .]את] אדﬓﬔ שמעת . שלם
4. ו﬒עת.] ש﬑ ----ר﬒ --- . הפקח
5. ----]. עין .] ע﬒בﬓדך . לספר . אשר .
6. שלﬖ . אדﬓ-- . לע﬒בﬓדך אמש . כי . לב
7. (ע﬐)בד﬐דך] . --- . מאז . שלחך . אל . עבד
8. ך . וכיאמר . אדﬓﬔ . לא . ידעתה .
9. ק﬑רא . ספ﬒רﬕ . חיהוה . אם . נסה . א
10. יﬖש . לק﬑ר﬒א לי ספר . לﬓצח . וגם .
11. כל . ספ﬒רﬕ אשר יבא . אליﬔ . אם .
12. קראתי . אתהﬕ --ר﬒ . אתנﬔ נﬕﬗ
13. -ל . מאוםﬓ-- . ו﬒עבדך . הגד .
14. לאמר . י﬒רד שר . הצבה .
15. כנﬔﬗ בן אלנתן לבא .
16. מﬖצרימה . ואﬓ-

---

* The reading *b*, although palaeographically probable and accepted by Torczyner and Dussaud, presents great difficulties in interpretation. Ginsberg has therefore suggested the reading 'ayin (this is now also accepted by Gordon, Albright, Hempel, De Vaux and others); if correct, the downstroke would be accidental. Reider suggested *n*, which is unlikely, as is also Torczyner's early reading of *z* (see also Cassuto).

Reverse

17. Ḥōdawyáhū son of Aḥiyáhū and

18. his men he sent to take . . . .

19. And as for the letter of Ṭōbyáhū servant of the king which came

20. to Shallum son of Yaddua' [[*A.*: through = the instrumentality of]] the prophet sayi-

21. ng: Beware! Thy ser[vant] hath sent it to my lord.

17. הודיהו בן אחיהו ו

18. אנשו שלח . לקחת . מֹ֯ה .

19. וספר . טביהו עבד . המלך . הבא

20. אל . שלם . בן ידע . מאת . הנבא . לאמ

21. ר . השמר . שלחה . עבו]ד[ך . אל . אדני .

LETTER IV

Field No. 4025—PM 38.128

TRANSLATION	TRANSLITERATION

Obverse

1. May *YHWH* let hear my lord this very day

2. tidings of good! And now, according to everything my lord hath sent (= written)

3. thus hath thy servant done. I have written on the door(?) according to all

4. that [my lord] hath sent to me. And concerning what my lord hath sent

5. about *BYTHRPD* (?), there is nobo-

6. dy there. And Semakhyáhū, him hath taken Shema'yáhū and

7. brought him up to the city, and thy servant . . .

8. ¹

1. ישמע . יהוה]. את אד]נֹ֯י עת כיֹם /

2. שמעת טב, ועת ככל אשר שלח אדנִ֯י .

3. כן . עשה ֿ עבדך].[כתבתי על הֿדלת ככל .

4. אשר שלחֿ ‒ ‒ ‒ ‒ לי . וכי . שלח אֿ

5. דני על . דבר . ביתֿ . הרפד . אין . שם ֿ. א

6. דֿם וסמֿכיהוֿ . לקחה . שמעיהו . וֿ

7. יעלהוֿ . העירה ועבדך . אֿי נֹ֯?

8. יֿ ‒ ‒ שלח . שמה . אֿ֯יֿה‒
   תֿ

Reverse

9. ¹

10. and will know that for the signals of Lachish we

11. are watching, according to all the indications which

12. my lord hath given, because we do not see (the signals of (?) Aze-

13. qah.

9. כי אם . בתסבתה ‒ בקר?

10. וידעֿ . כי . אל / משֿאת . לכֿשֿ . נחֿ

11. נוֿ . שמרם / ככֿל . האתת . אשֿר . נתן .

12. אדֿנֹ֯י . כי ֿ. לאֿ . נֿראֿה את . עֿז

13. קה .

---

¹ May rightly points out that "Lines 7–10 bristle with unsolved problems" both as concerns reading and interpretation. Albright is "convinced that a piece has been broken off the lower left-hand corner (which would be the upper left-hand corner of the reverse)". Also in May's opinion "Examination seems to substantiate this". I fully agree with this suggestion. Albright's latest tentative read-ing and translation (BASOR 97, p. 26) is as follows:

7. . . . *w'bdk'y*(!)*n*/*n*/ . . . And as for thy servant, I am
8. *y*[.]*šlḥ šmh m*(?)*y h*['] [*hy*(*w*)*m*] not sending thither anyone(?)
9. *ky'm btsbt hbqr* ['*šlḥ*] [today(?)] but in the course of the (com-ing) morning [I will send(?).]

Field No. 4026—B.M. 125703

<table>
<tr><td colspan="2" align="center">TRANSLATION</td><td align="center">TRANSLITERATION</td></tr>
</table>

	TRANSLATION	TRANSLITERATION
1.	May *YHWH* [let hear] my [lord]	ישמ֑ע יהוה]את . אד[נ֗י֗[.1
2.	[tidings of peace and good, this very	שמעת ֗. שלם֗ וטב]ועת . .2
3.	day, this very day !] Who is thy servant	כים . עת . כים[מ֗י . עבדך .3
4.	(but) a dog, that thou [hast sent to thy ser-	כלב ---]שלחת .[אל ֗. עבד .4
5.	vant the letters . . . .]?	-- את֑ -ס֗ ------- .5
6.	[Now] thy servant hath returned the let-	-- השב֗ . עבדך . הספר .6
7.	ters to my lord. May *YH*-	ם , אל . אדנ֗י . י֗]ראך[י .7
8.	*WH* let [see]	הו֗ - -֗. ------- .8
9.	*h*. What hath thy servant that he [could]	ה . מה . לעבדך . י- .9
10.	[[*A*.: benefit or injure]] the king?	טב֗ ? הו֑ . ירע . למ֗לך֑ .10
		חא

Field No. 4027—PM 38.129

	TRANSLATION	TRANSLITERATION
1.	To my lord Ya'ôsh. May *YHWH* let	אל אדנ֗י יאוש ֗. ירא֗ . יהוה ֗. א .1
2.	my lord see [[*A*.: this season in good health !]] Who is	ת ֗. א ֗ד ֗נ֗י אתהעתהזה . שלם מ֗י , .2
3.	thy servant (but) a dog, that my lord hath sent the [lett-	עבדך ֗. כלב֗ כי . שלח . אדנ֗ י֗ א[--?[.3
4.	er of the king and the letters of the prince]s, say-	ר המלך]ואת[ספרי֗ השר֗ --- .4
5.	ing : Read ! I pray thee(?) And behold, the words of the . . .	ר קרא נ֗ א֗]ו[הנה֗, דברי֗ . ה --- .5
6.	are not good, (liable?) to weaken (?) . . . . hands	א֑ טבם לרפת ידיך ---- .6
7.	. . . . . the hands [of the ?]	קט ידי הא֗ --- ה֗ ֗יך֗ ע֗ -- .7
8.	. . . . My lord, wilt thou not wri-	ב֗ ------- אדנ֗י הלא֗,תכ֗ .8
9.	te to . . . . why should ye do	תב א ------- ה תעשו ֗, .9
10.	thus [[*G*.: in Jerusalem]]	כזאת --- י֗-של֗מ֗ה-הל .10
11.	[king]	]מ֗[לך -----]ע֗]ש֗ו֗ - ה֗[-- .11
12.	. . . . As *YHWH* liveth, thy god	----- ֗. חי . יהוה אלה .12
13.	. . . . thy servant	יך - ------ קרא]עב֗ .13
14.	. . . . . read [the] letter	דך?]את[?הספ֗ר --- ה- .14
15.	to [thy] servant]	-------]נ֗ע֗ ב֗[.15

LETTER VII

Field No. 4028—B.M. 125715

TRANSLITERATION
Reverse

3. ‏– – – – ש– – – – –‏

4. ‏– – הו – – – – – – –‏

5. ‏בשלם‎ – – – – – – –‏

This ostracon is almost completely effaced. According to Torczyner's *Lachish I*, p. 124, "On the obverse are traces of about ten lines, and on the reverse about four lines are visible." However, on the obverse only a few letters here and there are partly legible, such as *sh* in l. 4, the letters *hw* in l. 5, the word *bshlm* in l. 6.
Interpretation of this document is hopeless.

LETTER VIII

Field No. 4029—B.M. 125704

TRANSLATION		TRANSLITERATION
	Obverse	

1. May [*YHWH* let hear my] lord

2. Tidings of good, this very day . . . . .

3. . . . .

4. . . . .

5. . . . .

Obverse

1. ‏ישמע‎ – – – – אֺת . אֺד‎– – – –‏

2. ‏עֺת טֺב עֺת כֺי‎ – – – – –ה‎‏

3. ‏ה –טֹ[טֺ]‎– [אֹא]‎ – – – – . מֶנ‎‏

4. ‏ב . דֺחֺ‎ – – –יהוֹ‎–‏

5. ‏אֺת לֺ‎ – – – – – –‏

Reverse

1. . . . . [shall I lie?] (or) [Akzib, *n. l.*]

2. . . . . . my lord . . . .

Reverse

1. ‏אכזֺב‎

2. ‏אדני‎

N.B. The reading of most of this ostracon is hopeless; as Professor Torczyner remarks, "No translation of this fragmentary letter can be given".

LETTER IX

Field No. 4030—B.M. 125705

TRANSLATION		TRANSLITERATION
	Obverse	

1. May *YHWH* let hear my lor-

2. d tidings of peace ! . . . .

3. . . . . . thou hast sent [[*A.*: 10+?]

4. . . . .

5. thy servant hath returned (?) . . . . .

6. . . . .

Obverse

1. ‏ישמע יהוה . אֺת . [אד]‎‏

2. ‏נֺי שֺומעת [. שלם . מ‎– – –‏

3. ‏– – – – –לחֺ‎– – – – – –‏

4. ‏ה – שֺ‎‏

5. ‏ב . עֺבֺדך‎ –‏

6. ‏פֺֺר‎ –‏

Reverse

7. hand of . . . yáhū [[*A.*: (telling us)]]

8. what we shall do [[*A.*: tomor-

9. row]].

Reverse

7. ‏ידשֺלֺמֺ‎ –יהו א‎‏

8. ‏שר . נעֺשה . מֺ‎‏

9. ‏חֺֺר‎‏

LETTER X

Field No. 4031—B.M. 125709

As Professor Torczyner says (*Lachish I*, p. 141), "Only very indefinite traces of this letter containing about thirteen letters are preserved; here and there one can make out distinct letters—ל stands out particularly clearly—and many seductive possibilities suggest themselves, but no word can be read with certainty."

LETTER XI

Field No. 4032—B.M. 125712

TRANSLITERATION

3. אֵל‾------‾

4. ‾מכיהו‾-----‾

5. סמֵכיהו

6. ר--צֵ

7. ‾---

"Traces of about thirteen lines can be seen on the sherd" (Torczyner). Only the name Semakhyáhū in line 5 seems to be certain, although it is quite possible that the same name appears in line 4. At the beginning of line 3 traces of the letters *aleph* and *lamed* are visible.

LETTER XII

Field No. 4033—B.M. 125713

According to Professor Torczyner, "This letter showed very faint traces of writing, most of them now unfortunately lost in the unavoidable cleaning. Thus there was only the first photograph, taken while the sherd was still partly covered with mud, as a basis for its reading. From the traces such fragments as 'my lord', 'letter', 'Yhwh lives', 'I have read it', etc. could be recognized."

Only very few and indistinct letters are now visible.

LETTER XIII

Field No. 4034—B.M. 125714

Obverse

Only very faint traces of a few letters can be recognised.

Reverse

TRANSLATION

According to Torczyner:

1. **Stand up to do work**

2. **and Semakhyahu shall dig it out**

3. **. . . . . quivers.**

According to Albright:

1. **They did [not] want to work . . . . .**

2. **And as for Semachiah . . . . hath hidden him.**

TRANSLITERATION

1. קֻֿם, לעשת מֵלאכֵה,

2. וֿחֿסֿנֿמֿכֿיֿהֿו--הפרהו

3. ‾--------את אֿשֿפֿת

LETTER XIV

Field No. 4035—B.M. 125711

"Many traces of single letters are visible, some of them are quite clear. However, as so many signs resemble each other, what looks like כ may also be ב or even מ. About the left centre of the potsherd יהוה.א seems to stand out distinctly, which may be the remains of 'may Yhwh . . . my lord' [יהוה א]ת אדנ'י or 'Yhwh lives . . . . if' [חי יהוה א]ם" (Torczyner).

LETTER XV

Field No. 4036—B.M. 125710

"This is the largest ostracon; unfortunately the writing upon it is no longer legible. The traces remaining in line 3 at the left-hand corner suggest single words as שלח עבדך, but these readings are very doubtful" (Torczyner).

LETTER XVI

Field No. 4037—B.M. 125705

TRANSLITERATION

Obverse

1. . . . . . חמ – . . . . . .
2. . . . . . ה הי . . . . . .
3. . . . . . עֶ?שֶׁלחה? . . . . .
4. . . . . . בְֿנִי . בַּר . . . . .
5. . . . . . הנבא הֹו . . . . . .
6. . . . . . – – – – – . . . . .

Reverse

1. . . . . . . – אֵ – . . . . . .
2. . . . . . – – – – – . . . . .
3. . . . . . שלח . ת . . . . . .
4. . . . . . . והֹו דבר – . . . . .

In this tiny fragment there seems to be (l. 5) a reference to . . . הו הנבא, ". . . *áhū*, the prophet", but the identification of this "prophet" either with Uriah or with Jeremiah, would be hazardous, though both these hypotheses have been suggested. Indeed, there were at that time many "prophets" whose names ended in -*yáhū*.

LETTER XVII

Field No. 4038—B.M. 125707

TRANSLATION	TRANSLITERATION
1. . . . . . [thy] servant	. . . . . עֶבֿד 1
2. . . . . . my lord	. . . . . אֵדֹנִי 2
3. . . . . . my lord (?)	. . . . . . דֹנִיֹי רֹבֹה? 3

Torczyner suggests in his Hebrew edition of the Lachish ostraca that this fragment is a palimpsest. He thinks that the older text was inscribed while the vessel was still whole, and concerned the contents of the vessel.

Torczyner reads the letters *r* and *ḥ* and restores [*by*]*rḥ*, "in the month of . . ." I think that more letters can be detected in different lines, a *t*, a *sh*, a *y*, and a *m*.

Re-examination of the actual sherd reveals that the marks which stand out so clearly in the photograph are lighter in colour than the potsherd; if they are deliberate signs, the ink has faded leaving a whitish trace.

LETTER XVIII

Field No. 4039—B.M. 125708

TRANSLATION	TRANSLITERATION
1. **Until the evening . . . . shall send . . . .** the letter which	1. עד? הערבֿ. ----שלֹםֿ.[י]שֹׁלח----הֿספֿר ‏ =‏ אשֹׁר.
2. **my lord hath sent from here (?) unto the city (?)**	2. שֿלח. אֿדֹנֹי. – ז. – ה. העֿירֹ[ה]

OSTRACON XIX (Pls. 48 A, B: 2)

SW. corner, Field No. 6899—PM 39.799

This inscribed sherd was found in 1938, at the base of the south-west corner of the mound, among the burnt masonry on the roadway.

Body: grey-pink in. and out. Hard fire; grits[1]. Form: irregular, nearly trapezoid. Maximum length and breadth: 14·7×9·8 cm.; thickness: 9–10 cm.

Inscription: The ostracon originally contained nine lines, of which the first four only are partly decipherable.

TRANSLATION	TRANSLITERATION
1. **Son (of) or Ben ʿUṣ (or ʿAzzûr[1])**	1. בן עץ (עֿזֹר) . 10
2. **Peqaḥ[2] 11**	2. פקח . 10 (+) 1
3. **[ʿAm]midal[3] 5 (?)**	3. עֿמדי . 5 (?) (50 ? .T)
4. **Shemaʿyáhū[4] 5 (?)**	4. שמעֹיהו . 5 (?) (50 ? .T)
5.[5]	5. עֿבֿשֿ. . . .

---

[1] Torczyner and Ginsberg, like myself, consider the fourth letter of the line as *ṣ*, whereas Albright considers it as "a perfectly distinct and characteristic *z*, followed by a shaft which can scarcely belong to any letter but *r*". While accepting the possibility of reading ʿ *z r*, ʿAzzur, I do not think Albright is right in considering the reading ʿ *ṣ* as out of the question. The aforementioned shaft is very clear and is perhaps too crooked to be part of an *r*.

[2] As Ginsberg has pointed out, this name is identical with that of the last king of Israel, Pekah.

[3] Torczyner, Ginsberg and Albright do not take the traces of the first letter into consideration. The remaining three letters seem to be certain. They are also read by Torczyner as well by Ginsberg as *mdl*. In Albright's opinion "it looks like *Mbl*, but such a name would be unparalleled and intrinsically improbable. The reading *Nbl* (Nabal) is graphically difficult, as is also *Mkl* (Michal)".

[4] My reading is very probable. In Ginsberg's opinion "The name in l. 4 is unfortunately uncertain. As I read it, it recalls the sinister Ishmael who was a contemporary of our ostracon (Jer. 40–41)." According to Albright, however, Shemaiah "is distinct".

[5] As for the remaining lines, no readings have been suggested by Torczyner, Ginsberg or Albright, except for the numerals at

the end of line 7: 10+?, which may be 10 and 1, or 10 and 5. Ginsberg provisionally assumes for the second numeral the value of "5", "though the resemblance between it and the figure '5' of the Samaria ostraca is not too close". My readings are:

L. 5: After some very uncertain traces of a letter, there are ʿ*ayin*, oval in shape, or traces of a *shin*; *bet* or *nun*, and *shin*, which is rather uncertain. There follow slight indecipherable traces. The meaning is very uncertain.

L. 6: Traces of two or three indecipherable characters, of which the last one may be a *mem* or *ṣade*, followed by a dot.

L. 7: Indecipherable traces; at the end of the line two signs, probably numeral signs 10 and 1, as in line 2.

L. 8: Indecipherable traces.

L. 9: Faint traces of some letters: perhaps a *ṭet* or *taw*, a *shin* and a *bet*. If the reading *taw*, *shin* and *bet* is right, we have the word *toshab*, "foreign inhabitant"(?). It could be a very important indication for the purpose of this document. The word *toshab* appears also in a jar handle (as a *n.p.*?): see D. Diringer, Iscrizioni antico-ebraiche palestinesi, Florence, 1934, stamp No. 21, p. 141.

In conclusion, the ostracon contains a list of names (like Ostracon I) with numerals against them.

OSTRACON XX (Pls. 48 A, B: 1; and Pl. 96: 495 (pot form))

L.12: 1065. Level II; Field No. 6820; now at the Institute of Archaeology (University of London).

This ostracon consists of seven fragments, part of the shoulder of a water jar, much of which was found in the room. These fragments were lying blackened on the floor among the ashes of the huts erected on the eastern side of the palace destroyed in the burning of the last phase of Level II, *c.* 586 B.C.

Body: light red in. and out. Hard fire. Size: 5–13·3 × 14–20·4 cm.; thickness: 0·35–0·55 cm.

Inscription: there were originally at least two lines, of which the first one seems to be nearly complete, and the characters mostly clear, while the second line is almost indecipherable. An isolated *taw* exists half-way down the sherd, with a possible *he* (?) on the lowest edge.

TRANSLATION	TRANSLITERATION
1. **In the ninth (year)**[1] . . . . *yáhū*	1. בתשעית בי׳ות[ן – – – –]וֹ׳הו
	2. הׄוֹלֵׄךָ – – – ז – – –רל

OSTRACON XXI (Pl. 48 A: 3)

L.12: 1065, Field No. 6821; now at the Institute of Archaeology (University of London). This tiny fragment was found on the east side of the palace below the floor of the same room where Ostracon XX was found, and possibly—as Ginsberg has pointed out—"alone among all the Lachish ostraca (except perhaps No. XIX), antedates the reign of Zedekiah".

Form: irregular, nearly trapezoid; size of the sides: 4·9 (bottom) × 2 (top) × 4·7 (left side) × 4·4 (right side) cm.; maximum height: 4·6 cm.; thickness: 0·45–0·55 cm.: all approx. Hard fire. Rough surface. Buff wash outside; inner half grey; contains fine crushed limestone.

Inscription: The fragment is inscribed on both sides. A suggested reading of the obverse is given below.[2]

TRANSLATION	TRANSLITERATION
Reverse	1. ז אל ? ׃ •
Originally there were six lines of writing, but only one letter is certain, viz., *samek*, the first letter of line 5.	2. ה . ן אֵׄת[
	3. שׄתכל בֵָׄׄ – ׳
	4. וצאה – –
	5. והא –

---

[1] Torczyner and Thomas remark that *b tsh ʿy t* standing alone for "in the ninth (year)" would be unusual. The former suggests that it is an abbreviation, while Thomas considers it a colloquialism. The second word is read and restored by Torczyner: *byw*[*m* . . . . *byrh*], i.e. "on the . . . day of the month of . . .", whereas Ginsberg suggests *byr*[*ḥ* . . .], and his reading is accepted by Albright. Ginsberg also suggests the possibility that the letters *yr* "combine with l. 2 to yield an ancient Hebrew month-name *yrḥ kl*". Obviously neither he, Torczyner, nor Albright take the last letters of the line into consideration, written on the fragment which is missing in the photograph published by Torczyner. These last letters of the line consist of the ligature *hw*, which seems to be quite clear, possibly preceded by a *y*, and may be the end of a *n.p.* ending in . . . *yahū*.

The letter read by Ginsberg as *r* is *certainly* not an *r*. Torczyner suggested reading it as *w*, but in Ginsberg's opinion, "that letter is even graphically more probably *r* than *w*. The spot to the upper right is obviously extraneous, and the head of the letter seems to be closed". Also Albright considers this reading as "obviously correct". The letter in question has the form of an irregular X, but its "head" (at the left side) is not quite clear. On the whole, it looks like a *w*, but it may also be a *taw*, as I suggested in my article in PEQ.

The second line offers many problems. The first sign can be either *ḥ*, as suggested by Torczyner, or a ligature of *h* and *w*, as suggested by Albright. The latter's opinion that "the following two letters are absolutely certain" is obviously suggested by the photograph published by Torczyner, but on the original, between the first sign and the letters read as *kl*, there is space for another letter (this distortion of the space in the photograph is due to the curved surface of the original).

The following letter is read ʿ*ayin* by Torczyner and *b* by Albright: both suggestions are possible, but the latter is preferable, and Albright's tentative reading *b*[*n* *Y*ʾ]*z*[*nyhw*], "son of Jaazaniah" is ingenious, especially considering as it is based only on two letters.

[2] Ginsberg translates as follows, his interpretation being also accepted by Albright: "To my lord . . . May *YHWH* cause my lord to hear tidings of peace. Who is thy servant, a dog, that he should bring forth (?) the (?) . . .?" Ginsberg also remarks on the resemblance between the opening sentences of this letter and Letters II and V, which, however, may be slightly later. "Some of the letters provide excellent examples of the penmanship of the scribes of Tell ed-Duweir" (Thomas).

JAR HANDLE STAMPS

The Archaeological Context

It is significant that among some four hundred stamps from Tell ed-Duweir, only one was not found on the mound itself. Moreover, the jar type 484—a form so far exclusive to "royal" or *la-melekh* stamps—was similarly lacking from the cemeteries, except for sherds from Cave 6003–4 which had been used as a dwelling.

Most jar handles came from a mass of sherds at the southern end of the podium or platform of the citadel; they were stamped with private seals or with "royal" marks, and others were found under the walls of the post-exilic Residency. Nearly every room attributed to city Level III contained fragments of the distinctive jars and broken handles, and it can be said that both seem to be exclusive to that level.

The best group of stamps came from Room 1089; there were impressions of three personal seals and of "royal" stamps classes ii and iii. If class iii was introduced in or after 615 B.C., as suggested in the following pages, that room would have been occupied in the final years of the pre-exilic city, but stratigraphical evidence for a chronological difference between the classes is by no means clearly defined.

Dr. C. C. McCown has expressed a wish for statistics on the handle cross-sections (TN I, p. 157), and examination has shown that the double ridge, his type A, is almost universal on jar type 484: in general, it is deep and extends the whole length of the handle (Pl. 77: 11). There are a few examples of type D, but the oval section, type F, is completely lacking. In the case of the reconstructed jar type 484 (H.15: 1003), three handles are markedly type A, while the fourth can be classed with type D. As the stamp belongs to group i, it would have been logical to find that the cross-sections of the handles were oval, or only slightly ridged. The jar was found apart from the other contents of Room 1003 (Pl. 115 and Fig. 9) in a denuded area, so that it cannot be definitely attributed to Level III, and may well be earlier, though the room itself was possibly reoccupied as late as Level II.

The majority of *la-melekh* stamps belong to class ii, and they come from rooms or areas on the mound attributed to Level III. On the hypothesis that Level III was destroyed in 700 B.C., can it now be shown that the few stamps grouped in class i and class iii were found in positions which would not be incompatible with an earlier or later date? Accepting the conclusion that classes i–iii show an epigraphic development, and placing class ii on archaeological grounds not later than 700 B.C., class i should belong to the early eighth century and class iii to the seventh century B.C.

Of the three stamps attributed to class i, the first, from the jar near Room 1003, as already mentioned, came from a denuded area, while the other two were found on open spaces, the roadway 1072 and near the palace steps, 1066, so that in each case they cannot be associated with a particular room, and could be dated earlier in the eighth century.

Of ten stamps attributed to class iii, four are from roadways 1072 and 1087, and other open spaces, one is from Room 1060, which is undoubtedly in Level II, two are from burnt levels in Rooms 1015 and 1017, which may be associated with the final destruction, and three are from Rooms 1073 and 1089, which do appear to belong to Level III. However, an element of doubt exists in both cases for 1073 (Pl. 115), sloped steeply over the ramp of the palace, and Room 1089 was close to an alley 1095 (Pl. 114), which may have been used later than the rooms.

O.T.

Jar handles with private seal impressions

The majority of the forty-eight stamps bearing private names have the form of the common Early Hebrew oval seal, divided horizontally by double lines and consisting of one line of inscription above and another below. Some seals are represented by three or more impressions.[1]

---

[1] For further details, see D. Diringer, "On Ancient Hebrew Inscriptions discovered at Tell ed-Duweir (Lachish)", PEQ, 1941, 38–56.

	Name	Tell Rooms	Palace Floors	Miscellaneous		Total	PEQ 1941 pp. 38 ff., no.
Pl. 47A: 1–2	Ṣafan (son of) 'Azaryáhū	H.17: 1089, F. No. 7166, PM.39.824 (1)	— —	M.14, 268·01 m. (1) D/X, F. No. 6116 (1)		3	1
3	Hosh'a (son of) Ṣafan	—	K.14/J.14: AG, 271·60 m. (2)	L.15: 46, F. No. 6366 (1)		3	2
4–6	Meshullam (son of) Aḥimelek	H.17: 1089, F. No. 7167, PM.39.825 (1)	K.14/J.14: AG (1)	J.16; L.14; L.15; Q.17 (4) D/X, F. No. 6115 (1)		7	3
7	Tanḥum (son of) Magen	H.17: 1072, F. No. 7070 (2)	—	D/X, F. No. 6118 (1 in H.17) (4) R.16 (1)		7	4
9	Shallum?(son of)Aḥisamak	G.14: 1008, F. No. 5400 (1)	—	K.17 (1)		2	5
10, 11	Naḥum (son of) 'Abdî	H.17: 1089, F. No. 7168, 259·68 m. (1)	K.14/J.14: AG (3)	D/X (3)		7	6
8	'Abdî	—	—	P.17, 255·50 m. (1)		1	7
Pl. 47B: 1	Shebnā (son of) Sh(aḥar)	—	K.14/J.14: AG, 271·60 m. (1)	—		1	8
2	Sokoh (?) (son of) Shebnā	J.16: 1028, PM.38.717, F. No. 6236, PEQ 1941, p. 90 (1)	—	J.15, F. No. 6119 (1)		2	9
3	Naḥum (son of) Hiṣilyáhū	—	—	D/X, F. No. 6117 (1)		1	10
4	Sh. . . (son of) Shebenyáhū	—	—	L.15 (1)		1	11
5	Shebenyáhū (?) . . .	—	—	D/X (1)		1	12
—	Naḥum (?)	—	—	D/X (1)		1	13
6	Pn bn yḥnî (?)	—	—	H.17 (1)		1	14
7	Karmî (son of) Yofiyáhū	—	—	Q.17, 251·30 m. (1) D/X (1)		2	15
—	See 5	—	—	D/X (1)		1	16
—	Uncertain	—	—	D/X (1) G.17, 268·50 m. (1)		2	17 / 18
10	Yrshlm? Uncertain	—	K.14: Rm.B, 272·20 m. (1)	—		1	19
—	Uncertain	—	—	D/X (1)		1	20
8, 9	Samkî (son of) Ṣefanyáhū(?) (4-winged serpent)	—	—	D/X, F. No. 6120 (1) D/X (2)		3	21–22
Totals		(7)	(8)	(33)		48	—

Notes

Pl. 47B: 1. The impression of this specimen is incomplete: in the lower line, only the first two letters and the upper right-hand part of the third letter are preserved. The reading, however, is confirmed by Dr. McCown's publication of three specimens from Tell en-Naṣbeh (TN I, pp. 161, 163). In McCown's opinion, "A comparison of the three impressions leaves no doubt as to what the characters are: *l š b n t š ḥ r* is the only possible reading"; a point apparently confirmed by his photographs (TN I, Pl. 57: 9, 11, 12).

The Tell ed-Duweir impression presents many similarities with the Tell en-Naṣbeh stamps. The preserved letters of the former, which are very clear, and even the word-divider after the first letter of the lower line, as well as the whole disposition of the inscription, seem to correspond with those of the Tell en-Naṣbeh impressions, if we do not consider the value of the final letter of the first name. However, it must be emphasised that on the Tell ed-Duweir impression all the strokes of the *aleph* are very neat. McCown bases his suggestion of a *taw* on the evidence of one stamp (M 2432, No. 12). Certainly the connexion between the Tell ed-Duweir and the Tell en-Naṣbeh stamps cannot be excluded. If, therefore, McCown rules out the possibility of his *taw* being a defective *aleph*, we might assume, as he suggests, that the name "Shebnath" may be parallel with "Shebnā", rather than a feminine. Otherwise, as the similarities between these stamps can hardly be a coincidence, the person in question would have had to be a sister of the individual mentioned in the Tell ed-Duweir impression, which it is difficult to believe unless the name Shebnā may also have been feminine.

With reference to my attempt to construct a "dynasty" of potters, mainly based on the name "Shebenyáhū—Shebenyáh—Shebni—Shebnā—Sheben" (see PEQ, 1941, pp. 89–90), Dr. McCown thinks my suggestion is uncertain: so do I. At the same time, I still prefer to consider that the stamps are potter's marks rather than, as McCown suggests, "the marks of an owner whose slaves, or women, made his pottery for him" (TN I, p. 162).

341

Pl. 47B: 3. Professor Sukenik's reading is acceptable (PEQ, 1942, p. 57).

Pl. 47B: 8–9. Decoration: Scarab with four outspread wings, or four-winged serpent.

La-melekh Stamps

Of all excavated sites in Palestine, Tell ed-Duweir produced by far the most remarkable collection of the much-discussed *la-melekh* stamps. Out of about 550 "royal" stamps which have come to light, some 300 were found at Tell ed-Duweir, of which nearly 250 are at the Institute of Archaeology in London. One hundred and seventy-two stamps were published in PEQ, 1941, pp. 99–101.

La-Melekh Stamps

CITY NAME	TELL ROOMS			PALACE FLOORS, RESIDENCY ROOMS AND MISCELLANEOUS		
	Class i	*Class ii*	*Class iii*	*Class i*	*Class ii*	*Class iii*
HEBRON	H.15: 1003, F. No. 5461, 262·45 m. G.17: 1072, 260·78 m.	M.13/14/15, L.14 J.15: 1015, F. No. 6211, 265·30 m. K. 16: 1031 H.15: 1035, F. No. 6253, 263·40 m. J.17: 1044, 261·65 m. L.13: 1059, F. No. 6781, 268 m. L.14/K.14: 1061, F. No. 6796(2) L.12/13: 1064, 269·5 m. L.13: 1060, F. No. 6783 — L.12: 1069, 268·8 m. H.18: 1081, F. No. 7104, 261·10 m. H.18: 1081, F. No. 7104A, 261·10 m. H.18:1049 H.18: 1084, F. No. 7119 H.17: 1087, F. No. 7145, 259·62 m. G.17: 1089, F. No. 7163, 260·34 m.	H.17: 1089, F. No. 7164, 260·01 m.	K.12, F. No. 5280 K.12 Section S. Gate D/X	Res. Rm. K, F. No. 5274 K.12, Ct. P., F. Nos. 5275–5280 L.13 K.12 L.12, F. No. 2693 K.14, F. No. 2690 K.14/J.14: AG L.14 M.14 L.15: 48, 55, 84, 87 F.18B, F. No. 5238 D/X	K.14/J.14: AG J.17 Road D/X
ZIPH	L.12/14: 1066, F. No. 6831	G.14: 1009, F. No. 5519	J.15: 1015, F. No. 6212, 265·30 m. J.15: 1017	L.15: 51 K.14/J.14: AG D/X	D/X P. 17	K.14/J.14: AG K.15 D/X
SOKOH		L.11: 1052, F. No. 6764, 268 m. L.13: 1060, F. No. 6784 — G.17: 1072, F. No. 7068, 260·77 m. H/G.17: 1087, F. No. 7147, 259·62 m.	G.17, F. No. 7078 G.17: 1072 H/G.17: 1089, F. No. 7165, 259·50 m.		Pal. AG: F. No. 5280 L.12 K.12 L.13: Res. Rm. AD L.15: 45 D/X, F. No. 3049 D/X	G.17 P.17 K.14/J.14: AG D/X, F. No. 3049 D/X
MMSHT			L.13: 1060, F. No. 6785 H.17:1072, F. No. 7071, 260 m. J.15: 1073, F. No. 7080, 264·6 m. H/G.17: 1087, F. No. 7146, 259·62 m.		D/X	J.15, F. No. 7081 D/X

The *la-melekh* stamps, as known, fall into two groups: one consisting of oval stamps containing a symbol with four wings, and the other of stamps with a two-winged symbol. The former group divides into two classes: (i) partially stylised stamps, showing greater detail in the execution of the body of the symbol; and (ii) completely stylised stamps representing the symbol with summary treatment.[1]

It is now generally agreed that the four-winged type represents the flying scarabeus or beetle, whereas the two-winged symbol seems to represent a flying scroll or "winged scroll",[2] a peculiar winged sun-disk, or else a crested bird; indeed, a few specimens have the feathers of the tail clearly indicated.

---

[1] For interpretation of these symbols see Diringer, Iscrizioni antico-ebraiche palestinesi, 1934, pp. 155 ff.; see also Watzinger, Denkmäler Palästinas, I, 1933, pp. 116 f.; Sukenik, Kedem I, 1942, pp. 32 ff.; Albright, AASOR XXI–XXII, 1943, pp. 74 f.; McCown, TN I, 1947, p. 156.

[2] The Biblical *m*-gillah 'aphah, "flying roll", Zech. V: 1 f., comes readily to mind.

The stamps are generally impressed on the upper part of the handle, though at times they are impressed upside down. The scarab type is always impressed longitudinally, while the flying scroll is sometimes impressed in the length of the handle (i.e. with head at the top and wings left and right, or upside down).

Some handles have in addition a stamp consisting of two concentric circles with a central dot. See in this connexion PEQ 1941, p. 99 and McCown's comments (TN I, p. 159, n. 11), but it seems useless to give statistics, when only two examples were recovered from Duweir.

In each class the oval generally also contains an inscription consisting of two lines, one above the symbol and the other below. The upper line consists of the letters *l-m-l-k* (*la-melekh*, "to the king", "of the king", "belonging to the king", or "royal"). The lower line contains one of the following words: *ḥ b r n, z p* or *z y p, sh k w h* and *m m sh t*. The first three represent the names of the towns Hebron, Ziph and Sokoh. The fourth is an unknown place-name, MMSHT. In a few examples of the winged-scroll type (in specimens found at Jerusalem, Gezer, Tell el-Fûl and Tell en-Naṣbeh, but in none found at Tell ed-Duweir), the city name MMSHT, and in one case at Tell en-Naṣbeh, the name Ziph, occupies the place where *la-melekh* is usually found, the lower register being blank.

On a certain number of stamps the town name is completely missing, owing to fracture, disintegration, or imperfect impression. In a few of these the upper line is also gone, and nothing remains except the symbol, which is more or less distinct.

All the other specimens show traces of one of the four town names. In many of the Tell ed-Duweir stamps a given name may be made out clearly; in others, however, the position of one or more letters suggests identification with one of the four city names.

Epigraphically the stamps can be divided into three groups which coincide with the typological classes. Two of the most distinguished Palestinian archaeologists (Albright and McCown) having accepted the writer's suggestion that the "royal" stamps should be subdivided into the three classes mentioned above, this subdivision may now be considered established.

There appears to be such an epigraphic cleavage between the first and the second class that a complete specimen of the first class and a complete specimen of the second may serve as typical of the evolution of the Early Hebrew alphabet.

In the inscriptions of class i all the letters are long and thin and partly irregular, whereas the letters of class ii are generally more squat, wider and shorter. In class ii the main stems of the letters *lamed, kaph, mem, nun,* and *pe* are curved and rounded at the bottom, and in the *heth* the vertical strokes go beyond the horizontal ones. On the whole the letters are much more accurate and regular than those of the first class. It is therefore suggested that class i should be assigned to the first half or middle of the eighth century, and class ii to the late eighth or early seventh, but not to the sixth century B.C. The main epigraphic difference between the second and the third class, which shows still further development, is that the short vertical strokes of the head of the *mem* are sometimes not joined to the main stem, and this letter is otherwise more advanced than the *mem* of the inscriptions in the second class. The third class may, therefore, be assigned to the late seventh or early sixth century B.C.

These general remarks concern mainly the Hebron and Ziph series. Regarding the latter, the following points should also be observed:

(*a*) In a few specimens of the first class the third letter of the upper register bears a correction: the inexperienced craftsman had probably first incised a *kaph* which he then altered to a *lamed*.

(*b*) The lower register is written in "mirror-writing".

(*c*) The lower register of the first class consists of three letters, *z y p*, while the second class has no *y*, and the third class contains the *y*, though it seems to be missing in one or two cases.

(*d*) In the second class both words are followed by a dot.

343

No specimens of the Sokoh and MMSHT series present the characteristics of the first class. The Sokoh stamps are interesting for the following peculiar features:

(1) In the second class the *he* is very oblique, has four horizontal strokes—a unique feature in North-West Semitic epigraphy, though there are Etruscan parallels.

(2) In the third class the *waw* is characteristic (a vertical stem curved above towards the left is cut by a hook); there is an elegant ligature between the *kaph* and *he*, and the latter has three horizontal strokes which are usually of different lengths, the upper one not going beyond the vertical stroke; as in Ziph ii, each word is followed by a point.

At Tell ed-Duweir only one specimen of the MMSHT series belongs to the second class, and in that only two *mem* remain of MMSHT. In the third class the *mem* appears sometimes in slightly different forms, and the city name is sometimes followed by a dot, but it is uncertain whether a dot was also in the upper register.

Conclusions

The table on p. 346 shows the distribution of *la-melekh* stamps at Tell ed-Duweir compared on the following chart with those from other sites.

The epigraphic conclusions are partly based on a comparison of the styles of writing employed in the three classes of "royal" stamps in relation to the style of the Siloam inscription.[1] For all practical purposes they belong to the same epigraphic type, written by the same kind of people, living in the same territory, and perhaps having much the same kind of education. This being so, there is nothing more instructive in the history of Early Hebrew writing than a comparison between the individual letters of the various types of "royal" stamps and of the Siloam inscription. Between classes i and ii the style of the Siloam inscription is much nearer the latter class. It is generally agreed that the inscription belongs to the reign of Hezekiah; class i, therefore, may be assigned to early or middle eighth century and class ii to its end. Class iii is clearly a later development.

There are a few specimens which may be considered as transitional between classes i and ii. In four or five examples the scarab symbol seems to be only partly stylised, and the letters are slightly more evolved than in class i, but the classification is by no means certain.

On the evidence available from Starkey's preliminary reports, which ascribed the destruction of city Level III to the early sixth century, Albright dated class i to Hezekiah's reign, class ii to Manasseh's time and class iii to Josiah and his successors. It is indeed likely that the change of symbol from class ii to iii may be assigned to King Josiah, the great religious reformer, who, in his determination to stamp out all pagan cults and symbols, and to free his country from all foreign influence, may have also ordered a significant alteration in official seals, replacing the scarabaeus by a bird, or perhaps by the representation of the winged Scroll of the Law. In this connexion it is worth remembering that the discovery of a "Law Scroll" (II Kings XXII: 8; II Chronicles XXXIV: 15) during repairs to the Temple led to Josiah's drastic reforms. This hypothesis would perfectly agree with the epigraphic evidence.

Jar Handles impressed with Symbols or engraved or scratched with Marks

This may not be a suitable place for a discussion of the objects in question, which are not inscribed, but on the other hand they should perhaps be considered with the other jar handle stamps.

(*a*) Nineteen stamps: Gate N. wall; Pal. East Wall, 266·5 m. (Pl. 53: 4); L.12: 1067, F. No. 6835 (Pl. 53: 1); L.14/M.14 (Pl. 53: 2); L.14; PQR.17: 252·25 m.; Q.12: 106, F. No. 5254; G.17: 1072, F. No. 7067; D/X (11 ex.) (Pl. 53: 3).

---

[1] See paper on the Royal Stamps read to the XXIst International Congress of Orientalists, Paris, 1948. In the discussion following the paper, Professor Albright agreed with the conclusions and produced further evidence in their favour.

The emblem is a rosette in various forms and sizes. The four main patterns are reproduced full size on Pl. 53: 1–4. All are circular, their diameter being approximately 1·2–2 cm., except one which is oval (approximate size, 1 × 1·5 cm.).

		SILOAM	ROYAL JAR STAMPS		
			CLASS i	CLASS ii	CLASS iii
B	ב	ℐ (ℐℐ)	ℐ (ℐ)	ℐ ℐ ℐ	ℐ
Ḥ	ח			ℯ	ℰ
W	ו			↑ ↑ (↑w)	↑
Z	ז		⊤ (⊤)	ℨ	⊤ ⊤
Ḥ	ח		⊟	⊟	⊟ ⊟
Y	י	℥	∿ (∿)		℥
K	כ	ש ℣℣	y y y	y y	ש (ℯℳ)
L	ל		ℓ ℓ	ℓ	ℓ ℓ
M	מ		y y	y y	y y y
N	נ		y	y y	y y
P	פ		) (ℐ)	ℐ ℐ	ℐ
R	ר	ℐ	ℐ	ℐ	ℐ
Š	ש	⋎⋎		w	w w
T	ת	✗			✗

FIG. 34. Letters of *la-melekh* compared with Siloam inscription

Similar stamps were found at Tell ez-Zakariyeh and are published in BM, Pl. 56: 35–43; they are rightly defined as "different patterns conventionally developed from a flower".

According to I. Mendelsohn (Guilds in Ancient Palestine, BASOR No. 80, December 1940, p. 21), "the various forms of the rosette, pentagram, wheel, cross, and the letter *tau* cannot be regarded as ownership marks". He suggests that "these potters' marks are trade marks, each design belonging to a particular guild of potters".

Earlier W. F. Albright had written (AASOR XII, § 121): "One wonders whether there may not have been two rival groups of potters' guilds, one employing variations of the rosette theme, the other variations on the *tau* and *samek* themes." On the other hand, in 1940 Albright wrote (BASOR No. 80, p. 21, n. 51): "The rosette may possibly have had royal significance in Judah at this time, as it undoubtedly had possessed in Hittite Asia Minor about 1300 B.C." and "it originally seems to have symbolised the Hittite belief that the great king was the incarnation of the sun-god".

The archaeological data of Tell ed-Duweir seem to agree with that of Albright, who writes as follows (op. cit.): "At Gibeah of Benjamin (Tell el-Fûl), I found in 1933 some half a dozen still unpublished examples of the rosette stamp . . . which was unquestionably contemporary with the royal stamp."

(*b*) Two stamps: D/X.

The symbol is a cross in relief stamped in a hollow surround, and the diameters of the two stamps are approximately 1·25 cm. and 1·2–1·4 cm. These specimens may be contemporary with the rosette stamps and the "royal" stamps, but according to Albright (op. cit.): "It may further be asked whether the royal monogram of the Persian period, which consisted of a circle with a cross inside dividing it into four sectors . . . is not also derived from the same rosette . . . simplified in the same way at Bogazköy. . . ." See also what has been said in connexion with the rosette stamp.

(*c*) Five specimens: 120; J.15: 1015; D/X (3 ex., cooking pot type 442).

A cross or *taw* of different shapes and dimensions, engraved or scratched before or after firing. See above for suggested explanation.

(*d*) One stamp: D/X.

A circle with a central dot in relief stamped in a hollow ground. Diameter: 1·3 cm.

(*e*) One stamp: D/X.

In an irregular field, a kind of rectangle with rounded corners (approximately 1·3 × 1·4 cm.), two vertical lines in relief cut by two horizontal lines, also in relief.

(*f*) Two specimens: D/X.

These have an irregular geometrical figure, one being a kind of trapezoid (1·8 × 1·7 × 1·3 × 1·6 cm.) incised before firing, the other (1·1 × 1·3 cm.) scratched after firing. They are, perhaps, attempts to represent a "shield of David".

(*g*) One potter's mark (L.14) in the shape of a Greek *psi* (π).

(*h*) One potter's stamp: D/X.

This is quite unusual. It consists of one thick vertical stroke and three small ones, either vertical or oblique or horizontal, on both sides of the stamp, all in relief in a hollow oval surround (approximately 1 × 1·4 cm.).

Distribution of La-Melekh Stamps

(*a*) TELL ED-DUWEIR

		Hebron		Ziph		Sokoh		MMSHT		Broken		Uncertain		Totals	
		No.	%	No.	%	No.	%	No.	%	No.	%	No.	%	No.	%
Four-winged scarab	i. Script archaic; figure partly stylized	30	9·68	4	1·29	—	—	—	—	1	0·32	4	1·29	39	12·58
As above	ii. Script more evolved; figure fully stylized (some transitional specimens are included⁴)	156	50·32	6	1·94	28	9·03	1	0·32	8	2·58	27	8·71	226	72·90
	Totals i–ii	186	60·00	10	3·23	28	9·03	1	0·32	9	2·90	31	10·00	265	85·48
	Two-winged symbol iii	12	3·87	9	2·90	12	3·87	7	2·26	2	0·65	3	0·97	45	14·52
TOTALS		198	63·87	19	6·13	40	12·90	8	2·58	11	3·55	34	10·97	310	100·00

	Duweir		Sandaḥannah		Judeideh		Ṣâfi		Zakarîyeh		'Ain Shems		Naṣbeh		Totals	
	No.	%	No.	%	No.	%	No.	%	No.	%	No.	%	No.	%	No.	%
Hebron i	30	9·68	—	—	—	—	—	—	—	—	—	—	3	3·49	33	6·70
ii	156	50·32	—	—	—	—	—	—	—	—	—	—	5	5·81	161	32·72
i or ii	—	—	3	17·65	2	5·41	—	—	3	17·65	11	57·89	—	—	19	3·86
iii	12	3·87	—	—	3	8·11	—	—	1	5·88	1	5·26	5	5·81	22	4·47
Total	198	63·87	3	17·65	5	13·52	—	—	4	23·53	12	63·15	13	15·11	235	47·76
Ziph i	4	1·29	—	—	—	—	—	—	—	—	—	—	—	—	4	0·81
ii	6	1·94	—	—	—	—	—	—	—	—	—	—	—	—	6	1·22
i or ii	—	—	—	—	2	5·41	—	—	2	11·76	—	—	—	—	4	0·81
iii	9	2·90	2	11·76	2	5·41	—	—	1	5·88	—	—	9	10·47	23	4·67
Total	19	6·13	2	11·76	4	10·82	—	—	3	17·64	—	—	9	10·47	37	7·52
Sokoh i	—	—	—	—	—	—	—	—	—	—	—	—	—	—	—	—
ii	28	9·03	—	—	—	—	—	—	—	—	—	—	—	—	28	5·69
i or ii	—	—	2	11·76	2	5·41	2	33·33	5	29·41	—	—	—	—	11	2·23
iii	12	3·87	4	23·53	5	13·52	—	—	—	—	—	—	4	4·65	25	5·08
Total	40	12·90	6	35·29	7	18·93	2	33·33	5	29·41	—	—	4	4·65	64	13·01
Mmsht i	—	—	—	—	—	—	—	—	—	—	—	—	—	—	1	0·20
ii	1	0·32	—	—	—	—	—	—	—	—	—	—	—	—	1	0·20
i or ii	—	—	—	—	—	—	—	—	1	5·88	—	—	—	—	1	0·20
iii	7	2·26	3	17·65	6	16·23	—	—	—	—	1	5·26	10	11·63	27	5·49
Total	8	2·58	3	17·65	6	16·23	—	—	1	5·88	1	5·26	10	11·63	29	5·90
Uncertain } i	5	1·61	—	—	—	—	—	—	—	—	—	—	3	3·49	8	1·62
or broken } ii	35	11·29	—	—	—	—	—	—	—	—	—	—	4	4·65	39	7·93
i or ii	—	—	1	5·88	5	13·52	4	66·67	2	11·76	4	21·05	—	—	16	3·25
iii	5	1·65	2	11·76	10	27·03	—	—	2	11·76	2	10·53	43	50·00	64	13·01
Total	45	14·52	3	17·64	15	40·55	4	66·67	4	23·52	6	31·58	50	58·14	127	25·81
Totals i	39	12·58	—	—	—	—	—	—	—	—	—	—	6	6·98	45	9·15
ii	226	72·90	—	—	—	—	—	—	—	—	—	—	9	10·46	235	47·76
i or ii	—	—	6	35·29	11	29·73	6	100·00	13	76·47	15	78·95	—	—	51	10·37
iii	45	14·52	11	64·71	26	70·27	—	—	4	23·53	4	21·05	71	82·56	161	32·72
GRAND TOTALS	310	100·00	17	100·00	37	100·00	6	100·00	17	100·00	19	100·00	86	100·00	492	100·00

Note: Stamps found in early excavations, which could not be assigned to a definite chronological class, are placed under "i or ii". The last column contains approximate percentages in relation to 492 stamps, the total number from all sites being about 550.

SEALS AND SEAL IMPRESSIONS

The Archaeological Context

Six out of eleven seals and seal impressions bearing Early Hebrew inscriptions or designs were found loose in the soil in or around the mound, and must therefore be considered on their own merits. Of the remaining five, two scaraboids, 168 and 171, came from Tomb 106, and should name two of the occupants of this late and crowded tomb. A seal in a bronze mount, with loop attachment, was unfortunately too corroded for decipherment, and efforts to remove the accretions were unavailing. It came from Tomb 1002 and is illustrated on Pl. 57: 14. That it belongs to the series is clear from the traces of the double dividing line across the middle of the seal, and from the indications of letters which remain. Apart from this seal, and the fine steatite scarab 167, the material falls into two classes: the scaraboids 168–171, made of malachite, bone, carnelian and pink limestone respectively, and the clay seal impressions 164–166 and 172–173, showing marks of the papyrus documents to which they were affixed on the reverse. That five of these tiny impressions have been recovered testifies to a fairly common use of papyrus rolls at Tell ed-Duweir. It is likely that the names of Hilqiah and Gedaliah belonged to persons who lived elsewhere, and in this connexion the suggestion that Gedaliah was the ruler appointed by Nebuchadrezzar is very attractive, while the names on the scarab and scaraboids should be those of inhabitants of, or visitors to, Tell ed-Duweir.

All that can be said about the archaeological evidence for chronology is that the scaraboids 168 and 171 came from the filling of Tomb 106, which is the latest large group, beginning in Iron II and apparently extending into Iron III, while the seal impressions 166 and 172 came from rooms of Level III, which were in use up to the burning of the city attributed to the Assyrian campaign in 700 B.C. For illustrations see Pls. 44, 45.

O. T.

No.	Locus	Material	Remarks	Field No.
167	500	Steatite	Scarab (PM.36. 1829) *Upper register*: four-winged beetle, holding disk (?), with Hebrew letters *s m k* above, and the *ankh* between wings. *Lower register*: *l'ḥ m l k* (See PEQ, 1941, p. 102, No. 2)	4041
168	106	Malachite	Scaraboid *Upper register*: two stars *Lower register*: probably . . . *ḥ*(?) *y h w*, the end of a name	371
169	D/X	Bone, burnt	Scaraboid *Upper register*: *l sh l m*(?) *Lower register*: *'ḥ ' sh*(?) (See PEQ, 1941, p. 104, No. 6)	5353
170	4000	Carnelian	Scaraboid (PM.38. 123) *Upper register*: winged uraeus and *ankh* *Middle register*: *l sh p ṭ y h* *Lower register*: *w ' ś y h w* (See PEQ, 1941, p. 103, No. 4)	6114
171	106	Pink limestone	Scaraboid *Upper register*: *l sh b n '* *Lower register*: *' ḥ ' b* (See PEQ, 1941, p. 103, No. 3)	328
172	H.15: 1003	Clay	Sealing from document, marks of papyrus and thread on reverse. PM. 36.2258 *Upper register*: *l ḥ l q y h w* *Lower register*: *b n m ' p s* (See PEQ, 1941, p. 102, No. 1)	5352
173	D/X	Clay	Sealing from document, marks of papyrus and thread on reverse. *Upper register*: *l g d l y h w* *Lower register*: *' sh r ' l h b y t* (See PEQ, 1941, p. 103, No. 5)	4040

WEIGHTS[1]

A false balance is abomination to the Lord: but a just weight is his delight. Proverbs, XI: 1.

Besides the large number of jar stamps, Tell ed-Duweir produced a most remarkable collection of weights, comprising six specimens inscribed with Early Hebrew letters, twelve marked with numerical or metrological signs, and forty unmarked specimens. Many more small pebbles and pieces of stone were found which may have been used as weights, but the excavators of the site prefer to err on the side of caution, and therefore only those unmarked objects are discussed which it is reasonable to assume, from their shape or metrological value, should be included in the series.

---

[1] This section deals with the Tell ed-Duweir weights and their contribution to the knowledge of Early Hebrew metrological standards. For fuller details on the single specimens the reader is referred to the article by D. Diringer in PEQ, 1942, pp. 82–103.

The list of weights in this volume includes all those published in PEQ, with their group numbers, which generally agree with the numbers as given in the classification below. The numbers in brackets after group III refer to the article in PEQ.

The Archaeological Context

Most of the weights were not associated with any particular building. Twenty-seven are consequently marked D/X, and three (F.7, L.12 and L.13) have grid references, making a total of thirty weights found on the mound. There are also five weights from the topsoil of the adjoining areas 500 and 7000, leading to the city gate, and it is perhaps significant that they should be found where there was doubtless considerable trade activity in the past. No. 39 is the only stone found in a tomb which bears any resemblance to a weight, but its irregular shape and the later re-use of the site as a quarry make it almost certain that it never formed part of the funerary equipment of the tomb.

Eight stones listed as weights were found in rooms attributed to Level III, but only half are typically dome-shaped specimens. Also there are No. 13, a very doubtful specimen, and No. 50, an interesting square weight, both of which were found in rooms provisionally attributed to Level II.

It will be noted that no specimens inscribed with Hebrew words were found in tell rooms; No. 49 is the only marked weight from H.18: 1084, and it bears a single letter or sign similar to that on No. 50.

Perhaps the most interesting group of marked weights is that comprising Nos. 2, 3, 4 and 5, for these were found in a context which makes it probable that they were either contemporary with Level II or, on the evidence of No. 5, from the Solar Shrine, as late as the post-exilic reoccupation. This accords with the general opinion that the series belongs to the Persian or Hellenistic period, but the former attribution is preferable (see Diringer, Iscrizioni, pp. 284–285). O. T.

The difficulties of classifying these objects are many and great. In the first place, Palestine had so many systems of weights during her long history, and the archaeological data connected with the finds are so uncertain, that any classification based on a metrological system alone must be considered as provisional.

Various Biblical passages (Lev. XIX: 35 f.; Deut. XXV: 13 ff., Prov. XI: 1, XX: 10, etc.) show that "divers" weights were employed, "just and unjust", and the inscribed weights found at Tell ed-Duweir and on other sites confirm this fact.

Although the inscriptions must have been intended as a guarantee of the exactness of the weights, there are no two Early Hebrew specimens bearing the same inscription which have exactly the same weight.

Dating of Inscribed Weights

On epigraphic and archaeological grounds, it is impossible to assign exact dates to the weights. However, with regard to the inscribed specimens, a comparison with the inscriptions of the royal jar handle stamps would suggest that while there is no parallel among them for la-melekh stamps, class i, the letters of classes ii and iii have their counterparts in nearly all examples of the inscribed weights. With due reserve their script may, therefore, be dated to the seventh–sixth century B.C.

Weights Inscribed in Early Hebrew: Provenance and Metrological value in grammes*

Neṣeph	Duweir	Zakariyeh	Samaria	'Anata	Jerusalem (?)	Zakariyeh	Jerusalem (?)	
	10·515	10·210	10·160[1]	10·105[2]	10·044	9·998	9·946	
	Naṣbeh	Ṭubeiqah	Jerusalem	Ṭubeiqah	Zakariyeh	Naṣbeh	Gezer	
	9·935	9·800	9·760	9·540	9·447	9·324	9·280	*Average:* 9·840
Pîm	Naṣbeh	Duweir	Duweir	Silwân	Jerusalem (?)	Gezer	Ṭubeiqah	
	8·591	8·130	7·805	7·750	7·610[3]	7·270	7·180	*Average:* 7·762
Beqaʿ	Ṣalaḥ	Duweir	Gezer	Duweir	Jerusalem (?)	Ṭubeiqah	Duweir	
	6·650	6·150	6·110	6·095	5·870	5·800	5·660[4]	*Average:* 6·110 (or 6·050)

* The table shows that the *beqaʿ* series practically covers the whole scale between 5·8 grammes (or even perhaps 5·66) and 6·65 grammes; the *pîm* weights between 7·18 and 8·59 grammes; and the *neṣeph*, between 9·28 and 10·515 grammes. In other words, the difference between the heaviest and the lightest specimens of the same series are much greater than the difference between the heaviest *beqaʿ* and the lightest *pîm*, or between the heaviest *pîm* and the lightest *neṣeph*. In addition, the specimen marked "¼ *neṣeph*" shows that there also existed fractions at least of the *neṣeph* unity of weight.

The Early Hebrew system of weights was thus far more complicated than had been supposed. We must assume that there were independent systems which probably varied according to the goods for sale, just as nowadays the chemist, the grocer and the jeweller use different standards; and also that these systems varied locally. We have it on the authority of the Bible that the *beqaʿ* (the only weight known from the Bible of which examples have survived) was used for weighing gold (Genesis XXIV: 22), that it was the poll tax (Exodus XXXVIII: 26) and that it was "half a sheqel according to the sheqel of the sanctuary", i.e. half of the "sacred" sheqel. The metrological value of the latter was therefore 11·32 or 11·6 to 13·3 grammes.

The *neṣeph* was perhaps the "common" sheqel (although etymologically it seems to indicate a "half"); and the *pîm* seems to have been originally two-thirds of the sheqel, whose metrological value would have been 10·77 to 12·2 grammes.

Finally, in the opinion of the present writer, it is a mistake to assume (as many scholars do) that the differences in the same system are variations of the average value, because this does not explain the weights which are heavier than the average.

[1] This specimen, inscribed *rebaʿ neṣeph* (¼ *neṣeph*), weighs 2·540 grammes, giving thus a unity of 10·160 grammes.
[2] This specimen actually weighs 8·680 grammes, but the hole bored through it, to make a bead or charm, accounts for the probable loss of 1·425 grammes.
[3] Some scholars indicate the weight of this specimen as 7·777 grammes.
[4] It is uncertain whether this weight represents a *beqaʿ*.

Provisional Classification

Even in the same metrological system, there must have been different local standards in early Palestine, as there were until recent times in modern Palestine. Also, ancient balances did not conform to modern standards in accuracy and sensitiveness.

For these and other reasons, it is preferable to subdivide the weights into the following groups:

I. Inscribed weights.
II. Weights with numerical signs or other marks.
III. Unmarked weights.

This classification, however, does not prevent a provisional classification based on the metrological values of the objects (see below), in which we must disregard the chronological co-ordination of the metrological systems of ancient Palestine, at least as far as the Early Hebrew and Jewish periods are concerned.

In conclusion, as in the case of all the other extant Early Hebrew weights, no definite system can be deduced from the series found at Tell ed-Duweir. A standard metrological system of early Palestine has yet to be discovered, if, indeed, it ever existed. Nevertheless, the Tell ed-Duweir weights, with their high metrological standard in comparison with other specimens, are extremely important both to Biblical archaeology and to metrology in general.

I. *Inscribed Weights*

i. One specimen (Pls. 50: 7; 51: 7): D.7000, F. No. 7253, List No. 31.

Inscription: n-ṣ-p, probably "neṣeph". The *nun* and the *pe*, with their shafts rounded at the bottom, are characteristic of the Early Hebrew script of the classical period; so is also the squat form of the *zayin*, although its shape, as a whole, is rather peculiar. This *neseph*, weighing 10·515 grammes, is the heaviest known example, differing from the lightest specimen by 1·235 grammes.

ii, 1. One specimen (Pl. 51: 8): D/X, F. No. 1505, List No. 35.

Inscription: p-y-m, probably "pîm". The *pe*, rather tall, is nearly rectangular at the top. In the *yodh* the lowest stroke is oblique and forms a V with the main stem. In the *mem* the two prongs of the head are not connected with the main stem. This is not a very common characteristic, but it appears in many "royal" jar handle stamps of the third group.

ii, 2. One specimen (Pl. 51: 9): D/X, F. No. 6157, List No. 37.

Inscription: p-y-m ("pîm"). The shape of the *pe* and the *mem* are quite different from that of the preceding weight. The *pe* has the characteristic Early Hebrew form, with a rounded base, similar to the *pe* of the Siloam inscription. The *mem* is also similar to that of Siloam; the two prongs of its head are connected to the main stem by a horizontal stroke across the middle of the prongs instead of at the base. The *yodh* is similar to that of the preceding weight.

Both the Tell ed-Duweir specimens, weighing 8·13 and 7·805 grammes respectively, are heavier than the other *pîms* found in Palestine, with the exception of that from Tell en-Naṣbeh. The difference in weight is even more marked than in the *neṣeph* series; indeed, the lightest *pîm* weighs 7·18 grammes, that is 1·41 grammes less than the Tell en-Naṣbeh specimen.

iii, 1. One specimen (Pl. 51: 12): D/X, F. No. 500, List No. 38.

Inscription: b-q-ʿ = "beqaʿ". The letters are neat, but two are unusual, especially the *qoph*, which consists of a vertical stem with a very oblong oval at the top, narrowing to the right and ending in a tail parallel to the main stroke; it may be compared somewhat with the *qoph* of the seal of "Yeqamiah (son of) Ishmael" (Diringer, Iscrizioni, p. 210).

iii, 2. One specimen (Pls. 50: 9; 51: 13): L.12, F. No. 5349, List No. 40.

Inscription: b-q-ʿ = "beqaʿ". All the letters differ from those of the preceding specimen. While the first two are extremely tall, the *ʿayin* is very small and rather irregularly shaped. The *qoph*, which resembles those of the Siloam inscription, is nearly connected to the preceding *beth*, but they do not constitute a real ligature. On the whole, this inscription is rather slender; it measures 6×6 mm., as compared with the 5·5×11·5 mm. of the preceding specimen.

iii, 3. One specimen (Pl. 51: 14): D/X, List No. 42.

Inscription: beth, perhaps standing for *b-q-ʿ* ("beqaʿ"). The letter is rather irregular, especially at its base.

While this specimen, possibly not a *beqaʿ*, weighs 0·14 gramme less than the lightest of this series found in Palestine, the preceding two are amongst the heaviest of the Palestinian examples. Indeed, No. 38, which weighs 6·15 grammes and is slightly damaged at the base, is not much lighter than the heaviest specimen, weighing 6·65 grammes; No. 40, weighing 6·095 grammes, is similarly chipped.

II. *Weights marked with numerical signs*

i. *The ४ -marked weights*

Six specimens: D/X, F. No. 6156, List No. 1 (Pl. 51: 1);
L.14: 1061, F. No. 6794, List No. 2 (Pl. 51: 2);
K.14: Pal. East Wall, F. No. 1491, List No. 3 (Pl. 51: 3);
K.14: Pal. East Wall, F. No. 1491A, List No. 4 (Pls. 50: 3; 51: 5);
Q.12: 106, F. No. 5261, List No. 5 (Pl. 51: 4);
D/X, F. No. 1512, List No. 6 (Pl. 51: 6).

One specimen (PQR.17, F. No. 7240A, List No. 9), probably belonging to the same series, is unmarked and slightly lighter than the other examples.

All these weights, except the last one, bear two marks which are, with minor variations, a T-shaped sign or a kind of circumflex (^), and a mark similar to the Arabic numeral 8, without the top curve (४). The former is probably a numeral, perhaps representing the number 8, the latter probably indicates the metrological unit. Some fifteen other weights belonging to the same series were unearthed in Palestine and one in Egypt.

Metrological value: The seven specimens cover the whole scale between 87·735 and 92·465 grammes. If the numerical sign represents the numeral 8, i.e. eight units, the value of the unit would be 11·56, 11·50, 11·43, 11·39, 11·38 and 11·08 grammes respectively. If No. 9 is considered to belong to this series, 10·97 grammes would be the lowest unit. Whatever the origin of the mark ४ may be, it probably represents the "standard" sheqel. *Dating*: On archaeological and epigraphic grounds, it is suggested that this series belongs to a later phase than the inscribed weights.

ii. *Weights with numerical signs*

1. One specimen: D.500, List No. 45 (Pl. 51: 11).

Mark: A horizontal stroke and a vertical one in the form of T, but the strokes are not connected. It is not clear whether this mark represents a single numerical sign, two strokes, or the metrological value. *Metrological value*: If we disregard the mark, or consider it as indicating the metrological value, the most reasonable suggestion would be to consider this specimen, which weighs 5·13 grammes, as half a *neṣeph*.

ii, 2. Three specimens: D/X, F. No. 7254, PM. 39, 830, List No. 46 (Pl. 50: 10);
H.18: 1084, F. No. 7124, List No. 49 (Pl. 51: 10);
J.17: 1042, List No. 50 (Pl. 51: 15).

Mark: The sign is not clear. It may consist of two hooks or it may be an incomplete or irregular *zayin*; it is not even certain that the mark of the first specimen is the same as the other two, especially as there seems to be a considerable difference in weight (if the weight of the Palestine Museum specimen is correct, which cannot at present be checked). The weights of the three specimens are 4·879, 3·820 and 3·770 grammes respectively. The metrological value is uncertain: No. 46 may be half a *neṣeph*, and Nos. 49 and 50 may be half a *pîm*, assuming that the first does not belong to the same series as the other two.

ii, 3. One specimen: D.500, List No. 54.

Marks: Some indecipherable traces of marks written in ink. *Metrological value*: This specimen, weighing 3·12 grammes, is probably half a *beqaʿ*, i.e. a quarter of the "sacred" sheqel.

ii, 4. One specimen: D/X, List No. 55 (Pl. 51: 16).

Mark: Two small strokes, probably indicating "two parts, two fractions" or "a whole unit divided into two fractions", i.e. "a half". It is not clear, however, to which unit this specimen refers. Its metrological value seems to have been a quarter of a *beqaʿ*, i.e. an eighth of a "sacred" sheqel.

352

III. *Unmarked Weights*

The other weights do not bear any inscription or mark. They are listed below, together with the inscribed and marked specimens.

List of Weights

No.	Locus	Group	Inscription or Mark	Plate No.	Grammes	Size in mm. (height, width, diameter at base; in some cases also measurements of top and base)	Material	Shape	Field No.
1	D/X	II, i, 1	Mark	51: 1	92·465	36×40×27	black and brown mottled limestone	dome	6156
2	L.14: 1061	II, i, 2	Mark	51: 2	91·985	35×40×31	white limestone	dome	6794
3	K.14: Pal. East Wall	II, i, 3	Mark	51: 3	91·430	35·6×40×29–30	pink limestone	dome	1491
4	K.14: Pal. East Wall	II, i, 4	Mark	50: 3 51: 4	91·115	35·5×39×33	yellow limestone	dome	1491A
5	Q.12: 106	II, i, 5	Mark	51: 5	91·055	35·5×39×33	yellow limestone	irreg. dome	5261
6	H.17: 1089	III	—	—	88·750	32×37·5×25	grey limestone	dome	7159
7	D/X	II, i, 6	Mark	51: 6	88·645	30·5–34·5×41×29	dk. gy. limestone	irreg. dome	1512
8	D.7000	III(1)	—	—	88·480	61×24·8–30·5×22·5–24	grey limestone	oblong, irreg. solid	—
9	PQR.17 (Great Shaft)	II, i, 7	—	—	87·735	30·5–32·5×40×33	pink and yellow mottled limestone	irreg. dome	7240A
10	D.7000	III(2)	—	—	75·740	35×17×40	grey dolerite	irreg. cone	—
11	J.15: 1039	III(3)	—	—	57·155	43·5×32×17·5–22·5	dk. gy. limestone	"pillow-form" with edges rounded	—
12	J.17: 1017	III(4)	—	—	49·355	36·5×40×24·5	blackish-brown limestone	half-dome	6227
13	J.17: 1044	III	—	—	48·210	27×34·5×23×29·5	grey limestone	irreg. cone with flattened top	—
14	D/X	III(5)	—	50: 4	48·030	18×33·5×25·5	white barytes	domed top	6158
15	D/X	III(6)	—	—	47·270	23–25×24–28	lt. gy. barytes	irreg. cylinder	—
16	D/X	III(7)	—	50: 5	46·280	36·2×35·2×9·5×20×18·2×23	black haematite	barrel or spindle	3072
17	K.14: Res. C	III	—	—	45·450	23·5×37×42·5×24×13	fine-grained greenish-black dolerite	irreg. duck form	—
18	H.14: 1002	III(8)	—	50: 6	45·365	21·5×30·7×29	white barytes	dome	5447
19	D/X	III(9)	—	—	44·340	31×31×15	white limestone	dome	—
20	K.15: 94	III	—	—	44·180	29×32·5×23	white limestone	dome	6360
21	G.18: 32	III(10)	—	—	42·640	26·7×31·5×21	white limestone	dome	6354
22	D.7000	III(11)	—	—	41·970	24–27×21×18	dk. bn. haematite	irreg. cylinder	—
23	H.14: 1002	III(12)	—	—	33·750	24–29	brownish-black limonite	spherical irreg.	—
24	D/X	III(13)	—	—	29·980	20–22×29×18	white limestone	irreg. dome or cone	—
25	D/X	III(14)	—	—	25·345	36×20·5×17	pink and white mottled limestone	oblong, irreg. solid	—
26	D/X	III	—	—	23·380	21·5×28·5×26·5×20	limonite	v. irreg. cone	—
27	D/X	III(15)	—	—	22·950	29×21×17·5	brownish-black limonite	irreg. barrel	—
28	D/X	III(16)	—	—	22·856	20×22·2×18	brownish-black limonite	dome	—
29	D/X	III(17)	—	—	19·530	24×20×15×12	brownish-black limonite	barrel, roughly made	—
30	H.18: 1084	III	—	—	11·230	13·5–10·5×25·5×22·5	yellowish limestone	irreg. very flat cylinder	7123
31	D.7000	I, i	n-ṣ-p	50: 7 51: 7	10·515	14–16×22×16–19	pink limestone	irreg. dome	7253
32	PQR.17, 251·25 m.	III	—	—	10·390	16–18·5×19–20·5×15·5	dk. gy. limestone	v. irreg. dome	—
33	D/X	III(18)	—	50: 8	9·690	29×12×10×18×7	black haematite	spindle	1580

No.	Locus	Group	Inscription or Mark	Plate No.	Grammes	Size in mm. (height, width, diameter at base; in some cases also measurements of top and base)	Material	Shape	Field No.
34	D/X	III(19)	—	—	8·975	7·5–11 × 16·5 × 14·8–15·2	lt. gy. limestone	irreg. dome or cylinder	—
35	D/X	I, ii, 1	p-y-m	51: 8	8·130	16·5 × 18 × 12	pinkish-white limestone	dome	1505
36	D/X	III(20)	—	—	7·870	24 × 14 × 11 × 17·3 × 10 × 5	bk. to brownish-bk. haematite	spindle	—
37	D/X	I, ii, 2	p-y-m	51: 9	7·805	14·5 × 18 × 13·5	yellow limestone	dome	6157
38	D/X	I, iii, 1	b-q-ʿ	51: 12	6·150	14 × 17 × 15·5	pinkish-white limestone	dome	500
39	219	III(21)	—	—	6·135	12·5 × 19 × 13–16	dk. gy. limestone	irreg. dome	4876
40	L.12	I, iii, 2	b-q-ʿ	50: 9 / 51: 13	6·095	15·5 × 16 × 13·5	pink limestone	dome	5349
41	F.7	III(22)	—	—	5·870	32 × 11·5 × 7 × 4 × 2·5	reddish-black haematite	—	
42	D/X	I, iii, 3	beth	51: 14	5·660	15 × 15·5 × 8	hard pink limestone	dome or ball flattened at base	—
43	D/X	III(23)	—	—	5·450	11 × 16 × 13	white barytes	irreg. dome	—
44	G.14: 1012	III	—	—	5·280	10 × 16·5	green soapstone (steatite)	v. flat cylinder	5533
45	D.500	II, ii, 1	Mark	51: 11	5·130	12·5 × 16·5 × 15	white limestone	dome	—
46	D/X	II, ii, 2	Mark or zayin	50: 10	4·879	?	limestone (?)	dome	7254
47	D/X	III(24)	—	—	4·580	20·5 × 14·6 × 11 × 11	gn. and gy. mottled serpentine	duck-form	1515
48	PQR.17	III(31)	—	—	4.020	8 × 29 × 5	haematite	spindle	7241
49	H.18: 1084	II, ii, 2	{ Mark or	51: 10	3·820	11 × 14·5 × 11·5	grey limestone	dome	7124
50	J.17: 1042	II, ii, 2	{ zayin	51: 15	3·770	13 × 12–12·5 × 8	yellow limestone	cuboid	—
51	L.13	III(25)	—	—	3·550	16·8 × 9·8 × 5·5	reddish-brown limonite	irreg. cylinder	—
52	L.14: 65	III(26)	—	50: 11	3·380	11·8 × 13·2–14·2 × 11·8 × 6·8–9·0	dk. gy. limestone	cylinder with flattened base and domed top	6398
53	D/X	III(27)	—	—	3·185	9 × 11·2 × 9·5	black haematite	dome	—
54	D.500	II, ii, 3	Traces of marks	—	3·120	9·8–10·2 × 14 × 11	white limestone	dome	—
55	D/X	II, ii, 4	Mark	51: 16	1·705	9·5 × 9·5 × 7	white limestone	cuboid	—
56	D/X	III(28)	—	50: 12	1·445	8 × 9 × 7	black haematite	dome	3074
57	D.7000	III(29)	—	—	1·330	7·9 × 10·2 × 8·2	grey limestone	cylinder flattened at base, domed at top	—
58	D/X	III(30)	Mark?	—	17·310	12 × 14·5	lead	irreg. cylinder flattened at base, slightly domed at top	3075

Suggested Metrological Values (*in grammes, unless otherwise indicated*)

1–9   It seems that the weights of this group represent eight units of the "standard" sheqel. If this suggestion is correct, the value of the units would be: (1) 11·558; (2) 11·498; (3) 11·429; (4) 11·389; (5) 11·382; (6) 11·094; (7) 11·081; (8) 11·060; (9) 10·967. There is also a possibility that each of the weights is ten units of the *neṣeph* system, and the value of each unit would range from 9·25 to 8·77.

10   It is uncertain whether this object is a weight; if so, its metrological value would be seven sheqels, its unit being 10·820, or else eight *neṣeph*, based on the unit of 9·416.

11   Five sheqels, its unit being 11·431.

No.	
12	Broken in antiquity, its original weight and metrological value is uncertain. There is a possibility that it belonged to the same series as the group 1–9; it is slightly more than half the weight of those specimens.
13–16	The weights of this group seem to represent five *neṣeph*, their units being: (13) 9·357; (14) 9·337; (15) 9·241; (16) 9·142.
17–20	Probably four "standard" sheqels, their units being: (17) 11·3625; (18) 11·341; (19) 11·085; (20) 11·045.
21–22	Probably four *neṣeph*, their units being: (21) 10·66 and (22) 10·49.
23	Probably three "standard" sheqels, based on the unit of 11·25.
24	Probably three *neṣeph*, based on the unit of 9·99.
25–26	Probably four *beqaʿ*, i.e. two "sacred" sheqels, their units being: (25) 6·3365 for a *beqaʿ* or 12·673 for a "sacred" sheqel, and (26) 5·854 for a *beqaʿ* or 11·690 for a "sacred" sheqel.
27–28	Probably three *pîm*, their units being: (27) 7·65 and (28) 7·619.
29	Probably two *neṣeph*, based on the unit of 9·765.
30	Probably a "standard" sheqel (11·230).
31–34	A total of 13 weights from various Palestinian sites are inscribed "*neṣeph*", including No. 31 and two weights from Tell en-Naṣbeh; between them they range from 10·515 to 9·28. Thus Tell ed-Duweir Nos. 32 and 33 fit into this scale, whereas No. 34, weighing 8·975, would be rather light.
35–37	The three weights (35) of 8·13, (36) of 7·87 and (37) of 7·805, are *pîms*; the fact that the first and the last of them are inscribed makes it certain that the second also belongs to this series.
38–42	These weights, (38) of 6·15, (39) of 6·135, (40) of 6·095, (41) of 5·87 and (42) of 5·66, belong to the *beqaʿ* series. Indeed, Nos. 38 and 40 are inscribed, and No. 41 weighs exactly the same as another inscribed specimen, probably found at Jerusalem (see p. 350). The only doubt may arise about No. 42, which would be rather light, and is inscribed only with the letter *beth*.
43–47	These weights seem to represent a half-*neṣeph* (provided we leave out of consideration the marks of Nos. 45 and 46, which defy explanation) based on the following units: (43) 10·90, (44) 10·56, (45) 10·26, (46) 9·758 and (47) 9·16. As to No. 46, see also Nos. 49–50 below.
48	Probably half a *pîm*, weighing 8·04.
49–50	Both the weights bear the same marks and represent the same standard and unit, which are, however, unknown. The significance of the mark is also uncertain. It must be noted that No. 46 bears the same mark, but perhaps represents another unit or standard. No explanation can be given for the mark if it is a letter, probably a *zayin* (although there is a possibility that it may be an irregular *shin*, in which case it would stand for *sh-l-sh* or *sh-l-sh-t*, *shelishith*, "one-third"; see the weights inscribed *shlsht* (Diringer, Iscrizioni, p. 281) and *ḥmsh* (ibid., p. 282)). It may, however, represent two hooks or strokes, indicating two fractions of a unit perhaps two-thirds of a *beqaʿ* (the units being 5·73 and 5·655 respectively) or two-fourths, i.e. one half of a *pîm* (the units being 7·64 and 7·54 respectively) or else two-fifths of a *neṣeph*, 9·55 and 9·425 respectively. No. 46 represents probably the same fraction, but of another unit or standard.
51–52	Probably half a *pîm*, (51) 7·10 and (52) 6·24 respectively. The latter, however, may represent a *beqaʿ*.
53–54	Probably half a *beqaʿ*, i.e. a quarter of the "sacred" sheqel, of 6·37 and 6·24 respectively for the *beqaʿ*, i.e. 12·74 and 12·48 respectively for the "sacred" sheqel.
55–56	No. 55 is probably a quarter of a *beqaʿ* weighing 6·82, i.e. one-eighth of the "sacred" sheqel weighing 13·64. No. 56 may also be a quarter of a *beqaʿ*, the unit, 5·78, being rather a rare one.
57	Probably one-fifth of a *beqaʿ* or one-tenth of the "sacred" sheqel, the unit being 6·65 for the *beqaʿ*, i.e. 13·30 for the "sacred" sheqel.
58	This certainly belongs to a much later period than the foregoing specimens; it probably represents two *stater*, its unit being 8·655.

Professor F. E. Zeuner has provided the following remarks on the raw materials of the weights:

1. The term *limestone* as used in the list includes many varieties with relatively small amounts of calcite. At least some of them (e.g. No. 15) contain barium sulphate and thus provide a transition to the specimens made of pure barytes (Nos. 14, 18, 19). All are relatively hard.

2. The *limonites* are outwardly indistinguishable from the haematites.

3. A distinct tendency to use heavy rocks for the weights such as lead, haematite and limonite, barytes and barytic limestones, and basic igneous rocks, is apparent.

4. The numerical distribution of the weights over the major classes of raw materials is as follows:

Barytes, barytic and other limestones	38
Limonites and haematites	14
Basic igneous rocks	3
Pure metal	1
Soapstone	1

5. As to the origin of the raw materials, I am not competent to hold an opinion.

MISCELLANEOUS

The "Royal Bath" Inscription

H.17: 1078, F. No. 7066 (Pl. 49: 1).

The inscription was incised before firing on the upper part of a storage jar which measured from 7·5 to 8·15 cm. at the rim. The pocked surface was buff inside and pink outside, with a grey core, while the ware was rather hard and had contained limestone and flint grits. The vessel resembles, but is not identical with, the *la-melekh* jars.

Inscription:

בת למלך   *b-t l-m-l-k* (*bath la-melekh*), "royal bath".

The letters are very irregular, but the reading is clear. Only the head (1·3×0·9 cm.) remains of the first letter, *beth*, with a small part of the main stem. The *taw* has the shape of an irregular X (1·6×1·4 cm.). The first *lamed* is very tall (about 4·8 cm.) and its base is very irregular. The form of the *mem* is rather archaic and is not complete (the preserved portion of the stem is 2·0 cm. high, while the head measures 1·3 cm.). The second *lamed* is much taller than the first; it measures about 6·4–6·5 cm. The *kaph* consists of a long stem (5·6 cm.) which may have been even longer, for a small part may be missing from the base. The latter is rounded; at the top, two irregular strokes branch off from the main stem, one about 2·4 cm. long, and the other measuring about 1·8 cm.

The inscription indicates the Biblical liquid measure *b-t*, *bath*, corresponding to the *ephah*. There is no indication of the form of the lower part of the inscription, and too few fragments remain to make a check on the value to be attributed to the unit of a bath or a "royal" bath. C. H. Inge tried to identify (PEQ, April–July 1941, pp. 106–109) the standard of the "royal" bath with that of the jars bearing the "royal" stamps (see pp. 342–347). On the other hand, W. F. Albright, dealing with a sherd found at Tell Beit Mirsim and inscribed *b-t* ("bath"), arrived at the conclusion that the stamped jars "must represent two baths if the standard of capacity is the same, which seems likely" (AASOR XXI–XXII, p. 58, n. 7). Albright, however, accepts Inge's solution of the metrological question, though referring it to a double "royal" bath, and thus attributing to the latter measure the metrological value of about 22 litres.

Concerning the date of the inscription, nothing definite can be said from the archaeological point of view, the fragments having been found in the burnt debris over Room H.17: 1078, which was one of the shops by the side of the road, destroyed in the burning of city Level III. It could have been deposited later when the area was an open space, before or at the time of the second destruction, but such an hypothesis is not tenable on epigraphic grounds.

Inge suggested that the inscription should be attributed to "the late Jewish period", whereas the writer, for strictly epigraphic reasons, places it much earlier. Albright, agreeing with the latter suggestion, gave an additional reason (op. cit., p. 59, § 36) for its attribution to the eighth century B.C. Indeed, as Albright points out, the tendency to exaggerated prolongation of the shafts of the letters, and particularly the archaic form of the head of the *mem*, are characteristic of the eighth century B.C. (perhaps even of the early eighth century). Lastly, Albright's opinion that the "royal" stamped jars probably begin after the disuse of the *bt lmlk* inscribed jars also seems reasonable.

Fragmentary Inscription engraved on Jar Handle

PQR.17, 254 m. Part of jar handle (Pl. 52: 8).

The inscription was engraved in the clay before firing: only four letters are preserved. None of them is quite regular, this irregularity being due to the difficulty of engraving in the clay. The second symbol is not complete, nor perhaps the fourth, but the reading of all four letters does not present any difficulty. The letters are: *lamed*, *beth*, *nun* and *he*.

The first letter is the possessive *lamed*, "of, (belonging) to". The following three letters (*bnh*) may represent an abbreviated theophorous name, such as the Biblical Ben, Benayah(u) or something similar, or else the first part of *ben ha-melek* or the like.

Remains of an Inscription

E.18:A: Outside the outer gate, F. No. 5248 (Pl. 52: 10).

This was a pinkish fragment, irregular in shape, measuring 5·6–6·6 × 3·9 cm., with a thickness of 0·6–0·8 cm.

The inscription was incised in the clay before firing. Only the first letter is preserved—slightly damaged at the top—and the main stem of the following character, which could have been a *mem*, or a *kaph*, or else a *pe*. The preserved letter is a *resh*; its head, like the preserved part of the following letter, is not regular in line, which is easily explained by the difficulty of engraving curved lines in the clay. It is useless to attempt a reconstruction of the original inscription. Its probable date is the sixth century B.C.

The First Five Letters of the Alphabet

L.13: 1063 (Fig. 10, Pls. 48B; 18: 2–4).

The rise of a limestone step, part of a stairway underlying the exposed flight L.13: 1063, east of the palace. The height of the rise was 15 cm., and the original width of the step was about 4 metres, but the Figure is constricted, omitting a blank space between the alphabetic letters and the outline of a lion: the drawing of the letters is, however, to the actual size. All the signs and the animal are very lightly scratched in the soft howr limestone.

Discovered on the last day of the excavations, the letters were so faintly made that they could only be seen in a side light. Sitting on a lower step with his back to the palace wall, the writer must have stretched out his arm to scratch the letters diagonally across the corner of the rise. Professor H. Torczyner, on seeing the drawing, at once recognised the inscription as the first five letters of the Early Hebrew alphabet in their conventional order, "perhaps the work of a schoolboy airing his knowledge, writing the equivalent of ABCDE until he reached the top of the step" (Inge). It was also pointed out, and rightly, that this is actually the earliest archaeological evidence for the order of the alphabet in Palestine, and the first example of the Hebrew alphabet being learnt systematically. There are a few other signs, including a *resh* and also perhaps a *daleth*; three signs in the form of two vertical strokes and a kind of Roman numeral, X, may represent some numerical figures. Finally, there may be traces of a *yodh* in mirror writing, but all this is rather uncertain.

On the other hand, the importance of the partial alphabet is not to be underestimated. On palaeographic grounds the letters may be assigned to the late ninth or early eighth century B.C. This dating, with which Professor Albright agrees, is mainly based on the *daleth*, with its short tail, on the tall form of the *beth*, and on the *he*, in which the upper horizontal stroke does not pass the vertical line of the letter. If this palaeographic evidence can be taken into consideration for such a short and casual inscription, it should be placed between the Mesha' stone and the Siloam inscription, and much nearer to the former than to the latter. In this case the Lachish partial alphabet could be considered as the earliest preserved North Semitic alphabetic inscription, preceding by some decades the Marsiliana Tablet of the eighth century B.C. (see Diringer, The Alphabet, p. 494).

Aramaic Inscription on an Altar

Group 534, F. No. 3668A (Pls. 49: 3 and 68: 1).

The following note on the Aramaic inscription found on a limestone altar in Group 534 has been contributed by Professor A. Dupont-Sommer (Université de Paris, à la Sorbonne):

"Cette inscription, gravée sur l'une des faces latérales du petit cube de pierre, ne compte que trois lignes, qui, dans leur état actuel, présentent respectivement six, cinq et six signes. Les caractères, nettement gravés, sont typiquement araméens; ils sont tout à fait comparables à ceux des inscriptions d'époque perse (voir notre exemple, Pl. 49). De ce fait, cette nouvelle inscription constitue un témoin fort intéressant concernant la diffusion de l'araméen en Judée vers le V–IV siècle avant J.C.

"Un fragment important de la pierre a disparu à la partie gauche de la face où figure l'inscription, ce qui a entraîné la suppression de deux ou trois signes à la fin de chaque ligne. Mais, en dehors de cette mutilation, l'inscription est complète. Voici comment nous la lisons:

לבנתא[ן] 1

שבנמח[ן] 2

ליהמרא[ן] 3

"A la ligne 1, bien que les mots dans cette inscription ne soient pas séparés les uns des autres, le premier mot se détache nettement, grâce à la désinence de l'état emphatique: לבנתא; ce mot ne peut guère se traduire ici autrement que 'l'encens'. C'est le mot araméen לְבוֹנְתָא, syriaque ܠܒܘܢܬܐ, correspondant à l'hébreu לְבוֹנָה; on le rencontre dès le V siècle avant J.C. dans les papyrus d'Eléphantine: לבונה (Cowley, No. 30, l. 21, No. 31, l. 21, No. 33, l. 11), לבונתא (Cowley, No. 30, l. 25, No. 32, l. 9). Le mot est écrit défectivement, ce qui ne fait pas difficulté, vu l'époque de notre inscription. Un tel nom est parfaitement en situation ici, étant donné qu'il s'agit d'un petit autel à encens. Notons que sur deux autels semblables trouvés dans le Yémen sont gravées de courtes inscriptions en sud-arabique mentionnant divers parfums, notamment 'l'encens' (לבני); cf. Ryckmans, *Muséon*, t. XLVIII (1935), pp. 176–177 (Nos. 136, 137).

"Ce qui suit est d'une interprétation difficile, étant donné que, pour sept lettres certaines, il y a cinq lettres plus ou moins douteuses et environ six ou sept lettres manquantes. En outre, nous ne possédons aucune autre inscription araméenne gravée sur un autel de ce type. Dans ces conditions, nous ne pouvons malheureusement proposer que des conjectures plus ou moins probables.

" Il nous semble d'abord qu'au milieu de la ligne 2, on peut distinguer le mot בן 'fils de'. Le ב est partiellement mutilé: le haut de la lettre a disparu dans une échancrure de la pierre, comme le montre assez clairement la photographie; sinon, il faudrait lire un ס ou, à la rigueur, un ו (à queue un peu longue). Si le mot בן est bien à lire, on doit avoir avant et après ce mot, deux noms propres. Le premier pourrait se lire י[הוא]ש ou יו[אש] 'Joas'. Le second, qui commence par un מ et se continue par une lettre mutilée qui est probablement ה (plutôt que ד ou ר), pourrait se lire par exemple מְחִיר (cf. I Chroniques IV: 11) — défectivement מחר — ou encore מחסה (nom fréquent à Eléphantine, abrégé de מַחְסְיָה). Ce 'Joas (?) fils de Meḥir (?)', un Juif, ce serait l'auteur même de l'ex-voto, dont il est naturel que le nom figure dans l'inscription. Le mot hébreu בן, au lieu de l'araméen בר, peut surprendre dans cette inscription araméenne; mais rappelons qu'à l'inverse, la grande inscription de Kilamû, bien qu'entièrement phénicienne, conserve le mot araméen בר dans la généalogie du roi, parce que la famille était araméenne: ici, on aurait gardé le mot בן, parce que l'hébreu restait la langue maternelle, la langue domestique de ce Juif. Si, toutefois, la présence du mot בן dans cette inscription araméenne semblait à certains impossible, on pourrait peut-être lire à la rigueur ו au lieu de נ et supposer ici deux noms propres reliés par la conjonction 'et'; le premier nom serait alors Y--ŠB (= Yôyôsîbh?). Il y aurait ainsi deux offrants, au lieu d'un; pour le reste, l'interprétation serait la même·

"A la ligne 3, les trois lettres ליה pourraient être la fin du second nom propre; ce nom serait alors non pas de trois ou quatre lettres, comme מחי)ר(, mais de six lettres, comme par exemple dans le type מבטחיה. Toutefois, nous ne voyons pas au juste quel nom propre serait à lire ici; et surtout nous serions assez embarrassés pour donner ensuite un sens aux trois lettres מְרָא qui suivent. Aussi pensons-nous que ליה est plutôt ici un mot indépendant, signifiant: 'à Yah', c'est-à-dire à Yahvé; on sait que la forme abrégée יָהּ, pour יהוה, se rencontre dans l'Ancien Testament, surtout dans les formules liturgiques, et aussi que le même nom divin est écrit tantôt יה tantôt יהו sur des estampilles de Jéricho (cf. M. Lidzbarski, Ephemeris..., III, p. 45). Nul ne contestera que le nom du dieu ait à figurer dans une inscription votive.

"Les trois lettres qui suivent ליה sont plus ou moins mutilées. L'examen attentif de la photographie, nous a convaincu que la lecture מרא était épigraphiquement possible et même probable: le premier signe ne peut guère se lire autrement que מ; le second semble être la tête d'un ר (ou d'un ד); le troisième semble être la partie supérieure d'un א, du type de l'א de la ligne 1. Le mot מרא est excellemment araméen: מְרָא 'seigneur'. On peut compléter, semble-t-il: ou bien מראה 'son seigneur', ou bien מרא שמיא, 'seigneur du ciel'. A l'appui de cette seconde hypothèse, rappelons l'expression מרא שמיא ליהו, 'à Yahô, seigneur du ciel', dans un papyrus d'Eléphantine (Cowley, No. 30, l. 15) et aussi מָרֵא־שְׁמַיָּא, désignant Yahvé, dans Daniel (V, 23). Le mot שמיא, il est vrai, paraît un peu long pour la lacune; mais le graveur a pu, sur la fin, serrer un peu les lettres, ou bien déborder un peu sur la face voisine.

"Sous les réserves indiquées plus haut, nous aboutissons donc à la traduction suivante:

1 *L'encens J[oa]*
2 *s* (?) *fils de Meḥ*[ir] (?)
3 *à Yah, maître* [du ciel]

"Il manque manifestement un verbe, tel que קרב, 'a offert'. Etant donné la liberté de l'ordre des mots dans la phrase verbale araméenne, on peut supposer que ce verbe se trouvait tout à la fin de l'inscription et a disparu dans la lacune; en ce cas, on rétablirait la dernière ligne plutôt comme suit: ליה מרא [הקרב]. Mais il nous paraît plus probable que le verbe est resté sous-entendu: cette omission du verbe קרב, notons-le, est extrêmement fréquente dans les inscriptions gravées sur les pyrées palmyréniens (voir Corpus Inscriptionum Semiticarum II, Nos. 3981, 3989, 4006, 4009, 4010, 4016, 4017, etc.).

"L'inscription ainsi interprétée offre un sens plausible, et bien en accord avec la destination de ce petit autel telle qu'on pouvait la déterminer du point de vue archéologique. La mention de Yahvé — si ליה signifie bien ici 'à Yah' — est, il est vrai, un peu étonnante; elle semble indiquer, en effet, qu'en dépit des prescriptions du Deutéronome et du Code Sacerdotal sur l'unité de sanctuaire, s'était maintenu à Lakish, à quelque quarante kilomètres de Jérusalem, au V–IV siècle avant J.C., un sanctuaire consacré à Yahvé, un sanctuaire où des Juifs offraient l'encens à leur Dieu. Mais on sait que, vers le même temps, les colons juifs d'Eléphantine avaient leur propre temple de Yahô, tout en restant en communion avec les autorités juives de Jérusalem. On sait aussi qu'au II siècle avant J.C., le grand-prêtre Onias construisit un temple de Yahvé à Léontopolis, en Egypte. Il semble donc que l'application de la loi sur l'unité de sanctuaire ne fut pas aussi stricte qu'on aurait pu le penser. L'inscription de Lakish, si notre interprétation est recevable, constituerait à cet égard un nouveau témoignage, d'un réel intérêt historique.

"Paris, 30 Octobre 1948."

CHAPTER 11

HIEROGLYPHIC AND ORNAMENTAL SEALS

By MARGARET A. MURRAY, D.LIT.

SCARABS

THE sphragistic material published in the present volume was found either in an undoubted Iron Age context in tombs and in the tell rooms, or it was recovered from the surface soil and cannot be dated stratigraphically. In the latter case, scarabs or scaraboids which appear to belong to the Iron Age have been included on the basis of style. All the tombs except 110, 160, 191 and 194 contained many burials and covered a long range of time.

Enough material is now available from Palestine to warrant an attempt at a closer division of scarabs, scaraboids and seals within the Iron Age, when the popularity of the scarab, at least, had passed its zenith, and shared the honours equally with the simple scaraboid. It is, of course, necessary to begin with the scarabs of Egyptian origin or influence, though it must be admitted that after the close of the New Kingdom these are neither clearly defined nor found in groups of chronological value. Indeed, the problems of royal descent and succession in the following dynasties are obscure, and in Egypt are complicated still further by the existence of contemporary lines, ruling respectively from Tanis and Thebes (CAH II, p. 703).

In Palestine the attempt at exact dating is obscured by the common practice of placing many interments in one tomb, the contents of which may cover many years, whereas in Egypt individual burials were the rule.

The scarabs engraved with hieroglyphs from Tell ed-Duweir can be divided into three categories:

(*a*) Royal names and titles.
(*b*) The God Amen and his attributes.
(*c*) Designs and symbols.

(*a*) *Royal Names and Titles*

Scarabs bearing royal names were often used as seals on official documents. It is, however, difficult to distinguish between the official scarabs and those which, though bearing a royal name, were regarded as amulets. It would seem that the Pharaoh's name had as great a power of protection against spiritual enemies as he himself had against his physical foes.

Six scarabs bear the throne name of Thotmes III (1501–1447 B.C.), *Mn-ḫpr-Rʿ*: Nos. 3 and 4 came from groups 107 and 120, Nos. 1 and 6 from Tomb 218, and Nos. 2 and 5 from Tomb 116. With them can be placed No. 9 (cf. TN I, Pl. 54: 16), possibly reading *Rʿ-mn-ḫpr-sʾ-ymn*, and No. 44, reading *Rʿ-ḫpr*.

There is no doubt that the pottery is far removed from the forms and technique associated with the time of the great conqueror (cf. L. II, Pl. XXXII: 8, 9 and Pls. XXXVIII ff.), and it has long been assumed that such scarabs were either heirlooms or reissues to commemorate this king. It would be surprising if local memory in south Palestine had so far venerated Thotmes III as to reproduce his scarabs in some quantity after a lapse of five hundred years, for few, if any, scarabs of the more spectacular Ramesside monarchs are to be found in an Iron Age context.

There are, however, at least two other Pharaohs who bore the throne name *Mn-ḫpr-Rʿ*. The first of these was the third king of the xxist dynasty, whose rule is guaranteed by a bandage wrapping to have lasted forty-nine years. The second is a very nebulous person of the xxvth dynasty, *circa* 700 B.C., who is known only by a partly erased name on a stela and by some scarabs which are said to be common (see Petrie's History of Egypt, vol. III; cf. CAH III, p. 254, ed. 1929).

Mn-ḫpr-Rʿ of the xxist dynasty was a secular ruler of some power, who had long been absent from Thebes, and needed to establish his authority before the god. His return in the twenty-fifth year of his reign to restore order in southern Egypt shows that he was normally domiciled in the north. Only one of his scarabs is recorded from Egypt (PSC XLIX: Cairo 37426), naming also his queen Isi-em-kheb, but it is very possible that others have been incorrectly attributed to Thotmes III in museum collections. This lack of scarabs in a reign of half a century would be explained if his suzerainty extended from the Delta to south Palestine, where *Mn-ḫpr-Rʿ* scarabs are common and are almost exclusively associated, as far as the Iron Age is concerned, with pottery ascribed to the eleventh–ninth centuries B.C.

Besides the six scarabs from Duweir, there are three from T.32 at Tell en-Naṣbeh, which some Egyptologists assign to the xxvth dynasty, 712–663 B.C. (TN I, p. 148), though it was noted in the publication that so late a date "does not agree with the graph or pottery evidence" (op. cit., p. 99). Examples came from Tomb 1 at 'Ain Shems (RES 500, 501 and APEF II, Pl. XXIX). There are others from the filling of Stratum IV at Megiddo (M. I, Pl. 69: 36) and from Stratum V (M. I, Pl. 71: 76). All are associated with pottery which includes a good proportion of hand burnished wares, and forms such as the strainer-spouted jug.

On the basis of style and cutting, Nos. 1 and 2 may well be original Thotmes III scarabs, possibly rediscovered and re-used in the Iron Age. With regard to the others, some backs are poorly executed, though in Egypt scarabs dated to the same period show that good cutting continued as late as 925 B.C.

The name of *Mn-ḫpr-Rʿ*, with an additional group of hieroglyphs, is to be seen on No. 6 from Tomb 218. There are comparable scarabs in Petrie's catalogues (PSC, Pl. LIII: 19–23 and BDS, Pl. XXV: 25c 22a), and though the signs included in the second group are not always identical, the variants have much in common.

Petrie has attributed the scarabs which he illustrates to *Mn-ḫpr-Rʿ* of the xxvth dynasty. Whether they should not preferably be transferred to the holder of that name in the xxiind dynasty remains uncertain, but the personal name of whatever king is commemorated would seem to be contained in the second group of signs.

The following variants may be read:

No. 6				*Mn-ḫpr-Rʿ*	*Rʿ-mny*[1]	*k tʿw*
BDS, Pl. XXV: 25c 22a		.	.	*Mn-ḫpr-Rʿ*	*Rʿ-mny*	*k tʿwi*
PSC, Pl. LIII: 22	.	.	.	*Mn-ḫpr-Rʿ*	*Rʿ-mny*	*k(y)rn* (?)
PSC, Pl. LIII: 23	.	.	.	*Mn-ḫpr-Rʿ*	*Rʿ-mny*	*k(y)rn* (?)

The first two examples read, "(the king) *Mn-ḫpr-Rʿ*, *Rʿ-mny* (is the) other name". The signs following the *k* in the last two examples have rounded ends, suggesting the sign *tʿ*.

Other scarabs are attributed to the xxvth-dynasty king by Petrie (PSC, Pl. LIII: 7–21), but the majority are not so well made as those noted above.

There is a duplicate of No. 20 from Tell en-Naṣbeh (TN I, Pl. 54: 3) found in Tomb 32 (cf. RES 876, 878, 879). Another scarab illustrated in PSC. Pl. XXXIX: 36, could also give the same reading, though the signs are differently disposed.

No. 9, already noticed with the *Mn-ḫpr-Rʿ* scarabs, bears a resemblance to the scarabs attributed to *Si-amen* jointly with *Mn-ḫpr-Rʿ* (PSC, Pl. XLIX: 3, 9); it has a parallel from Lahun (Lahun II, Pl. LXIII: 13), while examples with some similar elements come from Koptos (BDS, Pl. XVII: 1244–1245) and from Tell en-Naṣbeh (TN I, Pl. 54: 11).

The broken scarab No. 43 is reminiscent of those attributed to Sheshenq IV, ninth king of the xxiind dynasty (PSC, Pl. L:12–16), and it comes from group 107, which contained burials and part of the ossuary deposit.

No. 8, *Ḫpr-Rʿ*, in a cartouche, was a surface find, but No. 44 from Tomb 218, with the same symbols flanked by hawks, may belong to Sheshenq IV or Osorkon III, second king of the xxiiird dynasty (PSC, Pl. LI: 1–14, RES, 866–869). A duplicate of this scarab comes from Lahun (Lahun II, Pl. L, bottom right, Tomb 603) and

---

[1] The two lines after the sign *Rʿ* show that the word is to be repeated, i.e. read in the two names.

from 'Ain Shems, Tomb 1 (APEF II, Pl. XXIX), and there are also in both groups more than one example of scarabs bearing the title *Tyt-n-Ymn*. Cf. also No. 11 from Tomb 218 reading *Tyt-Ymn* and No. 131. The sign is not unlike *štp*; but in *štp*, which represents an adze, the handle turns down; in *tyt*, which is part of the conventional sacred eye, the end curves up, often into a spiral.

Other scarabs which may eventually prove to be readable when more is known of the dark period covered by the xxiiird–xxvith dynasties are Nos. 29, 34, and 37. No. 36 may possibly read *Nfr-Nub-Rʿ*, a petty ruler at the rise of Saite domination, *c.* 700 B.C. (Petrie's History of Egypt III, p. 300, Fig. 124).

The large scarab No. 156 was found in the floor of a post-exilic building north of the Great Shaft. The size and style of cutting show that it was contemporary with Amenhetep III, whose name it bears.

It is unusual to find the double cartouche of Amenhetep III placed side by side on a scarab; when two cartouches occur, they contain the king's throne name (*Nb-Mʾ 't-Rʿ*) and the name of his queen Tyi. Otherwise the whole inscription, with the exception of the words after the second cartouche, contains only the usual formulae: (right): "The good god, *Nb-Mʾ 't-Rʿ*, beloved of *Ymn*"; (left): Son of the Sun, *Ymn-ḥtp*, Ruler of Thebes, King of all Lachish (*ni-śwt Rḫš nb*)". The last three words may have been cut later than the rest in a space left for the purpose. The large size of the *R* in relation to the following signs suggests that the craftsman concerned miscalculated the space at his disposal.[1]

(b) The God Amen and his Attributes

Nos. 11–18 are scarabs bearing the name of the Theban god *Ymn-Rʿ*; they come from Tombs 107, 120, 218 and 116, to which groups the *Mn-ḫpr-Rʿ* scarabs are also confined. The name of *Ymn-Rʿ* is one of the most popular motifs on scarabs, both in Egypt (BDS, 659–675) and south Palestine ('Ain Shems APEF II, Pl. XXIX; Megiddo I, Pl. 69: 11, from Stratum V).

The name flanked by *nb* signs like Nos. 14–16 and the variety encircled by a lotus bud (like No. 17), are both introduced in the xviiith dynasty (IKG, Pl. XXVI: 23, 10 "Maket Tomb" which is attributed to the xxth dynasty though it contains base-ring ware juglets, which now place the group in LB II, *c.* 1400 B.C. Note also the delicate workmanship of the xviiith-dynasty *Mn-ḫpr-Rʿ* scarabs in the group). The lotus-bud variety certainly survived until Shishak's reign, for it occurs in a tomb 651 from Lahun (Lahun II, Pl. LV: 8) which contained scaraboids bearing that king's name. The evidence from Palestine suggests that in the early part of the Iron Age *Ymn*-scarabs, with the name followed by strokes, circles and *tyt* or *štp*, were plentiful.

Though it is clear from the eleventh-century account of Wen-Amen's adventurous journey up the Syrian coast that local rulers could challenge the authority of the god (CAH III, p. 423), excavations have shown that the people attached some value to scarabs bearing the name of Amen in the tenth–ninth centuries, though they were extinct in tombs at Duweir before 800 B.C.

No. 10, *Wsr-Mʾ 't Rʿ štp-n-Rʿ*, is from the plastered area east of the palace; it may well come from the underlying burnt city of the Bronze Age and commemorate Rameses II, though it must be borne in mind that several kings of the xxii–xxiiird dynasties also held this title. It was found near No. 57, which rather supports an attribution to the later date.

(c) Scarabs with Designs and Symbols based on Hieroglyphs

Nos. 20, 21 and 41 from Tombs 116, 1002 and 106 respectively, maintain the tradition of a class popular in MB II, in which the hieroglyphs *rnw*, reading "names" are repeated (see M. A. Murray, PEQ 1949, p. 96);

---

[1] Dr. Murray's tentative but attractive solution of these signs must be viewed in relation to the only possible known reference to the city transcribed in hieroglyphs. It occurs on the reverse of papyrus 1116, A Hermitage Museum, Pl. 15, line 2, and the transliteration reads: *Rakis(a)*. Golenischeff (Pap. Ermitage, p. 5) has identified it with Lakiš in Palestine, a Canaanite stronghold. Professor P. E. Newberry has seen the original scarab, but was unable to suggest a reading.—O.T.

possibly they are survivors from the period. The curious bird on No. 41 is reminiscent of those painted on "Philistine" pottery.

Scarabs and seals which appear to be heirlooms from the second millennium are Nos. 20, 21, 23, 38, 40, 43, 59 and 157 (MB), and Nos. 1, 2, 22, 24, 25, 27, 28, 31, 33, 45, 47, 60, 125 and 138 (LB).

For individual descriptions of other scarabs in the class, see pp. 368–370.

SCARABOIDS, SEALS AND CONOIDS

The number of scarabs and scaraboids found at Tell ed-Duweir is almost equal, but few of the latter group were inspired by Egyptian motifs or hieroglyphs; Nos. 109–114 and 116 certainly show some influence, and No. 110 can be compared with the plaque No. 131 and the scarab No. 11.

Among the few scaraboids bearing a royal name is one of blue glaze, with a slightly domed back, from Lahun (Lahun II, Pl. LV: 4). It bears the name of Sheshenq (Shishak), Libyan founder of the xxiind dynasty of Egypt. The backs of the scarabs in the same group, which is dated by the presence of the scaraboid to the second half of the tenth century B.C., are carefully detailed and well-made; No. 7, for instance, on Pl. LV resembles No. 6 from Tomb 218 at Duweir. On the whole the scaraboids from Duweir are thicker in section and more angular and domed than that of Shishak, a difference which may place them somewhat later in date.

The motifs of the scaraboids are very simple and seem to be derived from originals of great antiquity.[1] While Egyptian scarabs continued to reach Palestine regularly during the Iron Age, few scaraboids bearing the simple designs described in the following classes have been found in Egypt.

Nos. 62–66

The bone scaraboids depicting men, drawn with triangular bodies and semicircular heads, and occasionally accompanied by a lion or other animal, are distinctive. The angular precision of the figures, filled in with hatched lines, is uniform throughout; they are allied in style to Nos. 89, 103 and the small group 106–107 showing the crested bird or phoenix, so that they can well be considered together.

At Tell ed-Duweir all stratified examples came from the large Tomb 1002, and were evenly divided among the layers. The only example (No. 106) attempting to reproduce a cartouche came from the surface, but the result of the attempt is not clear enough to make certain of the reading.

As the list of comparisons will show, there are parallels from Gezer, Megiddo, Tell en-Naṣbeh, but Tell el-Fara provides the largest selection, all from relatively small groups in the same cemetery (BP I, Pls. XXXI: 298; XXXV: 408, 423; XXXIX: 444; XL: 458; XLI: 291; XLIII: 515). Petrie placed them mostly in the xxiind dynasty, on the scarab evidence, but a scarab of *Men-k'-R'*, vassal of Shabaka, among others, suggests that the series may extend into the period of Ethiopian domination.

At Gezer, Macalister found an example with a man and cartouche (Gezer I, p. 334 and Fig. 173) in a tomb, but here again the reading is not clear and it can be attributed to Psametticus I or II or Amasis II.

Nos. 67–75

Made of stone, bone or paste, these scaraboids show figures of men. Though they are executed in a primitive style with blobs for the heads and bodies and lines for the arms and legs, they are distinct from the wooden and geometric attitudes of the previous group, and they manage to convey a great effect of carefree movement. Nos. 72, 73 and 75 were found in tombs which had later contained ossuary deposits, so that their date cannot be firmly established, but No. 68, with two men only, came from Tomb 1002 attributed to the eighth century.

The motif of the three men is missing from Tomb 218, from Tomb 1 at 'Ain Shems, and Tomb 32 at Tell

---

[1] The balanced design of a central object with a supporter on each side is Mesopotamian, and though known in Egypt in predynastic times, it seems to have been foreign.

en-Naṣbeh. At Megiddo there are examples from Strata V and IV (Megiddo I, Pls. 67: 56 and 69: 30). The best comparison for No. 73 is No. 2262 from Ajia Irini, Period 4 (GSCE II, p. 849), *c.* 650–600 B.C.

The foremost figure on scaraboid 71 is carrying an object which appears to be a trident, otherwise there is nothing to show whom these men represent.

No. 76

The seal represents a seated figure, holding a child by the hand, executed in blob style. There are close parallels for it from Tomb 32 at Tell en-Naṣbeh and from Illahun.

Nos. 77–80

Four seals show a man and a quadruped, apparently intended for a horse. The design is popular at other sites and is usually executed in the blob style.

Nos. 81, 82, 84–86 and conoid 143

All these show two ostriches, either with a blob-style man in the centre, or disposed in pairs, with one bird inverted. Only Nos. 84–85 are well made, and both came from Tomb 218; No. 86, from an open area on the mound, was not in its true context. There are comparisons from Tomb 1 at 'Ain Shems and Tomb 32 at Tell en-Naṣbeh, and a close parallel comes from Stratum B₃ at Tell Beit Mirsim, which Albright places before the end of the tenth century B.C. A later example is from Megiddo Stratum III (Megiddo I, Pl. 67: 38), but as it is made of haematite it may belong to an earlier level.

Nos. 87–99, 105

The antelope, ibex or gazelle, shown with or without another object, which is often a tree, is one of the most popular designs on scarabs and scaraboids alike. Nos. 91 and 92 demonstrate how a transformation can take place from a scorpion to a plant.

Nos. 100–102, 104

The first two scaraboids are large and boldly cut, and they came from Tomb 224, which is intermediate in date between Tombs 218 and 1002. The third example from Tomb 1004, which is only slightly later, shows less successful work. The shaggy-necked animal is matched in Tomb 1 at 'Ain Shems (RES: SO 36).

No. 103

See group 62–66.

Nos. 106–108

The three seals are made of bone; the first two show a crested bird or phoenix, the third may be a degradation of the design. The hatched style, bands on the back, and the small cartouche, links No. 106 to the general class discussed under Nos. 62–66.

Nos. 111–112

Both examples are somewhat out of place among the scaraboids; the signs are Egyptian and the shape is more closely allied to the cowroids (of which No. 157 is the only example in an Iron Age context at Duweir). Similar examples came from Megiddo, and from Tomb 1 at 'Ain Shems.

No. 114

See No. 142.

Nos. 118–122

The five seals of bone or limestone are decorated with the ring-and-dot circles, poorly cut and badly spaced. They were found in those tombs which contained the bone pendants similarly decorated.

No. 123

The glass scaraboid with a faintly impressed design of a mermaid or nereid finds its inspiration in the gem seals of the Greek world. It came from Tomb 4005 which was re-used for burials in the post-exilic period.

No. 124 (Fig. 35)

It is unfortunate that this unique scaraboid was a surface find, for it represents the Great Goddess, associated with several elements which date from the Late Bronze Age, and were revived centuries later, and it is no doubt to the period of renewed interest that the scaraboid should belong.

FIG. 35. Scaraboid 124

The goddess is nude, and her hair is elaborately dressed, with a ringlet spraying out on each side. Possibly she wears some kind of diadem. Her attitude is reminiscent of the pottery figurines of the *dea nutrix* type (Pls. 27, 28). Above her head hovers a bird (or the sun-disk) with outstretched wings. The long-robed worshipper with raised hand on the right of the goddess stands above an altar or footstool. On the left of the goddess is a tree on which is a monkey.

B. W. Buchanan, who has seen the scaraboid, remarked that the motif of the naked woman and monkey represents an interesting survival of one of the popular subjects of Syrian glyptic in the middle of the second millennium. In his opinion the woman is presented full face with her hands to her breasts in the manner usually associated with old Babylonian glyptics, and she has been so drawn that her figure assimilates itself to the form of the offering table which is commonly placed before a worshipper in glyptic of the first millennium. By contrast the monkey is quite unusually depicted in the naturalistic posture, sitting on a tree. With the presentation of the Persian worshipper in the usual style of the period, he found the elements of the design made an interesting eclectic ensemble.

No. 135

The attitude of the kneeling king, holding a staff, and the cross hatching, are reminiscent of such figures on Middle Bronze Age scarabs. The striding lion on the reverse of the plaque conforms to a decorative idiom which is foreign to Egypt.

No. 136

Both in material and design, this plaque shows a marked similarity to a cylinder from Megiddo, attributed to LB I by the excavators, who note its resemblance to cylinders from Nuzi and Kirkuk (MT, pp. 182 ff.). The plaque from Tomb 218 had probably survived as an heirloom.

No. 141

The carnelian seal is beautifully cut and polished, and shows a lion trampling on an antelope. It was found in a large cave 504, in which a rectangular grave, 525, had been cut, which probably belonged to a dignitary of the post-exilic period. It seems reasonable to assume that the seal came from this burial.

No. 142

One of three seals from Level III–II areas on the mound. The unpierced cone 142 is incised with a stylised design of a gazelle and trees, indifferently executed. With the scaraboids 86 and 114, it represents a late phase of degradation.

No. 143

See Nos. 81, 82 and 84–86.

No. 150

Possibly owing to the nature of the material, the three haematite seals—scarab 54 from Tomb 1002, scaraboid 96 from the undisturbed Tomb 521 and the conoid from Tomb 218—were all cut in the drilled blob style. Each one depicts a varied fauna, carefully observed, characteristic of the style and the material. See especially the fine bull's head from Tell el-Fara (BP I, Pl. XXXV: 389), where haematite seals are more common than at other sites.

No. 152

This steatite cylinder is the only one which exhibits any Egyptian influence, and yet all three elements in the design acquired most popularity in Palestine and in the Delta region during the xxiind dynasty. The rope pattern border was revived (previously common in the Middle Bronze Age), dancing figures of Bes were common, both as linear representations and as amulets, and the bird (or scarab) with outstretched wings became the emblem of sovereignty in Judah. Though cylinders are uncommon in the Iron Age, and seldom bear motifs which are distinctively Egyptian, the elements on the present example do suggest a date in the xxiind dynasty or later.

Nos. 153–155

No. 153 shows affinity with the Nuzi cylinders dated to the Late Bronze Age. The patterns of Nos. 154 and 155 can both be matched on Palestinian sites. No. 154, for instance, seems to be a degradation of the design on a glass cylinder from Tell el-Ajjul (AG III, Pl. IV: 127), while the pattern of linked circles on No. 155 is comparable to designs on cylinders from Megiddo (MT, Pl. 94: 3) and Tell Abu Hawam (QDAP IV Pl. XXXVIII: 406).

No. 156

See under *Royal Names and Titles*.

Nos. 159–164

The common factor in the design of these scaraboids and impressions is that they are all divided into two or more registers, either vertically or horizontally, and the signs engraved on them appear completely formal and meaningless. They are doubtless imitations of the old Hebrew seals like Nos. 168–173, in which complete mastery of the lapidary's art and orthography had been obtained. Who, then, among the peoples of south Palestine, were sufficiently uninstructed in the language to produce these scaraboids, and were yet anxious to compete with the Hebrews in the production of these characteristic seals?

Perhaps the group should be attributed to the makers of the bone scaraboids incised with human figures, Nos. 62–66, for the native-born Palestinians could normally do better in orthography. Scaraboids of this kind have not so far been noted from other sites.

Conclusions

The scarabs assembled on Pl. 43 are almost all comparable with Egyptian examples, and are not inferior to them in execution.

Nine scarabs are attributed to Middle Bronze Age inspiration or tradition, though they were not necessarily made at that time. Nearly a score follow Late Bronze Age models and some may have survived from that period. The remainder seem to be contemporary with the tombs in which they were found.

The only royal names enclosed in a cartouche are those of *Mn-ḫpr-Rʿ* (Nos. 1–3, 5) and of *Ḫpr-Rʿ* (No. 8), and while the consensus of opinion would give them merely an amuletic significance, traditional from the time of Thotmes III, an alternative suggestion might attribute them to one or other of the later bearers of that name, one of whom was a powerful Delta king who reigned for more than half a century. In the same early groups are examples of designs incorporating the name of the god Amen (*Ymn*) (Nos. 12–18).

The only scarabs from Tell ed-Duweir which appear to be of non-Egyptian inspiration are Nos. 24, 32, 34, 41 and 50.

Arranging the main groups in order of the pottery sequence, it will be seen from the schedule below that both scarabs and scaraboids were mostly made of stone, up to and including the occupation of Tomb 218, but that in later groups, paste and especially bone had become the common material.

A decrease in average length of scarabs in the later groups helps to confirm the approximate chronological order of the tombs and marks a steady degradation of the glyptic arts.

The scaraboids on Pl. 44 cover the same range as the scarabs. While the example from Lahun shows that they can be as early as Shishak's reign (Lahun II, Pl. LV), there is no guarantee that they originated in Egypt, and the well-made haematite scaraboid from Tomb 521 (No. 96), with which the series at Tell ed-Duweir begins, may suggest that they emanated from the same source as other iron ore products.

Distinctive motifs in Tomb 218 are the ostriches (Nos. 84, 85 and conoid 143) and a quadruped resembling a horse with a man or tree (Nos. 79, 88 and the conoid 151). In Tomb 224 the shaggy-necked beasts (Nos. 100, 101) are followed by a degenerate imitation in Tomb 1004 (No. 102).

A design of two "blob" style men was found in Tomb 1002, but the characteristic group of three men is less certainly placed in tombs which are associated with the ossuaries. From the vitality of their design, it would seem that the "blob" style men in stone precede the conventional hatched renderings of the same subject in bone, which are exclusive to Tomb 1002.

The antelopes with plants or other motifs in the field (No. 92), made of paste, follow an earlier tradition than Nos. 93–95, which all occur in Tomb 1002, and this favoured design is also to be found in the ossuary group 120, recurring in a debased form on a conoid (No. 142) associated with Level III.

Of the five scaraboids found in Tomb 106, three are too worn to be legible. No. 78 alone is a tolerable production, while the poor design in paste of No. 109 is based on an Egyptian model. No. 129 has reached an advanced stage of degradation.

	Egyptian Scarabs				Scaraboids					
	Average length (mm.)	Material			Average diam. (mm.)	Material			
Locus		Stone	Paste	Total		Stone	Paste	Bone	Total
Houses II	—	—	—	—	14	—	—	1	1
Tomb 106	13	2	2	4	14	1	1	1	3
Houses III	—	—	—	—	14·50	—	—	2	2
Ossuary 120	10	1	—	1	14	1	—	2	3
Tomb 1002	13·50	11	5	16	14·41	2	4	11	17
Tomb 1004	—	—	—	—	14·50	—	—	2	2
Tomb 224	13·50	2	1	3	19	2	—	1	3
Tomb 116	14·57	7	—	7	14·66	—	1	2	3
Tomb 218	14	10	—	10	15	5	—	—	5
Burials 120	16·50	6	—	6	—	—	—	—	—
Tomb 521	18	1	—	1	13·50	1	—	—	1
TOTALS	—	—	—	48	—	—	—	—	40

Plate 43

No.	Locus	Material	Remarks	Field No. Mus. No.
1	218	Steatite	*Mn-ḫpr-R'* in cartouche. *Ḏḥwtĭ-ms* Thothmes III. The god's name written with ape, which suggests Upper Egypt. Cf. PSC XXVIII: 120. LB I (dyn. xviii).	4851
2	116	,,	*Mn-ḫpr-R'* in cartouche. S-spirals at each side. Debased design top and bottom. LB I (dyn. xviii).	562 PM. 33.1947
3	107	,,	*Mn-ḫpr-R'* in cartouche. Snake and *M''t* feather at each side. (Colt). Dyn. xxii or later.	405
4	120	,,	*Mn-ḫpr-R'*. Dyn. xxii or later.	5163 PM. 36.1573
5	116	,,	*Mn-ḫpr-R'* in imitation cartouche. *M''t* feather with stroke above on each side. (Colt). Dyn. xxii or later.	569A
6	218	,,	*Mn-pḫr-R'* at top. *R'-Mny-k-t'w* below. Cf. PSC LIII: 22, 23; RES XXII: 876. Dyn. xxii or later.	4852
7	1002	Paste	*Mn-M''t-ḫpr* flanked by *n[u]b* signs. (Colt). Dyn. xix or later.	1329
8	D/X	Blue paste	*Ḫpr-R'* in cartouche. *M''t* feather on left, snake on right. Possibly Osorkon III or dyn. xxii–xxiii.	5364
9	120	Steatite	*Mn-ḫpr-R'*. Possibly Siamon? Cf. Lahun II, LXIII: 13. Dyn. xxii.	5161 PM. 36.1571
10	K.15: 1033	,,	*Wsr-M''t-R', śtp-n-[y]mn*. Cf. PSC p. 30 and Pl. L: 22.8: 1–4; AS Tomb 11, RES 864, possibly Pamay. See No. 57. Dyn. xxii, c. 769 B.C.	6252A
11	218	,,	*Tyt-[y]mn* "Integral part of Amen", *nb* on each side. Cf. AS Tomb 1, RES 769 and Nos. 110, 131 in list.	4846
12	218	,,	*Ymn* with five strokes below. Lotus stem springing from *nb* on left curves over top to bud on right. Cf. AS Tomb 1, RES 860. Dyn. xxii or later.	4847
13	218	,,	As 12 with four strokes below. Cf. AS Tomb 1, RES 860. Dyn. xxii or later.	4845
14	218	,,	*[Y]mn-R'*, stroke and circle below. *Nb* on each side. Cf. Lahun II, LXIII: 18; AS Tomb 1, RES 862. Dyn. xxii or later.	4856
15	116	,,	*[Y]mn-R'*, with four strokes below. *Nb* on each side. Dyn. xxii or later.	569
16	107	,,	As 15 (Colt). Dyn. xxii or later.	404
17	116	,,	*[Y]mn-R'*, as 12, 13. Dyn. xxii or later.	565
18	218	,,	*[Y]mn-R'*, with three strokes below. Vertical. Dyn. xxii or later.	4857
19	106	,,	*Ḥtp-mn-yr-M''-(?)-Nb*. Dyn. xxv–xxvi(?).	368
20	116	,,	*Rn-rn* between uprights, *rn* on each side. Above, *nfr*. MB II or later.	570
21	106	Paste	*Rn-rn-rn* in two vertical columns divided by line. Reads: "names" (Colt). MB II or later.	346
22	120	,,	King smiting an enemy with curved blade. Rope-pattern border. Late Ramesside.	5162 PM. 36.1572
23	120	,,	Woman holding branch, another branch behind her; snake in front. MB II.	5165 PM. 36.1576
24	D/X	,,	Man with outstretched arm; debased sacred eye and other signs in field. Geometric work. Cf. BP II, LII: 158, LV: 285. LB II, dyn. xix or later.	6111
25	6006	,,	Hawk-headed figure, holding *w's*-sceptre. LB II, dyn. xix or later.	6525
26	1002	,,	Hawk-headed, long-coated figure, preceded by snake wearing Red Crown; *nb* below. Cf. NS XXV: 12; see SS III, No. 4831 for similar back (Colt). Dyn. xxiii–xxv.	1451 1451
27	218	,,	Two captives on either side of a central chain of linked spirals. Poor work. LB II, dyn. xix or later.	4861
28	L.15: 50	,,	Ptah in shrine, before him two *dd* pillars, on each of which is a human-headed bird, with circles above their heads. Cf. AG IV, XI: 438; RES XVIII: 718. LB II, dyn. xix.	6379 PM. 38.731

Plate 43 (*cont.*)

No.	Locus	Material	Remarks	Field No. Mus. No.
29	116	Steatite	Hawk, preceded by snake; *nb* below, hieroglyphs—*Yry-m' 't* "Doer of righteousness"(?). Dyn. xxiii–xxv.	566
30	107	,,	Above: sphinx with *ḥs* vase over back; below: figure holding two palm branches. Reading: *Ḥs-nb-ḥḥ* "Praise the Lord eternally"(?). LB II, dyn. xix or later.	403
31	1002	,,	*R'* seated. LB II, dyn. xix or later.	1328
32	1002	,,	Feather-crowned winged kneeling figure holding 2 lotuses. Below wings on right, sacred eye; on left, two unreadable signs. Dyn. xxv–xxvi(?).	1143
33	1002	,,	Hathor-head; crowned snake on each side; *nb* below. Cf. BDS IX: 317, XVIII: 1365–66; Gezer II, p. 316, No. 101; III, CCVI: 2. LB I, dyn. xviii.	1444 PM. 33.2097
34	1002	,,	Sacred eye and unreadable hieroglyphs; *nb* above and below (Colt). Dyn. xxiii–xxvi(?).	1294
35	120	,,	Design divided into two parts horizontally by two sacred eyes. Above, plant of North (partly destroyed) with *'nḥ* on each side; below, *nfr* with *s'* on each side. Reading "Good protection"(?). Cf. AG III, III: 112. Dyn. xxii.	5168 PM. 36.1575
36	106	,,	In centre, falcon wearing Red Crown, *nfr* in front, *nb* below, *R'-M' 't* behind. Possibly *Nfr-n[u]b-R'*, a Delta king of the xxvth dyn. Cf. History of Egypt III, p. 300, Fig. 124.	367
37	1002	,,	Snake facing left; above, *ḥprw*; behind, *nfr*; below, *nb*. Suggested reading "Good of all existences" (or "forms"). Dyn. xxiii–xxvi.	1310
38	K.13: Res.K	,,	Hook spirals surrounding unreadable hieroglyphs. Cf. BDS IX: 356, 357 (Colt). MB II.	1478
39	1002	Paste	Above, Boat of the Sun; below, roughly made *ntr-nfr* "The good god". Cf. NS XL: 25. Dyn. xxii.	1450
40	218	Steatite	In centre, alphabetic sign *ḥ*; above, lotus flower(?); below, double rectangle; at each side debased C-spirals. MB II(?).	4848
41	1002	,,	Centre, bird; above *'nḥ*; below, *rn-rn-rn* preceded by *nfr*; *nb* at right side (Colt). MB II(?).	1345
42	1002	,,	Crocodile on right, *ḥpr* between snakes on left, surrounded by rope-pattern border (Colt). Cf. BDS X: 485, 486. MB II or later.	1335
43	107	,,	Broken. Centre, moon sign with *ḥpr* below. Inner border of half circles, for which cf. BP I, X: 87. Surrounded by rope-pattern outer border. MB II or dyn. xxii.	398
44	218	,,	*Ḥpr* flanked by *R'*, winged snakes or hawks on each side. Cf. Lahun II, L, Tomb 603, bottom left; AS Tomb 1, RES: 855. Dyn. xxii.	4850
45	224	,,	*'nḥ* between notched lines; *nb* on each side. LB II, dyn. xix.	5055
46	1002	Paste	*'nḥ* between snakes facing outwards. Dyn. xxii.	1452
47	1002	Blue paste	*'nḥ* between *M' 't* feather facing outwards. LB II, dyn. xix.	1259
48	515	Blue glaze	Centre, two *M' 't* feathers facing outwards, *nb* on each side. Suggested reading "Lord of righteousness". Dyn. xxv or later.	3480
49	1002	Steatite	Two lions and heron (*b' bird*). Cf. BP I, XXXIX: 439; AS Tomb 1, RES: 851. (Colt). Dyn. xxii.	1334
50	218	,,	Stag, with branch or tree in front; for back cf. No. 26. Dyn. xxiii–xxvi.	4849
51	521	,,	Kneeling Nile figure, partly erased, and animal. Cf. PSC XLIX: 3–4 for figure. Dyn. xxi(?).	3567
52	218	Limestone	Antelope, facing left towards two palm-trees. Dyn. xxii.	4844
53	1002	Paste	Antelope. Undefined object in front, tree behind. Cf. Nos. 93–94 (Colt).	1281
54	1002	Haematite	Animal, couchant, facing left. (Colt).	1445
55	1002	Steatite	Monkey (for derivation see BDS II: 89). Cf. BP I, XL: 457. Dyn. xxii.	1296
56	116	,,	Monkey. Dyn. xxii.	567
57	K.15: 1033	,,	Right, snake; left, scorpion. Dyn. xxiii–xxvi(?).	6252B
58	106	Paste	Bird; above, *hrw nb* "Every day" (Colt). Dyn. xxiii–xxvi(?).	330

Plate 43 (cont.)

No.	Locus	Material	Remarks	Field No. Mus. No.
59	120	Steatite	Lotuses with looped stems. MB II.	5164 PM. 36.1574
60	224	Blue paste	Flower with bent stem. Cf. NS XLII: 15. LB II, dyn. xix.	5056
61	120	Limestone	Two branches.	5167 PM. 36.1599

Plate 44

No.	Locus	Material	Remarks	Field No. Mus. No.
62	1002	Bone	Man standing, semicircular head. Iron I–II.	1295
63	1002	,,	Man, arm raised, semicircular head; in front, *nb* sign on end (or debased crocodile). Cf. Gezer I, p. 334, Fig. 173. Iron I–II.	1308
64	1002	,,	Man, arm raised, square head, facing lion. Cf. Megiddo I, 67: 40; AG I, XIV: 164 (Colt). Iron I–II.	1440
65	1002	,,	Two men, one inverted. Semicircular heads. Cf. BP I, XXXV: 423; TN I, 54: 38; BDS I: 43 for derivation(?). Iron I–II.	1330
66	1002	,,	Two men side by side, arm upraised. Semicircular heads. Cf. Megiddo I, 67: 51; BP I, XL: 458; TN I, Pl. 55: 73 (Colt). Iron I–II.	1260
67	1002	,,	Man on right, two indeterminate objects on left, "blob" style (Colt). Iron II.	1307
68	1002	Limestone	Two men, "blob" style (Colt). Iron II.	1442
69	D/X	Steatite	Two men, "blob" style. Iron II.	6106
70	6000	Serpentine	Tree in centre, figure on each side. Cf. AS Tomb 1, see RES: SO 23; Megiddo I, 69.13. Iron II.	6932
71	H.14: 23	Bone	Three men, "blob" style, the foremost holds a trident(?). Iron II.	6344 PM. 38.730
72	116	Paste	Three men, "blob" style. Cf. Megiddo I, 67: 21, 56; Gezer II, p. 316, No. 104; III, CCVI: 5 (Colt). Iron II.	563
73	107	Limestone	As 72. Cf. GSCE II, CCXLVI: 10 (Colt). Iron II.	399
74	D/X	,,	As 72. Iron II.	5367
75	107	,,	As 72. Iron II.	402
76	120	Bone	Man seated, holding boy by the hand. Cf. TN I, 54: 18, Tomb 32; IKG, Pl. XXIX: 28. Iron I–II.	5169 PM. 36.1578
77	120	Limestone	Man leading horse. Circle above horse's back to represent load(?). Iron I–II.	5170 PM. 36.1579
78	106	,,	Man arms raised, inverted animal, "blob" style. Iron II.	372
79	218	,,	Man and horse. Hawk(?) in background, "blob" style. Cf. AS Tomb 1, see RES: SO 25; TN 1, 54: 7, Tomb 32; Megiddo I, 69: 43. Iron II.	4838
80	D/X	Steatite	Man standing above (upon?) an antelope or horse, holding a stick. Cf. AS Tomb 1, see RES: SO 26; TN I, 54: 34; SS III, period IV, No. 2397. Iron II.	6101
81	D/X	Limestone	Man holding creatures in each hand. Cf. AS Tomb 1, see RES: SO 15, 16; AASOR XXI–XXII, Pl. 29: 7 from TBM Stratum B; TN I, 54: 23, Tomb 32. Iron II.	6921
82	D/X	Paste	As 81. Very worn. Iron II.	6921
83	224	Limestone	Man holding branch. Iron II.	5054
84	218	,,	Man between two ostriches, "blob" style. Cf. TN I, 54: 23, Tomb 32. Iron I–II.	4837
85	218	,,	Two ostriches, one inverted, "blob" style. See No. 143. Iron I–II.	4836

Plate 44 (*cont.*)

No.	Locus	Material	Remarks	Field No. Mus. No.
86	J.15: 1030	Bone	Two ostriches, plant (or man) between them; "blob" style. Iron I–II.	6239
87	1002	Limestone	Two animals, one with head turned back, "blob" style. Iron II.	1453
88	218	,,	Antelope and plant. Cf. Megiddo I, 69: 40, Stratum V; AS Tomb 1, see RES: SO 21, 31. Iron I–II.	4835
89	1002	Bone	Antelope. Cf. BP I, XLIII: 515; RES: SO 8; AS Tomb 1, see RES: SO 20. Iron I–II.	1309 PM. 33.2061
90	120	,,	Antelope facing left, with plant. Iron I–II.	5166 PM. 36.1577
91	D/X	,,	Antelope facing left, with scorpion. Cf. Megiddo I, 69: 22, Stratum V; TN I, 54: 19, Tomb 32. Iron I–II.	6103
92	1002	Paste	Antelope facing left, with plant or debased scorpion. Iron II.	1446
93	1002	,,	Antelope, with plants, cf. No. 53; Megiddo I, 69: 17, Stratum IV. Iron I–II.	1441
94	1002	,,	Antelope with conventional plants. Iron I–II.	1449
95	1002	,,	Antelope with conventional plants. Cf. Megiddo I, 69: 17, Stratum IV (Colt). Iron I–II.	1336
96	521	Haematite	Antelope facing left, with plant, drilled style. Cf. TN I, 55: 66 and p. 150.	3567A
97	D/X	Glass	Quadruped. Iron II or later.	3068
98	D/X	Paste	Quadruped. Iron II or later.	3067
99	D/X	Limestone	Antelope couchant. Iron I–II.	4092
100	224	Bone	Two horned animals, long shaggy necks, heads turned back. Iron II.	5051
101	224	Limestone	Two horned animals, long shaggy necks, heads turned back. Iron II.	5052
102	1004	Bone	Two animals, long shaggy necks, one inverted. Cf. AS Tomb 1, see RES: SO 36. Iron II.	7285
103	1002	,,	Lion, large *nb* below. Cf. AS Tomb 1, see RES: SO 35. Iron I–II.	1315
104	D/X	,,	Stylised fish and column(?); cf. 105 for column. Iron II.	4088
105	D/X	Limestone	Antelope jumping to left. Star above, column(?) behind the animal; cf. 104.	4091 PM. 36.1830
106	100	Bone	Stylised crested bird, spread wings. Above, imitation cartouche, reading *Yr-yb-R'*(?). Cf. BP I, XXXI: 298 for a similar cartouche; Bittel and Guterbock: Bogazkoy Taf. 31: 11B. Iron II.	5374
107	1002	,,	Stylised crested bird, spread wings. Cf. Megiddo I, 69: 28, Stratum IV; Gezer II, p. 325 and III, CCIIIA; APEF II, p. 73 and XL: 4; TN I, 54: 56; Iron II.	1454
108	1002	,,	Design possibly derived from 106 and 107. Iron II.	1455
109	106	Paste	Hawk-headed figure, right arm raised, snake(?) in left hand, signs unreadable. Dyn. xxii or later.	323
110	160	Steatite	*Tyt-ymn.* Cf. Nos. 11, 131. Dyn. xxii or later.	2666
111	218	,,	*M' 't-s' t-R'.* Cf. Gezer II, p. 326, No. 326, and III, CCVA: 15. Iron I–II.	4854
112	218	,,	*M' 't-s' t-R'* with snake in front. Cf. BDS, XII: 714, 715 and p. 21; AS Tomb 1, see RES: 854. Iron I–II.	4855
113	D/X	Paste	Monkey seated, *nb* below. Not pierced. Dyn. xxii.	—
114	H.14: 1002	Bone	Crude representation of sacred eye. Iron II.	5448
115	6000	Limestone	Conventional design. Iron II.	6933
116	107	,,	Cross pattern, perhaps derived from four Red Crowns(?). See BDS VIII: 261 seq. Iron I–II.	400
117	224	,,	Pattern derived from two *s'* signs with snakes on each side(?). Iron I–II.	5053
118	1002	Bone	Nine ring-and-dot circles; eight radiating from central circle. Cf. BP II, LIII: 202. Iron II.	1439
119	107	,,	As 118 (Colt). Iron II.	401
120	1004	,,	Five ring-and-dot circles. Cf. AG I, XIV: 184. Iron II.	7286
121	218	Limestone	Five ring-and-dot circles, divided by line ending in blob. Iron II.	4842

Plate 44 (*cont.*)

No.	Locus	Material	Remarks	Field No. Mus. No.
122	116	Bone	Eight ring-and-dot circles (Colt). Iron II.	570A
123	4005	Glass	Mermaid and star. 5th cent. B.C. or later	5855
124	D/X	Limestone	Nude goddess. Above, winged sun(?); left, clothed priest or devotee; below, a footstool; right, tree with climbing monkey. 6th–5th cent. B.C.	6097

Plate 45

No.	Locus	Material	Remarks	Field No. Mus. No.
125	218	Blue paste	King seated before *m' 't* feather, *R'* above. Much worn. LB II, dyn. xix.	4866
126	218	Steatite	Round seal. Obverse, cross pattern derived from four Red Crowns. See No. 116. Back decorated. Iron I–II.	4858
127	D/X̣	Faience	Amulet, emblem of resurrection. Cf. RES, XXIV, p. 215; Amulets, pp. 24–25, XI: 92. Dyn. xxvi or later.	5365
128	218	Steatite	Triangular object between snakes, *n* above, *nb* below. Lower half only.	4853
129	106	Bone	Quadruped *t* or *R'* above (Colt). Iron II or later.	374
130	191	Steatite	Plaque. Obv. lion; rev. geometric design. For back, cf. BP I, XXXV: 392–394. Dyn. xxi.	3020 PM. 34.3086
131	116	„	Plaque. Obv. hawk and hieroglyphs; rev. *tyt-Ymn*. See Nos. 11, 110 (Colt). Dyn. xxii(?).	568
132	194	Green glaze	Hathor head between snakes. Fish back. LB I, dyn. xviii.	—
133	223	Paste	Plaque. Obv. in relief, antelope kneeling; rev. cross pattern. Cf. Megiddo I, 71: 72 for animal. LB II or later.	4942
134	223	Faience	Plaque. Obv. winged shake over *mn* sign; rev. sacred eye. Dyn. xxii or later.	4941
135	110	Steatite	Plaque. Obv. king kneeling holding staff, *nfr* behind; rev. lion; sun disk above, hieroglyph behind. Dyn. xxii.	476A
136	218	„	Plaque. Obv. winged griffin couchant; rev. winged and horned animal couchant. Cf. Megiddo Tombs 95: 34. LB II.	4843
137	106	Paste	Circular plaque. Obv. *nfr m' 't*; rev. 8-petalled rosette. (Colt).	322
138	106	Porphyry	Bird "displayed" Hedgehog back. Cf. OIP XL, 58: 103 (Colt). *c.* 730–700 B.C.	370
139	106	Blue glass	Antelope, bird in flight. Traces of bronze pin in pierced conoid. Dyn. xxvi or later.	369
140	116	Paste	Conoid, illegible. Iron I–II.	567A
141	504	Sard (carnelian)	Conoid. Lion trampling on antelope. Cf. NS XXV 35. 6th–5th cent. B.C.	3437
142	J. 16: 1038	Limestone	Conoid. Long-necked antelope in front of tree. Not pierced. 7th cent.(?)	7293
143	218	Serpentine	Conoid. Two ostriches, one inverted. See No. 85. Iron I–II.	4860
144	K.12	Jasper	Conoid. Two horned animals. Iron I.	5283
145	106	Steatite	Conoid. Stylised tree with winged sphinx on each side. Cf. Megiddo I, 71: 74, Stratum IV. 1000–800 B.C.	366
146	D/X	Green jasper	Conoid, not pierced. Antelope(?). Iron II.	5368
147	116	Paste	Conoid. Antelope, facing left (Colt). Iron II.	564
148	D/X	Limestone	Conoid. Antelope, facing left (Colt). Iron II.	1437
149	D/X	Pink limestone	Conoid. Antelope. Drilled style. Iron I.	6920
150	218	Haematite	Conoid. Bull, sun sign above. Drilled style. Cf. TN I, 55: 66, and p. 150. Iron I.	4859
151	218	Limestone	Conoid. Long-necked animal, head turned back. Traces of figure on left. Type of 101 and 102. Cf. Gezer II, p. 323, No. 233; III, CCIIIa, No. 10. Iron II.	4839

Plate 45 (*cont.*)

No.	Locus	Material	Remarks	Mus. No. Field No.
152	116	Steatite	Cylinder. Two figures of Bes between hawks with spread wings. Rope-pattern border. Dyn. xxii or later.	561
153	110	Paste	Cylinder. Two long-coated figures adoring tree. Two animals rampant (Colt). Middle of 2nd millennium B.C.	475A
154	106	,,	Cylinder. Stylised birds. Cf. AG III, IV: 127; Hittite Seals, p. 80, Fig. 91. 8th–7th cent.(?).	365
155	106	Glazed paste	Cylinder. Design of circlets linked by tangents in two registers. Cf. Megiddo I, Pl. 66: 4; Megiddo Tombs, 94: 3; Hittite Seals, p. 71, Fig. 73 (Colt). Late 2nd millennium B.C.	364
156	R.15: 13	Steatite, blue glaze	Large scarab of Amenhetep III. For reading and translation see p. 362.	5351
157	106	Steatite	Cowroid. *dy-n-R'* between *'nkh* signs reversed (Colt). MB II.	329
158	106	Green jasper	Scaraboid. Rear part of rampant lion, right, initial letter *sin* below line (and on Pl. 54: 43) (Colt). Iron II.	320
159	218	Bone	Scaraboid, imitation script. Iron I–II.	4840
160	100	,,	Scaraboid, imitation script. Iron I–II.	5370
161	116	,,	Scaraboid, imitation script. Iron I–II.	568A
162	218	,,	Scaraboid, imitation script. Iron I–II.	4841
163	D/X	Steatite	Scaraboid, zigzag lines above and below central division, imitation script. Iron I–II.	3055
164	D/X	Clay	Impression on conical lump, afterwards burnt. Imitation script. Iron I–II.	5366
165	D/X	,,	Sealing from document, marks of papyrus and thread on reverse. Design derived from four Red Crowns(?).	—
166	H.17: 1088	,,	Sealing from document, marks of papyrus on reverse. Four rows of *'nkh* signs between horizontal registers.	7150 PM. 39.820

For descriptions of Nos. 167–173 see Chapter 10: Seals and Seal Impressions, p. 348.

CHAPTER 12

CULT OBJECTS

Pottery Models

Tomb or group	Vases and figures Birds and animals		Pillar-base figurines Mould-cast face		Beak face		Horses and riders		Furniture Bed, couch or chair		Rattles		Tota
Houses II 106	Pl. 27: 7	1	Pl. 27: 4	1	Pl. 27: 1, 3	2	Pl. 27: 2, 5	2	F. No. 114 NP (as Pl. 29: 20)	1	Pl. 27: 6	1	8
Houses III	—	—	F. No. 7094, 7144, 7247 NP	3	—	—	—	—	—	—	—	—	3
120	Pl. 30: 28	1	Pl. 27: 8	1	—	—	—	—	—	—	Pl. 27: 9	1	3
107	F. No. 383 NP (Colt)	1	—	—	—	—	—	—	—	—	F. No. 393 NP	1	2
1002 layers 1–5	Pl. 28: 12	1	F. No. 1254 NP (Colt)	1	Pl. 28: 14	1	Pl. 29: 18 (beak-faced rider)	1	Pl. 29: 19, 20	2	Pl. 28: 15, 16	2	11
	F. No. 1270 NP	1	Pl. 28: 11	1									
	F. No. 1271 NP (as Pl. 27: 7)	1											
layers 6–10	F. No. 1290 NP (as Pl. 28: 12)	1	Pl. 28: 10	1	—	—	—	—	Pl. 29: 22	1	F. No. 1291 NP	1	8
	F. No. 1301 NP (as Pl. 27: 7)	1	Pl. 28: 13	1							F. No. 1299 NP	1	
											F. No. 1300 NP	1	
layers 11–13	Pl. 30: 23, 26	2	—	—	—	—	—	—	Pl. 29: 21	1	—	—	
	Pl. 30: 24	1					Pl. 29: 17	1	—	—	—	—	5
218	Pl. 30: 27	1	—	—	—	—	—	—	—	—	—	—	1
223	Pl. 30: 25	1	—	—	—	—	—	—	—	—	—	—	1
TOTAL		13		9		3		4		5		8	42

Shall the clay say to him that fashioneth it, what makest thou? Isaiah XLV: 9

IN condemning the idolatrous tendencies of the nation the Prophets have described in opprobrious terms the images of stone, metal or wood which the people worshipped (Isaiah XL: 20, Jeremiah X: 3–5). According to the standards of the time, these idols, cunningly carved or moulded and frequently overlaid with gold, were works of art, made to order by experienced craftsmen. It is unlikely that many figures of the kind survived the recurrent phases of iconoclastic zeal, apart from the natural hazards of time and climate, and it is rare, indeed, to find even fragments which could have formed part of such images.

On the other hand, city deposits and tombs in Judah contain many broken pottery models which are but crude playthings or homely symbols of no intrinsic worth. In some groups of the second millennium there were plaques or tablets bearing the clay impression of a nude recumbent figure decked with ornaments. Either the hands rest against the sides, or they offer the full breasts in the gesture associated with the *dea nutrix*, a position also adopted by the standing figures modelled in the round, which became popular in the later Iron Age.

Between the two periods, during the twelfth to tenth centuries B.C., votive plaques took the form of a woman in labour, and the best fragment of the kind is illustrated on Pl. 32: 4. The comparative desertion of the site at that time is in marked contrast to the situation at Tell Beit Mirsim, where those plaques were common (Melanges Syriens I, p. 119).

No plaques of any kind were found in groups of the ninth century at Tell ed-Duweir, and it was apparently not until the latter part of the eighth century that standing pillar-base figurines were introduced.

Pillar-base figures, mould-cast face (Pls. 27: 4, 8; 28: 10, 11, 13; 31: 1–14)

Modelled by hand, or more rarely thrown on the wheel, the body of the figurine ended in a slightly splayed but otherwise plain pillar base. Rolls of clay were attached to represent arms supporting very prominent breasts. Ending in a peg, which fitted into the neck, the head was made separately from a ball of clay; the rough finish

374

of the back shows that it was not intended to be seen. The face, side-curls and head-dress were cast in an open clay mould, a method which ensured a detailed portrayal without the need for individual skill. Indeed, the superior modelling of the moulds and impressions to that of the figures, and the similarities of heads from other sites in Judah, may suggest that the moulds were made elsewhere and distributed from a common source, while the bodies were modelled locally.

The best figure is illustrated on Pl. 28: 10. The body is wheel-turned and hollow; the features are clear and pleasant and the expression is free from the stereotyped "oriental" smile. The cheeks were once painted red on a chalky white face, but only traces remain of the colour, as it was applied after the model was baked. The careless way in which the head was fixed to the body by forcing the clay up around the neck mars the effect of an otherwise successful achievement.

For full details of manufacture, see Kelso and Thorley in AASOR XXI–XXII, § 140.

Some idea of fashionable hair styles can be derived from a study of the broken heads, mostly found on the surface of the mound or on the surrounding slopes, which are illustrated on Pl. 31.

Nos. 1, 2, 5, 11 and 13. The hair or wig is arranged in three or more rows of stiff little curls, which pass horizontally across the front of the head and hang down the sides of the face. The base of the hair or wig stands out from the head.

Nos. 3, 4, 10 and 12 show a similar arrangement of curls, but the base line follows that of the head and does not project, a variation which may be due to careless manipulation of the clay around the neck.

Nos. 6 and 8 have similar rows of curls, surmounted by a high pointed cap. No. 7 does not show the curls above the forehead clearly, and it is possible that a bandeau is intended. No. 10 is presumably the head of a woman, but it is covered by a shawl and no hair is visible around the face.

Pillar-base figures, beak face (Pls. 27: 1, 3; 28: 14)

There is little to distinguish the bodies of these figures from those with mould-cast faces, though they are possibly smaller and even more crude. The tiny heads were formed by the simple expedient of pinching the clay up between the fingers to make the nose and eye sockets—a primitive convention, which was widely used throughout the ancient world from India to Egypt, as early as the fourth and third millennia B.C., and is not altogether unknown in modern art today. Compare the beak faces of horsemen, which are similarly made (Pl. 29: 17, 18).

Other human figures (Pl. 31: 15–19)

These heads are the products of different artistic traditions and techniques.

No. 15 is the head of a man, wearing an unusual cap, which is flat on top and projects behind. No hair is visible, but the ears are clearly indicated. That both men and women wore pointed caps is demonstrated by the figure of a horseman on Pl. 29: 17 and the heads on Pl. 31: 6–8, where the features are markedly feminine.

No. 16 was found on the surface of the courtyard east of the palace. In all probability, the head once formed part of a large and elaborate vessel. The brown burnish of the fragment is comparable to that of the Duweir Ewer and other pieces from the last structure of the Fosse Temple.

No. 17 is a vigorous sketch or caricature of a bearded man, in unbaked clay. The profile is like those of the figures on the Kara Tepe reliefs (ILN May, 1949, pp. 665–668).

The technique of Nos. 16 and 17 is comparable. In both cases separate pieces of clay were added to represent the eyes and other features, a practice commonly used by the makers of the statuettes in the mainly Iron Age shrine of Ajia Irini in Cyprus (GSCE II, Pls. CCXXIX, CCXXX). Both pieces may belong to the close of the second millennium B.C.

No. 18 was part of an anthropomorphic vessel. Built up round a hollow wheel-turned neck, the details of the elaborate wig and ear-rings were apparently hand-modelled, but the face—like those of the pillar-base figurines—was cast from a mould. The piece is late post-exilic.

No. 19 was probably part of a large decorative vessel, associated perhaps with the disturbed deposits on the eastern courtyard. The fragment represents a hero wearing a lion's head helmet.

Horses (and Riders) (Pls. 27: 2, 5; 29: 17, 18)

Fragments of model quadrupeds were very common on the site, but in most cases it is hard to identify the species which the artist intended to portray. Both heads and legs were often missing and only the solid back had survived; which is straight and rather flat and seems to be equine rather than bovine, a supposition confirmed, perhaps, by the representation of harness in paint or incisions on some of the heads. In two examples there is a boss or decoration on the forehead, probably reproducing a metal or leather ornament.

Three reasonably complete models from Tombs 1002 and 106 are spirited figures of bare-back horsemen. The rider in each case sits forward on his mount and appears to grasp its ears or mane. If not naked, he wears tight-fitting garments and in one instance a pointed cap, while his steed is ridden without harness or trappings. Compare the horsemen of the following centuries (Pl. 33), with full beards and cloaks, astride much smaller mounts.

Furniture (Pl. 29: 19–22)

Five models of a bed, couch or chair, of which four are illustrated, were found in Tombs 1002 and 106. They vary somewhat in detail; those like a divan bed have foot and/or head boards, and the chairs are low and wide with sloping backs. There is nothing to indicate the material of the originals, but the models were no doubt copies of furniture in domestic use during the eighth and seventh centuries.

Rattles (Pls. 27: 6, 9; 28: 15, 16)

Five out of a total of nine rattles came from the upper part of Tomb 1002. The others were from ossuary deposits and from Tomb 106. They are pottery cylinders turned on the wheel and the average length is 9 cm.; the diameter of 5 cm. is of convenient size to be held in the adult hand. The ends of the cylinder were closed with disks of clay pierced in the centre by one or more holes. A pebble or clay pellet inside was sufficient to produce a satisfactory sound. For a full description of the method of manufacture, see AASOR XXI–XXII, Section II, § 142. Though rattles were found in Stratum A at Tell Beit Mirsim, it is unusual to find fragments in town deposits; none were found in city levels at Tell ed-Duweir, and the single example from Megiddo (MRMC, Pl. XXII: P. 3596) was also found in a tomb. Rattles at Gezer (Gezer II, 306) were also exclusive to burial groups.

Rattles of a different shape were found at Tell Zakariyeh and Tell es-Ṣafi (BM Pl. 45: 3, 8, 16).

Animal and Bird Vases and Models (Pls. 27: 7; 28: 12; 30: 23–30)

Zoomorphic vessels occur sporadically at all periods at south Palestinian sites, and numerous fragments attest that they were more common than would appear from the number of nearly complete vases of the kind. Whether complete or fragmentary, the birds and beasts are seldom identifiable, and both are highly conventionalised. The bodies are cylinders of clay turned on the wheel, with heads and legs modelled by hand and added to the body. Various inlets and outlets for liquid are provided, in which the fantasy of the artist has had full play. The surface of the vessels is frequently burnished, and details are sometimes added in black or red paint.

Similar vessels were in use during the Islamic period as pipe bases.

When fragments are found in unstratified contexts, the quality of the ware and finish is the only indication of date. Examples from Tombs 223 and 218, and from the bottom layers of Tomb 1002 show that the existence of such vessels was maintained from the Bronze Age during the early tombs of the series, and continued throughout the eighth and seventh centuries.

Among the solid models, the delightful bird on a stand (Pl. 28: 12) should be noted.

Comparisons

The pillar-base and equestrian figurines, the model furniture, the rattles and zoomorphic vases are mainly concentrated in Tombs 1002 and 106. They are closely contemporary and they may have fulfilled a ritual or votive purpose in the same cult.

The closest parallel to the group as a whole is afforded by the contents of Tomb 1 at 'Ain Shems (APEF II, Pls. XX, XXII). On the whole, it is somewhat earlier in date than the later part of Tomb 1002, which contained the models, for the black burnished juglet, Class D.7 (q.v.), was still paramount. Grant and Wright (AS V, p. 7) have dated the use of Tomb 1 *c.* 900 B.C., which is probably the period of the first deposits, but the figurines should belong to later burials in that cave.

According to the same authorities, Tomb 5 at 'Ain Shems is little earlier than the seventh century (AS V, p. 8). It contained two beak-faced figures associated with pottery typical of Stratum II at Tell ed-Duweir (Classes B.13, J.8 and D.5). There were no figurines in city deposits prior to Stratum II or IIc (AS V, p. 155).

At Tell en-Naṣbeh pottery models of all kinds were common, and "with only a very few chronologically insignificant exceptions" they were all attributed to Stratum I from 700–450 B.C. (TN I, p. 246).

At Gezer the figurine in Tomb 7 (Gezer I, p. 306, Fig. 162) is an early example in the round. Macalister suggested that this type superseded the plaques "towards the end of the fourth Semitic" and continued through Persian and Hellenistic times (Gezer II, p. 417, Fig. 502).

Figurines with mould-cast and beak faces came from Stratum A at Tell Beit Mirsim (AASOR XXI–XXII, Pls. 55–57 and Pl. 31). "None can be dated with confidence before the eighth century", wrote Albright, "and the majority come from the last century of Stratum A" (op. cit., p. 69, § 41).

Conclusions

It is thus generally agreed that the pottery models, and in particular the pillar-base figurines, are confined to deposits of the eighth and seventh centuries.

H. G. May in "Material Remains of the Megiddo Cult" has noted many analogies between the figures of Assyria and Babylonia and those of Palestine, and he considers that "there are enough close parallels to make accidental resemblance improbable" (MRMC, p. 29). He states, however, that the "pillar form of the mother-goddess figurine had little influence at Megiddo" (op. cit., p. 31 and Pl. XXVI: M 1776). Nevertheless, Albright attributes all the heads from Megiddo on Pl. XXIII (op. cit.) to this class (Melanges Syriens, p. 120), but in view of the difference in manufacture, it would seem that May is right in making a distinction.

Mrs. E. D. van Buren has described the position of hands clasping the breasts as one of the most usual adopted by Assyrian and Babylonian clay figures, but she notes that it did not become common in those lands until the early ninth century (CFBA, p. xlvii).

With other oriental characteristics the gesture had spread to Greece and Asia Minor by the middle of the eighth century. Müller, discussing Greek examples adopting arm position 7 (i.e. hands clasping the breasts), wrote:

"All these figures look extremely Semitic, and notwithstanding the appearance of the last-named motif already in the second millennium, one must accept a new influence from the Continent, confirmed by the fact that the gesture seems to be missing in the intervening period" (FPGK, p. 161).

If, as it appears, the revival of a long dormant manifestation of the *dea nutrix* occurred at the same time in south Palestine and in the Greek world, it is reasonable to suppose that the inspiration derived from a common source, which had reached Assyria in the previous century.

The simultaneous introduction of equestrian figures is a further sign of northern pressure, commemorating, perhaps, those bands of horsemen from northern steppes whose descendants had reached Egypt by the middle of the seventh century. At some royal burials in Scythian lands the stuffed bodies of warriors on horseback were placed around the grave, and it would be natural to replace the sacrifice by token models for less important people (CMH I, p. 354).

In the last centuries of the pre-Christian era the popularity of equestrian and other figures increased greatly in the eastern Mediterranean world, and, despite the decrease of population at Tell ed-Duweir, that interest is reflected in a great number of crude figurines, made without skill or artistic ability.

Post-exilic figurines

The pottery models illustrated on Pl. 33 are only a selection from among those which were found in rock cavities or in surface soil near the south-western approaches to the city.

The main group consists of many heads so crudely cast or modelled that they are not identifiable. A little pottery was found with other deposits, including a mortarium, of about the fifth century, and a lamp (type 138) of a kind which is dated in Mesopotamia from the second century B.C. to the second century A.D.

Pl. 33: 1, 4, 5 illustrate equestrian figures, which are very different to those of the eighth–seventh centuries (p. 376). The rider sits back near the tail of his mount and he is wrapped in a cloak worn over a pointed cap or helmet. The animal wears some kind of cloth or breast-plate, which hangs down almost to the ground.

Though trappings of the sort are not shown in Mrs. van Buren's "Clay Figurines of Babylonia and Assyria", she notes that "men on horseback are very common enveloped in their great cloaks and wearing a pointed hood" (CFBA, p. xlvii). For an illustration of a horse wearing an apron or horse-cloth dated to the ninth century in Assyria, see "Evolution of the Domestic Horse" by M. Hilzheimer (Antiquity, Vol. IX, Pl. VI).

Among the figurines of foreign peoples found by Petrie at Memphis there were cloaked and bearded horsemen (Memphis I, Pl. XL: 42, 46 and Pl. XLIV: bottom left). He considered that the solid figures ranged from 500 to 300 B.C., and that those cast in a double mould were made in the following century.

In describing the "Terracottas from Nippur", L. Legrain distinguished Persian riders, c. 500 B.C., Greeks, c. 300 and Parthians, c. 100 B.C., but the horsemen from Tell ed-Duweir are not identical with any of these groups.

FAIENCE AMULETS

By MARGARET A. MURRAY, D.LIT.

Tomb or group	Sekhmet		Isis and Horus, Horus the Child		Uzat		Bes		Miscellaneous		Total
Houses II 106	—	—	F. No. 345 (as Pl. 36: 51)	1	—	—	—	—	Pl. 34: 1, 2	2	3
Houses III 1002 layers 1–5	—	—	—	—	F. No. 1282 NP	2	F. No. 1275, 1263, NP	2	Pl. 36: 49, 50	2	6
layers 6–10	—	—	Pl. 36: 51	1	F. No. 1286 NP	1	Pl. 36: 48	1	—	—	3
layers 11–13, unstratified	—	—	—	—	F. No. 1337 NP F. No. 1594 NP	2	F. Nos. 1447, 1448 NP	2	F. No. 1343 NP F. Nos. 1595–6 NP	3	7
224	F. No. 5061 NP (as Pl. 34: 29)	1	—	—	Pl. 35: 37	2	—	—	Pl. 35: 38	1	4
116	F. No. 560 NP	1	—	—	—	—	Pl. 34: 7	1	—	—	2
218	Pl. 34: 18–21, 28, 29 F. No. 4820 NP	6 1	Pl. 34: 22, 23	2	—	—	—	—	Pl. 34: 24–27 Pl. 35: 30–35	4 6	19
120 (Burials)	F. No. 5181–2 NP	2	—	—	Pl. 34: 8–10	8	Pl. 34: 12–14	3	Pl. 34: 11, 15–17	4	17
107 (Burials)	Pl. 34: 3 F. Nos. 425–427, 429 NP	1 4	Pl. 34: 5 F. No. 423 NP (as Pl. 36: 51)	1 1	F. Nos. 419–422 NP (as Pl. 35: 37)	4	F. No. 418 NP	1	Pl. 34: 4, 6 F. Nos. 430, 431 NP	2 2	16
223	Pl. 35: 36	1	—	—	—	—	—	—	—	—	1
TOTAL		17		6		19		10		26	78

Faience amulets were introduced into Palestine as a result of Egyptian expansion in the xviiith dynasty, from about 1500 B.C. They became more frequent in the following centuries of Ramesside rule, xix–xxist dynasties, and they achieved great popularity under the Libyan kings of the xxiind dynasty, both in Egypt and in Palestine.

The amulets with a Delta connexion greatly outnumber those from Upper Egypt. In order of popularity, those found at Tell ed-Duweir in Iron Age groups represent the deities Sekhmet (or Bast) in various forms, and Bes, who was of Mediterranean origin. Figures of Isis are not very common, though she was universally venerated; but Harpocrates (Horus the child) has a close connexion with the Delta, for, according to legend, he was hidden by his mother in the marshes to save him from the enemy. Ptah-Sokar and Nefertum are Memphite gods. The only figures which appear to belong to the Thebaid are those of Mut, the goddess of Thebes, and the Ram, representing Amon, though the actual figure of the latter may have been used by the people of the Delta-town of Mendes to represent their local god.

The same result is found when classifying the animal-amulets, for the greater number have a Delta connexion: the cat (sacred animal of Bast), the lion (from Leontopolis), the ape (sacred to Thoth, originally a Delta god), and the falcon (sacred to Horus, originally chief god of the North).

Though it is sometimes difficult to distinguish between the two Delta goddesses, *Bast* the cat and *Sekhmet* the lioness, two examples are inscribed down the back with the name of Sekhmet (Pls. 34: 19 and 35: 36). All seventeen examples were found in tombs which were in use during the earlier part of the period under review. No figures of Sekhmet were found in Tombs 1002 or 106, which suggests that the popularity of this goddess had waned before the eighth century B.C.

Small figures of *cats* (Pl. 34: 16, 17) became common in Egypt when Shishak of Bubastis, first king of the xxiind dynasty, made himself Pharaoh.

The god *Bes* (Pls. 34: 7, 12–14; 35: 45, 46 and 36: 48) was originally the protector of the mother and new-born child. Later he became the protector of all women and children. Five out of ten examples from Tell ed-Duweir came from Tomb 1002. The remaining five amulets came from Groups 107, 116 and 120, all of which had two periods of use.

Figures of *Isis* (Pls. 34: 23; 36: 51, and two unpublished from Groups 106 and 107), seated, with the infant Horus on her knee, were for the protection of mother and child. The best example, from Tomb 1002, has an inscription down the support of the back (cf. two figurines published by Rowe: *Catalogue of Egyptian Scarabs*, A.25 and A.26, from Beisan and 'Ain Shems respectively). These amulets are very common at Lahun (Lahun II, Pl. XLIX).

Harpocrates (Horus the child) was, as the son of Isis, the protector of children (Pl. 34: 5, 22). He is represented as a nude child sucking his finger and wearing the side-curl of youth.

There are no figurines of Isis from Megiddo, and only four were found at Duweir; two are illustrated from Tomb 1 at 'Ain Shems, but figures of Isis are said to be only second to Bes in number in that group (op. cit., p. 60). It seems that the cult of Isis was less widespread in Palestine than in Egypt.

The sacred eye (Pls. 34: 8–10; 35: 37, 41, 42, 43) is a combination of the human eye and the marks on the feathers round the eye of the falcon. It is therefore an emblem of Horus in both his human and his falcon forms. The Eye of Horus also represented the Sun or Moon; when duplicate, i.e. when the Eye appears on the back as well as the front of the amulet, the wearer is placed under the protection of the god during the night and the day.

There is no doubt that an analysis of the varieties of Horus eyes would show a chronological sequence, for it is one of the commonest amulets both in Egypt and in Palestine. Here it must suffice to say that they were frequent in Strata IV–III at Megiddo, were found in Tombs 1002 and 224 and ossuary groups 107 and 120 at Duweir, and most common in Tomb 1 at 'Ain Shems. A fine example comes from Tomb 651 at Lahun, dated to Shishak's reign (Lahun II, Pl. LV: 18), but probably the peak period of popularity was reached in the ninth–eighth centuries (see Guy Brunton (QB III, p. 24) on the sacred eye).

The so-called *Aegis of Bast* (Pls. 34: 26, 27; 36: 50) is not in any sense a shield; it consists of the head of a lioness, surrounded with necklaces forming a semicircle. The head clearly belongs to Sekhmet, but the object is always associated with Bast, who, when cat-headed, carries it in her hand.

Ptah-Sokar (Pls. 34: 11; 35: 44; 36: 49) combines in his name, though not in appearance or attributes, two of the great gods of Memphis—Ptah, god of the living, and Sokar, god of the dead. He is represented as a new-born child, with a large head, protuberant stomach, and short fat limbs. He embodies the idea of resurrection or reincarnation.

Amulets of Ptah-Sokar are also found in Bronze Age context (cf. L. II, Pls. XVI: 4 and XXI: 51) and in tomb deposits to be published in *Lachish IV*.

Though *Nefertum* (Pl. 35: 38, 39) was one of the ancient gods of Memphis, he was completely overshadowed in the official religion by the more modern deity, Ptah. One of the figures came from a brick building on the mound, which had been overlaid by, or built into, a structure of Level III. Therefore, the attribution of similar figures to the xxvith dynasty made by Petrie (Amulets, p. 38) would accord with the Palestinian evidence from Duweir and Megiddo, where an example came from Stratum II (M. I, Pl. 76: 3).

Mut (Pl. 34: 15) was originally the great goddess of Thebes. She was the personification of the White Crown of Upper Egypt, which was itself a divinity. Part of a broken figure was found in Tomb 120, but it is not possible to say if it belonged to the earlier phase of burials or to the ossuary deposits.

The *Sphinx* (Pl. 35: 30), when reproduced as an amulet, usually has a cat's body and a woman's head. There is, however, no proof that it was connected with the worship of Bast. The well-modelled amulet comes from Tomb 218 at Duweir, and the head is particularly interesting on account of the distinctive hair style. The whole head is shaved, leaving four circular tufts of tight curls, a style which is typically negroid (cf. PAC, Fig. 40).[1] A duplicate was found in Tomb 4 at Tell er-Retabeh (Raamses) with a figure of Ptah-Sokar (like Pl. 35: 44), a small cat (like Pl. 34: 6) and two Horus eyes. There was in addition a juglet (HIC Pl. XXXVI: 17) which Petrie described as "foreign", similar to Duweir Class D.3a.

It is uncertain whether the *Barbary Ape* (*Cercopithecus macaca sylvana*) can be interchanged with the baboon (*Papio Anubis*) as the sacred animal of Thoth (Pl. 35: 31–32). Realistic representations of both animals were found in Tomb 218, but they are not very common either in Palestine or Egypt. The best dated *Papio* is one from Stratum VA at Megiddo, for which there is a good parallel from Tomb 1 at 'Ain Shems. Petrie places figurines of *Cercopithecus* from xxvith dynasty to Ptolemaic, though *Papio* was known in the Old Kingdom (Amulets, p. 43).

The *falcon* (Pl. 35: 34) is the form of the god Horus, and is known as an amulet in Egypt from the pre-historic period down to Ptolemaic times. The example from Duweir comes from Tomb 218, and there is a stone figure of a falcon from the Solar Shrine (Pl. 36: 56).

The *lion* (Pl. 34: 25) as an amulet is rare in Egypt, and lion-gods are also rare and their cult is obscure, though the lioness in the form of Sekhmet was common.

The amulet of the *ram* (Pl. 35: 33) represents the sacred animal of Amon of Thebes, for it invariably shows the peculiarity of the Theban breed in the horns which curve down and forward. The amulets are certainly uncommon in Palestine, and there is no close parallel illustrated in Petrie's Amulets, Pl. XXXVIII.

The *pig* (Pl. 35: 35) was originally the sacred animal of Osiris, to whom it was sacrificed. In course of time the legend to explain the sacrifice was changed, and the pig then represented Sutekh the enemy of Osiris. The sow from Tomb 218 is well made in comparison with one from Tomb 1 at 'Ain Shems. It is also a better representation of the animal than any of those illustrated by Petrie from Egypt in the xxvith dynasty (Amulets, p. 47).

The *menyt* (Pl. 34: 24) is often wrongly called the counterpoise of a necklace, whereas it is in reality a stylised reproduction of the tasselled ends hanging down the back; it became an apotropaic amulet for that part of the person which could not be guarded by the eyes. One specimen came from Tomb 218, but the type is uncommon in Palestine.

---

[1] Note the Ptolemaic development, where the tuft is retained in front, and the sides and back grow into long ringlets (Amulets, Pl. XXXIII: 185 k, l; see also IKG, Pl. XIX: 43).

Conclusions

The best group of amulets was contained in Tomb 218. Tombs 107 and 120 also made substantial contributions; it would appear, however, that like the scarabs and bone pendants in both groups, the amulets should belong to the phase of normal burials, rather than to the later ossuary deposits. Though there were sixteen amulets in Tomb 1002, they were few in comparison with the amount of pottery.

The subject should be viewed in relation to the distribution of amulets on Egyptian sites, with particular reference to the Delta gods and their range of influence. Meanwhile, it is perhaps permissible to suggest, in the light of evidence from some Palestinian sites, that Ptah-Sokar led in popularity at the end of the Bronze Age and in the first centuries of the Iron Age (cf. M. I, Pl. 74 and M. II, Pls. 205–206, Strata VII–V).

As in Egypt, the conquest of Shishak, who founded the xxiind dynasty, and ruled from Bubastis, brought figures of Bast and Sekhmet into prominence, and it is these which are prominent in the early tombs at Duweir. Indeed, no examples were found after the closure of Tomb 224.

Figurines of Isis and Horus were uncommon, despite the importance of the cult in Egypt, but the Sacred Eye (of Horus), and Bes, who was of Mediterranean origin, were the chief amulets of the ninth and eighth centuries.

BONE PENDANTS

Group or tomb	Calendars	Gavels	Club-shaped rods			Flat pieces, disks, etc.	Total
			Plain	Hatched	Ring-and-dot		
Houses II	—	—	—	—	—	—	—
Tomb 106	—	—	—	—	—	Pl. 54: 36, 37, 39, 55, 56 (5)	5
Houses III	—	—	—	—	Pl. 63: 21 (1)	Pl. 63: 15 (1) (and Pl. 41: 10)	2
Tomb 1002							
layers 1–5	—	—	Pl. 57: 30 (1)	—	—	—	1
layers 6–10	—	—	—	—	—	Pl. 57: 32 (1)	1
layers 11–13	—	—	—	—	Pl. 57: 31 (1)	—	1
Unstratified	Pl. 57: 28 (1)	—	—	—	—	Pl. 57: 29 (1)	2
Tomb 224	—	—	—	—	Pl. 56: 14 (2)	—	2
Tomb 116	—	—	—	Pl. 54: 77 (1) (and ring-and-dot)	Pl. 54: 76, 78 (2)	—	3
Tomb 218	—	Pl. 55: 48–50 (3) (and Pl. 37: 24, 25)	Pl. 55: 47 (1)	Pl. 55: 44 (1) (and ring-and-dot)	Pl. 55: 45, 46 (8)	Pl. 55: 51 (1)	14
Tomb 120 (Burials)	Pl. 55: 27, 28 (2)	Pl. 55: 25, 26 (and Pl. 37: 13, 8) (2)	Pl. 55: 17 (1)	Pl. 55: 18–21 (4)	Pl. 55: 22–24 (15)	Pl. 55: 29 (1)	25
Tomb 107 (Burials)	—	—	Pl. 54: 66–67 (2)	Pl. 54: 65 (1)	—	Pl. 54: 64 (1)	4
Tomb 521	Pl. 56: 23 (and Pl. 37: 3) (1)	—	—	—	—	—	1
	4	5	5	7	29	11	61

The use of three classes of bone objects, so far found exclusively in Palestine, has never been satisfactorily explained. These are:

(a) Club-shaped rods, varying in length from 5 to 8 centimetres. The tapered end is pierced for suspension, and all corners are rounded off, giving a somewhat oval section. (Pls. 37: 7, 9, 12, 14, 19–23, 26, 27; 54: 76–78; 55: 17–24, 44–47; 56: 14; 57: 30, 31).

(*b*) Flat pieces, rectangular in shape, with a projecting piece, pierced for suspension at one end. The variety with thirty pierced holes has been described as a calendar (Pls. 37: 3, 15, 17; 55: 27, 28; 56: 23; 57: 28).

Less carefully made pieces decorated with an irregular number of ring-and-dot circles, and only pierced at the top for suspension (Pls. 37: 16, 18; 54: 64; 55: 51; 57: 29).

Very crude slats or disks, also with a projection pierced for suspension, decorated with ring-and-dot circles or with incised lines (Pls. 41: 10 and 63: 15; 54: 36, 37, 39, 55, 56).

(*c*) Gavels, made in two parts, one end of the shaft being inserted into the head, and the other pierced for suspension (Pl. 37: 6, 8, 10, 11, 13, 24, 25).

A few pieces are undecorated, some have incised bands of diagonal hatching round the shaft, but the majority are decorated with a varying number of ring-and-dot circles, while occasionally a piece bears both types of ornament.

Macalister suggested (Gezer II, p. 452; III, Pl. CCXXVI: 35, 41–56, 61, 62) that the clubs with hatched bands came early in the series, and McCown supports this view from the limited evidence available from Tell en-Naṣbeh (TN I, p. 272), where six examples with bands of diagonal lines came from Tombs 32 and 54, while three with ring-and-dot design came from the later cisterns and rooms. Both kinds occur at Megiddo (M I, Pl. 97; M. II, Pls. 216, 218).

The distribution of examples found at Tell ed-Duweir in the various groups suggests at least that the ring-and-dot motif survived longer than the hatched bands; a transitional period is perhaps represented by the clubs on Pls. 54: 77 and 55: 44.

Nearly half the total of club-shaped rods came from the groups 120 and 107, which had two periods of use, but as only two rods and a fragment of a calendar came from the large Tomb 1002, it is assumed that the bulk of examples from groups 120 and 107 should be associated with the earlier burial phase, like the faience amulets illustrated on Pls. 34–36, and many of the scarabs and scaraboids on Pls. 43–45.

The following table assembles some similar bone objects from sites in Palestine; they do not seem to occur in surrounding countries.

Site	Rods	Flat pieces		Gavels	Reference
Tell ed-Duweir	41	4	11	5	—
'Ain Shems	21	—	—	5	APEF II, Pl. XXX
Gezer	—	—	—	—	Gezer III, Pl. CCXXVI: 35, 41–56, 61, 62
Tell en-Naṣbeh	16	—	—	—	TN I, Pl. 112: 29–36
Megiddo	43	—	1	—	M I, Pl. 97; M II, Pls. 216, 218
Tell Abu Hawam	1	—	—	—	QDAP IV (1935), Pl. XXXII: 32
Tell Jemmeh	8	1	—	—	Gerar, Pls. 33, 34
Tell el-Fara	1	1	—	—	BP I, Pls. XL: 481, XLI: 292; BP II, Pl. LXXIV: 116

It will be seen that where stratification is available, most examples fall within the earlier part of Iron II. At 'Ain Shems the whole group comes from Tomb I, at Megiddo more than half the total comes from Stratum V, and at Tell Jemmeh the few stratified examples came from Levels 190–194, with one as low as 186 feet.

The rods outnumber the gavels by ten to one, and the latter were only found at two sites: Tell ed-Duweir and 'Ain Shems. The purpose of both rods and gavels remains obscure.

The most plausible explanation as to the use of these objects is that they were for divination by rods or rhabdomancy, a method well known in Palestine and elsewhere. The Matabele method of foretelling the future by means of "divining bones" is strongly suggestive. In Matabeleland the rods were generally made from the teeth of elephants, hippopotami and wild pig, and always have the same shape and designs. They are long and narrow, and are decorated on one side with the ring-and-dot design. The number of rings varies considerably, ranging from three to sixteen. The method was to unstring the "bones", shake them and throw them down, interpreting the result according to their position on the ground.[1]

It is possibly significant that the introduction of these rods and gavels coincided at Tell ed-Duweir with many new influences and that among them were some people of African strain, as suggested by the little sphinx on Pl. 35: 30.

ALTARS

By this therefore shall the iniquity of Jacob be purged . . . when he maketh all the stones of the altar as chalkstones that are beaten in sunder, the groves and images shall not stand up. Isaiah XXVII: 9.

Tapered Stands (Pls. 42: 4, 5; 64: 1; 68–71)

The majority of the so-called stands or altars from Lachish were roughly cut in soft local howr limestone. They varied in height from 12 to 85 cm.; their size at the base was 10 to 12 cm. square, and they tapered to a squared or rounded depression on top, which seldom showed traces of burning or discoloration. Most of the stands were undecorated, a few were denticulated or horned round the top depression, and others had red paint applied on the sides; only one fragment was painted but not incised.

The usual form of decoration consisted of lightly scratched motifs set below a geometric border. On one or more sides of the stand there were representations of birds, animals, palms, snakes, ladders, suns and outlined human figures (Pls. 68–70: 1–16).

Altogether there were more than 200 stands, and they were found in three main deposits, apparently unconnected with burials or domestic quarters, but in association with mortaria such as type 568 and pottery figurines (Pl. 33). There were thirteen examples in Area 506, thirty examples in Cave 515, and 170 in Cave 534. Except in the cases of 515 and 534, where the altars were found in caves with collapsed roofs, they were scattered all over the 500 Area, a few centimetres below the present ground level.

Cuboid Stands on Feet (Pls. 49: 3 and 68: 1; for inscription, see p. 358; 64: 7)

One altar or incense stand from Cave 534 was inscribed. Unlike the tapering pillars found in the same context, it was a cuboid of soft howr limestone, standing at least 16·5 cm. high, with much damaged sides, each between 11 and 12 cm. wide. The four stump feet were missing, and the shallow depression on the top surface did not show signs of fire.

The lightly scratched inscription occupied most of one face, below two zigzag lines which were continuous round the remaining three sides. Opposite the inscription was a palm tree with unidentifiable objects on each side, and a ladder pattern with vertical strokes was a poor attempt to fill the space with decoration.

Analogies in form and design were found by Macalister at Gezer (Gezer II, pp. 442–447 and III, Pl. CCXXV), and though they were attributed at the time of discovery to the Hellenistic period, the amended chronology for that site would date them to about 550 B.C.

Petrie found cuboid altars between 195 and 203 ft. at Gerar (Gerar, Pls. XL, XLI and pp. 18–19) and saw in them the growth of Assyrian influence from 750 B.C., culminating in attacks on Egypt between 675 and 669 B.C. The guilloche pattern present on the well-designed examples from Gezer and Gerar is missing at Tell ed-Duweir, and the crudity of the decoration would place the inscribed altar, and the pillar stands similarly decorated, late in the series. Analogous designs are published from Tell Fara (BP II, Pls. LXXXVIII, XCIII).

Perhaps even later in development are the cuboid altars from the Moon Temple of Hureidha (TMTH, Pl. XVII: 1, 3, 5), where those found by Miss Caton-Thompson were merely decorated with bands of crisscross lines.

---

[1] H. W. Garbutt, "Native Witchcraft and Superstition in South Africa", Journal of the Royal Institute of Anthropology, XXXIX (1909), pp. 537 seq., fig. 4; Pl. XLVIII, Figs. 3, 4.

Jaussen and Savignac (Mission Archéologique en Arabie, Fig. 196) report that crude drawings were scratched on altars and tombs at various sites. Drawings of the same kind were found at Dura-Europos, scratched on the walls of Room 14 in the Temple of Azzanathkona (Rostovtzeff, Bellinger, Hopkins and Wells, Excavations at Dura-Europos, Sixth Season, 1932–1933, Fig. 34).

In assessing the value of these comparisons, it should be remembered that they are no doubt typical of untrained primitive draughtsmanship in the Near East at all periods, though an inventory of the fauna depicted might prove instructive.

Incense Stand (Pls. 42: 6 and 64: 11)

Made of soft howr limestone, a stand from the Solar Shrine is 13 cm. in height and 10×9 cm. square at the base. That it was used for burning incense is clear from the cracked and charred top surface, which formed a hollowed receptacle 7×6 cm. square. The solid panel at the back of the stand and the two pillars in front are grooved as if to imitate a house or shrine.

Offering Tables? (Pls. 71: 17, 22; 64: 10)

It would appear that the stone with three hollowed cup marks in the middle of the long side may once have been part of a pillar stand, for a depression remains on the square short end. A rectangular design was scratched on another face. The fragment, No. 22, was provided with two small cup marks. Both these crude pieces may be compared with a fragment of a marble palette or offering table from the Solar Shrine, which once had at least four such depressions.

Horned Altar (Pl. 42: 8, 9)

The only large altar was found overturned near the entrance to the sanctuary of the Solar Shrine. Originally the pedestal would have been nearly half a metre high, but the base and sides were chipped and broken. It appears to have had projections at each of the four corners on the top, which was slightly hollowed (cf. Gezer II, Fig. 507). The upper part, which flared out, was surrounded by a plain moulding, some 3 cm. in depth. All four vertical sides of the altar were originally carved with emblems in relief, but only two are now recognisable—a life-size hand, occupying all the space available, and on the opposite face the figure of a man with hands upraised in the attitude of worship.

Conclusions

On epigraphic style, Professor Dupont-Sommer dates the inscription on the cuboid incense altar to the fifth to sixth century B.C.; his note on the religious implications of the reading which he gives is transcribed in full on pp. 358–359.

While the surface deposits, which include a majority of tapering stands, do not provide any stratigraphical evidence, the pottery with the groups is quite consistent with Professor Dupont-Sommer's date for the inscription.

No altars or incense stands of any kind were found in pre-exilic contexts, and part of a limestone pillar which was inscribed (Pl. 64: 1) with rough marks or signs came from the courtyard of the Residency. Very crude undecorated altars on a bench in the Solar Shrine (Q.12: 104) show that they were still being made in the second century B.C.

The use of the altars, stands or symbols could be explained in various ways and identified with named objects in Hebrew ritual. While avoiding the difficulties which such an attempt would bring, it can be said that the cuboid altars are those on which incense was burnt. The word is used in the short votive inscription, and there are traces of fire on the stand on Pl. 42: 6. The stands may be the *ḥammānīm* which Ingholt has identified with incense altars (MS II, pp. 795–802).

With the exception of the trachyte altar (Pl. 64: 7), all examples are of limestone, the Hebrew word for which is translated "chalkstones" in the words from Isaiah quoted at the head of this section.

CHAPTER 13

UTENSILS AND ORNAMENTS

METAL

Weapons (Pls. 54, 56, 60, 61, 63)

THOUGH the city of Lachish is known to have been the focus of at least two military campaigns during the Iron Age, both of which were backed by all the force and equipment of a powerful foreigner, the site of Tell ed-Duweir has not so far yielded the expected variety of swords and shields, spears and chariot wheels, which were so precisely depicted on the Lachish reliefs.

And yet the evidence of armed attack does exist in the hundreds of iron arrowheads which had been aimed against the walls, many having their tips embedded in the masonry or curled and twisted by their impact with the stone. That the defenders used much the same type of arrowhead is indicated by the collections found within the city, notably in Rooms H.17: 1003 (40 examples), J.15: 1070 (12 examples) and H.17: 1046 (53 examples). Like those around the Bastion and near the roads leading to the gate, the clusters of arrowheads in the rooms were lying in the burnt ashes of destruction, often fused by the intensity of heat into a solid mass.

All the arrowheads are now corroded and broken, so that it is impossible to recognise any fine distinction of form. However, it is clear that the majority had leaf-shaped blades with tangs of varying length, and that the average size was about 7 cm.

Some examples showed a swelling at the base of the blade (Pl. 60: 5, 32, 58–60, 65, 75), a peculiarity noted at Tell Beit Mirsim (AASOR XXI–XXII, § 46 and Pl. 63: 27), at Megiddo (M. I, Pl. 80: 33, 34, etc.) Stratum III, 780–650 B.C., and at 'Athlit (QDAP II, p. 56, Fig. 14a).

There is nothing to show in the distribution of examples at Duweir that the form was more favoured by the defenders of the city, for it seems to be evenly divided between the rooms and the outside walls.

Despite the corrosion, it was possible to distinguish some specimens (Pl. 60: 13, 55–57) with a central rib down the blade; they came from the gate or road, which would conform to Petrie's observation (PTW, p. 34 and Pl. XLI: 32) that the type was not early, though the proportion is not high enough to show decisively that it is Assyrian. Analogous forms from Megiddo (M. I, Pl. 80: 29, 30, 33, 35) are from Stratum III (780–650 B.C.) which covers the period of Assyrian control. Albright considers that blades with a central rib were rare in Palestine before the Persian period (AASOR XXI–XXII, § 46 and Pl. 61: 20). In this connexion it may be noted that a central rib is common at Hama in the cremation cemetery during Periods I–IV (Hama, p. 122) and that arrowheads of iron did not achieve equity with bronze until Period III (*c.* 925–800 B.C.).

Examples of a less common type were described by Petrie as "armour piercing" bolts (Gerar, p. 15 and Pl. XXVIII: 13–20), and they occur between the seventh and fifth centuries B.C. Specimens of the type at Duweir came from the road and Bastion area (Pl. 60: 71–73), but two were found in Tomb 106 (Pl. 54: 48) and another was recovered from the floor of the Solar Shrine (Pl. 60: 70), thus supporting a date no earlier than the seventh century for these missiles.

The few leaf-shaped bronze arrowheads from Tell ed-Duweir (Pl. 60: 15, 25, 46, 68, 69) were found in open areas on the mound. No. 25 had actually stuck between two stones of the wall of Palace C, and must therefore be later than that construction. Nos. 68 and 69 came from a post-exilic building and a pit respectively. One specimen was found at the 250-metre level in the Great Shaft (Pl. 61: 13) and another was the only bronze blade among several iron arrows from Tomb 106 (Pl. 54: 46, 49–53). The excavations by R. W. Hamilton at Tell Abu Hawam produced examples of the same kind of slender bronze blade (QDAP IV, Pl. XXXIII: 360–362) in Stratum V, but these date from the second millenium.

It can therefore be said that iron was almost exclusively employed for arrowheads from the tenth to the seventh centuries B.C. at Tell ed-Duweir, and it was after 600 B.C. that bronze came into use once more for such weapons, as it had been used up to the close of the Bronze Age.

The triple-bladed socketed arrowhead, common in Scythian graves, and diffused, as a result of Scythian expansion and the use of northern mercenaries, through Syria and Palestine to Egypt, is rare at Tell ed-Duweir. An example, found in the post-exilic building, RQS.15/16: 10–21, can be compared with triple-bladed socketed arrowheads from 'Athlit (QDAP II, pp. 52–56, Fig. 14c), where C. N. Johns discusses their probable European origin and association with the fibulae. At Sheykh Zuweyid (Anthedon, Pl. XIX: 74–100) and at Gerar (Pl. XXIX: 1–22) they are unusually common. An early dated arrowhead of this kind may be from the Adoni Nur deposit at Amman (APEF VI) c. 650 B.C.

At Defenneh, a fort in the Egyptian Delta occupied between 665 and 565 B.C., Petrie found quantities of tanged iron arrowheads (Tanis II, Pl. XXXVII: 12–16), both with and without the central rib and the swelling at the base of the blade. Bronze arrowheads were almost as common and include varieties (op. cit., Pl. XXXIX: 9–16) like those on Pl. 60: 53, 54 of the present volume. Another late kind is the bronze arrowhead illustrated on Pl. 61: 14, which occurs in varying shapes and sizes (cf. PTW, Pl. XLII: 195–210). It came from the filling of the Great Shaft and could be as late as the third century B.C.

Associated with the arrowheads in H.17: 1003 and H.17: 1046 were several iron spikes, oval in section; the shortest complete example was 12 cm. long, while others measured over 26 cm., though incomplete (Pl. 60: 8 and Pl. 61: 12). From their presence among the arrowheads it may be assumed that they were weapons, though nothing like them is shown in the Assyrian reliefs.

The only large weapon recovered from the burnt debris in the vicinity of the gate was a heavy lancehead (Pl. 63: 8), but as the lower part was missing, it is uncertain whether it was tanged or socketed. Another lance or spearhead came from a pit (Pl. 56: 30). It was socketed and had been attached to the shaft by rivets. It is comparable to a spear from the fort of Defenneh (Tanis II, Pl. XXXVII: 4). There is also a rather similar iron spearhead from Stratum II at 'Ain Shems (AS IV, Pl. LIII: 59).

At the opposite north-east corner of the mound, in a burnt layer at the bottom of the well attributed to the final destruction, fragments of what appeared to be an iron sword were recovered, but its state of preservation was unsatisfactory, and no drawing was possible (cf. the well-preserved sword from a cistern at Tell Beit Mirsim (AASOR XXI–XXII, Pl. 61: 12)). See p. 93.

Two curious objects are drawn on Pl. 58: 34, 37 (photographs on Pl. 41: 7, 8). Both are made of bronze, and both appear to be metal terminals for a shaft of 2–2½ cm. in width. They seem to belong to Level III, for No. 34 was found below the plaster court attributed to Level II (K.15: 1033), and No. 37 came from Room H.18: 1082, but it must be admitted that the room has no clearly marked floor and is very close to the un-excavated scarp; K.15: 1033 has also been subjected to much disturbance. Compare No. 34 with a bronze spear-butt from Beth-Shan, Level IV (BS I, Pl. 39: 3), and with those illustrated in PTW, Pl. XL: 179–187, none of which is a close parallel.

Armour (Pls. 39, 41, 57, 58)

There were altogether seventeen pieces of scale armour. Seven were made of bronze and ten of iron; nearly all can be equated, directly or indirectly, with the period of destruction of Level III. The pieces on Pl. 58: 12, 14 from Room J.15: 1019, for instance, were probably associated with the layer of destruction known to lie beneath the floor. The same may apply to the pieces found below the bench and plaster floor in K.14: 1033 (two examples on Pl. 58: 6), though this open space did contain earlier objects and there is a good parallel for the scale armour at Megiddo in Stratum V. Only the fragment from Road 1087 (Pl. 58: 11) was in an apparently undisturbed position on the surface. All these examples were found with arrowheads and other objects, such as the butt on Pl. 58: 34 and the knife on Pl. 59: 12. The scale from Room J.15: 1039, illustrated on Pl. 58: 8, was found well above the floor of the building, which may be a construction of Levels IV–III. Three fragments were found in the casemate foundations of Palace A (Pl. 58: 7, 9, 13), but they cannot be confidently attributed to the building owing to the disturbed condition of the area.

Two bronze armour fragments from Tomb 1002 came from layers 3 and 11 (Pl. 57: 16, 17 and Pl. 39: 8, 9). It is perhaps significant that the only square-ended bronze scale is among the earlier fragments. Two bronze examples came from a partly excavated cistern 7005 (Pl. 58: 4, 5 and Pl. 39: 7). Two iron scales (Pl. 56: 11, 12) from the top filling of the earlier Tomb 224 are comparable to Cypriote scales from Idalion (GSCE II, Pl. CLXXII), though on ceramic evidence they are not later than the bronze pieces.

Scale armour is represented in Egypt from the times of Rameses II and III, and actual bronze scales, two of which bear the name of Shishak, were in the Abbott collection.[1] Possibly the history of scale armour begins elsewhere, but Goliath's coat-of-mail with "brass" scales was a novelty in south Judah (I Samuel XVII) and both contestants in that trial of strength wore helmets of "brass". Bronze seems to have remained long in favour for personal armour despite the introduction of iron.

At the time of the destruction of Level III, or possibly later, parts of a helmet, the crest-mount illustrated on Pl. 39: 1 and the cheek-piece on Pl. 41: 5, were in use, all cast in bronze. In the Lachish Reliefs a very close parallel to the crest-mount (Pl. 39: 3) can be seen, but it remains uncertain whether the example found is a relic of Sennacherib's campaign or of the Babylonian attack in the following century. The circumstances of the find are more fully described on p. 98. The cheek-piece can be compared with one found at Idalion in Cyprus (GSCE II, Pl. CLXXVI: 3) which is dated to 600–475 B.C. The same objects are described as blinkers in GSCE IV, pt. 2, p. 148, but sculptured horse trappings sometimes show a similar piece hanging between the eyes.

Knives (Pls. 54, 56–59)

The knives can equally well be classed with the weapons or with the tools, and no doubt they were on occasion used for either purpose. Examples from the tombs are illustrated on Pl. 54: 28–31, 44, 45, 69; Pl. 56: 10, 22, 26, 34; Pl. 57: 15, 38 and Pl. 58: 1; and from the tell rooms and Residency and pits on Pl. 59: 11–19. They are, for the most part, incomplete, and so heavily corroded that a general description must suffice. The blades, which are oval or ovate in section, vary in length from about 7 to 17 cm. Some had wooden handles, as is shown by traces of wood and iron rivets still in position. In Tomb 224 there was an iron blade fixed with bronze rivets (Pl. 56: 10). Nearly all can be classed with the straight-backed knives dated by Petrie to the late Iron Age (PTW, p. 23). Exceptions, having a curled or looped end to the handle, came from a tell room and a Residency pit respectively, and are illustrated on Pl. 59: 9, 10. Another variety of blade or sickle, riveted to the handle along the length of the blade, is shown on Pl. 57: 25 and Pl. 59: 7, 8.

The earliest group of iron weapons or implements from the sealed Tomb 521 is undoubtedly the most valuable. Of the three knives on Pl. 56: 22, 26 and 27, the last is especially interesting for it belongs to a class with recurved tip which is best known in the Iron Age culture of Europe (PTW, Pl. XXVI: 124–128 and p. 25) and is dated there to about 1000 B.C. Such distinctive and graceful blades are rare in Palestine, but there is a fine bronze knife of comparable shape from Gerar (Gerar, Pl. XXIII: 9 and I: 19) and a more developed iron blade from a higher level (Gerar, Pl. XXXI: 41) which Petrie has dated to about 750 B.C. (op. cit., p. 16).

Trident (Pls. 8: 3; 40: 7 and 56: 38)

In Tomb 521, with the knives described above, there was a trident measuring 60 cm. in length, with prongs 40 cm. long and measuring 15 cm. from outer tip to tip. It seems to have been made in three parts, with the central prong extended to form the main part of the handle; the other two were then shaped and welded to it, or separately attached, though the details are by no means clear owing to heavy corrosion.

It cannot be completely fortuitous that tridents, like the knife on Pl. 56: 27, are also an element in the Iron

---

[1] Iron scale armour attached to a leather corselet from Defenneh is dated to 665–565 B.C. (Tanis II, p. 78 and Pl. XXXVII: 19, 19A, 19B).

Age culture of Europe, and a magnificent example comes from an Etruscan tomb at Vetulonia (Déchelette, Manuel d'Archéologie, Vol. III, Fig. 322).

Rarely found in excavations, the trident is nevertheless one of the best known weapons of antiquity, as the attribute of Poseidon, god of the eastern Mediterranean. It passed to his Roman successor, Neptune, to reappear after a lapse of two thousand years on the coinage of another sea power. And yet this weapon is not exclusive to maritime sites. A trident (or bident?) was found in the fort at Defenneh (Tanis II, Pl. XXXVII: 3) and another came from Beth-Shan (BS III, Pl. XXXVIII: 33), but both examples appear in a later context.

Much closer in date are the forks or bidents from Sialk Necropolis B; though they are mostly made of bronze, Tombs 15 and 52 contained examples made of iron (Fouilles de Sialk II, Pl. LVII: S.845a, b and Pl. LXVIII: S.723a, b) and Tomb 15 also produced part of a trident in the same metal (Pl. LVII: S.845c). Instead of the date of 1000–800 B.C. proposed by the excavator for Necropolis B, Schaeffer would prefer 1250–1100 B.C. (Stratigraphie Comparée, p. 477).

The excavator of Sialk has found these forks in tombs of both men and women, and has established that they were used in the preparation of the funerary feast. It is therefore significant, perhaps, that the trident from Tell ed-Duweir was found just inside the threshold of the tomb, which was a favourite place for the deposit of food and drink. That tridents were used in the preparation of sacrifices is confirmed in the first Book of Samuel:

"And the priest's custom with the people was, that, when any man offered sacrifice, the priest's servant came, while the flesh was in seething, with a flesh-hook of three teeth in his hand;

"And he struck it into the pan, or kettle or caldron or pot; all that the flesh-hook brought up the priest took for himself" (I Samuel II: 13, 14).

Tools and Agricultural Implements (Pls. 41, 56, 59, 61, 62)

The introduction of iron into Palestine about the eleventh century B.C., and its speedy replacement of bronze for all practical purposes, has been very fully discussed (AJA, 1939, pp. 458–463; AASOR XXI–XXII, § 20; AS V, p. 153; TN I, p. 255, etc.). That metal of all kinds was comparatively rare in Judah during the three centuries under review is indicated both by the scarcity of iron and bronze implements and by evidence of repair.

Four iron implements which may be classed as ploughshares or plough-points were found in rooms of Level III and at the gate of the city, and ranged in length from 15 to 25 cm. (Pls. 61: 1–4 and 41: 11). Parallels to No. 1 were found at Tell Beit Mirsim (AASOR XXI–XXII, Pl. 61: 3, 4) from Stratum A and Megiddo (M. I, Pl. 83: 21), Stratum III, 780–650 B.C. Points resembling Nos. 2 and 3 also occur at Tell Jemmeh (Gerar, Pl. XXVI: 2, 5, 6) at levels 186, 188 and 190, dating to about the tenth century (AJA, 1939, p. 460). A plough-point from Tell en-Naṣbeh (TN I, Pl. 96: 1) is comparable to No. 3, and was found with pottery of the eighth-century B.C.[1]

Some ambiguity seems to exist about the definition of an ox-goad, and the distinction between these and plough-points is by no means clear. Both Albright (AASOR XXI–XXII, § 20) and McCown (TN I, p. 255) view them as somewhat shorter and narrower versions of the plough-point, but the present writer would submit that the two points illustrated on Pl. 61: 9, 11, both from tell rooms, are possibly lighter and more practical, though much less humane, for the purpose. The only parallel seems to be the iron spike from Sheykh Zuweyid (Anthedon, Pl. XXIII: 60), found in town HB 380, dated by Petrie to 805–625 B.C. Unlike the example from Tell ed-Duweir, the end is socketed.

Three iron sickles came from rooms occupied during Level III (Pl. 59: 3–5). These essential implements are found on almost every Iron Age site. At Tell Jemmeh (Gerar, Pl. XXVII) they are chiefly found between levels

---

[1] With regard to the discovery of a bronze plough-point at Tell en-Naṣbeh in association with pottery which appears to date after 600 B.C. (TN I, p. 255), present evidence goes to show that for some reason the source of iron ore was no longer available to the Palestinians in the sixth to fourth centuries B.C., and that bronze was again in use for many practical purposes (cf. the section on arrowheads, pp. 385 f. and QDAP II).

189 and 200, from the ninth to sixth centuries, at 'Ain Shems (AS V, p. 153 and AS IV, Pl. LIII: 57) they are late eleventh or tenth century; and at Megiddo (M. I, Pl. 82) they occur in Strata IV–II (1000–600 B.C.). There is an incomplete sickle or pruning hook (cf. PTW, Pl. LIX) from the Solar Shrine (Pl. 59: 6), which should be dated to the second century B.C. or later.

An iron sheath for a spade or hoe is illustrated on Pl. 62: 1. Enough metal remained to allow chemical treatment for the removal of corrosion, and it was then revealed that the spade had been carefully repaired on both sides by patches of the same metal riveted to the cracked blade. A fork found in the same locality near the gate is drawn on Pl. 62: 4. Two of the three prongs are missing, and the circular hole in the width of the tool was no doubt intended to take the wooden handle. Both tools may be compared to agricultural tools published by Petrie (PTW, Pl. LXVII) and both may have been abandoned on the mound by a peasant tilling the soil in the Roman period, for examples of spades have not so far been noted prior to that time.

The iron bar on Pl. 62: 2 measures over 46 cm. in length, both ends and part of the middle being missing. The iron object on Pl. 62: 3 is not easily comprehensible, and the reconstruction is very tentative. Both bear some resemblance to balance beams at present used in Palestinian villages.

Some other small tools are shown on Pl. 61. No. 5 may be an iron wedge or chisel, and No. 6 is a well-made tool of bronze of the same kind, found near the east wall of the palace. It may therefore be placed in a fifth- to fourth-century context. It somewhat resembles an iron tool from Tell Jemmeh (Gerar, Pl. XXXII: 34 from DH 194), which could be contemporary. Another similar fragment, also of iron, came from the top layers of Tomb 106 (Pl. 54: 34), with a nail (Pl. 54: 33). Nails were fairly common on the site. One example was recovered from the burnt patch inside the Level II inner gate (not published), and others came from the Residency (Pl. 63: 10, 11) and from an adjoining pit (Pl. 63: 5).

Personal Ornaments (Pls. 54–57, 63)

Anklets, Bracelets and Bangles

When the contents of the tombs are disturbed it is often impossible to distinguish between anklets and bracelets, and if uncertainty exists, as it does in most cases, the term "bangle" has been used.

In two single graves 110 and 147, a pair of bronze anklets were in position on each leg (Grave 147 and its contents are illustrated on Pls. 5: 2; 36: 58–60 and 55: 30). In Tomb 4005, also, where many burials had been pushed aside for later interments, one fairly thick bronze anklet was still in place (Pls. 9: 3 and 57: 45). There were altogether in this group about thirty bangles, most of them complete, in sets of three or four. The diameter ranged from a half to one centimetre, and the section was round. In most cases the ends of the bangle overlapped and were decorated with incised lines, a reminder, perhaps, of the Middle Bronze Age fashion, when gold bangles were graded and marked according to the order in which they should be worn. A single bronze bracelet (Pl. 56: 17), in place on the left arm, was the only object found with the burial in Grave 236, and two bracelets (Pl. 55: 33), together with some beads and shells, were the sole contents of a child's grave 193.

Tomb 223 had six bangles (Pl. 56: 4) and four larger ones (Pl. 56: 9) in which a flattened side is first seen, typical of the thick and heavy anklets which are a feature of Tomb 218.

All three chambers of Tomb 218 and the deposit near the door included bronze bangles. Thirty-eight were heavy and thick (Pl. 55: 35) with a flattened side, and ten were somewhat lighter in weight (Pl. 55: 36–38). Pl. 55: 34 and 39 are bangles which could only have belonged to a child.

It should be noted that in the earlier large groups, Tombs 223 and 218, there were many fragments of iron bangles which were mostly too broken and corroded for illustration, and a few were found in the lowest layer of Tomb 1002. It therefore appears that iron was seldom used for bangles in the later groups which date from about 800 B.C., either because it became unfashionable after the first novelty of the metal had waned, or because economic and military necessity diverted supplies to the manufacture of weapons.

The fact remains that among forty bangles, both heavy and light, from Tomb 116 (Pls. 54: 75, 79 and

55: 1–3), not one is made of iron, and the same situation prevails in Tomb 224 (Pl. 56: 15) and in layers 1–10 of Tomb 1002 (Pl. 57: 18–20, 24). There are, indeed, many fragments of iron bracelets in the ossuary group 120 (Pl. 55: 9, 10), but they no doubt belonged to an earlier burial phase, in common with the faience amulets and the bone pendants. Eleven bronze specimens (Pl. 55: 4, 6–8) were few in contrast to the profusion in previous groups. They were small and light and round in section, without overlapping ends, possibly a further indication of the growing shortage of metal. A bangle from the associated group 107 (Pl. 54: 57) falls within the same category.

It is interesting to note that in Tomb 1 at 'Ain Shems (APEF II, p. 59 and Pl. XXVII: A (item 12)), "Of the thirty bracelets photographed, only one was of iron". At Tell en-Naṣbeh (TN I, p. 270), Tomb 32 contained eight bronze and ten iron bangles.

Heavy and light bronze bangles, with or without overlapping ends, from layers 7–11 of Tomb 1002 are illustrated on Pl. 57: 18–20, 24. There are comparisons from Gerar (Gerar, Pl. XXIV: 76, 77), both from 194 ft., which should belong to the seventh century.

In the last large group, Tomb 106, there were altogether only ten bangles, hair-rings or rings (Pl. 54: 2, 13, 14, 16, 20–26) mostly made of bronze. They came from the top layers of chambers A, B and C, and chiefly belong to the intrusive burials of the third to fourth centuries A.D. (see QDAP XIV). The style of Nos. 16, 23 and 26, made of twisted bronze wire, is considered to be Roman by Petrie (ODU, p. 8). Another twisted bangle (Pl. 54: 75) came from Tomb 116, which also had a later period of occupation, and a third example (Pl. 63: 3) came from a Residency pit.

A thin bangle with overlapping knobbed ends is illustrated on Pl. 56: 18; it came from Cave 504 and may have belonged to the post-exilic grave 525 cut in the floor. Two examples of Pl. 56: 28 were found with some cooking pots in group 540, but they cannot be very closely dated.

Rings (Pls. 54–57)

Plain bronze rings with overlapping ends are a legacy from the earlier part of the Iron Age, when they were very common. There is no doubt that some were finger-rings, for examples have been found at Tell Fara (Petrie Collection, Institute of Archaeology, London), where the rings were still in position on the finger bones. They have a uniform diameter of 2 cm.—the average size of a woman's finger.

Bronze and silver swivel rings in which scarabs were mounted are rare (Pl. 54: 15), and in view of the numbers of scarabs and scaraboids in the earlier tombs it seems likely that it was then usual to string them on necklaces instead of mounting them in rings.

The only example of an iron ring from a group which was partly early came from Tomb 4005, where it was in place on the finger-bone between two shell rings (Pl. 57: 43, 44).

A silver ring from the ossuary pit 107 (Pl. 54: 59) was a complete circle hammered flat, and it was probably deposited late in the history of the group. Silver, bronze and iron rings were recorded from Tomb 106 (Pl. 54: 12–15). Nos. 12 and 13 are definitely associated with the intrusive burials of the fourth century A.D., and the other two rings came from the filling and should belong to the same period.

The bronze ring on Pl. 57: 34 was found with the mirror and kohl-sticks belonging to Tomb 1007, which should be dated to the sixth to fourth centuries B.C.

The latest bronze examples are illustrated on Pl. 57: 52; they occurred with iron fragments, and bronze coins dated to the fourth century A.D., all from the quarry 4035.

Ear-rings (Pls. 54–57)

Silver ear-rings were very common in the earlier large tomb groups. The majority were simple ovate rings, open at the side. One end was slender and pointed to facilitate insertion in the ear, the other was thickened at the lower part. The average length varied between 1 and 1·70 cm.

Locus	Ear-rings				Rings, overlapped ends	
	Silver or gold		Bronze		Bronze	
Great Shaft	Fig. 15	1	—	—	—	—
Tomb 4021	Pl. 57: 47 (AV)	1	—	—	—	—
515	—	—	Pl. 56: 20	1	—	—
4005	—	—	Pl. 57: 40	11	—	—
			Pl. 57: 42	1		
			Pl. 57: 41	2		
106	Pl. 54: 1	2	Pl. 54: 7, 8	2	Pl. 54: 11	1
	Pl. 54: 2	5	Pl. 54: 4	1		
	Pl. 54: 3	1	Pl. 54: 5	1		
	Pl. 54: 6	1	Pl. 54: 9	1		
1002						
layers 1–5	Pl. 57: 5, 11	3	Pl. 57: 6, 13	2	Pl. 57: 21	1
	Pl. 57: 9	1				
layers 6–10	Pl. 57: 3	1	Pl. 57: 8	5	—	—
			Pl. 57: 12	1		
layers 11–13	Pl. 57: 4	1	—	—	Pl. 57: 22, 23	2
	Pl. 57: 7	12				
	Pl. 57: 10	1				
224	Pl. 56: 16	1	—	—	—	—
116	Pl. 54: 71	16	Pl. 54: 72	3	Pl. 54: 74	2
	Pl. 54: 73 (electrum)	1				
218	Pl. 55: 40	20	—	—	Pl. 55: 42	1
	Pl. 55: 41 (AV and electrum)	2				
	Pl. 55: 43	1				
120 (Burials)	Pl. 55: 15	1	—	—	Pl. 55: 5	1
107 (Burials)	Pl. 54: 58	5	Pl. 54: 58	2	—	—
223	Pl. 56: 6	2	—	—	Pl. 56: 8	1
TOTALS		79		33		9

Forty-five out of a minimum total of fifty-two came from Tomb 223, Tombs 107 and 120 and Tombs 218 and 116: it is perhaps of some interest to note the distribution of examples throughout the groups. There were also a few gold and electrum ear-rings in Tombs 218 and 116. Bronze ear-rings of the same shape were less common and were confined to the later groups.

Some embellishments to the simple silver ovate ear-rings were introduced in Tomb 116 and onwards. They usually consisted of one or more pendant drops (Pl. 54: 73; Pl. 57: 9, 10), but the most striking variation was a group of at least a dozen examples, many of them fused into a mass (Pl. 40: 1, Pl. 57: 7) which came from the lowest levels of Tomb 1002. They represent the head and torso of a woman, but owing to corrosion the finer details of the work cannot be distinguished.

The last development appears in Tomb 106, where the ovate silver ring is provided with a heavy ball drop, sometimes with a row of pellets round the join (Pl. 54: 1–3). The same form was also made in bronze (Pl. 54: 4, 5). All were recovered from the sieving of the tomb and most of them appear to belong to the original burials, though the flat beaten ear-ring (Pl. 54: 6) may date to the sixth century B.C. (cf. Gezer III, Pl. CXXXV, Fig. 32a and Gerar, Pl. XX: 47). The iron ring with the beads shown on Pl. 54: 9 could be placed with the fourth-century A.D. intrusions.

The ball drop ear-ring is characteristic of "Second Semitic" at Gezer (Gezer II, p. 101 and Pl. CXXXVI: 1). It is common at 'Ain Shems in Tombs 5, 8 (APEF II, Pl. XLIII: 24, 25; Pl. LIX: 11–15) and occurs at Megiddo

(M. I, Pl. 86: 21) in Stratum III, 780–650 B.C., and at Tell Jemmeh, with the jewellers' hoard (Gerar, p. 10 and Pl. I).

Another comparison from the last-named site is the stone mould for an ear-ring (Gerar, Pl. XX: 45) from AFF 193. It resembles an electrum ear-ring from Tomb 116 (Pl. 54: 73) and both may well belong to the ninth to eighth centuries B.C. There is also an ear-ring with ball drops from Hama (Hama, p. 129, Fig. 159), Period I, dated at about 1200–1075 B.C.

Fibulae (Pls. 54, 56, 57, 58)

The fibulae found at Tell ed-Duweir can be divided into five main classes:

		Locus	Plate	Total
1.	Plain semicircular arc with coiled spring, made in one piece. Round section. Iron. (Blinkenberg's class II). Left-handed.	223 1002	56: 7 57: 27	2
2a.	Semicircular arc decorated with ball mouldings. Traces of iron pin, inserted. Bronze.	1002, layer 10	57: 26	1
2b.	Plain or ring-decorated bow, approaching "knee" type. Coiled spring and pin inserted. No. 21 has iron pin, No. 20 has a pin of bronze.	L.12: 1069 H.18: 1081 Bastion L. 15: 55	58: 20 58: 21 58: 17 58: 22	4
2c.	"Knee" type (Blinkenberg's class XIII), decorated with coiled wire, chased rings and/or balls. Coiled spring and pin inserted. Bronze.	106 (2 ex.) 534 560 562 Pal. walls: M.14, L.13 L.12: 1058 K.13: Res. Rm.N PQR.17	54: 40 56: 29 56: 36 56: 37 58: 15, 16 58: 18 58: 19 58: 26	10
3a.	Plain, undecorated. Pin separately made and riveted to bow. Bronze.	4005 PQR.17	57: 39 58: 27	2
3b.	Plain, undecorated. Square in section, pin attachments missing. Bronze.	M.14: 44 M.15: 75 PQR.17	 58: 24 58: 25	3
4.	"Cross-bow" fibula. Bronze.	700	58: 23	1
5.	Penannular fibula or buckle. Iron.	106 (2 ex.)	54: 17, 18	2
				25

It will be seen from the analysis that two fibulae were found in contexts which associated them with Level III, though the greatest number were found in groups or areas which are later than that destruction; and six fibulae were found in tombs, of which two were made of iron, which was very rarely used for such things.

Though the use of the fibula has long been attested all over Palestine, by Macalister at Gezer (Gezer II, p. 81 and Gezer III, Pl. CXXXIV), Mackenzie at 'Ain Shems (APEF II, p. 59), and more recently by Petrie at Tell Jemmeh (Gerar, p. 11 and Pl. XVIII), Lamon and Shipton at Megiddo (M. I, Pls. 78 and 79) and Badè at Tell en-Naṣbeh (TN I, p. 268 and Pls. 109–111), it appears certain that they were an imported fashion which only came into common use in Syria, Egypt and Palestine late in the seventh century, though isolated examples have been found in Palestine from the Bronze Age onwards.

On the evidence of eighth- to seventh-century groups, it would seem that the "knee" or "elbow" fibula (Blinkenberg's class XIII) only begins in a tentative way in about 750 B.C., and does not reach full development for a century or more, a conclusion which does appear to link them with incursions from the north in the seventh century.

The earlier "arc" or "bow" fibulae are by no means common in Palestine, and it may be worth following the comparisons in greater detail.

1. Illustrations of iron fibulae are rare in excavation reports from Palestine.

Macalister states that at Gezer "the vast majority of fibulae are of bronze", but a few iron specimens were found (Gezer II, p. 81), and on Pl. CXXXIV, Fig. 5 he shows an example made of iron of the "knee" type, attributed to the "Hellenistic" stratum, which under the revised chronology should belong to the "Persian" period.

Iron fibulae are also mentioned in Tell en-Naṣbeh I, p. 265, but they are fragmentary and unclassified. Tomb 32, dated to the tenth to eighth centuries (TN I, Pl. 109: 4), produced part of a bow and two-coil spring in iron, which is close to the examples from Tombs 223 and 1002.

The best comparisons so far available came from Alişar Huyuk (OIP XXIX, Fig. 494), where a very similar example is dated to post-Hittite-Phrygian times, c. 1000 B.C.

The same shape is to be found at Maral Deresi in the Caucasus (Stratigraphie Comparée, Fig. 275), and typologically it is said to be later than most of the ornamental varieties from the Kouban (op. cit., Fig. 301), where the latest graves, with those of the cemetery at Maral Deresi, date between 1200 and 1000 B.C., and both places contain some objects of iron.

Turning to Mediterranean countries, the examples from Tombs 223 and 1002 are close to Blinkenberg's Class II. Owing to the simplicity of the form, Blinkenberg considers that it remained long in use. There are one or two iron fibulae from Crete (Vrokastro, Tomb 2, p. 140 and Pl. XIXd) dated between the twelfth and tenth centuries, but they are not round in section.

Those few comparisons which are available for the fibulae from Tombs 223 and 1002 are dated about 1000 B.C. in their place of origin, but the burial chambers in which the iron fibulae were found at Duweir did not come into use until somewhat later.

2a. The use of an iron pin inserted into a bronze bow is possibly a device made expedient by a growing shortage of iron, and a pin of this metal was used whenever possible to provide greater strength.

A close parallel comes from Megiddo (M. I, Pl. 79: 13), Stratum III (780–650 B.C.), which was also provided with an iron pin. A similar fibula, with pin missing, was found in Tomb 1 at 'Ain Shems (APEF II, Pl. XXVIII: 10), and there were two fibulae (Nos. 8 and 9 on the same plate) of Class 2c. The group is placed by Grant and Wright in the late tenth or early ninth century B.C. (AS V, p. 136), while Tombs 2–8, in which single examples of the "knee" fibulae were found, are "probably to be dated little earlier than the 7th century B.C." (AS V, p. 8).

2b. The fibulae on Pl. 58: 20–22 lack the angular bend which is characteristic of Class 2c. Nos. 20 and 21 are definitely placed: No. 20 was found below the cobbled floor of a Level II room, and must therefore be associated with the previous city, and No. 21 came from a room flanking the road and Bastion which is attributed to Level III. A fibula of the same shape came from Tomb 2 at 'Ain Shems (APEF II, Pl. XXXVIII: 6) which is contemporary with Level III, and there is also a parallel with xxvith-dynasty groups at Tell Yehudiyeh.

2c. Blinkenberg has placed the fibulae described as "elbow"- or "knee"-shaped in his Class XIII. He includes in it examples found in Syria, Assyria and Palestine, which he thinks were all, or nearly all, imported from Cyprus (FGO, p. 231). He considers that the class as a whole was a local offshoot, developing independently from the original Greek type. He states that the local offshoots (his Group IV ff.) do not appear before the ninth century B.C. (op. cit., p. 17).

As far as south Palestine is concerned, a later date is suggested for the common use of fibulae in this class by the evidence from Tell Jemmeh (Gerar, p. 11 and Pl. XVIII), where one example only occurs below 192 ft., equivalent to about the seventh century B.C. Albright has suggested that the "knee" type fibula replaced the "bow" type "not far from 900 B.C." (AASOR XXI–XXII, § 47), though if the Gerar dating is now unassailable this would seem to be rather early.

In contrast to the situation at Tell Jemmeh, it will be seen that few fibulae illustrated from Megiddo (M. I, Pls. 78, 79) belong to the fully developed Class 2c, an asymmetrical arc with ball mouldings being far more common. The position of these fibulae in Stratum III, therefore, would seem to favour an earlier closing date for that stratum.

At 'Ain Shems both an arc with ball mouldings and two fibulae of the "knee" type were found in Tomb 1 (see Class 2a), while subsequent tombs only contained single examples of the "knee" type. As far as one can tell from the photographs, though the angle of the bend is marked, both seem to belong to the coiled wire variety which Petrie places fourth in the order of progression.

In support of the suggestion that the "knee" fibula is no earlier than the last decades of the eighth century, there is evidence that the type is missing from the cremation burials at Hama ending at about 720 B.C. (Les Cimetières à Crémation, p. 133), though it occurs in Level E of the citadel there.[1]

The bronze pin attached to a chain and signet from Nimrud (ILN, July 29, 1950, p. 182, Fig. 12) is an early example closely dated to 722–705 B.C.

At Carchemish the contents of House D are instructive, for they provide two "knee" fibulae with iron pin inserted (BM collection) besides iron arrowheads of the kind used at the attack on Lachish, and an almost equal number of bronze triple-bladed examples, with or without barbs. The group is dated by Woolley to the final destruction of Carchemish in 605 B.C. (Carchemish II, Pl. 22 (the fibulae are not illustrated)). The extension of the "knee" fibula into the following centuries is attested at Deve Huyuk (AAA VII, Pl. XVIII: J), a site which centres on the fifth century B.C. Where comparisons of Type II from Tell en-Naṣbeh are found in datable loci, they are mainly in the seventh to sixth centuries, extending in a few cases into the fifth century (TN I, p. 269).

3a. Both examples can be placed in a late context. One fibula, from Tomb 4005, belongs to a group which is, in the main, tenth to ninth century, though there are a few objects which seem to have come from a post-exilic interment. The other was found in the filling of the Great Shaft. Petrie places the class after 600 B.C. (Gerar, p. 11 and Pl. XVIII: 31, 32). Macalister dates a similar pin later than 550 B.C. (Gezer III, Pl. CCXXIV: 1). At Megiddo, fibulae of the same kind came from the surface (M. I, Pl. 78: 1–2).

3b. The three pins in this class came from Residency pits and the filling of the Great Shaft. The characteristic feature is the square section. Their presence in the pits dates them to between the fifth and fourth centuries B.C., which compares with Wampler's date for fibulae of Type III at Tell en-Naṣbeh (TN I, p. 269).

4. The "cross-bow" fibula is well known throughout the Roman world. The example from Tell ed-Duweir was found with coins of the fourth century A.D. and later, on the surface of the Roman road 700 (Fig. 17). Cf. J. P. Bushe-Fox's second Richborough Report, pp. 44–45, Nos. 14 and 15, dated to the late third or early fourth, rather than the fourth century A.D.

5. Penannular fibulae or buckles came from Tomb 106, and are made of iron. They are both about 3 cm. in diameter, with an iron pin attached to the ring by a simple loop. Though much corroded, they appear to have no decoration. Plain penannular brooches are a speciality of the La Tène culture of the Iberian peninsula where they were very common from the third century B.C. They are rare in Palestinian sites: Macalister noted their presence at Gezer and illustrates the best specimen (Gezer III, Pl. CXXXIV: 29), though he does not

---

[1] Ingholt, Rapport preliminaire sur la première campaigne des Fouilles de Hama, 1934, Rapport II, p. 114 and note 4.

specify whether it is made of bronze or iron. A very similar bronze buckle came from 'Athlit (QDAP II, p. 65, Fig. 23), which C. N. Johns considers to be medieval.

Several brooches of iron are illustrated from Gheyta (HIC, Pl. XLIII: 33–37), which are dated by Petrie to the Roman period.

Toilet Articles (Pls. 54: 27; 57: 33–35, 37)

The completely circular mirror with a tang for insertion into an ivory or wooden handle did not become established in Egypt as the sole form until the seventh century B.C. (ODU, p. 29). With kohl tubes and sticks and stone palettes, mirrors then came to be a standard part of funerary equipment between the sixth and fourth centuries, wherever tombs of that period have been found in Syria, Egypt and Palestine.

The simplest essential equipment, consisting of a mirror, kohl stick and ring, is illustrated on Pl. 57: 33–35, and another kohl stick is drawn on Pl. 57: 37. Bronze bowls were commonly included with these burials, either plain or ornamented with repoussé decoration, and broken and corroded fragments have been found in association with the nearby Pit 1009. The bowls were most probably for toilet purposes (NP).

For comparative material, see the groups from Deve Huyuk, "A North Syrian Cemetery of the Persian Period" which centres on the fifth century B.C. (AAA VII); 'Athlit, Tomb L.21 (QDAP II, Pl. XXIII: 551), fifth to fourth century; the so-called "Philistine" graves at Gezer (Gezer I, pp. 289–300), now dated to the Persian period by J. H. Iliffe (QDAP IV, p. 185), and Tell el-Yehudiyeh, Tomb 320 (HIC, Pl. XXA) which is attributed to the xxvith dynasty, seventh century B.C., but which certainly belongs to the same cultural phase.

A pair of tweezers or forceps came from Chamber A of Tomb 106 (Pl. 54: 27). They were made of iron bent into shape and were broad at the shoulder. One end was broken. Comparable tweezers from Gezer (e.g. Gezer III, Pl. CXXXV: 1) were all made of bronze, and the same distinction applies to those from Tell en-Naṣbeh (TN I, Pl. 105: 13–14) and Megiddo (M. I, Pl. 84: 21). It is therefore more likely that the pair from Tomb 106 belongs to the intrusive burials of the fourth century A.D. when iron was more freely used. See also Déchelette II, p. 368, where the examples illustrated are all made of bronze.

Wine Strainers or Siphon Ends (Pls. 36: 55; 58: 38)

A charming representation of a gazelle's head cast in bronze comes from a strainer or siphon-end, which was found in surface debris on the mound. The internal diameter of the hollow end was 1·5 cm. which would take an inserted reed, and there were two projecting loops of bronze (not visible on Pl. 36: 55) to bind the head to the shaft. The neck and muzzle of the animal were pierced with holes, but most of the curved horns were missing. See the plain examples with loops for attachment illustrated by Petrie (FFSV, Pl. XL: 46–47).

Other incomplete and corroded cornets of bronze or iron, made from thin sheet metal, were recovered, and the best example is illustrated on Pl. 58: 38. It came from a tell room of Level III and was associated with a deposit of over fifty arrowheads. A bronze strainer (F. No. 4114, NP) was among the objects in the recess or cupboard of the sanctuary in the Solar Shrine.

The purpose of these perforated cornets is illustrated in a funerary stele from Tell el-Amarna, depicting a Syrian warrior drinking wine through a siphon (cf. Zeitschrift für Ägyptische Sprache, Pl. XXXVI: 126–129), as M. E. L. Mallowan has noted in his account of excavations at Chagar Bazar, where similar objects were found in the bottom of large vases dated to 1900–1600 B.C. (Iraq IV, Pl. 14 C and p. 99).

That the use of such strainers was widespread over a long period is shown by their appearance at Tell er-Retabeh (HIC, Pl. XXXIV A, Tomb 24 and Pl. XXXV B); at Tepe Giyan (G. Contenau and R. Ghirshman, Fouilles de Tepe Giyan, Pl. 35) from Stratum 3; and at Deve Huyuk (AAA VII, Pl. XXII: 26).

Bells (Pls. 54: 19; 58: 28)

The two bells illustrated are the only ones from the site. Both were found in contexts which may well be Roman; the smaller one on Pl. 54: 19 is from Tomb 106 and is most probably associated with the intrusive burials of the fourth century A.D., and the larger and heavier one, which was probably a cattle bell, came from the surface of the Roman road.

Lamp (Pls. 42: 2 and 63: 1)

Cf. the bronze lamp from Idalion, Period 6, Cypro-Archaic II, 600–475 B.C. (GSCE II, Pl. CLXXIX: 18).

Bronze Fittings (Pls. 41: 2 and 63: 2; Pl. 41: 4, 6, 9)

The fluted bronze terminal found in a rubbish pit (Pl. 41: 2) has no obvious comparisons, though the fifth to fourth centuries was a period when bronze furniture such as beds and chairs became popular. Three other bronze articles appear to be handles from bowls or cauldrons.

STONE

Slingshots (Pl. 40: 5)

Among many fragments of stone used and fashioned by man which were picked up on and around the tell, none were more common than round balls of flint with a diameter of about 6 cm. and weighing about 256 grammes. From the quantity and uniform nature of these spheres, their preparation must have formed a considerable industry, though if it is correct to see in them the missiles of the slingers attached to the Assyrian army —the rear rank shown on the Lachish Reliefs—the industry was not necessarily a local one. Indeed, the absence of flint in the near vicinity suggests that such stone was imported.

Crude Figures (Pls. 36: 56; 41: 1, 3)

The hawk carved from schist is provided with a loop on the back cut from the same piece, and pierced for suspension. Though the body is crudely formed, some care was taken to indicate the feathers on the breast and wings. It is rather large, 6 cm. in length from head to tail, and heavy for use as a personal ornament, and as it was found on or above the floor of the sanctuary in the Solar Shrine, it can most probably be associated with the service of the cult.

Both the animals illustrated on Pl. 41: 1, 3 are made of the softest quality limestone and are somewhat leonine in appearance. The larger one, 11 cm. in length, was found on the surface, and the smaller one, 7 cm. in length and pierced through the body, came from a Residency pit. They cannot be closely dated, though they presumably belong to the occupation of Level I. Compare the earlier scratched drawing of a lion on the palace steps (Fig. 10).

Dishes, Palettes and Querns

Pls. 42: 7 and 57: 36. The dish of crystalline limestone from the post-exilic burial 1007 has its closest affinities with the tripod saucers from the Cave Tombs at Hureidha (TMTH, Pl. XXXVII: 5–10) which have a maximum range from the seventh to the fourth century B.C.

Pls. 57: 49 and 64: 2, 3. These three solid dishes of banded alabaster are very similar to each other in shape and size, and can be attributed to the post-exilic period. Two examples were found in the Residency building and the third came from a pit 4021 which contained, besides other things, a coin dating from the third century A.D. However, the true horizon of such dishes is to be found somewhat earlier. A good example comes from the fifth-century B.C. cemetery at Deve Huyuk (AAA VII, Pl. XXVI: 5).

Pl. 64: 8. The marble, or close-grained limestone, palette, 6·3 cm. in diameter when complete, which came from the road north of the gatehouse in G.18, is the largest fragment of a class which is rather common at Tell Beit Mirsim, and even more usual in Strata II–I at Megiddo. The examples from Duweir seem to be without any decoration on the rim, though much is broken away, and this would place them early in the series. For

Albright's remarks, see AASOR XXI–XXII, § 48, and for Lamon and Shipton's comments, see Megiddo I, opposite Pl. 111.

Pls. 64: 6, 9, 10 and 65: 7. These four palettes or querns all came from rooms in the Solar Shrine. Nos. 6 and 9 are roughly made for utility rather than ornament, but No. 10 is somewhat more elaborate and can be matched rather closely at Deve Huyuk (AAA VII, Pl. XXVI: 7). No. 7 on Pl. 65 is complete, 23 cm. in diameter, with a well-made ring base.

Pl. 65: 6, 8, 9. Other basalt querns are from tell rooms of Levels III–II.

Lids or Stoppers (Pls. 42: 1; 64: 4; 65: 11)

Jar stoppers are not commonly found in excavations, for such necessary adjuncts to domestic life were normally made of perishable material such as fibre or clay; cf. the drawing on Pl. 52: 12.

A stone stopper for a storage jar grooved across the top is shown on Pl. 42: 1, and another is drawn on Pl. 64: 4. The large one, measuring 11 cm. across, has a bung of 8 cm. which would fit a storage jar. The stopper on Pl. 65: 11 was intended for a small jug.

Flask (Pl. 55: 16)

The slender flask of gypsum or very poor alabaster which came from the ossuary group 120 has lost its rim and neck, and is much worn on the surface. The form of body does not appear among those classed by I. Ben-Dor (QDAP XI, pp. 93–112) from Palestinian sites, and there is nothing closely parallel illustrated by Petrie from Egypt (FFSV, Pl. XXVIII: 558 and Pl. XXIX: 644 are the nearest).

Hones (Pls. 55: 52; 56: 19, 21)

The first hone is a rectangular slab 12·5 cm. by 3 cm., very well finished, which can hardly have served any other purpose. It came from Tomb 218.

Both the other examples were pierced for suspension.

BONE

Spatulae or Pattern Sticks (Pl. 63: 22–27)

So much has already been written about the use of the thin bone spatulae which are to be found on most Palestinian sites, that it is hazardous to attempt yet another interpretation of their use. Lamon and Shipton have summarised the suggestions already made, in Megiddo I opposite Pl. 95, and have added their own idea that they were used for the application of cosmetics.

No explanation so far put forward is wholly compatible with the facts. While there is a considerable range of length from 17·5 cm. to 7·5 cm., the width is uniform at 4 cm. All the spatulae are very fragile—more so, of course, than when they were new—and the examples from Tell ed-Duweir, at least, show signs of wear and polish on the pointed end.

Weaving was an art practised in many places and at all periods, and the present writer suggests that the bone spatulae may be pattern sticks, as used to pick up threads and hold them apart while working an intricate pattern on the loom. Mrs. Crowfoot considers that they were quite suitable for that purpose.

Handles

Pls. 41: 13 and 63: 12; 63: 13. On the authority of W. F. Albright (AASOR XXI–XXII, § 52), these two bones, one decorated with punch marks and grooved lines, and the other plain, are described as fan handles. Both are incomplete and are made of sheep's bone in its natural state, sawn off at the narrow end. The length of the plain one illustrated on Pl. 63: 13 is 37 cm. Both pieces came from a room of Level III, and should therefore be dated to 700 B.C.

Pl. 57: 1 appears to be the bone inlay from the top of a dagger, decorated with an incised pattern. Found in a bell-shaped cistern 1001, it should belong to the post-exilic reoccupation, or Hellenistic period.

Pl. 63: 14 may be part of the handle of a knife or mirror. It was found in one of the Residency pits, and should belong to the post-exilic reoccupation. There is a comparable fragment from Gerar.

Kohl-pots

Pl. 54: 70. The pot is apparently made of ivory, the surface of which has become soft and flaky. It is 9 cm. in height, but the rim and lid are missing. It came from Tomb 114, and can be dated probably to the early sixth century B.C.

Pl. 56: 3. Most probably the lid of a double kohl tube of Egyptian inspiration. It came from Tomb 223 and should date to the late tenth to early ninth century.

Pin (Pl. 56: 1)

The upper part of a bone pin, with the terminal shaped like a *M''t* feather, was found in a tomb which had been cleared of its original burials.

Inlay (Pl. 63: 28)

Part of an inlay. The slat is decorated with a lotus flower and buds, and has a hole where a rivet fixed it to a box. It came from a Residency pit and may be as late as the fourth century B.C.

Fish-hook (?) (Pl. 54: 38)

Part of a hook, though it seems to be too large for fishing purposes. It came from Tomb 106, and may well be associated with the intrusive burials of the fourth century A.D.

Arrowheads (Pl. 63: 16–20)

There were altogether thirteen bone arrowheads from the site, found in a deposit near the palace steps and on the burnt roadway. In both cases iron arrowheads were found with them. Petrie suggests that similar bone points from Gerar were brought in by those whose supplies of metal were scarce (Gerar, p. 16 and Pl. XXXIII: 30–35).

STONE, BONE AND CLAY

Spindlewhorls (Pls. 54: 42; 55: 11, 14, 32; 56: 33; 65: 2–5)

The way in which spindlewhorls were used is well illustrated at Megiddo (M. I, Pl. 95: 38), with whorls in position on the spindle, and nearly a hundred and fifty examples were recorded from that site, equally distributed in Strata I–IV, with a few from Stratum V.

At Tell ed-Duweir they were not nearly so common, and though it would be more likely to find them in houses than in tombs, only three examples were recorded from Level III (Pl. 65: 2, 3 and F. No. 6205 from J.15: 1013, NP).

Single bone whorls came from the Grave 189, and from a Pit 558 (Pl. 55: 32 and Pl. 56: 33), and another bone whorl was in the ossuary group 120 (Pl. 55: 14). A pierced stone object from the same group is also described as a whorl, though it is elliptical and not round (Pl. 55: 11).

It remains to note a steatite whorl from Tomb 106 which is comparable to domed whorls with grooved lines from Gerar (Pl. XLIV: 32–35) which are exclusive to the upper levels of the site, and should perhaps be dated no earlier than the seventh century.

GLASS

There are only two interesting glass pieces to be recorded from the site, besides collections of fragments.

Pls. 40: 3 and 55: 13. The neck and handle of a small glass jug was recovered from the ossuary tomb 120. The method of construction is unusual, for the copper wire is in the centre of the handle and forms the core round which the glass is moulded. Mr. D. B. Harden has seen the drawing and photograph and describes it as follows:

"I presume this is the neck of a sand-core jug or oinochoe. The handle technique is very interesting and, so far as I know, unparalleled; but it is a very natural technique for early glass makers to adopt if they were not sure how a pure glass handle would stand up to use, and I am only surprised that it has not been recorded before. To judge from its shape alone, this fragment might be as late as the 4th or 3rd century B.C., but since this handle technique has never been recorded amongst the hundreds of glass oinochoai of that date, I suspect this piece is much earlier, and perhaps even belongs as far back as the later 2nd millennium B.C. The horizontal band round the neck looks like paint rather than an applied trail, but I cannot be sure which it is without inspecting the original. If it is paint, this, too, would argue for an early date (cp. the oinochoe in the British Museum bearing a cartouche of Thotmes III (Fossing, *Glass before Glass-blowing*, fig. 3))."

Pl. 40: 2. This double unguentarium is a form which is quite common on Palestinian sites, and comparisons are to be found at Tell en-Naṣbeh (TN I, Pl. 105: 1), and at Gezer (Gezer III, Pls. CII and CXIII), all in Roman contexts. Cf. also Harden, Iraq, XI, p. 156, where this shape is referred to as a 'type-fossil' of the fourth–fifth centuries A.D. From the personal recollection of the writer, the body was greenish-blue though all the colour was faint and faded. It is decorated with vertical ribs.

Pl. 54: 54. The body and part of the neck of a glass vase, with the globular base indented. It can be compared to similar vases, also of fourth-century A.D. date, from Gezer.

BEADS

	Oblate Nos. 1–6		Disk Nos. 13, 27, 28, 30		Short barrel Nos. 14–20		Long barrel Nos. 21–26, 56–59		Cylinder Nos. 31–37		Segmented Nos. 38–43		Bicone Nos. 44–50		Bicone Nos. 51–55		Total
		%		%		%		%		%		%		%		%	
Houses I	6	6	—	—	2	0·3	4	4	1	0·5	—	—	1	1·5	1	2	15
Bastion	—	—	—	—	—	—	—	—	—	—	—	—	—	—	—	—	—
Houses II	—	—	—	—	—	—	—	—	—	—	—	—	—	—	—	—	—
Tomb 106	16	17	43	4·2	37	6·7	13	12	8	4	4	7	2	3	4	9	127
Houses III	4	4	—	—	1	0·1	1	1	1	0·5	—	—	—	—	1	2	8
Tomb 120	12	13	11	1	69	12·5	2	2	8	4	13	21	2	3	12	27	129
Tomb 1002	29	30	5	0·7	267	48·6	16	16	27	13	7	11	51	74	21	47	423
Tomb 1004	—	—	—	—	—	—	—	—	—	—	—	—	—	—	—	—	—
Tomb 224	17	18	9	0·9	15	3	25	24	4	2	5	8	2	3	—	—	77
Tomb 116	—	—	1	0·1	9	2	—	—	7	3	2	3	1	1·5	—	—	20
Tomb 218	11	11	416	41·1	134	24·4	42	41	140	72	24	39	10	14	6	13	783
Tomb 223	1	1	527	52	15	3	—	—	2·7	1	7	11	—	—	—	—	553
Tomb 521	—	—	—	—	—	—	—	—	—	—	—	—	—	—	—	—	—
TOTAL	96		1,012		549		103		199		62		69		45		2,135

There were over 3,000 beads in the tombs and houses of the Iron Age. They are described opposite Pls. 66 and 67 according to H. C. Beck's system, which is given in his article, The Classification and Nomenclature of Beads (Archaeologia LXXXVII, 1928).

The above table gives numbers and percentages of the common beads in the groups, according to the tomb order which has been determined independently on pottery evidence. It will be seen that in the space of three centuries (excluding the post-exilic reoccupation) there was a slow but progressive change in fashion.

Disk beads (Nos. 13, 27, 28, 30), of bone or blue composition, comprised over 50 per cent. in one of the earliest tombs, Tomb 223, a percentage which fell to 41 in Tomb 218, and never exceeded 4 per cent. in any later group. Apparently this type of bead did not long survive the tenth century.

Cylinder beads (Nos. 31–37) and long barrel beads (Nos. 21–26), which are predominant in Tomb 218, give place in the course of a century to all varieties of bicone (Nos. 44–55) in Tomb 1002. While cylinder and bicone forms are normally made of carnelian, it will be seen that those forms common in the latter group are smaller and require less stone—another indication, it appears, of the scarcity of supplies.

The short oblates (Nos. 1–6) are characteristic of Tombs 1002 and 106, together with the short barrels (Nos. 14–20). They include a proportion of glass and glazed beads.

Segmented and granulated beads (Nos. 38–43), all of faience or composition, are more common in the earlier Tombs 223 and 218, and the large percentage of such beads in Tomb 120 is accounted for by the probability that they belonged to the original Iron Age burials. They were made on a core of copper wire.

L. Harding's corpus of beads from Tell el-Fara (Bethpelet) is to be found at the end of the Corpus of Palestinian Pottery; there are more varieties of cylinder and barrel beads, which is in accordance with the earlier trend of that cemetery.

G. Brunton's corpus of xxiind–xxivth dynasty beads from Lahun (Lahun II, Pl. LXII), where the same shapes are represented under different names, shows that the same kind of beads were being made in Egypt.

Of the beads 60–70, which are mostly of blue or yellow composition, the crenellated disk 62 is chiefly found in Tomb 218, while the short melon 63 is common in Tomb 1002. The glass beads 75–99, with coloured spots or bands, have not survived in quantity in any one group; while they are to be found throughout the series, they tend to concentrate in Tombs 1002 and 106.

Among the fancy beads and drop pendants on Pl. 67, the triangular pendant 115, and the banded agate beads 119 and 120 are comparable to those of Hissar III C (Excavations at Tepe Hissar by E. F. Schmidt, Pl. XXXV).

SHELLS

By D. BADEN-POWELL

Tomb 218

Cypraea annulus or *C. turdus* or *C. moneta*

A large number of cowries with body-whorl worn away, so that they could be strung as ornaments. As the shells are bleached of all colour, it is not easy to decide between these three species, though only one species seems to be present. As both *C. annulus* and *C. turdus* now live in the Indian Ocean area, it would seem that these cowries were imported from the south or south-east.

Cerithium vulgatum Linne.

Two broken individuals, extremely water-worn, which seem to be of this species. They now live in the Mediterranean.

? *Murex brandaris* Linne.

One extremely worn and broken shell which agrees with this species in shape and ornament, but as the canal is broken away, identification is most doubtful.

Nerita polita Linne. or *N. albicella* or *N. yoldii*

Four individuals with part of body-whorl removed, presumably for use as ornaments. Derivation probably from Red Sea or similar southern area.

Conus spp.

One small water-worn shell has its spire removed, and cannot be identified specifically. If it was an adult, it is more likely to be a Pacific type than Mediterranean, but this conclusion is little more than a guess without a more complete specimen.

One disk was made by sawing off the top of a *Conus* which has had a very low spire when complete. A number of species now living in the Indian Ocean have spires like this, but it is difficult to decide between five species. Derivation of this specimen from the south is more likely than from the Mediterranean, where flat-topped cones do not seem to occur living.

Identification of these shells is difficult, largely owing to the way in which they have been made into ornaments. Among those which can be identified with reasonable certainty, the Cowries, Cones and *Nerita* shells appear to have been imported from the Red Sea or Persian Gulf, but the *Cerithium* shells may have come from the Mediterranean, or possibly as fossils from a Palestine raised beach.

Tomb 224

Ampullaria sp. (possibly *Ampullaria ovata* Olivier)

One individual. This fragile shell is of freshwater origin, and it is thought unlikely that it was derived from a marine raised beach. It is very difficult to give specific names to shells belonging to this genus, but all known species are from sub-tropical or tropical waters. The shell in question closely resembles *A. ovata*, which lives at the present time in Egypt. (I have not been able to discover whether it is also found living in Palestine, but it is, on the whole, a southern form). It is reported to be edible.

Conclusions

Mr. Baden-Powell, whose report on the shells is given above, has also seen cowries from Nubian cemeteries in the Pitt-Rivers Museum. It is perhaps worth considering, therefore, whether the apparent influx of shells in Egyptian Delta and south Palestinian groups should be associated with the entry of African mercenaries into Palestine under Shishak, founder of the xxiind dynasty, *c.* 925 B.C. Their popularity in Palestine might also be the result of good southern trade connexions during the reign of Solomon.

Cowrie shells are, of course, widely distributed, and are frequently worn by Bedouin women to this day, but there is some indication that the use of these shells as ornaments varied in popularity at different times. G. Brunton, for instance, remarks on the number found in the xxiind dynasty tombs in Egypt and close parallels to the Palestinian examples, comprising twelve varieties, are illustrated in Lahun II (p. 37 and Pl. L, bottom left). The same authority states (QB III, p. 23) that cowrie shells were very common about two centuries later, in the xxvth–xxvith dynasties.

APPENDICES

APPENDIX A

THE HUMAN AND ANIMAL REMAINS

THE CRANIA

By MADELEINE GILES, B.A., F.R.A.I.

(From the Duckworth Laboratory, University Museum of Archaeology and Ethnology, Cambridge)

Introduction

THE original study of the Iron Age crania and other bones from Lachish, now preserved in the British Museum (Natural History), was made by Commander D. L. Risdon (1939). His material was recovered from Tombs 107, 108, 116 and 120, the greater part of it from Tomb 120. The series now under review came from Tombs 239 (No. 807), 521 (No. 800), 1004 (No. 834), 4002 (No. 829), 4005 (Nos. 801–803, 813–815, 817–820, 827, 843), 4029 (Nos. 822, 823, 828), 6006 (No. 804). The object of the present study is to place a description of this series on record, and to ascertain whether or not it differs from the Iron Age population of Lachish as represented by Risdon's far larger samples. The remains comprise the whole or fragmentary crania of twenty individuals; nineteen adult (four with associated mandibles) and one child of indeterminate sex, aged about twelve. Anatomical sexing shows that ten of the adult crania appear to be male and nine female. Two of the mandibles can be associated with the male and two with female crania. Estimates of the age distribution of the adults, based on the degree of closure of the principal calvarial sutures (the coronal, sagittal and lambdoid), indicate that it is close to the original series examined by Risdon.

Pathological conditions

Four of the male skulls, Nos. 800, 807, 815 and 817, show signs of disease. No. 800 has an extensive irregular area of roughened bone in the supraglabellar region, which is probably due to periosteitis following infection of a traumatic injury to the left frontal. There are two holes in the frontal bone of No. 807. The first, some 2·7 cm. in diameter, lies about 3 cm. from the bregma in the median sagittal plane, and its endocranial margins are considerably thinned. The second hole lies below and to the right of the first, and has a diameter of about 1·5 cm. There is also a small cavity on the left side of the occipital, which, with the two holes in the frontal, may probably be attributed to metastatic growths of the brain, secondary to a carcinoma elsewhere in the body. The left parietal of the same skull also exhibits two parallel cuts a centimetre apart and each about 1·5 cm. long, on the outer table, which seem to have been made by a sharp instrument. They suggest an attempt at trepanation which, had it been completed, would resemble the openings in skulls Nos. 114 and 115 of the series described by Risdon (1939, p. 116 and Pl. V). No. 815 has an expanded brain-case which could be due to a rather late onset of hydrocephalus. The sagittal suture of No. 817 is closed prematurely, but not so as to distort the shape to any marked degree. Of these specimens, only No. 815 was considered to be sufficiently affected by the conditions it displayed for its measurements to be excluded in calculating the means. Carious teeth are present in the dentitions of Nos. 804 and 814 (both male), and of Nos. 822 and 823 (both female). No pathological features were observed in the female crania or in any of the mandibles.

Cranial and dental anomalies

Slight traces of a metopic or persistent frontal suture were observed in three skulls, Nos. 802 (male) and 818 and 823 (both female). In the first two the coronal, the sagittal and the lambdoid sutures are still open, and in the third the extremities of the coronal have begun to close. Supernumerary bones occur in five skulls, Nos. 802

and 815 (both male) and Nos. 823, 829 and 834 (all female). Nos. 815 and 823 have ossicles of lambda, the second with three small Wormian bones in the sagittal suture immediately above the ossicle and a fourth in the left half of the lambdoid suture. Both Nos. 802 and 834 also have a large Wormian bone in the left half of the lambdoid suture, and No. 829 has an epipteric on the left side. The upper dental arcade is preserved in only eight specimens, two adult male and six adult female. No. 802 (male) has its right P^2 greatly reduced in size, with a single root. In No. 818 (female) both M^2s are tricuspid and the left M^3 has both a small tubercle of Carabelli on the lingual aspect of the protocone, and, apparently, another larger accessory cusp on the lingual aspect of the hypocone. This unusual pattern is not reproduced in the corresponding tooth on the right side, which bears the usual four cusps. The M^3s of No. 823 are incompletely erupted, though the specimen is fully adult. No anomalies were found in the teeth of any of the four mandibles.

Metrical characters

The greater part of the measurements on the present series of Iron Age skulls from Lachish were made by Dr. I. G. Cunnison, now of the Rhodes-Livingstone Institute, to whom the writer is indebted for leave to use them; but in a number of instances she has added to these. Apart from the cranial capacity, which was determined directly with mustard-seed by Breitinger's method (Breitinger, 1936; Tildesley and Datta-Majumder, 1944), the technique adopted was the biometric, which is also that of Risdon. The definitions of points and planes given by Buxton and Morant (1933) for the cranium, and by Morant, Collett and Adyanthāya (1936) for the mandible, as summarised, with some additions, by Trevor (1950), have been followed. The symbols used to denote the various characters are:

Cranium: C, capacity in cm.^{3}; L, maximum glabello-occipital length (in median sagittal plane); B, maximum biparietal breadth (perpendicular to L); B', minimum frontal breadth; H', basi-bregmatic height; OH, auricular height; S'_1, frontal chord; S'_2, parietal chord; S'_3, occipital chord; S_1, frontal arc; S_2, parietal arc; S_3, occipital arc; S, total sagittal arc; βQ, transverse biporial arc (through bregma); U, maximum horizontal perimeter (through supraglabellare); FL, foraminal length (opisthion to basion, *not* endobasion); FB, maximum foraminal breadth; LB, basinasal length; GL, basialveolar length (basion to alveolare, *not* prosthion); $G'H$, upper facial height; GB, bimaxillary breadth (between zygomaxillaria); J, maximum bizygomatic breadth; NH, nasal height (nasion to nariale, left); NB, maximum nasal breadth (between anterior surfaces of lateral margins of pyriform aperture); O_1, maximum orbital breadth (from maxillofrontale, left); O_2, maximum orbital height (perpendicular to O_1, left); G'_1, palatal length (staphylion to orale); G_2, palatal breadth (between endomolaria); $N\angle$, $A\angle$ and $B\angle$, nasal, alveolar and basal angles of upper facial triangle having nasion, alveolare and basion as apices.

Mandible: G_oG_o, bigonial breadth; C_rC_r, coronial breadth; W_1, bicondylar breadth; C_yL, maximum condylar length (in any direction, left); RB', maximum rameal breadth (in any direction, left); M_2P_1, molar-premolar chord (ectomolare to ectopraemolare, left); ZZ, bimental breadth (between anterior margins of foramina mentalia); H_1, symphyseal height (intradentale to subsymphyseale); C_pL, projective length of corpus (left); RL, projective length of ramus (left); ML, maximum projective length of mandible; C_pH, projective height of coronoid process (left); M_2H, projective height of corpus (to ectomolare, left); $M\angle$, mandibular angle; $R\angle$, rameal angle (left).

With the exception of the Pearsonian occipital index (*Oc. I*) of the cranium, $100\,S_3/S'_3\,\sqrt{\{S_3/24(S_3-S'_3)\}}$, the values of which were found from the table of this function prepared by Tildesley (1921), the indices need not be defined. Table I provides the male and female means of the present series of crania from Lachish, together with those of Risdon's larger samples. No means were calculated for the mandibular characters, since only three mandibles were measurable, but their individual measurements for linear characters and angles are given in the appendix to Table III.

Discussion

Owing to the smallness of the samples now considered, it seemed advisable to restrict their quantitative comparison with the larger series measured by Risdon to characters based on at least five observations for both male and female crania. In addition, it was decided to omit the capacities, which had been determined in different ways, and the absolute values of the frontal, parietal and occipital chords and arcs. Apart from capacity, then, there remain for comparison the male and female means of twenty-four characters, viz. sixteen absolute and eight indicial, of the forty in Table I.

TABLE I

Mean Measurements of Two Series of Iron Age Crania from Lachish*

Character	Male		Female		Character	Male		Female	
	Giles	Risdon	Giles	Risdon		Giles	Risdon	Giles	Risdon
$C\dagger$	1,395·0 (7)	1,425·1 (108)	1,330·3 (6)	1,286·5 (89)	J	132·6 (3)	128·4 (49)	118·5 (2)	121·3 (40)
L	188·6 (9)	184·5 (322)	179·1 (9)	176·8 (259)	NH	51·7 (6)	51·4 (136)	48·2 (6)	48·9 (116)
B	137·2 (9)	136·5 (327)	133·7 (9)	133·3 (261)	NB	24·5 (7)	25·2 (123)	23·1 (6)	24·5 (88)
B'	94·6 (9)	95·5 (319)	91·8 (8)	92·2 (245)	O_1	41·4 (8)	41·5 (148)	40·2 (6)	40·6 (111)
H'	132·6 (8)	133·8 (263)	131·3 (8)	128·4 (213)	O_2	33·3 (8)	32·9 (152)	32·4 (6)	33·2 (112)
OH	114·9 (8)	115·1 (108)	112·0 (5)	109·4 (89)	G_1'	46·9 (5)	46·7 (101)	42·9 (6)	44·8 (90)
S_1'	111·4 (9)	112·9 (299)	110·0 (9)	108·7 (248)	G_2	39·9 (3)	40·3 (57)	36·9 (6)	39·2 (68)
S_2'	116·0 (9)	116·0 (323)	113·5 (9)	112·1 (251)	—	—	—	—	—
S_3'	94·7 (8)	96·3 (280)	97·7 (7)	94·0 (216)	100 B/L	72·4 (9)	74·3 (310)	74·7 (9)	75·5 (252)
S_1	122·8 (9)	129·2 (296)	126·1 (9)	124·7 (248)	100 H'/L	70·2 (8)	72·7 (257)	72·7 (8)	72·7 (209)
S_2	128·9 (9)	129·9 (321)	127·1 (9)	124·9 (249)	100 B/H'	103·1 (8)	102·4 (256)	101·9 (8)	103·8 (206)
S_3	117·3 (8)	116·9 (279)	116·5 (7)	113·3 (215)	100 $(B-H')/L$	2·2 (8)	1·7 (246)	1·4 (8)	2·8 (202)
S	374·4 (8)	375·5 (255)	367·5 (7)	363·0 (212)	Oc. I.	58·5 (8)	59·5 (278)	61·1 (7)	60·0 (215)
$\beta Q'$	307·4 (9)	308·6 (306)	296·6 (8)	297·8 (234)	100 FB/FL	82·2 (7)	82·7 (222)	80·5 (7)	81·4 (167)
U	518·7 (9)	518·1 (304)	501·3 (9)	500·4 (214)	100 $G'H/GB$	73·7 (4)	74·6 (63)	73·2 (2)	72·9 (59)
FL	36·7 (8)	37·0 (247)	35·9 (7)	35·8 (193)	100 NB/NH	48·0 (6)	49·4 (114)	47·9 (6)	50·2 (84)
FB	30·1 (7)	30·4 (244)	28·6 (8)	28·9 (192)	100 O_2/O_1	79·3 (7)	79·4 (141)	80·7 (6)	82·0 (100)
LB	103·6 (8)	100·7 (243)	96·8 (8)	96·4 (206)	100 G_2/G'_1	79·2 (2)	85·9 (44)	86·6 (6)	86·9 (55)
GL	97·8 (5)	94·3 (89)	89·2 (4)	90·6 (76)	$N\angle$	64°·7 (5)	64°·0 (89)	63°·7 (4)	64°·5 (75)
$G'H$	70·0 (5)	70·1 (98)	65·3 (4)	66·9 (87)	$A\angle$	75°·1 (5)	73°·9 (89)	74°·9 (4)	73°·7 (75)
GB	94·0 (5)	94·4 (107)	90·2 (4)	91·8 (81)	$B\angle$	40°·2 (5)	42°·0 (89)	41°·4 (4)	41°·8 (75)

* The sample size is given in parentheses after each mean, and the values of NH, O_1, O_2, 100 NB/NH and 100 O_2/O_1 are for characters measured on the *left* side.

† The mean capacities of Risdon's series were determined by reconstruction formulae and were not found directly as in the case of those of the present series.

If it is assumed that the means and standard deviations of Risdon's series are equivalent to the corresponding parameters of the Lachish Iron Age population instead of being estimates of them, it becomes possible to consider whether the mean values of the characters in the writer's samples of male and female crania differ significantly from those in Risdon's series. In view of the large size of the samples studied by Risdon, such assumptions are not unreasonable. If n is the number of observations on which the mean of any cranial character x for one sex in the present series is based, and μ and σ are the respective values of the mean and standard deviation of the same character in the corresponding Lachish Iron Age population, and d is the difference between x and μ irrespective of sign, then the standard error of that difference s_d may be expressed as $s_d = \sigma \sqrt{(1/n)}$.

Table II gives for males, and Table III for females, in the first place, the difference d between the two means (either $\bar{x} - \mu$ or $\mu - \bar{x}$); secondly, the standard error of the difference s_d; and thirdly the value of the difference in terms of its standard error, d/s_d. If the last value is 2·00 or more, then the difference may be regarded as statistically significant at the 5 per cent. probability level; in other words, the odds are of the order of nineteen to one against its occurring by chance alone.

Three of the male "standardized differences" in Table II are significant, but not highly so. Two of these, L and 100 H'/L, involve the maximum glabello-occipital length, and the third, LB, is the basinasal length, which is as a rule closely correlated with L. None of the differences for females in Table II are statistically significant,

407

but one of them, *NB* or nasal breadth, is almost so. This situation is to be expected when dealing with samples of the size of those available, and it could be argued that, in view of the assumptions made above, a more stringent test should be applied to indicate real differentiation between the various characters. Little weight should therefore be accorded to the few cases in which the differences exceed the level of probability adopted, taking into account the many more in which they do not. It is thus possible to conclude that, on the basis of the available evidence, there are no grounds for believing that each of the series now treated could not have been drawn at random from the Iron Age population of Lachish represented by Risdon's material.

TABLE II

Differences between Means of Series of Iron Age Crania from Lachish*

Character	Male			Female			Character	Male			Female			Character	Male			Female		
	d	s_d	d/s_d	d	s_d	d/s_d		d	s_d	d/s_d	d	s_d	d/s_d		d	s_d	d/s_d	d	s_d	d/s_d
L	4·1	1·96	*2·09*	2·3	1·70	1·35	FL	0·3	0·89	0·34	0·1	0·81	0·12	100 B/L	1·9	1·03	*1·84*	0·8	1·00	0·80
B	0·7	1·70	0·41	0·4	1·52	0·26	FB	0·3	0·82	0·37	0·3	0·70	0·43	100 H'/L	2·5	1·04	*2·40*	0·0	1·03	0·00
B'	0·9	1·42	0·63	0·4	1·55	0·26	LB	2·9	1·35	*2·15*	0·4	1·50	0·27	100 B/H'	0·7	1·67	0·32	1·9	1·81	1·05
H'	1·2	1·77	0·68	2·9	1·79	*1·62*	NH	0·3	1·08	0·28	0·7	1·10	0·54	100 (B–H')/L	0·5	1·15	0·43	1·4	1·24	1·13
OH	0·2	1·39	0·44	2·6	1·89	*1·38*	NB	0·7	0·66	1·06	1·4	0·71	*1·97*	Oc. I.	1·0	0·92	1·09	1·1	0·94	1·17
S	1·1	4·50	0·24	4·5	4·34	1·04	O_1	0·1	0·58	0·17	0·4	0·67	0·60	100 FB/FL	0·5	2·20	0·23	0·9	2·01	0·45
βQ'	1·2	3·20	0·37	1·2	3·29	0·36	O_2	0·4	0·72	0·56	0·8	0·82	0·98	100 NB/NH	1·4	1·63	0·86	2·3	1·56	*1·47*
U	0·6	4·50	0·13	0·9	4·16	0·22	G'_1	0·2	1·25	0·16	1·9	1·22	*1·56*	100 O_2/O_1	0·1	1·87	0·53	1·3	1·84	0·71

* Differences which are statistically significant are shown in *italics*.

Acknowledgements

The writer is indebted to the authorities of the British Museum (Natural History) for permission to bring the series from South Kensington to Cambridge for study, and to Dr. J. C. Trevor, University Lecturer in Anthropology, for much valuable advice and assistance. Her thanks are also due to Dr. A. M. Barrett, University Morbid Anatomist and Histologist to Addenbrooke's Hospital, for examining and commenting on the pathological specimens; to Dr. John Wishart, University Reader in Statistics, and his research students Messrs. A. S. G. Ehrenberg of Trinity College, and H. Mulhall of King's College, for advice on statistical procedure; to Mr. W. B. Denston, Assistant in the Duckworth Laboratory, for help rendered in various ways; and to the Trustees of the Estate of the late Sir Henry Wellcome, F.R.S., for their financial support of the research.

REFERENCES

BREITINGER, EMIL (1936). "Zur Messung der Schädelkapazität mit Senfkörnen." Anthrop. Anz., XIII.

BUXTON, L. H. DUDLEY, and MORANT, G. M. (1933). "The essential craniological technique. Part I. Definitions of points and planes." J. R. Anthrop. Inst., LXIII.

MORANT, G. M., COLLETT, MARGOT, and ADYANTHĀYA, N. K. (1936). "A biometric study of the human mandible." Biometrika, XXVIII.

RISDON, D. L. (1939). "A study of the cranial and other human remains from Palestine excavated at Tell Duweir (Lachish) by the Wellcome-Marston Archaeological Research Expedition." Ibid., XXXI.

TILDESLEY, MIRIAM L. (1921). "A first study of the Burmese skull." Ibid., XIII.

—— and DATTA-MAJUMDER, N. (1944). "Cranial capacity; comparative data on the techniques of Macdonell and Breitinger." Amer. J. Phys. Anthrop., N.S., II.

TREVOR, J. C. (1950). *s.v.* "Anthropometry", Chambers's Encyclopedia (new ed., 15 vols.), I. London, Newnes.

TABLE III

Individual Measurements of Iron Age Skulls from Lachish*

No.	Sex	C	L	B	B'	H'	OH	S_1'	S_2'	S_3'	S_1	S_2	S_3	S	$\beta Q'$	U
800	♂	—	190	141·5	95	136·5	116	109	123	99	125	138·5	121	385	314	528
801	,,	1410	191·5	139·5	101	134?	113	112·5	105	96	137	114	115·5	368	312	525
802	,,	1304	186·5	133·5	89·5	134	109	108	114	94	121·5	127·5	114	363	293	507
803	,,	1413	192·5	136	97	130·5	115	119	118	92	135	130	116·5	382	308	524
804	,,	1620	192	144·5	99	139	118·5	115·5	120	97	130·5	137	125	392	318	534
807	,,	—	186	139	94·5	—	120	116	119·5	—	134	132·5	—	—	323	520
813	,,	1252	186	134·5	90	133	115	106·5	112	—	119	123	130	372	303	505
814	,,	1525	190	140	94·5	135·5	113	112	114·5	100·5	132	127	120·5	379	312	527
815	*,,*	*—*	*195*	*150?*	*99*	*—*	*—*	*120·5*	*128*	*96*	*144·5*	*146·5*	*122*	*413*	*322*	*556*
817	,,	1241	183·5	125	91	119	—	109	118	84	126·5	131·5	96	355	285	498
818	♀	1321	183·5	128·5	90·5	131	106	106	115	102·5	121	127	128	376	286	501
819	,,	1454	185	133·5	96	130·5	112	112·5	115	103	130	128	123·5	368	302	509
820	,,	1302	180	131	87·5	127	106	107	117·5	91	118·5	134	111·5	364	287	495
822	,,	1254	170·5	132·5	88·5	130	—	107	103·5	96	121	115·5	110	346	286	483
823	,,	1353	179	137·5	88·5	126·5	118	111	118	—	128	132	—	—	297	502
827	,,	—	180	135·5	—	138	—	114	115	103·5	130	129	119·5	379	306	511
828	,,	1298	170·5	136·5	95·5	131	—	111	108	88	128·5	121	102·5	352	298	496
829	,,	—	181·5	135·5	93·5	137	118	111·5	111	100	129·5	123·5	121	374	311	502
834	,,	—	181·5	133·5	95	—	—	110	119	—	128	133·5	—	—	—	513
843	Juv.	—	171	140	90·5	—	—	102	110	90	109	124	112	357	303	495

No.	Sex.	FL	FB	LB	GL	$G'H$	GB	J	NH	NB	O_1	O_2	G_1'	G_2
800	♂	37·0	31·0	102	—	—	—	—	—	—	39·1	35·0	—	42·0
801	,,	38·0	31·2	106·5	98	74·5	103	139	53·0	27·5	44·9	35·5	46·4	38·4
802	,,	37·1	—	105·5	—	—	—	—	52·5	22·6	43·5	35·7	—	—
803	,,	39·1	30·0	103	96·5	68·5	—	130	53·4	27·0	42·1	33·0	45·4	—
804	,,	34·1	30·0	106	95	73	95·5	129	53·0	25·4	40·3	33·4	43·7	—
807	,,	—	—	—	—	—	89	—	—	22·9	40·2	31·9	—	—
813	,,	34·1	28·1	100·5	97·5	61	89·5	—	45·2	24·2	40·2	28·2	46·9	—
814	,,	34·1	30·6	106·5	102	73	93·5	—	53·0	22·0	40·5	33·7	52·0	39·3
815	*,,*	*38·1*	*—*	*—*	*—*	*—*	*—*	*—*	*—*	*—*	*—*	*—*	*—*	*—*
817	,,	40·4	29·5	98·5	—	—	—	—	—	—	—	—	—	—
818	♀	36·0	29·4	93·5	—	—	86	115	47·0	22·9	38·2	30·5	44·8	34·5
819	,,	33·6	28·2	97	90	66·5	86	—	50·0	24·0	40·5	33·2	42·2	35·1
820	,,	35·0	29·5	98	93·5	65	—	—	47·5	21·9	41·5	32·2	47·4	36·0
822	,,	40·2	29·5	97·5	88·5	63	—	—	46·4	23·0	40·3	33·8	41·1	39·7
823	,,	—	26·7	90·3	85	67	97	—	49·2	23·8	40·5	33·9	42·0	38·9
827	,,	37·0	30·7	99	—	—	—	—	—	—	—	—	—	—
828	,,	35·0	28·2	96	—	—	—	—	—	—	—	—	—	—
829	,,	35·0	26·9	103	—	—	92	122	49·1	23·0	40·5	31·3	40·0	37·9
834	,,	—	—	—	—	—	—	—	—	—	—	—	—	—
843	Juv.	—	—	—	—	65	—	—	—	—	—	—	—	—

No.	Sex.	$\frac{100\,B}{L}$	$\frac{100\,H'}{L}$	$\frac{100\,B}{H'}$	$\frac{100\,(B-H')}{L}$	Oc. I.	$\frac{100\,FB}{FL}$	$\frac{100\,G'H}{GB}$	$\frac{100\,NB}{NH}$	$\frac{100\,O_2}{O_1}$	$\frac{100\,G_2}{G_1'}$	N∠	A∠	B∠
800	♂	73·9	71·8	103·6	2·6	58·5	83·8	—	—	89·5	—	63°	75°	42°
801	,,	72·8	69·9?	104·1?	2·8?	59·8	82·1	72·3	51·9	79·1	82·8	—	—	—
802	,,	71·6	71·8	99·6	−0·3	59·2	—	—	43·0	82·1	—	—	—	—
803	,,	70·6	67·8	104·2	2·9	56·3	76·7	—	50·6	78·4	—	65°	75°	40°
804	,,	75·2	72·4	103·9	2·9	55·6	88·0	76·4	47·9	82·9	—	61°	77°	42°
807	,,	74·7	—	—	—	—	—	—	—	79·3	—	69°	75°	36°
813	,,	72·3	71·5	101·1	0·8	55·4	82·4	68·1	53·5	70·1	—	65°·5	73°·5	41°
814	,,	73·7	71·3	103·3	2·4	56·8	89·7	78·1	41·5	83·2	75·6	—	—	—
815	*,,*	*76·9*	*—*	*—*	*—*	*56·2*	*—*	*—*	*—*	*—*	*—*	*—*	*—*	*—*
817	,,	68·1	64·8	105·0	3·4	66·1	73·0	—	—	—	—	—	—	—
818	♀	70·0	71·4	98·1	−1·4	57·1	81·7	—	48·7	79·8	77·0	63°	76°	41°
819	,,	72·2	70·5	102·3	1·6	60·0	83·9	77·3	48·0	82·0	83·2	66°·5	73°·5	40°
820	,,	72·8	70·5	103·1	2·2	58·4	84·3	—	46·1	77·6	75·9	62°·5	78°·5	39°·5
822	,,	77·7	76·2	101·9	1·5	65·6	73·4	—	49·6	83·9	96·6	—	—	—
823	,,	76·8	70·7	108·7	6·1	—	—	69·1	48·4	83·7	92·6	63°	72°	45°
827	,,	75·3	76·7	98·2	−1·4	64·4	83·0	—	—	—	—	—	—	—
828	,,	80·1	76·8	104·2	3·2	63·3	80·6	—	—	—	—	—	—	—
829	,,	74·7	75·5	98·9	−0·8	59·2	76·9	—	46·8	77·3	94·7	—	—	—
834	,,	73·5	—	—	—	—	—	—	—	—	—	—	—	—
843	Juv.	81·9	—	—	—	57·5	—	—	—	—	—	—	—	—

No.	Sex.	G_0G_0	C_rC_r	W_1	C_yL	RB'	M_2P_1	ZZ	H_1	C_yL	RL	ML	C_pH	M_2H	M∠	R∠
800	♂	103	107·5	124	22·7	36·0	26·9	45·1	30·2	77	63·0	98·5	69·9	26·0	113°	83°
807	,,	85·5	—	—	19·3	30·9 (R)	27·3 (R)	43·0	36·7	72	57·5	107	67·2 (R)	30·4	125°·5	76° (R)
819	♀	86·5	87·5	110·5	16·2 (R)	31·9	25·4	40·0	30·4	58	50·4	96	50·4	20·6	125°·5	64°

* No. 815 ♂ is a pathological specimen and its measurements have been omitted in calculating the means.

THE ANIMAL BONES

By DOROTHEA M. A. BATE

The mammal remains were found in tombs used as ossuaries, and they had evidently been thrown in after most of the space had already been filled with human remains (Risdon, Biometrika XXXI, 1939). It is noticeable that the collection consists almost entirely of skull remains, but this may have no significance since it may be the result of selective collecting. Remains of five species are present, and each probably represents a domestic form. They are:

Canis sp.	Domestic Dog
Bos sp.	Ox
Sus sp.	Domestic Pig
Camelus sp.	Camel
Equus cf. *caballus*	Horse

Canis sp.: Domestic Dog

A domestic dog is represented by three skulls, one of which has a total length of 19 cm., and the largest of 20·5 cm. This last is slightly larger than the EB skulls, but otherwise it appears to be similar.[1]

It should be noted that no remains of large fighting dogs, such as were used by the Assyrians, were found at Tell ed-Duweir.

Bos sp.: Ox

An ox is represented by a single nearly complete skull with the associated lower jaw. It is flat-fronted and of medium size, that is, larger than the small Celtic short-horn, but its horn cores are very small compared with the size of the skull, and they are much smaller than the horn core preserved in the collection of animal remains from the Middle Bronze Age level of Tell Ajjul (Ancient Gaza). Horn cores from Megiddo are also slightly larger. The Tell ed-Duweir horn cores have a length of 9 cm. along the outer curve, and a circumference at the base of 10 cm. The length of the lower cheek tooth row is 14 cm.

It is of interest that this ox with very small horns is evidently quite distinct from the long horned animals depicted in the bas-reliefs of Sennacherib's siege of Lachish. If these reliefs picture the spoil from Lachish, then it must be inferred that the people of the town possessed two races of cattle.

Remains of a *Bos* were found in the Middle Bronze level of Tell Ajjul, but this appears to be of a different race to that of Tell ed-Duweir.

Sus sp.: Domestic Pig

There are seven almost complete skulls with the cheek teeth, portions of several other skulls, and a number of lower jaws of pig. Compared with the skull of a sub-adult wild boar from Persia, the Tell ed-Duweir skulls are found to be rather smaller, and with snouts much shorter, and also stouter. Since the skulls of pigs under domestication are extremely plastic, some difference in size and shape would be expected, but a very curious fact about these Iron Age skulls is that each one is more or less deformed by pachyostosis, particularly on the frontal portion. I have not yet been able to discover a possible cause for this condition, and I have been informed by the Royal Veterinary College, London, that the modern domestic pig skull is not affected by this disease.

Had the population of Tell ed-Duweir in those times been of Hebrew race it would have been curious to find the remains of pig so plentiful, but after an intensive study of the Lachish human skulls, Mr. Risdon (Biometrika XXXI, 1939, p. 142) writes:

"The relationship of the Lachish series (of human skulls) may now be considered. All its closest connections are with

---

[1] A full report on the Early Bronze domestic dog at Tell ed-Duweir will appear in *Lachish IV*. Miss Bate notes that only the largest of these dogs was equal in size to a small wolf, and comparisons show that it was probably a seluki type though it had not attained the highly specialised character of the modern breed.

series of the Lower Egyptian type, and these are close enough to suggest that the population in the Palestinian town was entirely, or almost entirely, of Egyptian origin."

This conclusion regarding the racial identity of the owners of the Lachish skulls has been challenged by Sir Arthur Keith, who considers them as "members of the Mediterranean family of peoples".[1] Their resemblance to the inhabitants of Lower Egypt was due to an infiltration of the Mediterranean type in that area.

It may be of interest to note that in excavations at Alişar in south-eastern Anatolia remains of pig were found in all levels, and were particularly plentiful in the Hittite deposits.

Camelus sp.: Camel

The camel is represented by an imperfect skull, portions of jaws with teeth, and a number of limb bones of considerable size.

Equus sp.: (?) Horse

There are several portions of skulls and fragmentary jaws, which equal in size those of the medium-sized horse found in the Middle Bronze level of Tell Ajjul. However, in the absence of foot bones, it is not possible to say with certainty whether it is a true horse or a "half-ass" which is represented. There are no remains of donkey from this level.

---

[1] PEQ, 1940, pp. 7–12.

APPENDIX B
LIST OF COINS

REFERENCES to coins are to the relevant section in the relevant volume of the British Museum Catalogue (B.M.), the Catalogue of Imperial Byzantine Coins (I.B.C.), Catalogue of the Hunterian Collection (Hunt.), Newall: Western Seleucid Mints (New.), Babelon: Les Monnaies de Syrie (Bab.), Historia Numorum (Head), Cohen: Medailles Romaines (C.), Svoronos: Coinage of the Ptolemies (Svor.) and Sabatier: Monnaies Byzantines (S.). Dates are taken from the Cambridge Ancient History and the Cambridge Medieval History, Vol. I.

No.	Field No. Palestine Museum No.	Area	Metal and size or denomination	Authority and mint	Date of reign	Type	Reference
1	6872 C.2140	J.14	AR Tetradrachm	City, Athens	400 B.C.	Archaic Head of Athena/ Owl	B.M. 41
2	6122 C.2020	700	,, ,,	,, ,,	,,	,, ,,	,,
3	—	DX	,, ,,	,, ,,	,,	,, ,,	,,
4	6898 C.2144	,,	Æ 15 mm.	Abdashart I, Sidon	370 B.C.	Galley/Great King in Car	BM. 46
5	7051a C.2202	G.17: 1072 1072	,, 9 mm.	,, ,,	,,	Galley/King in running attitude	B.M. 53
6	7269	Q.13	,, 17 mm.	Alexander the Great	336–323 B.C.	Young Head/Horseman	Hunt. 327
7	7270	DX	,, 20 mm.	,, ,,	,,	Young Head/Club and Bow	Hunt. 296
8	—	R.17	,, 18 mm.	,, ,,	,,	,, ,,	,,
9	6897 C.2143	DX	,, 14 mm.	,, ,,	,,	Illegible/Helmet	Head pp. 227–8
10	6892	,,	,, 18 mm.	Seleucus I, Antioch	−280 B.C.	Head of Apollo/Athena Alkis	New. 912
11	6873 C.2141	L.15	,, 18 mm.	,, ,,	,,	Head of Apollo with countermark horse's head	—
12	6874	DX	,, 16 mm.	,, ,,	,,	Head of Apollo/Tripod Lebes	New. 919
13	—	,,	,, 14 mm.	Ptolemy I	−283 B.C.	Head of Alex. with long hair/Eagle, wings open	Svor. 239
14	—	,,	,, 17 mm.	Ptolemy I or II	,,	,, ,,	,,
15	7051 C.2203	G.17: 1072	,, 20 mm.	,, ,,	,,	Head of Alex. in skin/ Eagle, wings open	—
16	—	DX	,, 20–23 mm.	,, ,,	,,	,, ,,	—
17	6855	4000	,, 27 mm.	,, ,,	,,	Head of Ammon/Eagle, wings closed, club in field	—
18	6856	DX	,, 27 mm.	,, ,,	,,	,, ,,	—
19	6879	,,	,, 27 mm.	,, ,,	,,	,, ,,	—
20	6858 C.2138	4000	,, 20 mm.	Ptolemy I, II, or III	,,	Head of Alex. in skin/ Eagle, wings open	—
21	6878	K.16	,, 15 mm.	City, Side in Pamphylia	300 B.C.	Head of Athena/Pome- granate	B.M. 59
22	6857	4000	,, 30 mm.	Ptolemy II, Tyre	285–246 B.C.	Head of Ammon/Eagle, wings closed, club in field	Svor. 707
23	—	DX	,, 19 mm.	,, ,,	,,	,, ,,	Svor. 709
24	—	,,	,, 20 mm.	,, ,,	,,	,, ,,	,,
25	—	,,	,, 17 mm.	,, ,,	,,	,, ,,	Svor. 710
26	—	,,	,, 23 mm.	,, ,,	,,	Head of Ammon/Eagle, wings open	—
27	—	PQR.17	,, 16 mm.	,, ,,	,,	,, ,,	—
28	—	DX	,, 14 mm.	Ptolemy II or III	,,	Head of Alex. in skin/ Eagle, wings open	—
29	—	,,	,, 23 mm.	,, ,,	,,	,, ,,	—

No.	Field No. Palestine Museum No.	Area	Metal and size or denomination	Authority and mint	Date of reign	Type	Reference
30	6894	DX	Æ 18 mm.	Antiochus I	280–262/1 B.C.	Shield/Elephant	New. 942
31	6896	,,	,, 10 mm.	Antiochus III	223–187 B.C.	Head of Ant. III/Apollo standing	New. 1082
32	6875	,,	,, 10 mm.	,,	,,	,, ,,	,,
33	6877	7000	,, 11 mm.	,,	,,	,, ,,	,,
34	6123	700	,, 12 mm.	,,	,,	,, ,,	,,
35	—	PQR.17	,, 10 mm.	,,	,,	,, ,,	,,
36	5259	Q.12: 106	,, 12 mm.	,,	,,	,, ,,	,,
37	—	DX	,, 22 mm.	Ptolemy IV	221–203 B.C.	Head of Ammon/Two Eagles, wings closed	Svor. 1158
38	6895	,,	,, 13 mm.	Antiochus IV	175–163 B.C.	Head of Ant. IV/Hera standing; serrated	Bab. 572
39	—	Q.12: 102	,, 16 mm.	,,	,,	Head of Ant. IV/Apollo seated	Bab. 576
40	6876	R.12	,, 10 mm.	Uncertain, Seleucid	—	—	—
40a	6322	R.15: 14	,, 14 mm.	Antiochus IV	175–163 B.C.	Head of Ant. IV/Hera standing	—
41	6124	700	,, 10 mm.	Alexander Jannaeus	103–76 B.C.	Illegible/Double Cornucopiae	B.M. Ser. C.
42	6880	7000	,, 16 mm.	,,	,,	Illegible/Anchor	B.M. Ser. F.
43	5257	Q.12: 106	AR Tetradrachm	City, Tyre	47 B.C.	Head of Melqarth/Eagle	B.M. 168
44	6868	DX	15 mm.	Procurators (Augustus) Caesarea	31 B.C.–A.D. 14	Ear of Barley/Illegible	B.M. 1 f
45	6129	700	15 mm.	Procurators (Tiberius) Caesarea	A.D. 14–37	Wreath/Palm branch	B.M. 31 f
46	—	DX	,, 15 mm.	,, ,, ,,	A.D. 27	Lituus/Wreath	B.M. 69 f
47	6130 C.2022	,,	,, 17 mm.	Procurators (Nero) Caesarea	A.D. 54–68	Wreath/Palm branch	B.M. 1 f
48	6860	4000	,, 16 mm.	,, ,, ,,	,,	,, ,,	,,
49	6841	DX	,, 15 mm.	,, ,, ,,	,,	,, ,,	,,
50	—	,,	,, 15 mm.	Procurators (Claudius) Caesarea	A.D. 41–54	Shields/Palm tree	B.M. 21
51	6125–6128 C.2021	700	,, 15 mm.	Herod Agrippa I	A.D. 37–44	Umbrella/Three Ears of barley	B.M. 1
52	6867	DX	,, 16 mm.	,,	,,	,, ,,	,,
53	6861	4000	,, 15 mm.	Illegible, Procurators or Herod Agrippa I	—	— ,,	
54	6132	700	,, 23 mm.	Roman Provincial, Antoninus Pius, Ascalon?	A.D. 138–161	Bust r./Two draped figures standing	—
55	6131	700	,, 30 mm.	Roman Provincial, Antoninus Pius, Gaza	—	Bust r./Bust of City Goddess	B.M. 65
56	6869	DX	,, 23 mm.	Roman Provincial, Lucius Verus, Neapolis	A.D. 161	Bearded Bust/Two figures	B.M. 72
56a	6333 C.2023	S.16: 19	,, 23 mm.	Ascalon	—	Head r./City Goddess standing	—
56b	6334	S.16: 19	,, 22 mm.	Titus, Ascalon	A.D. 169–181	,, ,,	—
57	6133	700	,, 24 mm.	Roman Provincial, Geta, Ascalon	A.D. 211–212	Bust r./Illegible	—
58	—	—	,, 21 mm.	Roman Provincial, Alexander Severus Caesarea	A.D. 222–235	Bust r./Eagle with wreath	B.M. 118
59	6859	4000	,, 15 mm.	Illegible Roman Provincial	—	—	—
60	6047	4021	,, 30 mm.	Roman Provincial ?	—	Radiate Bust/Emperor as founder ploughing	—
61	6881	DX	,, 21 mm.	Constantine I	A.D. 306–337	Soli Invicto Comiti	C. 546
62	7267 C.2204	4035	,, 20 mm.	Licinius I	A.D. 311–323	,, ,,	C. 161
63	6136	700	,, 18 mm.	Constantine I	A.D. 306–337	Gloria Exercitus (2 Standards)	C. 254
64	—	DX	,, 15 mm.	Constantine II (as Caesar) Constantinopolis	Caesar A.D. 317, Augustus 337–340	Gloria Exercitus (1 Standard)	C. 113
65	6870	,,	,, 18 mm.	Constantius II (as Caesar) Antioch	Caesar A.D. 323, Augustus 337–340	—	C. 92
66	6137	700	,, 17 mm.	Constantius II (as Caesar)	—	,, ,,	,,

No.	Field No. Palestine Museum No.	Area	Metal and size or denomination	Authority and mint	Date of reign	Type	Reference
67	6883	DX	Æ 16 mm.	Constantine I	A.D. 306–337	Bust of Constantinopolis/ Victory on prow	C. 2
68	6884	,,	,, 14 mm.	Constantius II, Alexandria	—	Vot xx Mult xxx	C. 335
69	6882	,,	,, 14 mm.	Constantius II	Augustus A.D. 337–340	,,	,,
70	—	,,	,, 14 mm.	,,	—	Vot type	—
71	—	,,	,, 19 mm.	Constantius II, Rome	—	Fel Temp Reparatio (Emperor and Horseman)	C. 44
72	6845	,,	,, 15 mm.	Constantius II	—	,, ,,	,,
73	6846	,,	,, 15 mm.	,,	—	,, ,,	,,
74	—	,,	,, 15 mm.	,,	—	,, ,,	,,
75	6884 C.2142	,,	,, 18 mm.	Valens or Valentian I	A.D. 364–375	Gloria Romanorum (Emperor and Captive)	—
76	—	700	,, 18 mm.	,, ,,	,,	,, ,,	—
77	—	DX	,, 18 mm.	,, ,,	,,	,, ,,	—
78	6135	700	,, 11 mm.	,, ,,	,,	,, ,,	—
79	—	DX	,, 18 mm.	,, ,,	,,	Victory type	—
80	6144	700	,, 13 mm.	Arcadius	A.D. 395–408	Gloria Romanorum (Emperor and Captive)	S. 36
81	6862 C.2139	4000	,, 14 mm.	Arcadius Nicomedia	,,	Vot type	—
82	—	DX	,, 12 mm.	Barbarous	—	Emperor and captive type	—
83	6138	700	,, 15 mm.	Valentinian III, Alexandria	A.D. 425–455	Victory type	C. 5
84	6139	,,	,, 12 mm.	Uncertain	Late 4th or early 5th cent.	,,	—
85	—	,,	,, 12 mm.	,,	,, ,,	,,	—
86	6847	DX	,, 13 mm.	,,	,, ,,	,,	—
87	6849	,,	,, 11 mm.	,,	,, ,,	,,	—
88	6886	244	,, 13 mm.	,,	,, ,,	,,	—
89	6863	4000	,, 14 mm.	,,	,, ,,	,,	—
90	6138–6143	700	,, 12 mm.	,,	,, ,,	,,	—
91	6864	,,	,, 12 mm.	,,	,, ,,	Victory and captive type	—
92	6865	4000	,, 10 mm.	,,	,, ,,	Vot type	—
93	—	DX	,, 11 mm.	,,	,, ,,	Gloria Reipublice (Camp gate)	—
94	6885	6000	,, 11 mm.	,,	,, ,,	Illegible	—
95	7268	4035	,, 14–10 mm.	,,	,, ,,	,, (13 coins)	—
96	7271	700	,, 11 mm.	,,	,, ,,	,, (2 coins)	—
97	6850	DX	,, 12 mm.	,,	,, ,,	,,	—
98	6871	,,	,, 11 mm.	,,	,, ,,	,,	—
99	6848 C.2136	,,	,, 13 mm.	Leo I (in name of Verina)	A.D. 457–474	Bust of Empress/Victory seated	S. 3
100	—	,,	,, 10 mm.	Justin I	A.D. 518–527	Bust of Emperor facing/ 5 Nummia	I.B.C. 40
101	6851	,,	,, 30 mm.	Tiberius II	A.D. 578–582	Bust of Emperor facing/ 40 Nummia	—
102	—	,,	,, 26 mm.	Maurice Tiberius	A.D. 582–602	,, ,,	—
103	—	,,	,, 20 mm.	,,	,,	Bust of Emperor facing/ 20 Nummia	—
104	6866	4000	,, 15 mm.	Heraclius, Alexandria	A.D. 610–641	Bust of Emperor facing/ 12 Nummia	I.B.C. 276
105	6887	DX	,, 24 mm.	Heraclius or Constans II	—	Illegible	—
106	6852 C.2137	,,	,, 26 mm.	Constans II	A.D. 641–668	Bust of Emperor facing/ 40 Nummia	—
107	—	,,	,, 20 mm.	,,	,,	,, ,,	—
108	—	,,	,, 20 mm.	,,	,,	Emperor standing/ 40 Nummia	—
109	6888	,,	,, 24 mm.	Uncertain, Byzantine	—	Illegible	—
110	—	,,	,, 15 mm.	Ummayad Raqqah	A.D. 670	Sprig and Kalima in margins	B.M. 50
111	—	,,	,, 12 mm.	Uncertain Ummayad	—	Illegible	—
112	—	,,	,, 20 mm.	al-Ashraf Shaaban, Cairo	A.D. 1363	Legend, title and mint	B.M. 591

No.	Field No. Palestine Museum No.	Area	Metal and size or denomination		Authority and mint		Date of reign	Type	Reference
113	—	DX	Æ	21 × 16 mm.	Uncertain Mameluk		—	Legend in 3 lines divided by dots: . . . . *al-malek al-Na. . . .aa nas. . . .?/* fleur-de-lis, illeg. marginal legend	Not in B.M.
114	—	,,	AR	15 mm.	Murad II, Misr		A.D. 1421	Legend, title and mint	—
115	6146	700	Æ	18 mm.	Illegible Islamic		—	—	—
116	6889	L.15	,,	—	Illegible, probably Islamic		—	—	—
117	6890	M.13	,,	—	,,	,,	—	—	—
118	6891	DX	,,	—	,,	,,	—	—	—
119	6853	,,	,,	—	,,	,,	—	—	—
120	6854 38.774	,,	,,	—	,,	,,	—	—	—
121	7272	700	,,	—	,,	,,	—	—	—
122	6145	,,	,,	—	,, (4 coins)	,,	—	—	—

415

APPENDIX C

OBJECTS IN THE PALESTINE ARCHAEOLOGICAL MUSEUM, JERUSALEM

Museum No.	Field No.	Plate No.	Museum No.	Field No.	Plate No.
33.1886	5	80: 80	33.1926	179	93: 462
33.1887	6	83: 152	33.1927	180	93: 452
33.1889	10	83: 151	33.1928	187	79: 51
33.1890	17	83: 148	33.1929	189	85: 218
33.1891	21	83: 153	33.1930	196	80: 63
33.1892	35	93: 445	33.1931	198	90: 384
33.1893	38	88: 286	33.1932	213	84: 194
33.1894	41	88: 312	33.1933	226	84: 193
33.1895	42	87: 275	33.1934	234	91: 424
33.1896	49	88: 283	33.1935	243	79: 39
33.1897	45	93: 458	33.1936	244	91: 411
33.1898	50	89: 353	33.1937	250	88: 310
33.1899	53	88: 311	33.1938	254	88: 311
33.1900	64	Frag. NP	33.1939	258	89: 360*
33.1901	68	88: 309	33.1940	267	89: 366
33.1902	73	93: 449	33.1941	268	87: 280
33.1903	80	88: 320	33.1942	269	85: 210
33.1904	82	81: 106	33.1943	552	55: 2
33.1905	83	83: 144	33.1944	553	55: 1
33.1906	84	88: 321	33.1945	554	55: 3
33.1907	92	84: 187	33.1946	555	54: 79
33.1908	95	87: 269	33.1947	562	43: 2
33.1909	97	85: 206	33.1948	571	54: 72
33.1910	102	91: 410	33.1949	572	54: 73
33.1911	116	83: 150	33.1950	573	54: 78
33.1912	117	84: 199	33.1951	575	54: 77
33.1913	120	88: 292	33.1963	819	88: 283
33.1914	123	80: 70	33.1964	821	85: 223
33.1915	125	81: 95	33.1965	823	83: 150
33.1916	127	79: 45	33.1966	826	84: 178
33.1917	130	79: 48	33.1967	829	87: 267
33.1918	131	79: 49	33.1968	830	84: 190
33.1919	134	80: 73	33.1969	831	93: 458
33.1920	136	88: 309	33.1970	837	79: 2
33.1921	140	86: 243	33.1971	838	83: 148
33.1922	142	88: 331	33.1972	839	84: 185
33.1923	144	80: 64	33.1973	844	86: 247
33.1924	158	95: 485	33.1974	845	83: 151
33.1925	176	84: 187	33.1975	846	93: 457

* Underlined numbers indicate type specimens.

Museum No.	Field No.	Plate No.	Museum No.	Field No.	Plate No.
33.1976	849	88: 283	33.2028	1062	93: 455
33.1978	854	84: 203	33.2029	1064	84: 180
33.1979	857	87: 271	33.2030	1065	84: 186
33.1980	860	93: 454	33.2031	1068	84: 170
33.1981	868	88: 309	33.2032	1069	79: 37
33.1982	869	80: 75	33.2034	1077	85: 228
33.1983	874	84: 189	33.2035	1080	87: 265
33.1984	877	83: 146	33.2036	1088	84: 166
33.1985	878	84: 190	33.2037	1092	93: 450
33.1986	880	84: 174	33.2038	1123	89: 369
33.1987	882	88: 303	33.2039	1128	84: 168
33.1988	888	79: 9	33.2040	1129	85: 215
33.1989	893a	79: 41	33.2041	1130	86: 252
33.1990	899	79: 4	33.2042	1140	87: 266
33.1991	906	84: 196	33.2043	1148	79: 13
33.1992	907	87: 261	33.2044	1158	81: 95
33.1993	914	85: 218	33.2045	1165	86: 231
33.1994	924	84: 176	33.2046	1169	85: 208
33.1995	929	91: 420	33.2047	1173	92: 431
33.1996	930	89: 361	33.2048	1177	90: 381
33.1997	942	81: 102	33.2049	1178	87: 257
33.1998	944	84: 178	33.2050	1186	83: 161
33.1999	946	79: 40	33.2051	1195	84: 167
33.2000	950	84: 171	33.2052	1207	88: 296
33.2001	951	81: 98	33.2053	1224	84: 201
33.2002	955	79: 11	33.2054	1231	81: 89
33.2003	958	92: 434	33.2055	1255	28: 11
33.2004	965	88: 311	33.2056	1255a	28: 14
33.2005	970	88: 305	33.2057	1262	36: 50
33.2006	974	84: 169	33.2058	1265	28: 15
33.2007	975	88: 300	33.2059	1297	36: 51
33.2008	978	88: 287	33.2060	1303	NP
33.2009	979	88: 336	33.2061	1309	44: 89
33.2010	982	79: 48	33.2062	1311	36: 48
33.2011	986	88: 286	33.2063	1322	30: 26
33.2012	991	88: 286	33.2064	850	Frag. NP
33.2013	996	91: 421	33.2065	984	93: 462
33.2014	999	84: 172	33.2067	1093a	87: 262
33.2015	1002	80: 62	33.2097	1444	43: 33
33.2016	1012	79: 3	33.2098, 2099, 2100	1457	NP
33.2017	1013	84: 184			
33.2018	1015	84: 203	33.2101	1487	NP
33.2019	1026	86: 250	33.2103, 2104, 2105	1541	NP
33.2021	1029	87: 258			
33.2022	1037	84: 190	33.2106	1542	NP
33.2023	1044	93: 462	33.2107	1543	NP
33.2024	1045	84: 190	33.2108, 2109	1544	NP
33.2025	1046	88: 293	33.2110, 2111	1545	NP
33.2026	1049	85: 227	33.2112	1546	NP
33.2027	1058	86: 237	33.2113	1547	NP

Museum No.	Field No.	Plate No.	Museum No.	Field No.	Plate No.
33.2114	1548	NP	35.3069	3887	33: 15
33.2115	1549	NP	35. 3070	4119	42: 8, 9
33.2116	1554	84: 191	35.3071	4173	32: 1
33.2117	1573	87: 256	36.1491	4709	82: 126
33.2118	1581	87: 268	36.1492	4710	81: 97
33.2119	1589	NP	36.1493	4711	86: 244
33.2120	1590	36: 49	36.1494	4721	79: 22
33.2121	1592	NP	36.1495	4734	81: 119
34.106	436	85: 218	36.1496	4755	84: 172
34.107	437	88: 327	36.1497	4772	89: 370
34.108	438	88: 300	36.1515	4902	88: 296
34.109	439	84: 180	36.1516	4920	83: 164
34.110	440	80: 76	36.1517	5091	83: 141
34.111	441	NP	36.1518	5094	84: 176
34.112	442	NP	36.1519	5097	84: 172
34.123	1050	93: 442	36.1520	5098	81: 117
34.124	1258	39: 8 and 57: 17	36.1521	5110	88: 304
34.125	1268	28: 12	36.1522	5116	88: 297
34.126	1269	29: 18	36.1523	5132	88: 330
34.127	1289	29: 22	36.1524	5133	82: 123
34.128	1318	28:10	36.1525	5134	80: 86
34.129	1321	29: 21	36.1526	5135	81: 120
34.130	1325	40: 1 and 57: 7	36.1527	5136	55: 15
34.132	1483	Fig. 13	36.1528	5137	55: 10
34.133	1504	39: 1	36.1529	5138	55: 9
34.2923	2569	94: 470	36.1530, 1531	5139	55: 6
34.2924	2570	88: 322	36.1532–1536	5140	55: 7
34.2925	2571	88: 337	36.1537	5141	55: 8
34.2926	2572	88: 338	36.1538, 1539	5142	55: 4
34.2927, 2928, 2929, 2930	2573	36:58,59,60 and 55: 30	36.1540	5143	55: 5
			36.1541	5144	55: 12
34.3083	3017	94: 476	36.1542	5145	NP
34.3084	3018	88: 296	36.1543, 1562	5146	37: 12 and 55: 20, 21
34.3085	3019	82: 132			
34.3086	3020	45: 130	36.1544	5147	55: 19
34.3097	2854	84: 183	36.1545	5148	55: 18
35.2927	3487	33: 5	36.1546	5149	55: 17
35.2928	3490	33: 12	36.1547	5150	55: 24
35.2929	3493	33: 9	36.1548	5151	55: 22
35.2930	3495	33: 8	36.1549–1561	5152	37: 7, 14 and 55: 23
35.2931	3496	33: 7	36.1562, 1543	5146	37: 12 and 55: 20, 21
35.2932	3502	33: 3			
35.2933	3506	33: 14	36.1563	5153	37: 11, 13 and 55: 25
35.2934	3509	33: 11			
35.2935	3514	33: 10	36.1564	5154	37: 8 and 55: 26
35.2936	3517	33: 6	36.1565	5155	37: 6 and 55: 11
35.2937	3523	33: 13	36.1566	5156	37: 16 and 55: 27
35.2959	3656	70: 16	36.1567	5157	37: 15 and 55: 28
35.2960–2978	3672	NP	36.1568	5158	37: 9 and 55: 29
35.3068	3880	NP	36.1569	5159	55: 14

418

Museum No.	Field No.	Plate No.	Museum No.	Field No.	Plate No.
36.1570	5160	40: 3 and 55: 13	38.718	6237	NP
36.1571	5161	43: 9	38.719	6238	42: 1
36.1572	5162	43: 22	38.722	6254	41: 11 and 61: 4
36.1573	5163	43: 4	38.725	6271	90: 386
36.1574	5164	43: 59	38.726	6282	84: 179
36.1575	5168	43: 35	38.727	6283	41: 10 and 63: 15
36.1576	5165	43: 23	38.728	6287	80: 59
36.1577	5166	44: 90	38.729	6310	82: 136 and 36: 61
36.1578	5169	44: 76	38.730	6344	44: 71
36.1579	5170	44: 77	38.731	6379	43: 28
36.1580	5171	NP	38.742	6572	90: 389
36.1581	5172	34: 8	38.743	6574	90: 393
36.1582	5173	34: 10	38.744	6579	90: 398
36.1583	5174	34: 14	38.745	6580	83: 155
36.1584	5175	34: 13	38.748–750	6591	41: 12, 14 and 58: 2
36.1585	5176	34: 12	38.751	6593	NP
36.1586	5177	34: 17	38.768, 777	6774a	98: 558
36.1587	5178	34: 16	38.769	6827	63: 18
36.1588	5179	34: 11	38.770, 771	6832	NP
36.1589	5180	34: 15	38.774	6854	No. 120 on List of Coins
36.1590	5181	NP			
36.1591–1596	5183	34: 9	38.775	7233	19: 7
36.1597	5184	38: 2	38.776	7234	NP
36.1598, 1599	5185, 5167	NP; 43: 61	38.777, 768	6774a	98: 558
36.1600	5186	55: 16	39.792	6592	31: 17
36.1601	5188	27: 9	39.795	6697	p. 254
36.1603	5214	91: 404	39.798	6825	63: 16
36.1604	5232	39: 7 and 58: 4	39.799	6899	48: 2
36.1621	5346	90: 390	39.815	7049	79: 30
36.1814	3658	70: 15	39.816	7050	89: 374
36.1815	3668a	68: 1	39.817	7065	36: 57
36.1816	3669a	42: 5	39.818	7085	94: 465
36.1817	3670a	42: 4	39.819	7094	31: 6
36.1828	3881	31: 19	39.820	7150	45: 166
36.1830, 1829	4091, 4041	44: 105, 45: 167	39.821	7151	90: 387
36.2245	5187	27: 8	39.822	7160	p. 125
36.2258	5352	45: 172	39.823	7162	41: 13 and 63: 12
36.2259	5354	47A: 1	39.824	7166	47A: 1
37.729	5474	90: 396	39.825	7167	47A: 4
37.833–840	5848	57: 45	39.826	7186	NP
38.51	5496	89: 350	39.827	7187	41: 2 and 63: 2
38.71	5850	57: 39	39.828	7197	
38.123	6114	45: 170	39.830	7254	50: 10 (No. 46 on List of Weights)
38.710	6201	94: 466			
38.711	6202	88: 311	39.832	7261	90: 382
38.712	6203	89: 368	39.833	7274	31: 14
38.713	6204	91: 425	C.2020	6122	No. 2 on List of Coins
38.714	6205	65: 14	C.2021	6126	No. 51 ,, ,,
38.716	6235	61: 7	C.2022	6130	No. 47 ,, ,,
38.717	6236	47B: 2	C.2023	6133	No. 56a ,, ,,

Museum No.	Field No.	Plate No.		Museum No.	Field No.	Plate No.
C.2136	6848	No. 99 on List of Coins		C.2142	6897	No. 75 on List of Coins
C.2137	6852	No. 106 ,, ,,		C.2143	6897	No. 9 ,, ,,
C.2138	6858	No. 20 ,, ,,		C.2144	6898	No. 4 ,, ,,
C.2139	6862	No. 81 ,, ,,		C.2202	7051a	No. 5 ,, ,,
C.2140	6873	No. 1 ,, ,,		C.2203	7051	No. 15 ,, ,,
C.2141	6873	No. 11 ,, ,,		C.2204	7267	No. 62 ,, ,,

APPENDIX D

BIBLE REFERENCES

422

INDEX

Bowls (*cont.*)
    in Tomb 1004: 236, 237
    in West Section, 73, 74
    Miscellaneous, 321, 322, 323
    total number examined, 267
Bracelets, see Bangles.
Breastwork, 99
Brick(s), 84, 85n., 86, 89, 91, 92, 97, 117, 118, 119, 120, 121, 122, 123, 124, 125, 126, 150, 151, 153, 154, 156, 157, 159
British Museum, 55, 142, 331, 399
    Collection, 394
    (Natural History), 62n., 405, 408
Broneer, O., 137, 148, 155
Bronze, 46, 55, 57, 98, 142, 146, 152, 181, 197, 205, 212, 215, 220, 229, 230, 240, 253, 347, 385, 386, 387, 388, 389, 390, 391, 392, 393, 394, 395, 396
Bronze Age, 34, 35, 46, 47, 51, 52, 60, 63, 71, 219, 227, 246, 250, 266, 269, 281, 376, 380, 381, 386, 392
    drainage, 179
    history of the site, 51. See also Level VI.
    sherds, 91, 112, 114, 116
    tombs re-used, 171, 242
Bronze Age, Early, 38, 219, 221, 249, 250, 260, 410, 410n.
    tombs, 178
Bronze Age, Late, 192, 282, 365, 366
    burnt layer, 71, 74, 77
    city, 51, 52, 58, 77–78, 80, 104, 149, 181, 268, 362
    decoration, 264, 265, 280
    forms, 223, 234, 242, 243, 253, 267, 271, 305, 306, 307, 308
    scarabs, 363, 366
    sherds, 76, 78, 79, 137, 179, 212, 218, 222, 242, 245, 247
    tombs, 178, 193, 210, 211, 226, 227, 228, 236, 241, 243, 253
Bronze Age, Middle, 51, 60, 240, 267, 282, 362, 366, 389, 410, 411
    fosse, 91, 92, 196, 200, 219, 239, 244
    scarabs, 221, 363, 365, 366
    sherds, 92, 212, 228
    tombs, 178, 236, 239, 242
Brunton, G., 400, 401
Buchanan, B. W., 365
Buckle(s), 181, 392, 394, 395
Building R/Q/S/.15/16: 10–21: 56, 146–149, 163, 304, 311, 315, 386
    Classified Summary of Pottery, 149
    comparisons, 147
        architectural, 147
    contents, 148, 149
    date, 147, 148
    scarab, 362
Buildings, the, 61
Buren, Mrs. E. Douglas van, 377, 378

Burial, 64–66
Burning, see Fortifications, Level II, Level III, Solar Shrine and Tomb 1002.
Burnish, hand, 47, 53, 149, 191, 205, 215, 220, 221, 222, 223, 228, 229, 230, 231, 233, 234, 236, 237, 240, 247, 250, 252, 260–264 *passim*, 269, 271, 272, 273, 274, 275, 287, 288, 289, 290, 292, 294, 295, 296, 298, 301, 302, 303, 305, 306, 321, 361
    in bowls, Analysis of, 261, 262
    in Tomb 106, Analysis of, 182
    in Tomb 116, Analysis of, 191
    in Tomb 218, Analysis of, 206
    in Tomb 224, Analysis of, 215
    in Tomb 1002, Analysis of, 231
    red, 46, 55, 73, 80, 191, 213, 215, 216, 223, 224, 233, 250, 268, 269, 270, 272, 276
Burnish, wheel, 47, 57, 73, 117, 229, 230, 231, 236, 237, 261–264 *passim*, 265, 272, 273, 274, 275, 276, 277, 292, 296, 307
    in bowls, Analysis of, 261, 262
    in Tomb 106, Analysis of, 182
    in Tomb 1002, Analysis of, 231, 232
    introduction of, 47, 215, 220, 229, 261, 262, 272, 274, 292, 296
Burnt layer(s), 55, 95, 120, 159, 238, 246, 386
    See also Bronze Age, Late, Burning and Level VI.
    deposits, 74
Bushe-Fox, J. P., 394
Butler, Samuel, quotation from, 45
Byzantine coins, 167, 168
    period, 39, 59, 164, 179, 180, 246

Camel, 63, 411
Camp buildings, 32, 219, 229, 238
    garden, 32
Canaan, 51, 52
Carchemish, 57, 61, 101, 102, 394
Carmel, 34
Cassuto, Professor U., 332n.
Caton-Thompson, Miss G., 66n., 383
Cave 6024: 46, 233, 250–252
    clay head, 250
    date and comparisons, 250
    loomweights, 250
    pottery, 250, 252, 261, 269, 294, 298
Cavern 101: 91, 178, 179
Cemeteries, 171–254
    industrial and domestic constructions in, 177
    See also Cave 6024, Cavern 101, Cemetery Areas, Graves and Tombs.
Cemetery Area 500: 219, 349, 383
Cemetery Area 1000: 228, 229
Cemetery Area 4000: 33, 239
Cemetery Area 6000: 33, 246, 247
Cemetery Areas 100, 200: 178, 179

PRINTED IN
GREAT BRITAIN
AT THE
UNIVERSITY PRESS
OXFORD
BY
CHARLES BATEY
PRINTER
TO THE
UNIVERSITY